# The Beatles
# on
# Apple Records

Compiled
by
## Bruce Spizer

*To Michael –
Best BEATLE wishes.
Bruce Spin
4-3-2004*

Foreword
by
## Ken Mansfield

Copyright ©2003 by 498 Productions, L.L.C.

498 Productions, L.L.C.
P.O. Box 70194
New Orleans, Louisiana 70172
Fax: 504-524-2887
email: 498@beatle.net

Library of Congress Control Number: 2002095729
ISBN 0-9662649-4-0

Printed in Singapore
1 2 3 4 5 6 7 8 9 0

# Contents

# Foreword

Apple was magic–it sizzled, it sailed, it stormed and it soared. One thing for sure–it seldom slept. It was poignant, it was madness, it was beautiful and it was absurd. One undeniable fact–it was never dull. It gathered into its heart and halls one of the wildest assemblages of ducks and drifters, executives and eccentrics, geniuses and gutterballs, and the leading lords and loonies of the day. Amid the magic and madness were four very fine young men–my bosses for a while, and friends forever–the Beatles. Only their simplicity and genius could have created Apple.

I walked through the doors of 3 Savile Row (Apple headquarters, London) for the first time on a muggy summer's day in 1968. That was long ago. And though we've all gone our separate ways, somewhere behind those fabled portals, parts and pieces of each of us who had purpose there will always be tightly tucked away in the recesses and corners of that space in time. Pieces remain on the roof when we were the fortunate few who got to see the greatest band of all time perform for the last time. Parts remain in our memories in the form of the echoes of a magical music that will never go away. Most importantly there will always remain pieces of us in the deep parts of each other's hearts because for a brief moment we occupied what has to be the most privileged place in rock and roll history– the corps of that sweet Apple. There we savored the depth and passion of John's moods, the vigor and milieu of Paul's ideas, the serenity and warmth of George's gentleness and the joy and delight of Ringo's wit and laughter.

The Beatles were easy to be with! When you closed the doors to the Apple building and it was just the four of them alone with the Apple staffers it was all so very normal–in a mad sort of way. If the creativity in that building could have been harnessed as electricity we could have lit London for days. Actually some of the after hours antics of a few of the staffers did keep a lot of lights on all night in the streets, clubs and pubs of London. I'm not sure it is appropriate here to name names, but the initials J. Oliver and T. Bramwell seem to come to mind. Aah yes, lovely, lively London had become the new geographical center of the rock and roll universe because of these four lads, their cohorts and the goings on inside that curious white building.

My job was a challenging experience in that as U.S. manager of Apple Records, I had to keep in balance the overseas aspirations of four very adventuresome young men who were not only the very Beatles themselves, but who were also the co-owners of the company I was to manage in their most important market—America. At that time this quartet of longhaired virtuosos accounted for about one half of Capitol Record's sales. When Capitol's president Stanley Gortikov and the label's general manager Bob York called me up to the executive floor of the Hollywood Capitol Tower, I had no idea what was about to transpire. To my surprise and delight I was told that Apple president Ron Kass had informed them that the Beatles wanted me, Capitol's National Promotion Manager and Director of Independent Labels, to assume the responsibility for running Apple in North America.

I was to leave immediately for London. My instructions from Bob York were simple, clear and to the point. "When it comes to the Beatles Ken, keep it together!" Stanley Gortikov wanted to interject even a little more clarity into that admonition so he restated the instruction. "When it comes to the Beatles and Apple Records Ken, not only must you keep it totally together, *there is no margin for error!*" Not much leeway for my management style, right? There was an operational perk in all this though. With the density of the responsibility they gave me the corresponding levity to function without the normal formal restrictions of corporate policy. These were my unique ground rules: I did not have to get prior approvals as to my activities, whereabouts or expenditures in terms of Apple and the Beatles–as long as I kept them informed and *kept it together*! Talk about a ticket to ride!

This is a foreword, but I can't help but look backward. And as I do, something begins to stir from the deep because it is starting to get a little lonely. So many are gone and yet I can still see, hear and feel the vision, sound and presence of Ron Kass, Maurine Starkey, Derek Taylor, John Lennon, Linda McCartney, Mal Evans and George Harrison. There are others too, and I miss them all as I know you do. It was like family and it was fun and it sure didn't last as long as we would have liked. But the results of that awesome assemblage will live forever.

While much has been previously written about Apple, this book focuses on what the Beatles and Apple did best– make music. After all, Apple's legacy should not be how much liquor was consumed in Derek Taylor's office or how many typewriters and televisions were stolen from 3 Savile Row. Nor should it be the bickering and legal entanglements that brought it down. Apple's legacy is the fabulous music left behind by the Beatles and its other artists. This book tells how the music was created and marketed to America.

That is why I am so proud to have been invited to lead you into this incredible work. You can now know what we knew and see what we saw through this wonderful book. Bruce Spizer is the ultimate presenter of the historical phenomenon known as the Beatles. If this is the first of his books you have read, then take my advice and journey backward through his previous works. It is amazing to realize how much there was to all this.

There were only a few of us there and it was special. Now you too can walk through those doors as you join the Apple Corps in the exciting pages ahead.

God bless us all.

Ken Mansfield
September, 2002

*Ken Mansfield served as Apple's first U.S. manager. He is the author of the critically acclaimed book* The Beatles, The Bible and Bodega Bay.

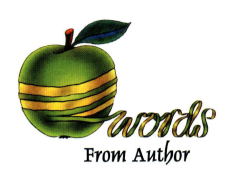

# From Author

It was a cool Sunday August night in the summer of 1968, the last night of camp. I was in my bunk at Camp Zakelo in Harrison, Maine, trying to listen to WABC out of New York. The reception faded in and out, but this evening there was magic in the air. The disc jockey introduced a new song by the Beatles called *Hey Jude*. At first, it was only Paul's voice and piano, but then the others joined in. After a few minutes, when I was certain the song was about to end, I heard a glorious sing-along that stretched out for several minutes. And when it was over, I couldn't get that "Na, na na na na na na, na na na na, Hey Jude" out of my head.

On the plane ride back to New Orleans, that ending hook kept playing over and over in my mind. The next morning I had my mother drive me to the neighborhood record store, Studio A. I quickly went to the Beatles album section, looking for the group's new album containing *Hey Jude*, but there were only albums I already owned. I asked the store's owner, Bill, if he had the new Beatles album. Bill told me there was no new album, but that a single would be released in a few days. That surprised me because the song I had heard on the radio was too long to be a single. It had to be seven or eight minutes long. But Bill insisted that the next Beatles record was a 45 containing two songs: *Hey Jude* and *Revolution*. I called the store every day until the record arrived. That Friday, my mother rushed me there so I could buy the group's incredible new single.

Even before I got home I was impressed. The record came in a classy-looking black sleeve with a simple message — "The Beatles on Apple." And the labels were different, too. A bright green apple on one side and a white sliced apple on the other. And yes, I was right about the length of the song. The label listed the running time for *Hey Jude* at 7:11. Upon reaching home, I raced to my room and played the record over and over again. Of course, *Hey Jude* was fabulous, but so was the flip side, the powerful rocker *Revolution*. Both songs not only had great music, but also had lyrics I could relate to. At the time I didn't know anything about Apple, but I knew the label had given me my money's worth. For less than a dollar I had purchased what had to be ten to eleven minutes of the greatest music ever recorded.

A few months later it happened again. On the evening of Monday, November 18, 1968, I began hearing songs from the Beatles new album on New Orleans radio station WTIX. The variety in the music was incredible. I heard bits of rock, folk, heavy metal, reggae and country. There were parodies of the Beach Boys and Bob Dylan. There were raunchy rockers and lush ballads. And there was a long sound collage that sounded unlike anything I had ever heard before. In 1968, WTIX played the top ten requested songs at 10:00 p.m. each evening. By Wednesday night, all of the top ten songs were from the new Beatles album. Unfortunately I did not write down the names of the ten songs played that evening, but I do remember *Back In The U.S.S.R.*, *Cry Baby Cry*, *Bungalow Bill* and *Ob-La-Di, Ob-La-Da* were in that number.

That Friday I ran from the school bus stop to get home as quickly as possible so my mother could drive me to Studio A to purchase the record, which was simply titled *The Beatles*. Upon returning home, I played the double album three straight times on the family stereo. I studied the photo collage on the album's poster and read the lyrics along with the songs. It took over ninety minutes to play all four sides. Although the double album wiped out my allowance, the Beatles had once again given me tremendous value.

Had Apple only released those records, דַּיֵּנוּ — *dayenu!* (that would have been enough). But there were other releases to follow. And while every record did not capture the magic of the first two Beatles releases, there were many fine moments.

This book covers the records issued by the Beatles on their Apple label in America, beginning with the 1968 releases *Hey Jude* and *The White Album,* and continuing through the final Beatles releases of Apple's initial phase, the red and blue "hits" collections from 1973. The book also covers the label's triumphant return in the nineties and goes through the release of *Beatles 1*. This book does not cover the solo records released by band members on the Apple label. Those records are detailed in a companion volume titled *The Beatles Solo on Apple Records*. And while many of the original Apple albums were also available on cassette, 8-track, 4-track and reel-to-reel tapes, these formats are not detailed here. This book is *The Beatles on Apple Records*, not *The Beatles on Apple Records and Tapes*.

As an attorney, I could have written an exposé detailing the complex and bitter legal entanglements involving the Beatles during the Apple years, but I chose not to do so. Instead, I focused on what always was and always will be the most important thing about the Beatles on Apple–the quality and variety of the music resonating from those records with the colorful Granny Smith apple on the label.

Section One of this book is titled *A is for Apple*. It covers Apple's origins and features the initial press kits issued by Apple in America.

Section Two is titled *S is for Singles*. It details the 45 RPM (revolutions per minute) Beatles records released from August, 1968, through May, 1970. While the first Beatles single on Apple was issued in mono, all subsequent American 45s, beginning with *Get Back*, were pressed in stereo.

The Apple Beatles singles are detailed in chronological order in separate chapters. For records issued without custom picture sleeves, the chapter opens with an image of the disc inside its Apple sleeve. For the three singles packaged in custom sleeves, an image of the picture sleeve is shown. The text contains release dates, chart action and sales information followed by stories of the recording of the songs. Details regarding the picture sleeves (if applicable) and label variations are followed by images of the sleeves (if applicable) and labels. The section also covers the reissued singles *I Want To Hold Your Hand* through *Lady Madonna* pressed with Apple label backdrops as well as chapters on the Canadian and Mexican 45s. There is also a chapter on the rare pocket disc singles.

Section Three, *L is for LPs*, explores the long playing (LP) albums. These 12" records play at 33⅓ revolutions per minute. By the time Apple began issuing albums in late 1968, Capitol had completely phased out mono LPs. Thus, all of the Beatles Apple albums in America were pressed only in stereo.

The Beatles Apple albums appear in chronological order. A picture of each album's front cover jacket is provided, followed by a list of the record's track selections and details of release dates, chart positions and sales performance. Stories regarding the recording of the songs are presented for each release. Apple's promotional posters and displays, album covers and record labels are described, followed by pictures of the front and back covers and label variations. The section also contains chapters on the two unreleased *Get Back* albums and on the LPs issued in Canada and Mexico on Apple.

Section Four is titled *T is for Triumphant Return*. It covers the albums released by the revitalized Apple label, including *Live At The BBC*, *Anthology 1, 2 & 3*, *Yellow Submarine Songtrack* and *Beatles 1*.

Section Five, *B is for Bibliography*, provides a pictorial bibliography of essential books covering the Beatles during the Apple era. Section Six, *C is for Checklist*, lists the albums and singles detailed in this book.

Section Seven is titled *V is for Vendors*. It contains advertisements from reliable dealers and entertaining publications to assist the reader in expanding his or her Beatles collections and knowledge about the group.

As with my previous books, *The Beatles Records On Vee-Jay* and *The Beatles' Story on Capitol Records*, there are no values assigned to the records and other collectibles pictured in the book. This is because prices for collectibles constantly change. This book is designed to be a permanent reference book and companion piece to the Vee-Jay and Capitol books. Those seeking to value their records and other Apple collectibles or to obtain information on what to pay for a particular item are urged to purchase the most recent editions of the Beatles price guide by Perry Cox and Joe Lindsey and *The Beatles Memorabilia Price Guide* by Jeff Augsburger, Marty Eck and Rick Rann.

Although Capitol Records in America chose not to issue the last two Beatles albums covered in this book on vinyl, EMI pressed special vinyl editions of *Yellow Submarine Songtrack* and *Beatles 1*. And while both collections sound great on CD, the elaborate packaging of these records makes them worth seeking out. *Yellow Submarine Songtrack* has a colorful gatefold cover and is pressed on yellow vinyl. *Beatles 1*, with its huge poster and Richard Avedon photos of John, Paul, George and Ringo, brings back memories of the excitement generated by the poster and pictures included with the Beatles first Apple album.

I will never forget the magic I felt when I first removed my copy of *Hey Jude* from its black Apple sleeve on Friday afternoon, August 23, 1968. While researching this book, I realized that Bill had sold me *Hey Jude* and *The White Album* on the Friday before their official Monday release dates. My persistent calling to his record store must have paid off! As for *Hey Jude*, I still remember placing the needle on the spinning black disc and hearing Paul's voice come out of the tiny speaker to my record player, which was built into a curved carrying case covered with red and black plaid cloth. My old record player was thrown out in the early seventies, but my original copy of the single remains and is pictured left. I still can't get that "Na, na na na na na na, na na na na, Hey Jude" out of my head.

# Acknowledgments

Ever time I see a new Woody Allen movie, I'm always amazed at how many of the names shown during the credits are the same film after film after film. Woody Allen has assembled a great team of creative people and knows not to break up a winning combination. I am also a firm believer in sticking with what works. If you take the time to read these acknowledgments, you will see many names that were listed in my previous books.

First and foremost, I must give credit to my pre-press person, Diana Thornton of Crescent Music Services. She's the one responsible for converting the images in my brain to the images on the page. I can't imagine doing a Beatles book without her.

Other key people returned to assist me on the production end. Michael Ledet lined up the printer and Rick Randall of Harvey Press provided support and expertise. Jim Filo and Tom Bennett of Garrison Digital Color handled the photography of some of the larger items such as posters and displays.

Once again, several dealers came to my aid by either sending me digital files or lending me records, posters and other items. Key contributors include Jeff Augsburger, Randy Cates, Perry Cox, Marty Eck, Paul and Staci Garfunkle of Blackbird Records, Paul Grenyo, Tom Grosh of Very English and Rolling Stone, Jim Hansen of Blue Jay Way Galleries, Gary Hein, Gary and Wayne Johnson of Rockaway Records, Louisiana Music Factory, Rick Rann, Bob Richerson, Rock 'n' Roll Collectibles in New Orleans, Jim Russell's Rare Records in New Orleans, John Tefteller, Thomas Vanghele of Fab 4 Collectibles and Cliff Yamasaki of Let It Be Records.

Many collectors also provided valuable assistance. Mark Galloway was kind enough to lend me a hefty portion of his impressive Beatles and Beatles solo singles collection for scanning and examination. David Rau sent me images from his extensive collection of foreign picture sleeves. Jim Marien sent me images from his run of All Rights labels.

Other collectors aiding in this project include Jason Anjoorian, Ricardo Aranda, Dave Askamit, Bob Avellino, Kevin Ball, Belmo, Bojo, Bozo, Bob Burt, Frank Caiazzo, Lou Calitri, Barry Chasin, Sherman Cohen, Thomas Cook, Kevin Curran, Dennis Dailey, Frank Daniels, Thomas Deak, Bill DeMartini, Dave Dermon, George "Still The King" Edmonds, Mark Erbach, Howard Fileds, Tom Fontaine, Chris Fonville, Michael Fortes, Al Frazza, Rob Friedman, Andy Geller, Joe Giardina, Kenny Grazioso, Steve Green, Denise Gregoire, Mike Greif, Rod Griffith, John Guarnieri, Steven Hakeman, Dan Hilderbrand, Joe Hilton, Lin Hol-

land, Greg Homan, Troy Hubbard, Philip Hunott, Geoff Jacobs of Glass Onion, Todd Jackson, Larry Jaffee, Seth Kaplan, Christopher Kennel, Bill Kern, Harry Klaassen, Donald Lanza, Mark Lapidos, Bill Last, Russ Lease, Jeff Leve, Jeffery Levy (author of *Applelog*), Martin Lewis, Bud Loveall, Gilbert Luque, Jeff Marcus, Phillip Marks, Ron Martin, Mitch McGeary, Mark McManus, Doug Miller, Sam Mitchell, Maury Mollo, Charles Moore, Steve Moore, Jeff Morris, Mark Naboshek, Peter Nash, Tim Neely of *Goldmine*, Bob Nichols, Dave Nichols, Jerry Osborne, Stanley Panenka, Tony Perkins of *Good Morning, America*, Jeff Petshow, Cary Pollack, John Posner, Simon Postbrief, Wayne Rogers, Mike Sarafian, Craig Satinsky, Tom Schalk, Piet Schreuders, David Schwartz, Rob Shackleton, Pat Smith, Barry Spizer, Suellen Stewart, Mike Tartamella, Jeffrey Tilem, Edward Tovrea, Mark Vaquer, Collin Weaver, Jonathon White, Michael White, Tony Wilson, John Winn, Robert Wolk, Chris Wood, Michelle Wood and Bob York. I apologize in advance to anyone I may have inadvertently failed to mention.

The Canadian and Mexican chapters were greatly enhanced by help from my friends from north and south of the border. The Canadian gang includes Steve Clifford, Andrew Croft (publisher of *Beatlology*), Tom Elliott, Piers Hemmingsen, Brad Howard (publisher of *The Beatles World Forum*), Bob Kodak, Peter Miniaci, Gilles Pépin, Brian Schofield, Peter Stone, Yvan Tessier, Doug Thompson and Giles Valiquette. Piers once again exhibited the determination of a Canadian Mountie in gathering information. Doug again assisted me with interviews. Ricardo Calderón provided guidance and lent me records from his collection of Apple singles, EPs and LPs pressed by Discos Capitol de Mexico. Ricardo Rodríguez Castaño gave me background information on Mexican releases.

Assistance regarding British releases and magazines was provided by Chad Craddock of Tracks, Andy Davis of *Record Collector* and Alan Ould of Good Humour. Peter Nash of *The Beatles Book* provided Apple and Capitol press releases.

Record Research, publisher of the wonderful series of *Billboard* chart books, allowed me access to magazines from its extensive *Billboard* library. This enabled me to provide images of Apple trade advertisements. Information from various *Billboard* record charts appears through the courtesy of Billboard Productions, Inc. (BPI) and Joel Whitburn's Record Research Publications. Mark Wallgren, who is working on an updated version of his book *The Beatles On Record*, provided data on the Beatles chart listings in *Cash Box* and *Record World*.

Much of the information regarding the Beatles activities in the studio comes from Mark Lewisohn's *The Beatles Recording Sessions* and *The Complete Beatles Chronicle*. Mark's well-researched books set the standard for Beatles books and belong in every Beatles library. Mark frequently gave me quick answers when I needed to resolve conflicting dates and other information. Additional details about the recording of the songs came from Walter Everett's *The Beatles As Musicians* and George Martin's *All You Need Is Ears* and *With A Little Help From My Friends*. Andy Babiuk's *Beatles Gear* provided fasinating information regarding the instruments and amplifiers used by the band.

Although (through the magic of bootleg CDs) I was able to hear many of the songs and rehearsals recorded during the *Get Back* sessions, I did not have access to the unedited Nagra tapes from Twickenham and the Apple basement studio. I did, however, have Doug Sulpy and Ray Schweighardt's *Drugs, Divorce and a Slipping Image* and Doug Sulpy's *The 910's Guide to The Beatles' Outtakes Part Two, The Complete Get Back Sessions*. Doug was kind enough to proof the chapters in this book involving the *Get Back* Sessions.

William Brown once again shared his vast knowledge of pressing plants and printers. Frank Daniels assisted me in presenting the minute details that fascinate collectors. Beatles historian Matt Hurwitz, as well as Al Sussman and Bill King of *Beatlefan*, helped me with my research regarding the *BBC* and *Anthology* releases.

Many people involved with the Beatles, Apple and Capitol Records shared their memories with me. Although I did not interview any of the Beatles, I learned a lot about the members of the group from those who were part of the inner circle, including Tony Barrow, former Beatles press agent; Tony Bramwell, who did promotional work for the group and Apple; Barry Miles, author and friend of Paul McCartney; and Alistair Taylor, long-time confidant of the group and Apple's first office manager. George's sister, Lou Harrison, provided meaningful insights regarding her brother.

I obtained valuable information from Capitol employees from the Beatles era, including Wayne Bridgewater, Roy Calhara, Anne Davis, Roy Davis, Mickey Diage, Roy James, Curt Kendall, Alan Livingston, Jay Ranellucci and Bill Richter. Former Queens Litho employees Eric Kaltman and Richard Roth provided details of the printing and packaging of the Beatles albums and singles. David Picker, former United Artists executive, and Bruce Markoe, a vice-president with MGM-UA, gave me details regarding the film and soundtrack deals for *Yellow Submarine* and *Let It Be*. Kurt Dean provided information on Specialty Records, the company that pressed vinyl for Capitol in the nineties.

Ken Mansfield, who served as Apple's first U.S. manager, gave me wonderful stories about those crazy times and, equally important, words of encouragement. Allan Steckler, who handled the production and marketing of the Beatles Apple releases during the Allen Klein era, provided insights and details of Apple in the seventies. Alan Parsons, who served as an engineer during the *Get Back* and *Abbey Road* sessions, shared his studio experiences.

Cathy Sarver was kind enough to share her candid photos of the Beatles at Apple, Abbey Road and Trident Studios. These pictures appear on pages 10 and 115. Paul Saltzman provided his photo of the Beatles in Rishikesh that appears on page 103. The incredible shot of John and Paul on *The Tonight Show* set (page 3) is from the collection of Paul Goresh. Susan Petersen shared her pictures of the show taken off the television screen on the night of May 14, 1968. They appear on page 4. The photo of me on the next page was taken by Jose Garcia.

I also wish to thank the many people I have met at Beatlefest (now known as the Fest for Beatles Fans) and other Beatles conventions and events, including my assistant booksellers, Eloise Keene, Lisa Wagner and Ann Rausher. I must also thank fellow authors Mitch Axelrod, Andy Babiuk, Regina Burch, Richard Buskin, Howard DeWitt, Kristofer Engelhardt, Walter Everett, Dr. Bob Hieronimus, Mark Lewisohn, Ken Mansfield, Wally Podrazik and Paul Saltzman for their encouragement, insights and knowledge.

Many of my friends and colleagues provided much appreciated moral support. Trish Morgan and other members of the Audubon Park morning crew not only encouraged me to do this project, but also encouraged me to keep up my jogging. My new administrative assistant, Roblynn Sliwinski, helped keep things going at 498 Productions and my law practice while I put the finishing touches on this book. Good listeners include a gang of characters known as DC, the Burgs, Junior, Scrunge, Big Puppy, the bears, Doc, Kili and others too numerous and crazy to mention.

My gang of "assistant editors" included Frank Daniels, Doug Sulpy, Perry Cox, Andrew Croft of *Beatlology*, Matt Hurwitz, Bob Koenig, Maury Mollo, Al Sussman of *Beatlefan*, Diana Thornton of Crescent Music Services and Trish Morgan of the East Jefferson Hospital Emergency Room. Once again, I received guidance from Susan McDaniel on marketing matters.

I would also like to thank all those who purchased my previous books and encouraged me to press forward with the Apple project. And, of course, I must thank my sisters, Dale Aronson and Jan Seltzer, and my parents, David and Jean Spizer, for their love, understanding and guidance.

## About Author

Bruce Spizer is a first generation Beatles fan and a life-long native of New Orleans, Louisiana. A tax man by day, Bruce is a board certified tax attorney and non-practicing certified public accountant. A paperback writer by night, he is the author of the critically acclaimed books *The Beatles Records on Vee-Jay* and the two-book set *The Beatles' Story on Capitol Records*. He is also a regular feature writer for *Beatlology Magazine*, *Beatlefan* and *Goldmine*.

Bruce was eight years old when the Beatles invaded America. He began listening to the radio at age two and was a diehard fan of WTIX, a top forty station that played a blend of New Orleans R&B music and top pop and rock hits. His first two albums were *The Coasters' Greatest Hits*, which he permanently "borrowed" from his older sisters, and *Meet The Beatles!*, which he still plays on his vintage 1964 Beatles record player.

During his high school and college days, Bruce played guitar in various bands that primarily covered hits of the sixties, including several Beatles songs. Due to the limited range of his baritone voice, his singing was primarily restricted to Ringo songs such as *With A Little Help From My Friends*. He was allowed to sing *Like A Rolling Stone* because his band mates didn't think Bob Dylan had a good voice. He was given the task of singing the Rolling Stones' *Get Off My Cloud* because he was the only one who could remember the words.

Although Bruce was the photography editor for the Newman High School yearbook, he decided against a career in photography because he didn't want to do weddings and bar mitzvahs. He wrote numerous album and concert reviews for his high school and college newspapers, including a review of *Abbey Road* that didn't claim Paul was dead. While at Tulane University, he served on the Board of Directors of the Mushroom, which was a highly-successful student-run record store.

Bruce received his B.A. (in economics), M.B.A. (concentrating in marketing and finance) and law degree from Tulane University. Upon graduation, he clerked for a judge at the Louisiana Supreme Court. During his tenure at the Court and for the first part of his legal career, he managed the Cold, which was a pop rock band that dominated the New Orleans music scene in the early eighties. Two of the group's singles, *You* and *Mesmerized*, received extensive airplay on New Orleans' top rated radio stations, including B-97, WQUE-FM and his childhood favorite WTIX.

Bruce has had his own law practice for nearly 20 years, specializing in tax and estate planning and administration. He has given numerous lectures on tax, retirement plans and estate planning matters. In his other life, Bruce is a frequent guest speaker at The Fest for Beatles Fans (the event formerly known as "Beatlefest") and other Beatles conventions. He has appeard on numerous national and local television and radio programs as a Beatles historian.

Bruce has an extensive Beatles collection, concentrating primarily on United States and Canadian first issue records, record promotional items, press kits and posters. His varied interests, background and training have made him uniquely qualified to detail the history of the Beatles American records.

---

### ERRORS AND OMISSIONS POLICY

Although every effort was made to ensure that the information contained in this book is accurate and complete, errors, omissions and typos do occur. At an early age, my extensive comic book reading taught me that writers often make mistakes. Marvel Comics addressed this problem by awarding a "no prize" to the first reader to write a letter informing the editor of the mistake. For those readers of this book unfamiliar with this marvelous tradition, a "no prize" is just what it sounds like—you get no prize. However, the person receiving a no prize is given credit for spotting the error.

In continuation of the errors and omissions policy adopted by me for my previous books, I will award a no prize to each person who is the first to inform me of a particular mistake. I will also award no prizes for new information and variations of records and promotional items pertaining to the subject matter and time frame covered by this book. I have already sent out dozens of no prizes to astute readers of the Vee-Jay and Capitol books. I am proud to say that nearly all of these no prizes were for new discoveries and typos rather than outright errors.

I must caution readers that you will not get a no prize merely by informing me that my book has information in it contradictory to what you have read in every other book on the Beatles. This book will have some facts different from what has previously been written. For example, the Apple discography on page 23 lists the release date for *Two Virgins* as January 6, 1969, rather than November of 1968. My research indicates that although the LP was scheduled for November release, it did not hit the stores until the following January. To get a no prize, you must prove me wrong. Also, you must be the first person to inform me of the error.

Because this book is over 300 pages, I am sure alert readers will find some typos and other glitches. Don't worry. I recently purchased a new stash of no prizes, so there is no danger of me running out of these coveted awards. Please write or email me (bruce@beatle.net) if you think you have what it takes to earn a no prize.

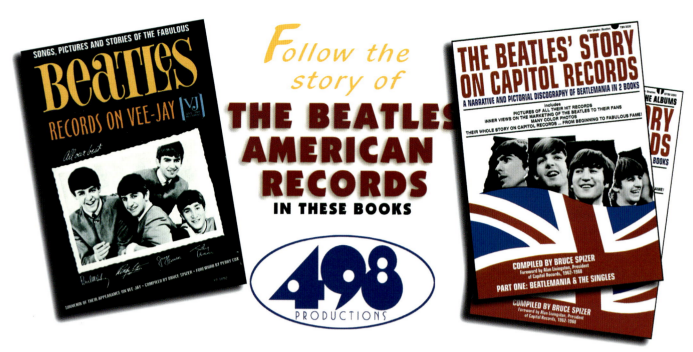

is for Apple

Beatles, Electronics, Films,
Merchandising, Publishing,
Records, Television.

3 SAVILE ROW/LONDON, W.1.

# "WE'VE GOT THIS THING CALLED APPLE, WHICH IS GOING TO BE RECORDS, FILMS AND ELECTRONICS."

On Tuesday evening, May 14, 1968, John Lennon and Paul McCartney were guests on NBC TV's *Tonight Show*. The plan was for the pair (shown in the above photo seated next to annoucer Ed McMahon) to promote the Beatles homegrown business venture, Apple Corps. Unfortunately, guest host Joe Garagiola (a former baseball player subbing for Johnny Carson) and guest Tellulah Bankhead (an actress past her prime) (both shown behind the desk) did little to facilitate discussion about the business. It wasn't until after a commercial break that Garagiola got around to asking, "How about this new organization, Apple?"

John explained that their accountant told them they could give their money to the government or do something with it. "So we decided to play businessmen for a bit, because we've got to run our own affairs now. So we've got this thing called Apple, which is going to be records, films and electronics, which all tie up. And to make a sort of an umbrella so people who want to make films about ... grass ... don't have to go on their knees in an office, you know, begging for a break. We'll try and do it like that. That's the idea. I mean we'll find out what happens, but that's what we're trying to do."

Lennon's remarks summarize how Apple came about and why the Beatles were becoming businessmen. The company was not created for Utopian reasons. It was formed to shelter the Beatles sizable income from British taxes. As for the Beatles running their own affairs, this was necessitated by death of manager Brian Epstein in August, 1967.

John and Paul told the TV audience what their company planned to do. It was to be a place where people with talent could go, rather than begging for a break from big business. Paul explained that "Big companies are so big that if you're little and good it takes you like 60 years to make it. And so people miss out on these little good people." John provided a metaphor based on George saying he was "sick of being told to keep out of the park." According to Lennon, "That's what it's all about, you know. We're trying to make a park for people to come in and do what they want." So that explained what the Beatles were trying to do. It wouldn't take long for the Beatles to "find out what happens." But on that idealistic evening in May, 1968, it sounded like a noble venture that the Beatles could pull off. After all, they were the Beatles.

**The above pictures of John and Paul on** *The Tonight Show* **are actual screen shots taken by Beatles fan Susan Petersen from a television set on the night the program aired.**

On June 20, 1963, The Beatles Limited was incorporated in the United Kingdom and assigned Company No. 764797. The corporation's shareholders were John Winston Lennon, George Harrison, James Paul McCartney and Richard Starkey, each owning 25 of the company's 100 ordinary £1 shares. In a move to reduce the huge tax burden facing the individual members of the group, a partnership named Beatles and Co. was established on April 19, 1967. Under the Deed of Partnership, each Beatle owed a 5% interest in the company, with the remaining 80% owned by The Beatles Limited. The partnership agreement provided that all of the income earned by the Beatles, with the exception of songwriting royalties, would be paid into The Beatles Limited. This substantially reduced taxes as the British corporate tax rates were significantly lower than the individual tax rates. Furthermore, income flowing into the corporation could be offset by corporate expenses. At the time this arrangement was set up, the Beatles had no idea how big those expenses would become.

By resolution dated November 17, 1967, the members of The Beatles Limited (John, George, Paul and Ringo) voted to changed the corporation's name to Apple Music Limited. The name change took effect on December 4, 1967, with the filing of the appropriate corporate documents. A special resolution adopted by the members on January 12, 1968, changed the name again, this time to Apple Corps Limited, the company's current name. This change took effect on February 9, 1968.

Paul is given credit for naming the company Apple. In an Apple press release, managing director Neil Aspinall stated: "Paul came up with the idea of calling it Apple, which he got from René Magritte...[who] painted a lot of green apples. I know Paul bought some of his paintings in 1966 or early 1967." This is confirmed by Barry Miles in his book *Paul McCartney, Many Years From Now*. Miles states that art dealer Robert Fraser delivered Magritte's *Le Jeu de mourre* to McCartney in the summer of 1966. The painting was one of Magritte's last works and features a large green apple. Alistair Taylor, who at the time was with Brian Epstein's NEMS Enterprises, recalls McCartney telling him in 1967 that the Beatles company was going to be called Apple. According to Taylor, Paul explained that "A is for Apple" is one of the first things a child learns. Apple Music quickly developed into Apple Corps, which is a pun blending apple core and Apple Corporation. When Ken Mansfield asked Paul why the company was named Apple, McCartney replied "Have you ever heard anyone say anything bad about an apple?"

**LOOK WHO'S JOINED THE APPLE CLUB NOW!**

**END A MEAL WITH AN APPLE
IT'S NATURE'S TOOTHBRUSH**

While the Beatles did not begin calling their company Apple until 1967, the seeds for the Apple brand name had been planted long before. The above ad with the Beatles plugging the dental benefits of eating apples appeared during the height of Beatlemania. At the end of the video *The First U.S. Visit*, George is shown eating an apple and singing "An apple for the teacher."

The first widespread appearance of the Apple name came in June, 1967, with the release of *Sgt. Pepper's Lonely Hearts Club Band*. The back of the album's jacket contains the following credit: "Cover by M C Productions and The Apple." This reference gave no clue as to what Apple was or hint that the Beatles would soon be operating as Apple.

The Apple name surfaced in November, 1967, with *Magical Mystery Tour*. An Apple logo, surrounded by the phrase "apple presents," appears above the group's name on the inside gatefold covers to the British EP and the Capitol LP. The accompanying booklets list Neil Aspinall and Mal Evans as "Editorial Consultants (for Apple)." The sleeve to the 1967 Beatles Christmas record refers to the company in its production credit, which reads "Another little bite of the Apple: Produced by George (Is Here Again) Martin."

The image of the Apple logo appearing on the *Magical Mystery Tour* package was inspired by Magritte's *Le Jeu de mourre*. The painting's translated title is *The Guessing Game*, which seems appropriate as one could only guess what the Beatles planned to do with their company.

As early as Spring, 1967, the group began meeting regularly with their advisors to discuss ways of spending their money to defer immediate recognition of income. Initial plans for the business followed traditional investment ideas associated with tax shelters, such as real estate, including a four-story building at 94 Baker Street that would later serve as Apple's first office. Other ideas, such as establishing a chain of card shops, were shot down by the group because they didn't want their name associated with "bloody greeting cards." Consideration was given to setting up a chain of record stores, but this idea was abandoned.

After rejecting a series of investment suggestions made by their accountants and other advisors, the group decided to enter into an area promoted by Paul–music publishing. Due to the numerous recordings and performances of Lennon-McCartney songs, Paul was well aware of how much money music publishers could make with hit tunes. Years later, Paul would increase his own massive fortune by obtaining the publishing rights to several songs, including the Buddy Holly catalog. But in 1967, the idea was for the Beatles company to develop new songwriting talent.

Although Beatles manager Brian Epstein had little involvement with Apple, his death on August 27, 1967, changed everything. John was the one who best understood the serious effect that Brian's death would have on the group. Shortly thereafter, Lennon confided in Alistair Taylor, "We've fookin' had it now."

The first changes came within Brian's management company, NEMS Enterprises. Brian's younger brother, Clive Epstein, was quickly appointed head of the company. Robert Stigwood, who had brought in new bands such as Cream and the Bee-Gees, left NEMS and took his acts with him, forming his own company, Robert Stigwood Organization. Stigwood's departure was prompted by the Beatles informing him that they would not accept him as their manager.

Unlike Brian and Stigwood, Clive had little interest in developing new talent, an idea embraced by the Beatles. In response to rumors that the Beatles would be leaving NEMS, the company's press officer, Tony Barrow, issued a statement in October that "NEMS continues to handle the management, agency and other business interests of the Beatles." The relationship would not last much longer.

Barrow also made a tantalizing announcement that the Beatles and Rolling Stones were considering a business merger. The October 28, 1967, *Record World* reported that under the plan, "both groups would retain their own identity and continue recording separately for different labels, but would become joint owners of recording studios, possibly joint film producers, and act as a launching pad for new groups and artists." Barrow was quoted as saying that "Nobody contemplates the boys ever issuing a 'Rolling Beatles' disc, but we look upon any merger as a fusion of nine people's business talents in a new and exciting project." Although nothing came of the proposed merger, the Beatles own company, Apple, did set up a recording studio, produce films and sign and promote new groups and artists.

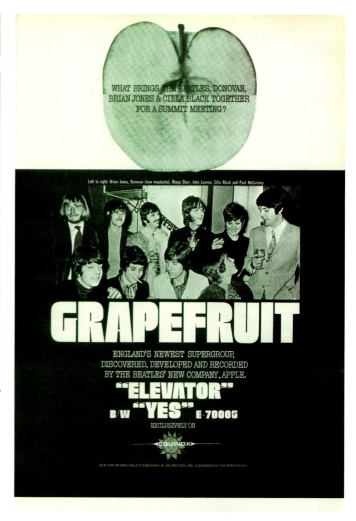

The above slipsheet to the Japanese issue of *Hey Jude* (Apple AR-2120) shows the Beatles practicing their dance steps for the grand finale of *Magical Mystery Tour*. The April 20, 1968, *Billboard* contains an ad for Grapefruit's single *Elevator* b/w *Yes*. It features a picture of Brian Jones, Donavon, Ringo Starr, John Lennon, Cilla Black and Paul McCartney standing behind the group, which is billed as "England's newest supergroup, discovered, developed and recorded by the Beatles new company, Apple."

The first Apple project was *Magical Mystery Tour*, a psychedelic fantasy film featuring the Beatles. The movie was shot in segments without benefit of a script during September, October and November of 1967. Although Apple Films head Denis O'Dell wanted the movie to debut on American television (and was in negotiations with NBC and ABC), Paul insisted that the BBC be given first bite of the apple. The move backfired when the BBC showed the color film in black and white on the evening of December 26, 1967. The movie was savagely panned by the critics, causing NBC and ABC to drop their pursuit of the film. Rather than receiving a million dollars or so for U.S. broadcast rights, Apple had to settle for meager rental revenues from limited American screenings at college campuses. While the film was dubbed a failure at the time, it is now regarded as an interesting period piece depicting the free-wheeling spirit of the sixties.

Paul had pitched his idea for the movie in April, 1967, to Brian Epstein, who would have coordinated the project had he been alive. With Brian gone, Paul took charge to ensure that his idea would become reality. Many of the logistical details were handled by Beatles road manager Neil Aspinall. His successful handling of this chore influenced the Beatles decision to hire Aspinall as Managing Director of Apple. This action was not made based upon his experience or qualifications. It was based on his loyalty and the total faith and trust that each of the Beatles had in Aspinall. The group hired Alistair Taylor away from NEMS to serve as Apple's General Manager.

Meanwhile, the Beatles were anxious to get their publishing company up and running. They hired another former NEMS employee, Terry Doran, to head Apple Music Publishing. Although Doran had no experience in the music publishing business, he had contacts and knew young and upcoming songwriters. Doran quickly signed George Alexander to a songwriting contract with Apple. Shortly thereafter, Alexander and three other musicians formed a band. John Lennon named the group Grapefruit in recognition of a poetry book written by Yoko Ono. As Apple had not yet established its record division at that time, the group had to look elsewhere to get a recording contract. In England, the band was signed to EMI's Stateside subsidiary. In the U.S., Grapefruit was signed to Equinox Records. Although the Beatles helped promote the group, Grapefruit had only moderate success in England (a number 21 hit with its debut single, *Dear Delilah*).

Apple Music Publishing signed other songwriters, including Jackie Lomax, who would later record for Apple Records. His performance of George Harrison's *Sour Milk Sea* (Apple 1802) was one of the first singles released by the company.

The Beatles also ventured into electronics, placing their faith and money with a 27-year-old Greek television repairman, Alexis Mardas. John was particularly infatuated by Mardas and his inventions and dubbed him "Magic Alex." At first, they formed a company with him named Fiftyshapes Ltd. It was later renamed Apple Electronics and became part of Apple.

The Fool painted a colorful mural over the exterior walls to the Baker Street building that housed Apple, the group's clothing store (shown above on an Apple postcard). Invitations to the store's December 5, 1967, opening (right) were also designed by the Fool.

Magic Alex impressed the boys with his electronic toys. Some had potential, such as a device that enabled a person to listen to a record player through a portable transistor radio, while others had absolutely no practical value, such as a small metal box with 12 small lights that did nothing and was called a "nothing-box."

Mardas was always coming up with ideas. He claimed he could invent a force field that would cause a house to hover above the ground. Alistair Taylor recalls Magic Alex creating a device that enabled a person to reach another person by phone merely by saying the individual's name. This was an early form of voice-recognition technology. Alistair also remembers Mardas demonstrating wallpaper that could serve as a stereo system's speakers. He attracted the attention of record companies by working on a method to prevent home taping of vinyl records. By August, 1968, Apple Electronics had patented eight of his inventions, though none ever went into production.

The Beatles faith in Magic Alex led to them requesting that he build a recording studio in the basement of Apple headquarters. Mardas boasted that his studio would have a 72-track recorder. This was at a time when 16 tracks was state-of-the-art and EMI was still limited to eight. The result was a total disaster (as detailed on pages 148-149).

Apple Retail's first endeavor, a clothing store called "Apple," opened towards the end of 1967 on the ground floor of the group's Baker Street building. The store was initially run by Pete Shotton, who had no retail clothing experience, but had played with John in his pre-Beatles band, the Quarry Men. He was quickly replaced by a more-experienced John Lyndon in early 1968.

The bulk of the boutique's clothing was designed by a trio of Dutch fashion designers, Simon Posthuma, Marijke Koger and Josje Leeger. The three hooked up with British publicist Barry Finch and began calling themselves The Fool. The Beatles became aware of The Fool through their costume designs for productions held at Brian Epstein's Savile Theatre. This led to The Fool designing outfits for the band's *Our World* television broadcast of *All You Need Is Love*. The Fool was also hired to paint George's fireplace in his Esher bungalow and John's Bechstein piano. When they approached the band about setting up a boutique using the Beatles money, the Beatles, looking to get into retail, eagerly agreed.

While The Fool may have been good fashion designers, they were even better at spending Apple's money. They hired 30 art students to paint an elaborate mural over the outside walls of the Baker Street building.

The Fool's excessive spending was not limited to visuals. Even though inside labels would remain unseen, The Fool insisted that their clothing be adorned with expensive handmade silk tags. And, of course, Apple was expected to provide sufficient funds for The Fool to live a lifestyle appropriate for world class fashion designers.

The Apple boutique was launched with a splashy party on December 5, 1967, and opened for business two days later. Employees quickly noticed the lack of business controls and began raiding the cash registers on a regular basis. Customers came by to look at the beautiful clothes and the beautiful people, browse and shoplift. When neighboring businesses complained about the mural, Apple was forced to paint over it. The combination of The Fool's excessive spending, employee pilferage, shoplifting and sluggish sales led to losses approaching a half million dollars in six months. The Beatles decided to end the financial bleeding by closing the shop. At John's suggestion, the store opened its doors one last time on July 30, 1968, inviting the public to take what they wanted in a free-for-all orgy of legal shoplifting.

Having set up film, publishing, electronics and retail divisions, the Beatles finally turned their attention to what they did best–make records. Apple Records was set up with the same philosophy as the company's other divisions. It would discover and development new talent. In addition, the Beatles hoped that many of their musician friends would switch labels and sign with Apple when their existing contracts expired.

Apple hired Ron Kass, an American who headed Liberty Records' British operations, to be president of Apple Records. Peter Asher, who had gained fame in the midsixties as half of Peter and Gordon, was brought in by Paul McCartney to serve as Apple's A&R (artists and repertoire) man. His job was to discover and develop recording artists for the label. His first significant signing was James Taylor.

Rather than hire an expensive ad agency, Paul decided that he could fashion a campaign to launch Apple Records. One evening he dropped by Alistair Taylor's home to kick around ideas. Paul came up with the concept of a one-man band who would be touted as an Apple success story. McCartney convinced Alistair that he would be perfect for the role.

Later that week, the pair went to a photography studio to shoot the ad. Alistair sat on a stool with a bass drum strapped on his back. He wore a harmonica around his neck and strummed a guitar. He was surrounded by a microphone, tape recorder, washboard tub, brass instruments and books. And, for the crowning touch, Paul purchased a bowler hat for Alistair. To add to the authenticity of the proceedings, McCartney insisted that Taylor sing. When Alistair protested that he was a lousy singer, Paul reminded him that he was being photographed, not recorded. As the photographer shot away, Alistair crooned *When Irish Eyes Are Smiling*.

The completed ad (shown left) was placed in a number of music magazines and distributed as a handbill poster throughout London and the surrounding provinces. In America, the ad ran in the May 25, 1968, issue of *Rolling Stone*. Apple received over 400 tapes in two weeks. Hundreds more arrived in the following months. Although many tapes were ignored, Peter Asher did hire a staff to listen to them. According to Asher, "None of it was much good unfortunately. Out of the myriad of tapes we got in the mail, we didn't sign anyone." A discography of the records released by Apple appears on pages 22-24.

# This man has talent...

One day he sang his songs to a tape recorder (borrowed from the man next door). In his neatest handwriting he wrote an explanatory note (giving his name and address) and, remembering to enclose a picture of himself, sent the tape, letter and photograph to *apple* music, 94 Baker Street, London, W.1. If you were thinking of doing the same thing yourself–do it now! **This man now owns a Bentley!**

M.P.Co.

Negotiations for the rights to manufacture and distribute Apple product in America began in February, 1968, with Neil Aspinall flying to New York to meet with representatives of several U.S. record companies. The June 1, 1968, *Billboard* reported that five companies were vying for the rights. Capitol's relationship with the Beatles gave the company the edge.

On June 20, 1968, exactly five years after the formation of the corporation that became Apple, Capitol Records issued a series of press releases about the Beatles new venture. Capitol proudly proclaimed: "Beatle Paul McCartney and Ronald S. Kass, Head of Apple Corps Music, today jointly announced with Alan W. Livingston, President, Capitol Industries, Inc., and Stanley M. Gortikov, President, Capitol Records, Inc., the completion of negotiations and the signing of an agreement whereby Capitol Records will manufacture and distribute all Apple Records product for the United States and Canada. Climaxing the prolonged negotiations between representatives of Apple Corps in London, New York and Los Angeles, and Capitol Records, is the announcement that The Beatles themselves will in the future be released on their Apple label." Another press release stated that Apple Music would be a "fully functional record company with facilities planned for all major countries of the world," and that Apple was "pledged to seek out, produce and promote young unknown talents to star status."

Other announcements dealt with planned record releases. One stated that the first Apple Records album would be the George Harrison score for the film *Wonderwall* and that the next two albums tentatively set for release were "The Beatles 1968 successor to 'Magical Mystery Tour' and an LP featuring the voice, guitar and songs of former New Yorker, James Taylor." Another stated that the first Apple single would "feature Mary Hopkin, a young Welsh girl hailing from the same village as Richard Burton and Dylan Thomas," and that the "Arrangement and production on this first Apple single was handled personally by McCartney." The announcement regarding Apple's film division stated that Apple hoped to have four major productions in progress by the end of the year. In addition, the company was planning to make another Beatles picture as well as film versions of John Lennon's two books, *In His Own Write* and *A Spaniard in the Works*. Many of the details from the press releases were reported in the June 29 *Billboard*.

At the request of the Beatles, Capitol Records executive Ken Mansfield, shown below seated between Paul and Ringo in a meeting with Ron Kass (seated left) and Capitol president Stan Gortikov (standing), was given the title of U.S. Manager of Apple Records. He had met the group during their 1965 visit to Los Angeles, which included a visit to the Capitol Tower and two concerts at the Hollywood Bowl. Under the arrangement set up in the summer of 1968, Capitol continued to pay Mansfield's salary. Although his duties included the oversight of all independent labels distributed by Capitol, Apple took up nearly all of his time.

Mansfield became the Beatles and Apple's liaison in America. He was in charge of all aspects of the American operation, including release dates, promotion, mastering and art work. This was quite a responsibility as America was the Beatles biggest and most important market.

3 Savile Row London W.1.

**In 1968, Apple moved its headquarters to 3 Savile Row, London. The company prepared a postcard (center) showing off its new building. The above pictures of George (left) and Ringo (right) at the front door to 3 Savile Row were taken in 1969 by Beatles fan Cathy Sarver.**

The August 17 *Billboard* reported that the Beatles Apple project was set to roll in America on August 25 with the release, through Capitol, of five discs. The initial releases would be George Harrison's *Wonderwall* soundtrack album and four singles, including a new Beatles disc featuring "two new songs written by them, *Revolution* and *Hey Judge*." (The latter song was really titled *Hey Jude*, and the release of *Wonderwall* was pushed back to the end of the year.) The article reported that the Beatles were deeply involved in all of Apple's divisions, namely music, films, electronics and merchandising, and that a recording studio was being built in Apple's new London headquarters.

Propelled by huge sales of the Beatles *Hey Jude* single and *The White Album*, as well as Mary Hopkin's *Those Were The Days*, Apple got off to a tremendous start. The February 1, 1969, *Billboard* reported that Capitol presented the Beatles with $2,500,000 in royalties for the last three months of 1968.

While Apple's success in America was cause for celebration, things in London were a different matter. At an executive board meeting at Apple, Alistair Taylor gave the Beatles a heavy dose of reality. He informed the group that Apple was losing about £50,000 a week. The group's substantial revenue could not keep pace with the company's out-of-control spending. Salaries were too high, and employees were ordering expensive art and furniture for their offices and running up outrageous expense accounts. The Beatles were also guilty of excessive spending. And then there was the outright theft. People were stealing records, office equipment and even the copper stripping off the roof of Apple's Savile Row headquarters.

Alistair warned the group that if things continued as they were, the Beatles would lose their money within a year. He admitted that he and Neil Aspinall were not up to the task of running a complicated business such as Apple and told them that the company needed an experienced businessman such as Lord Beeching to take over and set things right. Beeching was the former head of British Railways.

Alistair got through to John, who, in a brutally frank interview with Ray Coleman in *Disc and Music Echo* maga-zine (January, 1969), spilled the beans. Lennon stated that Apple needed streamlining and that if things carried on, "all of us will be broke in six months." He elaborated, "[W]e can't let Apple go on like this. We started off with loads of ideas of what we wanted to do...it didn't work out because we aren't practical and we weren't quick enough to realize we needed a businessman's brain to run the whole thing.."

Although Alistair's naming of Lord Beeching as someone who could run Apple was only an example and not a suggestion, John met with him just the same. Beeching was not interested in sorting out the mess and advised Lennon that the group should get back to what they were good at–making music.

Paul was also looking for answers. He was now seriously involved with Linda Eastman and discussed the problems at Apple with her father, Lee Eastman. Contrary to erroneous stories published over the years, Lee Eastman had no connection with the Eastman Kodak company. He had changed his last name from Epstein to Eastman in his early twenties. Lee Eastman was a successful attorney and expert in international copyright law. He owned some valuable music publishing copyrights and was an art collector. He brought his son, John, into his law practice, which was known as Eastman and Eastman. When Paul asked Lee Eastman who he would recommend to fix Apple, Lee suggested his son John.

With Paul's blessings, John Eastman flew to London to survey the situation. He made some tax suggestions and advised the Beatles to buy NEMS, which was now owned primarily by Brian's estate. Eastman explained to the group that under their contract with EMI, 25% of their royalties were paid directly to NEMS. By purchasing the company, the Beatles would in effect receive their full royalties from EMI. Clive Epstein, who was handling Brian's estate and serving as chairman of NEMS, was interested in selling the company to obtain cash needed for payment of the substantial estate taxes due at the end of March. Eastman began negotiations with Clive, suggesting a purchase price of one million pounds. The transaction was to be financed by advance royalty payments from EMI.

Meanwhile, Allen Klein was getting ready to make his play to become the Beatles manager. Klein was an accountant who got his start in the music industry by auditing the books of record companies on behalf of musicians. Klein was aware that labels consistently underreported royalties owed to their acts. He became an expert at finding money already owed to artists. After successfully aiding Bobby Darin, Klein began picking up other clients. He became Sam Cooke's manager. This led to him securing the music publishing of Cooke's catalog for his management company, Abkco.

Although Klein had a questionable reputation, he got results. Not only was he getting his clients the royalties they were really owed, but also he was negotiating new recording contracts with higher royalty rates. Klein became the manager of British acts such as the Rolling Stones and Herman's Hermits. While he got the Stones a higher royalty rate than the Beatles, his acquisition of the American publishing of the band and other dealings left a sour taste with Mick Jagger and the other Stones. They parted ways, but not until Abkco had locked up the Stones sixties catalog.

Although Allen Klein had fantasized about managing the Beatles when the group first made its mark in America, he was a realist and knew nothing could happen as long as Brian Epstein was in charge. After Brian's death, he began his quest by meeting with Clive Epstein and Peter Brown.

In his memoirs, *The Love You Make*, Brown found Klein "so foul-mouthed and abusive that I ended the meeting in a few moments and had him shown the door."

After hearing reports from London of John's claim that the Beatles were going broke, Klein renewed his efforts, this time going for the direct approach by securing a meeting with Lennon, which took place at the Dorchester Hotel in London on the night of January 27, 1969. Allen Klein made the most of his time with John and Yoko, impressing both with his knowledge of the music industry, the Beatles music and Yoko's art. John immediately hired Klein to handle his financial affairs and informed the other Beatles of his decision the next day. He sent the following letter to Sir Joseph Lockwood, head of EMI: "Dear Sir Joe: I've asked Allen Klein to look after my things. Please give him any information he wants and full cooperation. Love, John Lennon." Similar letters, dated January 29, 1969, were sent to Clive Epstein, music publisher Dick James and the Beatles accountants.

When Mick Jagger heard that Klein had met with John, he decided to brief the Beatles on the Rolling Stones' experiences with Klein, who was the band's manager. The Stones were in the process of terminating their relationship with Abkco, and Jagger apparently wanted to warn his friends about Klein. He agreed to drop by Apple to give a firsthand account of the Stones' dealings with Klein.

**Apple prepared a colorful assortment of promotional items, including the paperweight, lighter, necklace, box and stuffed apple radio (show left), set of garden stickers (shown right) and dartboard (shown center above).**

The details of Jagger's Apple appearance vary among those telling the story; however, all agree on one thing. Mick did not advise the Beatles to stay away from Allen Klein. Paul speculates that Jagger felt intimidated by the presence of the Beatles and was reluctant to give them advice. Peter Brown recalls John warning Klein of the meeting with Jagger and allowing him to attend. If Allen Klein was in fact at the meeting, it would have been very awkward for Jagger to give a candid account of his dealings with Klein, particularly since the Stones were still involved with Abkco.

After completing the *Get Back* sessions, the Beatles met to decide who would manage their affairs. John convinced Ringo and George that Allen Klein was the man for the job. On February 3, 1969, the Beatles hired Klein to review their finances. Although Paul was against this decision, he chose not to fight the others, recognizing that the group needed to hire someone to straighten things out. McCartney was able to get Eastman and Eastman hired as counsel for the group. The February 15 *Billboard* reported that Klein had taken over the business affairs of the Beatles and Apple and that his function was to review and negotiate various business activities of the group.

In addition to reviewing Apple's finances, Klein also became involved with the proposed purchase of NEMS. He pointed out to the Beatles that the group would have to generate approximately two million pounds of pre-tax revenue to purchase NEMS for one million pounds. He hoped that an audit of the payments made to the group by NEMS would reveal that NEMS had shortchanged the Beatles in prior years. He would use this as leverage to reduce the purchase price. Klein contacted Clive to request that he defer any decision regarding the sale of NEMS for three weeks.

John Eastman also had issues with NEMS, believing that Brian had acted improperly by inserting the 25% royalty clause into the band's contract with EMI. The effect of this provision was to give NEMS 25% of the Beatles royalty income for the entire nine-year length of the contract even though NEMS was no longer providing

management services. On February 14, 1969, John Eastman sent a letter to Clive Epstein referring to Klein's audit and "the propriety of the negotiations surrounding the nine-year agreement between E.M.I., the Beatles and Nems." Clive was offended by the insinuation that Brian had acted unfairly. He had also grown tired of conditions and warrantees that Eastman wanted attached to the proposed sale. Without calling Klein or Eastman, he abruptly sold the NEMS stock to a group of investors known as the Triumph Trust. When Klein tried playing hardball with Triumph by instructing EMI to pay all royalties directly to Apple, EMI wisely froze the Beatles royalty payments until the parties settled their differences.

A series of tough negotiations between Klein and Triumph eventually led to a settlement under which NEMS forfeited all its rights to income from the Beatles except as provided for in the deal. The Beatles paid £750,000 plus 25% of the royalties frozen by EMI (approximately £300,000). In addition, Triumph would receive 5% of the Beatles royalties under the EMI contract from 1972 through 1976 (rather than the 25% originally called for). The Beatles also paid £50,000 to buy out NEMS' 23% ownership interest in their film company, Subafilms. The agreement gave the Beatles an option to buy NEMS' 4.5% ownership in Northern Songs at a fixed rate well below the stock's market value. Finally, the Beatles exchanged their 10% interest in NEMS for 226,000 shares of Triumph. Although the Beatles paid more than the one million pounds originally negotiated by John Eastman, the group obtained total ownership of Subafilms and received stock in Triumph as well as an option to purchase additional shares in Northern Songs at a bargain rate.

On March 21, 1969, Allen Klein was hired as business manager for Apple. He immediately cleaned house, firing nearly everyone in sight. Among the casualties were long-time Beatles confidant Alistair Taylor, Apple Records president Ron Kass and Magic Alex. Neil Aspinall was also on Klein's hit list, but the Beatles insisted that Aspinall keep his job with Apple. Derek Taylor was spared, apparently as a reward for helping set up Klein's initial meeting with John and Yoko.

Although Paul had reluctantly gone along with the decision to have Klein look into the group's financial affairs, he had yet to sign a management contract with Abkco. On Friday evening, May 9, 1969, the group met at Olympic Studios for what was intended to be a recording session. The other Beatles told Paul he needed to sign the agreement because Klein was heading back to New York the next day. Paul told the others that the Beatles were the biggest act in the world and therefore Klein would take 15% rather than the 20% management fee called for in the contract presented to the group by Klein. He wanted to have his lawyer review the agreement on Monday. The others accused Paul of stalling and stormed out of the studio.

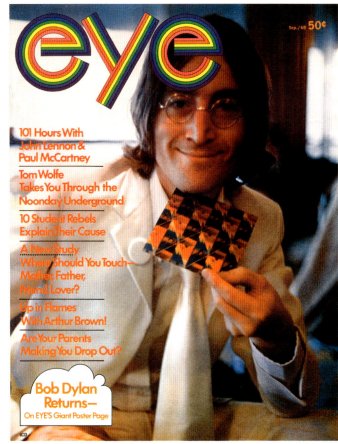

**Paul (pictured left) and John held a press conference at New York's Americana Hotel on May 13, 1968, to announce and answer questions about Apple. The September, 1968, issue of *eye* magazine featured a story on their New York adventures. The cover photograph of John (right) was taken by Linda Eastman (who would later marry Paul) at Kennedy Airport just prior to Lennon and McCartney heading back to England.**

Paul ventured over to another room at Olympic where Steve Miller was recording. After telling Miller of his battle with the others, he asked if he could take out his frustrations on the drums. Miller readily agreed and he and Paul completed a track for Miller's new album. After laying down the drums, McCartney added bass, guitar and backing vocals. The song was appropriately titled *My Dark Hour*.

The May 31, 1969, *Billboard* reported that Abkco, headed by Allen Klein, had signed a three-year contract to manage Apple and the Beatles. The article failed to mention that Paul refused to sign the agreement.

Ken Mansfield was disturbed by Allen Klein's firing of Apple Records head Ron Kass and informed Capitol and Apple that he was resigning. Kass was hired to run MGM Records and offered Mansfield a key executive position with the company. Although Klein had dismissed nearly everyone in Apple's London office, he flew to Los Angeles to discuss Apple's restructuring and attempt to reverse Ken's decision to leave Apple.

Klein informed Ken that Apple would triple his Capitol salary if he agreed to remain as U.S. manager of Apple Records. Mansfield found the salary tempting, but was leery of accepting the offer due to his loyalty to Ron Kass and uneasy feelings about Klein's reputation. As the meeting progressed, Mansfield realized it would be difficult to get Klein to accept his rejection of the offer. In a move as bizarre as the situation at Apple, Mansfield issued a challenge. He would remain with Apple provided Klein could beat him in one set of tennis.

Ken played tennis on a regular basis and was convinced that he could easily beat the heavyset Klein. When the game began, Mansfield realized he had underestimated Klein's competitive nature and that he was in for the game of his life. The two battled until Ken finally won fifteen games to thirteen. Afterwards they shook hands and it was over. Mansfield no longer worked for Apple or the Beatles.

Having failed to keep Mansfield aboard, Klein turned to his own company to fill the void. The running of Apple's day-to-day affairs was turned over to Abkco's Alan Steckler.

With his team in place, Allen Klein focused his attention to renegotiating the Beatles contract with the Gramophone Company Limited ("EMI"). Under the terms of the contract, which ran from January 26, 1967, through January 26, 1976, EMI had the exclusive right to manufacture, distribute, sell and exploit phonograph records and magnetic tapes of performances of the Beatles and the individual members of the group throughout the world. The Beatles were required to provide five singles and five albums. By the summer of 1969, the Beatles had all but completed their recording obligations under the agreement, thus giving the group leverage to renegotiate.

Klein informed EMI that the Beatles would not provide any new records unless the group was given a substantial increase in royalties. After months of tough negotiations, a new agreement was reached. Under the 1967 contract, the Beatles were getting 39 cents per album. The new contract provided for 58 cents per album through 1972 and 72 cents per album for the remainder of the term.

John and Paul (shown above with apples and Magic Alex) returned to London's Heathrow Airport on May 16, 1968, after announcing Apple to America. During their New York visit, they held an Apple directors' meeting on a Chinese junk sailing around New York Harbor, conducted interviews at their St. Regis Hotel suite with *Time*, *Newsweek*, *Business Week* and *Fortune* magazines, gave a press conference and did *The Tonight Show*.

As part of the agreement, EMI granted Apple Records, as licensee, EMI's rights to the Beatles for the United States, Canada and Mexico. This exclusive license covered all recordings made by the Beatles (either as a group or as individuals) during the term of the contract, as well as all records previously made by the Beatles owned by and available to EMI. Apple then entered into an agreement with Capitol under which Capitol manufactured and distributed the records and tapes for Apple. This brought significant revenue to Apple Records, who previously did not receive any income from the sales of Beatles records and tapes.

*Abbey Road* was the first album covered under the new agreement. Anxious to keep the money flowing, Klein had Apple (through Abkco) put together the *Hey Jude* album for the United States, Canada and Mexico.

Although Paul was pleased with the new recording contract negotiated by Klein, he never accepted Klein as his manager. By 1973, the other Beatles became dissatisfied with Klein, and their business relationship ended. They battled each other in court for many years, but those lurid stories are beyond the scope of this book.

Throughout all the craziness, Neil Aspinall remained. As of the 2003 publication of this book, he is still serving as Apple's Managing Director. Under his care, Apple made a triumphant return in the nineties, releasing six new albums, five of which sold in the millions.

"This thing called Apple" may not have worked out the way the Beatles intended, but Apple has ensured that the legacy of the Beatles music will be preserved for generations to come.

This colorful "A is for Apple" poster was designed by Simon & Marijke of The Fool. The 20" x 30" poster was printed in England by Trade Platemaking Services. It was available at the Apple boutique on Baker Street. Copies of the poster were sold in the United States exclusively through the Beatles fan club, Beatles (U.S.A.) Limited, for $1.25 each.

# The Fool is Four.

Four persons with mouths and minds who make fantastic sounds.

Three of them are Dutch.

One's a Briton.

Their names are Sea-moan, Yosha, Mar-eye-ka, and Barry.

That's not the way you spell them, it's the way they sound.

Except of course British Barry.

The Fool does everything, separately and together.

They're fashion designers, painters, poets, musicians, boutique innovators, and dancers.

They did some costuming for the Beatles, and later became their business partners.

Then the Fool moved on and made an utterly exciting record album.

Which is the whole point of this story.

You must hear it.

The latest of the new Creative Wave on their first LP from Mercury Records.

SR 61178

*mercury*

A Product of Mercury Record Productions, Inc.
35 East Wacker Drive, Chicago, Illinois 60601
A Conelco Corporation

After the Beatles tired of The Fool's extravagant spending, The Fool latched onto Mercury Records in the United States. In order to "vibrate with the engineer," they banned Mercury's head of A&R, Bob Reno, from their recording sessions. In *Apple to the Core*, Reno stated that The Fool "cost Mercury a bundle of money." Reno gave the following description of the album: "It was dreadful and it sold about three copies. Needless to say, the art work was gorgeous." So was the above ad, which ran in *Billboard*.

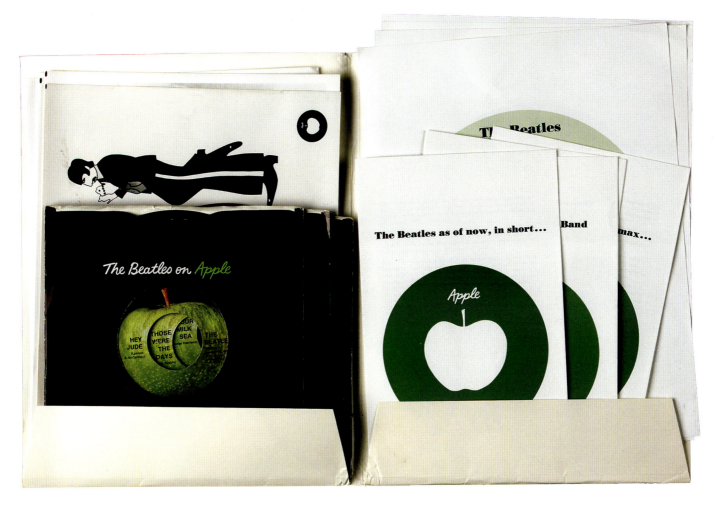

## APPLE'S FIRST FOUR

On August 22, 1968, employees of Capitol Records sent press kits to radio station program directors across the United States. The kits were packaged in white envelopes with an Apple logo in the upper left corner serving as the return address. The logo was a solid green circle with a white apple in the center with the word "Apple" in white script letters above the stem. The lucky recipients of these envelopes would be among the first people in America to read about and, more importantly, hear the initial offerings of the Beatles new venture, Apple Records.

For those disc jockeys who had been monitoring Apple's progress by reading trade magazine articles, the arrival of the classy looking white envelope with the Apple logo was truly a magic moment. Upon ripping open the envelope, the recipient encountered a glossy cream colored folder with a large Apple logo on its front side. Inside the folder was a treasure of sound, visuals and information.

In contrast to the white envelope and folder were four distinguished-looking black center cut record sleeves. One proclaimed "The Beatles on Apple" in an attractive script font. The group's name was in white and "Apple" in green. The other three sleeves merely said "Apple" in the same eye-catching green script letters. Peeking out of the center of each sleeve was a record label covered with a green Granny Smith apple.

The sleeves were not the only thing different about the singles. While most records had the same design on both sides, these discs had a full green apple on one side and a

sliced apple with its exposed white innards on the other side. The singles also had something new to most Americans–a slip guard consisting of 360 interlocking serrations surrounding the label. Although many people thought the tiny grooves were Apple's innovation, several British labels has been pressing discs with slip guards for years. By coincidence, Capitol had retooled its pressing plants for slip guard singles in August, 1968, so the Apple singles were among the first Capitol manufactured 45s to take on the new look.

For program directors, the most important part of the package was the first new Beatles single in over five months: *Hey Jude* b/w *Revolution*. The quality of both sides of the single assured that listeners would stay put when the songs were aired. Disc jockeys were delighted to see that the running time for *Hey Jude* was an incredible 7:11. At the time the 45 was released in 1968, singles normally contained songs running between two and three minutes long. This record would truly be a DJ's best friend when nature called or a groupie dropped by the station. Because the Beatles were under contract to Capitol Records, the single was assigned a record catalog number in the Capitol series, 2276.

As detailed in the chapter on the *Hey Jude* single, there are over a dozen different label variations for the 45. The press kit contained first label Los Angeles pressings, **APP 2276.01L(i)(as)**, packaged inside a tab cut "The Beatles on Apple" sleeve.

The other three singles included in the folder were also pressed by Capitol in Los Angeles and packaged in tab cut sleeves. Unlike the Beatles disc, they have Apple catalog numbers, beginning with 1800. The first of these was *Thingumybob* b/w *Yellow Submarine* by the John Foster and Sons Ltd. Black Dyke Mills Band. The text on both sides of the record is printed vertically. *Thingumybob* is credited to "McCartney & Lennon" rather than the normal "Lennon & McCartney." Both sides of the disc have a Paul McCartney production credit. Paul also produced Apple 1801, Mary Hopkin's *Those Were The Days* b/w *Turn, Turn, Turn*. All label information on this single appears horizontally. Apple 1802 paired *Sour Milk Sea* and *The Eagle Laughs At You* by Jackie Lomax. The record was produced by George Harrison, who is given production credit on the label. George is mistakenly listed as the writer of both songs. Although he wrote *Sour Milk Sea*, the B side was penned by Lomax.

The press kit also included two 8" x 10" black and white glossies of each of the artists featured on the records. The Beatles are represented by their cartoon images from the *Yellow Submarine* film, which had yet to be released in America. Paul and his sheep dog Martha are pictured with the Black Dyke Mills Band in the brass band's horizontal publicity still (shown on page 108). Jackie Lomax and the lovely Mary Hopkin are each featured in vertical pictures (shown on page 20). All four glossies have the artist's name printed below the picture towards the left side and the Apple logo in the lower right corner.

Recipients of the press kit learned about each artist through separate 8½" x 11" information sheets and 5½" x 8½" booklets. The text on the information sheets is cred-

ited to Apple press agent Derek Taylor. Although no credit is given in the booklets, the writing appears to be in the style of Derek Taylor as well.

The information sheet on the Beatles reads in part:

"It is The Beatles again, doing it again, doing our minds in again with the magical mystic Beatle mastery of their medium. They have written and produced two sides for this new single which you know, you know beyond the thinnest wisp of a shadow of a doubt, will engage the most profound admiration from the public, from the industry, from those in other groups, who strive to match The Beatles achievements. *Hey Jude* is lead sung by Paul McCartney and it is a long lovely loving lovesong offering hope ("Hey Jude, don't be afraid...take a sad song and make it better...") and beauty in the words and extraordinary melodic subtleties in the music. *Hey Jude* is the longest song ever recorded by The Beatles (seven minutes and five seconds), and I would say it was the best if it weren't for all those others that have gone before. I would say it was the best if, also, it were not that *Revolution* – main voice John – were not so breathtaking vital and insistent. This is the new Beatle peace – with strength message, with the voices forced out of the grooves by a backing as new for Capitol now as *Strawberry Fields* was for then. A theme for today, *Revolution*, written by revolutionary visionaries. The Beatles are without peer. Their music is magnificent. It can be said again and again as they sing and sing it again."

The booklet on the Beatles is full of optimism and tells a story of the Beatles quite different from the tensions that sometimes surfaced during the recording of the group's first Apple album:

THE BEATLES

"The Beatles are in good health, of sound heart and willing spirit, and by the Fall the new evidence of their continuing supremacy will be spinning on the world's turntables around the symbol of their own shimmering green Apple label.

"At his moment they are deeply involved in the twin responsibilities of recording the album-successor to the profoundly respected *Sergeant Pepper's Lonely Hearts Club Band* and of administering the Happy Apple complex of companies in London.

"John, Paul, George and Ringo, firmly united one for all and all for one as The Beatles, growing up and outwards, phasing their expansion so as to keep a hold on which might otherwise consume their precious careers and confuse the thread of their energy sources are confident and cheerful and the human condition will be thrilled by the coming results of their willing and enduring Beatle-bondage. Unhampered by the pressures of world stardom, entranced by their opportunities, stimulated by the blossoming of Apple, they will give us new wonders to soothe our pain.

"The end for now, but there is no end."

While the comments about "Happy Apple" and "willing and enduring Beatle-bondage" later rang hollow, the statements about the brilliance of the Beatles new single were on target. *Hey Jude* quickly topped the charts and remained in the number one spot on the *Billboard Hot 100*

for nine straight weeks during its 19-week run. *Revolution* charted separately for 11 weeks and peaked at number 12. The Beatles first Apple single sold over three million copies in its first two months of release.

The information sheet on the Black Dyke Mills Band urges readers (including radio program directors) to "come on and hear about the best band in the land." The opening text is a play on the lyrics from the tune *Alexander's Rag Time Band* ("Come on and hear the best band in the land"). The accompanying booklet is titled "The Black Dyke Mills Band and a Beatle." The reader learns that the band is 113 years old and is sponsored by John Foster and Son Ltd. of the Woollen Mills in the village of Queensbury, Yorkshire near Bradford. The band, which has 27 members plus a percussion section, won the National Champion Band of Great Britain award in 1967 for the seventh time since 1945. The sheet tells the following story:

"When Paul McCartney was faced with the challenge of producing his theme song for the London TV show 'Thingumybob' he decided to forget studio musicians, and the sophistication of formal studios and took himself up the trunk road which splits England from top to bottom. Up from exciting London to industrial Bradford in the north where, in an ancient city, he recorded The Black Dyke Mills Band in their home town. The results are strong and amazingly contemporary for within the song there are those

MARY HOPKIN

JACKIE LOMAX

strange, unique touches of the Beatle-flair. The 'B' side is Yellow Submarine, one of the great youth marching songs of all time played as a march as it is begged to be played. Be played by them. March to them yourselves across the living room, be young again, and brave."

Although the single was interesting and well produced, most program directors were not brave enough to play a brass band record on their stations. It failed to chart, and as Apple's first numbered single, is highly collectible.

The booklet on Mary Hopkin tells the tale of how supermodel Twiggy saw the young Welsh folk singer on the British TV talent show *Opportunity Knocks* and was so impressed that she told Paul McCartney of her talent. Paul signed her to be part of the launching of his dream organization, Apple. The information sheet boldly predicted that "Mary Hopkin will be #1 in the charts with *Those Were The Days*." According to Derek Taylor:

"The record is produced by Paul McCartney who is English, sung by Mary Hopkin who is Welsh, written by Gene Raskin who is American. It is for all ages, all tastes, all creeds, sensibilities, for anyone with the capacity to be stirred by music and is there anyone who has not this capacity? It is a long song: it builds, grips, embraces. It will be whistled, hummed, sung, translated, exploited, adopted all over the world. It will be one of the hits of the year."

All of the above proved true except for the prediction that the song would be number one. While *Those Were The Days* was number one in England, it had to settle for the second spot in the United States, where it could not get past *Hey Jude*.

Although the booklet on Jackie Lomax tells more of his background than most people would care to know, the information sheet gets straight to the point: "Jackie Lomax

is from Liverpool and it shows." Derek Taylor informs the reader that:

"George Harrison produced and wrote for this first Lomax solo effort on the fresh, new just-ripening APPLE label. It is called *Sour Milk Sea* – the sea we all find ourselves in from time to time. "Get out of that Sour Milk Sea, you don't belong there. Come back to where you should be..." A few words of Beatle-warning, Lomax delivered. The backing of the record is astounding–listen to the guitar solo and know that Britain can still play rock 'n' roll."

While the information sheet justifiably raves about the Lomax single, it tells the reader little about the song's history and recording. *Sour Milk Sea* was written by Harrison during the Beatles stay with the Maharishi Mahesh Yogi in Rishikesh, India, in March of 1968. The Beatles recorded a demo of the song in May of 1968 at Kinfauns, George Harrison's bungalow in Esher, Surrey. The song was one of over two dozen tunes recorded in demo form for consideration for the upcoming Beatles album. For reasons unknown, George decided against recording it for the Beatles LP. Instead, he gave it to Lomax for his first Apple single. The song was recorded in late June at Trident Studios with a lineup featuring three of the Beatles. Lomax sings lead and plays rhythm guitar along with Harrison on rhythm guitar, Paul McCartney on bass, Ringo on drums, Eric Clapton on lead guitar, Nicky Hopkins on piano and Eddie Clayton on conga drums.

*Sour Milk Sea* is a great rock single that should have been a hit. Unfortunately for Lomax, Harrison and Apple, the song was overshadowed by the Beatles and Mary Hopkin singles and did not chart. The song was reissued in July of 1971 on Apple 1834, this time paired with *(I) Fall Inside Your Eyes*. Once again, the song failed to chart.

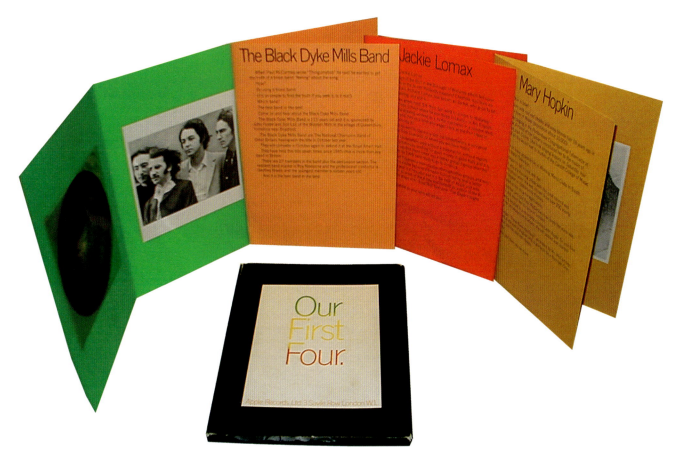

The Apple press kit mailed to U.S. radio stations in August of 1968 is the American equivalent of the elaborately packaged "Our First Four" box (shown above), which contained the same debut singles and was distributed to British radio stations and members of the press. While Apple in London hand-delivered copies of the boxes to the Queen and the Prime Minister, Capitol did not send a copy of the U.S. press kit to the White House.

A surviving Capitol Merchandising Project Authorization form dated August, 1968, provides details regarding the press kit. The Special Apple Presentation project was budgeted at $8,000 and classified as a "broadcast promotion" expense. Capitol's Los Angeles pressing plant was directed to supply 1,300 copies each of "the initial 4 single record releases on APPLE to be collated into the special mailing kit." The records were scheduled for August 20 pick up by Commercial Printing, who was instructed to collate the component parts of the kit and mail the 1,300 press kits.

Capitol ordered 5,000 white mailing envelopes and 5,000 press kit folders constructed of Kromekote cast-coated stock (the same paper later used for the cover of *The White Album*). These items would be used for the initial press kit mailings as well as for future press releases. The company also ordered 25,000 sheets of 8½" x 11" white bond paper imprinted with a light green Apple logo. The imprint was done in a 50% ghost effect to allow for overprinting of text. These sheets were used for the press kit's information sheets on each artist. In addition, Capitol ordered 5,000 prints of each of the four black and white glossies of the artists. The large order enabled Capitol to stock each press kit with two copies of each picture and still have a large leftover supply for later use.

The Project Authorization form also directed the preparation of 30 two-color 22" x 28" flip charts for use at an Apple presentation meeting. It is not known if any of the flip charts have survived.

Complete copies of the press kit are extremely rare. For those lucky enough to possess the package, it is still a thrill to go through the press kit, read its flowery Derek Taylor text, look at the pictures of the beautiful young Mary Hopkin, the cartoon Beatles and Paul with his sheep dog Martha posing with a brass band, and, of course, play the singles that launched Apple Records. One can only imagine the excitement generated by that white folder with the green Apple logo all those years ago.

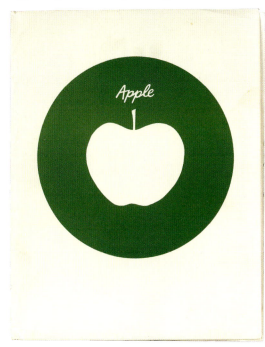

# BEYOND APPLE'S FIRST FOUR

## THE AMERICAN SINGLES DISCOGRAPHY

Beginning with *Hey Jude* and continuing through December, 1970, all Beatles singles and solo recordings by a Beatle (with the exception of the John Lennon/Yoko Ono discs) were assigned a number in the Capitol 2000 series. All non-Beatle singles, as well as Beatle solo singles issued from 1971 through 1975, have numbers in the Apple 1800 series.

| Record # | Artist | Title | Release Date |
|---|---|---|---|
| 2276 | The Beatles | Hey Jude/Revolution | 8/26/68 |
| 1800 | Black Dyke Mills Band | Thingumybob/Yellow Submarine | 8/26/68 |
| 1801 | Mary Hopkin | Those Were The Days/Turn, Turn, Turn | 8/26/68 |
| 1802 | Jackie Lomax | Sour Milk Sea/The Eagle Laughs At You | 8/26/68 |
| 1803 | The Iveys | Maybe Tomorrow/Daddy's A Millionaire | 1/27/69 |
| 1804 | Trash | Road To Nowhere/Illusions | 3/03/69 |
| 1805 | James Taylor | Carolina In My Mind/Taking It In [Cancelled] | 3/17/69 |
| 1805 | James Taylor | Carolina In My Mind/Something's Wrong | 3/17/69 |
| 1806 | Mary Hopkin | Goodbye/Sparrow | 4/07/69 |
| 2409 | The Beatles | Get Back/Don't Let Me Down | 5/05/69 |
| 1807 | Jackie Lomax | New Day/Thumbin' A Ride | 6/02/69 |
| 2531 | The Beatles | The Ballad Of John And Yoko/Old Brown Shoe | 6/04/69 |
| 1808 | Billy Preston | That's The Way God Planned It/What About You | 7/14/69 |
| 1809 | Plastic Ono Band | Give Peace A Chance/Remember Love | 7/21/69 |
| 1810 | Radha Krishna Temple | Hare Krishna Mantra/Prayer To The Spiritual Masters | 9/08/69 |
| 2654 | The Beatles | Something/Come Together | 10/06/69 |
| 1811 | Trash | Golden Slumbers-Carry That Weight/Trash Can | 10/15/69 |
| 1812 | The Hot Chocolate Band | Give Peace A Chance/Living Without Tomorrow | 10/17/69 |
| 1813 | John Ono Lennon/Yoko Ono | Cold Turkey/Don't Worry Kyoko | 10/20/69 |
| 1814 | Billy Preston | Everything's All Right/I Want To Thank You | 10/24/69 |
| 1815 | Badfinger | Come And Get It/Rock Of All Ages | 1/12/70 |
| 1816 | Mary Hopkin | Temma Harbour/Lontano Dagli Occhi | 1/29/70 |
| 1817 | Billy Preston | All That I've Got/As I Get Older | 2/16/70 |
| 1818 | John Ono Lennon/Yoko Ono | Instant Karma/Who Has Seen The Wind | 2/20/70 |
| 1819 | Jackie Lomax | How The Web Was Woven/(I) Fall Inside Your Eyes | 3/09/70 |
| 2764 | The Beatles | Let It Be/You Know My Name | 3/11/70 |
| 1820 | Doris Troy | Ain't That Cute/Vaya Con Dios | 3/16/70 |
| 1821 | Radha Krishna Temple | Govinda/Govinda Jai Jai | 3/24/70 |
| 1822 | Badfinger | No Matter What/Carry On Till Tomorrow | 10/19/70 |
| 2832 | The Beatles | The Long And Winding Road/For You Blue | 5/11/70 |
| 1823 | Mary Hopkin | Que Sera, Sera/Fields Of St. Etienne | 6/15/70 |
| 1824 | Doris Troy | Jacob's Ladder/Get Back | 9/21/70 |
| 2969 | Ringo Starr | Beaucoups Of Blues/Coochy, Coochy | 10/05/70 |
| 1825 | Mary Hopkin | Think About Your Children/Heritage | 10/12/70 |
| 2995 | George Harrison | My Sweet Lord/Isn't It A Pity | 11/23/70 |
| 1826 | Billy Preston | My Sweet Lord/Little Girl | 12/03/70 |
| 1827 | John Lennon/Yoko Ono | Mother/Why | 12/28/70 |
| 1828 | George Harrison | What Is Life/Apple Scruffs | 2/15/71 |
| 1829 | Paul McCartney | Another Day/Oh Woman, Oh Why | 2/22/71 |
| 1830 | John Lennon/Yoko Ono | Power To The People/Touch Me | 3/22/71 |
| 1831 | Ringo Starr | It Don't Come Easy/Early 1970 | 4/16/71 |
| 1832 | Ronnie Spector | Try Some, Buy Some/Tandoori Chicken | 4/19/71 |
| 1833 | [Not used] | | |
| 1834 | Jackie Lomax | Sour Milk Sea/(I) Fall Inside Your Eyes | 6/21/71 |
| 1835 | Bill Elliot and Elastic Oz Band | God Save Us/Do The Oz | 7/07/71 |
| 1836 | George Harrison | Bangla-Desh/Deep Blue | 7/28/71 |
| 1837 | Paul & Linda McCartney | Uncle Albert-Admiral Halsey/Too Many People | 8/02/71 |
| 1838 | Ravi Shankar | Joi Bangla/Oh Bhaugowan/Raga Mishra Jhinjhoti | 8/09/71 |
| 1839 | Yoko Ono | Mrs. Lennon/Midsummer New York | 9/29/71 |
| 1840 | John Lennon | Imagine/It's So Hard | 10/11/71 |
| 1841 | Badfinger | Day After Day/Money | 11/10/71 |
| 1842 | John Lennon/Yoko Ono | Happy Xmas/Listen, The Snow Is Falling | 12/01/71 |
| 1843 | Mary Hokpin | Water, Paper And Clay/Streets Of London | 12/01/71 |
| 1844 | Badfinger | Baby Blue/Flying | 3/06/72 |
| 1845 | Lon & Derrek Van Eaton | Sweet Music/Song Of Songs | 3/06/72 |
| 1846 | [Not used] | | |
| 1847 | Wings | Give Ireland Back To The Irish/Version | 2/28/72 |
| 1848 | John Lennon/Yoko Ono | Woman Is The Nigger Of The World/Sisters O Sisters | 4/24/72 |
| 1849 | Ringo Starr | Back Off Boogaloo/Blindman | 3/20/72 |
| 1850 | Chris Hodge | We're On Our Way/Supersoul | 5/03/72 |
| 1851 | Wings | Mary Had A Little Lamb/Little Woman Love | 5/29/72 |

| Record # | Artist | Title | Release Date |
|----------|--------|-------|--------------|
| 1852 | The Sundown Playboys | Saturday Night Special/Valse De Soleil Coucher | 9/26/72 |
| 1853 | Yoko Ono | Now Or Never/Move On Fast | 11/13/72 |
| 1854 | Elephant's Memory | Liberation Special/Madness | 11/13/72 |
| 1854 | Elephant's Memory | Liberation Special/Power Boogie | 12/04/72 |
| 1855 | Mary Hopkin | Knock Knock Who's There/International | 11/08/72 |
| 1856 | [Not used] | | |
| 1857 | Wings | Hi Hi Hi/C Moon | 12/04/72 |
| 1858 | Chris Hodge | Goodbye Sweet Lorraine/Contact Love | 1/22/73 |
| 1859 | Yoko Ono | Death Of Samantha/Yang Yang | 2/26/73 |
| 1860 | [Not used] | | |
| 1861 | Paul McCartney & Wings | My Love/The Mess | 4/09/73 |
| 1862 | George Harrison | Give Me Love/Miss O'Dell | 5/07/73 |
| 1863 | Wings | Live And Let Die/I Lie Around | 6/18/73 |
| 1864 | Badfinger | Apple Of My Eye/Blind Owl | 12/17/73 |
| 1865 | Ringo Starr | Photograph/Down And Out | 9/24/73 |
| 1866 | [Not used] | | |
| 1867 | Yoko Ono | Woman Power/Men Men Men | 9/24/73 |
| 1868 | John Lennon | Mind Games/Meat City | 10/29/73 |
| 1869 | Paul McCartney & Wings | Helen Wheels/Country Dreamer | 11/12/73 |
| 1870 | Ringo Starr | You're Sixteen/Devil Woman | 12/03/73 |
| 1871 | Paul McCartney & Wings | Jet/Mamunia | 1/28/74 |
| 1871 | Paul McCartney & Wings | Jet/Let Me Roll It | 2/18/74 |
| 1872 | Ringo Starr | Oh My, My/Step Lightly | 2/18/74 |
| 1873 | Paul McCartney & Wings | Band On The Run/Nineteen Hundred Eighty Five | 4/08/74 |
| 1874 | John Lennon | Whatever Gets You Through The Night/Beef Jerky | 9/23/74 |
| 1875 | Paul McCartney & Wings | Junior's Farm/Sally G | 11/04/74 |
| 1876 | Ringo Starr | Only You/Call Me | 11/11/74 |
| 1877 | George Harrison | Dark Horse/I Don't Care Anymore | 11/18/74 |
| 1878 | John Lennon | #9 Dream/What You Got | 12/16/74 |
| 1879 | George Harrison | Ding Dong;Ding Dong/Hari's On Tour | 12/23/74 |
| 1880 | Ringo Starr | No No Song/Snookeroo | 1/27/75 |
| 1881 | John Lennon | Stand By Me/Move Over Ms. L | 3/10/75 |
| 1882 | Ringo Starr | Goodnight Vienna/Oo-Wee | 6/02/75 |
| 1883 | John Lennon | Ain't That A Shame/Slippin' And Slidin' [ISSUED ONLY AS PROMO] | 6/02/75 |
| 1884 | George Harrison | You/World Of Stone | 9/15/75 |
| 1885 | George Harrison | This Guitar/Maya Love | 12/08/75 |

## SPECIAL PROMOTIONAL SINGLES

| Record # | Artist | Title | Release Date |
|----------|--------|-------|--------------|
| PRO-4675 | | More Apples Radio Co-Op Ads (one sided; small play hole) (Radio spots for James Taylor and the Modern Jazz Quartet) | 1969 |
| PRO-6498/SPRO-6499 | David Peel | F Is Not A Dirty Word/The Ballad Of New York City | 4/20/72 |
| PRO-6545/SPRO-6546 | David Peel | Hippie From New York City/The Ballad Of New York City | 6/16/72 |

## THE AMERICAN ALBUMS DISCOGRAPHY

Except as noted below, the Apple albums were assigned numbers beginning with 3350. The Beatles albums distributed by Capitol from 1968 through 1970 were given numbers in the Capitol album series, which restarted in fall, 1968, with 101, the number assigned to *The White Album*. The United Artists-distributed *Let It Be* LP was numbered AR 34001. When Capitol refused to distribute John and Yoko's *Two Virgins*, Tetragrammaton picked up the controversial disc and assigned it T 5001. George Harrison's *All Things Must Pass* was also given a number in the Capitol series. Z designates Zapple Records.

| Record # | Artist | Title | Release Date |
|----------|--------|-------|--------------|
| SWBO 101 | The Beatles | The Beatles (The White Album) | 11/25/68 |
| ST 3350 | George Harrison | Wonderwall Music | 12/02/68 |
| T 5001 | John Lennon and Yoko Ono | Unfinished Music No. 1. Two Virgins | 1/06/69 |
| SW 153 | The Beatles | Yellow Submarine | 1/13/69 |
| ST 3351 | Mary Hopkin | Postcard | 3/03/69 |
| SKAO 3352 | James Taylor | James Taylor | 2/17/69 |
| ST 3353 | Modern Jazz Quartet | Under The Jasmine Tree | 2/17/69 |
| ST 3354 | Jackie Lomax | Is This What You Want | 5/19/69 |
| ST 3355 | Iveys | Maybe Tomorrow [Not Issued] | |
| 3356 | [Not used] | | |
| ST 3357 (Z) | John Lennon and Yoko Ono | Unfinished Music No. 2: Life With The Lions | 5/26/69 |
| ST 3358 (Z) | George Harrison | Electronic Music | 5/26/69 |
| ST 3359 | Billy Preston | That's The Way God Planned It | 9/10/69 |
| SO 383 | The Beatles | Abbey Road | 10/01/69 |
| STAO 3360 | Modern Jazz Quartet | Space | 11/03/69 |
| SMAX 3361 | John Lennon and Yoko Ono | Wedding Album | 10/20/69 |
| SW 3362 | The Plastic Ono Band | Live Peace In Toronto 1969 | 12/12/69 |

| Record # | Artist | Title | Release Date |
|---|---|---|---|
| SW 385 | The Beatles | Hey Jude | 1/26/70 |
| STAO 3363 | Paul McCartney | McCartney | 4/20/70 |
| ST 3364 | Badfinger | Magic Christian Music | 2/16/70 |
| SW 3365 | Ringo Starr | Sentimental Journey | 4/24/70 |
| 3366 | [Not used] | | |
| AR 34001 | The Beatles | Let It Be | 5/18/70 |
| SKAO 3367 | Badfinger | No Dice | 10/15/70 |
| SMAS 3368 | Ringo Starr | Beaucoups Of Blues | 10/15/70 |
| SMAS 3369 | John Tavener | The Whale | 10/15/70 |
| ST 3370 | Billy Preston | Encouraging Words | 10/15/70 |
| ST 3371 | Doris Troy | Doris Troy | 10/15/70 |
| STCH 639 | George Harrison | All Things Must Pass | 11/27/70 |
| SW 3372 | John Lennon | Plastic Ono Band | 12/11/70 |
| SW 3373 | Yoko Ono | Plastic Ono Band | 12/11/70 |
| 3374 | [Not used] | | |
| SMAS 3375 | Paul & Linda McCartney | Ram | 5/17/71 |
| SKAO 3376 | Radha Krishna Temple | Radha Krishna Temple | 5/17/71 |
| SW 3377 | Original Soundtrack | Come Together | 9/17/71 |
| 3378 | [Not used] | | |
| SW 3379 | John Lennon | Imagine | 9/09/71 |
| SVBB 3380 | Yoko Ono | Fly | 9/09/71 |
| SMAS 3381 | Mary Hopkin | Earth Song/Ocean Song | 11/03/71 |
| 3382 | [Used to identify tape] | [Fly–tape #1] | |
| 3383 | [Used to identify tape] | [Fly–tape #2] | |
| SWAO 3384 | Original Soundtrack | Raga | 12/07/71 |
| STCX 3385 | George Harrison & Friends | The Concert For Bangla Desh | 12/20/71 |
| SW 3386 | Wings | Wild Life | 12/07/71 |
| SW 3387 | Badfinger | Straight Up | 12/13/71 |
| SWAO 3388 | Original Motion Picture Score | El Topo | 12/27/71 |
| SMAS 3389 | Elephants Memory | Elephants Memory | 9/18/72 |
| SMAS 3390 | Lon & Derek Van Eaton | Brother | 9/22/72 |
| SW 3391 | David Peel | The Pope Smokes Dope | 4/03/72 |
| SVBB 3392 | John & Yoko | Sometime In New York City | 6/12/72 |
| 3393 | [Used to identify tape] | [Sometime In NYC–tape #1] | |
| 3394 | [Used to identify tape] | [Sometime In NYC–tape #2] | |
| SW 3395 | Mary Hopkin | Those Were The Days | 9/25/72 |
| SVBB 3396 | Ravi Shankar | In Concert 1972 | 1/08/73 |
| 3397 | [Used to identify tape] | [Ravi Shankar In Concert–tape #1] | |
| 3398 | [Used to identify tape] | [Ravi Shankar In Concert–tape #2] | |
| SVBB 3399 | Yoko Ono | Approximately Infinite Universe | 1/08/73 |
| SW 3400 | Phil Spector | Christmas Album | 12/11/72 |
| 3401 | [Used to identify tape] | [Yoko Ono AIU–tape #1] | |
| 3402 | [Used to identify tape] | [Yoko Ono AIU–tape #2] | |
| SKBO 3403 | The Beatles | 1962-1966 (The Red Album) | 5/02/73 |
| SKBO 3404 | The Beatles | 1966-1970 (The Blue Album) | 5/02/73 |
| 3405 | [Used to identify tape] | [The Red Album–tape #1] | |
| 3406 | [Used to identify tape] | [The Red Album–tape #2] | |
| 3407 | [Used to identify tape] | [The Blue Album–tape #1] | |
| 3408 | [Used to identify tape] | [The Blue Album–tape #2] | |
| SMAL 3409 | Paul McCartney & Wings | Red Rose Speedway | 5/30/73 |
| SMAS 3410 | George Harrison | Living In The Material World | 5/29/73 |
| SW 3411 | Badfinger | Ass | 11/26/73 |
| SW 3412 | Yoko Ono | Feeling The Space | 11/02/73 |
| SWAL 3413 | Ringo Starr | Ringo | 10/31/73 |
| SW 3414 | John Lennon | Mind Games | 10/31/73 |
| SO 3415 | Paul McCartney & Wings | Band On The Run | 12/05/73 |
| SW 3416 | John Lennon | Walls And Bridges | 9/26/74 |
| SW 3417 | Ringo Starr | Goodnight Vienna | 11/18/74 |
| SMAS 3418 | George Harrison | Dark Horse | 12/09/74 |
| SK 3419 | John Lennon | Rock 'N' Roll | 2/17/75 |
| SW 3420 | George Harrison | Extra Texture (Read All About It) | 9/22/75 |
| SW 3421 | John Lennon | Shaved Fish | 10/24/75 |
| SW 3422 | Ringo Starr | Blast From Your Past | 11/20/75 |

## SPECIAL PROMOTIONAL ALBUM

| SPRO-6210/6211 | Paul & Linda McCartney | Brung To Ewe By | 5/71 |

# APPLE LABELS & SLEEVES

The labels to the Apple singles and albums have a full green apple on the A side (or side one) and a sliced apple on the B side (or side two). The labels were designed by Gene Mahon, an ad agency designer who worked on the cover to *Sgt. Pepper's Lonely Hearts Club Band*. Mahon proposed having different labels on each side of the record. One side would feature a full apple that would serve as a pure symbol on its own without any text. All label copy would be printed on the other side's label, which would be the image of a sliced apple. The white-colored inside surface of the sliced apple provided a good background for printing information.

The idea of having no print on the full apple side was abandoned when EMI advised Apple that the contents of the record should appear on both sides of the disc for copyright and publishing reasons. Although Mahon's concept was rejected for legal (and perhaps marketing) reasons, his idea of using different images for each side of the record remained.

Mahon hired Paul Castell to shoot pictures of green, red and yellow apples, both full and sliced. The proofs were reviewed by the Beatles and Neil Aspinall, with the group selecting a big green Granny Smith apple to serve as the company's logo. A sliced green apple was picked for the B side. Alan Aldridge provided the green script perimeter print for the British labels (see page 34) and, in all likelihood, the script "The Beatles on Apple" designation on the custom record sleeves.

After Apple signed its distribution agreement with Capitol, color transparencies of the label images and the record sleeves were sent to the Capitol Tower in Hollywood, California. Capitol paperwork indicates that the color separations for both the single and album labels were prepared by Barclay in Los Angeles at a cost of $486.13. On August 2, 1968, Barclay shipped the film for the Apple 45 labels to Bert-Co Press in Los Angeles and to Bill Mathias, manager of Capitol's Scranton factory, who then forwarded the film to Queens Litho in New York. Following its standard 80% East Coast and 20% West Coast allocation, Capitol ordered 80% of the Apple label backdrops from Queens Litho and the remaining 20% from Bert-Co.

The initial label backdrops prepared for Apple singles in America have "Mfd. by Apple Records, Inc." in light green upper case letters running along the lower perimeter of the sliced apple B side (although later label backdrops have this designation on the full apple A side or on both sides). This book's numbering system assigns **(as)** to labels with "Apple perimeter print" on the sliced apple side, **(af)** to labels with this print on the full apple side and **(ab)** to labels with this print on both sides.

Some of the later Apple label backdrops have B side perimeter print identical to the perimeter print appearing on the labels to Capitol albums issued in late 1968. These labels have "Mfd. by Capitol Records, Inc., a Subsidiary of Capitol Industries, Inc., U.S.A. • T.M." in white upper case letters to the left of a small white Capitol dome logo

The initial 45 label backdrops used by Capitol's Los Angeles and Scranton factories are glossy and have light green apples (top left). Later Los Angeles discs (beginning sometime in 1973) have dull light green apple labels, often with a slight yellowish tint (top middle). In the spring of 1969, Scranton began using glossy dark green apple labels (top right). The Jacksonville factory initially used either glossy light or dark green apple labels (from Bert-Co or Queens Litho) before switching to dull dark green apple labels (bottom left). Capitol's Winchester plant started with dull light green apple labels (bottom center) before changing to dull dark green apple labels (bottom right).

located to the right of six o'clock. This is followed by "Marca Reg. • U.S. Pat. No. 2,631,859" in white upper case characters. This book's numbering system assigns a **(c)** to labels with "Capitol logo perimeter print."

The first labels used for the singles have light green apples and are printed on semi-glossy paper. Later labels have varying shades of green, ranging from light to medium to dark. The paper stock also varies, ranging from glossy to neutral to dull finishes. The light green apple labels work best as their light background allows for the black text to be easily read. The dark green apple labels are difficult to read. The different appearances of the labels results not only from the different printers used, but also from changes in the film prepared for the label backdrops, the paper stock and the color settings selected by the pressman.

While the labels for the Apple singles are attractive, they presented challenges for typesetters, who often had trouble coming up with functional layouts for the label copy. Nearly all of the singles in the Apple catalog have multiple layout designs. All text was overprinted in black ink onto previously prepared label backdrops.

The label copy for West Coast records was normally overprinted by Bert-Co, although sometimes it was added in-house by Capitol's Los Angeles factory. The film for the label copy was often prepared by Barclay and sent to Bert-

Co and other printers. Labels printed by Bert-Co and/or overprinted with text from Barclay film are assigned an **L** in this book's numbering system. In most cases, the text on East Coast Queens Litho label backdrops was overprinted by Keystone Printed Specialties Co., Inc. of Scranton, Pennsylvania. Small quantities of labels were sometimes overprinted in-house at Capitol's Scranton plant. East Coast labels are normally assigned an **S** in this book's numbering system. Capitol's other factories also had in-house printing capabilities. This book assigns a **J** to labels found primarily on Jacksonville discs and a **W** to labels found primarily with Winchester records.

An August 19, 1968, Capitol memo estimated that three million side one and side two Apple album labels would be needed through the end of the year. This figure was revised upward when Capitol learned that the first Apple album would be a Beatles double LP set requiring twice the number of labels as a single disc release. The memo indicates that 80% of the labels would be printed on the East Coast by Queens Litho and the remaining 20% on the West Coast by Bert-Co.

The images on the label backdrops for Apple albums are identical to those used for the singles. However, because the album labels are 4" in diameter compared to the 3⁵⁄₁₆" labels for the singles, the apples are larger on the

The initial album label backdrops used by Scranton and Los Angeles have dark green apples (top left). Later labels printed by Bert-Co have lighter green apples (top middle). By the time the "all rights" language was added to Apple labels in 1975, the Bert-Co labels had light green apples with a yellow tint (top right). Special project Beatles albums were pressed with labels deviating from the standard label backdrops featuring green apples over a dark background. *Let It Be* has custom red apple labels (bottom left). *The Red Album* has green apples with a red background (bottom center), and *The Blue Album* has green apples with a blue background (bottom right). Some of the solo albums also had special apple labels.

album label backdrops. The initial labels printed for the first two Beatles albums on Apple (*The White Album* and *Yellow Submarine*) have Capitol logo perimeter print on the sliced apple side. Many of the later pressings of these albums have Apple perimeter print on the full apple side. Most first pressings of *Abbey Road* have Apple perimeter print on side two. Some later pressings have either Capitol logo perimeter print on side two or Apple perimeter print on side one. The initial labels for the *Hey Jude* LP have the album's original title, *The Beatles Again*, and Apple perimeter print on side two. Later labels have the correct title and either Capitol logo or Apple perimeter print. As with the labels to the singles, the apples on the album labels vary from light to dark green. The labels for the *Let It Be* LP have red apples and red Apple perimeter print on side one.

Some of the labels with Apple perimeter print were printed from film that originally had Capitol logo perimeter print. On these labels, the blacked out Capitol logo perimeter print is visible upon close examination.

The Apple singles were packaged in attractive glossy black sleeves with script text above a die-cut center hole. The sleeves for Beatles singles have "The Beatles on" in white and "Apple" in green. Sleeves for the other artists on the label merely state "Apple" in green. The sleeves were probably designed by Gene Mahon and Alan Aldridge.

The color separations for the "Apple" and "The Beatles on Apple" sleeves were prepared by Barclay at a total cost of $177.63. The initial batch of sleeves were printed and constructed by Queens Litho and Bert-Co, most likely in the same 80% to 20% allocation as the record labels.

The initial Queens Litho "Beatles" sleeves, **APP RS.01A**, have a straight cut top. The first batch of Bert-Co "Beatles" sleeves, **APP RS.01B**, have a small center tab cut on one side. Capitol probably hired additional printers for the sleeves in later years.

The initial "Apple" sleeves were also printed by the same two printers, with the Queens Litho "Apple" sleeves, **APP RS.02A**, having a straight cut top, and the Bert-Co "Apple" sleeves, **APP RS.02B**, having a tab cut top. During the later Apple years, Beatles singles were often packaged with "Apple" sleeves. By this time, Queens Litho was manufacturing sleeves that were rounded upward on one side and rounded downward on the other. These rounded top "Apple" sleeves, **APP RS.02C**, are often found with the Apple reissue Beatles singles.

Some "Beatles" sleeves have surfaced with no center hole. Collectors have speculated that these were special promotional sleeves. This is not the case. According to former Queens Litho employee Richard Roth, "If a black Apple sleeve left Queens without a center hole, it was a mistake."

# APPLE SLEEVES

 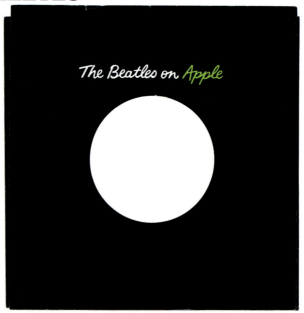

APP RS.1A

APP RS.1B

APP RS.2C

**S is for Singles**

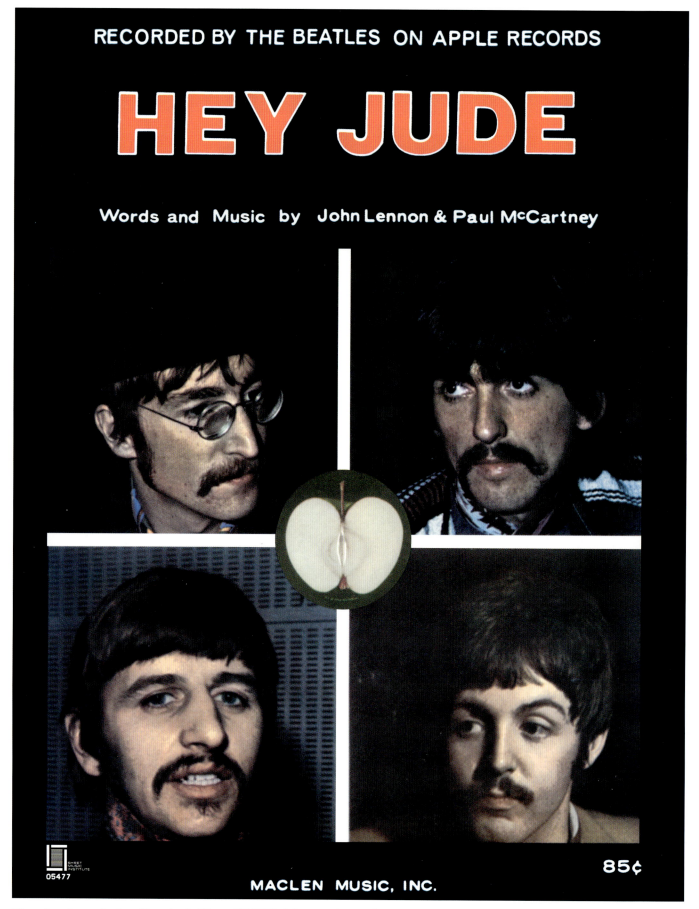

The sheet music for *Hey Jude* (Keys 05477) (shown above) features a sliced Apple label backdrop surrounded by the same four 1967 *Sgt. Pepper*-era portraits of the Beatles used on the sheet music for *All You Need Is Love* (Keys 05051). The first issue sheet music for *Revolution* (Keys 05476) has the same photos and layout, but the song title is in green and a full green Apple label backdrop appears in the center.

## HEY JUDE b/w REVOLUTION
## APPLE 2276

The all-important first Beatles record issued by the group on its Apple label was the single *Hey Jude* b/w *Revolution*. The disc was released by Parlophone in England as Apple R 5722 on August 30, 1968, and by Capitol as Apple 2276 on August 26. Nearly a half-year had gone by since the release of the Beatles previous single, *Lady Madonna*. And while that record had topped the British charts, the song peaked at number four on the *Billboard Hot 100*. Its flip side, *The Inner Light*, was ignored by both fans and radio stations, charting for only one week at number 97. This relatively poor performance caused some people to speculate that the Beatles popularity was finally beginning to fade.

*Hey Jude* quickly shattered any such thoughts. The song entered the *Billboard Hot 100* on September 14, 1968, at number ten. After jumping to number three the following week, it passed Jeannie C. Riley's *Harper Valley P.T.A.* (Plantation 3) and the Rascals' *People Got To Be Free* (Atlantic 2537) on its way to the top on September 28. *Hey Jude* remained the number one single for nine straight weeks before finally being replaced by Diana Ross & the Supremes' *Love Child* (Motown 1135). *Hey Jude* charted for 19 weeks, including 14 in the top ten. *Cash Box* and *Record World* also reported the song at number one for several weeks.

The single's B side, *Revolution*, also received significant airplay. It spent 11 weeks in the *Billboard Hot 100*, peaking at number 12 for three straight weeks. *Cash Box* reported it at 11. *Record World* accurately reflected the song's popularity by charting it at number two behind *Hey Jude*.

The October 12 *Billboard* reported that the single had been certified gold by the RIAA (Record Industry Association of America), indicating sales of over one million units. Two months after its release, *Hey Jude* had sold nearly three million copies. By mid-January, sales reached 3,773,000. Apple's Beatles debut went on to sell between four and five million copies in the U.S. and eight million worldwide.

Paul got the idea for *Hey Jude* while driving in his car to visit Cynthia and Julian Lennon. Although John had recently divorced Cynthia, Paul thought it wrong to end his friendship with her and John's son Julian, so he decided to visit and see how they were doing. At the time, Cynthia was still living in John's Kenwood house, so Paul was used to writing songs on the way to Kenwood, where he and John had collaborated on many songs in the past. In Barry Miles' *Paul McCartney Many Years From Now*, Paul explained:

"I started with the idea 'Hey Jules,' which was Julian, don't make it bad, take a sad song and make it better. Hey, try and deal with this terrible thing. I knew it was not going to be easy for him. I always feel sorry for kids in divorce. The adults may be fine but the kids...I had the idea by the time I got there. I changed it to 'Jude' because I thought that sounded a bit better."

Although Paul was probably not aware of it, the name change also fit in nicely with the theme of the song. Saint Jude is the patron saint of desperate cases.

Shortly thereafter, Paul finished the song at his Cavendish home. When John and Yoko visited him on July 26, 1968, he played the song for them. Although Paul had completed the lyrics, there was one line he viewed as filler that he intended to replace. When he got to the line "The movement you need is on your shoulder," he looked at John and told him he would fix it. Much to Paul's surprise, John told him to leave the words alone, calling it the best line in the song. In the *Anthology* video, Paul commented:

"So that was the great thing about John, where as I would have definitely knocked that line out, he said 'it's great,' I could see it through his eyes and go 'oh, OK.' So that is the sorta line now when I do that song, that's the line when I think of John, you know, sometimes I get a little emotional during that moment."

While John knew Paul had written the song for his son Julian, he thought Paul had subconsciously written it for him. In his interview for *Playboy* magazine, John stated:

"I always heard it as a song to me. If you think about it...Yoko's just come into the picture. He's saying, 'Hey Jude—hey, John.' I know I'm sounding like one of those fans who reads things into it, but you *can* hear it as a song to me. The words 'go out and get her'—subconsciously he was saying, 'Go ahead, leave me.' On a conscious level, he didn't want me to go ahead. The angel in him was saying, "Bless you.' The devil in him didn't like it at all, because he didn't want to lose his partner."

John viewed the song as one of Paul's masterpieces, as did millions of others. For many, the song is a message of inspiration: to adjust to a bad situation and make it better and to have the confidence to go out and do what you want to do.

Paul and John both recognized the song's potential, so it was destined from the start to be a single. This decision was made despite the song's length, which would ultimately stretch past seven minutes due to its long anthem-like sing-along ending. At a time when singles normally ran between two and three minutes long, the idea of having a 45 RPM single shatter the conventional time barrier was indeed revolutionary. But the Beatles never let rules interfere with their recordings. However, as told below, Paul later had concerns that disc jockeys might be reluctant to play the song due to its length.

Recording on *Hey Jude* began on July 29, 1968, at EMI's Abbey Road studio. While Ken Scott served in his usual function as engineer, George Martin did not attend the session. Because Paul was feeling his way through his latest composition, the six takes recorded that evening sound more like magnificent rehearsals rather than serious attempts to capture a master recording. The lineup for the live recordings featured Paul on piano and lead vocal, John on acoustic guitar and backing vocal, George on electric guitar and backing vocal and Ringo on drums. Although the song's glorious sing-along ending was in place from the start, the three completed takes were not as long as what would later become the finished master. Take 1 lasted 6:21, while Takes 2 and 6 ran for 4:30 and 5:25. *Anthology 3* contains a slightly edited version of one of the latter takes from this session.

The following evening the Beatles were joined by George Martin at Abbey Road for more recorded rehearsals of the song. Takes 7 through 23 were performed without George Harrison, who was stationed in the control room with George Martin and Ken Scott. Harrison had wanted to add lead guitar fills to the song, an idea that was shot down by Paul in a less than diplomatic manner.

The Beatles had earlier agreed to be filmed for a documentary by the National Music Council of Great Britain. This session, which was really a rehearsal, provided the perfect opportunity for the Beatles to keep their promise. The crew, led by producer James Archibald, shot several hours of film. The finished show, titled *Music!*, featured two segments (running 2:32 and 3:05) of the Beatles performing and talking about the new song. The color documentary was shown in British theaters on the same bill with Mel Brooks' comedy classic *The Producers* in October, 1969. In the United States, the film was broadcast as part of the NBC network television show *Experiment In Television* on February 22, 1970.

Although the Beatles had previously been filmed in the studio, this was the first time that a camera crew was allowed to capture the group running through take after take of a new song. The idea of filming the group's rehearsals appealed to Paul, who would soon come up with the concept of having the band perform a concert for television. As part of the program, the group would be shown rehearsing

Parlophone issued this picture disc (RP 5722) on the 20th anniversary of the release of *Hey Jude*. The B side (left) features a John Kelly photo taken during the filming of the *Revolution* promotional clip. The picture on the A side (right) was taken by Don McCullin on July 28, 1968. In addition to the standard 7" disc, Parlophone also issued a special 12" picture disc (12 RP 5722) for the Beatles biggest-selling single.

new songs for the concert. During the month of January, 1969, the group was filmed rehearsing and recording new songs and old favorites. Although the planned television concert never took place, the film of the group's rehearsals eventually evolved into the movie *Let It Be*.

On July 31, the Beatles were ready to record the master for *Hey Jude*. The session was booked at Trident Studios, a facility familiar to George and Paul, who had each produced Apple sessions there (George with Jackie Lomax and Paul with Mary Hopkin). Trident's main attraction was its then state-of-the-art eight-track recorder. Although EMI had purchased an eight-track recorder, it had yet to be installed. Thus, Abbey Road was still equipped only with four-track recorders.

The Beatles, with Paul on piano, John on acoustic guitar, George on electric guitar and Ringo on drums, ran through four takes of rhythm tracks designated Takes 1 through 4. Take 1 was deemed the best and was subjected to overdubs.

The Beatles completed the single on August 1 at a follow up session also held at Trident Studios. Paul overdubbed a bass part and his lead vocal. He was then joined by John and George for the backing vocals. Just before the first part of the song comes to an end at the three-minute mark, John realizes he made a mistake and lets out an expletive, which was not deleted from the finished master. Ringo also added a tambourine part. During the song's ending mantra, Paul gets carried away with his vocal, adding excitement with all his "Judy, Judy, Judy, wooh!" improvisations, which he later described as "Cary Grant on heat!"

After the Beatles completed their vocals, 36 classical musicians were brought in to add George Martin's score to the song's ending mantra. The instruments consisted of ten violins, three violas, three cellos, two flutes, one contra

bassoon, one bassoon, two clarinets, one contra bass clarinet, four trumpets, four trombones, two horns, two string basses and a percussionist. The latter portion of Paul's bass part was recorded over by the strings during this orchestral overdub session. After the music was completed, the orchestra members were asked to participate in the recording of additional hand claps and the ending vocal refrain ("nah, nah nah nah nah nah nah, nah nah nah nah, Hey Jude"). Although most were happy to join in and get extra pay, one musician thought himself above it all and reportedly stormed out the studio mumbling "I'm not going to clap my hands and sing Paul McCartney's bloody song!"

On August 2, three stereo mixes were made of Paul McCartney's bloody song at Trident Studios. Although stereo Remix 3 was collapsed to from a mono mix, this mix (mono Remix 1) was not used. Instead, three new mono mixes from the eight track tape were made on August 8 at Abbey Road. The final mix, mono Remix 4, became the master for the mono single.

In Miles' *Many Years From Now*, Paul tells an amusing story about the recording of what turned out to be the master take of *Hey Jude*. Just prior to the start of recording, Ringo snuck off to the bathroom. Paul was unaware that the drummer was not behind his set, so he started the song. Because the drums are not used in the first verses of the song, Paul was unaware of Ringo's absence until he noticed the drummer tiptoeing behind him trying to get to his drums. According to Paul:

"And just as he got to his drums, boom boom boom, his timing was absolutely impeccable. So I think when those things happen, you have a little laugh and a light bulb goes off in your head and you think, 'This is the take!' and you put a little more into it...what just happened was so magic! So we did that and we made a pretty good record."

**The labels for the British Apple singles have light green script perimeter print stating "Apple Records - All Rights of the Manufacturer and of the Owner of the Recorded Work Reserved" at the top and "Unauthorized Public Performance, Broadcasting and Copying of this Record Prohibited" at the bottom.**

Although that pretty good record ended up being the A side to the Beatles first Apple single, the song initially selected for that honor was *Revolution*. John's political statement set to music was the first song recorded by the Beatles after their return from India in the spring of 1968. John had pushed for the song to be the next Beatles single, but Paul and George objected, fearing that the song's slow tempo would prevent it from being a hit. A compromise was reached by John agreeing to rerecord the song as a rocker. For the story behind the original version of the song, later renamed *Revolution 1*, see the chapter on the group's first Apple album "*The Beatles*."

On July 9, 1968, the band recorded several takes of the fast version of *Revolution* after working on *Ob-La-Di, Ob-La-Da*. Because these runthroughs were considered rehearsals, the tape from this session was later recorded over.

The following evening the group went through ten takes of the song, with John and George on highly distorted guitars, Paul on bass and Ringo on drums. The guitars' unique hard-biting fuzz sound was achieved by running the guitars directly through the recording console. This overloaded the channels and caused tremendous distortion. Ringo's drums were highly compressed, adding to the song's hard and heavy sound. Hand claps and a second drum part were then superimposed over Take 10, which was given three reduction mixes (Takes 11 through 13) with Take 13 being the best. John then added his no-nonsense lead vocal to form Take 14. Another Lennon lead vocal, as well as the scream heard during the song's hard hitting introduction, was added as part of Take 15.

Work continued on the song the next night with Nicky Hopkins adding an electric piano solo to the song's instrumental break and another bit of fast-paced piano to the song's ending coda. This was then mixed down to form Take 16.

The fast and loud single version of *Revolution* was completed the following evening on July 12 with the addition of an another lead guitar part by John and a second bass part by Paul. The song was then mixed for mono; however, neither John nor Paul were satisfied with the results, so two more mono mixes (designated Remixes 20 and 21) were made on July 15. Mono Remix 21 was selected as the master. As the song was intended for release only as a mono single, no stereo mix was made at the time. The song was not mixed for stereo until December 5, 1969, when a stereo mix was needed for the *Hey Jude* album.

In addition to having a totally different sound than the original *Revolution 1*, the single version of the song has a slight change in the lyrics. On the album version of the song, John is ambivalent about his stance on revolutionary violence as he sings "But when you talk about destruction, don't you know that you can count me out/in." For the single John removes the ambiguity by singing "don't you know that you can count me out."

Although the Beatles selected *Hey Jude* to be the A side, Ken Mansfield, who served as manager of Apple Records' American operations, remembers Paul having serious misgivings about the acceptability of the song due to its length. In his book *The Beatles, the Bible, and Bodega Bay*, Mansfield tells of Paul's artistic insecurity and how he put Paul at ease. Mansfield, who was in London at the time, told Paul he would take an advance of the record with him and visit several key radio stations on his way back to Los Angeles. He would play the song for respected DJs to get their opinion on the single and phone Paul with the results upon arriving back at the Capitol Tower. As expected, the music directors were extremely enthusiastic about *Hey Jude*, so Paul could relax about Apple's first release.

To promote their new single, the Beatles recruited Michael Lindsay-Hogg to direct performance videos of the

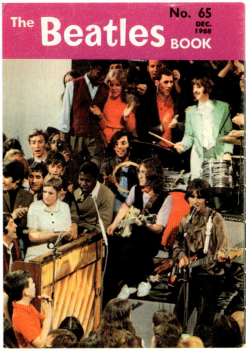

**The promotional clip for *Hey Jude* was taped at Twickenham Studios on September 4, 1968. The Beatles, backed by a 36-piece orchestra, performed the song three times. During the extended second part of the song, the Beatles were joined on stage by fans who sang and swayed along with the band. The back cover to issue number 65 of *The Beatles Book* (Dec. 1968) features a picture of the performance.**

two songs. The director had put together the promotional clips for *Paperback Writer* and *Rain* and would later direct the *Get Back/Let It Be* project. The promo clips were taped after the single's release at Twickenham Film Studios on September 4, 1968.

The Beatles ran through three performances of *Hey Jude*, with the most commonly shown video consisting of the first part of first performance edited with the second part from the third. The set consisted of a stage containing Paul's piano, three microphones and a Fender speaker cabinet. Ringo's drum kit and a Fender amplifier were on a separate and higher platform. George, armed with a Fender Bass VI, sat on the top edge of the speaker cabinet, while John, with his Epiphone Casino hollow body electric guitar, sat on the drum riser with his feet resting on the top of the cabinet to the left of George's body. A 36-piece orchestra was set up on three successively higher raised rows in the background. Behind and to the left of the platforms were 300 lucky extras, some of whom were fans invited by Beatles assistant Mal Evans. The Beatles and the orchestra played over the recorded single, with Paul singing along with his prerecorded lead vocal. During the second part of the song, Paul's vocal was recorded live for the video. For the extended mantra during the second part of the song, many of the extras climbed on the platforms, singing and swaying with the Beatles. Although really not a live performance, the video captured the excitement of the event.

Because the *Hey Jude* video was scheduled to make its debut on the September 8 *Frost On Sunday*, David Frost stopped by Twickenham Film Studios to introduce the song and give the impression the Beatles were appearing exclusively on his show. With Frost looking on, the Beatles performed a jazz version, complete with John and Paul vocals ("hear the beat of David Frost"), of the show's theme song,

*By George! It's The David Frost Theme*. The song actually was by George in that it was composed by George Martin. Frost then commented:

"Beautiful. Absolute poetry. Welcome back to part three, as you can see with the greatest tearoom orchestra in the world....Making their first audience appearance for over a year, ladies and gentlemen, the Beatles."

John then gives a salute to the host and George lowers his microphone to say "Thank you David." The introduction was then edited to the front of the *Hey Jude* clip for broadcast on Frost's show. The video of the song, without the Frost intro, was shown three times (September 12 and 26 and December 26) on the BBC's *Top Of The Pops*. All British broadcasts were in black and white. The video was shown in America in color on the October 6 *Smothers Brothers Comedy Hour*. The Frost introduction and the performance of the song appear on the *Anthology* video, although the second half of the song is interrupted three times, twice by comments from George and Paul superimposed over the video and once by a Lennon voice-over. Ringo follows the song by comparing the group's eventual break up to a divorce. Unfortunately the negative comments of the individual Beatles destroy the exuberance and excitement of the original unaltered video.

The *Revolution* video is even more straightforward, with the Beatles shown on stage with Ringo in the rear on a raised platform. John is with his Casino guitar, George with a red Gibson Les Paul guitar and Paul with his Hofner bass. Although the Beatles play over a backing instrumental track of the single, the vocals are entirely live and different from the released single. Paul handles the song's introductory scream and sings harmony with George on some of the lines to the verses. In addition, Paul and George sing the "shoo-be-do-wop-bow, shoo-be-do-wop-bow" refrains heard on

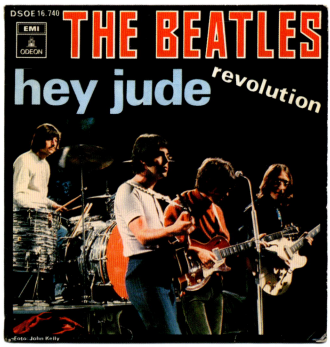

The laminated jacket to the Spanish single *Hey Jude* (Odeon DSOE 16.740) features a John Kelly picture of the Beatles taken during the filming of the *Revolution* performance video.

the album version of the song. John also draws from his initial rendition of the song by singing "But when you talk about destruction, don't you know that you can count me out/in." This exciting performance combines the best elements of the album and single versions of the song.

The *Revolution* promo clip was shown in England in black and white on the September 19 *Top Of The Pops*. In America, it appeared in color on *The Smothers Brothers Comedy Hour* on October 13, one week after the broadcast of the *Hey Jude* film. The *Revolution* performance appears in the *Anthology* video; however, the song is briefly interrupted by a Lennon voice-over during the second chorus.

Apple did not prepare a picture sleeve for *Hey Jude*, making it the first Capitol-distributed Beatles single issued without a picture sleeve. Instead, the record was packaged in "The Beatles on Apple" sleeves. East Coast singles were issued in straight cut sleeves manufactured by Queens Litho. The West Coast discs were initially packaged with Bert-Co tab cut sleeves (example shown on 31).

Because the Beatles were under contract to Capitol and EMI, the band was unable to sign a recording agreement with its own Apple company. However, both Capitol and EMI agreed to press the group's records with Apple labels. As all releases by the group were part of the catalogs of Capitol and EMI, the companies assigned their own record numbers to the Beatles singles and albums. This is why *Hey Jude* and the other Beatles 45s released with Apple labels in America have record numbers in the Capitol 2000 series rather than in the Apple 1800 series.

At the time *Hey Jude* was released in August, 1968, Capitol was pressing singles at its factories in Los Angeles, California, and Scranton, Pennsylvania. The Los Angeles records have a machine stamped asterisk (✳) in their trail off areas. The Scranton discs can be identified by the logo

of the International Association of Machinists (⬣) stamped in their trail off areas. Sometime in 1969, Capitol's factory in Jacksonville, Illinois, began manufacturing singles. These records have either a hand etched "O" or a machine stamped "0" in their trail off areas. In late 1969, Capitol opened a new factory in Winchester, Virginia. The trail off areas to the Winchester discs have a hand-etched drawing that is supposed to resemble a Winchester rifle, but looks more like a crudely drawn long-stemmed wine glass. Nearly all of the Apple singles pressed at Capitol factories have a slip guard consisting of 360 interlocking serrations surrounding the label.

In order to meet the huge demand for Beatles records, Capitol often subcontracted with other companies, such as RCA, to manufacture singles. These non-Capitol pressings do not have the serrations.

All of the Beatles Apple singles issued in the United States have more than one layout design. *Hey Jude* has four different layout variations.

The first pressings of the single, **APP 2276.01**, were pressed with light green apple label backdrops and have "HEY JUDE" and "(Lennon & McCartney)" to the left of the center hole at nine o'clock, and "THE BEATLES," "Maclen Music Inc., BMI," the running time 7:11 and record number 2276 to the right. The B side has "REVOLUTION" and "(Lennon & McCartney)" printed vertically to the left of the center hole, and "THE BEATLES," "Maclen Music Inc., BMI" and the running time 3:22 printed vertically to the right. The record number 2276 is printed vertically in the lower left portion of the apple.

The labels for the Los Angeles discs were printed by Bert-Co Enterprises of Los Angeles. The label backdrops for the Scranton records were printed by Queens Litho in New York, with the label copy overprinted by Keystone Printed Specialties Co., Inc. of Scranton. The print on the Los Angeles labels is slightly larger than the print on the Scranton labels. For example, "THE BEATLES" is 1⅛" on the Los Angeles B side and 1¹/₁₆" on the Scranton B side.

The first Los Angeles labels, **2276.01L(i)(as)**, have only the information listed above. They do not have master numbers, the production credit or "Recorded in England." These first labels have Apple perimeter print on the B side.

The second batch of Los Angeles labels, **2276.01L(ii)**, have production and recording information, but do not have master numbers. On the A side, "Produced by: George Martin" and "Recorded in England" appear on separate lines below the center hole. On the B side, "Produced by: George Martin" is printed vertically to the immediate left of the center hole. The recording location does not appear on the B side. This variation appears on labels with either Apple perimeter print, **01L(ii)(as)**, or Capitol logo perimeter print, **01L(ii)(c)**.

The initial Scranton labels, **2276.01S(i)(as)**, also lack master numbers and production and recording information. These first labels have Apple perimeter print on the B side.

The second batch of Scranton labels, **2276.01S(ii)(as)**, have master numbers, but do not have production or location credits. On the A side, the number 45-X-46434 is below the record number 2276. On the B side, 45-X-46435 is

**Shortly after the release of** *Hey Jude* **by the Beatles, Capitol issued an instrumental version of the song by The Sounds Of Our Times (Capitol 2291) (left). Incredibly, the label lists the songwriters as "Paul Lennon - John McCartney." In Mexico, the initial** *Hey Jude* **discs were pressed with Capitol swirl labels (right) because Apple had yet to secure its trademark in the country.**

printed vertically to the right of the record number. The B side has Apple perimeter print.

The third batch of Scranton labels, **2276.01S(iii)**, have master numbers and production and recording location information. On the A side, "Produced by: George Martin" and "Recorded in England" appear on separate lines below the center hole. On the B side, "Produced by: George Martin" is printed vertically to the immediate left of the center hole and "Recorded in England" is printed vertically to the far right after the running time 3:22. This variation appears on labels with either Apple perimeter print, **01S(iii)(as)** (Scranton ⚠ pressings confirmed), or Capitol logo perimeter print, **01S(iii)(c)** (RCA Rockaway pressings without serrations confirmed).

Subsequent layout variations do not have vertical label copy on the *Revolution* side of the disc. Apparently Capitol decided to switch to a more conventional layout for marketing and/or artistic reasons.

The second layout variation, **APP 2276.02L(c)**, has the song title and "(Lennon-McCartney)" in the upper left part of the apple on both sides. On the A side, "THE BEATLES" is below the center hole, shifted slightly off-center to the left. On the B side, the group's name appears in the lower left part of the apple. All other information, including publishing, time, record number, master number, production credit and recording location, is to the right of the center hole on both sides. These discs were pressed by Capitol's Los Angeles factory with light green apple label backdrops with Capitol logo perimeter print.

The third layout variation, **APP 2276.03**, is similar to the second, but emphasizes the song title and group's name on the A side. "HEY JUDE" is printed in thick bold print to the left of the center hole and "THE BEATLES" appears in thick bold print below the center hole. The B side is virtually identical to the B side of the second variation, except

for the placement of "McCartney" in the songwriters credit. The following label variations have been confirmed: (1) glossy light green apple Los Angeles pressings with Apple perimeter print on the B side, **2276.03L(as)**; (2) glossy light green apple Los Angeles pressings with Capitol logo perimeter print, **2276.03L(c)**; (3) glossy dark green apple Scranton pressings with Capitol logo perimeter print, **2276.03S(c)**; and (4) dull dark green apple Jacksonville pressings with Apple perimeter print on the A side, **2276.03J(af)**.

The fourth layout variation, **APP 2276.04W(af)**, is similar to the third, except that the B side has "REVOLUTION" and the songwriters credit in the lower left part of the apple, and "THE BEATLES" in the lower right part of the apple. In addition, the printing of the song title and group's name on the A side is not as thick as the printing on the third variation. This layout variation has been confirmed only with dull light green apple Winchester pressings with Apple perimeter print on the A side.

Beginning in September, 1975, the following legend was added to the Apple labels: "All rights reserved. Unauthorized duplication is a violation of applicable laws." There are two confirmed variations of *Hey Jude* with the all rights language. Los Angeles pressings, **APP 2276.11L(ar)**, have the same layout as **2276.04**, with the all rights language appearing on two lines at the top of the apple on the A side and on five lines in the upper left part of the apple on the B side. They have light green apple labels with Apple perimeter print on both sides. Jacksonville pressings, **APP 2276.12J(ar)**, have the same layout as **2276.03**, with the all rights language appearing on five lines to the lower left of the center hole on both sides. They have dull dark green apple labels with Apple perimeter print on the A side.

*Hey Jude* holds the distinction of being the most successful single debut for a new record label.

APP 2276.01L(i)(as)
First Label

APP 2276.01L(ii)(as)

APP 2276.01L(ii)(c)

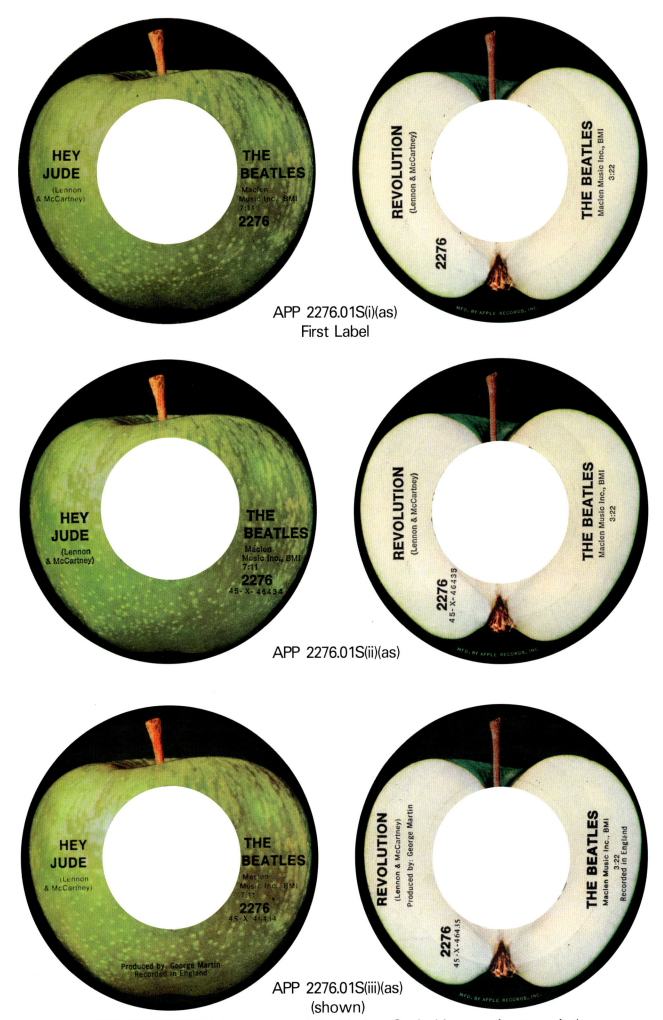

APP 2276.01S(i)(as)
First Label

APP 2276.01S(ii)(as)

APP 2276.01S(iii)(as)
(shown)
APP 2276.01S(iii)(c) (same, except B side has Capitol logo perimeter print)

APP 2276.02L(c)

APP 2276.03L(as)
(shown)
APP 2276.03L(c) (same, except B side has Capitol logo perimeter print)

APP 2276.03S(c)
(shown)
APP 2276.03J(af) (same, except dull dark green apple Jacksonville pressing with Apple perimeter print on A side)

APP 2276.04W(af)

APP 2276.11L(ar)

APP 2276.12J(ar)

# The Beatles
# as nature intended.

"Get Back" is the Beatles new single. It's the first Beatles record which is as live as can be, in this electronic age.

There's no electronic watchamacallit.

"Get Back" is a pure spring-time rock number.

On the other side there's an equally live number called "Don't let me down".

Paul's got this to say about Get Back... "we were sitting in the studio and we made it up out of thin air...we started to write words there and then... when we finished it, we recorded it at Apple Studios and made it into a song to roller-coast by".

P.S. John adds, It's John playing the fab live guitar solo.

And now John on Don't let me down. John says don't let me down about "Don't let me down".

In "Get Back" and "Don't let me down", you'll find the Beatles, as nature intended.

**Get Back / Don't let me down (Apple 2490)**

**Apple Records**

Apple's ad for the Beatles second Apple single stressed the pure nature of the recordings. *Get Back* was described as a "spring-time rock number ... to roller-coast by." *Don't Let Me Down* was called "an equally live number." Although there was no "electronic watchamacallit" on the recordings, both sides of the single have minor edits. The ad appeared in London's *Daily Mirror* on April 15, 1969, and in the April 26, 1969, *Billboard*.

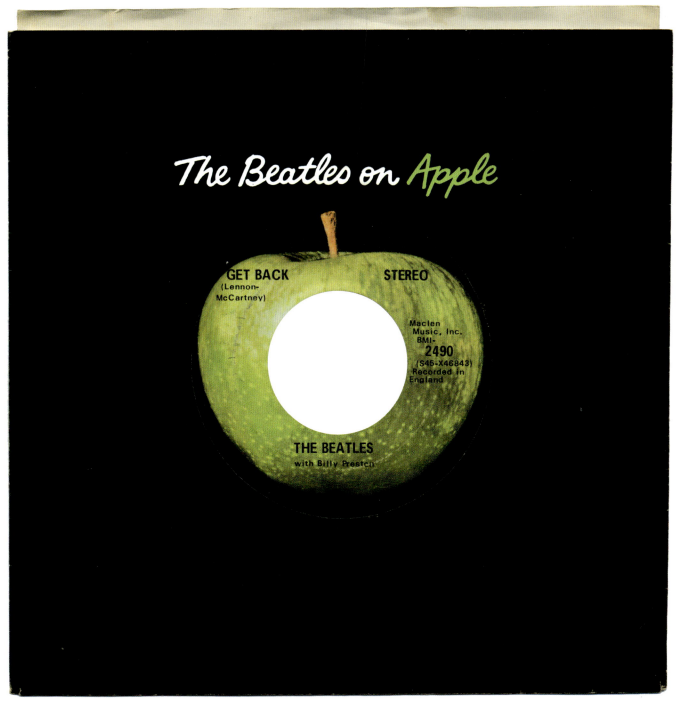

## GET BACK b/w DON'T LET ME DOWN
## APPLE 2490

Shortly before Easter, 1969, the Beatles decided it was time for a new single. Although they had released a double album in November, 1968, and the *Yellow Submarine* LP in January, 1969, the group had not issued a single since *Hey Jude* in August, 1968. The songs selected for the new 45 were Paul's *Get Back* and John's *Don't Let Me Down*.

In England, the Beatles supplied an acetate of *Get Back* to BBC Radio 1 for surprise broadcast of the new single on Easter Sunday, April 6. Apple announced a rush release date of April 11, although the disc (Apple R 5777) did not appear in stores until the following week.

Things proceeded at a more leisurely pace in America, where the single was officially released by Capitol as Apple 2490 on May 5, although it probably came out earlier. *Get Back* entered the *Billboard Hot 100* at number ten on May

10. The next week *Billboard* charted the song at number three and reported that the single had been certified gold by the RIAA. On May 24, it leaped past two records containing songs from the rock musical *Hair*: the Fifth Dimension's *Aquarius/Let The Sunshine In* (Soul City 772) and the Cowsills' *Hair* (MGM 14026). *Get Back* spent five weeks at the top before falling to number three behind Henry Mancini's rendition of *Love Theme From Romeo & Juliet* (RCA 74-0131) and *Bad Moon Rising* by Creedence Clearwater Revival (Fantasy 622). *Billboard* charted *Get Back* for 12 weeks, including nine in the top ten. *Cash Box* and *Record World* also charted the song at number one.

*Billboard* charted *Don't Let Me Down* for four weeks, showing a peak at number 35 on May 24. *Cash Box* and *Record World* did not separately track the song.

The single's 20th anniversary picture disc (Parlophone RP 5777) has a black and white picture from the Beatles last photo session (August 22, 1969) on the A side (left) and a color photograph (with a square insert photo of Ringo) from the band's last public performance (January 30, 1969) on the B side (right). The Beatles performed *Get Back* three times and *Don't Let Me Down* twice during the rooftop concert.

*Get Back* quickly proved to be a worthy follow-up to *Hey Jude*, topping the charts throughout the world. In the United States, the record sold over two million copies.

Although the British disc was mono, Capitol pressed the 45 in stereo, making *Get Back* the group's first stereo single.

Both sides of disc were recorded during January, 1969, as part of the sessions that would eventually form the basis for the *Let It Be* movie and its soundtrack album. From January 2 through January 14, the group was filmed by director Michael Lindsay-Hogg on a Twickenham Film Studios soundstage in London rehearsing new material and loosely performing some of their favorite oldies. On January 21, the Beatles resumed work on the project in a makeshift studio in the basement of Apple's Savile Row headquarters. Recording and filming continued through the end of the month. Although the sessions were full of tension, bickering and overall bad vibes, the initial songs issued from the project gave listeners no indication of the troubled conditions under which they were recorded.

The genesis of *Get Back* dates to the morning of January 7, when Paul introduced the song prior to John's arrival. McCartney's initial rendering of *Get Back* consisted of thumping bass and loose scat vocals. Although George played a few open chord notes at the start, this embryonic performance was essentially all Paul. George joined Paul for the next attempt, which opened with Paul singing the chorus and some incomplete lyrics that would later serve as the second verse. Although Ringo did not play drums, he sang with Paul on the choruses and later verses.

The first real runthrough of *Get Back* was performed as a simple rocker with Ringo supplying a straightforward beat and George adding some wah-wah guitar fills. Paul sings the song in the style of Apple recording artist Jackie

Lomax, perhaps realizing that the "get back to where you once belonged" chorus is similar to the "get back to where you should be" line from Lomax's recording of George Harrison's *Sour Milk Sea* (Apple 1802). Paul acknowledges his Lomax imitation by shouting "C'mon Jackie" during the second chorus.

The group returned to the song two days later on January 9, this time with John present and accounted for. Early run-throughs sound more like a jam than a finished song, but elements of the story line, such as references to Arizona and California, begin to appear. Paul then switches direction by temporarily changing the lyrics to political satire aimed at Parliament member Enoch Powell, who was in the news at that time spouting his beliefs that too many nonwhite citizens of the British Empire were immigrating to England and taking away limited jobs. Before launching into this political version of the song, Paul sings "Don't want no black man. Don't dig no Pakistanis taking all the people's jobs." The song's improvised lyrics include references to Puerto Ricans and Mohicans for the United States and Pakistanis for England. The group jams behind Paul, who shouts "get back" over and over again in a voice that mocks the hatred behind Enoch Powell's beliefs. After a few political versions of the song, the band returned briefly to the song's original story line, with Jo and Theresa serving as the principal characters.

The following day, January 10, the band spent a significant portion of the morning session working on *Get Back*. Prior to the start of band rehearsals, Paul performed the song on piano. After McCartney switched to bass, he led the group through a raucous version of *Get Back*. At Paul's suggestion, the song was rearranged to open with crashing guitars (somewhat reminiscent of the beginning to *A Hard Day's Night*) and a building drum roll from Ringo.

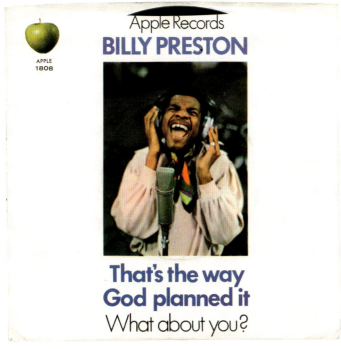

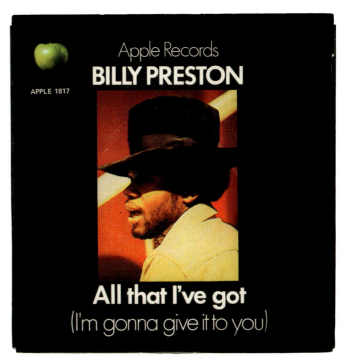

At the time Billy Preston joined the *Get Back* sessions, he was under contract to Capitol Records. The Beatles were so impressed by Preston that they had Apple buy out his Capitol contract. George Harrison produced several of Preston's songs for Apple, including the singles *That's The Way God Planned It* (Apple 1808) and *All That I've Got* (*I'm Gonna Give It To You*) (Apple 1817).

The band performed several rocking run-throughs of the song, with some containing bits of the "No Pakistanis" lyrics from the previous day. One of the more spirited performances features John joining Paul on the verses, a jamming wah-wah guitar solo and a Ringo drum fill leading into a third verse, which was later discarded. This verse contains references to living in a council flat (government-subsidized housing) and statements from the candidate for Labour (one of Britain's political parties). The verse about Sweet Loretta is substantially complete, but serves as the first rather than second verse. The middle verse features Jo Jo, Arizona and California, but is not in final form.

Although the group's progress with *Get Back* gives the impression that things were finally coming together for the band, things were about to fall apart. Shortly after the group's break for lunch on January 10, George announced he was quitting the group and walked out of Twickenham.

On January 13, the three remaining Beatles returned to *Get Back*, with Paul refining the lyrics. Loretta's last name alternated between Marsh and Marvin after Paul rejected John's "suggestion" of "Sweet Loretta Meatball." Although the group completed a few rocking takes of the song, Ringo's drum fills during the breaks threw the band's timing off. John's guitar solos, which borrow elements from Dale Hawkins' *Suzie Q*, range from passable to pitiful.

By the time the Beatles returned to *Get Back* on January 23, George had rejoined the band and the sessions had moved to the basement of Apple's Savile Row headquarters. In addition, Billy Preston was providing keyboards. Preston, who the Beatles met in 1962 when he was in Little Richard's touring band, was invited to the sessions by George. His presence not only added musical depth to the band's live performances, but also helped the group to behave in a more civil manner.

Most of the day's session was devoted to *Get Back*. Although the group did not perfect the song, its structure, lyrics and instrumentation, including Ringo's galloping snare drum part, George's chopping rhythm guitar, John's guitar solos and Billy Preston's electric piano fills and solo were taking shape.

The group continued to rehearse the song on January 24, at first without Preston, who did not arrive until mid-afternoon. The most interesting version recorded that day comprises of the group playing back to back performances of the song, complete with spirited improvisations from Paul during the final coda.

On January 27, the group ran through over 30 takes of *Get Back*. During one of the early performances, Paul sings the first verse with Japanese characters and cities; however, most of the versions of the song recorded this day were serious attempts at a suitable master take. The performances are fairly similar, with the main differences being the tempo, John's guitar solos and the codas. During one of the codas, Paul sings "it's five o'clock, your mother's got your tea on." He ends another with the "One, two, three o'clock, four o'clock rock" opening line from Bill Haley's *Rock Around The Clock*. On the take that would later be chosen as the master for the single and the *Let It Be* album, the group fails to play a coda, causing Harrison to comment, "We missed that end, didn't we?"

Due to the flubbed ending of this performance, the group continued work on the song. The later recordings are entertaining, but do not match the perfection of the master. The most interesting of the bunch has Paul singing pseudo-German lyrics until he switches to pseudo-French for the final chorus. During an instrumental break, Paul once again acknowledges the Jackie Lomax influence on the song by saying, "Yah, that's good Jackie" in a German accent.

The Beatles recorded additional takes of *Get Back* the following day. The extended coda from one of these January 28 performances was put to good use. A segment containing the first 35 seconds of the coda was edited to the end of the January 27 performance chosen for the single. A later segment of the coda was used as the *Get Back* reprise that ends both unreleased *Get Back* albums as well as the *Let It Be* film. The full coda runs 1:22 and ends with John singing, "Shoot me when I'm evil, shoot me when I'm good, shoot me when I'm hungry, and shoot me when I'm...." The later performances of the song are ragged and have Billy Preston on organ rather than electric piano.

On January 29, the Beatles rehearsed the songs slated for the rooftop concert, including *Get Back*. Because Billy was not present, John vocalized Preston's piano solo.

The Beatles, accompanied by Billy Preston on electric piano, gave their last public performance on January 30. The impromptu concert was staged on the roof of Apple headquarters and included three complete performances of *Get Back*, two of which appear in the *Let It Be* film. The group's final take on the song was the closing number to the concert and the film. This historic performance, complete with Paul's ad-libbed reference to playing on the rooftops, is included on *Anthology 3*.

On March 10, 1969, Glyn Johns made stereo mixes of a January 23 and a January 27 performance of *Get Back*. These mixes were transferred to an acetate for the Beatles to review.

On March 26, *Get Back* was mixed for mono at Abbey Road by EMI engineer Jeff Jarratt. The finished master combines the January 27 coda-less performance previously mixed by Glyn Johns with the first 35 seconds of a coda recorded on January 28. An acetate of this mix was played on Easter Sunday (April 6) on BBC 1 by disc jockeys John Peel and Alan Freeman. Because Paul was not satisfied with the mix, the song was remixed for mono on April 7 by Glyn Johns and Jerry Boys at Olympic Sound Studios. This is the mix used on the British single. Johns and Boys also prepared a stereo mix for the American single. Paul was the only Beatle who attended these sessions. It is not known whether George Martin was present.

*Get Back* was the perfect choice for a single. As stated in the Apple ad shown on page 42, the song is "A pure springtime rock number." The Beatles quickly recognized the song's potential during the recording sessions. On January 26, Ringo called it the best of the new songs and George referred to *Get Back* as the group's next single.

*Don't Let Me Down* was written by John as an expression of his love for Yoko Ono. In late 1968, he recorded a demo containing most of the elements of the finished song.

John introduced *Don't Let Me Down* on the morning of January 2, 1969, as his initial offering for the project. The first run-throughs of the song, with John playing chords and George adding some lead guitar lines, took place prior to Paul's arrival. After McCartney arrived, he rearranged John's composition and suggested that it open with the title being sung twice. The group devoted a portion of the next day's session to additional rehearsals of the song.

When the band returned to the song on January 6, a considerable amount of time was spent on the middle eight. The group experimented with different rhythms, lyrics, harmonies, falsetto voices and call and response vocals, none of which proved satisfactory. About the only new idea surviving the day's extensive and frustrating rehearsals was John's decision to open the song with a guitar introduction rather than vocals. And while much of time devoted to the song was unproductive, the group did manage to work its way through a few near-satisfactory performances that showed the song's potential. At this stage, the instrumentation of the song was still open to discussion, with consideration being given to adding piano. Although George was willing to play bass to allow Paul to move to piano, John wanted the song to have two guitars. During the initial rehearsals of the song, and for the next few days, George used a wah-wah pedal to alter the sound of his guitar.

The group returned to the song on January 7, once again working on the middle eight. Performances from the next two days show the band making progress in spite of John's constant inability to remember the lyrics.

Prior to the start of rehearsals on January 10, Paul played several tunes on piano, including *Don't Let Me Down*. By the time the group returned to the song that afternoon, George had quit the band. The performance by the remaining Beatles was an embarrassing mess.

The first session at Apple's basement studio took place on January 21. *Don't Let Me Down* was one of the songs rehearsed that day. During the middle eight of one of the performances, John resorts to laughter and Little Richard improvisations. Another runthrough is tighter, but once again spiked with inappropriate vocal ad-libs. George is no longer using his wah-wah pedal and is playing his rosewood Fender Telecaster through a Leslie speaker.

Billy Preston joined the Apple *Get Back* sessions on January 22. One of the first songs shown to him was *Don't Let Me Down*. On his first take of the song with the band, Preston starts tentatively, but quickly falls into a groove with his blues-sounding electric piano riffs. John plays organ on this performance, perhaps to help Billy learn the chords to the song. After a bit of rehearsals, the group performs a fairly solid rendition of the tune, although John has trouble with the lyrics to the first verse and gets a bit silly during the second bridge. As the song reaches what had previously been its ending, John says "Take it Billy" and the band starts up again with Preston taking a piano solo while John ad-libs "Can you dig it?" and "I had a dream this afternoon." When the song comes to a halt, John says the song's title and the band adds a brief coda. One of the later takes from this day was selected by Glyn Johns for inclusion on the unreleased *Get Back* album.

When the Beatles returned to *Don't Let Me Down* on January 27, they rehearsed specific sections of the song and recorded two complete takes. While the song was beginning to come together, there were still vocal glitches.

By January 28, the band had finally mastered the song, turning in two near perfect performances. The best of these was selected to serve as the flip side to *Get Back*, although part of John's vocal from another take was dropped in to cover up some flubbed lyrics during the first verse. In addition, some vocal ad-libs and screams by John and Paul from another take were added to the end of the song.

The following day the group, without Billy Preston, rehearsed *Don't Let Me Down* for the rooftop concert. To avoid straining his vocal chords, John sang in a deeper and more relaxed voice than on previous performances. Paul stopped the song midway through the first verse to work on his harmony part with John. During some of the choruses, John sang the title to *Keep Your Hands Off My Baby*, which was a 1962 hit for Little Eva and was recorded by the Beatles as one of their early BBC performances. Towards the end of the song, John calls out, "Go Bill," and does a brief vocalization of the missing pianist's solo.

The group played *Don't Let Me Down* twice during the January 30 rooftop concert. During the first performance, John forgot the opening lyrics to the second verse, forcing him to ad-lib some gibberish. When the group returned to the song later in the show, John muffed the lyrics to the first verse. The earlier take of the song is tighter and appears in the film.

The January 28 version of song selected for the single was mixed for mono and stereo on April 7, 1969, at the same mixing session as *Get Back*. Glyn Johns and Jerry Boys served as engineers.

Apple prepared 16 mm color promotional films for both sides of the single using footage shot by Michael Lindsay-Hogg during the sessions. The *Get Back* clip features scenes from a rooftop performance of the song synchronized to the master tape of the released single. The film aired in England in black and white on *Top Of The Pops* on April 24 and May 8, 15 and 22, 1969. It appeared in color on *Top Of The Pops '69* on December 25, 1969. In America, the promo film was shown in color on *The Glen Campbell Goodtime Hour* broadcast by CBS on April 30, 1969. The film for *Don't Let Me Down* combined studio and rooftop performances of the song synchronized to the released single. This promo film was not broadcast in England, but was shown in the United States on the same Glen Campbell show that featured *Get Back*.

For the second single in a row, neither Apple nor Capitol prepared a picture sleeve. This is unfortunate, as an attractive and interesting sleeve for *Get Back* could have been made with pictures from the rooftop concert. Instead, the record was packaged with "The Beatles on Apple" sleeves.

The first layout variation, **APP 2490.01**, has "GET BACK" on one line followed by the songwriters credit in the upper left part of the apple. "THE BEATLES with Billy Preston" is below the center hole. This single marked the first and only time an outside musician was given credit on the label to a Beatles record. On the B side, the song title is on three lines followed by the songwriters credit in the upper left part. "THE BEATLES with Billy Preston" is in the lower left part. Both sides have "STEREO" is in the upper right and all other information to the right of the center hole. The master number is preceded by "S45-X," indicating a stereo 45 and a foreign recording. Although the label states "Recorded in England," there is no production credit,

perhaps due to the dual involvement of George Martin and Glyn Johns. All label copy is in thin print.

The first labels printed for the single, **2490.01L(i)(c)**, have light green apple labels with Capitol logo perimeter print and are missing the running times for the songs. The second batch of labels, **2490.01L(ii)(c)**, are the same, except that the running times have been added after "BMI." The initial press run of the single used up all of the first batch and many of the second batch of labels. Thus, when the record first went on sale, it could be found either with or without the running times on its labels. This label variation appears on singles pressed by Capitol's Los Angeles, Scranton and Jacksonville factories, as well as non-Capitol plants (identified by the lack of serrations).

The film for this variation was also used by Scranton and Jacksonville on later pressings of the single. The later Scranton discs have dark green apple labels with Capitol logo perimeter print. The later Jacksonville records were pressed with dull medium green apple labels with Apple perimeter print on the A side, **2490.01J(ii)(af)**.

The second layout variation, **APP 2490.02**, is similar to the first, except that the print for the song titles, group name, stereo designation and record number is thicker, and the font for the record number is different, particularly noticeable on the 9 and 0. The first labels with this variation have glossy light green apples and Capitol logo perimeter print, **2490.02L(c)**. Later pressings have light green apples with Apple perimeter print on the A side, **2490.02L(af)**, or on both sides, **2490.02L(ab)**. All of the records with this variation examined for this book were L.A. pressings.

There is a third layout variation, **APP 2490.03S(c)**, that has "GET BACK" on two lines followed "(Lennon & McCartney)" in the upper left part of the apple. The most striking characteristic of this variation is its thin font. Unlike the other variations, "THE BEATLES with Billy Preston" is located in the upper right part of the apple, "STEREO" is to the left of the center hole and "Recorded in England" below the center hole. All other information is to the right of the center hole. The layout is similar for the B side. The uneven typesetting for the song titles, group's name, stereo designation and record number is so tightly compressed that some of the characters touch each other. On some copies of the record, Billy Preston's last name appears as "Presto" on the A side. These amateurish-looking labels were printed in-house by Capitol's Scranton factory on glossy light green apple label backdrops with Capitol logo perimeter print supplied by Queens Litho. Because they do not list the running times for the songs, the labels were most likely used with first pressings of the single.

There are two all rights variations. Both have a layout similar to **APP 2490.02**, except that the placement of the "Lennon-McCartney" credit on the B side is slightly different. The all rights language appears on two lines at the bottom of the apple on the A side and on five lines in the lower right part of the apple on the B side. The Los Angeles pressings, **APP 2490.11L(ar)**, have light green apple labels with Apple perimeter print on both sides. The Jacksonville pressings, **APP 2490.11J(ar)**, have dull dark green apple labels with Apple perimeter print on the A side.

APP 2490.01L(i)(c)

APP 2490.01L(ii)(c)
(shown)
APP 2490.01J(ii)(af) (same, except dull medium green apple Jacksonville pressing
with Apple perimeter print on A side)

APP 2490.02L(c)

APP 2490.02L(ab)
(shown)
APP 2490.02L(af) (same, except Apple perimeter print only on A side)

APP 2490.03S(c)

APP 2490.11J(ar)
(shown)
APP 2490.11L(ar) (same, except light green apple labels and Apple perimeter print on both sides)

# The Beatles

## Ballad of John and Yoko

## Old brown shoe

Apple
Records
#2531

Apple's trade ad for *The Ballad Of John And Yoko* ran in the June 14, 1969, *Billboard.* The ad features the same Linda McCartney photo of the Beatles and Yoko Ono appearing on the single's American picture sleeve.

## THE BALLAD OF JOHN AND YOKO b/w OLD BROWN SHOE
## APPLE 2531

During spring, 1969, the Beatles continued to surprise their fans. Although the group's current single, *Get Back*, was firmly planted at number one, the Beatles rush released a new single featuring *The Ballad Of John And Yoko* b/w *Old Brown Shoe*. In 1964, with a half dozen American record companies having the rights to certain Beatles songs, it was not unusual for several of the group's records to be on the charts at the same time. However, those days of fast and furious releases were long gone. Over eight months had separated the release of *Hey Jude* and its follow up single, *Get Back*. But, less than one month after issuing *Get Back* in America, the Beatles had a new 45.

*The Ballad Of John And Yoko* was released in England by Parlophone as Apple R 5786 on May 30, 1969. Capitol issued the record on June 4 as Apple 2531. Although the song topped the British charts, things were different in America as several radio stations refused to play the song due to its lyrical content. The single entered the *Billboard Hot 100* on June 14 at number 71. By July 12 it reached its peak position of number eight, where it remained for three weeks. During the song's nine week chart run, the number one songs were *Get Back*, *Love Theme From Romeo & Juliet* by Henry Mancini (RCA 74-0131) and *In The Year 2525* by Zager & Evans (RCA 74-0174). *Cash Box* charted *The Ballad Of John And Yoko* at number ten, while *Record World* gave the song its highest ranking at number seven. None of the magazines charted the disc's B side, *Old Brown Shoe*. Despite having limited airplay, the single sold over one million copies, giving the Beatles yet another RIAA certified gold record.

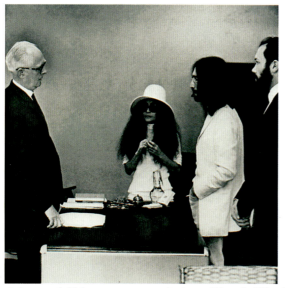

**John and Yoko were married on March 20, 1969, at the British Consulate in Gibraltar. The ceremony was performed by registrar Cecil Wheeler (left in left photo) while Peter Brown looked on. The couple then traveled to the Amsterdam Hilton, where they invited the press to attend their Bed-In for peace.**

The June 7, 1969, *Billboard* reported that the Beatles had released a controversial single that "mentions Christ in a manner considered blasphemous by some critics." The article stated that the song had been banned by a flock of radio stations. In New York, WMCA and WABC refused to play the disc. WABC's program director said he banned the record "because I'd be talking to more monsignors in two minutes than I've talked to all year." WNEW-FM added the song to its playlist. In Chicago, ABC-owned WLS refused to play the record, while WCFL placed the song in heavy rotation. The same issue reviewed the single, erroneously naming it *"The Battle Of John And Yoko." Billboard* correctly predicted that regardless of the controversy over the song, it would follow in the footsteps of *Get Back* from a sales standpoint.

Although limited airplay kept *The Ballad Of John And Yoko* from topping the charts in the United States, the single reached number one in several countries, including England, Canada, Holland, Denmark, Norway, Belgium, Austria, Spain and Mexico, where the song was identified as *La balada de John y Yoko*. The single reached number two in Switzerland and Malaysia, number three in Germany and New Zealand and number four in Argentina. It was also a top ten hit in Israel.

In mid-March of 1969, John and Yoko decided to get married. They headed to the port of Southampton with visions of having the ceremony take place at sea. This plan fell through and the couple flew to Paris hoping to wed in France. After their attempt at a quick wedding in Paris failed, John asked Peter Brown, the Beatles personal assistant, to check out other possible locations. While John and Yoko were honeymooning down by the Seine, Peter Brown called to say they could get married in Gibraltar near Spain. The wedding took place on March 20.

After the ceremony, the couple returned to France and went from Paris to the Amsterdam Hilton to stage their week-long Bed-In for peace. This was followed by a lightning trip to Vienna, where they held a press conference (and ate chocolate cake) while inside a large white bag. On April

Fool's Day, the newlyweds caught the early plane back to London, where they held a press conference at Heathrow Airport. John and Yoko sent acorns to heads of state throughout the world, asking each leader to plant an acorn for peace. All of these events were covered extensively by the men from the press.

*The Ballad Of John And Yoko* chronicles the chaotic events surrounding the couple's wedding. John accurately describes the lyrics as both a "piece of journalism" and a "folk song." On April 14, 1969, John dropped by Paul's house for help in completing the song. That afternoon they headed over to Abbey Road to record what would be the Beatles next single. Because Ringo was busy filming *The Magic Christian* and George was out of the country, John and Paul were the only Beatles at the studio.

They went through 11 takes (four of which were complete) with Lennon on lead vocal and acoustic guitar and McCartney on drums. It was a good natured and productive session. Prior to the start of Take 4, John called out to Paul, "Go a bit faster, Ringo!" to which Paul replied, "OK, George!" Take 10 was determined to be the best backing track. After Paul added bass, John overdubbed two separate guitar parts on his Epiphone Casino. Paul then contributed piano and backing vocals for the bridge and last two verses. The track was further embellished with Paul shaking maracas and John thumping the back of his guitar. The song was then mixed for stereo. No mono mix was made because the single was to be issued in stereo in both the U.S. and England, making the disc the group's first British stereo 45.

The finished master is an infectious rocker with clever, but controversial, lyrics. The song's chorus quickly caught the attention of radio program directors, with many refusing to play a record with John singing: "Christ you know it ain't easy, you know how hard it can be/The way things are going, they're gonna crucify me."

John knew that the song's chorus would cause problems, particularly coming from the man who previously said the Beatles were more popular than Jesus. In a note to

The 20th anniversary picture disc (Parlophone RP 5786) features the photo from the *Old Brown Shoe* side of the American picture sleeve on the B side (left) and a picture from the group's final photo session of August 22, 1969, on the A side (right).

Apple promo man Tony Bramwell, Lennon gave the following instructions: "<u>No</u> pre-publicity on Ballad Of John & Yoko especially the Christ! bit–So don't play it round too much or you'll frighten people–Get it <u>pressed first</u>." The song was originally titled "*The Ballad Of John And Yoko (They're Gonna Crucify Me)*." John wisely decided to drop the subtitle.

Apple prepared two similarly-edited color films to promote the song. The clips have the feel of a travelog, with sequences of John and Yoko in Paris, Amsterdam, Vienna and London and driving through the English countryside in John's Rolls-Royce. There is also a brief sequence of the Beatles rehearsing at Twickenham. In England, the film was shown in black and white on *Top Of The Pops* on June 5, 12 and 26, 1969, and in color on December 26. In the United States, the film aired on the September 22, 1969, debut of the ABC-TV show *Music Scene*, though the sound was edited out over the word "Christ" on each chorus. The October 4, 1969, *Billboard* reported that one of the highlights of the new show was a special film segment of the Beatles performance of "You Know It Ain't Easy."

The single's B side, *Old Brown Shoe*, was written by George on piano after returning home from the group's January 26, 1969, *Get Back* session. In his book *I Me Mine*, Harrison states that he "began writing ideas for the words from various opposites," focusing on "the duality of things – yes-no, up-down, left-right, right-wrong, etc." This approach is evident in the song's opening lines: "I want a love that's right, but right is only half of what's wrong/I want a shorthaired girl who sometimes wears it twice as long." Other opposites include pick me up-drag me down, smile-frown, love-hate and early start-late. Harrison's song is a rocking extension of the Eastern philosophy of yin-yang.

Upon arriving at Apple studios on the morning of January 27, George told the group that he had written a great new song the night before, which he described as a happy rocker. Although the song was complete, Harrison had yet to come up with a title. George played his new composition on piano for Billy Preston to teach him the chords.

After the group performed some oldies and extensively rehearsed *Let It Be* and *The Long And Winding Road*, George was given the opportunity to work on *Old Brown Shoe*. He played the song on piano and was joined at times by Ringo, who was experimenting with different drum beats, and John on bass (which he had been playing while Paul was on piano for *Let It Be* and *The Long And Winding Road*). When the performance broke down towards the end of the song, George commented "Pianos are very difficult, aren't they?" He then picked up the tune and finished it with Ringo and John. On the next runthrough, Ringo began to find his groove, and Billy Preston added organ. During the next few takes, Paul played guitar.

The following day George returned to the song, once again playing it on piano and this time teaching John the chords for him to play on guitar. For these rehearsals Paul is back on bass. Although parts of the performances show progress, George, John and Ringo often stumble. After John abandons his guitar for an organ-sounding instrument called an Ominichord, Preston plays piano, thus freeing George to switch to guitar. Because George wrote the song on piano and played it on piano for all previous performances, he jokes that he will have to learn the song on guitar. Some of George's guitar riffs are reminiscent of what he would later play when the group returned to the song in April.

On February 25 (his 26th birthday), Harrison recorded demos of *Old Brown Shoe*, *All Things Must Pass* and *Something* at Abbey Road. Engineer Ken Scott was the only person joining the birthday boy. For *Old Brown Shoe,* George recorded a live track of his vocal and piano and then overdubbed two lead guitar parts. This demo is on *Anthology 3*.

**The Danish and Swedish sleeves to the single (Apple R 5786) feature a Don McCullin color picture from the July 28, 1968, "Mad Day Out" photo session.**

George taped another demo version of the song on the afternoon of April 16. A few hours later the group joined him at Abbey Road for the tune's first proper recording. The backing track, with George on lead vocal and slide guitar on his Fender Telecaster, Paul on piano, John on rhythm guitar and Ringo on drums, was completed in four takes. Paul overdubbed his Fender Jazz Bass and George added a second guitar part on his Telecaster, matching Paul note for note on the bridge. John and Paul provided backing vocals and George rerecorded his lead vocal.

Two days later, at a session held with Chris Thomas subbing for George Martin, Harrison added a lead guitar solo on his Telecaster, played through a Leslie speaker and treated with ADT (artificial double tracking). He also recorded a Hammond organ part, which wiped out John's rhythm guitar. The song was then mixed for stereo.

In the United States, the single was issued in a white background picture sleeve featuring a different color photo of the Beatles and Yoko Ono on each side. The pictures were taken in the garden of Paul's Cavendish Avenue London home in spring, 1969, by Linda McCartney. The *Ballad* side of the sleeve has "The Beatles" in orange towards the upper left corner, a lime green border surrounding the center-placed photo and the record number 2531 and song titles in black towards the upper right corner. A circled "PRINTED IN U.S.A." appears in the lower left corner and a black Apple logo is to the right of the picture at the bottom of the sleeve. The picture has John and Yoko sitting among knee-high stone figurines, with Paul, Ringo and George standing behind them. The somber facial expressions give the impression that Paul, George and Ringo resented having Yoko included in the group photo. The *Old Brown Shoe* side has "The Beatles" in lime green towards the upper left corner, an orange border around the center-placed photo and the song titles in black towards the upper

right corner. The photo has a much more relaxed atmosphere than the picture on the *Ballad* side. The lower right corner shows an old brown shoe wedged between the branches of a flowered bush, indicating that the pictures were taken specifically to promote the new single. The East Coast sleeves, **APP 2531.PS1A**, which were printed and manufactured by Queens Litho in New York, have straight cut tops. The West Coast sleeves, **APP 2531.PS1B**, were made by Bert-Co Enterprises in Los Angeles and have a large rounded tab across the top of the *Ballad* side.

Apple's decision to rush release the single gave Capitol little time to send advance copies of the record to radio stations. Rather than wait for labels to be printed, Capitol's L.A. factory pressed hundreds of discs with blank white labels. Basic information regarding the songs was hand written onto the labels in blue ink. These promotional copies, **APP 2531.DJ1**, were then distributed to radio stations and reviewers. Stations were given a May 23, 1969, air date.

The first layout variation, **APP 2531.01**, has the song title and songwriters credit to the left of the center hole on both sides. The group's name is centered below the center hole on the A side and is in the lower left part of the apple on the B side. "Recorded in England" is below the group's name on the A side and in the lower right part of the apple on the B side. Both sides have "STEREO" in the upper right part of the apple and all other information to the right of the center hole. For the second straight single, there is no production credit even though George Martin produced the A side and was the primary producer for the B side. Perhaps this was merely an oversight.

The first pressings have Capitol logo perimeter print, **2531.01L(c)**. The discs pressed by Capitol's Los Angeles factory have light green apple labels, while the Scranton records, **2531.01S(c)**, have dark green apple labels. There are also non-Capitol East Coast pressings (no serrations surrounding the labels) with the dark green apple labels. Later pressings of the single have Apple perimeter print on the A side. There are Los Angeles pressings with light green apples, **2531.01L(af)**, and Jacksonville pressings with dark green apples, **2531.01J(af)**.

The second layout variation, **APP 2531.02S(c)**, has the song title, songwriters credit and "STEREO" to the left of the center hole, and the group's name, publishing information, time and record and matrix numbers to the right. On the A side, "Recorded in England" and "Manufactured by Capitol Records, Inc." appear below the center hole. On the B side, the same information is printed directly under the center hole. These labels have glossy dark green apples and Capitol logo perimeter print. They appear on records pressed by Capitol's Scranton factory. These labels may have been used for first pressings of the single, along with standard Keystone-printed labels.

The confirmed all rights variation, **APP 2531.11L(ar)**, has the same layout as **APP 2531.01**. The all rights language appears on five lines in the lower right part of the apple on the A side and in the upper left part of the apple on the B side. The labels to these Los Angeles pressings have light green apples and Apple perimeter print on both sides.

APP 2531.PS1B

APP 2531.PS1A

APP 2531.DJ1

APP 2531.01L(c)
(shown - glossy light green apple Los Angeles pressing)
APP 2531.01L(af) (same, except later Los Angeles pressing with Apple perimeter print on A side)

APP 2531.01S(c)
(shown, glossy dark green Scranton pressing)
APP 2531.01J(af) (same, except later Jacksonville pressing with Apple perimeter print on A side)

APP 2531.02S(c)

APP 2531.11L(ar)

## SOMETHING b/w COME TOGETHER
## APPLE 2654

On October 1, 1969, the Beatles issued the album *Abbey Road*. The two opening songs from the record were pulled for release as a single on October 6. Apple 2654 paired George's ballad *Something* with John's rocker *Come Together*. The same songs were later issued as a single in England on Apple R 5814 on October 31.

Although *Something* was designated the A side, each song received extensive airplay, with both entering the *Billboard Hot 100* on October 18. *Something* debuted at number 20 and *Come Together* at 23. The following week *Something* was at 11 and *Come Together* at 13. The November 1 chart showed *Something* remaining at 11 with *Come Together* pulling ahead at number ten. The next week *Something* crept into the top ten at number nine while *Come Together* jumped up to number three. The November 15 chart listed *Come Together* at number two and *Something* at three. The following week *Something* remained at three while *Come Together* fell to seven. Effective November 29, *Billboard* began a policy of reporting singles as a sole entry rather than listing each side of a double-sided hit separately. The Beatles single benefited from this new policy and topped the *Hot 100* that week, moving past the Fifth Dimension's *Wedding Bell Blues* (Soul City 779). In all, the Beatles 45 from *Abbey Road* spent 16 weeks on the charts, including nine in the top ten. While *Record World* charted *Come Together/Something* at number one, *Cash Box* continued its policy of separate reporting, listing *Come Together* at one and *Something* at two. As expected, the single quickly went gold, selling 1.6 million copies by mid-November. The RIAA certified sales of over 2 million units.

The single's 20th anniversary picture disc (Parlophone RP 5814) features the Abbey Road album cover on the B side (left) and a color photo shot by Ethan Russell at the Beatles last photo session of August 22, 1969, at John's Tittenhurst estate on the A side (right).

George began writing *Something* during the recording of *The White Album*. The song's opening line, "Something in the way she moves," came from the title to a selection from James Taylor's first album, *James Taylor* (Apple SKAO 3352). According to George, he composed the song on piano in an empty studio while waiting for Paul to complete overdubs. Chris Thomas, who served as producer for some of *The White Album* sessions, recalls George playing his new composition on harpsichord prior to recording *Piggies* on September 19, 1968.

Harrison, while playing his Fender Telecaster through a Leslie speaker, presented *Something* to the group towards the end of the *Get Back* sessions on January 28, 1969. After teaching the band the chords, George led the group and Billy Preston through a few loose rehearsals of the song. The lyrics were not finished, with Harrison looking to complete the second line. John advised George to "just say whatever comes into your head each time...until you get the word," and used "attracts me like a cauliflower" as an example. Following Lennon's advice, George sang "pomegranate" to fill the empty spot. Although Harrison had arranged the song's bridge, its lyrics were also incomplete. While John often ignored George's offerings for Beatles albums, he showed interest in the song and added backing vocals.

When George began playing an instrumental version of the song during the next day's rehearsals, Lennon comments "Just going through the requests." After the rest of the band joins in, John ends up singing whatever he can remember of the words. When the song falls apart after the third verse, John asks "OK, should we get on with the rock 'n' roll show?"

George recorded a demo of *Something* at Abbey Road on February 25, 1969. This recording, which features George on electric guitar and vocal, is on *Anthology 3*. It contains the following extra lyrics not present on the fin-

ished master: "You know I love that woman of mine/And I need her all of the time/You know I'm telling you/That woman, that woman don't make me blue."

The Beatles first serious attempt at *Something* took place at Abbey Road on April 16, 1969, with 13 instrumental takes being recorded. The performances featured Harrison on guitar, George Martin on piano, Paul on bass and Ringo on drums. Although John was present, he did not participate.

Apparently dissatisfied with the instrumental track from April 16, the group returned to the song on May 2 at an Abbey Road session produced by Chris Thomas. The remake performances were designated Takes 1 through 36, with the final take being the best. The backing track featured George playing rhythm guitar on his Les Paul played through a Leslie speaker, John on piano, Paul on bass, Ringo on drums and Billy Preston on Hammond organ. At this stage, the song had a long and monotonous coda consisting of George's lead guitar, Paul's bass, Ringo's drums and John's piano, which is similar to the style of piano he would play on *Remember* from his *Plastic Ono Band* album. The coda inflated the song's running time to 7:48, nearly four minutes longer than the 3:00 finished master. Once again, no vocals were recorded.

Additional work was done on the backing track on May 5 at Olympic Studios, with George Martin serving as producer and Glyn Johns as engineer. Harrison added his lead guitar solo and fills and Paul rerecorded his Rickenbacker bass onto Take 36.

The remaining work on the song was done at Abbey Road with George Martin at the helm. On July 11, George recorded his lead vocal onto Take 36. The song was given a reduction mix down and edited down from 7:48 to 5:32, eliminating much of the instrumental coda. An early mono mix of Take 37 has John's piano (which all but disappears in the final mix) and Preston's organ prominently featured and Ringo's excellent drumming buried deeper in the mix.

**The opening line to *Something* comes from the title of James Taylor's *Something In The Way She Moves*, which appears on the singer's first album, *James Taylor* (Apple SKAO 3352) (open outside gatefold cover shown above). The record was released on February 17, 1969.**

On July 16, the following overdubs were added: a new Harrison lead vocal; Paul's backing vocals; and hand claps from George, Paul and Ringo. Two reduction mix downs, numbered Takes 38 and 39, were made, with the latter marked the best.

On August 4, Harrison, assisted by engineers Phil McDonald and Alan Parsons, prepared a rough stereo mix of the song from Take 39 for the purpose of cutting an acetate. The acetate was given to George Martin for preparation of an orchestral score.

On August 15, George rerecorded his guitar solo for the instrumental break and assisted George Martin with the recording of the orchestra, which consisted of 12 violins, four violas, four cellos and one string bass. The song was mixed for stereo on August 19 and edited down to 3:00, completely deleting the unnecessary instrumental coda.

Beatles historians have speculated that Allen Klein selected *Something* as the A side to attract George's favor; however, Allan Steckler, who worked with Klein at Abkco, has a different explanation. According to Steckler, "Klein believed in George's talent and wanted to enhance his reputation as a songwriter." Whatever the reason, the song was a worthy choice. Frank Sinatra called *Something* one of the greatest loves songs of the past fifty years, but erroneous credited it to Lennon and McCartney!

John got the title for *Come Together* from Timothy Leary, who visited John and Yoko in early June, 1969, at the couple's second and final Bed-In for Peace held at the Queen Elizabeth Hotel in Montreal, Canada. Timothy and his wife Rosemary sang on the chorus of John's hotel room recording of *Give Peace A Chance* and were mentioned in the lyrics of the song. Leary, who was an outspoken proponent of LSD, asked Lennon to write a song titled *Come Together–Join The Party* for his bid to become governor of California. John quickly responded with lyrics such as: "Come together right now/Don't come tomorrow, don't

come alone/Come together right now over me." Lennon recorded a demo for Leary, who adopted it as his campaign song and had the tape played on California radio stations. After being imprisoned for possession of marijuana in late 1969, Leary dropped out of the gubernatorial race, which was won by Ronald Reagan.

Meanwhile, unbeknownst to Leary, John reworked and expanded the song for recording with the Beatles. When Leary later heard the Beatles version of *Come Together* on the radio, he felt a bit miffed, but admitted that "the new version was certainly a musical and lyrical improvement over my campaign song."

John's improved arrangement of the song opens with him repeatedly singing "Shoot me," an idea borrowed from *Watching Rainbows*, an uncompleted song from the *Get Back* sessions. While these words took on a morbid twist when John was shot and killed in 1980, their meaning in 1969 was most likely drug related as John was shooting heroin at that time.

The song's opening line, "Here come old flat top, he come groovin' up slowly," is similar to a line from Chuck Berry's *You Can't Catch Me,* "Here come a flat top, he was movin' up with me." Although Lennon's *Come Together* has a totally different feel than the Berry rocker, he was sued for copyright infringement by the song's publisher. A settlement was reached when John agreed to record three songs controlled by the publisher. He satisfied this requirement by recording Lee Dorsey's *Ya-Ya* and Chuck Berry's *You Can't Catch Me* and *Sweet Little Sixteen* for his *Rock 'n' Roll* album (Apple SK-3419).

The remainder of the lyrics are Lennon at his nonsensical best–phrases that sound good, but may or may not mean anything. There are obvious references to himself such as "He Bag Production, he got walrus gumboot, he got Ono sideboard." The line "He shoot coca cola" is most likely an acknowledgment of his drug habit of shooting heroin and cocaine. There are probable references to George in the first verse: "He one holy roller, he got hair down to his knees." The final verse appears to cover Paul. "He roller coaster" may refer to Paul's *Get Back*, which an Apple ad described as "a song to rollercoast by." The "muddy water" and "mojo filter" references may reflect Paul's fondness for Muddy Waters' guitar riffs. The "Got to be good looking, 'cause he's so hard to see" line pokes fun at Paul's reputation as the "cute" Beatle. Whether "He got early warning" was John intimating Paul had bad breath is not known.

The Beatles recorded eight takes of *Come Together* on July 21, 1969, at Abbey Road. These performances feature live vocals from John backed by Paul on his Rickenbacker bass, George on his Les Paul guitar and Ringo on drums. Take 1, which is on *Anthology 3*, reveals how the song sounded before the addition of echo and overdubs. On the finished master, John's vocal is given heavy echo treatment, but on Take 1 his voice is pure and playful. John can clearly be heard singing "shoot me," while on the master the "me" is lost in the mix. Because he did not play guitar or piano, John was able to clap his hands to accentuate the beat, most often used to accompany him singing "shoot me." During the song's instrumental break, John plays tambourine and sings some of the lyrics from the first verse. He also plays tambourine towards the end of the song. The first take also reveals slight lyrical variations and that John had yet to come up with an acceptable last line for the final verse. Although the song would be refined during the next few days, Take 1 is a fascinating first performance that demonstrates the magic the band was still capable of delivering without studio wizardry or, in the case of the *Get Back* sessions, excessive rehearsals.

Because *Come Together* was recorded on a four-track tape machine, the best performance (Take 6) was copied to an eight-track to allow for overdubs. The eight-track tape was identified as Take 9. On July 22, Lennon rerecorded his lead vocal and added a guitar part. At John's request, Paul provided "swampy and smokey" piano fills. A maraca was added during the middle and ending instrumental portions of the song. Additional vocals were recorded on July 23 and 25, including Paul's backing harmony during the latter session. George contributed his double-tracked lead for the instrumental break and guitar solo for the song's ending, as well as the tone-pedal guitar chords leading into his solo, on July 29 and 30. The song was mixed for stereo on August 7.

The promotional film for *Something* features home movie-style clips of the Beatles and their wives. Fittingly, the film contains no images of the Beatles together with each other. By the time it was broadcast in England on *Top Of The Pops* on November 13, 1969, and in the States on *Music Scene*, the Beatles had each gone off to be with their wives. The promotional film is on the *Anthology* video.

Neither Apple nor Capitol prepared a picture sleeve for the single, so it was issued in America with "The Beatles on Apple" sleeves.

There are four layout variations for Something. All four variations may have been used with first pressings of the single.

The first variation, **APP 2654.01**, the song title, songwriters credit and the group's name below the center hole on the A side. The B side has the song title and songwriters credit in the lower left part of the apple and the group's name in the lower right part. Both sides have publishing information, time, record and master numbers, production credit and "Recorded in England" to the right of the center hole and "STEREO" at nine o'clock. The first pressings have light green apple labels with Apple perimeter print on the B side, **2654.01L(as)**. Later pressings have Apple perimeter print on the A side. There are Los Angeles pressings with light green apples, **2654.01L(af)**, and Jacksonville pressings with dark green apples, **2654.01J(af)**. Some non-Capitol pressings (identified by the lack of serrations) also have this layout.

The second layout variation, **APP 2654.02S(as)**, has the song title followed by the songwriters credit to the upper left of the center hole, the group's name below the center hole and all other information, including the stereo designation, to the right of the center hole. On the A side, the song title is hyphenated as "SOME-THING" and appears on two lines. On the B side, "THE" and "BEATLES" are separated by the center stem of the apple. The text to the right of the center hole has more space between the lines than on other labels. This variation appears on records pressed by Capitol's Scranton factory and has glossy light green apple labels with Apple perimeter print on the B side.

The third variation, **APP 2654.03S(as)**, has a layout similar to that of the second variation, but with the following minor differences: the spacing between the lines on the right side of the label is tighter; the group's name below the center hole is off-center to left; and the song titles are printed with a different font (the "O" and "M" being noticeably different). This variation appears on labels with Apple perimeter print on the B side, and has been confirmed on Scranton discs and non-Capitol pressings (without serrations). The first run records have glossy light green apple labels; later pressings have glossy dark green apple labels.

The fourth variation, **APP 2654.04J**, appears on glossy dark green apple labels and has the following characteristics: the song titles, followed by the songwriters credit, are in the top part of the apple (with the B side having "COME" in the upper left part of the apple and "TOGETHER" followed by the songwriters credit in the upper right part); the group's name, "Recorded in England" and "Manufactured by Apple Records, Inc." below the center hole; "STEREO" at nine o'clock; and all other information to the right of the center hole. These Jacksonville pressings have either Apple perimeter print on the A side, **2654.04J(af)**, or Capitol logo perimeter print on the B side, **2654.04J(c)**. The latter pressing is the only variation of the Something single with Capitol logo perimeter print and is treasured by collectors.

The confirmed all rights variation, **APP 2654.11L(ar)**, has the same layout as **APP 2654.01**. The all rights language appears on two lines at the top of the apple on the A side and on five lines in the upper left part of the apple on the B side. These Los Angeles pressings have light green apple labels and Apple perimeter print on both sides. They have "Mastered by Capitol" stamped in the trail off areas.

APP 2654.01L(as)
(shown)

APP 2654.01L(af) (same, except later Los Angeles pressings with Apple perimeter print on A side)
APP 2654.01J(af) (same, except later Jacksonville pressings with Apple perimeter print on A side)

APP 2654.02S(as)

APP 2654.03S(as)
(earlier pressings of this variation have glossy light green apple labels)

APP 2654.04J(af)

APP 2654.04J(c)

APP 2654.11L(ar)

THE BEATLES 'Something' 'Come Together' OUT NOW Apple Records

The Swedish pressing of the single (Apple R 5814) (above left) was issued with a picture sleeve featuring a black and white photo of the group on an apple.

The Japanese 45 (Apple AR-2400) (above right) features a different Bruce McBroom picture from the same April 9, 1969, photo session.

Apple prepared a 17½" x 22½" poster (left) to promote the *Something* single. The poster, which was also made available to members of the Beatles fan club, features a black and white photo taken by Ethan Russell on August 22, 1969, at the Beatles last photo session.

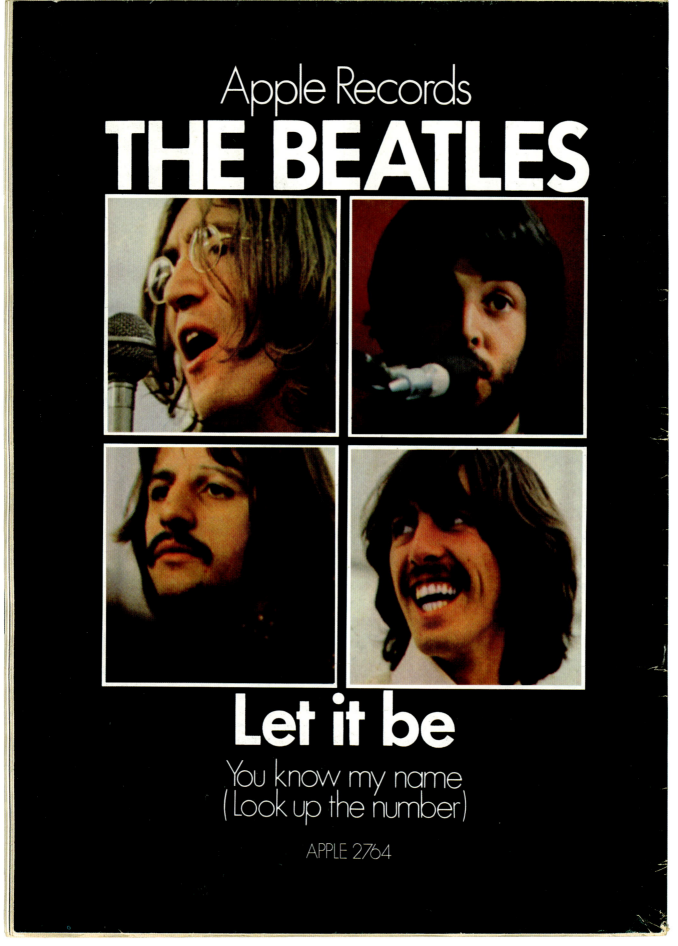

The above ad for the *Let It Be* single appeared on the back cover to the March 21, 1970, *Billboard*.

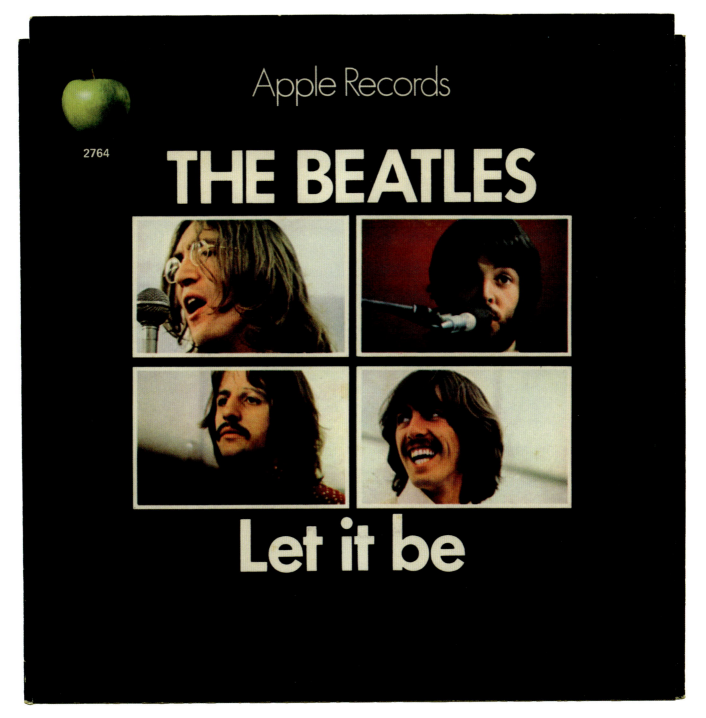

## LET IT BE b/w YOU KNOW MY NAME (Look Up The Number) APPLE 2764

As 1970 began, the Beatles still had not released their *Get Back* album that had been recorded a year earlier in January, 1969. Although John had informed the other Beatles in September, 1969, that he was quitting the group, the public was unaware of this development. Apple announced that the *Get Back* sessions would finally be released in the spring as both an album and a documentary film distributed through United Artists. To generate interest in the upcoming projects, the decision was made to issue *Let It Be* as the Beatles first single of the new year.

On March 6, 1970, Parlophone released *Let It Be* b/w *You Know My Name (Look Up The Number)* on Apple R 5833. The same songs were issued by Capitol on Apple 2764 on March 11. *Let It Be* entered the *Billboard Hot 100*

at number six on March 21. After spending two weeks at number two behind Simon & Garfunkel's *Bridge Over Troubled Water* (Columbia 4-45079), the song spent two weeks at the top before being replaced by the Jackson 5's *ABC* (Motown 1163). *Let It Be* was on the *Billboard* charts for 14 weeks, including 11 in the top ten. *Cash Box* and *Record World* also listed the song at number one. The April 18 *Billboard* reported that the single had been certified gold by the RIAA. Sales later passed the two million mark.

*Let It Be* was written by Paul during a difficult time in his life. John had become obsessed with Yoko, putting a strain on his relationship with Paul. The drugs, the stress, the tiredness were taking its toll on John and Paul. In Miles' *Many Years From Now,* Paul tells of the genesis of the song:

"One night during this tense time I had a dream I saw my mum, who'd been dead ten years or so. It was so wonderful for me and she was very reassuring. In the dream she said, 'It'll be all right.' I'm not sure if she used the words 'Let it be' but that was the gist of her advice, it was 'Don't worry too much, it will turn out okay.' It was such a sweet dream I woke up thinking, Oh, it was really great to visit her again. I felt very blessed to have that dream. So that got me writing the song *Let It Be*. I literally started off 'Mother Mary,' which was her name, 'When I find myself in times of trouble,' which I certainly found myself in. The song was based on that dream."

Although the reference to Mother Mary was to Paul's mother rather than the Virgin Mary, many people took it as a religious statement. This interpretation doesn't bother Paul. "Mother Mary makes it a quasi-religious thing, so you can take it that way. I don't mind. I'm quite happy if people want to use it to shore up their faith." Paul also acknowledged that the song helped get him through some tough times. "I was really passing through my 'hour of darkness' and writing the song was my way of exorcizing the ghosts."

Paul began writing *Let It Be* towards the end of the sessions for *The White Album*; however, he did not attempt to record the song at that time because the album was nearing completion. Instead, he chose to save the song for the group's next project.

On the morning of January 3, 1969, while waiting for the other Beatles to arrive at Twickenham Film Studios, Paul ran through the first verse and part of the chorus of *Let It Be*. Five days later on January 8, he introduced his new ballad to the group. During an equipment setup, Paul played the song on piano, accompanied at times by a disinterested John on guitar and Ringo on drums. John was not initially impressed with the song, kidding Paul that he should change Mother Mary to Brother Malcolm (a reference to the group's loyal assistant Mal Evans). Although Paul did not replace his mother with the Beatles former roadie in the song's lyrics, he did at times resort to singing "Brother Malcolm" when he found himself in times of trouble during a botched performance of the song. After a break for lunch and runthroughs of several other songs, including *I Me Mine* and *The Long And Winding Road*, Paul returned to *Let It Be*, calling out the chords for George. Ringo worked on his drum part and John occasionally sang on the choruses.

During rehearsals held on January 9, the song began to take shape. The most accomplished performance starts with Paul on piano and vocal for the first verse, with John and George supplying backing vocals on the chorus. During the second verse, Ringo falls into place, starting with his bass drum and tambourine kit before going to a tom-tom fill leading into the chorus and moving to his high-hat. John adds bass on the Fender Bass VI during the second chorus, which is followed by an instrumental break featuring a George Harrison guitar solo and backing vocals by John, George and Paul. At this stage Paul had not completed the lyrics, so some of the performances contained ad-libs and lines such as "read the *Record Mirror*, let it be." The following morning Paul played the song on piano for music publisher Dick James.

By the time Paul returned to *Let It Be* on January 23, the sessions had moved to the basement studio at Apple headquarters and Billy Preston had been invited to sit in on keyboards. While no group rehearsals of the song took place, Paul sneaked in two solo performances on piano, thus providing an opportunity for Preston to hear the ballad.

Even though Billy Preston was not present on January 25, Paul decided that it would still be productive for the group to rehearse the song, reasoning that Preston would pick up on it quickly. The initial rehearsals of the song were dreadful, marred by poor bass playing by John among other problems. Ringo still hadn't perfected his drum part and the backing vocals were erratic and too loud. In an attempt to rally the troops, Paul offered the following directive: "OK, you watch us, we're gonna do this now. OK, boys now, come on. Pull yourselves together." After John replies with "You talkin' to me?," George kick-starts the band into an impromptu performance of Chuck Berry's *I'm Talking About You*. Paul, wanting to carry on with *Let It Be,* brings things to a halt by interrupting with "Come on now, back to the drudgery." When John angrily reacts with "It's you that's bloody making it like this," Paul sarcastically replies "The real meaning of Christmas" and calms things down with the soothing opening chords to *Let It Be*. This is followed by a few mediocre rehearsals of the song.

Despite the degenerating mood of the session, Paul is confident the band can pull it together and instructs Glyn Johns to record the next take. *Anthology 3* contains this performance, which is introduced by Paul's assurance that "this here's gonna knock you out." Although Paul had yet to complete the lyrics, he turns in an excellent performance, highlighted by graceful piano playing and soulful vocals, backed by John and George on the choruses. During the second verse, the others join in with Ringo starting on his high-hat, John playing rudimentary bass on a Fender Bass VI and George playing his Telecaster through a Leslie speaker. George's guitar solo during the song's instrumental break is simple but effective. Although the band continued on with a few additional takes of the song before abandoning the day's session, these were unproductive as the group's energy level and interest were all but fully depleted.

On January 26, Billy Preston rejoined the sessions and played Hammond organ on the numerous rehearsals and recorded takes of the song. By this time, the song's structure had been settled, but Paul was still uncertain of what to sing for the last verse. This sometimes led to bizarre ad-libs, including one take where Paul sings "Now somewhere out in Weybridge is a cat whose name is Banagy." After Paul sings the usual "And in my darkest hour, she is...," George adds "sitting on the lavatory," causing John to repeat the phrase in a chuckling voice. On another take, Paul mumbles his way through the first line of the final verse before coming up with "You will be a good girl, let it be."

Although most of the performances recorded this day were substandard, one take was mixed by Glyn Johns on March 10, 1969. Johns included this version on an acetate containing songs from the *Get Back* sessions. Lennon's copy of the acetate was played by American radio stations and was the source for the *Get Back* bootlegs issued in 1969.

The 20th anniversary picture disc (Parlophone RP 5833) features the Ethan Russell photos from the 1970 picture sleeve. The A side (left) has unaltered color photos, while the B side images (right) are color tinted.

Paul led the group through additional rehearsals of the song on January 27. At times, John added inappropriate vocal ad-libs, perhaps out of boredom. On some performances, George and John played guitar and bass riffs during the early part of the song. Billy Preston experimented with different organ parts and George worked out his lead solo over the final chorus of the song. Paul sometimes sang scat vocals during the still unwritten third verse. The group did not rehearse the song the following day and turned in a pathetic performance on the 29th.

The day after their January 30 rooftop concert, the Beatles and Billy Preston returned to Apple's basement studio to record (with cameras rolling) proper takes of songs not suitable for the previous day's rocking performance. The group went through numerous takes of *Let It Be* (designated Takes 20 through 27 to coincide with take numbers from the film's clapper board). Some of the clapper board takes actually consisted of more than one performance as there were some false starts and breakdowns. Take 27 contains two complete performances of the song.

Shortly after a member of the film crew shouts "Take 20," the group begins a fine performance that is called off towards the end of the first chorus by Glyn Johns. After Johns explains that the vocals were popping, Paul responds "This isn't very loud, Glyn," and John adds "Poppin's in, man." A false start is followed by a fairly decent performance, although John muffs his bass part before the instrumental break and spews off an expletive. As the song concludes, John admiringly asks, "Let it be, eh?" After Paul says "Yeah," John adds "I know what you mean."

Take 21 breaks down after the chorus following the instrumental break, leading Paul to sing a few words in the voice of a drunkard. Although Take 22 was showing promise, Paul apparently realized it wasn't going to be the final take. Thus, for the last verse, he sings, "When I find myself in times of heartache, Brother Malcolm comes to me."

Prior to the start of Take 23, John asks "Are we supposed to giggle in the solo?" to which Paul replies "Yeah," followed by John's "OK." This bit of dialog was edited in before the start of *The Long And Winding Road* on both Glyn Johns versions of the *Get Back* album and also before the start of *Let It Be* on *Anthology 3*. Although John doesn't giggle during the solo of this spirited take, at the end of the performance he admits "I lost a bass note somewhere."

Take 24 gets into trouble during George's guitar solo, although Paul encourages him on by singing "Let it be, yeah, whoah." After Paul hits a sour chord going into the final verse, he sings "When I find myself in whoah," which prompts Billy Preston to play some soulful swirling organ. After a few gospel tinted lines, John calls the song off with an "OK, OK." Without missing a beat, Paul sings "OK, she stands right in" before admitting defeat by stopping the song.

When Take 25 unravels at the start of the chorus, John lets out a few expletives and engages with Paul in brief pseudo-German banter, including a unique count-in to a fresh start for Take 25. At the conclusion of the second Take 25, which is another "Brother Malcolm" version, the following conversation takes place:

John (sarcastically): I think that was rather grand. I'd take one home with me.

Glyn: No, that was fine.

John (in a voice mimicking the computer HAL 9000 from *2001: a space odyssey*): Don't kid us, Glyn. Give it to us straight.

Glyn: That was straight.

Paul: Ah, what do you think, Glyn?

Glyn: I don't think it's yet.

Paul: C'mon.

John: OK, let's track it. [Sharply intakes breath creating a "Huh!" sound.] You bounder, you cheat!"

John's last remark mocks the group's normal practice of overdubbing or tracking additional parts to their recordings, a definite "no no" for the *Get Back* project, which was originally intended to present the group live without any studio enhancements. Ironically, *Let It Be* would be the first of the *Get Back* session songs to receive overdubs. The first and last of John's above comments were edited to the end of *Let It Be* on *Anthology 3*.

Take 26 begins with Paul quickly abandoning the song and hitting the first few notes to *Twelfth Street Rag*. The next attempt at the song lasts longer, but falls apart at the start of the final verse.

After a film crew member announces "Take 27, sync to second clap," Paul follows with "Sync to second clap, please" before starting the performance that would later be used as the basic master for the single and album versions of the song. The take is near perfect, flawed only by a few sour notes during the middle of George's guitar solo.

Although Paul thought the take was "very fair," he still wanted to go "one more time." As Paul begins his piano introduction to the song, George asks Paul to hold briefly to allow him to tune a guitar string. After Harrison gives him the "OK," Paul remarks "Second clap," which causes George to break out in laughter during the start of the song. This excellent performance brought an end to the *Get Back* sessions and was featured in the film after being edited with a portion of the chorus from an earlier take.

After sifting through numerous recordings of *Let It Be*, Glyn Johns ultimately determined that the first Take 27 was the best version of the song and made a stereo mix of the tune on March 10, 1969. Although it was an excellent performance, George's guitar solo was substandard. To correct this problem, an exception was made to the "no overdubs" policy of the *Get Back* project. At the start of a session held on April 30, with Chris Thomas serving as producer, George overdubbed his guitar solo onto the eight track tape of Take 27. The augmented tape was mixed for stereo on May 28 and included on the master tape to both versions of the unreleased *Get Back* album.

Additional overdubs were added to Take 27 at a George Martin-produced session held on January 4, 1970, which was attended only by Paul, George and Ringo. John was on vacation in Denmark. McCartney and Harrison added backing vocals to Take 27. George Martin prepared a score for brass instruments (two trumpets, two trombones and a tenor saxophone), which was overdubbed live during three separate tape reductions designated Takes 28, 29 and 30. Take 30 was marked "best" and given further enhancements: a slightly raunchy lead guitar solo by George, additional drums by Ringo and maracas by Paul. Martin also scored a part for a few cellos, which was added towards the end of the song. Two stereo mixes were then made, with Remix 2 being used for the single. On this mix, George's January 4 guitar solo was mixed out and the brass was kept in the background. Although the overdub sessions went against the original concept of the *Get Back* project, the finished master is a refined improvement over the original January 31, 1969, performance. It remains one of the group's most popular songs.

While *Let It Be* is a tightly structured serious ballad, the single's flip side is the complete opposite—a free-spirited piece of nostalgic night club nonsense. *You Know My Name (Look Up The Number)* was recorded in several parts that would later be edited together. John lifted the title from a phrase appearing on the front cover to the 1967 London telephone directory: "You have their NAME? Look up their NUMBER." Although John envisioned the song as nothing more than the title repeated over and over again in the style of the Four Tops' *Reach Out I'll Be There*, the end result was more reminiscent of Goon Squad lunacy than Motown soul. In his *Playboy* interview, John described the song as "a piece of unfinished music that I turned into a comedy record with Paul."

The Beatles began work on Part One on May 17, 1967, during the time they were knocking out songs for the *Yellow Submarine* cartoon. The group recorded 14 takes consisting of Paul on piano and bass, John and George on guitars and Ringo on drums, supplemented by bongos, tambourine, hand claps and vocals. The group returned to the madness on June 7, adding overdubs to Take 9 and recording a separate rambling rhythm track that would not be used. The following evening the group recorded Parts Two through Five of the song. In addition to the usual instruments, the song contains George on vibraphone and Brian Jones of the Rolling Stones on tenor saxophone. The next evening (June 9) the song was edited together and numbered Take 30. The 6:08 rhythm track consisted of Take 9 of Part One, Take 12 of Part Two, Take 4 of Part Three, Take 6 of Part Four and Take 1 of Part Five. The song was mixed for mono and left alone while the group moved on to a more important project—the recording of *All You Need Is Love*.

After ignoring *You Know My Name* for nearly two years, John and Paul entered Abbey Road studio on April 30, 1969, to overdub vocals, percussion and sound effects, including crowd noise, applause and Mal Evans shoveling a bucket full of gravel. To add to the night club atmosphere, John asks the crowd for a big hand for Denis O'Bell, a name obviously derived from Denis O'Dell, who produced the *Magical Mystery Tour* TV film. Paul then takes on the persona of fictional crooner Denis O'Bell for the lounge act segment of the song. *You Know My Name*, still running 6:08, was mixed for mono at the end of the session.

Earlier that evening, George overdubbed a new improved guitar solo onto Take 27 of *Let It Be*. At that time, the group had no idea that the two songs would be issued together as the Beatles last British single nearly one year later in March, 1970.

In November, 1969, John decided that if the Beatles wouldn't release *What's The New Mary Jane* (a *White Album* reject) and *You Know My Name*, he would issue the songs as a single credited to the Plastic Ono Band. He booked a session at Abbey Road on November 26 (serving as co-producer with Geoff Emerick) to remix and edit the songs. Mono Remix 3 from April 30, 1969, of *You Know My Name* was copied and renamed Remix 4. It was then edited down to 4:19. *What's The New Mary Jane* was mixed for stereo and edited.

Apple quickly made test pressings of a single containing the songs, assigned a British catalog number (APPLES 1002) and announced a rush release date in England of December 5, 1969. An Apple press release stated that the disc featured John and Yoko backed by "many of the greatest show business names of today." This, however, was not to be as the single was put on hold on December 1 and was never released. Because the recordings were really Beatles songs, the release of the single was probably objected to by EMI and/or the other Beatles.

While *You Know My Name* would have been difficult to program onto a Beatles album, it was interesting enough to merit release. John finally succeeded in getting the song issued when it was placed on the B side to *Let It Be*.

*Anthology 2* contains a new version of the song that restores much of what John edited out in November, 1969. For the first time the song is in stereo and runs 5:42. The additional running time allows more of the song's infectious comedic aspects to surface.

The single was mastered at Bell Sound in New York by Sam Feldman. The trail off areas of the single have hand etched master numbers, a machine stamped Bell Sound logo and Sam Feldman's hand etched "sf" initials.

Apple prepared a promotional clip for the *Let It Be* 45 by synchronizing the master tape of the single with a performance of the song filmed on January 31, 1969. The promotional film made its debut on the March 1, 1970, *Ed Sullivan Show* and was shown twice in England on the BBC's *Top Of The Pops* (March 5 and 19). Volume 8 of the *Anthology* video contains a performance of the song.

*Let It Be* was the first British Apple single to be issued with a picture sleeve. (While Capitol prepared picture sleeves for all of its Beatles singles, the only Parlophone single to have a picture sleeve was *Strawberry Fields Forever* b/w *Penny Lane*.) The British and American sleeves are virtually identical.

The sleeve features the same Ethan Russell color photos of the faces of John, Paul, George and Ringo and has the same basic design as the black background cover to the deluxe picture book prepared in the summer of 1969 for the *Get Back* album (see page 243). With the exception of the song titles and manufacturing information, the two sides of the sleeve are identical. All of the text is white. "Apple Records" and "THE BEATLES" appear above the photographs. A green Apple logo and the record number 2764 are located in the upper left corner. The song titles appear below the pictures. There are two sleeve variations, both of which were probably printed by Queens Litho. The straight cut top sleeve, **APP 2764.PSA**, has "You know my name (Look up the number)" in thin letters on the open side and "Let it be" in thick letters on the other side. The second variation, **APP 2764.PSB**, has a curved down top on its open side and a curved up top on the other. "You know my name (Look up the number)" appears on the open side and "Let it be" on the other. The sleeves have "Manufactured by Apple Records, Inc. 1700 Broadway, New York, N.Y. 10019" in small upper case letters centered along the bottom of the open *You Know My Name* side. A circular "PRINTED IN U.S.A." appears in the lower right corner.

There are three layout variations of the single. The first variation, **APP 2764.01**, has the song title, songwriters credit and group's name centered below the center hole on the A side. The B side has the song title, mistakenly printed as *You Know My Name (Look Up My Number)* instead of "the" number, and songwriters credit to the left of the center and the group's name in the lower left part of the apple. "Recorded in England" is to the lower left of the center on the A side and in the lower right on the B side. "STEREO" is at nine o'clock on the A side, but does not appear on the flip side because *You Know My Name* is mono. All other information is to the right of the center on both sides. For the first time on a Beatles 45, the label lists an intro and total time for the songs. George Martin is credited as producer.

These Los Angeles pressings have glossy light green apple labels. The first run records have Apple perimeter print on the B side, **2764.01L(as)**, while later pressings have Capitol logo perimeter print, **2764.01L(c)**. This label variation also appears on later Jacksonville pressings with dull medium green apple labels with Apple perimeter print on the A side, **2764.01J(af)**, and later Los Angeles pressings with Apple perimeter on the A side, **2764.01L(af)**.

The second variation, **APP 2764.02**, has glossy dark green apple labels with the song title and songwriters credit to the left of the center hole. On the A side, the group's name and "*Recorded in England*" is below the center hole. The B side has the group's name in the lower left part of the apple and "*Recorded in England*" in the lower right part. Unlike the other variations, "(Look Up My Number)" is in upper and lowercase letters. "STEREO" is in the upper right part of the apple on the A side. All other information is to the right of the center hole on both sides. These Scranton labels have either Capitol logo perimeter print, **2764.02S(c)**, or Apple perimeter print on the B side, **2764.02S(as)**.

The third variation, **APP 2764.03**, has a layout similar to that of the second variation on the A side, but adds "Manufactured by Apple Records, Inc." at the bottom of the label and does not have the stereo designation. The B side is similar to that of the other variations, except that the group's name, "Recorded in England" and "Manufactured by Apple Records, Inc." are centered below the center hole. All copies of this variation examined for this book are Jacksonville pressings on glossy dark green apple labels with Capitol logo perimeter print, **2764.03J(c)**.

There are two all rights variations. The Los Angeles pressings, **APP 2764.11L(ar)**, are similar to **APP 2764.01**, except that the spacing between lines is different and the A side has the time information on the left rather than right side of the label. The all rights language is on two lines at the top of the apple on the A side and on five lines in the lower right part of the apple on the B side. These records have light green apple labels with Apple perimeter print on both sides. The discs have "Mastered by Capitol" stamped in the trail off areas. The Jacksonville pressings, **APP 2764.12J(ar)**, use the same film as **APP 2764.01**. The all rights language is on five lines to the upper right of the center hole on the A side and on two lines at the bottom of the label on the B side. These records have dull dark green apple labels and Apple perimeter print on the A side.

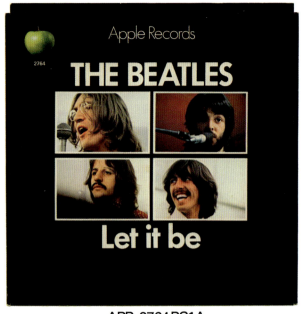

APP 2764.PS1A

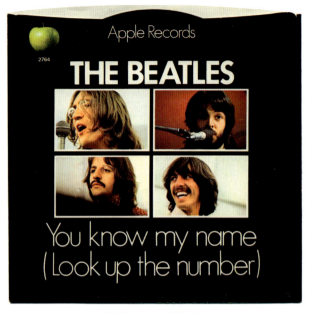

APP 2764.PS1B

APP 2764.01L(as)

APP 2764.01L(c)

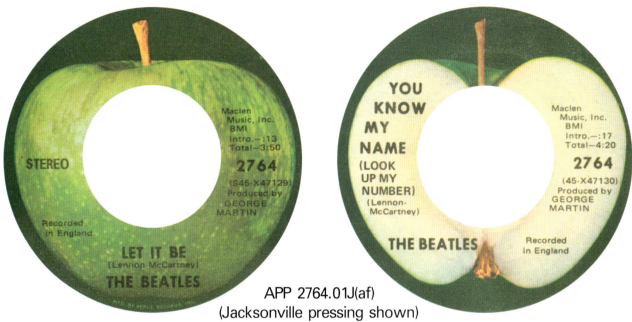

APP 2764.01J(af)
(Jacksonville pressing shown)
APP 2764.01L(af) (same, except light apple label Los Angeles pressing)

APP 2764.02S(c)

APP 2764.02S(as)

APP 2764.03J(c)

APP 2764.11L(ar)

APP 2764.12J(ar)

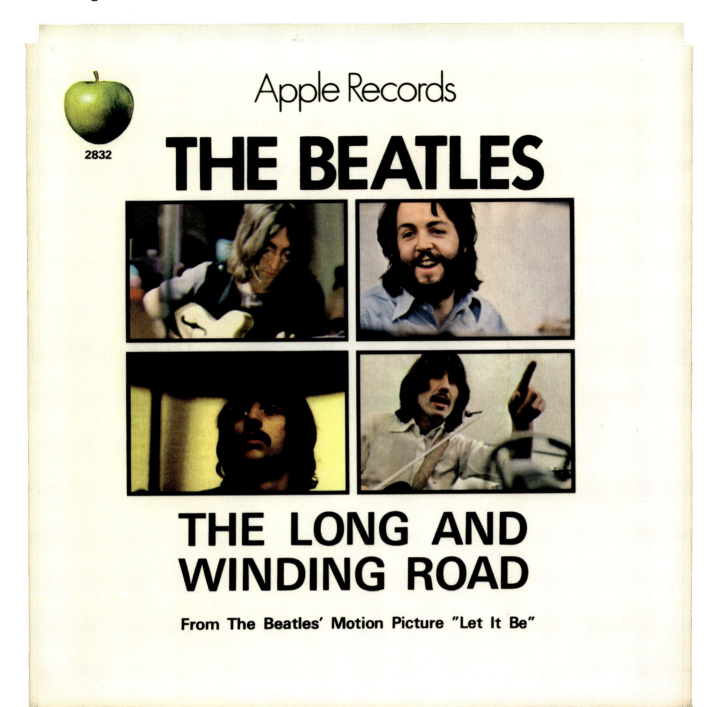

Apple Records

2832

# THE BEATLES

## THE LONG AND WINDING ROAD

**From The Beatles' Motion Picture "Let It Be"**

## THE LONG AND WINDING ROAD b/w FOR YOU BLUE
## APPLE 2832

On May 11, 1970, two months after the release of the *Let It Be* single and one week prior to the release of the *Let It Be* album, Apple issued an American single pairing two songs from the LP: *The Long And Winding Road*, a piano ballad by Paul in the same style as *Let It Be*, and *For You Blue*, an upbeat song by George. The record, which was distributed by Capitol as Apple 2832, was the last single containing previously unissued performances released by the Beatles until the mid-nineties. The 45 was not issued in England.

Although Paul's ballad was the A side and received the majority of air play, George's tune was popular enough to cause *Billboard* to track the 45 as a double-sided hit record. *The Long And Winding Road/For You Blue* entered the *Billboard Hot 100* at number 35 on May 23, while *Let It Be*

was still in the top ten at number six. After moving up to 12 and then to 10, the record topped the charts in its fourth week on June 13. It replaced Ray Stevens' *Everything Is Beautiful* (Barnaby 2011) and thankfully kept *Which Way You Goin' Billy* by the Poppy Family (London 129) from becoming a number one hit. After two weeks at the top, the single dropped to number four behind *The Love You Save* by the Jackson 5 (Motown 1166), *Mama Told Me (Not To Come)* by Three Dog Night (Dunhill 4239) and the Temptations' *Ball Of Confusion* (Gordy 7099), with its line "The Beatles new record's a gas." The Beatles new record spent two more weeks in the top ten before running out of gas and dropping to numbers 20 and 21 in its final weeks in *The Hot 100*. All told, the single charted for ten weeks, including six in the top ten.

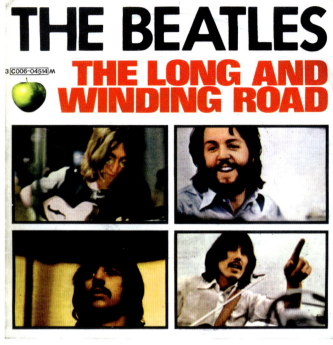

**Although *The Long And Winding Road* was not issued as a single in England, many countries in addition to the U.S. and Canada issued the 45. The Spanish single (Odeon J 006-04514) has a black background sleeve (left) with the same pictures as the American sleeve. The Italian sleeve (right) also has the same photos.**

*Cash Box* and *Record World* also reported the single at number one. This gave the Beatles 20 number one hits on *Billboard*, 22 chart toppers on *Cash Box* and 23 number ones on *Record World*. The RIAA certified sales of one million units.

As was the case with *Let It Be*, Paul began writing *The Long And Winding Road* during the sessions for *The White Album*. After Alistair Taylor told Paul of his fondness for the melody, McCartney recorded the unfinished tune and gave the tape to Alistair as a present for his wife Lesley. According to Paul, he wrote the tune with Ray Charles in mind, thus explaining the song's "slightly jazzy" chord structure. In Miles' *Many Years From Now*, McCartney recalled: "I was a bit flipped out and tripped out at that time. It's a sad song because it's all about the unattainable; the door you never quite reach. This is the road that you never get to the end of."

Paul played a brief segment of *The Long And Winding Road* on January 3, 1969, while waiting for the others to arrive at Twickenham. He returned to the song on January 7 under similar circumstances, this time spending nearly five minutes working through the tune. Although the chords and melody for the verses and bridge were in place, the lyrics had yet to be completed, with Paul only having one verse and a part of the bridge. After Ringo and George arrived, Paul played part of the song again, but made no effort to teach it to the others. He also slipped in a bit of the tune later in the day between rehearsals of other songs.

On January 8, Paul made his first efforts to teach the song to the band. John showed some interest in learning the chords when Paul briefly played the song during a break in rehearsals for George's *I Me Mine*; however, he did not participate when Paul returned to the song later that day. The next two mornings, Paul included the ballad as part of his piano warm up while waiting for the others to arrive

at Twickenham. He also played instrumental versions of the song on the afternoons of January 10 and 22. Paul slipped in two additional performances of the ballad on January 23.

By the time Paul finally got the band to rehearse the song seriously on January 26, he had completed the lyrics. The Beatles, joined by Billy Preston on organ, went through about a dozen performances of the song with Paul on piano, George on his Telecaster played through a Leslie speaker, John on the Fender Bass VI and Ringo on drums. After Paul taught the others the chords, the band plowed through a few dreadful performances before getting a feel for the song. John's initial bass playing was obtrusive and awkward. To add a touch of levity to the session, the group performed a cha-cha Latin-influenced version until Paul called it off with "All right lads, that's enough" after a minute and a half. Part of this segment appears in the *Let It Be* film. On one of the later performances, George experimented with playing a lead guitar melody line throughout the tune.

After a few stop and start runthroughs during which Paul instructed Ringo on how he wanted the cymbals played, McCartney asked Glyn Johns to record the song. Although this take began with two false starts, the completed performance was near perfect and was selected by Johns for inclusion on the *Get Back* album. It also served as the basic track for the version of the song released on the *Let It Be* album and as the group's last American single on Apple.

After the band listened to a playback of the performance at the end of the day's session, the group and George Martin discussed the possibility of adding brass and strings. Over 14 months later, Phil Spector would add brass, strings and a choir to the track. Details regarding Spector's overdubs are discussed below. The unaltered take, as nature intended, is on *Anthology 3*. This performance is somewhat unique in that it features Paul singing the words to the bridge over what is normally the instrumental break in the song.

The Danish and German singles (Apple C006 04 514) have the same sleeve (left) with different pictures than the American counterpart. The Japanese version (Apple AR-2611) (right) boasts a colorful sleeve also using a unique combination of Ethan Russell photographs from the *Get Back* book.

Apparently Paul was not satisfied with the January 26 performances of the song, so he ran the group through additional rehearsals the following day. The band turned in a few deliberately off-the-wall performances, including one in which John did most of the singing and Paul mimicked Al Jolson. Although one serious complete take was recorded, it was not as good as the best from the day before.

On January 28, Billy Preston, on electric piano, led the band through a blues jam reminiscent of T-Bone Walker's *Call It Stormy Monday*. The song is referred to as *The River Rhine* because Preston repeatedly sings that he's "moving along by the River Rhine." Shortly before the two minute mark, Paul, who is on bass, sings about a minute of lyrics from *The Long And Winding Road* in a bluesy voice. This performance is interesting in that it shows how the song might have sounded if Paul had followed his original idea of modeling the tune with Ray Charles in mind.

The following day the Beatles ran through most of the songs that they had been working on during the sessions, including *The Long And Winding Road*. The first attempt at the song broke down after the first verse. Paul then began singing the second verse and led the band through the rest of the song. After Paul comments that John's a bit heavy on the bass, he requests that they do the song again with John playing softer. On previous performances, Paul had been singing the line "Anyway you'll never know the many ways I've tried" during the bridge. This time he changed the lyrics to "Anyway you'll always know the many ways I've tried." Apparently Paul thought the change from "never" to "always" was an improvement as he sang "Anyway you've always known the many ways I've tried" for all subsequent performances during the sessions.

The final set of rehearsals and performances of *The Long And Winding Road* took place on January 31 in Apple's basement studio. After Paul rehearsed parts of the song for fine tuning, he led the group through several recorded takes (designated Takes 13 through 19 to coordinate with the film's clapper board). Some clapper board takes consisted of multiple performances as there were some false starts and break downs. During the song's instrumental break, Paul provided scat vocals over Billy Preston's Hammond organ solo. Takes 13B, 15B, 16C, 16D, 18 and 19 are complete, with the final take being the best. Take 19 is featured in both the *Let It Be* movie and the *Anthology* video.

On March 10, 1969, Glyn Johns took the session tapes to Olympic Studios and made a stereo mix of the best of the January 26 performances of *The Long And Winding Road*. He made additional mixes of the song over the next two days. In all likelihood his mixes included Take 19 from January 31. After comparing these two performances, Johns gave the nod to the January 26 take of the song and included it on an acetate. When Johns compiled his version of the *Get Back* album on May 28, 1969, he once again went with the January 26 performance.

As detailed in subsequent chapters on the *Get Back* and *Let It Be* LPs, the Beatles were not satisfied with the albums Glyn Johns prepared from the session tapes. In March of 1970, the project was turned over to Phil Spector, who had produced Lennon's latest single, *Instant Karma!*

On April 1, 1970, Spector, working with engineers Peter Brown and Richard Lush in Abbey Road's Studio One, augmented the Beatles sparse January 26 performance of *The Long And Winding Road* with 18 violins, four violas, four cellos, a harp, three trumpets, three trombones, two guitars, a choir of 14 singers and Ringo on drums. Richard Hewson arranged the score and conducted the orchestra and choir. During the song's instrumental break, Spector faded Paul's vocal out of the mix and replaced it with a heavy dose of strings and choir. This is the version of the song on the *Let It Be* album and on the single pulled from the LP.

Of all of Phil Spector's work on the project, *The Long And Winding Road* is by far the most controversial. Although some people believe Spector made necessary improvements to a dull and plodding song, most feel that he grossly overproduced the track. George Martin and Glyn Johns were shocked and disgusted. Paul was particularly upset with the use of the choir.

In his lawsuit to dissolve the Beatles partnership, McCartney stated that he received an acetate of the *Let It Be* album in early April, 1970, along with a letter from Phil Spector, which said that Paul should contact him if he wanted any alterations. After he was unable to contact Spector by phone, Paul sent Allen Klein a letter on April 14, 1970, requesting alterations be made to *The Long And Winding Road*. Although McCartney believed there was sufficient time to modify the track, the song was issued as re-produced by Spector on April Fools Day, 1970.

It has been argued that Spector needed to add orchestration to the song to cover up John's poor bass playing. This argument does not hold up as Paul could have been called in to overdub a new bass part.

Although conversations taped during the sessions indicate that Paul was not against adding strings and brass to *The Long And Winding Road*, Spector went way beyond what Paul had in mind. One can only wonder how the song would have sounded had George Martin been asked to score a subtle and tasteful orchestral arrangement similar to his enhancements to the *Let It Be* single.

George described *For You Blue* as "a simple twelve-bar [blues] song following all the normal twelve-bar principles except it's happy-go-lucky!" Harrison introduced the song to the band on January 6, 1969, by playing an instrumental version of the tune. Although he knocked off two more performances of the song on acoustic guitar the following day, the band showed little interest in his song.

George's persistence paid off on January 9 when he reintroduced *For You Blue* to the others as his "folk/blues" song. After doing a few solo performances of the tune on acoustic guitar, he was joined by Paul on piano and John on electric guitar before the group moved on to other songs. When the band returned to the song later in the day, they were in the standard lineup of John and George on electric guitars, Paul on bass and Ringo on drums. The group managed a few complete performances of the song amid false starts and jamming on oldies. At this stage, George had yet to complete the lyrics.

On January 25, the Beatles were ready to record *For You Blue*, which was initially titled *George's Blues* before temporarily being called *Because You're Sweet And Lovely*. The song was recorded prior to Billy Preston's arrival and featured George on his Gibson J-200 acoustic guitar, Paul on piano, Ringo on drums and John on a Hofner Hawaiian Standard lap-steel slide guitar. Although the *Get Back* sessions were full of dreary and uninspired performances, George's upbeat tune lifted the mood of the band. After a series of runthroughs, Glyn Johns rolled the tape to record Take 1. This performance, which opens with Paul on piano, is on *Anthology 3*. During Take 3, George mistakenly sings during the piano solo. When John lets George know

of his error by yelling "piano," Harrison ad-libs "I've loved that piano from the moment that I saw you." Take 6 is featured in the film *Let It Be*.

Take 7 opens with a ten-second false start followed by the sound of rattling ice cubes in a glass. After a second false start, John yells "Quiet please" before George and the band knock out an excellent performance. Glyn Johns selected this take, starting with the rattling ice cubes, for the side two opener of both versions of the unreleased *Get Back* album. An altered version of this performance, details of which are discussed below, was used for the *Let It Be* album and the single.

Although everyone was satisfied with Take 7, the group recorded five more performances. The instrumental break from Take 9 was used as the lead-in to the portion of the *Let It Be* movie featuring the Apple basement recording sessions. During the piano solo of Take 12, George shouts out "Mr. Blüthner" as a salute to Paul's fine playing on the studio's Blüthner grand piano. At the end of the song, George comments "It felt nice." After listening to playbacks of Takes 7 and 12, George Martin wanted to edit the two performances to form the master take, but Harrison objected because he was satisfied with Take 7. Unlike the other songs recorded during the *Get Back* project, *For You Blue* was essentially started and completed in one afternoon session.

On January 29, the Beatles ran through many of the numbers previously rehearsed and/or recorded during the month-long sessions. The group's performance of *For You Blue* sounds a bit heavier than the earlier versions.

Glyn Johns made a stereo mix of Take 7 on March 10, 1969. This is the mix included on both versions of the unreleased *Get Back* album.

Nearly one year after *For You Blue* was recorded, George had second thoughts about his singing and redid his vocal on January 8, 1970. During the instrumental break, Harrison added some vocal ad-libs, including "Go Johnny go" and "Elmore James got nothin' on this baby," to give the impression he was singing live with the band. These references to Chuck Berry's *Johnny B. Goode* and blues guitarist Elmore James pay tribute to Lennon's fine guitar work on the song.

Prior to Phil Spector's involvement in the project, Apple had Malcolm Davies, a former EMI engineer, produce stereo mixes of *For You Blue*. The session was held at Abbey Road on February 28, 1970, with Peter Brown and Richard Langham serving as engineers. Eight mixes were made, none of which was ever released.

Phil Spector, assisted by engineers Peter Brown and Roger Ferris, mixed the song for stereo at Abbey Road on March 25, 1970. After obtaining a generally suitable mix on the first try, Spector went through seven mixes (numbered Remixes 2 through 8) of the song's introduction. The final master appearing on the *Let It Be* album and issued as the single is an edit of introduction Remix 5 onto Remix 1.

The single was mastered by Sam Feldman at Bell Sound. The trail off areas to the disc have the Bell Sound logo, Sam Feldman's initials and a script "Phil & Ronnie." The last etching is producer Phil Spector's tribute to his then-wife Ronnie, former lead singer of the Ronettes.

APP 2832.PS1A

APP 2832.PS1B

The design of the picture sleeve issued with the record is similar to the sleeve for the *Let It Be* single; however, it features a different picture of each Beatle and has a white rather than black background. The black text includes the legend "From The Beatles' Motion Picture 'Let It Be'" below each song title. The *For You Blue* side of the sleeve has the following additional information: "Manufactured by Apple Records, Inc. 1700 Broadway, New York, New York 10019 an abkco managed company." The East Coast Queens Litho-produced sleeves, **APP 2832.PS1A**, have a straight cut top. The significantly rarer West Coast sleeves, **APP 2832.PS1B**, were manufactured by Bert-Co and have a tab cut on the *For You Blue* side.

There are four layout variations of the single. The first three are first pressings.

The first variation, **APP 2832.01**, has the song title and songwriters credit below the center hole, the group's name to the upper left of the center and "(From The Beatles Motion Picture "Let It Be")" to the lower left of the center on the A side. The B side has the song title and songwriters credit in the lower left part of the apple, the group's name in the upper left part and the film reference in the lower right part. Both sides have publishing information, time (intro and total), record and master numbers and "Reproduced for disc by PHIL SPECTOR-Record First Published: 1970" to the right of the center hole and "STEREO" at nine o'clock. These Los Angeles discs were first pressed with glossy light apple labels with Capitol logo perimeter print, **2832.01L(c)**. Later pressings have light apple labels with Apple perimeter print on the A side, **2832.01L(af)**.

The second variation, **APP 2832.02**, has the song title and songwriters credit in the upper left part of the apple, the group's name below the center hole (slightly off-center to the right on the A side and in the lower right part of the apple on the B side), the film reference in the lower left part of the apple, "STEREO" in the upper right part of the apple and all other information to the right of the center

hole. All copies of this variation examined for this book have glossy dark green apple labels and Apple perimeter print on the B side, **2832.02S(as)**. These labels appear on Scranton and non-Capitol East Coast pressings.

The third variation, **APP 2832.03**, has the song titles in small print and the group's name in micro print. The song title and songwriters credit runs along the top of the apple on the A side and in the upper left part of the apple on the B side. Both sides have the group's name below the center hole, the film reference to the left of the center and all other information to the right of the center. Neither side has the stereo designation. The "(J. Lennon-P. McCartney)" credit on the A side is too close to the top of the center hole, which cuts through the credit on many copies of the disc. These Jacksonville pressings have glossy dark green apple labels. All copies of this variation examined for the book have Apple perimeter print on the B side, **2832.03J(as)**.

The fourth variation, A**PP 2832.04**, is similar to the third variation, but with minor differences. To correct the problem of having the songwriters credit on the A side obliterated by the center hole, "J. Lennon" and "P. McCartney" are separated by an inch of space. In addition, the film reference is shifted from the middle left of the apple to the lower left. On the B side, the song title is on three lines rather than one. These corrected Jacksonville pressings have glossy dark green apple labels. The first labels of this variation have Apple perimeter print on the B side, **2832.04J(as)**, while later pressings have Apple perimeter print on the A side, **2832.04J(af)**.

The confirmed all rights variation, **APP 2832.11L(ar)**, has the same layout as **APP 2832.01**. The all rights language appears on two lines at the top of the apple on the A side and on five lines in the upper right part of the apple on the B side. These Los Angeles pressings have light green apple labels and Apple perimeter print on both sides. The copies examined for this book have "Mastered by Capitol" stamped in the trail off areas.

APP 2832.01L(c)

APP 2832.01L(af)

APP 2832.02S(as)

APP 2832.03J(as)

APP 2832.04J(af)
(shown)
APP 2832.04J(as) (same, except B side has Apple perimeter print)

APP 2832.11L(ar)

Apple Records

# THE BEATLES

# THE LONG AND
# WINDING ROAD

**From The Beatles' Motion Picture "Let It Be"**

2832        Manufactured by Apple Records Inc., 1700 Broadway, New York, N.Y. 10019        An abkco managed company

This ad for the Beatles last American Apple single appeared in the May 16, 1970, *Billboard.*

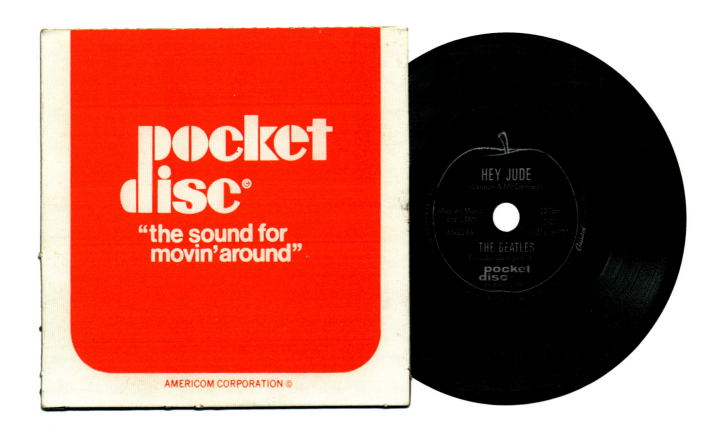

## THE BEATLES POCKET DISCS ON APPLE

In 1968, Americom Corporation of New York introduced a new music format for singles called the pocket disc. The thin, flexible discs were four inches as opposed to the seven-inch 45 RPM vinyl singles that had dominated the market since the mid-fifties, surpassing and eventually replacing the ten-inch 78 RPM shellac single. Each side of the pocket disc, which played at 33⅓ RPM, could hold approximately three and a half minutes of music.

The December 7, 1968, *Billboard* reported that Capitol Records was interested in the growth and development of the pocket disc. Bob Yorke, vice-president of Capitol Records Distributing Corp., observed that the singles business was "sick." While albums and 8-track tapes were showing increased sales activity, singles were not showing any significant growth. Yorke believed that the record business could not be healthy without a healthy singles business. He also believed that Capitol needed to adventurously pursue the future and saw the pocket disc as the salvation of slumping singles sales.

Yorke felt that the quality of a pocket disc was every bit as good as a regular 45 single. Unlike a vinyl record, it was not fragile and could be shipped in envelopes. Another advantage was Americom's ability to press 9,300 discs an hour. Yorke stated that he could hold 500 pocket discs in his hand and that a suitcase could hold enough stock to service 50 accounts.

Pocket discs were sold at counter displays for 49¢ and in vending machines for 50¢. The vending machines had separate slots for ten different selections and could be stocked with up to 75 copies of each title. *Billboard* reported that in test marketing in Seattle, customers preferred purchasing the discs in vending machines over counter merchandisers by a margin of two to one.

Some discs were packaged with four-inch by four-inch red and white or blue and white cardboard flip jackets. The front side of the red jacket (shown above actual size) calls the pocket disc "the sound for movin' around." The other side (shown on following page top) states:

- carry them in your pocket—they won't scratch
- todays stars and hits—today
- pocket money buys a pocketful of pocketdiscs

The inside of the red flap jacket (shown on following page bottom) boasts that the discs "can give you many hours of enjoyment if used properly" and contains instructions for their use. Unlike many new formats, pocket discs did not require the purchase of a new type of player. The discs were played on single automatic phonographs. Purchasers were told that if the discs slipped on the turntable, they should place a rubber mat, available through dealers, on the turntable.

Capitol was among the first companies to provide masters to Americom for the manufacture of pocket discs. Capitol's enthusiasm for the new format resulted in Americom receiving masters for the Beatles three singles issued in late 1968 and early 1969.

The first Beatles pocket disc was *Hey Jude* b/w *Revolution*. In keeping with Capitol's arrangement with Apple, the pocket disc was assigned a Capitol number, 2276P (the number was the same as the 45 and the "P" was for "pocket disc"), but had Apple images on both sides of the disc. The disc is marked M-221, which is its Americom catalog number. The black discs have silver print on both sides. The perimeter print is similar to that found on Capitol vinyl singles from 1968. It states "Mfd. by Capitol Records, Inc., a Subsidiary of Capitol Industries, Inc." and has the Capitol logo surrounded by "TM" and "Marca Reg." For obvious reasons, it does not have the patent number for the vinyl record that appears on the 45 labels. The A side has an full apple and the B side shows a sliced apple. The disc lists "Lennon & McCartney" as the song writers and George Martin as producer.

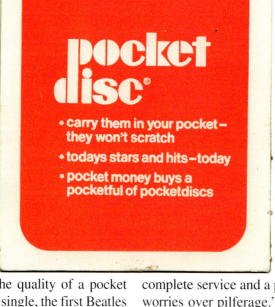

Although Yorke claimed that the quality of a pocket disc was every bit as good as a vinyl single, the first Beatles pocket disc demonstrated that Yorke's opinion was as flimsy as a pocket disc. The loud distorted sound of *Revolution* could not be captured on the thin disc. As every recording engineer knows, the sound is in the grooves. For pocket discs, the grooves were too narrow and shallow to produce high quality sound reproduction. *Hey Jude* also suffered, as it was edited down from its glorious 7:11 length to a mere 3:25 to fit within the time constraints of the format. The song fades out after only two "Nah, nah nah nah nah nah nah, nah nah nah nah, Hey Jude" refrains.

The second Beatles pocket disc (Apple 2490P and M-335), contains *Get Back* b/w *Don't Let Me Down*. The labels to the vinyl 45 list the artist as "THE BEATLES With Billy Preston." The pocket disc has the same designation. The songwriters credit is listed as "Lennon-McCartney." The disc is the rarest of the three Beatles pocket discs on Apple.

*The Ballad Of John And Yoko* b/w *Old Brown Shoe* (Apple 2531P and M-382) was the last Beatles pocket disc pressed for the retail singles market by Americom. The songwriters credit is "John Lennon-Paul McCartney" on the A side and "George Harrison" on the B side. The disc erroneously states

"Prod. by W. Miller" rather than giving producer's credit to George Martin. (W. Miller may be Bill Miller, a Capitol employee who, in 1966, took over Dave Dexter's job of handling the label's foreign artists.)

*Billboard* ran a follow-up article on the pocket disc in its April 19, 1969, issue. The magazine reported that after a test run of several months in Seattle, the disc would be introduced into the Detroit market on May 15, 1969. Americom planned to have distribution in 35% of the country by the fall, with full national distribution expected by April, 1970. Fred Hyman, chief of Americom, noted that "the introduction of Pocket Disc entails no cost to the retailer, who receives complete service and a percentage of sales and is free from worries over pilferage."

The June 28, 1969, *Billboard* reported that the pocket disc had shown strong sales during the first two weeks of its introduction into Detroit. Hyman indicated that sales for 14 days in 42 locations totaled 16,416 units, representing average sales of 390 discs per retail outlet. Some stores sold over 80 units per day. The discs were being sold in vending machines placed in department and record stores. Americom was particularly impressed with the sales figures for songs that had already peaked and were no longer on the charts.

For its July 12, 1969, issue, *Billboard* interviewed several retailers in the Detroit area. One store manager touted the pocket disc as "one of the most exciting developments in the record business in a long time." Others were impressed with the sales figures and the elimination of pilferage. The main complaint was the lack of participation by some of the key labels such as Columbia, RCA and Motown.

The August 9, 1969, *Billboard* reported that Americom was placing an order for a thousand additional vending machines at a cost of $500,000. The machines carried 18 selections, with 100 discs per title. The plan was to place two machines in each location. Market research showed that the pocket disc was

The above picture of a first generation pocket disc vending machine appeared in the January 4, 1969, *Billboard*. The *Hey Jude* single can be seen in the second position from the left on the top row. Some pocket discs were packaged in blue cardboard sleeves.

appealing to consumers who did not purchase or rarely purchased 45s.

*Billboard* ran another major article on the pocket disc in its November 29, 1969, issue. Americom announced that it was entering a new packaging and marketing phase that would make the discs available in variety stores and neighborhood locations on a non-vending basis. Stores would purchase the discs outright and display them on racks. The company initially was aiming for distribution in 10% of the estimated 600,000 nationwide variety store outlets. Americom's strategy was to make a cheap single (priced at 49 cents) available to the very young. According to Americom chief Fred Hyman, "Pocketdisc will compete with an ice cream soda, a package of candy, a magazine, etc., for the spendable dollar of the young buyer." The company would also continue distribution through vending machines in department and record stores.

While Capitol and 27 other labels cooperated in the pocket disc experiment, the format's progress was hindered by the holdout of most of the major companies, including

Columbia, RCA, Transamerica and MCA. Hyman complained that these company's lack of participation not only hurt the pocket disc, but also "hinders the development of every label in the industry which looks to the single record to introduce artists and repertoire." He added that sales data showed that the pocket disc was a supplementary market rather than a substitute market for the vinyl single.

Although Americom and Capitol both had high hopes for the pocket disc, the format fizzled out shortly after its introduction. The initial enthusiasm held by Capitol's Bob Yorke caused him to overestimate the format's appeal and to overlook its obvious shortcomings. His belief that the pocket disc would become a viable singles format with sales exceeding vinyl 45s was way off target. Without the participation of the other major labels, the pocket disc quickly went the way of other failed formats such as 2-track cartridge Playtapes. Because these tiny records were only sold for a limited time in limited markets, the Beatles Apple pocket discs are relatively rare and worth significantly more than their vinyl counterparts.

---

### FANTASTIC FAB FOUR FLEXI-FACTS

In 1964, the Capitol Record Club prepared a flexi-disc containing music by three of Capitol's most popular artists: the Beatles, the Beach Boys and the Kingston Trio. The Beatles segment of the disc contains a brief edit of *Roll Over Beethoven*. Details regarding this flexi-disc, which was manufactured by Eva-Tone in Deerfield, Illinois, are on pages 186-189 of *The Beatles' Story on Capitol Records, Part One: Beatlemania & The Singles*.

Capitol authorized the pressing of *Yellow Submarine* b/w *Eleanor Rigby* by Ameridisc. This rare flexi-disc, with Capitol catalog number 5715, is light blue with white print.

The 1968 and 1969 Beatles Fan Club Christmas Records were issued on two-sided flexi-discs manufactured by Americom. See pages 218-221.

In July, 1982, Capitol had Eva-Tone (which had relocated to Clearwater, Florida) manufacture three unique couplings of Beatles songs on 7" square soundsheets to promote its Beatles catalog. Each soundsheet contains a clear vinyl flexi-disc adhered to a photo of the group on thick stock paper. The back of the soundsheet has pictures of the Capitol Beatles albums, along with the Capitol logo and the name of one of three stores involved in the promotion (Sam Goody, Musicland and Discount).

The soundsheet titles are: *All My Loving* and *You've Got To Hide Your Love Away* (Eva-Tone 420826cs); *Magical Mystery Tour* and *Here Comes The Sun* (Eva-Tone 420827cs); and *Rocky Raccoon* and *Why Don't We Do It In The Road* (Eva-Tone 420828cs).

APP 2276.PD

APP 2490.PD

APP 2531.PD

APP 5112.21L(bs)

APP 5112.21W

APP 5112.21J(ar)

# APPLE REISSUE SINGLES

In early 1971, Abkco's Allan Steckler decided that all pre-Apple Beatles singles and albums should be pressed with Apple labels. This included the singles *I Want To Hold Your Hand* through *Lady Madonna*, which were at that time being pressed with Capitol red & orange target labels featuring Capitol's new circular logo. Steckler had always been conscious of label identity and saw the issuance of the Beatles extensive back catalog with Apple labels as a way of strengthening Apple's identity. After discussing his idea with Allen Klein and getting Klein's approval, Steckler asked Capitol to begin pressing all Beatles records with Apple labels. Realizing that this would not alter the terms of the existing record contract, and perhaps thinking that the move might increase back catalog sales, Capitol agreed.

Beginning in the spring of 1971, Capitol began pressing its Beatles 45s and albums with Apple labels. This was

done for nearly five years. As 1975 came to a close, so did Apple. That December, Capitol switched the Beatles record catalog over to its then-current orange labels.

There are no known typesetting variations for any of the Apple reissue singles. This is because each of the different printers used the same label copy film. Each of the singles is found in three different types: (1) Apple labels with a black star located in the lower right part of the full apple A side; (2) plain Apple labels; or (3) Apple labels with the all rights language printed on both the full apple and sliced apple sides.

The black star labels have light green apples printed on glossy paper and were used only on Los Angeles pressings. They are designated **.21L(bs)** in this book's numbering system. These records were pressed during the initial run of the series in the spring and summer of 1971.

The plain Apple labels appear on records pressed by Los Angeles (after dropping the black star), Jacksonville and Winchester. The Los Angeles discs, designated **.21L**, have glossy light green apple labels identical to labels used for the black star variation. The Jacksonville singles can be found on glossy and/or dull dark green apple labels. The earlier pressings, designated **.21J1**, have glossy labels, and the later pressings, designated **.21J2**, have dull finish labels. The crossover from the glossy to dull Jacksonville labels probably took place in early 1972. Winchester discs, designated **.21W**, were pressed with dull dark green apple labels. The plain Apple labels were used until around September, 1975, at which time Capitol switched to the all rights labels.

The all rights labels have only been confirmed with Los Angeles and Jacksonville pressings. The Los Angeles variation, designated **.21L(ar)**, has dull light green apple labels with a yellowish tint. The Jacksonville all rights discs, designated **.21J(ar)**, have dull dark green apple labels. There are two variations of Los Angeles all rights labels for *I Want To Hold Your Hand*.

Some records have been found with one or two sides pressed by stampers with the Scranton ⚠ logo. In all likelihood, these records were manufactured by another fac-

tory with old stampers transferred from Scranton. By the time the apple reissue singles were pressed, Capitol was no longer using the Scranton plant to press its records.

There are a few idiosyncracies in the series. Apple 5498 has *Act Naturally* on the full apple A side and *Yesterday* on the sliced apple B side. This is because *Act Naturally* was originally going to be the single's A side and has always been designated as such in Capitol internal documents. Similarly, Apple 5810 has *Strawberry Fields Forever* on the full apple side because it was the A side when the single was issued. (American disc jockeys and radio listeners preferred the more upbeat *Penny Lane*, which became a number one hit.) Apple 5964 is the strangest of the lot with *Baby, You're A Rich Man* appearing on the full apple side instead of *All You Need Is Love*, which always was the A side. This error occurred because *Baby, You're A Rich Man* has a lower master number (45-X-46047) than *All You Need Is Love* (45-X-46048). Because Capitol normally cataloged the A side first, it usually had a master number that was one number less than the master number assigned to the B side. Thus, the person preparing the Apple reissue singles mistook *Baby, You're A Rich Man* for the A side. Similarly, *Slow Down* (master number 45-X-45061) appears on the full apple side, with *Matchbox* (45-X-45062) on the sliced side.

| CONFIRMED APPLE REISSUE SINGLES Number & Title | Black Star | Plain | All Rights |
|---|---|---|---|
| 5112 I Want To Hold Your Hand | L | L, J1, W | L, J2 |
| 5150 Can't Buy Me Love | L | L, J2, W | L |
| 5222 A Hard Day's Night | L | L, W | L, J2 |
| 5234 I'll Cry Instead | L | L, J2 | L, J2 |
| 5235 And I Love Her | L | L, J1, J2, W | L |
| 5255 Matchbox | L | L, J2, W | L |
| 5327 I Feel Fine | L | L, J1 | L |
| 5371 Eight Days A Week | L | L, W | L |
| 5407 Ticket To Ride | L | L, J1, J2 | L |
| 5476 Help! | L | L, J2, W | L |
| 5498 Yesterday | L | L, J1, J2, W | L, J2 |
| 5555 We Can Work It Out | L | J2, W | L |
| 5587 Nowhere Man | L | L, J2 | L |
| 5651 Paperback Writer | L | L | L |
| 5715 Yellow Submarine | L | L, J1, J2, W | L, J2 |
| 5810 Strawberry Fields Forever | L | L, J1, J2 | L, J2 |
| 5964 All You Need Is Love | L | L, J2, W | L |
| 2056 Hello Goodbye | L | L, W | L |
| 2138 Lady Madonna | L | L, W | L |
| L=Los Angeles  J1=Jacksonville Glossy  J2=Jacksonville Dull  W = Winchester | | | |

Capitol pressed its entire Beatles catalog with Apple labels from the the spring of 1971 through the end of 1975. The Apple labels replaced the red and orange target labels (top) that Capitol was using in 1971. At the end of 1975, Capitol switched the Beatles records to its then current orange label (bottom).

APP 5150.21W

APP 5222.21L

APP 5234.21L(bs)

APP 5235.22L(ar)

APP 5255.21L

APP 5327.21L

APP 5371.21L                    APP 5407.21L(bs)                    APP 5476.22L(ar)

APP 5498.22J(ar)                    APP 5555.21J                    APP 5587.21L

APP 5651.21L

APP 5715.21L(bs)

APP 5810.21J

APP 5964.21L(bs)

APP 2056.21L

APP 2138.21L(bs)

# APPLE AROUND THE WORLD

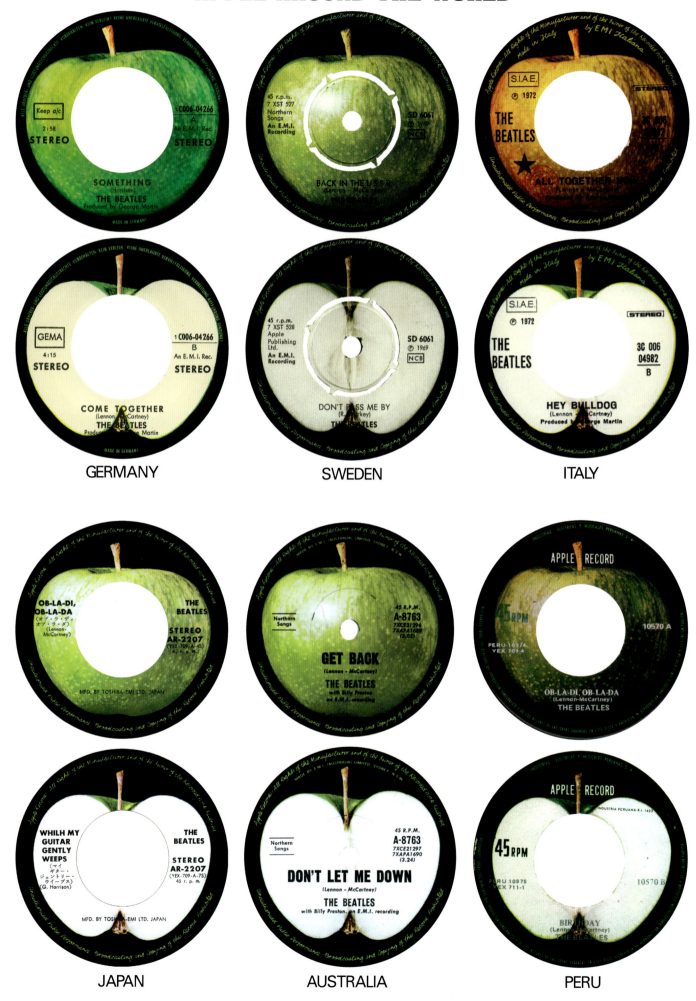

GERMANY  SWEDEN  ITALY

JAPAN  AUSTRALIA  PERU

## CANADIAN APPLE SINGLES

In June, 1968, Capitol Records entered into an agreement to manufacture and distribute all Apple Records product in the U.S. and Canada. As part of that agreement, the Beatles new records would be issued on discs with Apple labels. The six Canadian Beatles singles released from August, 1968, through May, 1970, have Apple labels and the same record numbers as their American counterparts.

The American and British singles were packaged in black sleeves with white and green text; however, the Canadian company took a Bizarro approach to the sleeves. Readers of Superman comics of the early sixties were treated to a series of stories in *Adventure Comics* featuring Bizarro Superman, an imperfect duplicate of Superman who was in many ways the opposite of Superman. Bizarro Superman lived on a square planet, Bizarro World, and was guided by

the Bizarro Code, which began "Us do opposite of all Earthly things!" For example, on Bizarro World, alarm clocks are not used to wake people up, but rather to let them know it's time to go to bed. And the government uses the Bizarro Income Tax Bureau to pay people an annual tax. Bizarro World autos, with square tires, stop for green lights and go when the traffic lights turn red. While Capitol's Canadian subsidiary was probably not aware of the Bizarro Code, its Apple sleeves are indeed Bizarro. Rather than being black with white and green text, the Canadian sleeves (shown above) are white with black and green writing.

While three of the six Apple 45s were issued with picture sleeves in the U.S., Capitol Records (Canada) did not prepare picture sleeves for any of its first issue Apple singles. Some 45s were sold with sleeves imported from the U.S.

The Canadian 45s are easily distinguishable from the U.S. singles. Because the Canadian records have no slip guard serrations, their labels are larger than the U.S. labels, measuring 3⅝" rather than 3¹⁵⁄₁₆". The text on the labels is printed in a font not used on any of the U.S. labels. All of the Canadian Beatles singles have the label copy printed vertically on the sliced apple B sides, which have "Mfd. by Apple Records, Inc." in upper case letters in the perimeter. The singles were pressed by the Compo Company, which maintained 86 pressing machines between its Montreal and Cornwall plants, and by RCA. The Compo singles (designated by an **A** in this book's numbering system) have the record number in thick print, whereas the RCA discs (designated by a **B**) have thin print record numbers.

As is the case with the U.S. records, *Hey Jude* is mono and all subsequent singles (with the exception of the song *You Know My Name*) are stereo. A limited number of the initial Compo pressings of Apple 2654 have *Come Together* on the green apple A side and *Something* on the sliced apple B side. These labels have the running time for *Come Together* erroneously listed as 2:16 rather than 4:16. Later Compo pressings and all RCA discs have *Something* as the A side and the correct 4:16 running time for *Come Together*. There are two versions of the Compo pressings of *Get Back*. RCA pressings for *Get Back* and *The Long And Winding Road* have not been confirmed and may or may not exist.

Beginning with its May 24, 1969, issue, *Billboard* published a top twenty chart titled *Canada's Top Singles*. The initial chart listed *Get Back* at number three. The following week the song moved up to number one, where it remained for five straight weeks. *Get Back* spent ten weeks on the charts, including eight in the top ten. *The Ballad Of John And Yoko* entered the *Billboard* Canadian chart at number eight on June 28, while *Get Back* was still number one. Although some Canadian stations banned the song, the single worked its way up to its first of two weeks at the top on July 19 and spent eight weeks in the top ten.

*Something* entered *Canada's Top Singles* chart at number 11 on October 25, 1969. The following week it moved up to number three and was joined by its flip side, *Come Together*, which debuted at ten. On November 8, the single spent its first of six straight weeks at number one. Beginning with the November 29 chart, both songs were listed as a single entry. The 45 charted for twelve weeks, including nine in the top ten.

Although *Billboard* ran its last *Canada's Top Singles* chart on March 21, 1970, the magazine reported the top ten Canadian singles as part of its *Hits Of The World* listings. *Let It Be* spent its first of two weeks at number one on April 18, 1970. *The Long And Winding Road* also charted at number one.

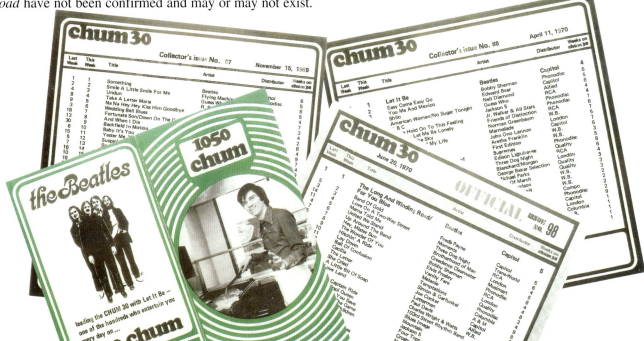

**ONTARIO RADIO STATION CHUM CHART ACTION FOR CANADIAN APPLE SINGLES**

| Peak Number | Weeks at #1 | Weeks on Chart | Song Title | Week of Entry | First Week at #1 |
|---|---|---|---|---|---|
| 1 | 7 | 11 | Hey Jude / Revolution | 8/31/1968 | 9/14/1968 |
| 1 | 5 | 11 | Get Back / Don't Let Me Down | 4/26/1969 | 5/17/1969 |
| 1 | 2 | 7 | Something | 10/18/1969 | 11/8/1969 |
| 1 | 4 | 8 | Let It Be | 3/21/1970 | 3/28/1970 |
| 1 | 2 | 9 | The Long And Winding Road / For You Blue | 5/23/1970 | 6/13/1970 |

**CHUM was one of several radio stations in the United States and Canada that initially banned the playing of *The Ballad Of John And Yoko* due to lyrical content. Accordingly, the station did not chart the song. The August 2, 1969, *Billboard* reported that CHUM had added *The Ballad Of John And Yoko* to its "forbidden" playlist. Although *Come Together* received airplay as the flip side of *Something*, CHUM did not list the song on its charts.**

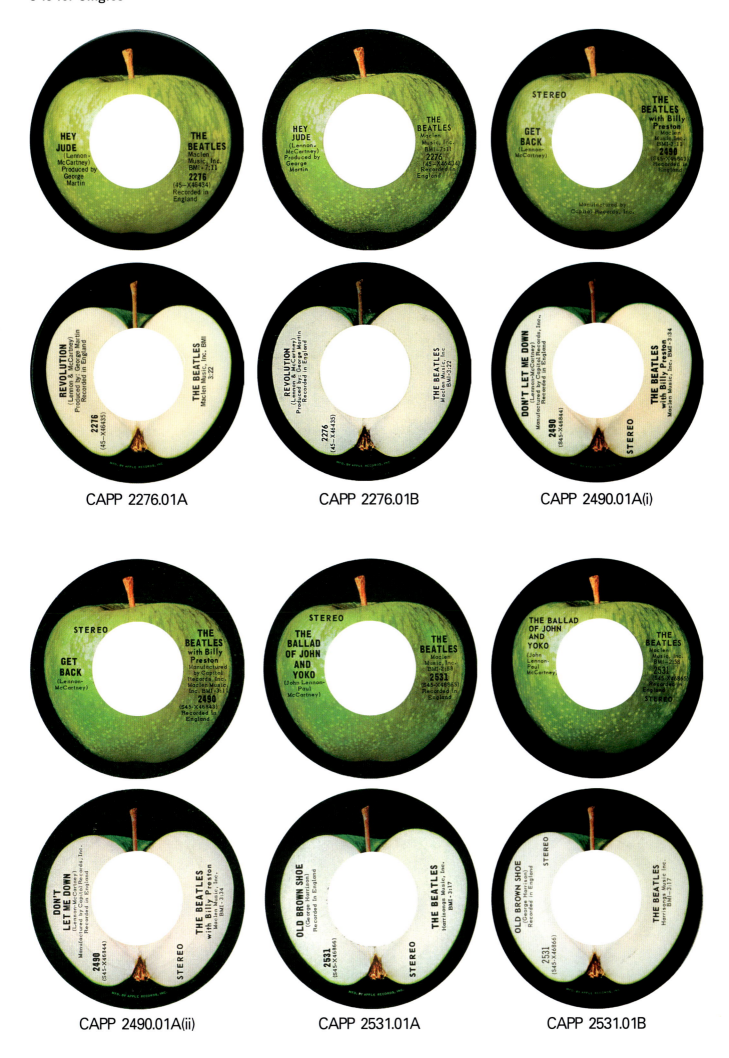

CAPP 2276.01A                      CAPP 2276.01B                      CAPP 2490.01A(i)

CAPP 2490.01A(ii)                  CAPP 2531.01A                      CAPP 2531.01B

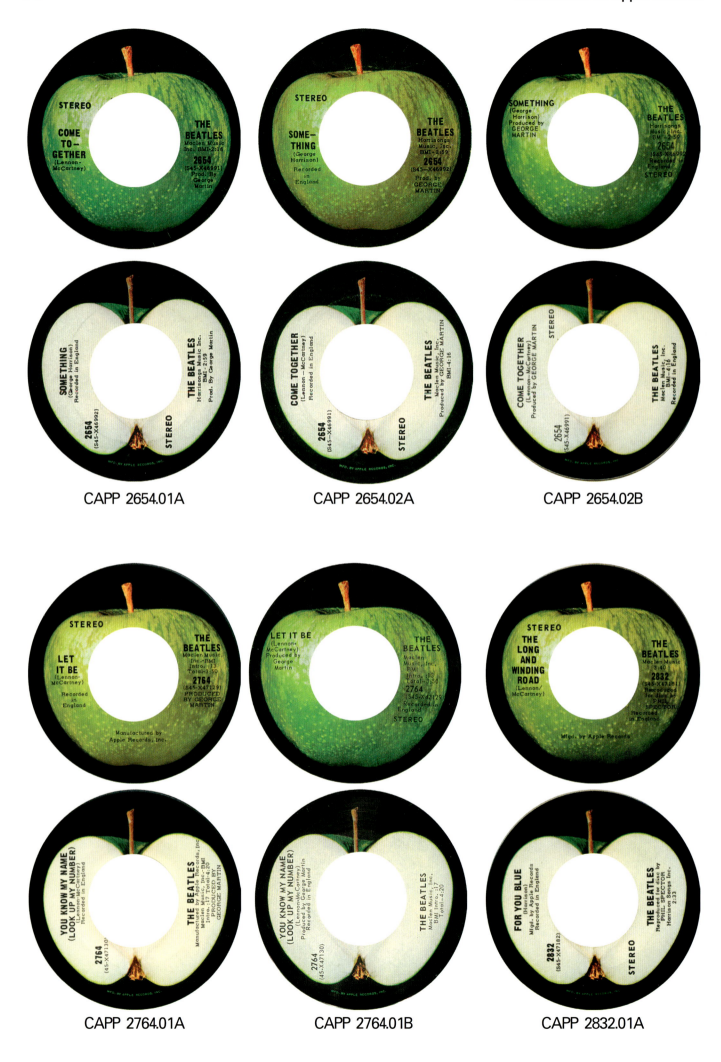

CAPP 2654.01A          CAPP 2654.02A          CAPP 2654.02B

CAPP 2764.01A          CAPP 2764.01B          CAPP 2832.01A

## MEXICAN APPLE SINGLES & EPs

At the time Apple Records began operations in North America in the summer of 1968, Capitol's south-of-the-border subsidiary, Discos Capitol de Mexico, had the exclusive right to distribute recordings of the Beatles in Mexico. Although the group's first Apple single, *Hey Jude*, was manufactured with Apple labels in the United States and Canada, initial pressings of the 45 in Mexico had Capitol labels (see page 37). This was because Apple had not secured its trademark in Mexico prior to the August, 1968, release of the single. Later pressings of the single have Apple labels.

The Beatles second single, *Get Back*, was manufactured with Apple labels from the start. Discos Capitol de Mexico issued the same Beatles singles in 1969 and 1970 as its U.S. parent and Canadian counterpart. *The Ballad Of John And Yoko*, *Something* and *Let It Be* were packaged in picture sleeves, while the other three singles came with ge-

neric Apple sleeves similar to the black U.S. sleeves. The sleeve for *The Ballad Of John And Yoko* is similar to the U.S. sleeve, except that it is entirely black and white. The *Something* sleeve features a blue-tinted image of the cover of *Abbey Road* on both sides. The *Let It Be* sleeve has the same basic layout as the U.S. sleeve and is also in color. Discos Capitol de Mexico issued promotional copies for *Get Back* and *The Ballad Of John And Yoko* with black and white Apple labels.

During the early seventies, Discos Capitol de Mexico manufactured a series of 14 Extended Play (EP) Beatles records with Apple labels. These EPs are unique to Mexico and were reportedly programmed by John Lennon. At the time the discs were put together, John was going through a phase where he viewed the group's recordings as a series of songs by John and the band, Paul and the band, George and the band and Ringo and the band. He was also engaged

Although *Hey Jude* was originally issued with Capitol labels (see page 37), later pressings have Apple labels (left). The Apple promotional records have black and white images of the apples (center). Several of the Extended Play discs have small play holes (right).

in a public battle with Paul, as evidenced by his McCartney putdown, *How Do You Sleep?* These factors influenced the track selections for the records, which generally showcase a particular Beatle. While John, George and Ringo are well represented, Paul is missing in action until the final two discs. All of the EPs were packaged with folded slip sheets rather than paper sleeves or cardboard jackets.

The first batch of records, Apple EPEM-10457, 10458 and 10459, contains classic Lennon songs from 1967 and beyond. The discs were packaged with slip sheets containing the same images and information on both sides. All three feature the Ethan Russell photos used on the *Let It Be* picture sleeve. The original issue discs have small play holes. The original slip sheet for the first disc has a white background, while the later issue has a red background.

The next three EPs follow the same pattern, but shift away from John. Apple EPEM-10503 contains four George lead vocals from 1963 and 1964. EPEM-10504 has three Ringo rockers rounded out with John's frantic *Little Child*. EPEM-10505 features Ringo's most charming vocals: *Yellow Submarine*, *Octopus's Garden*, *With A Little Help From My Friends* and *Good Night*. These records were packaged with colorful slip sheets and have large 1½" play holes.

The next six records in the series, Apple EPEM-10536 through 10541, exclusively contain George songs, except for 10538, which showcases Ringo. These records can be found with large and small play holes.

Paul finally makes an appearance on the last two discs in the series. Apple EPEM-10599 features four songs from *Let It Be*, three of which prominently feature Paul. EPEM-10600 opens with John's *Dig It* and its *"Hark, The Angels Come"* end-bit leading into Paul's *Let It Be*. Side two contains McCartney's *Paperback Writer* and *Lady Madonna*. These records have large play holes.

**MEXICAN SINGLES:**

**6365 Hey Jude b/w Revolution**

**6483 Get Back b/w Don't Let Me Down**

**6510 The Ballad Of John And Yoko b/w Old Brown Shoe**

**6565 Something b/w Come Together**

**6645 Let It Be b/w You Know My Name (Look Up The Number)**

**6680 The Long And Winding Road b/w For You Blue**

**MEXICAN EPs:**

**EPEM 10457 A Day In The Life/I Am The Walrus/ Strawberry Fields Forever/Come Together**

**10458 I Want You (She's So Heavy)/Don't Let Me Down/ Revolution/Yer Blues**

**10459 Lucy In The Sky With Diamonds/All You Need Is Love/Across The Universe/Ballad Of John And Yoko**

**10503 Do You Want To Know A Secret/Devil In Her Heart/ I'm Happy Just To Dance With You/Chains**

**10504 Honey Don't/Matchbox/Little Child/I Wanna Be Your Man**

**10505 Yellow Submarine/Octopus's Garden/With A Little Help From My Friends/Goodnight**

**10536 Taxman/Don't Bother Me/If I Needed Someone/ Think For Yourself**

**10537 Here Comes The Sun/For You Blue/While My Guitar Gently Weeps/Piggies**

**10538 Don't Pass Me By/What Goes On/Act Naturally/ Boys**

**10539 I Need You/You Like Me Too Much/It's Only A Northern Song/It's All Too Much**

**10540 Old Brown Shoe/Blue Jay Way/Long, Long, Long/ Savoy Truffle**

**10541 Within You Without You/The Inner Light/ Love You To/I Want To Tell You**

**10599 Get Back/One After 909/Two Of Us/I Me Mine**

**10600 Dig It/Let It Be/Paperback Writer/Lady Madonna**

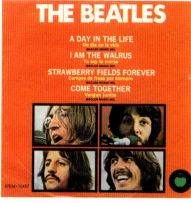

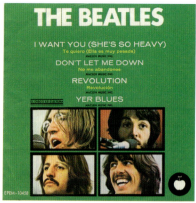

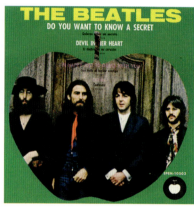

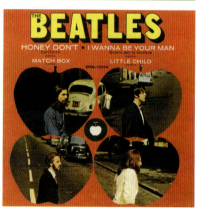

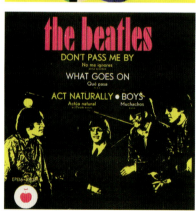

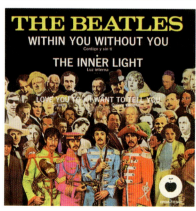

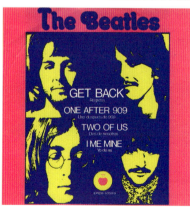

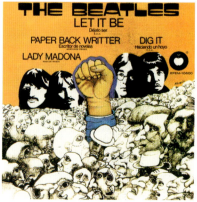

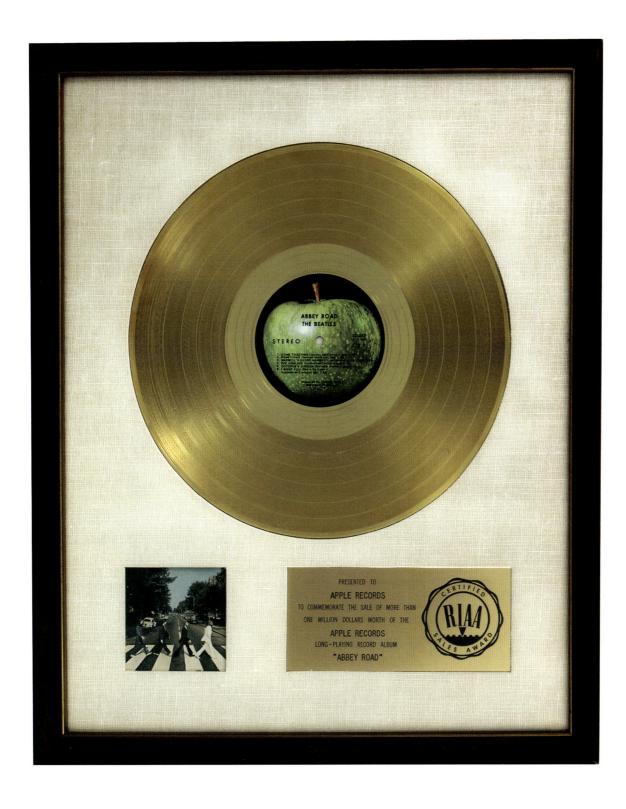

**L is for LPs**

# IT'S HERE!

Apple's 23" x 38" promotional poster for *The Beatles* LP features the collage included as an insert to the album. The simple message ''IT'S HERE!'' appears in red stylized letters at the top.

## THE BEATLES
## APPLE SWBO 101

The first album issued by the Beatles on their Apple label was simply titled *The Beatles*, although it is more commonly referred to as *The White Album* in recognition of its classy white cover. In England, the record was issued by Parlophone on November 22, 1968, exactly five years after the release of *With The Beatles*, as Apple PMC 7067-7068 (mono) and PCS 7067-7068 (stereo). Capitol issued the album as Apple SWBO-101 (stereo only) on November 25. The two record set contains 30 songs (plus an uncredited link track) and has a running time of over 93 minutes, in sharp contrast to the early Capitol Beatles albums that often had running times of less than 30 minutes. As was the case with the first Beatles single on Apple, the Beatles were giving their fans exceptional value for their money.

The December 7, 1968, *Billboard* called the LP "their most ambitious and impressive effort to date," stating that all the album's songs are "treated with the first rate performances one has come to expect of the quartet." In its December 6, 1968, issue, *Time* magazine recognized the high quality of the songwriting, but characterized the album's 30 tracks as "a sprawling, motley assemblage of the Beatles' best abilities and worst tendencies." The review went on to describe the two-disc set as "too much a virtuoso display of the quartet's versatility" in which "the foursome meander from style to style without any apparent guiding objective or urgency." Most listeners disagreed with *Time*'s assessment. For many fans, it is the album's scope and variety that makes the set their favorite Beatles album.

Side 1
1. BACK IN THE U.S.S.R. (Lennon-McCartney)
2. DEAR PRUDENCE (Lennon-McCartney)
3. GLASS ONION (Lennon-McCartney)
4. OB-LA-DI, OB-LA-DA (Lennon-McCartney)
5. WILD HONEY PIE (Lennon-McCartney)
6. THE CONTINUING STORY OF BUNGALOW BILL
   (Lennon-McCartney)
7. WHILE MY GUITAR GENTLY WEEPS
   (George Harrison)
8. HAPPINESS IS A WARM GUN  (Lennon-McCartney)

Side 2
1. MARTHA MY DEAR (Lennon-McCartney)
2. I'M SO TIRED (Lennon-McCartney)
3. BLACKBIRD (Lennon-McCartney)
4. PIGGIES (George Harrison)
5. ROCKY RACCOON (Lennon-McCartney)
6. DON'T PASS ME BY (Richard Starkey)
7. WHY DON'T WE DO IT IN THE ROAD?
   (Lennon-McCartney)
8. I WILL (Lennon-McCartney)
9. JULIA (Lennon-McCartney)

Side 3
1. BIRTHDAY (Lennon-McCartney)
2. YER BLUES (Lennon-McCartney)
3. MOTHER NATURE'S SON (Lennon-McCartney)
4. EVERYBODY'S GOT SOMETHING TO HIDE
   EXCEPT ME AND MY MONKEY (Lennon-McCartney)
5. SEXY SADIE (Lennon-McCartney)
6. HELTER SKELTER (Lennon-McCartney)
7. LONG, LONG, LONG (George Harrison)

Side 4
1. REVOLUTION 1 (Lennon-McCartney)
2. HONEY PIE (Lennon-McCartney)
3. SAVOY TRUFFLE (George Harrison)
4. CRY BABY CRY (Lennon-McCartney)
5. REVOLUTION 9 (Lennon-McCartney)
6. GOOD NIGHT (Lennon-McCartney)

---

*The Beatles* entered the *Billboard Top LP's* chart at number 11 on December 14, 1968. The following week it moved up to number two before passing Glen Campbell's *Wichita Lineman* (Capitol ST 103) to claim the top spot on December 28. After spending six straight weeks at number one, the double album was temporarily replaced at the top by *TCB* by Diana Ross & the Supremes with the Temptations (Motown 682). *The White Album* returned to the number one spot for three more weeks on February 15, 1969, before slipping down to number four on March 8 behind Campbell's *Wichita Lineman*, the Beatles *Yellow Submarine* and Cream's farewell album, *Goodbye* (Atco 7001). The album spent a total of 155 weeks on the charts, including nine at number one and 15 in the top ten. *Cash Box* and *Record World* also charted the LP at number one. The record topped the British charts for seven weeks.

Although the double album carried a list price of $11.79, most consumers recognized the quality of the music and were not deterred by the then-high cost of the set. One week after the album's release, Capitol reported dealer orders of 1.9 million units and over-the-counter sales of 1.1 million. The LP was quickly certified gold by the RIAA. As of February, 2001, the RIAA had certified sales of over 19 million units (meaning 9.5 million albums, as the RIAA certifies by the number of discs shipped).

*The White Album* was recorded primarily at Abbey Road Studios between May 30 and October 14, 1968, with mixing completed on October 17. The band's prior recording session had taken place at Abbey Road in early February, 1968, during which the Beatles recorded *Lady Madonna, The Inner Light*, *Across The Universe* and *Hey Bulldog*. Shortly thereafter, the group left for Rishikesh, India, to study Transcendental Meditation with Maharishi Mahesh Yogi. In his *Playboy* interview, John gave the following summary of the trip: "We got our mantra, we sat in the mountains eating lousy vegetarian food and writing all those songs. We wrote *tons* of songs in India." Many of those songs would appear on *The White Album*. A more detailed account of the Beatles Indian adventure can be found in Paul Saltzman's book, *The Beatles in Rishikesh*, as well as the group's *Anthology* video and book.

Prior to entering Abbey Road to record their new LP, the Beatles got together in late May, 1968, at Kinfauns, George Harrison's house in Esher, Surrey, to rehearse new material. Demo recordings of over two dozen songs were taped on Harrison's four-track Ampex recorder. Most of these songs ended up on *The White Album*. Two others, John's *What's The New Mary Jane* and George's *Not Guilty*, were recorded during the sessions, but were not selected for the album. Both recordings were eventually released on *Anthology 3*. Paul's *Junk* ended up on McCartney's first solo album in 1970. *Mean Mr. Mustard* and *Polythene Pam* were held back by John and ended up being part of the *Abbey Road* medley. John's *I'm Just A Child Of Nature* (also known as *On The Road To Rishikesh*) was given new lyrics and was recorded as *Jealous Guy* for his *Imagine* album in 1971. George's *Sour Milk Sea* was given to Apple artist Jackie Lomax and appeared in 1968 as Lomax's first single on Apple 1802, which was produced by Harrison. *Circles* was later recorded by George for his 1982 album *Gone Troppo* (Dark Horse 1-23734).

By the time the Beatles arrived at Abbey Road on May 30, 1968, the dynamics of the band had changed dramatically. Less than two weeks earlier, John had invited Yoko Ono to his home in Surrey. They taped a series of sound collages that would later be released on the album *Two Virgins* and then made love together for the first time. When John showed up at Abbey Road, he brought Yoko with him, breaking the unwritten rule that wives and girlfriends generally did not attend recording sessions. From that point forward, Yoko was nearly always at John's side. The group camaraderie of prior recording sessions was fading away.

**This photograph is one of many pictures featured in Paul Saltzman's book, _The Beatles in Rishikesh_. Shortly after the above picture was taken, Paul and John began singing _Ob-La-Di, Ob-La-Da_ with Ringo looking on.**

After the group's breakup became public, John offered the following view of _The White Album_: "Every track is an individual track–there isn't any Beatle music on it.... It was John and the Band, Paul and the Band, George and the Band." While most fans failed to notice the separate nature of the recordings, publisher Jann S. Wenner's perceptive review in the December 21, 1968, _Rolling Stone_ observed:

"There is almost no attempt in this new set to be anything but what the Beatles actually are: John, Paul, George and Ringo. Four different people, each with songs and styles and abilities. They are no longer Sgt. Pepper's Lonely Hearts Club Band and it is possible they are no longer the Beatles."

Although _The White Album_ is in many ways an elaborate compilation of solo-led recordings, the final product shows that John, Paul, George and Ringo recorded some incredible music.

The album's opening track, _Back In The U.S.S.R._, was written by Paul in Rishikesh. It is a clever parody of Chuck Berry's _Back In The U.S.A._ (Chess 1729), which peaked at number 37 on the _Billboard Hot 100_ and at 16 on _Billboard_'s _Hot R&B Sides_ chart in 1959. In the song, Berry sings about how good it feels having "just touched ground on an international runway, jet-propelled back home from overseas to the U.S.A." He sings about how he missed the cities, skyscrapers, drive-ins, hamburgers and juke boxes and how glad he is to be living in the U.S.A. Paul took the concept and wrote a tongue-in-cheek song about a Russian who flew in from Miami Beach and is glad to be back home. He may not have a lot, but he's still every bit as proud as an American would be. At Beach Boy Mike Love's suggestion, Paul added the bit about the Ukraine and Moscow girls, giving the lyrics a touch of the Beach Boys' _California Girls_. The song is full of in-jokes, including the line "That Georgia's always on my mind," which serves as a tribute to both the Soviet republic of Georgia and the Ray Charles tune _Geor-_

_gia On My Mind_. There is also a bit of irony in the lines "You don't know how lucky you are boys/Back in the U.S., back in the U.S., back in the U.S.S.R." Whether you're from the U.S. or the U.S.S.R., it's still great to be back home.

The Kinfauns demo of the song is propelled by acoustic guitars and the vocals of Paul and John. The demo arrangement is essentially the same as the later studio recording, except that Paul had yet to write the song's third verse.

The Beatles began recording _Back In The U.S.S.R._ on August 22. During the early stages of the session, Paul and Ringo got into an argument over the drumming, which prompted Ringo to quit the group for a few days. The band continued work on the song, laying down a rhythm track with Paul on drums, George on his Fender Telecaster guitar and John on the Fender VI bass guitar. The fifth and final take was deemed the best and given numerous overdubs the following evening, including piano, two guitar parts, bass by both Paul and George, additional drums (possibly by John and George) and vocals. According to Paul, he sang the lead in his "Jerry Lee Lewis voice." Beach Boys-style backing vocals by John, Paul and George were added on the bridge. As a finishing touch, the sound of a jet airplane was faded in and out of the mix, primarily to open and close the song. The track was mixed for mono at the end of the session and for stereo on October 13.

The sound of the landing jet from the end of _Back In The U.S.S.R._ cross fades into the opening guitar notes of the album's second track, _Dear Prudence_. John wrote the song in Rishikesh for Prudence Farrow, the sister of actress Mia Farrow. Prudence had become dangerously obsessive about practicing Transcendental Meditation and was spending all of her time meditating in her room. The opening line "Dear Prudence, won't you come out to play" was simply a plea by John for her to take a break from her excessive meditation and join the others.

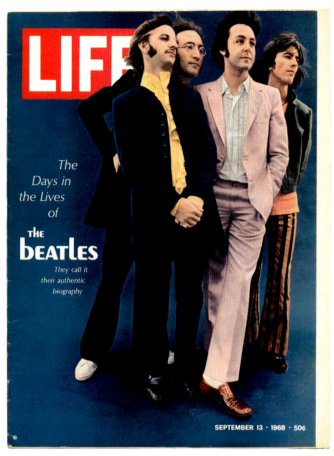

**The cover of the September 13, 1968, issue of *Life* magazine features a Don McCullin photograph of the group in mod clothing taken on July 28, 1968, during the so-called "Mad Day Out" photo session.**

The Kinfauns demo of the song has essentially the same lyrics and arrangement as the finished master. Towards the end of the performance, John gives the following explanation while continuing his guitar playing: "No one was to know that sooner or later she was to go completely berserk under the care of Maharishi Mahesh Yogi. All the people around were very worried about the girl because she was going insane. So, we sang to her." John later speculated that Prudence was "trying to reach God quicker than anyone else."

*Dear Prudence* was recorded in three straight days, beginning August 28, on Trident Studio's eight-track tape machine. The basic backing track was taped that first evening with John's finger-picking guitar style on his Epiphone Casino, George on his Gibson Les Paul guitar and Paul on drums because Ringo was still on his "vacation" from the group. John added a second Casino guitar and George overdubbed a distorted Fender Telecaster lead guitar part. The group's use of Fender Twin-Reverb amplifiers gave Lennon's guitar a sharp, clean sound and Harrison's Telecaster a tough, gritty sound. The next day more overdubs were superimposed to Take 1: Paul's distinctive Rickenbacker bass guitar, John's double tracked lead vocal and backing vocals, handclaps and tambourine from Paul, George, Mal Evans, Paul's cousin John McCartney and Apple recording artist Jackie Lomax. Finally, on August 30, Paul added the rippling piano heard at the end of the song and a brief bit of flugelhorn.

An initial mono mix of the song was made at Trident on October 5. The stereo and mono finished masters were mixed back at Abbey Road on October 13.

The album's next track, *Glass Onion*, was described by John Lennon in his *Playboy* interview as one of his "throwaway" songs. It is full of references to other Beatles songs (*Strawberry Fields Forever*, *I Am The Walrus*, *Lady Madonna*, *The Fool On The Hill* and *Fixing A Hole*) and interesting wordplay images (bent backed tulips, cast iron shore and dovetail joint). "Looking through the bent backed tulips to see how the other half live" refers to a floral arrangement featured at the posh London restaurant Parkes. The Cast Iron Shore is a name for Liverpool's beach and a dovetail joint is a type of construction wood joint.

The line that later drew the most attention was "And here's another clue for you all, the Walrus was Paul." When the "Paul is dead" rumor surfaced in late 1969, people claimed that John's revelation was a vital clue proving Paul's death because the walrus was a symbol of death. In the *I Am The Walrus* sequence from *Magical Mystery Tour*, John was the Walrus, not Paul. According to Lennon, "I threw the line in...just to confuse everyone a bit more." As for Glass Onion, it was one of the names suggested by John for the Iveys, an Apple act that changed its name to Badfinger.

The Kinfauns demo of *Glass Onion*, which appears on *Anthology 3*, shows that the song was far from being complete prior to *The White Album* sessions. With only a few lines to work with, John sings the first verse three times. And even its lyrics differ from the finished song as John opens with "I told you about Strawberry Fields, well here's a place you know just as real." Lennon's vocal is double-tracked throughout the song. Beginning with the second verse, he mumbles some gibberish-sounding phrases. The performance moves to shifting tempos for the third verse and a tambourine is heard in the background. Towards the end one of the Beatles yells "Help!" The tape concludes more Lennon vocal non-sequiturs.

*Glass Onion* was recorded at Abbey Road during a time in the sessions when Chris Thomas was subbing as producer for the vacationing George Martin. The Beatles ran through 34 takes of the song on September 11, with John on his Gibson Model J-160E "Jumbo" acoustic guitar, George on his Fender Stratocaster, Paul on his Fender Jazz Bass and Ringo on drums. The next day John's double-tracked lead vocal and a tambourine were superimposed onto Take 33. A second drum part by Ringo and piano by Paul were added the following day. Then, on September 16, Paul double-tracked a brief recorder part following the song's reference to *The Fool On The Hill*.

A somewhat bizarre mono mix of the song was completed on September 26, while George Martin was still on holiday. John assembled a four track tape of special effects including a ringing telephone, a sustained organ note, BBC soccer commentator Kenneth Wolstenholme shouting "It's a goal" over the sound of a roaring crowd and the sound of breaking glass. These effects were brought into the mix at various times during the song. The ringing telephone opens the song and is also heard after the middle break and during the ending coda. The soccer broadcast and breaking glass

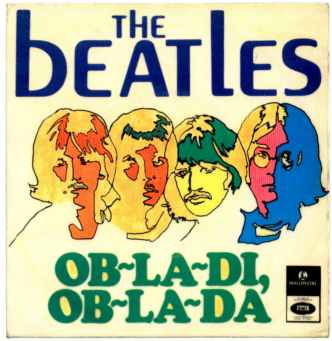

**Although Apple did not pull any songs from** *The White Album* **for release on singles in America or England during the sixties, songs from the album were featured on seven-inch discs in other countries. Sweden issued a single featuring** *Back In The U.S.S.R.* **and** *Don't Pass Me By* **(Apple SD 6061) (left). A Portuguese EP (Parlophone LMEP 1350) (right) features** *Ob-La-Di, Ob-La-Da* **along with** *Julia, While My Guitar Gently Weeps* **and** *Back In The U.S.S.R.*

tape loops are used to end the track. This version of the song is on *Anthology 3*.

Upon his return from vacation, George Martin was not impressed with the track and suggested adding orchestration in lieu of the special effects. On October 10, Martin's score of four violins, two violas and two cellos was superimposed onto Take 33. The song was mixed for mono and stereo later that day.

*Ob-La-Di, Ob-La-Da* was another song Paul worked on while in Rishikesh. In Miles' *Many Years From Now*, Paul recalls walking through the jungle with his guitar singing "Ob-La-Di, Ob-La-Da, life goes on, bra." Paul took the phrase from Jimmy Scott, a Nigerian conga player who had been part of the London music scene since the fifties. In Scott's native Yoruban language, "Ob la di ob la da" is an expression meaning "life goes on." The song was another of Paul's fantasy stories, this time inhabited by Desmond and Molly in their barrow in a Caribbean market place.

The rehearsal of the song at George's house reveals that Paul had completed his lyrics and initially envisioned the song as an acoustic guitar-dominated, Jamaican-flavored song. After the first line in the song's bridge, Paul vocalizes instruments with a "chick-a-boom, chick-a-boom, chick-a-boom, boom" refrain that was used in the first version of the song recorded at Abbey Road on three consecutive evenings beginning on July 3. The first session started with seven takes of a rhythm track featuring Paul on acoustic guitar and guide vocal, and Ringo on drums. Paul added another acoustic guitar and his lead vocal to Take 7, but then decided that Take 4 was a better performance. He added acoustic guitar to Take 4 before calling it a night. The following evening Paul recorded his lead vocal, with John and George adding background "la-la" vocals. The tape was given a reduction mixdown and designated Take 5, to which

Paul superimposed another lead vocal. The next day the track was embellished by outside musicians, including three saxophonists and Jimmy Scott on bongos. Later that evening, a piccolo was added, but Paul shortly thereafter recorded over the piccolo track with another guitar part played and recorded to sound like a bass.

Although this reggae version of the song is quite charming, Paul, in a move reminiscent of his handling of *I'm Looking Through You*, decided to rearrange the tune. The remake was started on July 8, with Paul on fuzz bass, George on acoustic guitar, John on piano and Ringo on drums. Ironically, it was John's resentment at doing a remake of the song that gave the tune its distinctive opening. John arrived at the studio late and somewhat stoned. He sat behind the piano and aggressively banged out the opening chords at a fast-pace that was carried throughout the performances. The group ran through 12 takes of the song before Paul was satisfied. After a reduction mix of Take 12 was designated Take 13, the group added lead and backing vocals and percussion onto the open tracks. Paul left the studio at 3:00 a.m. with a mono mix of the song.

Apparently dissatisfied with the remake, Paul worked on two takes of a re-remake (designated Takes 20 and 21) the following evening. Mark Lewisohn speculates that this version was recorded with Paul on drums prior to Ringo arriving at the studio. After spending five hours on the second remake, Paul decided to abandon the new version and return to the July 8 remake. Paul, John and George recorded over the vocals on Take 13, this time adding laughter and humorous asides. This lighthearted approach probably originated from Paul accidentally reversing the roles of Desmond and Molly in the last verse. Take 13 was then given a reduction mix, identified as Take 22, and embellished with handclaps and additional vocals and percussion.

On July 11, the recording resumed with overdubs of three saxophones by outside musicians and bass by Paul. The best of two mixdowns, Take 23, was further embellished before two mono mixes were made. The next night two new mono mixes were made. On July 15, after listening to an acetate of the best mono mix over the weekend, Paul decided to rerecord his lead vocal onto Take 23. Once this task was completed, ten mono mixes were made. *Ob-La-Di, Ob-La-Da* was mixed for stereo on October 12, at which time another mono mix was made.

The rejected reggae version of *Ob-La-Di, Ob-La-Da* was later slated to appear on the aborted *Sessions* LP of the mid-eighties and was nearly released as the B side to *Leave My Kitten Alone* (cancelled Capitol B-5439). It was finally released on *Anthology 3*. The *Anthology* version is preceded by Paul shouting "Yes sir, Take 1 of the Mighty Jungle Band" in a mock-Jamaican voice. At the song's conclusion, Paul adds "Ob-la-di, ob-la-da, brother."

*Wild Honey Pie* also had its origin in Rishikesh, starting out as a simple sing-along. Paul recorded the song by himself in Abbey Road's Studio Two on August 20, 1968, while George Harrison was in Greece, and John and Ringo were in Studio Three recording an edit piece for *Yer Blues* and supervising the mono mix of *Revolution 9*. Paul described *Wild Honey Pie* as "a little experimental piece" built up in the studio over one basic rhythm track. He started with acoustic guitar parts, featuring "a lot of vibrato on the strings." In addition to playing three guitars, Paul added harpsichord and drums, as well as three vocals. The 53-second track was mixed for mono at the end of the session and for stereo on October 13.

*The Continuing Story Of Bungalow Bill* is another song inspired by and written during the group's stay at Rishikesh. According to John, he wrote the song "about a guy [American Richard A. Cooke III] in Maharishi's meditation camp who took a short break to go shoot a few poor tigers, and then came back to commune with God." The Bungalow Bill name is a mutation of American showman Buffalo Bill and the bungalow living quarters in Rishikesh. In his *Playboy* interview John described the tune as "a sort of teenage social-comment song and a bit of a joke."

The Kinfauns demo, featuring John on lead vocal and acoustic guitar, has the same basic arrangement and lyrics as the finished master. The background handclaps and vocals of jungle sound effects give the performance a party atmosphere that carried over to the recording of the song at Abbey Road more than four months later. The tape ends with John asking, "What did Bungalow Bill kill?"

*Bungalow Bill* was started and completed in three takes at the end of an extremely productive 16 hour session held on October 8 that also produced John's *I'm So Tired*. The backing track consists of John and George on acoustic guitars, Paul on his Rickenbacker bass and Ringo on drums. Instrumental overdubs include John on organ, Chris Thomas on mellotron (mandolin tapes on the first part of the song and then bassoon, heard prominently during the ending breakdown of the song), Paul on a second bass part (heard only at the end of the third verse) and tambourine. John gives a spirited lead vocal performance and is backed by singing, handclaps and whistles provided by Paul, George, Ringo, Yoko and others present in the studio, including Ringo's wife Maureen. Yoko plays the role of Bungalow Bill's mommy by singing "Not when he looked so fierce" and "If looks could kill it would have been us instead of him." The flamenco-style guitar sound that opens the song was recorded separately and edited to the front of the master tape. The track ends with John enthusiastically shouting "Eh up!"

Lennon's vocal ad-lib effectively links *Bungalow Bill* to the album's next track, *While My Guitar Gently Weeps*. In his book *I Me Mine*, Harrison explains that he was reading the *I Ching*, the Chinese book of change, around the time he wrote the song. The book is based on the Eastern concept that everything is relative to everything else, as opposed to the Western view that things are merely coincidental. While visiting his parents, he decided to write a song on the first thing he saw upon opening a book "as it would be relative to that moment, at *that* time." George randomly opened a book and saw the phrase "gently weeps." He then laid the book down and began writing the lyrics.

George introduced the song to the group during rehearsals for the album. The Kinfauns demo, which lasts a mere two and a half minutes, is structurally similar to the finished master, but has a totally different feel. The stark arrangement features George on acoustic guitar and, beginning at the bridge, sustained Hammond B-3 organ probably played by Paul. George is also joined by Paul on some of the vocals. The lyrics to the second line of the first verse differ from the finished master. In addition, the demo contains a third verse absent from the finished master. The deleted lyrics are: "I look at the trouble and hate that is raging/while my guitar gently weeps/As I'm sitting here doing nothing but aging/still my guitar gently weeps."

The first studio recording of the song took place at Abbey Road on July 25. After several rehearsals, a beautiful solo performance of George singing and playing acoustic guitar was recorded, apparently for demo purposes. Paul added a simple but effective harmonium part towards the end of the song. This early acoustic take is one of the highlights of *Anthology 3*. It runs for about three and a half minutes and contains a third verse with lyrics different than the Kinfauns demo: "I look from the wings at the play you are staging/while my guitar gently weeps/As I'm sitting here doing nothing but aging/still my guitar gently weeps."

On August 16, the band made its first proper attempt at the song, recording 14 takes of a rhythm track consisting of George on guitar, John on organ, Paul on bass and Ringo on drums. Take 14 was then run at 42½ cycles per second to form Take 15. The following day George left for a long weekend in Greece, resulting in the song being ignored for a few weeks.

By the time the group returned to the tune in September, the Beatles had recorded *Dear Prudence* on Trident Studios' eight-track recorder. Upon learning that EMI had a 3M eight-track recorder being held for quality review, the Beatles persuaded engineer Ken Scott to arrange for the new recorder to be installed in Studio Two. *While My Guitar Gently Weeps* was the first song recorded on Abbey

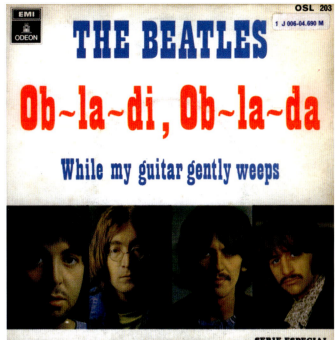

In Japan, EMI Toshiba released a single with *Ob-La-Di, Ob-La-Da* and *While My Guitar Gently Weeps* (Apple AR-2207) on March 10, 1969. The record came with a 7" square slip sheet (left). These songs were later issued on a 45 in Spain (Odeon OSL 203) (right). Dialog captured during the filming of *Let It Be* on January 10, 1969, reveals that Paul wanted the same two songs issued as a single in England and America.

Road's new eight-track machine. On September 3, Take 15 was transferred to eight-track tape and renamed Take 16. George then spent several hours recording a backwards guitar solo for the song.

On September 5, George was joined by the others at Abbey Road to record additional parts to Take 16, including two Harrison vocals, maracas, additional drums and another guitar solo. Upon hearing the playback, Harrison was not pleased with the direction the song was going, so he decided to start over again. This rejected version, which differs sharply from the final master, features Harrison's backwards guitar solo and more prominent organ.

For the full band remake of song, George led the group through 28 takes numbered 17 through 44. The new recording featured George on acoustic guitar and guide vocal, John on guitar, Ringo on drums and Paul on piano (or on some takes, organ). Take 25 was deemed the best.

The next day George got a ride into London with his friend, Eric Clapton. It was during this car ride that Harrison asked Clapton to play lead guitar on *While My Guitar Gently Weeps*. Although he was reluctant to accept George's invitation "because no one plays on Beatles sessions," Clapton's playing that evening was brilliant, giving the song the gently weeping guitar called for in its title. His presence inspired to group to be on their best behavior. In addition to Clapton's lead guitar (played on his Gibson Les Paul), other overdubs included: Paul's bass and backing vocal; Ringo's castanets and tambourine; and Harrison's organ (on the bridge) and double-tracked lead vocal.

Although stereo and mono mixes were prepared on October 7, the song was remixed a week later on October 14 to alter Clapton's lead guitar. Apparently the guitarist was concerned that his playing didn't have enough of a Beatles sound. Chris Thomas wobbled the oscillator during the mix, giving the guitar its distinct sound.

The final selection on side one, *Happiness Is A Warm Gun*, is one of the more interesting tracks on the album. It consists of three separate parts: *I Need A Fix, Mother Superior Jumped The Gun* and *Happiness Is A Warm Gun*. At the time the Kinfauns demo was recorded, John had only written what would be the ending lines for the *I Need A Fix* section and the one-line *Mother Superior Jumped The Gun* section. "Mother" was one of John's names for Yoko. After going through both existing elements of the song, John sings "Yoko Ono, oh no, Yoko Ono, oh yes" before returning to *I Need A Fix* and *Mother Superior Jumped The Gun*. This early rendition of the song is on *Anthology 3*.

The lyrics to the first part of the song came from phrases supplied primarily by Derek Taylor during an evening get together of Derek, John, Neil Aspinall and Pete Shotton. John told the gang he had a half-written song and needed help in finishing the lyrics. He wanted a way to describe a really smart girl and Taylor gave him the song's opening line, "She's not a girl who misses much." Taylor told of a man who enjoyed wearing moleskin gloves during sex and supplied the image of a lizard's quick movement on glass windows. This became "She's well acquainted with the touch of the velvet hand like a lizard on a window pane." "The man in the crowd with the multicolored mirrors on his hobnail boots" was lifted from a newspaper story about a soccer fan who had been arrested by the police for having mirrors on the tips of his shoes so he could look up ladies' skirts. The next line, "Lying with his eyes while his hands are busy working overtime," was drawn from a news story about a man who used a set of fake hands to divert attention away from his real hands, which he used to rob items from a counter case. The line about eating something and donating it to the National Trust was a reference to defecating on public property. John artfully tied all of these images together to complete the *I Need A Fix* segment.

**Paul and his sheepdog Martha take center stage with the John Foster & Sons Ltd. Black Dyke Mills Band in the above Apple publicity picture. Paul produced the brass band's Apple single, which paired McCartney's _Thingumybob_ with _Yellow Submarine_ (Apple 1800).**

The *Happiness Is A Warm Gun* section was the final piece of the puzzle. The phrase "Happiness is a warm gun" came from the cover of an American gun magazine shown to John by George Martin. (The NRA-inspired phrase was a takeoff on Charles Schulz's *Peanuts* comic strip line "Happiness is a warm puppy.") Part of this section was lifted from an unused half-spoken bit from *I'm So Tired*. Towards the end of the Kinfauns demo of *I'm So Tired*, John sings "When I hold you in your arms, when you show me each one of your charms, I wonder should I get up and go to the funny farm," before going "no, no, no" and returning to song's bridge. For *Happiness Is A Warm Gun*, John slightly altered the first line and rewrote the remaining lines to fit the warm gun motif. In his *Playboy* interview, John admitted that the line "When I hold you in my arms and I feel my finger on your trigger" had a double meaning as he was fresh in his relationship with Yoko and "very sexually oriented" at the time.

Recording on *Happiness Is A Warm Gun In Your Hand* (as it was initially titled) got underway on September 23 with Chris Thomas in charge. The song's changing tempos caused problems for the band, resulting in 45 unacceptable takes that evening alone. The next night Takes 46 through 70 were recorded. All of these takes featured John on guide vocal and his Epiphone Casino, George on his Fender Telecaster, Paul on his Rickenbacker bass and Ringo on drums.

After listening to the tapes, it was decided that the first two parts of Take 53 (up through 1:34) and the third and final part of Take 65 were the best performances. On September 25, these two takes were edited together and named Take 65. That evening the following parts were superimposed onto Take 65: John's lead vocal (triple-tracked in some places); "happiness, bang, bang, shoot, shoot" backing vocals by John, Paul and George; additional bass by Paul; organ; piano; tuba (all but mixed out in the final masters); tambourine; and Ringo's song-ending snare drum couplet.

The song was mixed for mono on September 25 and 26 and for stereo on October 15. At the mixing stage, the first "I need a fix 'cause I'm going down" line was deleted to provide a brief instrumental passage. A careful listen 57 seconds into the stereo version reveals John singing "down" as his vocal was brought back into the mix a tad too early.

John considered *Happiness Is A Warm Gun* one of his best songs. Paul and George reportedly said the track was their favorite on the album.

Side two opens with Paul's piano-driven ballad *Martha My Dear*. Although named after Paul's sheep dog, Martha, the song is a sentimental love song written for a woman.

The song was recorded at Trident Studios on October 4 in one take featuring Paul on piano and vocal. It is believed that Ringo played drums on the song, but the drums may have been provided by Paul as the session was pretty much an all-Paul affair that also involved overdubs to Paul's *Honey Pie*. That evening George Martin's score, consisting of four violins, two violas, two cellos, three trumpets, French horn, trombone, tuba and flugelhorn, was recorded onto Take 1. After the musicians left the studio, Paul rerecorded his vocal and added handclaps. The following night Paul added bass and guitar to the song. Mono and stereo mixes were made that evening, although the equalization was changed at Abbey Road on October 7 when the tapes were copied.

*I'm So Tired* is another of John's songs written in India. According to John, the all-day meditation regime in Rishikesh prevented him from sleeping at night. On top of that, he was missing Yoko. The line "You know it's three weeks, I'm going insane" indicates that the song may have been written at the three-week mark of John's stay in India.

The Kinfauns demo shows that the song was complete by the time the group began rehearsals for the upcoming album. As discussed above, the demo contains a spoken segment that was dropped from the song and rewritten to form the final section of *Happiness Is A Warm Gun*.

*I'm So Tired* was started and finished in 14 takes on October 8. The live basic track features John on lead vocal and electric guitar, George on his Fender Stratocaster, Paul on his Rickenbacker bass and Ringo on drums. Overdubs added to Take 14 include piano, organ and additional vocals from John and Paul. At the end of the recording, John mumbles "monsieur, monsieur, how about another one?" When played backwards, it sounded like "Paul is dead man, miss him, miss him" to those looking for clues of Paul's death. The song was mixed for stereo and mono on October 15. *Anthology 3* contains an edit of Takes 3, 6 and 9.

*Blackbird* was written by Paul at his Scotland farm. According to Paul, he developed the melody on guitar based on a Bach composition and took it to another level, fitting words to it. In Miles' *Many Years From Now*, McCartney states that he wrote the song with a black woman in mind, relating to the civil rights movement in the United States. He kept the song symbolic so that others could apply the song's empowerment message to their particular problems.

The Kinfauns demo has the same lyrics and arrangement as the finished master, except that its ending is a bit different. The song was recorded on June 11 by Paul alone in Abbey Road's Studio Two while John was over in Studio Three working on tape loop sound effects for *Revolution 9*. Paul sang and played acoustic guitar, accompanied only by a metronome, through 32 takes (of which 11 were complete) before being satisfied. An additional vocal, acoustic guitar and bird sound effects were then superimposed onto Take 32. The song was mixed for mono at the end of the session and for stereo on October 13. *Anthology 3* contains Take 4, an equally effective performance.

*Piggies* is another of George's social comment songs dating back to 1966. Its stinging lyrics bring back memories of *Taxman*. Although "pig" was a sixties derogatory term aimed at police, Harrison's target was the upper class, not figures of authority. His mother supplied the line "What they need's a damn good whacking" to rhyme with "backing" and "lacking."

The Kinfauns demo is on *Anthology 3*. It features George on acoustic guitar and double-tracked lead vocals. At that stage the song's last line was "Clutching forks and knives to cut their pork chops." John improved on this with "Clutching forks and knives to eat their bacon."

The rhythm track for *Piggies* was recorded at Abbey Road on September 19 with Chris Thomas subbing as producer. It was completed in 11 takes on a four-track machine. The backing track features George on his Gibson J-200 acoustic guitar, Thomas on harpsichord, Paul on his Rickenbacker bass and Ringo on tambourine. Apparently John did not attend the session. The next night the four track tape was copied to an eight-track tape (designated Take 12) to allow for overdubs. Three Harrison vocals were recorded onto some of the open tracks. John put together a tape loop of pig sounds taken from the EMI sound effects tape library. The pig sound effects (and possibly Beatle-made pig grunts) were then superimposed onto Take 12.

On October 10, George Martin's orchestral score of four violins, two cellos and two violas was added to Take 12 using the same musicians who would later play on *Glass Onion*. The mono and stereo mixes were completed the following night.

*Rocky Raccoon* was written in India by Paul, with a bit of help from John and Donovan. The song was originally titled "*Rocky Sassoon*," but was changed to *Rocky Raccoon* "because it sounded more cowboyish." According to Paul, "I like talking blues so I started off like that, then I did my tongue-in-cheek parody of a western and threw in some amusing lines."

At the time the Kinfauns demo was recorded, the song was lacking its talking blues intro as well as the verse about the doctor stinking of gin. The arrangement is similar to the finished master; however, the demo has more of a country and western feel to it, with George playing country-sounding lead fills after Paul's double-tracked vocal lines.

*Rocky Raccoon* was recorded in a single session held on August 15. The rhythm track, perfected in nine takes, features Paul on vocal and acoustic guitar, John on harmonica and Fender Bass VI and Ringo on drums. As was the case with *Hey Jude*, Paul did not want George playing lead guitar fills on the song, and Harrison was once again relegated to the control room.

The multiple outtakes of the song show that Paul was still formulating the words to the introduction and the doctor verse. Take 8, which is on *Anthology 3*, opens with John proclaiming "He was a fool onto himself." Paul uses this line early in his intro, in which Paul tells us that Rocky came from a little town in Minnesota. This is a tip of the hat to Bob Dylan, who grew up in Hibbing, Minnesota. During the start of the doctor verse, Paul flubs the lyrics, having the doctor "sminking" of gin. This causes Paul to laugh and ad-lib his way through the rest of the verse.

On Take 9, McCartney mimics Dylan's vocal style in his introduction. Paul was satisfied with this performance, so the group proceeded with overdubs. After Ringo added a second drum part and George contributed bass, the tape was given a mixdown reduction and designated Take 10. The following embellishments were then added: harmonica and harmonium by John, honky-tonk piano solos for the instrumental breaks by George Martin and backing vocals by John, Paul and George. The song was mixed for mono at the end of the session and for stereo on October 10.

Ringo's *Don't Pass Me By* was the oldest song recorded for the album. Although the drummer had bits of the song completed back in 1963, he had to wait five years to get the Beatles to record his first solo composition. Oddly enough, EMI recording sheets initially listed the song as "*Ringo's Tune (Untitled)*" and "*This Is Some Friendly*."

Paul and Ringo recorded the backing track, which consisted solely of Paul's piano miked through a guitar amplifier and Leslie speaker and Ringo's drums, in three takes on June 5. Paul then overdubbed a second piano part and sleigh bells. Two reduction mixes were made, with Take 5 being considered the best. Ringo added a lead vocal, which was recorded over by one of two bass overdubs by Paul. Although a reduction mix (Take 6) was made, it was decided to go back to Take 5 when recording resumed the following day. Ringo's vocal was double-tracked and recorded at a slower tape speed to raise its pitch when played back at the normal speed. A new reduction mix was made and designated Take 7. Paul then added a new bass part on his Rickenbacker.

*Anthology 3* contains the first 2:40 of the instrumental backing track of Take 3 with a Ringo vocal from Take 5. This stark version of the song has some later-mixed-out vocal ad-libs by Ringo and is missing the song's yet-to-be-recorded fiddle passages.

No additional work was done on the song until July 12, when Paul added bass, Ringo added piano and Jack Fallon played the tune's country fiddle violin part. The song was then mixed for mono, with the stereo mix being made on October 11. The mono mix differs noticeably from the stereo mix, having its ending fiddle solo running longer.

By the time Ringo entered Abbey Road on July 22 to rerecord his lead vocal to *Good Night*, a decision had been made to come up with an introduction for *Don't Pass Me By*. On this date, two totally different edit pieces were recorded. Paul ran through four takes of tinkling around on piano, with the 45 second Take 4 being considered the best. George Martin recorded a 48 second instrumental passage using the same musicians present for the orchestral overdub for *Good Night*. The two recordings met different fates. An eight second segment of McCartney's piano piece was edited to the mono and stereo mixes of *Don't Pass Me By* on October 11. George Martin's orchestral composition, titled *A Beginning*, was not used, but eventually appeared as the opening track on *Anthology 3*.

According to Paul, *Why Don't We Do It In The Road?* was "a primitive statement to do with sex or...freedom." The idea for the song came from Paul observing a male monkey hop on the back of a female monkey for sex in the Indian jungle.

The song was recorded by Paul, with Ken Townsend serving as engineer, at Abbey Road on October 9. McCartney sang and played acoustic guitar on five takes. All solo performances start with Paul tapping out the beat on the sounding board of his guitar. Although the finished master is an all-out raunchy rocker, the early takes consist of Paul alternating between gentle, high-pitched vocals and his gritty rocker voice. Take 4 is included on *Anthology 3*. Towards the end of the performance, Paul changes the line "No one will be watching us" to "People will be watching us." As the song ends, Paul asks Ken, "What do you think of all that; do you think I can do it better?" Apparently he thought Paul could do better as a fifth and final take was recorded. Paul then overdubbed piano onto Take 5.

The following evening, while John and George were involved with George Martin's string overdubs to *Piggies* and *Glass Onion* in Abbey Road's Studio Two, Paul had Ken and Ringo join him in Studio Three to complete his song. Vocals, handclaps, Rickenbacker bass and Ringo's drums were recorded onto Take 5, which was given a reduction mix to form Take 6. Paul then added an electric guitar part played on his Epiphone Casino. The song was mixed for mono and stereo on October 16.

Paul's raunchy rocker is followed by his gentle love song *I Will*. Paul recalls having the melody for the song prior to his stay in Rishikesh. While in India, he tried col-

laborating with Donovan, but was not satisfied with the lyrics they came up with. Because the song was far from completion in May, is was not rehearsed or recorded at Kinfauns.

The song was recorded on September 16 at an Abbey Road session attended by Paul, John and Ringo and produced by Chris Thomas. The trio went through 67 takes of the song with Paul on lead vocal and acoustic guitar, Ringo on maracas and cymbals and John on temple blocks. *Anthology 3* contains Take 1, which demonstrates that Paul had the basic arrangement worked out prior to entering the studio.

During the session, Paul drifted into a few spontaneous performances. One of these (Take 19) was a 2:21 ad-lib containing the words "Can you take me back where I came from, can you take me back?" A 28-second segment from the end of this recording was used as an uncredited link track between *Cry Baby Cry* and *Revolution 9*. Other songs included: *Step Inside Love*, a tune Paul wrote for Cilla Black in 1967; *Los Paranoias*, a 3:48 madcap jam with silly made-up-on-the-spot lyrics; and *The Way You Look Tonight*, whose lyrics came almost exclusively from *I Will*. An edit of *Step Inside Love* and *Los Paranoias* is on *Anthology 3*.

At the end of the session, it was decided that Take 65 was the best performance of *I Will*. The four-track tape was copied to another tape to allow for overdubs and was designated Take 68. The following evening Paul overdubbed additional vocals, including an imitation of a bass guitar, and an acoustic twelve-string guitar part. Paul's lead vocal was treated with ADT (artificial double tracking) when the song was mixed for mono on September 26 and for stereo on October 14.

The final track on side two is John's beautiful ballad *Julia*, which was written primarily in Rishikesh. Julia was John's mother, who died when he was 17 years old. The song's depiction of Julia as an "ocean child" is a reference to Yoko, whose name means "child of the ocean" in Japanese. In his *Playboy* interview, John described the song is "a combination of Yoko and my mother blended into one."

Some of the song's lyrics, including its opening couplet, were adopted from *Sand And Foam*, a collection of writings and drawings by Kahlil Gibran, a Lebanese poet and philosopher. Gibran's words are: "Half of what I say is meaningless; but I say it so the other half may reach you." and "When life does not find a singer to sing her heart she produces a philosopher to speak her mind." The song's imagery was inspired by Yoko, who sent letters to John while he was in India. According to John, "She would write things like 'I am a cloud. Watch for me in the sky." This blending of people and nature probably influenced John's use of phrases such as "seashell eyes," "windy smile," "hair of floating sky," "sleeping sand" and "silent cloud."

John learned the finger-picking guitar style used on the song from Donovan and/or Gypsy Dave while in Rishikesh. Donovan recalls that "John was keen to learn the finger-style guitar I played and he was a good student." This style was also used by John on *Dear Prudence*, as well as some of his post-Beatles recordings such as *Look At Me* and Yoko's *Remember Love*.

The Kinfauns demo shows that John had completed *Julia* prior to the start of the *White Album* sessions; however, he did not record the song until October 13, making it the last new selection recorded for the album. It is John's first and only solo recording for a Beatles record. *Julia* was completed in three takes featuring John on lead vocal and acoustic guitar (with a capo on the second fret). *Take 2*, which is on *Anthology 3*, is a mostly instrumental runthrough that breaks down past the midway point. On his third attempt, John plays the tune perfectly. His lead vocal was then recorded twice to allow for overlapping of the word "Julia" at the end and start of the verses. Afterwards the track was mixed for mono and stereo.

The album's third side opens with *Birthday*, a powerful rocker that was made up in the studio on September 18. Chris Thomas, who served as producer, recalls that the session was scheduled to start two hours earlier than normal at 5:00 p.m. to accommodate the group's desire to break in time to watch the 9:00 p.m. BBC broadcast of *The Girl Can't Help It* at Paul's nearby Cavendish Avenue home. The 1956 rock 'n' roll film stars Jayne Mansfield and contains performances by Little Richard, Fats Domino, Eddie Cochran, Gene Vincent, the Platters and the Treniers. Paul was the first to arrive at Abbey Road and quickly came up with the song's memorable riff. As the others arrived, the song began to take shape. The basic track consisted of Paul (on his Epiphone Casino) and George (on Fender VI bass) hammering out the *Birthday* riff, with Ringo on drums and John on tambourine. By the twentieth take, the backing track was completed and the gang headed for Paul's house to watch the film.

Upon their return, Take 20 was copied to form Takes 21 and 22. The following overdubs were added: John's Epiphone Casino matching Paul's riff an octave higher; Paul's piano through a Leslie speaker; Paul's scorching lead vocal; John's occasional matching lead vocal; and backing vocals and handclaps by the group, aided and abetted by Yoko Ono, George's wife Pattie (who apparently had gone to London with George so she could watch the movie with him) and Mal Evans. The party ended around 4:30 a.m. Take 22 was then mixed for mono. The stereo mix was made on October 14.

Although John later called the song "a piece of garbage," Paul considers it one of his favorites on the album because it was instantaneous and good to dance to. Most fans agree with Paul.

*Yer Blues* is another song written in India by John, who later described it as a case of being "up there trying to reach God and feeling suicidal." With its opening line "Yes I'm lonely, wanna die," the song is full of anguish and foreshadows the tone of Lennon's early solo recordings.

The Kinfauns demo is lyrically similar to the finished master, but there are subtle differences. In the demo he sings "My mother was of the earth, my father was of the sky, but I am of the universe and that's the reason why." By the time the song was recorded at Abbey Road, he had reversed the roles of his parents by singing "My mother was of the sky, my father was of the earth, but I am of the universe and you know what it's worth." There is also a change in the line

about Mr. Jones, the central character of Bob Dylan's *Ballad Of A Thin Man* (from his 1965 album *Highway 61 Revisited*). In the demo John sings "I feel so insecure, just like Dylan's Mr. Jones." In the finished master he feels suicidal.

At the request of John, *Yer Blues* was recorded in a small storage room next to the control room of Abbey Road's Studio Two. Lennon got the idea to record there when engineer Ken Scott jokingly complained to John about all the unconventional things the group was doing in the studio. Scott remarked, "Bloody hell, the way you lot are carrying on you'll be wanting to record everything in the room next door!" John thought it was a great idea and had the studio crew set up the band's amplifiers, microphones and instruments in the control room's tiny annex.

The session took place on August 13 with John on his Epiphone Casino, George on his Telecaster through a Leslie speaker, Paul on his Fender Jazz Bass and Ringo on drums. The group ran through 14 takes before preparing reduction mixdowns of Take 6 into Takes 15 and 16 and Take 14 into Take 17. The four-track tapes were then joined together with the opening minute or so of Take 17 being edited onto the end of Take 16 at the 3:17 mark of the finished master. No instrumental overdubs were made.

The following evening John recorded his lead vocal over the Take 16 part of the song. Paul added his backing vocal on the line "girl you know the reason why" beginning with the second verse. John chose not to rerecord his lead vocal over the Take 17 ending part of the song, instead allowing his bleed-through guide vocal of the previous evening to stand alone in the background. The song was then mixed for mono. A brief edit piece was recorded on August 20 featuring Ringo's slow "two, three" vocal and hi-hat count-in. This was then edited to the start of the mono master, which fades at the 4:10 mark. When the song was mixed for stereo on October 14, it was faded out ten seconds earlier.

While John viewed the words to the song as "pretty realistic," he felt self-conscious about singing it in the idiom of American blues artists. Musically *Yer Blues* became a parody of the English blues scene, particularly evident in its swing-time boogie-guitar instrumental passage and its simplistic guitar fills and solos.

The album's next track, *Mother Nature's Son*, may have also had its origin in India. John recalls a Maharishi lecture on nature that prompted him to write *I'm Just A Child Of Nature*. The song, with its opening line "On the road to Rishikesh," was given demo treatment at Kinfauns, but was not recorded during the *White Album* sessions. Lennon later resurrected the song's melody and rewrote the lyrics for *Jealous Guy* (which is on his *Imagine* album).

While John believed the same lecture inspired Paul to write *Mother Nature's Son*, McCartney remembers writing the song at his father's Liverpool home and that it was inspired by *Nature Boy*, one of Paul's favorite standards. Nat "King" Cole's recording of *Nature Boy* (Capitol 15054) was a million seller that topped the charts in America for eight weeks in 1948. Paul describes *Mother Nature's Son* as a "heartfelt song about my child-of-nature leanings."

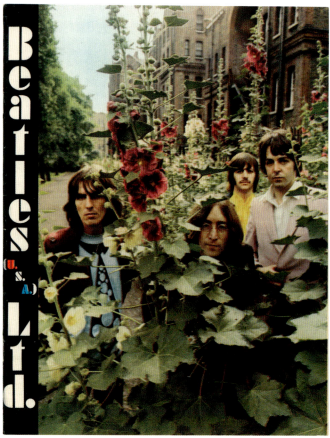

**The cover to the above photo book published by Beatles (U.S.A.) Ltd., the American fan club, features the boys posing as Mother Nature's sons in a Don McCullin photo taken during the "Mad Day Out" session.**

Although Paul had completed the lyrics and music to *Mother Nature's Son* by the time the Kinfauns demo was recorded, he had neither worked out the opening or closing of the song nor refined its scat vocal passages.

The song was recorded at Abbey Road as a solo McCartney piece on the evening of August 9 after the other Beatles had all gone home. Paul went through 25 live performances of the song, each featuring his vocal and his Martin D-28 acoustic guitar. Take 24 was selected as the best, although many of the other performances could have served as the basic track. *Anthology 3* contains Take 2.

On August 20, additional instruments were added to Take 24, which was then given a reduction mixdown and designated Take 26. Overdubs included George Martin's brass arrangement featuring four horns and Paul on bass drum, bongos, timpani and a second acoustic guitar. The drums were set up in an uncarpeted hallway to give them a natural echo staccato sound.

John's exuberant rocker *Everybody's Got Something To Hide Except Me And My Monkey* was written shortly after John began his relationship with Yoko in May, 1968. In his *Playboy* interview, John described the song as: "a nice line that I made into a song. It was about me and Yoko. Everybody seemed to be paranoid except for us two, who were in the glow of love." The song's opening line "Come on is such a joy" was, according to George Harrison, a favorite saying of the Maharishi.

The Kinfauns demo shows that although John had not come up with the song's introduction, the tune was essen-

tially complete. Even at this early stage, the song's infectious nature is apparent. One can sense that the group was looking forward to recording this one.

On June 26, the Beatles ran through several takes of the song, but these were later considered little more than rehearsals and the tape was erased. The following evening the backing track was recorded in six takes, with John on his Epiphone Casino, George on his Gibson SG, Paul on percussion (alternating between cowbell and chocalho) and Ringo on drums. During the song's mixdown to Takes 7 and 8, the tape was run at 43 cycles per second rather than the usual 50. Thus, upon playback at the normal speed, the song was in a higher pitch and considerably shorter. On July 1, Paul overdubbed two Rickenbacker bass parts. The song was given additional mixdowns to form Take 10, over which John added his lead vocal.

Although the track was thought to be complete, John apparently believed it could be improved upon. On July 23, he rerecorded his lead vocal onto Take 10. After reduction mixes formed Takes 11 and 12, backing vocals and handclaps were superimposed onto Take 12. The song was then mixed for mono, although it would receive an improved mono mix on October 12 when the stereo mix was made.

*Sexy Sadie* was another song that originated in India. In his *Rolling Stone* interview, John stated that the song was about the Maharishi, adding that he "copped out and wouldn't write 'Maharishi what have you done, you made a fool of everyone.'" John's disenchantment with the Maharishi started when he heard rumors that the holy man had made sexual advances towards some of the women at the compound. After John and George had heated discussions about whether it might be true, they decided to confront the Maharishi. When John told the Maharishi they were leaving, he asked why. John curtly told him, "Well, if you're so cosmic, you'll know why." Because the Maharishi was never told what he had supposedly done, he was unable to deny the allegations. John interpreted the Maharishi's non-denial as an admission of guilt. John reportedly wrote the song just before leaving Rishikesh.

Although John's initial lyrics were apparently quite crude and mentioned the Maharishi by name, by the time the Kinfauns demo was recorded, Lennon had cleaned things up and replaced "Maharishi" with "Sexy Sadie" at George's request. On July 19, the group ran through 21 takes of the song ranging in length from five and a half to eight minutes and featuring John's lead vocal, electric guitars, organ and drums. *Anthology 3* contains the first 4:05 of Take 6. John wasn't satisfied with any of the performances, so the group returned to the song on July 24. This time 23 more takes (designated Takes 25 through 47) were recorded. Although Take 47 was deemed the best, John still was not satisfied.

The band tried a new instrumental approach to the song on August 13, featuring John on acoustic guitar and lead vocal, Paul on piano (with echo), George on his Les Paul through a Leslie speaker and Ringo on drums. The group recorded eight takes, which were designated Takes 100 through 107. The final version was considered the best and given four reduction mixdowns. On August 21, additional reduction mixes were made to allow for the overdubbing

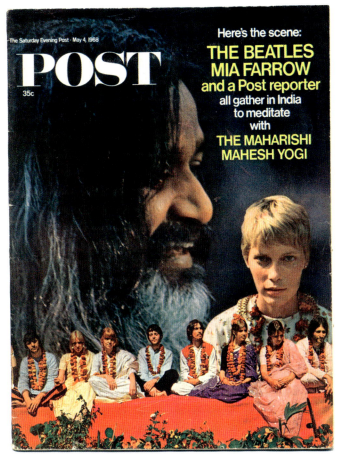 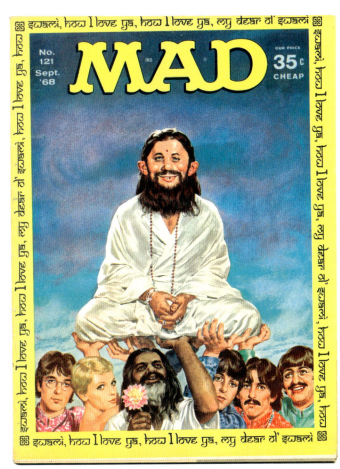

*The Saturday Evening Post* featured a cover story on the Beatles and the Maharishi Mahesh Yogi in its May 4, 1968, issue. The two-part story concluded in the magazine's May 18th issue. *MAD* magazine parodied the Beatles stay in Rishikesh on its September, 1968, cover. The text surrounding the picture reads "swami, how I love ya, how I love ya, my dear ol' swami."

of organ and an additional lead vocal by John, Rickenbacker bass by Paul, tambourine by Ringo and two sets of backing vocals by John, Paul and George. The song was then mixed for mono. The stereo mix was completed on October 14.

*Helter Skelter* was the product of Paul's desire to record a song with "the most raucous vocal, the loudest drums, et cetera, et cetera." According to Paul, he was inspired to make such a record after reading an interview with the Who's Pete Townshend in which the guitarist described his band's new single, *I Can See For Miles*, as the loudest, rawest, dirtiest and most uncompromising song the band had ever recorded. While this story may have been embellished a bit by Paul, it demonstrates McCartney's competitive nature, in this case wanting to out do the Who at their own game. Paul took the symbol of a helter skelter (a spiral slide at a British playground) as a "ride from the top to the bottom...and this was the fall, the demise, the going down."

The Beatles first attempt to record the song took place at Abbey Road on July 18. The band jammed its way through three extended performances featuring the standard lineup of two guitars, bass and drums backing Paul's lead vocal. The first two takes lasted over ten minutes each, and Take 3 went on for an incredible 27:11, making it the group's longest recording by far.

Realizing that none of the July 18 takes were of a suitable length, the group decided to rerecord the song on September 9. The session marked Chris Thomas' baptism of fire as producer, though by this stage in the Beatles career,

the group was often calling its own shots in the studio. The band ran through 18 chaotic takes of the song (designated Takes 4 through 21) before Paul was satisfied. The basic instrumental track consisted of Paul's rhythm guitar on his Epiphone Casino, George's distorted lead guitar on his Les Paul, John on Fender Jazz Bass and Ringo on drums. Overdubs were superimposed onto Take 21 the following night and included John on saxophone, Mal Evans on trumpet and backing vocals form John and George. The final result was just what McCartney had been aiming for: his "most raucous" vocal and Ringo coming through with his "loudest drums." After pounding away for 18 unrelenting performances of the song, Ringo shouted "I've got blisters on my fingers!" the end of the final take. His immortal words are preserved on the 4:29 stereo mix of the song, which was made on October 12. The mono mix, completed on September 17, runs nearly a minute shorter at 3:36 and is without Ringo's scream. Both versions begin fading out around the 3:30 mark, but where the mono mix completely fades out, the stereo mix fades back in and runs to the end of the recording.

The loudest song on the album is quickly followed by the set's softest selection, *Long, Long, Long*. Although its lyrics are about lost and regained love, George insists that the "you" in the song is God. He admits that the chords were taken from Bob Dylan's *Sad Eyed Lady Of The Lowlands,* which is on the singer's 1966 *Blonde On Blonde* double album.

The song, initially titled "*It's Been A Long Long Long Time*," was recorded on October 7 in 67 takes featuring George on vocal accompanied by his Gibson J-200 acoustic guitar, Paul on Hammond organ and Ringo on drums. Towards the end of the song, Paul hit an organ note that caused a bottle of Blue Nun wine to rattle. The group liked the effect, so microphones were set up to capture the sound for use at the end of the song. Ringo added some drums to complement the rattling sound. The next day Harrison added a second vocal and acoustic guitar part and Paul overdubbed his Rickenbacker bass. On October 9, Paul added his backing vocal and Chris Thomas contributed a piano part on the bridge. John did not participate in any of the sessions for the song, which was mixed for stereo on October 10 and for mono on October 12 and 14. *Long, Long, Long* was selected to close side three.

The fourth and final side of the album opens with the first song recorded for the disc, *Revolution*. John wanted the song released as a single to serve "as a statement of the Beatles' position on Viet Nam and the Beatles' position on revolution." According to John, the lyrics expressed his feelings about politics: "I want to see the plan....Count me out if it's for violence. Don't expect me on the barricades unless it is with flowers."

John began work on the song while in India. By the time the Kinfauns demo was recorded, John had only completed the first two verses. After singing the completed verses, John simulates an instrumental passage with scat vocals before repeating the first verse. John's antiviolence stance is clear as he sings the line "But when you talk about destruction, don't you know that you can count me out." The demo features acoustic guitars, hand claps, tambourine (on the last verse), John on lead vocal, Paul sometimes joining him on the verses and Paul and George on the "Don't you know it's gonna be" backing vocals.

The rhythm track for the song, with John on acoustic guitar, Paul on piano and Ringo on drums, was recorded in 16 takes at the first *White Album* session on May 30. All of the performances, with the exception of the final take, were about five minutes long. Take 18 (there were no takes numbered 11 or 12) ran for 10:17. Its final six minutes consisted of jamming and feedback, which came to an end with John shouting "OK, I've had enough."

The next day John added two vocal parts and Paul overdubbed his Rickenbacker bass onto Take 18. In rehearsal, John's stance on destruction alternated between "you can count me out" and "you can count me in." Although the lyric sheet included with the album reads "you can count me out," John actually sings "you can count me out, in." After a reduction mix created Take 19, Paul and George added their "shoo-be-do-wop-bow" backing vocals.

On June 4, John rerecorded his lead vocal. In an effort to alter the sound of his voice, Lennon sang while lying on his back on the floor of Abbey Road's Studio Three. Other overdubs included percussive clicks (heard during the song's intro) and a second drum part by Ringo, a tone-pedal distorted lead guitar by John and organ by Paul (not heard in the final mix). The song was given another reduction mix (Take 20) to accommodate the additions.

By the time work resumed on the song on June 21, John had done substantial work on *Revolution 9*. It was at this time that the song's title was changed to *Revolution 1*. After George Martin's brass arrangement (two trumpets and four trombones) was recorded, and the song given another reduction mixdown (Take 22), Harrison superimposed an electric guitar part. The song was mixed for stereo during this session and again on June 25.

*Honey Pie* is a nod to the vaudeville tradition Paul was raised on, following in the footsteps of *When I'm Sixty-Four* and *Your Mother Should Know*. It is also another of Paul's fantasy songs; this time written for a woman who sails to America and becomes a legend of the silver screen.

The Kinfauns demo, which is on *Anthology 3*, features Paul backed by acoustic guitars and percussion. The 1:18 recording lacks the song's spoken intro, although it has most of the lyrics of the finished master.

The backing track for *Honey Pie* was recorded in one take at Trident Studios on October 1. It consists of Paul on piano, John on his Casino, George on Fender Bass VI and Ringo on drums (with brushes). The next day Paul returned to Trident to superimpose his lead vocal and a lead guitar part. More overdubs were added on October 4, including George Martin's score of five saxophones and two clarinets. Paul recorded the line "Now she's hit the big time" in a manner mimicking the low fidelity recordings of the 1920s. To drive home the point, his vocal is backed by the sound of a scratchy record, duplicating the effect of listening to an old worn-out 78 RPM shellac disc. (Michael Nesmith of the Monkees had used the same scratchy record sound on his tune *Magnolia Simms*, from the group's May, 1968, album *The Birds, The Bees & The Monkees*.) *Honey Pie* was mixed for mono and stereo at Trident on October 5, although both mixes were copied and converted to a different equalization system two days later at Abbey Road.

George's fourth selection on the album, *Savoy Truffle*, was inspired by Eric Clapton's addiction to chocolate. The lyrics jokingly warn Harrison's friend that he'll have to have his decaying teeth pulled out if he doesn't cut back on the sweets. Most of the candies mentioned in the song, including Creme Tangerine, Montelimart, Ginger Sling, Coffee Desert and Savoy Truffle, are taken from Mackintosh's Good News double centre chocolate assortment box. Cherry Cream and Coconut Fudge are Harrison creations. The lyrics contain a cryptic reference to *Ob-La-Di, Ob-La-Da*.

The song's backing track, featuring George on electric piano, Paul on his Rickenbacker bass, John on his Epiphone Casino and Ringo on drums, was recorded in one take at Trident Studios on October 3. Two days later Harrison returned to Trident to add his lead vocal. Chris Thomas' score of two baritone and four tenor saxophones was recorded on October 11 at Abbey Road. At Harrison's request, the saxes were given a distorted sound. The song's final overdubs, consisting of Telecaster leads played by George, organ, tambourine and bongos, were added on October 14. These would be the last instruments recorded for the album. Ringo was not present as he left that morning for a two-week family vacation in Sardinia. The song was mixed for mono and stereo later that evening.

The above snapshots were taken by Beatles fan Cathy Sarver during the 1968 recording sessions for *The White Album*. Top row (left to right): George leaving Trident on August 29 at 6:40 a.m.; John and Yoko outside at Trident on August 30 at 8:00 p.m.; and John leaving Trident on August 29 at 6:41 a.m. Middle row (left to right): Paul leaving Trident on August 29 at 4:50 a.m.; John and Yoko leaving Abbey Road on August 8 at 5:30 a.m.; and John and Yoko outside Abbey Road on September 7 at 1:45 a.m. Bottom row (left to right): Ringo driving away from Abbey Road on August 16 at 1:00 a.m.; and John waving to fans outside Abbey Road on August 15 at 4:15 a.m.

John's *Cry Baby Cry* dates back to late 1967. Lennon's inspiration for the song came from an ad tag line, "Cry baby cry, make your mother buy." While in India, John refined the lyrics, which have a nursery rhyme quality. By the time the Kinfauns demo was recorded, the song was essentially complete.

On July 15, the Beatles recorded nearly two hours of unnumbered takes of the song. As these were considered rehearsals, the tapes were later recorded over. The next day the group began the proper recording of the song. *Anthology 3* contains Take 1, which features John's excellent guide vocal and acoustic guitar, Paul on his Rickenbacker bass, Ringo on drums and George with occasional lead fills. The tenth and final take was deemed "best" and given a mixdown reduction to form Take 12. During the mixing, John's acoustic guitar was given ADT treatment with variable tape speed to produce a phasing effect. John then added his piano and George Martin contributed harmonium.

After taking a day off to attend the premier of *Yellow Submarine*, the group completed its work on the song on July 18, with additional overdubs onto Take 12. These included John's lead vocal, backing vocals by John and Paul, an additional harmonium part by George Martin heard during the opening chorus, Harrison's lead guitar lines on a Gibson Les Paul, tambourine and tea party sound effects. The song was mixed for stereo and mono on October 15.

The final chord of *Cry Baby Cry* is followed by an uncredited link track, Paul's *Can You Take Me Back*. The ad-lib tune was recorded during the September 16 session that produced *I Will*. The 2:21 performance, which was logged in as Take 19 of *I Will*, features Paul on vocal and acoustic guitar, Ringo on maracas and John tapping the beat on a wood block. When the album was banded on October 16 and 17, a 28 second segment from the end of the song was placed immediately after *Cry Baby Cry*, giving listeners the impression that it was part of the song. Its words, "Can you take me back where I came from, can you take me back?," are not included on the album's lyric sheet.

*Revolution 9* is the most controversial track ever to appear on a Beatles album. It is not really a song, but rather a sound collage of multiple tape loops put together by John. In his *Playboy* interview, John recalled, "Yoko was there for the whole thing and she made decisions about which [tape] loops to use. It was somewhat under her influence." Although Paul had produced a similarly styled sound collage with the group on January 5, 1967, he did not participate in the making of *Revolution 9* and thought it inappropriate for a Beatles LP. At John's insistence, the track ended up on *The Beatles* despite objections from the other Beatles and George Martin.

The track took on a life of its own, springing out of the six minute instrumental jam at the end of Take 18 of *Revolution 1*. The extended ending of the song, which was started on May 30, is full of feedback and John screaming "alright" over and over again. Yoko also got into mix, speaking phrases such as "they look like they're naked" and "if you become naked." After overdubs were added on May 31 and June 4, *Revolution 1* was edited down to 4:15, thus freeing the chaotic six minute ending for other use.

On June 6, John began assembling tapes and loops of various sound effects, some of which would be incorporated into *Revolution 9*. Lennon prepared more tapes of sound effects on June 10 and 11.

The master version of the track was compiled during a 7:00 p.m. through 3:30 a.m. session held on June 20. According to John, "There were about ten machines with people holding pencils on the loops–some only inches long and some a yard long. I fed them all in and mixed them live. I did a few mixes until I got one I liked." To accommodate the simultaneous inclusion of multiple tape loops into the mix, all three of Abbey Road's studios were used. Prior to compiling the master version, John prepared several different tape loops that could brought into the mix when ever it suited his fancy.

The most memorable sound was lifted from the start of an EMI testing tape. It consists of an unknown engineer repeating the phrase "number nine." The "number nine" loop is brought into the mix nine times during the piece. George Harrison was the only other Beatle present at the session. He joined John on the studio floor to record a bizarre series of phrases and bits of strange conversation that were faded into the mix at various times. The master version was completed by the end of the session, although additional sound effects were superimposed onto the master tape the following evening. The stereo mix was also made that night, with John panning many of the sound effects across the left and right channels. On June 25, the 9:05 stereo master was edited down to 8:12. The mono mix, which was merely a mixdown of the stereo master, was made on August 20.

*Revolution 9* is preceded by a bit of a conversation (secretly recorded by John) in which Apple office manager Alistair Taylor apologizes to George Martin for forgetting to bring him a special claret. After Taylor asks, "Will you forgive me?," Martin replies, "Yes, son-of-a-bitch."

The track begins calmly enough with the "number nine" voice panning from left to right over a slow piano theme in B minor, which is also faded in and out of the mix throughout the piece. The serenity quickly yields to chaotic sound effects, including bits of symphonic music (some normal and some reverse looped), choral passages, crowd noises and crashing cymbals. John's dialog is brought to the front of the mix, revealing that "as time went by they'd get a little bit older and a little bit slower." The swirling symphonic sounds continue, leading into laughter, a crying baby, the "number nine" loop and George asking "Who wants to know?" Additional confusion persists and John's repeated screaming of "right" from the extended ending to *Revolution 1* is brought to the forefront of the mix. This is followed by the "number nine" loop, a ringing bell and the blended sounds of a choral passage, an unintelligible conversation, crowd noise, symphonic instruments, honking horns and other effects.

The voices of George and John come forward to reveal George saying "with the situation," John adding "they are standing still" and George mentioning a telegram. John's moans from the *Revolution 1* jam and the "number nine" voice return, leading into the following dialog from John:

"Who could tell what he was saying; his voice was low and his mind was high...." As the conversation fades, an "alright" from John leads into crowd noise and the return of "number nine" and chaotic music. John can be heard saying "so the wife told him he'd better go to see a surgeon" as the crowd noises and effects build up. John continues his prose with "so anyhow he went to see the dentist instead, who gave him a pair of teeth, which wasn't any good at all, so, so instead of that he joined the fookin' navy and went to sea." A tape loop of a crowd chanting "hold that line" and "block that kick" also enters the mix.

After the choral passage returns, John can be heard saying "my broken chair, my wings are broken and so is my hair, I am not in the mood for wearing blue clothing" over the sound of crackling flames. John's moaning voice from *Revolution 1* returns amid gunfire and other sound effects. As the choir returns, George says "only to find the night watchman unaware of his presence in the building."

The return of the "number nine" loop leads to more audible prose, including John's "industrial output, financial imbalance" and George's "thrusting in between your shoulder blades." As things calm down, the piano theme returns and John continues with "the Watusi, the Twist" and George adds "El Dorado." John then commands, "Take this brother, may it serve you well."

The mood of the piece abruptly changes and Yoko's soft conversation about exposure and nakedness competes with an operatic tenor and various sound effects. As the piano theme returns, the piece gets quiet for a brief moment to expose Yoko saying "you become naked." This leads into a crowd chanting "hold that line" a few times before switching to "block that kick." The track ends with "block that kick" panning between the left and right channels before moving to the center and fading away.

For most listeners back in 1968, *Revolution 9* was unlike anything they had ever experienced. Had the track appeared on a John and Yoko album, the piece would have been heard by a relatively small audience. But being part of a Beatles album meant that millions of listeners would hear the experimental recording whether they wanted to or not. For those who weren't initially turned off, the track made for fascinating listening. It is truly a recording that reveals new things with each listen.

The famous "number nine" loop gained notoriety beyond the song, with many listeners mimicking its sound. In addition, the number nine took on significance to Beatles fans. During the height of the Paul McCartney death rumor, the tape loop was a major clue supposedly pointing to Paul's death. By some incredible coincidence, when the record is played backwards, the phrase "number nine" sounds like "turn me on, dead man." The author remembers hearing its eerie sound and nearly ruining his turntable in the process!

The album's final selection, *Good Night*, was written by John for his then five-year-old son, Julian. Perhaps believing the tender lullaby would harm his image, John turned the song over to Ringo. Paul fondly recalls John teaching the song to Ringo. "[I]t was fabulous to hear him do it, he sang it great...he sang it very tenderly."

The Beatles initial attempt at the song took place on June 28, with rehearsals featuring John on either guitar or piano and Ringo on vocals. Five early takes were recorded, each starting with a different spoken introduction by Ringo. The *Anthology* video contains a segment of Ringo reciting the following prose over John's finger-picking-style guitar: "Come on, now, it's time you little toddlers are in bed. I'm having no more messing. You've been out to the park all day, you've had a lovely time. Now it's time for bed. Are we ready? Daddy'll sing." Another charming introduction has Ringo saying "Put all those toys away. Yes, Daddy will sing a song for you!" *Anthology 3* contains a lovely rehearsal of the song with Ringo backed by John on piano and George on percussion.

On July 2, Ringo rerecorded his lead vocal onto Take 5. Ten numbered takes, also featuring harmony backing vocals from John and Paul, were recorded, though none of the instruments or vocals from these sessions were used. George Martin had copies of Take 15 made to enable him to write an orchestral score.

The song's lush orchestral backing was recorded on July 22 in 12 takes, designated Takes 23 through 34. George Martin conducted the orchestra, which featured twelve violins, three violas, three cellos, three flutes, clarinet, horn, vibraphone, harp and double bass. Backing vocals by four male and four female members of the Mike Sammers Singers were then recorded over Take 34. Four of the singers had previously recorded with the Beatles, being part of the backing vocal shenanigans on *I Am The Walrus*. Finally, Ringo recorded his charming solo lead vocal, which ends with him whispering, "Good night, good night everybody, everybody, everywhere, good night." The song was mixed for mono and stereo on October 11.

At 5:00 p.m. on October 16, John, Paul, George Martin and engineers Ken Scott and John Smith met at Abbey Road to determine the running order of the thirty plus songs available for the album. Neither Ringo, who was on family vacation in Sardinia, nor George, who was in Los Angeles to produce Jackie Lomax's album *Is This What You Want?*, were present for what would be the Beatles only 24-hour session. Although Harrison's *Not Guilty* was mixed for mono, it was not given a stereo mix and probably not considered for the album. John lobbied for the inclusion of both of his experimental tracks, *What's The New Mary Jane?* and *Revolution 9*, but in the end only *Revolution 9* was included.

The wide variety and number of the songs presented a sequencing challenge for John, Paul and George Martin. Following the producer's practice of opening a record with a "potboiler," sides one and three open with powerful rockers. Three of the songs with animals in their titles are together on side two. Many of the hardest rocking songs are on side three. Each of George's four songs is on a different disc. By coincidence, the record's first two tracks feature Paul on drums rather than Ringo. *Revolution 9,* which is both a challenging listen and a difficult song to follow, appears where it belongs–towards the end of the album. And Ringo's charming *Good Night* is the perfect way to close the set.

**George Harrison's production of Jackie Lomax's _Is This What You Want?_ (Apple 3354) in October and November of 1968 proved fortuitous as it gave Harrison the opportunity to hear Capitol's mastering of _The White Album_. After expressing his displeasure with the album's compressed sound, George was allowed to work with Capitol's engineers to re-master the record.**

As was the case with the group's previous British LP, _Sgt. Pepper_, the songs run together without the normal three to six second gap between tracks. This was accomplished with cross-fades (_Back In The U.S.S.R._ into _Dear Prudence_), tight edits and even an uncredited link track (_Cry Baby Cry_ to the link track _Can You Take Me Back_ to _Revolution 9_).

Although George Harrison was in Los Angeles during the banding session for the album, he did play an important role in the sound of the American release. During a break from his production of Jackie Lomax's LP, Harrison dropped by the Capitol Tower to listen to the acetate pressings of the album. George did not like what he heard and insisted that he be allowed to work with Capitol's engineers to re-master the album.

According to Mal Evans, who was with George in Los Angeles, the Capitol engineers had "done all sorts of technical things to it that altered half the effects!" As was often the practice at the time, the engineers had run the sound signal through a limiter and compressed the volume range of the recording by cutting back the high volume peaks and bringing up the low passages. This would have been particularly noticeable on songs such as _Helter Skelter_, which is a loud raucous rocker that has a fade-out fade-in ending, and Harrison's _Long, Long, Long_, which has quiet passages throughout and loud distortion at the end. Evans observed that if George had not "returned it the way it should be the American LP records might have been a bit of a mess!" Capitol used Harrison's remastered version of _The White Album_ to make the metal parts for the discs.

The remastering of the album and cutting of new lacquers explains the high lacquer numbers found in the trail off areas to initial pressings of the album. The original lacquers cut by Capitol's engineers had low numbers, but these lacquers were scrapped at George's request. A review of early pressings suggests that 33 sets of lacquers were de-stroyed. The first lacquers made under Harrison's specifications were cut on the A/B Scully lathe at the Capitol Tower. The lowest confirmed number is A34, with subsequent low numbers being B35, A36 and B37. These lacquers were sent to Capitol's Los Angeles factory for the manufacture of metal parts to press the records. Additional lacquers were cut on the H/J lathe at the Tower and assigned numbers such as J40, J41, etc. up through J66. The initial records manufactured by Capitol's Scranton and Jacksonville plants originated from lacquers numbered in the 40s. Later Los Angeles pressings were made from lacquers with numbers such as H70 and H74. When Winchester came on line in late 1969, the factory was sent lacquer numbers A70 and A71. Additional lacquers for Winchester were later cut in New York, with numbers such as W5, X6, W7 and X8 and F72 and F77.

On most of the records pressed for the album there is the expected visible gap between songs; however, on some copies there is no visible separation between tracks. These unbanded records were pressed with metal parts originating from lacquers with numbers between J40 and J46.

The album's catalog number, SWBO 101, is not an Apple number, but rather is part of the Capitol series. During 1968, Capitol reached album number ST 2999 and decided to start over at 101. _The White Album_ holds the distinction of being the first album in Capitol's new series. The "S" stands for stereo, the "W" is a price code, the "B" indicates the album has two records and the "O" signifies that the gatefold cover has two openings.

Prior to embracing the minimalist concept of the all white cover, the Beatles considered different ideas, including a transparent cover that would expose a color photograph when the record was removed from the jacket. The group also considered naming the album after Henrik Ibsen's novel _A Doll's House_.

Many people assumed that John and Yoko were responsible for the album's all white cover; however, the idea came from pop artist Richard Hamilton, who was approached by Paul on the advise of Robert Fraser. Hamilton's concept was to do something that was the opposite of the elaborate cover to *Sgt. Pepper* by having the album issued in a plain white jacket. There was also discussion of having a simulated coffee cup ring or apple stain on the cover, but these ideas were dismissed as being flippant and difficult to print accurately. It was Hamilton's idea to title the album *The Beatles*, thus following an elaborate title (*Sgt. Pepper's Lonely Heart's Club Band*) with a simple one. After Paul expressed reservations about an all white cover, the artist came up with the idea to emboss "The BEATLES" onto the jacket. Hamilton also suggested that each cover be sequentially numbered "to create the ironic situation of a numbered edition of something like five million copies."

While Hamilton was pleased with his concept, he began to feel guilty about putting the group's double album out in a plain white jacket. He suggested that the package "could be jazzed up with a large edition print, an insert that would be even more glamorous than a normal sleeve." Paul was recruited to collect pictures of the Beatles to be incorporated into a huge collage. After selecting the images for the poster, Hamilton had many of the pictures re-sized. He then laid out the photos on a sheet of paper that was the same size as the poster insert. His composition was complicated by the fact that the poster would be a folded insert. This would create six separate squares, with the top right and top left sections needing to stand on their own, serve as a double spread and fit in with the four lower sections. The final product achieved the artist's goal of creating a print that "would reach and please a large audience" while including "some arcane touches which only the Beatles' more intimate associates were likely to smile at." Included in the poster are photos of Paul lying in a bathtub, John and Paul in black leather jackets (taken in Paris), a bearded Ringo Starr dancing with Elizabeth Taylor at London's Dorchester Hotel and the band performing for the *Revolution* video.

The Beatles followed their *Sgt. Pepper* practice of giving their fans good value for their money. *Sgt. Pepper* had the song lyrics printed on its back cover; *The White Album* had its lyrics on the back of the poster. *Sgt. Pepper* came with an insert sheet of cutouts; *The White Album* contained glossy John Kelly color portraits of each Beatle.

The album's cover and enclosures created a challenge for Capitol to complete the packaging in time for the record's late November release date. Internal documents indicate that the art work was not sent to the printers until October 22 and November 1, 1968. Curt Kendall, who was Capitol's national director of purchasing at the time, recalls that "*The White Album* was an enormous undertaking. The quality control involved in the printing of that job was incredible."

As usual, the bulk of the work was handled by Queens Litho in New York, with Bert-Co in Los Angeles also contributing. In addition, Capitol contracted with Gugler Litho in Milwaukee, Wisconsin. The three companies printed the inside and outside cover slicks, posters and photographs. The folded posters and collated pictures were then shipped directly to Capitol's pressing plants. The cover slicks were sent to Imperial Paper Box Corporation and Modern Album for construction of the double gatefold album jackets, which were then forwarded to the pressing plants.

The outside slicks were printed by Queens Litho and Bert-Co on 80 lb. pure white Kromekote cast-coated stock. (Gugler Litho used a Kromekote substitute, Albemar, for the slicks, posters and pictures.) The front of the jacket has "The BEATLES" embossed in raised block letters starting approximately 6" from the left and 5" from the bottom. The album's title takes up 2¾" and is on a slight upward angle. The "limited edition" number appears in gray on a slight downward angle towards the lower right corner. The back cover is completely blank except for the word "Stereo," which is printed in gray towards the upper right corner. The album's spine has "The BEATLES" in gray towards the top and "Stereo SWBO 101" towards the bottom.

The inside slicks were also printed on pure white Kromekote stock. The right panel of the open gatefold has the four John Kelly portraits running left to right (John, Paul, George and Ringo) about 1¼" from the bottom. Each picture measures 2½" x 3⅞" and is printed in black and white. The left panel has the titles to the album's songs in gray on 12 rows. Each row is left-margin justified, starting approximately 5⅞" from the left side of the inside jacket. The top row lines up with the top of the portraits. The initial slicks from the first run have SWBO 101 printed in gray towards the lower left corner. Beginning with the second press run, the inside slicks have the album number plus "© Apple Records, Inc." Sometime in 1970, the sequential numbering of the covers was discontinued. By 1975, the covers were no longer embossed. Instead, "The BEATLES" was printed on the front cover in either black or dark gray. Post-Apple era covers have "©℗ Capitol Records Inc." on the inside slick following the album number.

**Stereo**     **SWBO 101**

**SWBO 101**     **© Apple Records, Inc.**

**All jackets have "Stereo" printed towards the upper right corner of the back cover (top left). The first-run inner slicks have the album number "SWBO 101" printed in the lower left corner of the open cover (top right). Later inner slicks have the album number plus a copyright notice (bottom).**

Although Queens Litho had state-of-the-art printing presses, it did not have equipment for embossing or sequential numbering. The outside slicks, printed six to a sheet, were taken to Card Processing, which was located in the Brooklyn Naval Yard, for embossing and numbering. It is believed that the initial batch of Queens Litho slicks were run through two different machines, which numbered and embossed them. The embossed and numbered sheets were then taken back to Queens Litho, where they were trimmed to form single outside slicks.

Capitol's use of multiple printers required the company to assign separate blocks of numbers to Queens Litho, Bert-Co and Gugler Litho. The Capitol paper work regarding the allocation of number blocks is missing and presumed destroyed. Thus, it is impossible to give a precise accounting of how the numbers were assigned. The sequencing discussed below is based upon the review of hundreds of copies of the album and information obtained from former employees of Capitol and Queens Litho.

The first 25 cover slicks were printed by Queens Litho and numbered by Card Processing. After these special covers were paired with inserts and records, they were sent by Capitol president Stan Gortikov to the London Savile Row headquarters of Apple Records. The *Anthology* book contains the following letter from Gortikov to George Harrison: "I am sending under separate cover those copies of the new U.S. Beatles album that are serially numbered 'A0000001 through A0000025' as personal souvenirs for you and selected friends. I have personally stolen number 'A0000005,' because I am a friend too. Besides, I love the music!"

The first major block of numbers, starting with 26 and running near 590,000, was assigned to Bert-Co (album **027** is in the author's collection). After the Bert-Co numbered covers pass 100, the numbers are preceded by a series of zeros. Examples include **0000340, 0008008, 0025007** and **0202735**. At some point around 210,000, the Bert-Co numbered covers begin having a wide **A** and space preceding the numbers. Examples include **A 0218307** and **A 0578465**. These covers are usually found with Los Angeles pressings of the album.

Gugler Litho was assigned the second batch of numbers, which started at some number near 590,000 and probably ran through about 1,350,000. The numbers are preceded by a large dot. Examples include **● 0597774** and **● 1338912**. These covers are usually found with either Jacksonville or Los Angeles records.

The next major block was assigned to Queens Litho. It starts at some number around 1,350,000 and runs past 2,000,000. These covers have numbers directly preceded by a thin **A**. Examples include **A1383270** and **A1974983**. Covers with the thin **A** are usually found with discs pressed by Scranton.

At some point beyond 2,000,000, some batches of covers were assigned to Gugler Litho. Examples include **● 2010437, ● 2041490** and **● 2048324**. Other covers, such as **A2035679, A2057401, A2173734** and **A2246058**, were printed by Queens Litho as part of its **A** series.

The confusion continues for covers with numbers over 2,250,000. Many are preceded by the abbreviation for "Number," which appears in two variations (**No.** and **N⁰.**).

Covers with numbers in the approximate range of 2,250,000 to 2,500,000 were probably printed by Queens Litho as part of its second run of outside slicks. These covers have the **No.** abbreviation for number. Examples include **No. 2273151** and **No. 2498150**. Some covers in this range, such as **A2311447** and **A2444483**, have the thin **A**.

A review of covers suggests that Bert-Co was assigned a second batch of numbers beginning at about 2,500,000 and running up to 2,800,000. The covers printed in Bert-Co's second run have the **N⁰.** abbreviation. Examples include **N⁰. 2514324** and **N⁰. 2697658**.

Queens Litho's second run probably included covers numbered in the range of 2,800,000 to nearly 3,000,000. Examples include **No. 2807496, A2847103, A2858939, No. 2892246** and **No. 2965544**.

Bert-Co did a third and final run of numbered slicks in late 1969 or early 1970. These cover numbers begin around 3,000,000 and return to the wide **A** prefix. Examples of these last numbered covers include **A 3002698** and **A 3116706**.

Collectors have often wondered if the differing symbols preceding the numbers have any significance. Capitol initially required the three printers to use different symbols for quality control identification purposes. It has been speculated that the "A" stood for either America or Apple, but neither story has been confirmed. The **N⁰.** abbreviation used by Bert-Co for its second run matches the symbol appearing on the British jackets and on covers in many other countries. It is possible that Bert-Co and Queens Litho were instructed by Apple to use a number abbreviation symbol for their second runs to be consistent with the jackets printed in England and other countries.

Bert-Co printed approximately 26% of the initial run. Its slicks were probably sent to Modern Album in Terre Haute, Indiana, for cover construction. The bulk of these completed covers were shipped to Capitol's Los Angeles factory. This explains why the covers with no symbol or the wide **A** are normally found with Los Angeles discs.

Approximately 34% of the initial slicks were printed by Gugler Litho, who most likely delivered its slicks to Imperial Packing Co.in Indianapolis, Indiana. Imperial then shipped the bulk of its covers to Capitol's Jacksonville pressing plant, although some covers were sent to Los Angeles. This explains why the covers with the large dot are normally found with Jacksonville and Los Angeles records.

The remaining 40% of the initial slicks were printed by Queens Litho, which sent the bulk of its slicks to Capitol's New York manufacturers, Imperial Paper Box Corporation (Brooklyn) and Modern Album (Long Island). These factories sent most of their covers to Capitol's Scranton plant, which explains why covers with the thin A are usually found with Scranton discs.

The above guidelines are not absolute. When shortages occurred, available covers were sent where needed. There was no consicous effort to match a particular symbol with a specific factory. Such an undertaking would have been complex, confusing and inefficient.

Capitol and the printers did take steps to ensure that there would be no duplicate numbers. The assignment of separate large blocks of numbers to Bert-Co, Queens Litho and Gugler Litho prevented each printer from using any number used by the other.

While these simple steps prevented duplicate numbers, there was no serious attempt to have every available number on a finished cover. If a numbered slick was damaged during the manufacturing process, a new slick with the same number was not prepared. This accounts for some of the missing numbers. In addition, there may have been partial blocks of reserved numbers that were never used. As explained by former Queens employee Richard Roth, "The sequential numbering was viewed as part of the album cover's design. The numbers had no legal or inventory control significance, so there was no need to be precise."

Although the copyright notice was not added to the inner slicks until the second press runs, some covers with relatively low numbers have the copyright notice. This happened because the album fabricators were sent boxes of second run inner and outer slicks prior to running out of first run slicks. As no effort was made to match first run outer slicks with first run inner slicks or to match second slicks with each other, mismatches often occurred. The arbitrary pairing of outer and inner slicks caused anomalies such as cover number ● 0924124 having the copyright notice even though most covers with numbers below 2,250,000 do not have the copyright notice. Although most covers with numbers above 2,250,000 have the copyright notice, there are covers with high numbers such as No. 2928594 that do not have the copyright notice.

A mismatched cover is not a pure first run cover because one of its slicks is from the second press run. As a general rule, a first run cover should have a number below 2,250,000 and no copyright notice.

It is interesting to note that two numbers were deliberately used on multiple covers. Capitol was excited by the prospect of the double album selling in excess of two million units. Capitol's Curt Kendall instructed Queens Litho to make a dozen or so covers with the number A2000000 to commemorate this milestone. The A2000000 covers were given to key Capitol executives. An employee of Queens Litho was inspired by this Capitol idea and made about a dozen instant collector's item covers with the number A0000001 for himself and a few of his friends. The cover shown on page 101 is one of the surviving souvenir covers.

Kendall recalls Capitol considering a contest under which a number would be randomly selected, and a prize awarded to the person owning the cover with the selected number. Apparently the idea was abandoned when Capitol realized that not all numbers were used and that it would be difficult to communicate word of the contest to the two million plus purchasers of the album.

With the exception of "The BEATLES" embossed on the front cover, the word "Stereo" on the back and minimal information on the spine, the album's outside packaging tells nothing about its contents. While all previous Beatles LPs listed the song titles on the back and/or front cover, *The White Album* is totally devoid of any song titles. Apple correctly assumed that the Beatles reputation and the expected favorable buzz about the record would overcome the marketing deficiencies of the essentially blank cover. Capitol, however, was not so sure and affixed stickers to some copies of the album.

The most common sticker, **APP 101.S1**, has "The BEATLES" at the top followed by the track listing as it appears on the inside left gatefold of the cover. The white background sticker measures 4¾" x 4" and has either blue, **APP 101.S1A**, or black, **APP 101.S1B**, print. These stickers are most often found affixed to the top center of the front cover, although some stickers were attached to the back cover or the album's shrinkwrap. Some of these covers have staple holes. The black print sticker is the rarer of the two.

There is also a white background sticker with red print, **APP 101.S2**, that measures 5¼" x 4". This sticker has a red double-line wiggly border and "The BEATLES" and "SWBO 101 - - STEREO" centered at the top on two lines followed by the song titles. This sticker was also affixed directly to the top center of the front cover.

Another sticker has a black background with white text, **APP 101.S3**. This rare sticker measures 3½" x 3½" and has "BEATLES" centered at the top. The song titles are left and right margin justified and are separated on each line by a large dot. The phrase "(Includes lyrics to all the tunes plus four Beatles pictures)" is centered at the bottom on two lines.

A fourth variation listing the song titles has black print over a flourescent reddish-orange background, **APP 101.S4**. This 6½" x 5⅞" sticker has rounded corners. Its top line has an Apple logo followed by "THE BEATLES." The song titles are listed in two columns, with the tracks on sides one and two on the left and the selections on sides three and four on the right, although *I Will* and *Julia* incorrectly appear at the bottom of the right column.

There is also a 9" x 2½" flourescent reddish-orange background banner, **APP 101.S5**, containing information about the album's contents and packaging. The sticker states that the new album has 2 LPs, 30 great songs, complete lyrics, a giant full color poster and four color photographs of John, Paul, George and Ringo.

The initial run of the 7¾" x 10¾" John Kelly color portraits of the band were printed on Kromekote cardstock (Gugler Litho printed on Albemar) and have a circular

"Printed in U.S.A." in the lower right border. The pictures came with a same-size paper sheet that varied in color and thickness. These were separator sheets placed by the printers between each collated set of the four portraits to make it easier for Capitol's factories to add the photos to the album package. Because the sheets were not intended to be part of the album's packaging, the printers used available scrap paper without regard to style. The following different separator sheets have been confirmed: (1) the same Kromekote white paper used for the outside cover slicks; (2) yellow thick stock; (3) light green thick stock; (4) pink thin stock; (5) blue thin stock; (6) blue thick stock; (7) orange thin stock; and (8) tan thin stock.

On December 12, 1968, Capitol instructed its printers to add the phrase "© Apple Records, Inc." at the bottom left of each photo. This addition was not made until the second press run, so over two million sets of pictures and posters do not have the copyright notice.

The Richard Hamilton poster caused a bit of controversy at the Capitol Tower. Some of the company's employees were concerned about the sexual nature a few of the images. John's tiny drawing of he and Yoko standing naked was altered by removal of pubic hair. The small image of a naked woman appearing to the left of Ringo dancing with Elizabeth Taylor was also airbrushed to remove pubic hair. Oddly enough, the biggest concern was over a picture of John sitting naked in bed while talking on the phone. Although John's arm blocked the view of his crotch, some Capitol executives were disturbed by the closeness of Yoko's head to John's legs. After much discussion, Yoko was allowed to remain in bed. Although she was not airbrushed out of the poster, her face may have been darkened.

The first few runs of the posters were also printed on Kromekote stock (with Gugler Litho using Albemar). The copyright information on the song lyric side of the posters varies between different press runs. The first line on all posters reads "†© All lyrics copyright 1968 for the world by Northern Songs Ltd. England." The second line on the first issue posters states "*© Apple Records," while on the later posters the copyright notice reads "© 1968 Apple Music Publishing Co., Inc." The final information on the first and second runs of the posters states "EMI Records (The Gramophone Co., Ltd.) Hayes, Middlesex, England." The later posters merely state "EMI Records Limited."

Beginning during the later part of 1969, albums were packaged with either left-over first run portraits and posters, the newly-printed enclosures with the copyright notice or any combination thereof. For later press runs, beginning around 1973, the quality of the enclosures was reduced. The pictures and posters were printed on dull thin paper rather than expensive Kromekote stock. Later issues of the album from the eighties have the four photos printed on a single sheet with perforations to allow for separation.

To assist collectors and dealers with cataloging the various press runs of the album and its inserts, this book assigns identification numbers. The album covers are identified as follows: (1) **APP 101. SC1**, first run covers printed on Kromekote or Albemar stock with a number of 2,250,000

**Some promotional copies of the *White Album* have "FREE" drill-stamped in the upper right corner of the cover.**

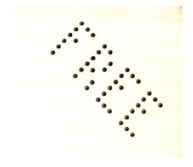

or less, a prefix other than one of the number abbreviations and no copyright notice; (2) **APP 101. SC2**, second run covers printed on Kromekote stock with a number higher than 2,250,000, a number abbreviation prefix and the copyright notice; (3) **APP 101. SC3**, later run covers printed on Kromekote stock with a number of 2,900,000 or higher, a wide **A** prefix and the copyright notice; (4) **APP 101. SC4**, later run covers printed on Kromekote stock with "The BEATLES" embossed, but no sequential number; and (5) **APP 101. SC5**, later run covers printed on dull white paper with "The BEATLES" printed in black or dark gray.

Transition covers are assigned the following designations: (1) **APP 101. SCT1**, transition covers printed on Kromekote or Albemar stock with a number of 2,250,000 or less, a prefix other than one of the number abbreviations and the copyright notice; (2) **APP 101. SCT2**, transition covers printed on Kromekote stock with a number higher than 2,250,000, a number abbreviation prefix and no copyright notice; and (3) **APP 101. SCT3**, transition covers printed on Kromekote stock with a number of 2,900,000 or higher, a wide **A** prefix and no copyright notice.

The John Kelly color portraits are identified as follows: (1) **APP 101. CP1**, first run pictures printed on Kromekote or Albemar stock without the copyright notice; (2) **APP 101. CP2**, second run pictures printed on Kromekote stock with the copyright notice; (3) **APP 101. CP3**, late run pictures printed on dull thin stock with the copyright notice; and (4) **APP 101. CP4**, late run pictures printed on a single sheet with perforations to allow for separation.

The album insert posters are identified as follows: (1) **APP 101.AP1**, first run posters printed on Kromekote or Albemar stock with the "*© Apple Records" legend; (2) **APP 101.AP2**, second run posters printed on Kromekote stock with the "© 1968 Apple Music Publishing Co., Inc." legend; and (3) **APP 101.AP3**, later run posters printed on thin dull stock with the "EMI Records Limited" legend. The promotional poster shown on page 100 is identified as **APP 101.P1**.

Although the labels for most Apple albums have multiple layout variations, there is only one basic layout for *The White Album*. This is because all labels for the album were overprinted in black from plates generated by the same film. The first labels have dark green apples with Capitol logo perimeter print and shorten *The Continuing Story Of Bungalow Bill* to *Bungalow Bill*, **APP 101.SR1(c)**. Later labels have the full song title, **APP 101.SR2(c)**. Some of these later pressings have Capitol logo label backdrops with light green apples. There are also Capitol logo labels that have an added record number designation, **APP 101.SR3(c)**.

**In England, the album was initially issued in a gatefold cover with top, rather than side, openings. While the inner sleeves for the American album were white, the British release initially had black dust jackets.**

These labels have "Record 1" printed on the upper right part of the apple on the first disc (sides one and two) and "Record 2" on the upper right part of the apple on the second disc. The copies examined for this book have dark green apple labels and are Jacksonville pressings.

Later copies of the record were pressed with labels having Apple perimeter print on either the sliced apple side, **APP 101.SR2(as)**, or the full apple side, **APP 101.SR2(af)**. The labels with the perimeter print on the sliced apple side were printed first and have medium green apples. The labels with the perimeter print on the full apple side have light green apples. Some of records with Apple perimeter print on the full apple side also have the record number designation, **APP 101.SR3(af)**.

Towards the end of the Apple run of the album, the all rights language was added to the labels. There are four confirmed variations: (1) **APP 101.SR4A(ar)**, with the all rights language in black on two lines at the top of the full apple and on five lines in the upper right corner of the sliced apple (light green apple labels) (Los Angeles pressings confirmed); (2) **APP 101.SR4B(ar)**, with the all rights language printed on two lines at the bottom of the apple on both sides (light green apple labels with the record number desination) (Jacksonville pressings confirmed); (3) **APP 101.SR4C(ar)**,

with the all rights language in green running along the lower right perimeter on the full apple side (dark green apple labels) (Jacksonville pressings confirmed); and (4) **APP 101.SR4D(ar)**, with the all rights language in green in the lower perimeter on both sides (light green apple labels) (Los Angeles pressings confirmed).

The U.S. copies of the album have the song *Rocky Raccoon* misspelled as "*Rocky Racoon*" on the label. This error was not the printer's fault as the Capitol label copy sheet was the source of the misspelling. The song title is correct on the album cover and lyric sheet. This error was not corrected until Capitol issued the remastered version of the album in 1995.

Some people, including George Martin, believe that the album would have been better had the group picked its best songs from the sessions and released them on a single disc. While there is some merit to this thinking, such criticism and speculation misses the point. It's the scope and variety of the music that makes the album what it is. In the *Anthology* video, Paul gave the perfect reply:

"I think it's a fine little album. And I think the fact that it's got so much on it, is one of the things that's cool about it... It was great. It sold. It's the bloody Beatles *White Album*. Shut up!"

It's here.

...and here.

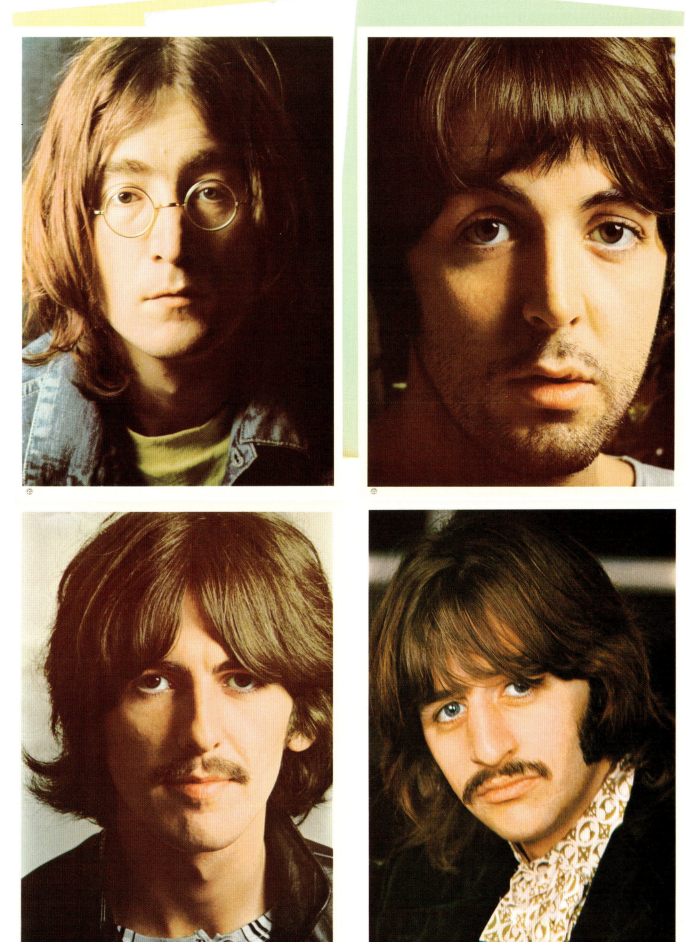

**ABOVE:** *The White Album* came with 7¾" x 10¾" color portraits of each Beatle photographed by John Kelly. Examples of the separator sheets packaged with the pictures are shown in the background.

**OPPOSITE PAGE:** *The White Album* also contained a 23" x 34" poster (top row) that featured a collage of photos on one side and the lyrics to the album's songs on the other. Apple placed two full-page ads (bottom row) in the November 30, 1968, issue of *Billboard* that ran on pages 63 and 65.

APP 101.SC1 (front)

APP 101.SC1 (back)

Back in the U.S.S.R. : Dear Prudence : Glass Onion :
Ob-La-Di, Ob-La-Da : Wild Honey Pie :
The Continuing Story of Bungalow Bill :
While My Guitar Gently Weeps : Happiness is a Warm Gun :
Martha My Dear : I'm so tired : Blackbird : Piggies :
Rocky Raccoon : Don't Pass Me By :
Why don't we do it in the road? : I Will : Julia :
Birthday : Yer Blues : Mother Nature's Son :
Everybody's Got Something to Hide Except Me and My Monkey :
Sexy Sadie : Helter Skelter : Long, Long, Long :
Revolution 1 : Honey Pie : Savoy Truffle : Cry Baby Cry :
Revolution 9 : Good Night

APP 101.SC1 (open gatefold)

Records in original sleeves

# The BEATLES

Back in the U. S. S. R.  :  Dear Prudence  :  Glass Onion  :
Ob-La-Di, Ob-La-Da  :  Wild Honey Pie  :
The Continuing Story of Bungalow Bill  :
While My Guitar Gently Weeps  :  Happiness is a Warm Gun  :
Martha My Dear  :  I'm so tired  :  Blackbird  :  Piggies  :
Rocky Raccoon  :  Don't Pass Me By  :
Why don't we do it in the road?  :  I Will  :  Julia  :
Birthday  :  Yer Blues  :  Mother Nature's Son  :
Everybody's Got Something to Hide Except Me and My Monkey  :
Sexy Sadie  :  Helter Skelter  :  Long, Long, Long  :
Revolution 1  :  Honey Pie  :  Savoy Truffle  :  Cry Baby Cry  :
Revolution 9  :  Good Night  :

APP 101.S1A (shown - blue print)
APP 101.S1B (same, except with black print)

# The BEATLES
## SWBO 101 -- STEREO

Back in the U. S. S. R. — Dear Prudence — Glass Onion —
Ob-La-Di, Ob-La-Da — Wild Honey Pie — The Continuing
Story of Bungalow Bill — While My Guitar Gently Weeps —
Happiness is a Warm Gun — Martha My Dear — I'm So
Tired — Blackbird — Piggies — Rocky Raccoon -- Don't
Pass Me By — Why Don't We Do It In the Road? — I Will
— Julia — Birthday — Yer Blues — Mother Nature's Son—
Everybody's Got Something to Hide Except Me and My
Monkey — Sexy Sadie — Helter Skelter — Long, Long,
Long — Revolution 1 — Honey Pie — Savoy Truffle —
Cry Baby Cry — Revolution 9 — Good Night.

APP 101.S2

APP 101.SR1(c)
First Label
(shortens *The Continuing Story Of Bungalow Bill* to *Bungalow Bill*)

APP 101.S3                                    APP 101.S4

APP 101.SR2(as)
(shown - Apple perimeter print on sliced side)
APP 101.SR2(c) (same, except Capitol logo perimeter print on sliced side)
APP 101.SR2(af) (same, except Apple perimeter print on full side)

APP 101.S5

APP 101.SR3(c)
(shown - Record 1 & 2 designations added)
APP 101.SR3(af) (same, except with Apple perimeter print on full side)

APP 101.SR4A(ar)

APP 101.SR4B(ar)

APP 101.SR4C(ar)
(All rights only on full apple side)

APP 101.SR4D(ar)
(All rights on both sides)

Selections by the Beatles plus original film music.

## YELLOW SUBMARINE
## APPLE SW 153

**Side One**
**THE BEATLES**

1. YELLOW SUBMARINE (Lennon & McCartney)
2. ONLY A NORTHERN SONG (George Harrison)
3. ALL TOGETHER NOW (Lennon & McCartney)
4. HEY BULLDOG (Lennon & McCartney)
5. IT'S ALL TOO MUCH (George Harrison)
6. ALL YOU NEED IS LOVE (Lennon & McCartney)

**Side Two**
**Original film music composed
and orchestrated by George Martin**

1. PEPPERLAND (George Martin)
2. MEDLEY: SEA OF TIME & SEA OF HOLES (George Martin)
3. SEA OF MONSTERS (George Martin)
4. MARCH OF THE MEANIES (George Martin)
5. PEPPERLAND LAID WASTE (George Martin)
6. YELLOW SUBMARINE IN PEPPERLAND (Lennon & McCartney/arr. George Martin)

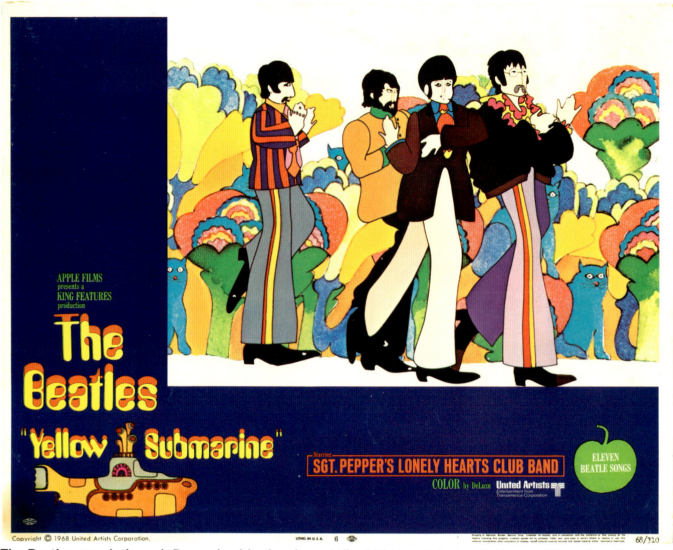

The Beatles march through Pepperland in the above 11" x 14" United Artists lobby card from the film. Most of the images appearing on the *Yellow Submarine* album cover, as well as the stylized font used for "The Beatles Yellow Submarine," were taken from the 27" x 42" onesheet United Artists poster (right) for the film.

Although the Beatles cartoon feature film *Yellow Submarine* premiered in England on July 17, 1968, and in the U.S. on November 13, 1968, the soundtrack album was not released until six months after the film's British release and seven weeks after *The White Album*. Parlophone issued *Yellow Submarine* as Apple PMC 7070 (mono) and PCS 7070 (stereo) on January 17, 1969, while Capitol released the LP as Apple SW 153 (stereo only) on January 13.

The album made its debut in *Billboard's Top LP's* chart on February 8, 1969, at number 86. On March 1 the album reached its peak at number two behind *The White Album*, which was in its last of nine weeks at the top. *Billboard* charted the soundtrack album for 25 weeks. *Record World* also charted the LP at number two, while *Cash Box* showed the album peaking at three. The disc was quickly certified gold by the RIAA and reportedly sold over one million units.

The story behind the *Yellow Submarine* movie begins in October, 1963, when United Artists entered into a three-film deal with the Beatles. The primary motivation of the company was to obtain the rights to the film soundtracks for its American record division, United Artists Records. The first film under the agreement, *A Hard Day's Night*, provided the company with both a hit movie and a soundtrack album that sold over two million units in 1964.

The group's second film, *Help!*, was also a box office hit; however, the soundtrack album was conceived, manufactured and distributed by Capitol Records rather than United Artists. No one interviewed for this book recalls why Capitol had the sountrack rights. Perhaps Capitol purchased the rights from United Artists, or maybe the film contract provided for three films but only two soundtrack albums. Capitol released its *Help!* LP on August 13, 1965. The disc accounted for sales of over one million dollars in less than one week, giving the Beatles another RIAA-certified gold record. The album sold over three million units.

After completing their first two motion pictures in two years, the Beatles had difficulty coming up with an appropriate vehicle for their third film. In February, 1965, it was announced that the group's next movie would be a Western named *A Talent For Loving*. It would be the first in a series of Beatles movies for Pickfair Films, a new company whose owners included Beatles manager Brian Epstein and Bud Ornstein, former European head of production for United Artists, who was instrumental in putting together the group's first film. The motion picture would not be part of the United Artists agreement. In June, 1965, a brief press release stated that plans for the Beatles to film *A Talent For Loving* had been cancelled.

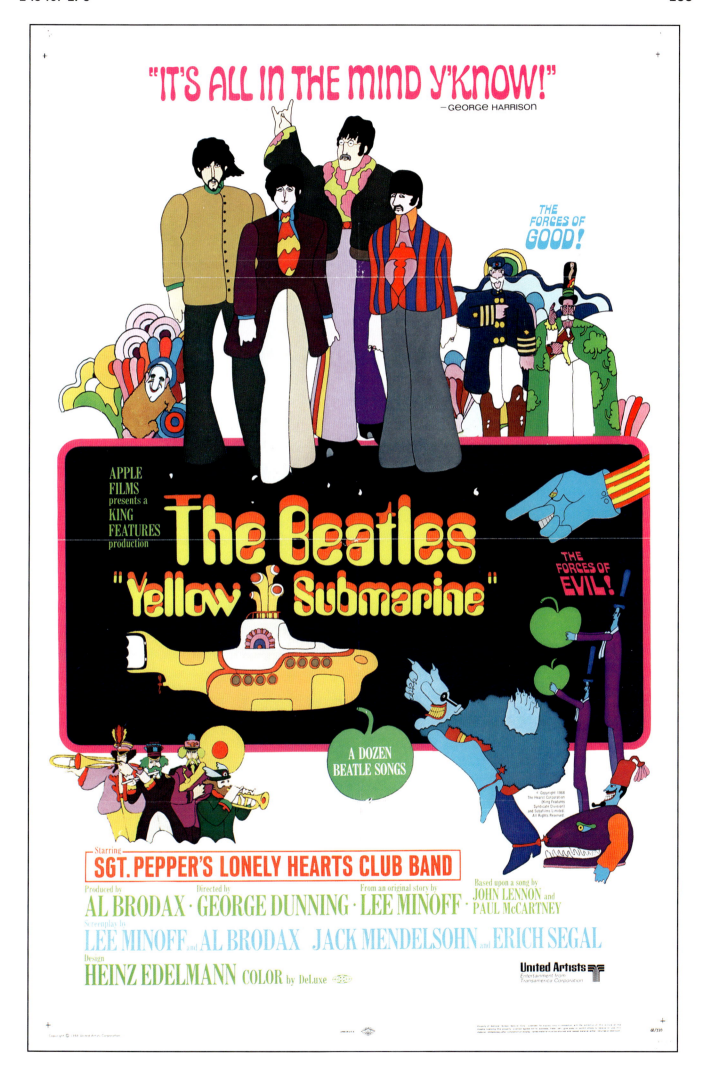

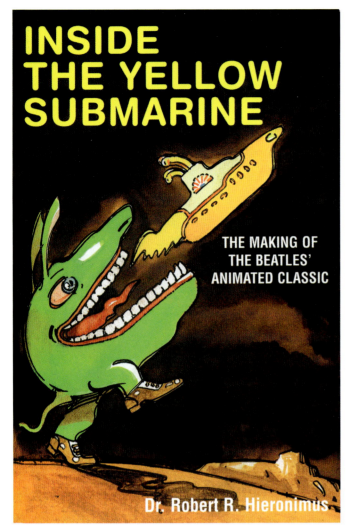

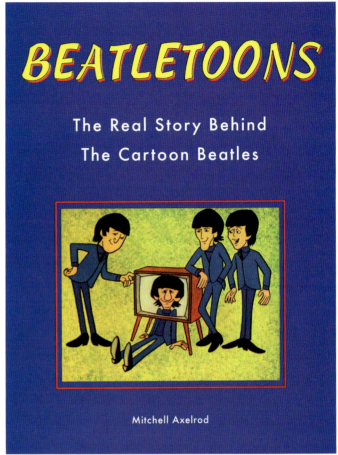

Dr. Robert R. Hieronimus' *Inside the Yellow Submarine* provides fascinating details about the making of the film. The definitive story behind the Beatles cartoons is told in the book *Beatletoons* by Mitchell Axelrod.

As for United Artists, the company planned to shoot its third Beatles film in the autumn of 1965, even though it had no script or title. These plans were put on hold as the Beatles concentrated their efforts on recording and touring. In April, 1966, Walter Shenson, who produced the first two Beatles films, confirmed that there would be no motion picture from the group in 1966. That summer, the word was that Owen Holder had been hired to script the next film, temporarily dubbed *Beatles 3*. Production was tentatively scheduled for January, 1967. The film would be about a man, played by John, who suffered from a personality disorder that gave him three different personalities in addition to his own. The other personalities would be played by Paul, George and Ringo. In June, 1967, it was announced that the film would be titled *Shades Of A Personality* and be directed by Michelangelo Antonioni of *Blow Up* fame. This, however, was not to be. With *Magical Mystery Tour* and the formation of Apple on the agenda, there were other projects deemed more important.

Another story under consideration in 1967 was a film scripted by Joe Orton titled *Up Against It*. Had the Beatles gone through with this project, they *would* have been up against it as it was a gay film. Paul's explanation for the group's decision not to do the film was, "It wasn't that we were anti-gay; just that we, the Beatles, weren't gay."

Another idea pitched to and rejected by the Beatles was a remake of *The Three Musketeers*. Although the Fab Four decided against doing a swashbuckler film, Richard Lester,

who directed the first two Beatles films, later took on the project. There was also talk of the Beatles obtaining the rights for and starring in a film adaptation J.R.R. Tolkien's fantasy masterpiece *The Lord Of The Rings*.

Unable to find the time to shoot or find an appropriate vehicle for a major motion picture, the Beatles attempted to fulfill their contractual obligation to United Artists by giving the company an animated film titled *Yellow Submarine*. There is disagreement as to whether the feature-length cartoon counted as the Beatles third and final movie owed to United Artists. *Yellow Submarine* producer Al Brodax and MGM/UA's Bruce Markoe believe that the cartoon did count; however, it most likely did not. Former UA executive David Picker indicated that the company refused to accept the cartoon as a Beatles film, but did agree to distribute the feature for Apple Films.

The idea of producing an animated moving starring the Beatles was pitched to Brian Epstein in 1966 by Al Brodax, who produced the group's King Features cartoon show for ABC-TV. After Epstein reluctantly agreed, it was decided that the film would be based on a Beatles song. Under the group's agreement with King Features, the company had the right to use up to 12 previously released Beatles songs and the band was to provide four new songs for the film.

While American Beatles fans enjoyed the ABC Saturday morning cartoon show, the group was not impressed with how they were portrayed. The Beatles were very skeptical about the full length cartoon and decided that their

The Beatles feature-length cartoon has long been a popular theme for magazines as demonstrated by the *Yellow Submarine* Special issued by *TeenSet* in Fall, 1968, and the first *Yellow Submarine* Annual published by *Beatlology* in the summer of 1999.

participation would be minimal. The group had no intention of wasting their best new songs on the venture when tunes were needed for their *Magical Mystery Tour* project as well as upcoming singles and albums. *Yellow Submarine* would get leftovers and throwaways. George Martin remembers that "whenever we were working on a song that we didn't like too much, or wasn't that brilliant a one, they would say, 'OK, let's put that one aside, that will do for the Yellow Submarine.' That was the attitude."

Although initially recorded for *Sgt. Pepper's Lonely Hearts Club Band*, George's psychedelic-sounding *Only A Northern Song* did not make the cut. The band and George Martin preferred his *Within You Without You*, so the *Pepper* reject was relegated to the film soundtrack. Brodax loves telling an elaborate story about how George Harrison composed the song in one night to fulfill the Beatles obligation to provide four new songs for the film. This misinformation has appeared in several Beatles books and articles. As detailed below, it was John's *Hey Bulldog* that completed the Beatles contribution to the soundtrack.

*Only A Northern Song* is a humorous jab at Northern Songs, a publishing company that was partially owned by John and Paul, although George's primary target was majority owner Dick James. According to George's lyrics, "It doesn't really matter what chords I play, what words I say...as it's only a Northern song." As George was under contract to the company, his tune truly was only a Northern song.

The band recorded nine takes of backing tracks on February 13, 1967. Instruments included George on organ, John

on piano, Paul on bass, Ringo on drums and all sorts of weird sound effects. The following evening Take 3 was mixed down three separate times forming Takes 10-12. Two George Harrison lead vocals were added to Take 12 and the song was mixed for mono for demo purposes. Apparently not satisfied with the Valentine's Day mix, the group came back to the song on April 20, wiping out previous overdubs on Take 3 and adding bass, guitar, trumpet (reportedly played by Paul) and glockenspiel. Vocals were then added to Take 11, which was a Take 3 reduction mix from February 14. On April 21 the revised Take 3 and the revised Take 11 were mixed together in sync to form a very strange discordant sounding mono master. As there was no way under the technology of the day to achieve a stereo mix, the soundtrack album version of the song is fake stereo.

For *Anthology 2*, producer George Martin and engineer Geoff Emerick created a stereo mix that features vocals with different lyrics from the February 14 session. According to Mark Lewisohn's booklet notes, the *Anthology 2* mix, "in stereo and slightly speeded up, is Take 3–the basic track from 13 February, with bass and guitar added on 20 April– with unused vocal tracks (yielding a number of lyric variations from the master) overdubbed on to a separate 'reduction,' Take 12, flown in." It was an awful lot of work for what George claimed was *only* a Northern song!

When the song was remixed for the re-release of the *Yellow Submarine* cartoon and the new *Yellow Submarine Songtrack* album in 1999, remix engineer Peter Cobbin was able to create a true stereo mix of the master recording by using state-of-the-art digital technology.

*Baby You're A Rich Man* was the first song specifically recorded for the *Yellow Submarine* soundtrack. It began life as two separate songs: John's *One Of The Beautiful People* and Paul's *Baby You're A Rich Man*. The song was recorded and mixed during a single productive session held at Olympic Sound Studios on May 11, 1967. As was typical of the group's recordings at the time, a wide variety of instruments was used. John played piano and clavioline, an electronic keyboard instrument. Paul gave the song its distinctive thumping bass sound and also added a piano part. George was at home on lead guitar as was Ringo on drums and tambourine. John, Paul and George supplied the vocals and George and Ringo added handclaps. The Rolling Stones' Mick Jagger attended the session and may have participated in the backing vocals at the end of the song.

The following evening, the Beatles returned to Abbey Road on May 12 to knock off another song for the movie, Paul's *All Together Now*. The simple sing along song was recorded in nine takes and subjected to numerous overdubs. Instruments included two acoustic guitars (probably Paul and George), bass guitar (Paul), bass drum (Ringo), harmonica (John), banjo (John), plastic sax, triangle, handclaps and a Harpo Marx-sounding horn. Paul sang lead and was joined by John, George and others present at the studio. The song's overall innocent feeling covers up its suggestive lyrics. ("Black, white, green, red, can I take my friend to bed?") Although not one of the group's more sophisticated efforts, the song is effectively used twice in the film, including the grand finale during which the phrase "All Together Now" appears in numerous languages.

The Beatles next contribution to the film was another George Harrison composition, *It's All Too Much*. According to George, the song "was written in a childlike manner from realizations that appeared during and after some LSD experiences and which were later confirmed in meditation." Recording took place on May 25 and 26, 1967, at De Lane Lea Music Recording Studios in London. Neither George Martin nor any of the usual Abbey Road engineers were present at the session, which was engineered by Dave Siddle and Mike Weighell. The first evening was spent rehearsing and perfecting the backing track of Lennon on guitar (including the song's soaring feedback opening), Harrison on organ, McCartney on bass and Ringo on drums. The group recorded four takes. The next night a reduction mixdown of Take 4 was overdubbed with George's lead vocal, John and Paul's backing vocals, handclaps and percussion, including cowbell, woodblock and tambourine.

The song is full of all sorts of vocal shenanigans. Towards the end the group sneaks in the opening line from *Sorrow*, "With your long blonde hair and your eyes of blue." The tune was originally recorded in 1965 by the American garage band the McCoys (of *Hang On Sloopy* fame) and became a number four hit in England in 1966 by the Merseys. As *It's All Too Much* rolls towards its finish, John and Paul begin chanting "too much, too much" until they switch to "tuba, tuba" and then to "Cuba, Cuba."

On June 2 the group returned to the song and De Lane Lea Studios, this time with George Martin, a bass clarinetist (Paul Harvey) and four trumpeters, including David Mason, who played the distinctive piccolo trumpet solo on *Penny Lane*. The riffs added by the outside musicians included bits of Jeremiah Clarke's *Prince of Denmark March*. By evening's end, the Beatles had completed four new songs for the film: *Only A Northern Song*, *Baby You're A Rich Man*, *All Together Now* and *It's All Too Much*. That obligation out of the way, they were free to pursue more important matters such as *You Know My Name*, *All You Need Is Love* and the recording and filming of *Magical Mystery Tour*.

On June 25, 1967, the Beatles recorded the vocals, bass, lead guitar solo and drums for *All You Need Is Love*, live before a world-wide audience of over 400 million people for the *Our World* television special. The decision was made to rush release the song as the group's next single. Because there was no time to record a B side, the group decided to put *Baby You're A Rich Man* on the flip side to *All You Need Is Love*. Accordingly, the song lost its status as a "new" song and does not appear on the soundtrack album.

Although the Beatles thought they were through with their commitment to the *Yellow Submarine* cartoon, there was still work to be done. On November 1, 1967, George Martin, assisted by engineers Geoff Emerick and Richard Lush, prepared a tape of songs to be used in the film. As most film exhibitors did not have elaborate sound systems in the sixties, movies normally had a mono soundtrack. Thus, the tape consisted strictly of mono mixes.

The first song prepared for the tape was *All You Need Is Love*, which was remixed for the movie. The new mix, designated Remix 11, was, like the mono single, made from Take 58. The next selection was a strange version of *Lucy In The Sky With Diamonds*. For this special remix, John's vocal was stripped from the song's opening lines and replaced with Dick Emery "singing" new lyrics in his voice for the film character Jeremy Hilary Boob. The new lines are:

"Picture yourself just of nuclear fission with library cards and a metaphor skies (ha ha ha ha)/Somebody quotes you, you read from a source book, a concept with microscope eyes (ha ha ha ha ha ha ha ha ha)."

The song then switches back to John singing about cellophane flowers of yellow and green. Fortunately, King Features decided against using the special Jeremy Hilary Boob mix. The film uses the unadulterated mono mix from *Sgt. Pepper*.

The tape also contains mixes of sound effects used during the recording of *Sgt. Pepper*, including the animal effects from *Good Morning Good Morning*, atmosphere into *Sgt. Pepper* (crowd noises and tuning instruments) and the applause into *With A Little Help From My Friends*. The remaining selections on the tape are transfers of previously mixed mono masters: the single *Yellow Submarine*, *It's All Too Much*, *All Together Now* and *Only A Northern Song*. Of particular interest is *It's All Too Much*, which clocks in at over eight minutes. Both King Features and George Martin thought the song was too much. Different edited versions of the tune appear in the movie and on the soundtrack album. The tape, which has been bootlegged, is currently the only place to find the Boob altered *Lucy* and the unedited, full-length *It's All Too Much*.

In February, 1968, the Beatles were told that they were one song short of the promised four new songs for the film. The shortage resulted from the release of *Baby You're A Rich Man* as the flip side to *All You Need Is Love* the previous summer. According to John, "They wanted another song, so I knocked off *Hey Bulldog*. It's a good sounding record that means nothing." John's demo tapes of the tune contain him playing the basic piano riff and singing "She can talk to me, if she's lonely she can talk to me." By the time John was ready to record the song with the Beatles, he switched to a more personal approach singing "You can talk to me, if you're lonely you can talk to me."

*Hey Bulldog* was recorded and mixed in mono during a ten hour session on February 11, 1968. The basic rhythm track consisted of John on piano, Paul on bass, George on guitar, Ringo on drums and a tambourine played by either George or Mal Evans. The group then overdubbed a distorted lead guitar solo by John, additional distorted guitar by George, fuzz bass, additional drums, John's double-tracked lead vocal and Paul's backing vocal onto Take 10. The finished master has a bass dominated heavy sound. Towards the end of the song John and Paul adlib barks, howls, shouts, gurgles and other vocal effects. And yes, John was right. It is a good sounding record.

Although the Beatles were not enthusiastic about the film, listening to the tunes they recorded shows they were having fun in the studio. Perhaps the good time feeling was the result of the group not being under pressure to be at their best. These songs were throwaways not intended for an album or a single. They were for a friggin' cartoon.

While the Beatles were off in India mediating with the Maharishi Mahesh Yogi, King Features was preparing *Yellow Submarine* for its July 17, 1968, British premiere. The following Beatles songs were featured in the movie: *Yellow Submarine*, *Eleanor Rigby*, *Love You To* (instrumental introduction), *A Day In The Life* (crescendo towards the end), *All Together Now*, *When I'm Sixty-Four*, *Only A Northern Song*, *Nowhere Man*, *Lucy In The Sky With Diamonds*, *Think For Yourself* (vocal rehearsal), *Sgt. Pepper's Lonely Hearts Club Band*, *With A Little Help From My Friends* (faded out during first verse), *All You Need Is Love*, *Baby You're A Rich Man* (introduction and first verse), *It's All Too Much* (movie edit), and *All Together Now* (edit). Some of the early prints of the film also contained *Hey Bulldog*, but this sequence was edited out of most of the prints and prior to the film's American debut. The 1999 re-release of the movie restored the *Hey Bulldog* sequence.

The edit of *It's All Too Much* featured in the film is different than the edit that would later be made for the soundtrack album. It features a verse that is not on the longer album version, "Nice to have the time to take this opportunity/Time for me to look at you and you to look at me." The song fades out 45 seconds after those lines for a total running time of 2:30.

As the sounds of *It's All Too Much* fade away, so do the cartoon images, leading to the real Beatles only appearance in the film. After John spots newer and bluer Meanies in the vicinity, the group goes out singing an edited version of *All Together Now*.

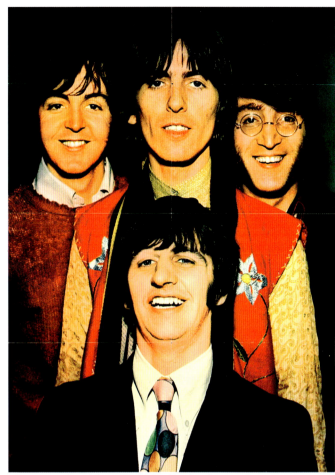

The Beatles Fan Club Bulletin from the summer of 1968 unfolded to reveal a color photo of the Beatles taken during the recording session that produced *Lady Madonna*, *The Inner Light*, *Across The Universe* and *Hey Bulldog*.

The cartoon film *Yellow Submarine* was scheduled for release in England in the summer of 1968. Capitol assumed that there would soon be a Beatles LP with songs from the movie and reserved number ST 2957 for the anticipated *Yellow Submarine* album. Capitol discs with similar numbers were issued in July, 1968. And though the film made its British debut on July 17, the soundtrack album was put on hold as the Beatles were too busy organizing the launch of Apple Records and recording their new album to devote any time to the project.

With the film set for U.S. release in mid-November, 1968, Capitol turned its attention back to the soundtrack album that fall. Capitol documents indicate that the art for the LP cover was approved on September 30, and that the album's number was changed to ST 3354, a number in Apple series, on October 14.

The switch of the album number from the Capitol series to the Apple series may have been due to Apple informing Capitol that the *Yellow Submarine* album would be a soundtrack without any Beatles songs. According to George Martin, the Beatles initial plan was to issue an EP containing the four new songs from the film. Martin was going to produce an album mixing his background score with narration and voices from the movie, done in the same style as *Peter And The Wolf*. Prior to Martin beginning the project, the Beatles, realizing that EPs did not sell well in America, decided that they wanted to issue an album. The decision was made to put Beatles music on one side and selections from George Martin's score on the other. With the soundtrack album now set to have Beatles recordings, Capitol assigned the LP its third and final number, SW 153 in the Capitol series, on November 15. (Apple later used number ST 3354 for its American release of Jackie Lomax's *Is This What You Want?*, which was issued in May, 1969.)

After completion of *The White Album* in mid-October, 1968, George Martin was free to turn his attention to the *Yellow Submarine* soundtrack LP. His first involvement on the project since the release of the film actually took place while he and John and Paul were putting the finishing touches on *The White Album* during a two-day session on October 16 and 17. Following Martin's instructions, EMI engineers Ken Scott and Dave Harries made mono and stereo mixes and edits of *It's All Too Much*. The song was shortened to 6:27 by removing one of the early verses and fading out during the lunacy at the end of the song. This explains why the movie version of the song has a verse not present on the album version even though it runs for less than half the time of the finished stereo master. Although the mixes were made from Take 2, the engineers identified it as Take 196.

For his side of the disc, George Martin decided to re-record selections from his score. According to Martin, "It was more convenient to do so–and no more costly since the original orchestra would have had to be paid twice anyway if we had used the soundtrack for the record." Six tracks were recorded at Abbey Road studios on October 22 and 23, with stereo mixing and editing taking place over the next two days. Out of the six songs, five were written by Martin and one was his arrangement of Lennon and McCartney's *Yellow Submarine*. Martin's comments on the songs (below) are taken from Dr. Hieronimus' book *Inside The Yellow Submarine*.

The first George Martin selection on the album is *Pepperland*, a majestic-sounding classical piece featuring strings and horns. Martin successfully matches the dream world setting of Pepperland with a theme that is light and lilting, with a happy feeling at the end.

The medley of *Sea Of Time & Sea Of Holes* is an eerie-sounding track that mixes Indian and classical music, much as George Harrison had done on his *Wonderwall Music* LP. The opening segment is reminiscent of Harrison's *Within You Without You*. Martin acknowledged Harrison's influence on the score, adding "I used a tanpura drone as the background, and I wrote my strings with bendy notes that sound like the Indian dilrubas."

*Sea Of Monsters* is a quirky-sounding piece that starts off with classical touches, throws in a spaghetti-Western theme and ends with backwards tapes to match the images of the Vacuum Cleaner monster sucking up everything in sight. Martin recalls writing an entire section of backwards music for the orchestra to get the desired effect.

*The March Of The Meanies* is a sinister-sounding song that switches between a staccato sound and swirling strings. Martin acknowledged that he was influenced by Bernard Herman's scores for Alfred Hitchcock films. "I was using all the brass instruments in the orchestra, tubas and trombones, and gave a very staccato feel to the strings, a very choppy beat to it...."

The theme of *Pepperland Laid Waste* is one of hopelessness and devastation. Martin used his score to "convey there was the kind of wasteland that was left after the war."

The album closes with a spirited George Martin arrangement of the title song named *Yellow Submarine in Pepperland*. The track is very upbeat, starting off in march tempo before slowing down for a poignant passage of verses. When the song returns to the chorus, the tempo increases and the full orchestra joins in to pound out the ending in the style of a marching band playing in unison. According to Martin, "It was a triumph in the end and everyone was happy and the *Yellow Submarine* was a good tune to blare out."

On October 29, Engineers Geoff Emerick and Graham Kirby completed stereo mixes for *Hey Bulldog*, *All Together Now*, *All You Need Is Love* and *Only A Northern Song* (fake stereo from the mono master). This would be the first stereo mix for *All You Need Is Love* as it appears in duophonic fake stereo on Capitol's *Magical Mystery Tour* LP. There was no need to do a stereo mix for *Yellow Submarine* as the song was mixed for stereo in 1966 for the *Revolver* album. The stereo album was cut at Abbey Road on November 22, with a mono master mixed down and cut from the stereo master on November 25. Capitol was sent a copy of the stereo master tape shortly thereafter.

Side One of the album contains *Yellow Submarine*, *Only A Northern Song*, *All Together Now*, *Hey Bulldog*, *It's All Too Much* and *All You Need Is Love*. Side Two has the re-recorded George Martin film score selections. Although Martin's score is excellent, most listeners rarely bothered to flip the album over to hear the second side.

For Beatles fans, the album was a bit of a disappointment. While the Beatles previous album contained 30 songs and over 90 minutes of new Beatles music, the soundtrack LP had only four new Beatles songs and two repeats (although one of these was the true stereo debut of *All You Need Is Love*). As for the new tunes, the Beatles didn't consider them worthy of appearing on their own singles or albums. Nonetheless, the album sold over one million units.

Capitol prepared a colorful motion display, **APP 153.MD**, to send to selected accounts. This eye-catching floor merchandiser (shown opposite) housed copies of the album. The lower portion of the display consists of two large X-shaped cardboard sections that are fitted together to form its base. These sections are adorned with colorful images from the cartoon, including head shots of each Beatle (at the bottom), Blue Meanies and yellow flowers over a bright reddish-orange background. A 14" square bin sits atop the base to hold the albums. The sides of the bin have black ovals over a white background representing the film's Sea of Holes. Alternating sides have either "Yellow Submarine" or "The Beatles" printed in the same style and colors that appear on the album cover. A 52" yellow cardboard tube (assembled from two pieces) runs from the ground through the center of the record bin to display a large cardboard Yellow Submarine. A three-piece motor mechanism fits inside the top of the tube and, when activated, causes the Yellow Submarine to rotate.

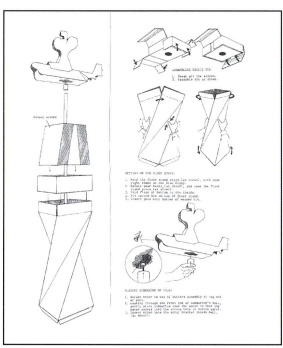

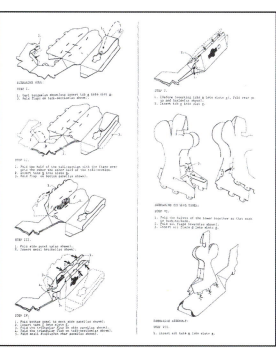

The display was sent unassembled to stores in a flat cardboard mailer, complete with motor and printed instructions. The package's contents were identified by a large white sticker with red print proclaiming: "HEY DEALER! This is Your MOTORIZED BEATLES YELLOW SUBMARINE Floor Merchandiser." This is followed by an Apple logo and the words "OPEN IMMEDIATELY AND TURN ON!" The sticker's instructions to "turn on" referred to both the motor and sixties activities often associated with the film.

There is also a 20" x 37" two-sided poster, **APP 153.P**, designed for window display. The front of the white poster features a large image of the Yellow Submarine with "The Beatles" appearing to the left of the periscope and "Yellow Submarine" to the right. The back shows each Beatle looking through a separate porthole. A variation of the poster, **APP 153.P2** (shown on page 142), was folded as an attachment to the January 25, 1969, issue of *Billboard*.

The album's colorful cover, **APP 153.SC**, features images of the characters and foliage from the cartoon, and, of course, the Yellow Submarine. Nearly all of the illustrations were taken from the film's one sheet poster shown on page 133.

The white background front cover shows the Beatles standing on top of a gray mountain, with Old Fred and Jeremy Hilary Boob to their left and the Lord Mayor of Pepperland to their right. The right side of the cover pictures, from top to bottom, the following forces of evil: a Butterfly Stomper, the Flying Glove, Apple Bonkers, the Chief Blue Meanie, a Snapping Turtle Turk and Blue Meanies. The lower portion of the cover has the Yellow Submarine to the left and Sgt. Pepper's Lonely Hearts Club Band to the right. "THE BEATLES" appears above the submarine in the same yellow and orange stylized font used on the poster. The submarine's periscope is surrounded by the words "YELLOW" and "SUBMARINE" in the same font. The upper right corner contains the phrase "Selections by the Beatles plus original film music." The following copyright notice appears to the left of Old Fred in upper case letters: "© King Features Syndicate-Subafilms Ltd. 1968." The color of the mountain is usually light or medium gray; however, there are a limited number of covers where the mountain is nearly black. Although the "black mountain" covers are merely the result a pressman using too much black ink during the printing of the front cover slick, some collectors pay a premium for these covers.

The back liner also has a white background with color images from the film. The upper portion features the Beatles and the Yellow Submarine surrounded by the list of the Side One selections to the left and the Side Two selections to the right. The middle section, surrounded above and below by a thick red line, contains liner notes giving a bit of world history from *Beowulf* to the *Magna Carta* to the *Declaration of Independence*. The lower section mixes a brief summary of the plot of the movie with images of Sgt. Pepper's Lonely Hearts Club Band and other characters from the film. The liner notes were written by Capitol employee Dan Davis. The upper right corner contains the record number

SW 153, "Stereo" and "Playable on Stereo & Mono Phonographs," all in upper case letters. The bottom of the cover has a circled "PRINTED IN U.S.A." in the left corner, "Manufactured by Capitol Records, Inc., a Subsidiary of Capitol Industries, Inc., Hollywood and Vine Streets, Hollywood, Calif. • Factories: Scranton, PA., Los Angeles, Calif., Jacksonville, Ill." in upper case letters in the center and the RIAA seal in the right corner.

The spine to the cover has (from top to bottom) "The Beatles • Yellow Submarine" in black upper case letters, "Stereophonic" in white upper case letters inside a black rectangle, a white Capitol logo and SW 153 in white. There is absolutely no reference to Apple Records anywhere on the cover.

The American front cover is virtually identical to that of the British album, except that the British cover has "NOTHING IS REAL" in green below the word "Submarine" and does not have the copyright notice or the "Selections" text. The back covers differ in that the British cover has a brief statement from Beatles press agent Derek Taylor followed by a favorable review of the recently released *White Album* from the *London Observer* by Tony Palmer instead of the Dan Davis liner notes.

*Yellow Submarine* was the first non-gatefold Beatles Capitol album cover to have color on its back liner. This addition of color changed the way the jacket was constructed.

Capitol primarily used Imperial and Modern Album to construct its covers. Both companies printed black and white back liners for Capitol at no additional cost over the charge for manufacturing the covers. Because Capitol was essentially getting the back liners printed for free, Capitol had its fabricators wrap the back liner over to the front of the cardboard jacket. This allowed for the use of a smaller front cover slick, which saved Capitol additional money as its printers, Queens Litho and Bert-Co, charged less for the smaller front cover slicks. Although covers look better when the front slick wraps over to the back, Capitol opted to keep its printing costs down by have its covers constructed with the back liner wrapping over to the front.

Because *Yellow Submarine* required color printing for both sides of the cover, Capitol contracted with Queens Litho and Bert-Co to print both the front slicks and back liners. Accordingly, it did not matter whether the front or back slick was the smaller of the two. Because no money would be saved by having the back liner wrap over to the front, Capitol opted to go with the more attractive construction having the front slick wrap over to the back.

Some of the albums used by Capitol for promotional purposes have the word "FREE" drill stamped into the upper right corner of the album jacket.

There are two typesetting variations of the first issue labels for the album. Both have the album, matrix and side numbers to the right of the center hole and the song titles, songwriters credits, BMI and running times below the center hole. The first issue labels were printed on label backdrops with Capitol logo perimeter print on the sliced apple side.

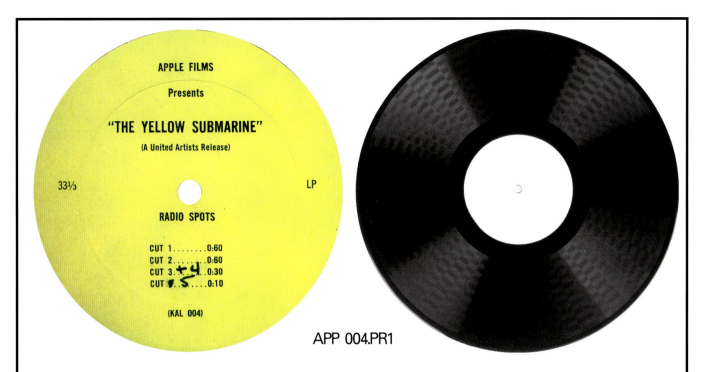

APPLE FILMS

Presents

"THE YELLOW SUBMARINE"

(A United Artists Release)

33⅓                                              LP

RADIO SPOTS

CUT 1........0:60
CUT 2........0:60
CUT 3.+4.0:30
CUT 4.5....0:10

(KAL 004)

APP 004.PR1

Apple Films and United Artists released a promotional 12" album (KAL 004) containing five radio spots to promote the film. The one-sided yellow label disc contains two 60-second spots, two 30-second spots and one 10-second spot. The upper part of the label states "APPLE FILMS Presents 'THE YELLOW SUBMARINE' (A United Artists Release)." The lower part of the label lists the radio spots. The printed label mistakenly lists only four cuts, accidently leaving out one of the 30-second spots. Apparently the error was discovered before the album was distributed and all copies were corrected by a pen mark to add "+4" after CUT 3 to indicate that CUT 4 was also a 30-second spot. In addition, the "4" in CUT 4 was crossed out and a "5" added to indicate that the the 10-second spot was the fifth track. The other side of the record has a blank white label and a checkered pattern on the vinyl.

The radio spots feature bits of George Martin's score and Beatles songs such as *Eleanor Rigby* and *All You Need Is Love*. One spot touts the film as "a movie that loves you." Others bill the cartoon as "The Beatles vs. the Blue Meanies." As *Hey Bulldog* was deleted form the film before its American debut, a radio spot proclaims that the movie features *three* new songs by the Beatles plus eight Beatles classics. Nearly all of the spots use the line "art work, photography, psychedelic landscapes painted with Beatles sounds" and close with "Love...from the Beatles."

The Los Angeles labels, **APP 153.SR1L(c)**, have light green apple labels printed by Bert-Co. Side one has the album title and the group's name in small upper case letters on two lines in the upper left part of the apple. Side two has the album title and "Original film music score composed and orchestrated by George Martin" in small upper case letters on four lines in the upper left part of the apple. "STEREO" is in the upper right part of the apple on both sides. These labels are found on Los Angeles and Jacksonville pressings, as well as discs pressed for Capitol by Columbia Records in Santa Maria, California.

The Scranton labels, **APP 153.SR1S(c)**, have dark green apple label backdrops printed by Queens Litho with label copy probably overprinted by Keystone. Side one has the group's name in small upper case letters in the upper left part of the apple and the album title in large upper case letters centered above the spindle hole. Side two has the album title in large upper case letters and the George Martin credit in small uppercase letters centered above the spindle hole. "STEREO" appears at nine o'clock on both sides. In addition to appearing on Scranton pressings, these labels have been confirmed on records subcontracted to Columbia in Terre Haute, Indiana.

The later labels have the same typesetting as the Los Angeles labels, but are printed on light green apple label backdrops with Apple perimeter print on the full apple side, **APP 153.SR1L(af)**. These labels have been confirmed with Los Angeles and Winchester pressings.

There are three confirmed all rights variations, all with Apple perimeter print on the full apple side and having the same layout design as **APP 153.SR1L**. The all rights variations include: (1) **APP 153.SR2A(ar)**, with the all rights language in black on two lines centered at the top of the apple on the full apple side and on five lines in the upper left part of the apple on the sliced apple side (light green apple labels) (Los Angeles pressings confirmed); (2) **APP 153.SR2C(ar)**, with the all rights language in green running along the lower right perimeter on the full side (dark green apple labels) (Jacksonville pressings confirmed); and (3) **APP 153.SR2D(ar)**, with the all rights language in green in the lower perimeter on both sides (light green apple labels) (Los Angeles pressings confirmed).

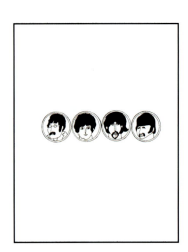
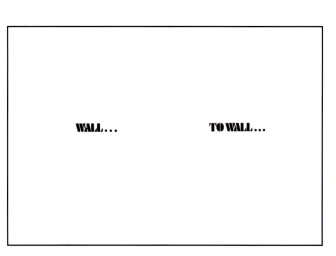

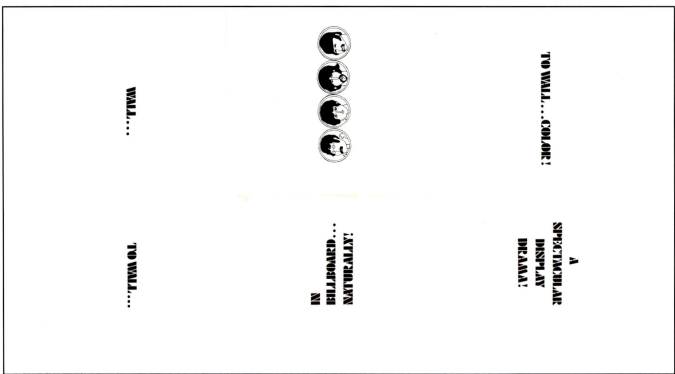

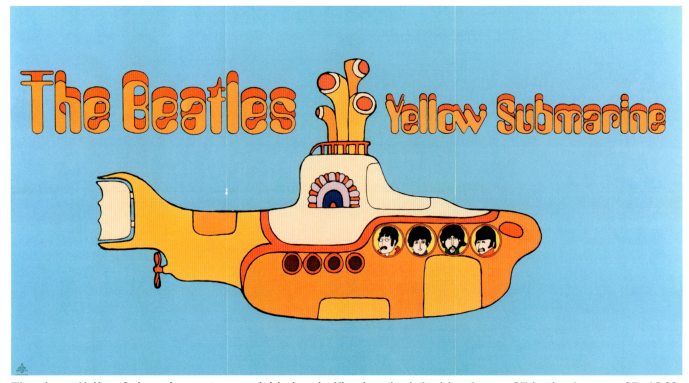

The above *Yellow Submarine* poster was folded and affixed to the left side of page 37 in the January 25, 1969, *Billboard*. The top row shows how the folded poster appeared in the magazine.

APP  153.SC1

APP  153.SR1L(c)

APP  153.SR1S(c)

APP 153.SR1L(af)

APP 153.SR2A(ar)

APP 153.SR2C(ar)
(All rights only on full apple side)

APP 153.SR2D(ar)
(All rights on both sides)

## THE BEATLES; GET BACK
## (UNRELEASED)

Side 1
1. ONE AFTER 909 (Lennon-McCartney)
   Link Tracks: ROCKER (Lennon-McCartney)
   SAVE THE LAST DANCE FOR ME (Pomus-Shuman)
2. DON'T LET ME DOWN (Lennon-McCartney)
3. DIG A PONY (Lennon-McCartney)
4. I'VE GOT A FEELING (Lennon-McCartney)
5. GET BACK (Lennon-McCartney)

Side 2
1. FOR YOU BLUE (Harrison)
2. TEDDY BOY (Lennon-McCartney)
3. TWO OF US ON OUR WAY HOME (Lennon-McCartney)
   Link Track: MAGGIE MAY (Public Domain)
4. DIG IT (Lennon-McCartney-Harrison-Starr)
5. LET IT BE (Lennon-McCartney)
6. THE LONG AND WINDING ROAD (Lennon-McCartney)
   GET BACK (Reprise) (Lennon-McCartney)

In February, 1969, less than three months after releasing the massive double album *The Beatles* and one month after issuing the *Yellow Submarine* soundtrack, Apple announced that the Beatles would be putting out a new LP within the next few months. At the time this optimistic report was issued, the Beatles had completed a recording session held from January 21 through 31, 1969, at their Savile Row Apple headquarters, but no record had been compiled. That would not occur until May 28, when the album that would eventually be titled *Get Back* was put together. Although Apple planned for a summer release, the *Get Back* album in its initial form was never issued.

The January, 1969, session during which the *Get Back* album was recorded grew out of a totally different concept. The initial plan, conceived by Paul McCartney in August, 1968, was to have the group give a concert in a small venue such as the Roundhouse in London. The show, which was later tentatively scheduled for January 18, 1969, would be the group's first public performance in over two years and would be filmed for a one-hour television special.

In late November, 1968, Apple announced that the concert would not take place at the Roundhouse, but did not name a replacement venue. The group would perform three separate shows for invited audiences, with each set recorded on color videotape. The television program would consist of the best performances from these shows. Most of the songs would be from the recently released *White Album*, with a few oldies thrown in.

The driving force behind the show was Paul, who wanted the group to return to live performances. Many of his ideas for the project can be traced back to the band's promotional clips for *Hey Jude* and *Revolution* (see pages 32-33). These performance videos were directed by Michael Lindsay-Hogg and were shot before an audience of invited fans on September 4, 1968, at Twickenham Film Studios. McCartney was pleased with the dynamic promotional films and reenlisted Lindsay-Hogg to serve as director for the television program.

Although the initial plan was to have the TV show revolve around and plug *The White Album*, the group later decided they should learn about eight new songs for the concert. This would require a week or two of rehearsals, which could also be filmed in a manner similar to the filming of the Beatles July 30, 1968, *Hey Jude* session (see page 32). According to Mal Evans, the plan was to make a "Beatles At Work" documentary separate from the TV special that could be viewed at a later date to show what goes on as the Beatles build up a new set of songs.

Apple Films president Denis O'Dell decided that the proceedings should be shot using 16 mm film rather than video tape, and booked Twickenham for rehearsals commencing on January 2, 1969. This fit in well with his schedule as O'Dell was serving as producer for *The Magic Christian* (starring Peter Sellers and Ringo Starr), which was set to begin filming at Twickenham on February 3. During the month-long Beatles project, cameramen shot approximately 475 rolls of film. Most of the proceedings were filmed by two cameras, although four cameras were used for the rooftop segment.

The sound crew used two Nagra mono reel-to-reel tape recorders, each of which was paired with a camera. The reels of tape were run at a high speed, thus resulting in a recording time of only 16 minutes per tape. Although each recorder would have down time to change reels, most of the proceedings were captured because while one machine was having its tape replaced, the other was still recording. Approximately 530 reels of tape were used, yielding about 141 hours of music and dialog. While some of this is duplicated between reels from the two recorders, there are probably over 100 hours of unique recordings. A significant portion of the Nagra tapes has been bootlegged.

In addition to tapes made by the sound crew, Glyn Johns recorded some of the performances on January 7, 8, 9, 10 and 13 so that the Beatles could listen to playbacks of the songs. Johns was recruited by McCartney to serve as balance engineer for the sessions. Johns' experience included work as either an engineer or producer for several high profile acts, including the Rolling Stones, the Who, the Kinks, the Steve Miller Band and Traffic. His membership in the filmmakers union enabled him to work with the film crew. While George Martin did not attend all of the Twickenham and Apple sessions, Johns was there from the start and was present throughout the entire proceedings, often serving as unofficial producer. It is believed that the tapes recorded by Johns at Twickenham were either recorded over or lost.

Although none of the Twickenham rehearsals were properly recorded on multitrack equipment, over ten hours of performances from the later January 21-31 sessions held at Apple were recorded on an eight-track unit. When the Beatles felt they were ready for a serious take of a song, they instructed Glyn Johns to roll the tape. Some of these performances were given rough mixes by Johns and were transferred to acetates so that the Beatles could evaluate their new songs. The *Get Back* and *Let It Be* albums were compiled solely from recordings made at Apple.

A complete chronological discussion of the rehearsals, loose jams, oldies, dialog and serious performances taped from January 2 through 31, 1969, would fill an entire book. This chapter is limited to a brief summary of the proceedings, with detailed information limited to the songs selected for the original *Get Back* album. Those seeking the full story are referred to Doug Sulpy and Ray Schweighardt's *Drugs, Divorce and a Slipping Image* (or its revised and updated edition published as *Get Back*) and its companion piece, Doug Sulpy's *The 910's Guide to The Beatles' Outtakes Part Two, The Complete Get Back Sessions*.

On the morning of January 2, 1969, the Beatles arrived at Twickenham to begin rehearsing songs for the show. On this first day they primarily worked on *Don't Let Me Down*, *I've Got A Feeling* and *Two Of Us*, although other songs were introduced. During discussions about the planned concert, Paul suggested it take place at Twickenham, but also expressed an interest in holding it outdoors.

During the next day of filming, the Beatles added George's *All Things Must Pass* and Paul's *Maxwell Silver Hammer* to the rehearsal rotation. The group also ran through bits and pieces of several oldies such as Little Richard's *Lucille* and the Coasters' *Three Cool Cats*.

During the *Get Back* sessions, the Beatles often resorted to playing songs from their old stage show. Sometimes they would turn in fairly complete and competent versions, but usually it was a case of no one really remembering the words. Many of these performances broke down after a verse or two. At one time there was talk of releasing an entire album of oldies performed during the sessions, but this idea was abandoned when the group realized that while some of these recordings were interesting and entertaining, the musicianship and singing sounded amateurish and was not up to their usual high standards.

The initial rehearsal sessions for the Beatles planned television special took place in Twickenham Film Studios' huge Stage One soundstage. The above Ethan Russell photograph appears on the inside gatefold to the *Let It Be* album cover.

The group also played a few contemporary songs such as Canned Heat's *Going Up The Country* and Janis Joplin's *Piece Of My Heart*. George showed his fondness for Bob Dylan and the Band by leading the group through songs such as *I Shall Be Released*, *The Mighty Quinn (Quinn The Eskimo)*, *Positively 4th Street* and *The Weight*.

After taking the weekend off, the Beatles returned to Twickenham on January 6. It was during these Monday through Friday sessions that things really deteriorated. The group went through tedious rehearsals but didn't seem satisfied with their performances of the new songs. They had numerous discussions about the live show but could not agree on a location. (Michael Lindsay-Hogg suggested that the show be filmed at an ancient outdoor Roman amphitheater on the shores of North Africa. Although this idea was

abandoned, it was given serious consideration, as demonstrated by plans to have Mal Evans fly to Tripoli on January 13 to inspect the theater.) John, who was often on strung out on heroin, was going through a phase where he preferred nonverbal communication to talking. His lack of participation in serious discussions frustrated both Paul and George. At times, Yoko would speak for John, and her constant presence at the rehearsals added to the tense atmosphere. George was becoming increasingly frustrated with the group's indifference towards his songs, his role in the band and John's failure to communicate. Ringo showed up to play drums, but did not participate in most of the talks about the upcoming concert or the band's future. By default, Paul was forced into the role of running the sessions, often leading to resentment from the others.

The *Let It Be* film contains a segment from January 6 showing Paul criticizing George's guitar playing on *Two Of Us*. Paul tells George his riffs are complicated and need to be made simpler. When George disagrees with Paul's assessment, McCartney says "I'm trying to help you, but I always hear as though I'm annoying you." He later adds "I'm not trying to get ya. What I am really trying to just say is 'Look lads...should we try it like this?'" To emphasize his point, McCartney says "This one is like 'Should we play guitar all through *Hey Jude?*' Well I don't think we should." This reference to Paul's previous ordering of George not to play lead guitar fills on *Hey Jude* causes Harrison to replay "Yeah, OK, well I don't mind. I'll play, you know, whatever you want me to play, or I won't play at all if you don't want me to play. Whatever it is that will please you, I'll do it."

That evening, the Beatles held a business meeting and discussed the planned live concert. The next morning, Paul expressed his continuing desire to do the show, but the others were less enthusiastic. John observed that even if they didn't do the show, they would still have a film about making an album. Paul discussed how pessimistic the group had become since the death of their manager, Brian Epstein. After Paul stated that they could either work to improve things or call it quits, George agreed and gave his opinion that the Beatles were coming to an end. Further discussions indicate that John and George not only had little enthusiasm for the concert, but also were losing their desire to put their creative energies into any group project. When George later suggested that the band break up, John asked who would get possession of the children. After Paul reminded them how stupid it would be to break up the group and unsuccessfully tired to engage in a serious discussion with John, the band returned to rehearsing new songs.

By the end of the week, George had had enough. He felt stifled by Paul telling him what to play and was feeling negative vibes from John and Yoko. On January 10, after the group's lunch break, he quit the Beatles. Although the exact incident triggering this decision remains unknown (the press reported it was a fight between he and John), the actual moment of George's departure was captured by one of the Nagra tapes. While John plays the opening riff to Chuck Berry's *I'm Talking About You*, Harrison calmly tells him "I'm leaving the band now." Lennon asks "When?" and George replies "Now." The sound of Harrison's footsteps is accompanied by his advising the others to "Get a replacement and write the NME [*New Musical Express*] and get a few people."

After George's departure, the remaining Beatles resumed rehearsals, but these were not terribly productive. The following Sunday (January 12) the group met at Ringo's house for a previously scheduled business meeting. Although George attended, he left the meeting early after becoming fed up with John's lack of input and Yoko's habit of speaking for John.

The following morning both George and John were no-shows at Twickenham. Although no music was played, the tape machines recorded a series of frank conversations involving, at different times, Paul, Neil Aspinall, Linda Eastman (Paul's future wife), Mal Evans and Michael Lindsey-Hogg. While Paul went out of his way not to condemn Yoko, he recognized her effect on John's behavior. By devoting himself to Yoko, John was no longer fulfilling his responsibilities to the group. Paul was concerned that if he confronted John on this matter and suggested that Yoko's involvement with the Beatles be curtailed, John would quit the group. Paul also acknowledged that George was no longer willing to put up with the situation.

When Mal later reached John on the phone, the call was put through to Paul, who talked John into returning to Twickenham. After Lennon's arrival, he and Paul discussed George's departure, with John believing that George was no longer satisfied with his role in the group. While John had previously been reluctant to talk about the band's current problems, he was much more open during this discussion. Lennon expressed his belief that Paul directed George and him on what to play because McCartney was concerned that he wouldn't like their playing if he left it up to them. After John discussed his and Paul's different approach to recording sessions (Paul in charge versus John wanting suggestions which he can take or leave), Paul wondered how he could avoid hurting George's ego when he tells Harrison how to play. The brief rehearsal session held that afternoon featured the three remaining Beatles working on *Get Back*, with the emphasis on completing the lyrics.

The January 14 session was extremely unproductive as George did not attend, and John did not arrive until after lunch and spent his initial time being interviewed by Canadian journalists. After a bit of jamming, the group decided that continuing at Twickenham without George would be a waste of time. At the end of the day, Mal packed up the group's instruments, thus bringing an end to the Beatles Twickenham sessions.

Although memories differ as to how and where things got patched up, George's recollection in the *Anthology* book was that he was called to a meeting at Ringo's house, where it was decided that the group should get back together and finish the record. "Twickenham Studios were very cold and not a very nice atmosphere, so we decided to abandon that and go to Savile Row into the recording studio."

The group had entrusted the job of turning Apple's basement into a state-of-the-art studio to Alexis Mardas, a friend of John's who supposedly was an electronic genius. Magic Alex, who was appointed head of Apple Electronics, boasted that he would build a studio vastly superior to EMI's facilities. It would have 72 tracks instead of EMI's measly eight. And rather than placing baffles (soundproof walls) around the drums to prevent leakage to microphones, Magic Alex would invent a sonic beam force field device that would magically stop the drum sounds from reaching the mikes. When the Beatles arrived at the basement studio on January 20, they were confronted with a total disaster. Magic Alex had put in 16 speakers for his 16-track recorder, but, as Harrison pointed out, "You only need two speakers for stereo sound." The speakers were quickly removed. Engineer Dave Harries described the mixing console as being made of "bits of wood and an old oscilloscope" and looking like the "control panel of a B-52 bomber."

When the sessions resumed on January 21, the Beatles moved to their basement studio at Apple headquarters. The control room (shown above) was augmented with equipment borrowed from EMI. The above Ethan Russell photograph appears on the inside gatefold to the *Let It Be* album cover.

When the Beatles tested the system, the playback tape was full of hums and hisses. George Martin had EMI send over two four-track consoles to pair with Apple's eight-track recorder. Because Magic Alex had neglected to put holes in the wall between the studio and control room, the cables had to be run through the door.

The building's heating and air conditioning system, which was located in the basement, provided additional problems. It had not been soundproofed, so the system had to be turned off when the tapes were rolling.

Despite its shortcomings, the makeshift basement studio provided a vastly superior atmosphere to Twickenham's soundstage. Rehearsals resumed on January 21, with some takes recorded that afternoon. The version of *She Came In Through The Bathroom Window* appearing on *Anthology 3* is probably from that session.

The switch from Twickenham to Apple was not the only change in the project. The prospect for doing a live concert was looking grim, so the focus shifted from learning eight new songs for the TV show to recording 14 tracks for an album. The other significant development was the addition of Billy Preston, who sat in on keyboards.

One evening George went with Eric Clapton to see Ray Charles' concert at the Festival Hall. Prior to Ray coming on stage, Billy Preston warmed up the crowd by singing, dancing and playing organ. After Charles introduced Preston to the crowd, George remembered meeting him in Hamburg in 1962 when Preston was in Little Richard's band. Harrison had Billy tracked down and invited to Apple. When

George was informed of Preston's arrival during the January 22 session, he met him at reception and asked him to come down to the basement studio and play electric piano. Billy's presence caused everyone to behave better leading to a "100% improvement in the vibe in the room." According to Harrison, "Having this fifth person was just enough to cut the ice that we'd created among ourselves." George Martin agreed that Preston a very good keyboard player who "helped lubricate the friction that had been there."

A portion of the January 22 session with Billy Preston was recorded by Glyn Johns. Paul's hand written comments on the back of the EMI tape box indicate that he was not impressed. Although McCartney wrote "Only good for conversation (if anything)," Johns placed the entire "Rocker & Conversation, Save the last Dance into Don't Let me Down" and the entire "Dig a Pony into I've Got a feeling" segments on the *Get Back* album.

Much of the January 23 session was spent rehearsing *Get Back*, which had become the top contender for the band's next single. The following day, prior to Billy Preston's arrival, John suggested that Preston be made a permanent member of the group. Although Paul wanted Preston to play during the sessions and on the television concert, he was against expanding the group's membership. Songs recorded that day included *Two Of Us*, *Teddy Boy*, *Dig It* and *Get Back*.

The Beatles decided that they needed to work through the weekend, so sessions were held on January 25 and 26. Highlights of the first day included the recording of *For*

*You Blue* and rehearsals of *Two Of Us* and *Let It Be*. The Sunday session included extensive work on *Let It Be* and *The Long And Winding Road*, although the group found time to run through several oldies. Glyn Johns prepared an acetate containing some of the day's recordings and titled it "Beatles Sunday."

The idea of performing an unannounced concert on the roof of Apple's Savile Row headquarters reportedly evolved on this day. According to Glyn Johns, the Beatles had expressed their desire to play to the whole of London. During the lunch break, the conversation turned to Apple's building, with Ringo commenting that the group was thinking of putting a garden on the roof. Johns suggested that they go up to the roof and told them his idea of having the band play up there, thus enabling the Beatles to play to a part of London.

Johns also takes credit for the concept of releasing an album containing loose performances and studio banter. "One night I took a couple of reels of the eight-tracks away with me to Olympic Studios and mixed two days of rehearsals with a lot of chat and humor and so on. I thought it would make the most incredible Beatles album ever, because it was so real." He gave copies of his rough mixes to each of the Beatles. The following day he was told that his concept for the album was a terrible idea, so he thought no more about it.

The January 27 and 28 sessions were highly productive, with solid performances of *Get Back* and *Don't Let Me Down* being recorded. The group's first single for 1969 was pulled from these recordings. Although it remains unreleased, the band also performed a rough version of their first single, *Love Me Do*.

On January 29, the group rehearsed songs intended for the rooftop concert, which was scheduled for the next day. The band also ran through songs that would later appear on George's first album (*All Things Must Pass* and *Let It Down*) as well as several oldies.

Taped conversations from the day's session reveal that the group thought they could not finish 14 songs for an album before Ringo began filming *The Magic Christian* in a few days. Only *Get Back* and *For You Blue* were considered good enough for release, with producer George Martin believing that the others were not beyond the rehearsal stage. Paul recognized that the project had shifted from the planned television concert to a documentary about the Beatles making an album, and was worried that without the live concert, there was no payoff. Fortunately for all concerned, the following day's rooftop concert would provide the payoff needed to end what would later become the *Let It Be* film.

During lunchtime on January 30, 1969, the Beatles, with Billy Preston, climbed to the roof of their Savile Row headquarters to give what would be their last public performance. On this cold and windy day, the group gave a 42-minute show to both the delight and frustration of London's busy business district. The band played, in order, *Get Back* (two performances), *Don't Let Me Down*, *I've Got A Feeling*, *One After 909*, *Dig A Pony*, *God Save The Queen*, *I've Got A Feeling*, *Don't Let Me Down* and *Get Back*.

Towards the end of show, the police arrived on the roof to put an end to the concert. During the final performance of *Get Back*, Mal became concerned that the group would be arrested if they didn't immediately stop, so he turned off the power to John and George's Fender Twin Reverb amps. While the others kept playing, George let Mal know the group would finish the song and flipped his amp back on. Mal then flipped the switch to John's amp and the band was full strength again. During the song's coda, Paul made fun of the incident by singing, "Oh, get back, you been out too long, Loretta. You been playing on the roofs again and that's no good 'cause you know your mommy doesn't like that. Oh she get's angry, she gonna have you arrested, get back." At the end of the song and concert, John stepped up to the mike and made his classic remark, "I'd like to say 'thank you' on behalf of the group and ourselves. I hope we passed the audition."

The next day the Beatles returned to the basement studio to record and film three songs that were inappropriate for their rooftop concert: *Two Of Us*, *The Long And Winding Road* and *Let It Be*. This brought an end to the *Get Back* sessions.

On February 5, Glyn Johns made stereo mixes of the songs performed during the rooftop concert. This session took place at Apple Studios with Alan Parsons serving as engineer. It is not known if George Martin was present. The mix of the rooftop version of *One After 909* was later used on the *Get Back* LP. Nothing further was done on the project for over a month.

After visiting the United States to work with Steve Miller, Johns returned to England and produced a February 22 session with the Beatles recording Lennon's *I Want You*. A few weeks later he received a call from Paul requesting that he meet John and Paul at Abbey Road. Upon his arrival, Johns was questioned about his idea to put together an album from the sessions. He was shown a big pile of tapes in the corner of the room and told "There are the tapes. Put them in your car. Take them away and do the album as you want to do it." Johns was extremely excited about having the extraordinary opportunity to put together a Beatles album as he saw fit.

On March 10, Johns began mixing songs for the new album at Olympic Sound Studios. He prepared an acetate for the Beatles containing the following tracks: *Get Back* (recorded January 23); *I've Got A Feeling* (brief intro from January 23 that immediately followed *Get Back*); *Teddy Boy* (January 24) (an edited version of this mix was included on the *Get Back* album); *On Our Way Home* (early title for *Two Of Us*) *(January* 24); *Dig A Pony* (January 22); *I've Got A Feeling* (January 22); *The Long And Winding Road* (January 26); *Let It Be* (January 26); *Don't Let Me Down* (January 22); *Because You're Sweet And Lonely* (alternate title of *For You Blue*) *(January* 25); *Get Back* (January 27 with pre-song banter used on the *Let It Be* album and without the January 28 coda edited to the single) (this take was used for the single and the album); and *The Walk* (January 27). Although the *Rocker* and *Save The Last Dance For Me* into *Don't Let Me Down* segment from January 22 was also mixed, it was not included on the acetate.

John Lennon's copy of the March 10 acetate was the source of several bootlegs. *Get Back To Toronto* (I.P.F. Records) (shown left) opens with a *Peace Message* from John recorded at a Toronto press conference. Lennon talks about Year One of Peace, his great hopes for the new year (1970) and a planned Toronto Peace Festival scheduled for July. Because the bootleg was released a few months ahead of the *Let It Be* album, some songs are identified with descriptive titles such as *On Our Way Home* [*Two Of Us*], *All I Want Is You* [*Dig A Pony*], *Sweet And Lovely Girl* [*For You Blue*] and *When You Walk* [*The Walk*]. The record does not contain *The Long And Winding Road*. The album's concluding *Christmas Message* is a bit of *Christmas Time (Is Here Again)* from the 1967 Beatles Fan Club Christmas record. The Lemon Records bootleg (shown right) was probably issued shortly after the release of the *Let It Be* LP. It came in a plain white jacket with a simple "GET BACK" stamp. The album contains selections from the March 10 acetate plus *Across The Universe* (from the British charity LP *Nothing's Gonna Change Our World*). Other early bootleg titles include *Come Back* and *Kum Back*.

Six months later, Lennon's copy of the March 10 acetate came into the possession of a Buffalo disc jockey, who played the disc on the air. Shortly thereafter, Boston's WBCN broadcast the acetate on September 22, 1969, erroneously describing it as the *Get Back* album. Tapes of the acetate were circulated among other American radio stations, thus leading to the songs being played in several cities across the country. The acetate became the source of several bootlegs, some of which were released on vinyl months ahead of the Beatles official *Let It Be* album.

On March 11, Johns continued his work on the project with new mixes of *On Our Way Home* and *The Long And Winding Road*. He also made an unreleased mix of *Lady Madonna* from January 31. The next day he made mixes of different versions of *Let It Be* and *The Long And Winding Road*, both from January 31. Neither of these mixes were released; however, the January 31 performance of *Let It Be* served as the basic master take for the single and all album releases of the song.

On March 13, Johns mixed a January 27 performance of *I've Got A Feeling* as well as two different versions of *Dig It* (January 24 and 26). He also mixed *Maggie Mae* (January 24), which would find its way onto every version of the *Get Back* and *Let It Be* albums. Finally, Johns mixed the following rock 'n' roll songs from January 26: a medley of *Rip It Up* and *Shake, Rattle And Roll*; a medley of *Miss Ann*, *Kansas City* and *Lawdy Miss Clawdy*; *Blue Suede Shoes*; and *You Really Got A Hold On Me*. None of these

cover tunes were selected for the album. An acetate was cut containing most of the March 13 mixes plus an alternate mix of the January 26 *Let It Be*.

After listening to the mix of the January 31 version of *Let It Be*, George realized that his lead guitar solo on the song was not up to his usual high standards. On April 30, Harrison entered Abbey Road Studio Three to overdub a new solo. While this was a violation of the "no overdubs, warts and all" concept behind the album, the new solo was a big improvement.

One week after Harrison tweaked his guitar on *Let It Be*, Glyn Johns and George Martin got together at Olympic on May 7 to begin putting together what was then known as the *Get Back* album. The first step was to select and mix bits of studio chatter from the sessions to give the album an at-home live-in-the-studio felling. This work continued on May 9. Martin and Johns then listened to the finished masters of the songs available for the album, which included the February 5 mixes of the rooftop concert and the March 10-13 mixes of tracks recorded in the Apple basement studio, as well as the unmixed April 30 enhanced *Let It Be*.

On May 28, Martin and Johns returned to Olympic to mix the April 30 overdubbed master of *Let It Be* and to select the running order of the record's songs. The finished masters, including the bits of studio dialog, were then banded and compiled into the master tape for the album. George, who was the only Beatle in the country at the time, reportedly attended the session.

Four cats
on a
London
roof

A TV documentary will
detail the making of
the Beatles'
new record album

The cats on the roof are, of
course, the Beatles. And what
they're up to up there is a
recording session, the entire
proceedings of which were,
coincidentally, filmed for a
television documentary.
    In the panel of pictures at
top are, from left to right:
Ringo Starr, George Harrison,
a hirsute Paul McCartney and
John Lennon. In the bottom
photo, the Beatles en masse
in a *furor poeticus*.
    The reason for making an
album is obvious. The reason
for filming the session is to let
the world—all over which the
Beatles hope to sell the documentary in a few months—
know just how the Beatles go
about their work. At least part
of the world, however, was
less than enchanted with the
opportunity. Their neighbors
(the recording studio just happens to be in London's elegant Savile Row) dispatched
bobbies to quell the noise.
Even bobbies couldn't do that.
14

**News of the Beatles planned television documentary detailing the making of their new record album hit mainstream America through *TV Guide*. The April 19-25, 1969, issue of the magazine ran a two-page spread featuring Ethan Russell photos of the group performing in the studio and on the roof.**

Word of the new Beatles album first surfaced in February, 1969, when it was reported that the record might be set for release in April or May. By April, Apple was reporting that the album's release had been delayed until late summer to allow for additional recording sessions and the design and preparation of a cover. The word in May was to expect the LP coming out in July. In June, Apple announced a late August release and the possibility that several additional tracks would be added to the finished product.

Issue No. 72 of *The Beatles Book* (July 1969) contained Mal Evans' report on the album, which was titled *The Beatles; Get Back*. The article described the LP cover and included track-by-track details of the songs. Evans described the new album as "The Beatles with their socks off, human Beatles kicking out their jams, getting rid of their inhibitions, facing their problems and working them out with their music." The article was reprinted in the September 20, 1969, *Rolling Stone*.

In America, Capitol Records was getting ready for the late summer release of the album. The company announced that *Get Back* would be packaged with a special book and list for $10.98.

By the end of July, Apple reported that the *Get Back* LP had been postponed and that the Beatles were in concentrated recording sessions to complete another entirely new album for rush-release. (The new album would be completed in August, titled *Abbey Road* and issued in England by the end of September.) Mal Evans told *The Beatles Book* that the group "realized that it would be much more appropriate to hold back this whole set of [*Get Back*] recordings so that they could form an LP which would go out the time their TV documentary is shown in Britain and America." *The Beatles Book* reported that *Get Back* would be released in November with the same recordings.

This, however, was not to be. As detailed in the *Let It Be* LP chapter, an album containing songs from the *Get Back* sessions would not be released until May, 1970, and would contain different mixes, recordings and songs than the *Get Back* album. It would also be renamed *Let It Be*. The original unreleased album, as compiled in late May, 1969, is described below.

The *Get Back* album opens with the sounds of the band ready to start their rooftop performance of *One After 909* (which is identified on EMI tape boxes as "*The One After 909*"). As the tape begins to roll, a chord from Billy Preston's electric piano and a few stray guitar notes are heard. This is followed by a member of the film crew shouting "All cameras four" (indicating Take 4), the sound of the clapperboard and John's count-in to the song. The Beatles then play an inspired performance with John and Paul sharing lead vocals. George's lead guitar and Billy Preston's piano riffs highlight the tight musical backing. At the end of the song,

THE BEATLES "LET IT BE"
AN APPLE FILMS LIMITED PRODUCTION
Produced by NEIL ASPINALL    Directed by MICHAEL LINDSAY-HOGG
COLOR by Technicolor (R)    UNITED ARTISTS, Entertainment from Transamerica Corporation

John sings what sounds like "Oh Danny boy, the old Savannah's calling." (The correct lyrics to *Danny Boy* are "Oh Danny boy, the pipes, the pipes are calling.") This leads into a bit of dialog taken from the end of the rooftop concert, with Paul saying "Thanks Mo" to Ringo's wife Maureen (because she was clapping the hardest) and John's classic line "I'd like to say 'thank you' on behalf of the group and ourselves. I hope we passed the audition."

The album's opening selection is literally a blast from the past. *One After 909* was one of the first songs written by John, dating back to 1957. The song's railroad theme and rhythm suggest that John may have been influenced by Lonnie Donegan's skiffle recording of Huddie "Leadbelly" Ledbetter's *Rock Island Line,* which charted in 1956 at number eight in England and at number ten in the U.S. (London 1650). In Miles' *Many Years From Now*, Paul recalls he and John "trying to write a bluesy freight-train song." Rehearsal tapes from 1960 and 1962 demonstrate that *One After 909* was a part of the band's early repertoire.

In the *Let It Be* film, Paul is asked about the tune and states that *One After 909* was from the days he and John used to "sag off every school day" and go to the McCartney house on Forthlin Road to write songs. After explaining that during this period they wrote about a hundred unsophisticated songs, Paul confesses "We always hated the words of *One After 909*" and recites its opening lines: "Baby said she's travelin' on the one after 909. I said move over honey, I'm travelin' on that line. I said move over once, move over twice, come on baby don't be cold as ice."

Although they may have hated the words, the Beatles recorded *One After 909* at one of their first EMI sessions. On March 5, 1963, after completing the songs for their third single (*From Me To You* and *Thank You Girl*), the band ran through five rough takes of the song. George's lead guitar was so mediocre that at the end of the second take, John asked "What kind of solo was that?" A comparison of that clunker with the rooftop performance shows how much Harrison improved over the years. Because none of the 1963 takes proved satisfactory, the song was passed over and forgotten until resurrected by the group in 1969. *Anthology 1* contains bits of Takes 3, 4 and 5 followed by a 1995 edit of Takes 4 and 5 of the 1963 recording.

*One After 909* was introduced to the *Get Back* sessions on January 3. In his *Playboy* interview, John admitted that the song was probably resurrected for lack of material. The early performances of the song feature John on rhythm guitar and vocals, Paul on bass and vocals, George on lead guitar through a wah-wah pedal and Ringo on drums. At this stage, the song retained a bit of a skiffle beat that would soon be replaced as the song evolved into an all-out rocker.

While the initial pair of January 6 performances were taken at a slow tempo, the group picked up the pace for its

*I'm Ready* was written by Fats Domino along with Bradford and Lewis. His January 29, 1959, recording of the song was released on Imperial 5585 in April of that year. The song peaked at number 16 in the *Billboard Hot 100* and at seven in the *Billboard Hot R&B Sides* chart. Domino recorded a version of *Lady Madonna*, which *Billboard* charted at 100 for two weeks in September, 1968. It appeared on the album *Fats Is Back* (Reprise RS 6304) along with *Lovely Rita*. The Drifters recorded *Save The Last Dance For Me* (written by Doc Pomus and Mort Shuman) during a May 19, 1960, session produced by Jerry Leiber and Mike Stoller. When released on Atlantic 2071 August, 1960, the song went on to top the *Billboard Hot R&B Sides* and *Hot 100* charts.

third and final run-through of the day. The January 7 and 8 performances show that the song's transformation to rocker was complete, with Paul and Ringo providing a solid backing. The *Let It Be* film contains an edited version of the January 9 rehearsals.

By the time the Beatles returned to the song on January 28, Billy Preston had joined the sessions. The addition of Preston on electric piano and George's decision not to use his wah-wah pedal improved the song. During one of the day's spirited performances, Paul encourages George during his solo by shouting "yeah, rock 'n' roll." When John muffs his vocal, he gamely carries on after singing "Oh I did it again, oh yeah." While the Beatles were bored with many of the songs they rehearsed during the sessions, there is no doubt that they truly enjoyed playing *One After 909*. The group's first January 29 rehearsal of the song was performed prior to the arrival of Billy Preston and is interesting in that George's guitar is more prominently featured. The band performed the song two more times later that day.

*One After 909* is followed on the *Get Back* album by a link track featuring a segment of the Beatles and Billy Preston jamming on two oldies. As the tape from January 22 begins to roll, Paul can be heard singing "I'm willing and I'm able to rock 'n' roll all night, I'm ready." Although the lines are from the Fats Domino song *I'm Ready*, the 33 second improvisation is identified by Paul on the session tape box as *Rocker*. After Paul says "Just a minute boys," the group discusses what to do next. They then launch into the first verse of the Drifters' *Save The Last Dance For Me*, which segues into John and Paul singing the first two lines of *Don't Let Me Down*. After this breaks down, John says "This time it's serious." He then jokingly gives members of the band separate instructions on the song's tempo: "Now remember, you're waltz, you're 3/4, I'm 5/6." George is heard in the background playing riffs from *Don't Let Me Down* and saying "There's a letter for you John." After Lennon laughs and says "It's Doris," Paul says "Do your thing man," to which John replies "I can't keep off it."

John then counts in for the start of *Don't Let Me Down*, which quickly breaks down when George asks, "Oh no, what are we doin'?" After he is told, Paul says "I was just into" and plays the bass riff from *Dig A Pony*. John then instructs Ringo to "Do a nice big 'cooshhh' [sound of a crashing cymbal] for me, you know, to give me the courage to come screaming in."

After another count-in, the group performs a bluesy full take of *Don't Let Me Down*. This version, also from January 22, is at a slower tempo than the single and is full of vocal ad-libs, including John's "goody, goody, goody, good" following the line "she done me good." Prior to the start of Preston's electric piano solo, John shouts "Hit it Bill" and continues with vocal ad-libs over the solo. The recording history of the song is detailed in the chapter on the single.

*Don't Let Me Down* is immediately followed by more studio banter, starting with John saying "Well ladies and gentlemen I'd like to change the [begins quickly strumming his guitar] tempo a little." Upon completing his rhythm guitar improvisation, Lennon adds "OK, let's do the next song then." After Paul asks "Is he [Glyn Johns] tapin' them?," John replies "Yeah, we'll do *Dig A Pony* straight into *I've Got A Fever* [meaning *I've Got A Feeling*]."

Glyn Johns used the above dialog to lead into the album's next selections, *Dig A Pony* and *I've Got A Feeling*, which were recorded back-to-back later that day. The segment starts with George practicing riffs from the song and John saying "OK...You never changed drumming now. Yeah, that's OK. OK. Alright Glynis, we're off again." In the background Paul is practicing his bass and George is singing the first song's "All I want is you" introduction over matching guitar notes. After John's count-in, a deliberate three note false start and John's second count-in, the group launches into acceptable but somewhat ragged performances of both songs. At the end of the first tune, the "All I want is you" vocal line is followed by John singing "Yes I do" just before the band goes straight into *I've Got A Feeling*.

*Dig A Pony* (which was sometimes referred to as *All I Want Is You* during the sessions) was written by John, who later dismissed the song as a "piece of garbage." Shortly after performing *Don't Let Me Down* for George at the start of the initial Twickenham session of January 2, Lennon performed a runthrough of the song on electric guitar. This was essentially a solo performance, although George added some lead guitar towards the end. While John had yet to complete the chorus, many of the lyrics to the verses were in place.

The group returned to the song on January 7 with an uninspired rehearsal that ended abruptly when John lost interest and asked "Has anybody got a fast one?" A portion of this performance is shown in the movie. Although John played bits of the song on January 13, no serious attempt to develop the song was made until the sessions moved to Apple's basement studio.

The initial January 21 rehearsals of the song were marred by sloppy playing and John's inability to remember the lyrics. From this point forward, the song begins and ends with "All I want is you" background vocals, which Phil Spector mixed out of the performance chosen for the *Let It Be* album. Later rehearsals from the day showed progress as Paul experimented with his falsetto harmony and George worked out his guitar solo. This encouraged Lennon to have Glyn Johns record two takes of the song, which are flawed, but played with spirit. After listening to a playback of Take 1, the band returned to the song, but only managed a few false starts before moving on.

The Beatles continued rehearsing the song on January 22, with Glyn Johns recording some of the performances. *Anthology 3* contains one of the better takes. Other runthroughs from this part of the session have Lennon goofing around with his vocals and even singing one verse in a staccato style. John also spent time instructing Ringo on where he should emphasize his cymbals.

Shortly after Billy Preston was brought to Apple's basement studio for the first time, the Beatles showcased the song for him. After running through other songs, the band returned to *Dig A Pony* with Preston, whose electric piano added musical depth. Although, as detailed above, one of these January 22 performances was selected for inclusion on the *Get Back* album, the group was not satisfied with the recordings and returned to the song on January 28. Of the eight takes recorded by Glyn Johns that day, only two were complete. At the end of Take 8, John sings "I think the other one was much better, let's do *Get Back*."

The group ran through *Dig A Pony* as part of its January 29 rehearsal for the rooftop concert. John's vocals were laid back because he did not want to strain his vocal chords. The rooftop performance of the song was included in the film and selected by Phil Spector for the *Let It Be* album. To overcome his tendency to muff the words, John read the lyrics from a clipboard.

*I've Got A Feeling* is a merger of two songs started separately by John and Paul. John's contribution, *Everybody Had A Hard Year*, was written sometime towards the end of 1968. During a visit by Lennon to McCartney's Cavendish Avenue home, the pair realized that John's song had the same tempo as Paul's *I've Got A Feeling*. The two unfinished songs were linked together and completed by the duo as an equal collaboration. The final arrangement of the song features John and Paul singing their separate contributions over each other during the last verse

Prior to Paul's arrival at Twickenham Studios on January 2, John played his contribution to the song for George, who unsuccessfully attempted to add lead guitar lines over Lennon's strumming guitar. After singing a bit of the *Everybody Had A Hard Year* section, John kept the same rhythm and sang "Well I've got a feeling, deep inside." This unique performance has a folk song feeling reminiscent of Bob Dylan and shows how the song might have evolved had McCartney not been involved.

After Paul arrived at the session, he led the group through several runthroughs of the song, sometimes calling out the chords for John and George. He often stopped the song to explain the arrangement and at one point switched briefly to acoustic guitar to demonstrate some of the changes. He also spent time working with George on the descending guitar riff. Even during these early rehearsals, the vocal interplay between John and Paul was present.

The Beatles resumed rehearsals of the song on January 3 with a mixture of runthroughs and work on selected segments. On January 6 they managed only one complete pass at the song. Rehearsals continued in earnest the following day with emphasis on the vocals. Paul also spent time working with Ringo to perfect his drum part.

The group turned in a very respectable take of the song on January 8, highlighted by Paul's scorching vocal. The *Let It Be* film contains an edit of this performance, including McCartney's enthusiastic shout of "Good morning" after the middle eight, mixed with bits of the January 9 rehearsals of the song. During this later performance, John messes with the lyrics and sings "Everybody got a face-lift" and George uses his wah-wah pedal. The movie also shows Paul explaining to John and George that the descending guitar riff after the middle eight is coming down too fast and should have no recognizable jumps.

Paul began the morning session of January 10 on piano while waiting for the others to arrive. During this time he played a unique piano performance of *I've Got A Feeling*. He also played a few improvisations of the song and was later joined by the others for a more or less familiar arrangement. After George quit the group midway through the day's session, the remaining Beatles turned in a horrendous attempt of the song.

The Beatles returned to *I've Got A Feeling* during their first session at Apple's basement studio on January 21. The only known surviving take from the day has the descending guitar riff replaced by a series of vibrato notes and John shouting "Can you dig it?" towards the end of the song.

The first near complete take from January 22 is fairly solid, but breaks down shortly into the final verse. During later rehearsals the group experimented with a softer and country & western swing approach to the song to "get more feeling."

In the 80s, a clever bootlegger put together a fantasy promotional piece for the unreleased *Get Back* album. The contents came in a white envelope with green text proclaiming "The Beatles as nature intended." In addition to a simulated album cover and record containing Glyn Johns' original *Get Back* mix, the package included a folded 22" x 33" promotional poster (shown open on the previous page) and an Apple memorandum dated July 17, 1969. The poster features a picture taken at the same location as the cover, but the Beatles appear in different clothing. The memo is a reprint of the Mal Evans report on the album that ran in Issue No. 72 of *The Beatles Book* (July 1969).

The bottom row on this page shows the record's labels and the back cover. Each of the envelopes has a mailing label addressed to someone associated with the Beatles. Examples include Klaus Voormann (shown right), Billy Preston, Ethan Russell and Mary Hopkin. Although the package is authentic looking and has fooled many a fan, the bootlegger left an obvious clue as to its dubious origin. The cancelled stamps in the upper right corner of the mailing envelope are from various foreign countries such as Germany, Spain, Austria and Italy (detail upper right).

John sings "I had a dream" and "I had a dream this afternoon" several times during rehearsals for *I've Got A Feeling* and other songs performed that day. He and Paul also engage in a discussion about Martin Luther King, Jr., which at times includes their attempts to quote from his "I have a dream" speech (delivered at the Washington, D.C. mall during a civil rights demonstration held on August 28, 1963). John and Paul's sudden interest in King was brought about by the two having viewed on the previous evening an ITV program titled *Deep South*, which explored rare relations in Mississippi and contained references to King and parts of his most famous speeches.

After the late morning arrival of Billy Preston, the group worked through a couple of separate extended rehearsals of the song. Once again, time was spent trying to perfect the descending guitar riff following Paul's middle eight.

Glyn Johns selected one of the performances from the afternoon of January 22 for the *Get Back* album. Although this version is a spirited take, the song breaks down at the 2:40 mark (just before the final verse) when Lennon realizes he's playing too loud. As the music stops, John admits "I cocked it up tryin' to get loud." After Paul says "Yeah," John retorts with "Nothin' bad though." Johns included the above dialog on the *Get Back* album. This spirited but aborted take of the song was also selected for *Anthology 3*.

On the morning of January 23, the group jammed on riffs from *I've Got A Feeling*, but did not rehearse or perform the song. Towards the end of the day's session, the group briefly played the start of the song, the first eight seconds of which are on the March 10 acetate.

The group continued rehearsing and recording the song on January 27. One of these takes was mixed by Glyn Johns and included on the March 13 acetate. Shortly after the song begins, John's guitar begins to feed back through his amplifier, bringing the performance to an end. He quickly starts over, singing "I'm so ashamed, I goofed again." While this performance is somewhat ragged, the group's enthusiasm makes it an enjoyable listen.

More *I've Got A Feeling* rehearsals and runthroughs were held the following day. One of these performances was taken a slower pace and contained extra vocal interplay between John and Paul. After McCartney left the session to attend a meeting, John led the group through a couple of passes at the song, singing Paul's vocal part as well as his own. These versions make for interesting listening due to Lennon's different singing style and phrasing. Additional work was done on the song after Paul's return.

The Beatles, without Billy Preston, performed the song as part of their rooftop rehearsal on January 29. This version is somewhat laid back as neither John nor Paul wanted to strain his voice prior to the upcoming concert.

*I've Got A Feeling* was performed twice during the rooftop concert. The first take appears in the movie and on the *Let It Be* soundtrack LP.

Immediately prior to the start of the *Get Back* album's next song, Glyn Johns edited in the following segment involving Ringo: "Glyn [sound of Ringo hitting his tom-tom twice], what does that sound like?" This dialog took place after the January 27 "I'm so ashamed" take of *I've Got A Feeling* mixed by Johns for the March 13 acetate.

Side one closes with the album's title track, *Get Back*. While the LP version of *Don't Let Me Down* is completely different than the previously released single, the album version of *Get Back* is the same as the stereo single released in America. The recording history of the song is covered in the chapter on the single.

Side two of the album opens with the sound of rattling ice cubes in a glass, followed by George's "OK?" This leads into a false start of *For You Blue*. After John yells "Quiet please," the band turns in an excellent performance of the song. This recording (Take 7 from January 25, 1969) also served as the master for the song as it appears on the *Let It Be* album and the single pulled from the LP. The primary difference between the versions on the *Get Back* and *Let It Be* albums is that the later mix does not have any of the pre-song banter and false starts and features George's rerecorded vocal from January 8, 1970. Otherwise, Phil Spector's mix for the *Let It Be* LP is similar to Glyn Johns' original work on the song. Details regarding the recording of *For You Blue* are contained in the chapter on the single.

The album's next selection, *Teddy Boy*, was started by Paul during the Beatles stay in Rishikesh, India, in March, 1968, and finished later that year in Scotland and London. Although he played a brief bit of the song at Twickenham on January 9, the band was not formally introduced to the tune until January 24 when Paul sang and played a mostly solo performance on acoustic guitar. After a brief rehearsal during which he taught the chords to John and George, Paul led the band through a complete performance. In order to liven things up (and perhaps out of boredom), John throws in square dance calls midway through the song: "Take your partner, doesey-doe, hold her tight and don't let go, when you've got it, jump up...." Glyn Johns selected this take of the song for the *Get Back* album. In keeping with the original "warts and all" philosophy of project, he even left in a bit of feedback squeal. As the song comes to an end, Paul can be heard saying "So goes that one for further consideration."

*Teddy Boy* was given further consideration on January 28 and 29, with Paul leading the way on acoustic guitar and vocal. During the first of these performances, Paul vocalizes instrumental solos midway through and at the end of the song and breaks into laughter during one of the verses. Ringo provides steady drumming, but John's guitar is at times erratic. Lennon also supplies brief vocal contributions and can be heard talking in the background. The January 29th take is the worst of the lot, ruined by John's poor guitar playing.

Although *Teddy Boy* was slated to appear on the original *Get Back* album and was later mixed by Phil Spector during his work on the *Let It Be* LP, the song did not appear on a Beatles album until 1996's *Anthology 3*. The *Anthology* version is an edit of 1:15 from January 28 followed by 2:00 from January 24. Paul included the song on his first solo album, *McCartney*, which was released one month prior to the *Let It Be* album.

Two foreign picture sleeves for *All Together Now* used photos from the *Get Back* sessions. The Italian sleeve (Apple C006-04982) (left) has eight studio shots. The Spanish sleeve (Odeon J 006-04.982) (right) features a rooftop photo along with four studio pictures.

*Two Of Us*, which was originally titled *On Our Way Home*, was written by Paul for Linda. He introduced the song to the group on January 2, playing acoustic guitar, teaching the chords to John and George and vocalizing drum parts for Ringo. At this stage the song's lyrics were essentially complete, although the arrangement had not been finalized. The next day Paul continued with stop and start rehearsals, this time playing bass. John began singing with Paul during the verses. Although John and Glyn Johns suggested an acoustic arrangement, the band initially rejected this idea and played the song with electric guitars, probably to facilitate its inclusion in the planned TV concert.

The Beatles returned to *Two Of Us* on January 6, with Paul playing a galloping bass riff to open the song and to lead into the bridge. During these tedious rehearsals Paul and George got into a lengthy argument over how songs should be developed. Part of this discussion appears in the film (and is quoted earlier in this chapter).

The group turned in an entertaining up-tempo performance of the song on January 8 with John and Paul standing up and sharing a microphone. During the middle eight, Paul resorted to an Elvis impersonation, and John ended the song singing "We're goin' home" in a deep bass voice. An edited version of this performance appears in the film.

The following day, the Beatles continued with rehearsals of the song. The arrangement retained the galloping bass and guitar riff and added vocal harmonies by George on the bridge and part of the verses and chorus. On January 10, the band tried several different approaches to the middle eight, including a bossa nova beat, drumming patterned after Buddy Holly's *Peggy Sue* and a shuffle beat.

Although snippets of *Two Of Us* were performed on January 23, rehearsals of the song did not resume until January 24. The initial runthroughs were horrendous, with the group taking the song at too slow a pace. After John suggested they play the song with acoustic guitars, the lineup was revised to feature Paul on his Martin D-28 acoustic guitar, John on acoustic guitar, George on his Telecaster (playing a bass part on the top strings) and Ringo on drums. The first performance with acoustic guitars featured a solo John vocal on the first verse and, while a bit ragged, showed that the "unplugged" approach was the way to go.

As the group continued with a series of runthroughs, the song's familiar features began to emerge, including Paul's bending notes used to open the song and lead into the verses. Paul began singing solo on the middle eight. George worked out a bass pattern on his Telecaster and Ringo perfected his drum part. The new arrangement with John and Paul sharing vocals and acoustic guitars reminded McCartney of the Everly Brothers (Phil and Don), whose vocal harmony style influenced the Beatles. *Anthology 3* contains a charming performance in which Paul acknowledges the duo by saying "Take it Phil" just after completing the first middle eight. On later takes John began whistling over the song's ending. Paul also ended one of the performances by singing a bit of the "Maori finale" from *Hello Goodbye*. The Nagra tapes captured John jokingly offering a variant for the lyric "spending some one's hard-earned pay." Lennon's new line was "smoking someone's hard earned grass." Glyn Johns selected a January 24 take of the song (one without Lennon's whistling) for the *Get Back* album.

The following day the group continued with a series of *Two Of Us* rehearsals, once again concentrating on the middle eight, with John working out a harmony part to sing on its second line. The band also performed a few complete runthroughs of the song. Paul led the band through additional rehearsals and performances on January 28 and 29.

The final runthrough of the song on January 29, distinguished by goofy vocals from John and Paul, marked the end of the sessions leading up to the rooftop concert.

On January 31, the Beatles returned to the Apple basement studio for filming of their acoustic and piano songs. They recorded three performances of *Two Of Us*, designated Takes 10, 11 and 12. The first take came to a quick halt when the group realized they were playing too slow. After a brief pause, the band completed a mediocre performance that slowly plodded along with out-of-tune guitars. For Take 11, Paul and Ringo picked up the tempo. This made all the difference in the world, inspiring the group to give their best performance of the song. Although Glyn Johns passed over this version in favor of an inferior recording from January 24, Phil Spector wisely chose this upbeat performance, which appears in the movie, for the *Let It Be* album. Take 12, which is played at a slightly slower pace, is almost as good.

The song was later turned over to Mortimer, a trio of New York teenagers who were signed to Apple by Peter Asher. Their McCartney-produced recording of the song was scheduled for release as an Apple single in June, 1969, but was never issued.

On the *Get Back* album, *Two Of Us* is immediately followed by Paul saying "And so we leave the little town of London, England." This leads directly into another link track, *Maggie Mae* (spelled *Maggie May* in initial reports on the album published in *The Beatles Book*). The song, about a Liverpool prostitute, was recorded by the Vipers Skiffle Group in 1957. The British version of the tune is based upon an American minstrel song from 1856, *Darling Nellie Gray*, credited to Benjamin Russell Hanby.

Three short versions of *Maggie Mae* were captured on January 24 in between performances of *Two Of Us*. The song features the same lineup of John and Paul on acoustic guitars and vocals, George on his Telecaster and Ringo on drums. The first attempt at the song lasted about a minute, but the second fell apart after ten seconds. Glyn Johns recorded the third performance and included it on both versions of the *Get Back* LP. This 38 second track also appears on the *Let It Be* album.

The *Get Back* LP's next selection, *Dig It*, is more of a jam than a structured song. Although it started life as one of John's creations, the improvised participation by the band led to the song being credited to all four Beatles (in the same manner as the instrumental track *Flying* from *Magical Mystery Tour*).

The group's first pass at the song on January 24 was little more than John repeatedly singing "Can you dig it?" over some delta blues-style guitar. Paul later joined in on the vocals with the pair exchanging variations of "dig it" lines such as "I can dig it" and "everybody dig it." Lennon's guitar playing on the song is similar to his playing on a delightful runthrough of *Singing The Blues* performed just prior to his introducing *Dig It*.

After a couple of brief stabs at the song, the group turned in a four minute romp in which John expanded his rudimentary lyrics to include references to insurance and the

need for a guarantee. Paul added some levity to the song by pretending to be a remote location DJ with his announcement "Coming to you from the heart of Chicago's blues land, Blind Lame Lennon." His also sings "I think you're out of tune, boy" to John towards the end of the song.

The next take of the song lasted nearly five minutes and featured Billy Preston on organ. At the end of the performance, John announces "That was *Can You Dig It* by Georgie Wood. And now we'd like to do *Hark, The Angels Come*." Lennon's remark was used to link a different version of *Dig It* to *Let It Be* on both the *Get Back* and *Let It Be* albums.

On January 26, after running through several takes of *Let It Be*, John began improvising with a bossa nova-type riff that led into the chorus of Bob Dylan's *Like A Rolling Stone*. The band kept playing behind John as he began singing the words to *Twist And Shout* at the 1:44 mark. At about this time, Paul's daughter Heather was handed a microphone. Her wailing, which is reminiscent of Yoko's vocal style, continues on until the ten minute mark, often drowning out John on the Nagra tapes. At 3:17 into the jam, John sings "Well can you dig it?" and moves the performance into an extended version of *Dig It*. Just as the song begins to wind down after ten minutes, Paul begins singing his own "dig it" lyrical improvisations as a counterpoint to John's singing. At the 11:35 mark, John sings "Like a rolling stone" three times, followed by "Like the FBI, and the CIA, and the BBC, B.B. King, and Doris Day, Matt Busby, dig it...." Paul then dominates the vocals for a minute or so before the group moves into an instrumental jam leading to John and Paul improvising vocals to the end of the song. The entire performance runs just over fifteen minutes.

Lennon's calling out of names is reminiscent of a blues jam from January 9 (known as *Get Off!*) during which Paul and occasionally John tossed out a total of 46 names, including James Brown, Judy Garland, Wilson Pickett, Malcolm Evans, members of the Quarrymen (their first group), Dusty Springfield, Richard Nixon, David Frost, Betty Grable, Clark Kent (Superman's secret identity), Sean O'Mahony (publisher of *The Beatles Book*), Bill Harry (founder of the Liverpool pop newspaper *Mersey Beat*), Tony Sheridan and Winston Churchill. For *Dig It*, John limited his list to the Federal Bureau of Investigation, the Central Intelligence Agency, the British Broadcasting Corporation, blues guitarist B.B. King, American actress Doris Day and Matt Busby (manager of the Manchester United soccer team).

Glyn Johns placed a four-minute edit from the last five minutes of the January 26 performance of *Dig It* on the *Get Back* album. He then tagged on the end of the final January 24 take of the song, including John's *Hark, The Angels Come* announcement to lead into *Let It Be*. The film contains a 3:25 edit from this part of *Dig It*, and the *Let It Be* album uses 51 seconds of the Glen Johns edit.

The reason the January 26 version of *Dig It* sounds so different from the earlier performances is that the group was playing different instruments. For the later performance the lineup was the same as that used on *Let It Be*, which

GET BACK
THE BEATLES

STEREO

SOAL-269
(SOAL-1-269)
SIDE 1

1. ONE AFTER 909 (Lennon-McCartney) BMI 3:13
   ROCKER (Lennon-McCartney) BMI 0:37
   SAVE THE LAST DANCE FOR ME (Pomus-Shuman) BMI 1:26
2. DON'T LET ME DOWN (Lennon-McCartney) BMI 4:09
3. DIG A PONY (Lennon-McCartney) BMI 4:10
4. I'VE GOT A FEELING (Lennon-McCartney) BMI 2:55
5. GET BACK (Lennon-McCartney) BMI 3:22

Produced by George Martin
Engineered by Glyn Johns
Recorded in England

GET BACK
THE BEATLES

STEREO

SOAL-269
(SOAL-2-269)
SIDE 2

1. FOR YOU BLUE (Harrison) BMI 2:50
2. TEDDY BOY (Lennon-McCartney) BMI 3:43
3. TWO OF US ON OUR WAY HOME (Lennon-McCartney) BMI 3:32
   MAGGIE MAY (Public Domain) BMI 0:44
4. DIG IT (Lennon-McCartney-Harrison-Starr) BMI 4:29
5. LET IT BE (Lennon-McCartney) BMI 3:59
6. THE LONG AND WINDING ROAD (Lennon-McCartney) BMI 3:42
   GET BACK (Reprise) (Lennon-McCartney)  BMI 0:41

Produced by
George Martin
Engineered by
Glyn Johns

Recorded in
England

MFD. BY APPLE RECORDS, INC.

**Had Capitol released the *Get Back* album as originally planned, the record's labels may have looked like the above computer-generated labels.**

featured Paul on piano, John on the Fender Bass VI (played like a guitar for *Dig It*), George on his Telecaster, Ringo on drums and Billy Preston on organ.

The Beatles, without Paul, turned in a brief performance of the song on January 28. The following day John led the group through an up-tempo performance of the song, propelled by Ringo's steady drumming, that lasted for nearly seven minutes. While John sang his basic "dig it" lyrics, Paul provided a scat vocal in the background. About half way through the song John began singing out the titles to the Beatles songs recorded during the sessions. The final minute of the song is at a slower pace and is exclusively instrumental after John belts out a few German phrases.

On the *Get Back* album, the song *Let It Be* is preceded by a member of the film crew announcing "Take 27 [the sound of a clapperboard]...Take 27, sync to second clap [the sound of the second clap]" and Paul's mimicking "Sync to second clap, please." The following performance of *Let It Be* is the same recording later used for the single, Take 27A. This rendition was the second-to-last song recorded during the January 31 session. Because this take contains a few sour notes during George's guitar solo, Harrison overdubbed a new solo on April 30. The song, with George's improved solo, was mixed for stereo on May 28. This mix, which has Billy Preston's organ featured more prominently than on the single, was used on the *Get Back* LP. Details of the writing and recording of the song appear in the chapter on the single.

The album's last full-length song, *The Long And Winding Road*, is preceded by John asking "Are we supposed to giggle in the solo?" McCartney replies "Yeah." This bit of dialog actually occurred prior to Take 23 of *Let It Be* and is heard on *Anthology 3*.

Glyn Johns selected a January 26 take of *The Long And Winding Road* (mixed on March 10, 1969) for inclusion on the *Get Back* LP. For the *Let It Be* album, Phil Spector augmented this basic track with lush orchestration and a choir. The Spectorized version of the song was issued as an American single on May 11, 1970. The unaltered performance of the song made is legitimate debut on *Anthology 3*. Details regarding the writing and recording of the song appear in the chapter on the single.

The *Get Back* album ends with a track identified as *Get Back (reprise)*, which is a 41 second edit from an extended coda of the song recorded on January 28. A different portion of the coda (its first 35 seconds) was edited to the end of the version of the song selected for the single. The segment ending the album is highlighted by Paul's playful scat vocals and laughter. It was also placed at the end of the *Let It Be* film.

In *The Beatles: An Oral History*, Glyn Johns recalls his excitement in putting the album together. "I'm extremely proud of it. Always have been. Everybody thought the album was wonderful. I presented it to them in the same manner that I'd done the first idea, and it went down very well."

The above statement from Johns provides insight into how he compiled the record. His desire to follow his "first idea" of putting together an album containing lots of chat and humor influenced his selection of the tracks. Although Paul McCartney thought the January 22 recordings were "Only good for conversation (if anything)," Johns liked the humor and charm of these early performances. While his use of *Rocker* and *Save The Last Dance For Me* as a link track into *Don't Let Me Down* is effective, Johns carried the concept too far with his selection of the rough January 22 runthroughs of *Dig A Pony* and *I've Got A Feeling* over the superior January 30 rooftop performances of these songs. This is particularly unfortunate in the case of *I've Got A Feeling*, which breaks down towards the end. Thus, the performance selected for the *Get Back* album is missing

The *Get Back* album cover was to mimic the cover to the Beatles first album, *Please Please Me* (Parlophone mono PMC 1202; stereo PCS 3042) (shown left). Both feature an Angus McBean photograph of the group looking over the railing of the inside stairwell at EMI's headquarters at 20 Manchester Square, London. The cover shown above right, and on page 145, is computer generated.

the final verse in which Paul and John effectively trade lines from their separate contributions to the song. Johns' bias towards recordings from the first part of the sessions also caused him to select a plodding January 24 version of *Two Of Us* over the vastly superior upbeat performance from January 31 shown in the movie. While the *Get Back* album compiled by Glyn Johns is full of charm and contains some wonderful performances, it would have been better had Johns selected more of the polished recordings from the later part of the sessions.

Beginning with *Sgt. Pepper*, the Beatles began giving their fans extra value for their money by providing elaborate packaging. *Magical Mystery Tour* came with a 24-page color booklet, and *The White Album* continued the trend with a poster and a color portrait of each Beatle. The new album was to be a super deluxe package featuring a book consisting of Ethan Russell color photographs taken during the sessions and text by David Dalton and Jonathan Cott. While no one objected to Russell's excellent pictures, the writing was another story. EMI insisted that curse words be edited out, and the Beatles wanted the text to be less artsy and focus more on the group. Although the original *Get Back* album was eventually scrapped, the revised *Get Back* book was packaged with the initial pressings of the *Let It Be* LP in all major markets except the United States. Images of the Canadian album, along with the book, are shown on pages 242-243.

While the book was apparently conceived as part of the project from the start, the concept for the album's cover was not developed until the summer of 1969. Because *Get Back* was originally intended to be an album of the Beatles getting back to their rock 'n' roll roots, the front jacket would mimic the cover to the group's first album, *Please Please Me*. The Beatles, along with photographer Angus McBean,

gathered at EMI's headquarters, 20 Manchester Square, London, to reenact their pose from the first album. McBean reshot his earlier picture of the group looking over the building's inside stairwell railing (although the angle differed slightly). The text on the proposed cover was in the same style and colors as the first cover. John Lennon was particularly fond of this approach. Although the cover was ultimately deemed unsuitable for the *Let It Be* soundtrack LP, the reenacted picture was later used effectively on the jackets for *The Red Album* and *The Blue Album*.

For a variety of reasons, the *Get Back* album, as compiled by Glyn Johns, was not released. Initially, it was delayed to allow time for the design of its cover. Then more time was needed to complete the accompanying book. By the end of July, 1969, the decision had been made to push back the album's release to coincide with the planned television special, which was then scheduled for the end of the year. When the planned TV show was converted into a theatrical release, Johns was asked to modify the album to conform with the songs featured in the film. His revised album (see pages 181-184) was also never released.

While packaging and scheduling problems were initially responsible for delaying the album's release, its final fate was sealed by the group's disenchantment with the project and the realization that the "warts and all" approach did not present the band in its most favorable light. As discussed in the chapter on the *Let It Be* LP, John and George brought in Phil Spector to reproduce the album and give it a more polished sound. This, of course, was a complete reversal of the original concept of making an honest recording with no editing or overdubs. Apparently, the Beatles sensed that they had progressed too far to truly get back to their roots. The band's next recording session would yield their slickest production, *Abbey Road*.

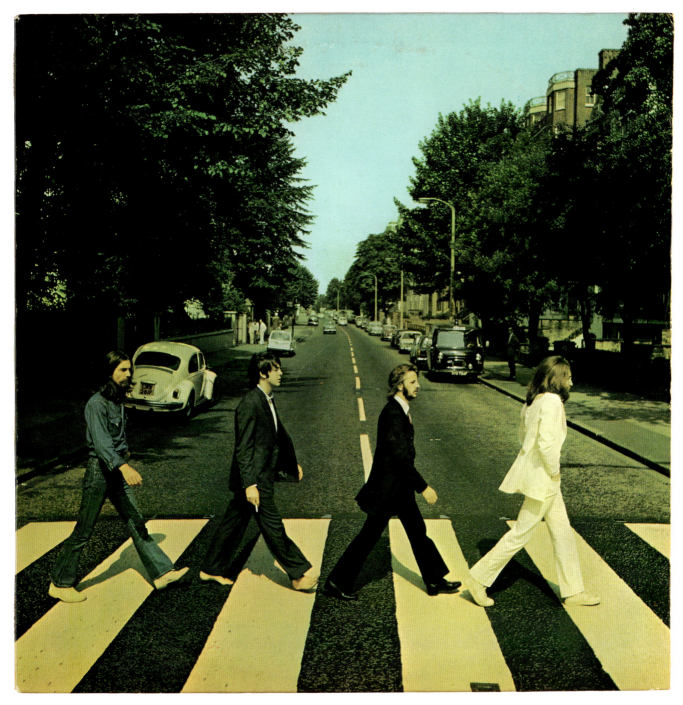

## ABBEY ROAD
## APPLE SO 383

Side 1
1. COME TOGETHER (Lennon-McCartney)
2. SOMETHING (George Harrison)
3. MAXWELL'S SILVER HAMMER
   (Lennon-McCartney)
4. OH! DARLING (Lennon-McCartney)
5. OCTOPUS'S GARDEN (Richard Starkey)
6. I WANT YOU (SHE'S SO HEAVY)
   (Lennon-McCartney)

Side 2
1. HERE COMES THE SUN (George Harrison)
2. BECAUSE (Lennon-McCartney)
3. YOU NEVER GIVE ME YOUR MONEY
   (Lennon-McCartney)
4. SUN KING (Lennon-McCartney)
5. MEAN MR. MUSTARD (Lennon-McCartney)
6. POLYTHENE PAM (Lennon-McCartney)
7. SHE CAME IN THROUGH THE BATHROOM
   WINDOW (Lennon-McCartney)
8. GOLDEN SLUMBERS (Lennon-McCartney)
9. CARRY THAT WEIGHT (Lennon-McCartney)
10. THE END (Lennon-McCartney)

Although *Abbey Road* was not the last album of new songs released by the Beatles, it was the last album recorded by the group. The record was issued in England by Parlophone as Apple PCS 7088 on September 26, 1969, and in America by Capitol as Apple SO-383 on October 1. The album was issued only in stereo.

*Abbey Road* entered the *Billboard Top LP's* chart at number 178 on October 25, 1969. The following week it jumped up to number four behind *Green River* by Creedence Clearwater Revival (Fantasy 8393), *Johnny Cash At San Quentin* (Columbia 9827) and the Rolling Stones' *Through The Past, Darkly (Big Hits Vol. 2)* (London NPS 3). The next week it reached the top on November 1 where it remained for eight straight weeks before being replaced for one week by *Led Zeppelin II* (Atlantic 8236). After returning to number one for two more weeks on January 3, 1970, the Beatles LP was once again displaced by *Led Zeppelin II* on January 17. The following week *Abbey Road* returned to the top for the last time on January 24. The next week it was once again behind *Led Zeppelin II* at number two, where it remained for five more weeks. All told, *Abbey Road* spent 129 weeks on the charts, including 11 weeks at number one, seven at number two and a total of 27 in the top ten. In addition, the album topped *Billboard's* 8-Track and Cassette charts. *Cash Box* and *Record World* also charted the album at number one for several weeks.

An unauthorized tape of the album began circulating among a limited number of American radio stations during the second week of September, 1969. This prompted Capitol to send copies of the album in a generic white cardboard jacket to 4,000 radio stations to level the playing field. The accompanying letter (shown right) requested that stations delay airplay until the record's scheduled release date of October 1, 1969.

*Abbey Road* was the first album issued under the terms of the group's new contract with Capitol Records. Due to the agreement's increased royalty rate and the appeal of the Beatles, Capitol distributed the album with a list price of $6.98 rather than the standard $5.98 list price for new releases. At that time, Capitol used the prefix "W" for single disc albums carrying a list price of $5.98. For example, *Yellow Submarine* was assigned number SW 153 (the "S" indicating a stereo disc). The "O" prefix signified a $6.98 list price. Thus, *Abbey Road* was given a "SO" prefix.

The one dollar price increase led to protests by some record stores, who accused Capitol of price gouging. Brown Meggs, Capitol's second-in-command who had spearheaded the Beatles Campaign back in late 1963 and early 1964, defended the action by describing the Beatles as a "high royalty act" and the "premier recording act in the world." Meggs called the album a "special case" and noted that Capitol was merely passing a cost increase on to the consumer. He explained that Capitol had to make money on its hits to enable the company to support new acts that often did not make back production costs.

Although consumers were not happy about the price increase, it had little, if any, impact on sales. The album was quickly certified gold by the RIAA (see award on

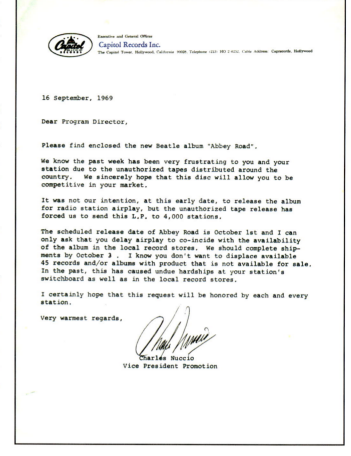

Capitol Records Inc.
Executive and General Offices
The Capitol Tower, Hollywood, California 90028, Telephone (213) HO 2-6252, Cable Address: Caprecords, Hollywood

16 September, 1969

Dear Program Director,

Please find enclosed the new Beatle album "Abbey Road".

We know the past week has been very frustrating to you and your station due to the unauthorized tapes distributed around the country. We sincerely hope that this disc will allow you to be competitive in your market.

It was not our intention, at this early date, to release the album for radio station airplay, but the unauthorized tape release has forced us to send this L.P. to 4,000 stations.

The scheduled release date of Abbey Road is October 1st and I can only ask that you delay airplay to co-incide with the availability of the album in the local record stores. We should complete shipments by October 3. I know you don't want to displace available 45 records and/or albums with product that is not available for sale. In the past, this has caused undue hardships at your station's switchboard as well as in the local record stores.

I certainly hope that this request will be honored by each and every station.

Very warmest regards,

Charles Nuccio
Vice President Promotion

page 99) and sold over three million copies in a little over a month. As of 2002, *Abbey Road* had certified sales in the U.S. of nine million units.

At the conclusion of the *Get Back* sessions on January 31, 1969, the Beatles were concerned that they did not have sufficient songs for a new album. But because Ringo was scheduled to begin filming *The Magic Christian* in February, the group could not continue recording. The return to the studio was also delayed by both Glyn Johns and Billy Preston being in America during the first part of February, and George Harrison being hospitalized from February 7 through 15 for tonsil surgery.

The Beatles first post *Get Back* session took place on Saturday, February 22. Ringo was available as he was not needed on the set of *The Magic Christian* that day. Two important elements from January were carried forward. During the recording of *Get Back*, Glyn Johns often acted as producer, even though he had been hired as a balance engineer. For this session, the Beatles made it official by naming Johns as producer. Apparently, George Martin was not invited. In addition, Billy Preston was brought back as a member of the recording band (although his career as the Beatles keyboard player would be short-lived). The Beatles recorded 35 takes of Lennon's *I Want You*, a song rehearsed during the *Get Back* sessions.

Because Apple Studios was going through a complete overhaul to recover from the Magic Alex phase, the group could not return to their basement studio. For reasons that are no longer remembered, the Beatles chose to record at Trident Studios rather than Abbey Road.

**Capitol ran an ad in the November 29, 1969, *Billboard* touting its new policy of issuing albums simultaneously in three formats. The upper portion of the ad (shown above) plugs *Abbey Road*. Capitol's multi-format distribution plan enabled the Beatles new album to explode to the top of the *Billboard* LP, 8-Track and Cassette charts. The December 6, 1969, *Billboard* showed *Abbey Road* at number one on its LP, 8-Track, Cassette and 4-Track charts.**

Perhaps the group felt awkward booking the EMI studio without George Martin's participation. Or maybe Paul's and George Harrison's use of Trident for non-Beatle Apple projects influenced the decision. Or maybe Abbey Road was not available. Whatever the reason, the first session for the album that would later be known as *Abbey Road* did not take place at the soon-to-be-immortalized studio.

The full group did not attend another recording session for nearly two months. On April 16, the Beatles got together again with George Martin at Abbey Road to work on two George Harrison compositions, *Old Brown Shoe* and *Something*. Subsequent April sessions were held at Abbey Road with Chris Thomas filling in for George Martin as producer. Additional recording took place in early May at Abbey Road with Chris Thomas and at Olympic Studios with George Martin and Glyn Johns. While most of the songs recorded during these sessions wound up on the *Abbey Road* album, the bulk of the sessions for the LP took place in July and August at Abbey Road.

In early 1969, it appeared that the relationship between George Martin and the Beatles was coming to an end. Martin's frustrations with the group began during the recording of *The White Album* and grew during the tension-filled *Get Back* sessions. He quickly became disenchanted with Lennon's no overdubs "play it till we get it right" recording philosophy. As for the Beatles, they seemed ready to make a change and go with Glyn Johns. Fortunately, the group had second thoughts about breaking up the successful combination. In an interview appearing in the July, 1987, issue of *Musician*, George Martin recalled:

"I never thought we would get back together again, and I was quite surprised when Paul rang me up and asked me to produce another record for them. I said, 'If I'm really allowed to produce it, I will. If I have to go back and accept a lot of instructions I don't like, I won't do it.' But Paul said they wanted me to produce it as I used to, and once we got back to the studio it really was nice."

While the atmosphere in the studio was much more relaxed than it had been earlier in the year, the *Abbey Road* sessions were not quite a return to the good old days. As had been the case with *The White Album*, many of the sessions took place with less than all four Beatles present. There were also times when George Martin found himself dashing between the three studios in the building as members of the group concurrently worked on different songs. For example, Paul and Ringo would be in one studio while John was in another. A few of the backing tracks were recorded without John's participation. There were also days when Paul would arrive before the others and record alone.

John was absent during the first week of July due to a car crash in which he, Yoko, Yoko's daughter Kyoko and his son Julian sustained injuries. When John arrived at Abbey Road on July 9, there was a new twist. Yoko, who was pregnant, had been ordered by her doctor to remain in bed until she recovered. Rather than be separated from Yoko, John had a double bed brought into the studio so Yoko could be by his side as he worked on the album. John had a microphone set up over Yoko's bed in case she wanted to participate, and when John roamed between studios, the bed was wheeled into the room where John was recording. Although John and Yoko and "The Bed" made for some interesting stories, the other Beatles and the studio crew, ever weary of offending John, kept quiet, worked around the distraction and carried on as if everything was normal.

In contrast to the no-overdubs policy of the January sessions, the Beatles made full use of the studio and spent considerable time embellishing the tracks. Under George Martin's supervision, the Beatles produced their most polished effort–an album that is the complete opposite of the "warts and all" *Get Back* album compiled by Glyn Johns. According to Martin:

"*Abbey Road* was kind of *Sgt. Pepper Mark II*–the last thing we ever did–and Paul went along with the idea, but John didn't. So it became a compromise, with one side of the album very much the way John wanted things–'Let it all hang out, let's rock a little'–and the other being what Paul had accepted from me: to try to think in symphonic terms, and think in terms of having a first and second subject, put them in different keys, bring back themes and even have contrapuntal work. Paul dug that, and that's why the second side sounds as it does."

Although *Abbey Road* contains some great individual songs such as John's *Come Together* and George's *Something* and *Here Comes The Sun*, the album's most striking characteristic is the eight-song medley that dominates side two. The stand-alone songs and the components of the medley are discussed in the order they appear on the album, followed by a discussion on the construction of the medley.

The album's first two tracks, *Come Together* and *Something*, were released as a single on October 6, 1969. The history of the writing and recording of these songs is covered in the chapter on the 45.

*Maxwell's Silver Hammer*, like *Ob-La-Di, Ob-La-Da*, is a song that Paul wanted released as a single. According to John, Paul "did everything to make it into a single." The numerous takes and overdubs on the track prompted Lennon to state that the group "spent more money on that song than any of them in the album." The final master is a slick, clever and catchy tune that many fans love and others abhor.

The upbeat vaudeville arrangement and cheery vocals belie the horrendous murders committed by the song's protagonist with his silver hammer. The lyrics are not intended to glorify a killer, but rather serve as a metaphor for when something goes wrong out of the blue, an instant karma experience. McCartney's explanation is "Just when everything is going smoothly, 'bang bang' down comes Maxwell's silver hammer and ruins everything." The line about Joan studying "pataphysical science" refers to "pataphysics," a term coined by avante-garde French playwright Alfred Jarry to describe a branch of metaphysics.

Paul began working on *Maxwell's Silver Hammer* in October, 1968, but held the song over as sessions for *The White Album* were coming to an end. He introduced the tune to the band during the *Get Back* sessions on January 3, 1969, leading the group through several stop-and-start rehearsals of the song he dubbed "the corny one." During the initial runthroughs, Paul played bass. The *Let It Be* film contains a segment with McCartney calling out the chords for John and George. Paul later followed Harrison's suggestion and switched to piano, leaving George to handle the bass on the Fender Bass VI. At this stage Paul had only written one and a half verses and the chorus.

The Beatles returned to *Maxwell's Silver Hammer* on January 7, working on the song's structure and adding new elements such as whistling to open and close the song and to fill instrumental breaks. George worked out a vocal harmony to accompany Paul on the chorus, and Mal Evans was given the task of striking a hammer on an anvil at appropriate times. Portions of these rehearsals appear in the film. The group continued fine-tuning the song the next day, with John joining Paul and George on the chorus, and Mal Evans perfecting his hammer part.

A few pitiful runthroughs of the song took place on January 10 after George quit the group. Paul played bass and sang as if he were drunk. The Beatles did not perform the tune during the Apple basement sessions.

The first proper recording of *Maxwell's Silver Hammer* took place at Abbey Road on July 9. The backing track of Paul on piano and guide vocal, George on Fender Bass VI and Ringo on drums was recorded in 16 takes, with the final take (designated 21 as there were no Takes 6 to 10) being selected as the best. *Anthology 3* contains Take 5, with Paul vocalizing the instrumental passages and singing nonsense syllables for the first few lines of the third verse. Towards the end of the day's session, two guitar parts (most likely John on his Gibson J-160E Jumbo acoustic guitar and George on his Telecaster) were overdubbed onto Take 21. Additional overdubs were made the following day, including Paul on piano, George Martin on Hammond organ, Harrison on Telecaster through a Leslie speaker, Ringo on hammer and anvil, Paul's lead vocal and backing vocals by Paul, George and Ringo. The next day Paul added an additional vocal and George overdubbed another Telecaster part. At this stage, the song contained a seven second instrumental introduction.

On August 6, Paul added five Moog synthesizer parts during tape reductions designated Takes 22 through 27. Stereo mixes were made that day and on August 12. On August 14, a stereo mix was made on an edit piece, which was then edited into Remix 34. The song's instrumental introduction was edited off the master tape on August 25, leaving Paul's vocal to start the song.

Paul's *Oh! Darling* also made its debut during the *Get Back* sessions. The song is a graceful piano-driven R&B number with influences from Fats Domino and Little Richard. Although McCartney played a bit of the tune on piano during his January 3 and 6 warm-ups, the band did not attempt the song until January 7. The two runthroughs from the day have Paul on piano, John on electric guitar, George on the Fender Bass VI and Ringo on drums. McCartney, joined by John and Ringo, played a bit of the song the next day during an equipment change. He also worked the tune into his morning piano warm-up on January 9. Paul did a complete solo performance of song towards the end of the Twickenham sessions on January 14. This version, which makes use of a Binson echo unit, has McCartney delivering an Elvis-styled rendition, complete with sneering vocal asides and a spoken passage during the bridge. A brief segment of Paul singing the introduction of the song from an early Twickenham session appears in the *Let It Be* film.

When the Beatles returned to *Oh! Darling* on January 23, Billy Preston had joined the sessions. The group played the song twice, with Paul on bass, John and George on electric guitars, Ringo on drums and Preston on electric piano. The same lineup did a 6½-minute extended performance on January 27, featuring Paul and John on vocals. When the song appears to have ended, John announces that he's just heard that Yoko's divorce has gone through and states "Free at last." As John sings "I'm free...this morning, Baby told the lawyer it's OK, " the band falls back into the song. *Anthology 3* contains a 4:07 edit of this performance.

During the final *Get Back* session of January 31, Paul led the band through two runthroughs of *Oh! Darling* between takes of *Let It Be*. These performances featured Paul on piano, John on Fender Bass VI, George on Telecaster, Ringo on drums and Billy Preston on Hammond organ. John joined Paul on the vocals during parts of the song.

The first serious attempt to record *Oh! Darling* took place at Abbey Road on April 20 with Chris Thomas serving as producer. The studio Recording Sheet listed the song as "*Oh! Darling (I'll Never Do You No Harm)*." The backing track was recorded in 26 takes, with Paul providing a guide vocal over his Rickenbacker bass, John's piano, George's Telecaster through a Leslie speaker and Ringo on drums. Although a Hammond organ part was superimposed onto Take 26, this was later taped over. On April 26, Paul overdubbed a lead vocal, which was also subsequently recorded over. Stereo mixes were made on May 1.

No additional work was done on the song until mid-July, when Paul rerecorded his lead vocal. This was done at four separate sessions during which Paul recorded only one take. The first attempt took place on July 17, with Paul singing over Take 16. On July 18, 22 and 23, Paul recorded his lead vocal over Take 26. McCartney was satisfied with his July 23 performance, which appears on the finished master. On August 8, Paul overdubbed lead guitar and tambourine. Paul, John and George added vocal harmonies on August 11. The song was mixed for stereo the following day, with Remix 9 from Take 26 selected for the album.

*Octopus's Garden* is Ringo's second solo composition on a Beatles album. Ringo got the idea for the song during his late August, 1968, "vacation" from the group, when he traveled to Sardinia. While on Peter Sellers' yacht, Ringo was told that octopus go round the ocean bed, pick up stones and shiny things and build gardens in front of their caves. The beauty of these images and his desire to get away from the pressures of the Beatles ("I just wanted to be under the sea, too") inspired him to write the song.

The *Let It Be* film contains a charming segment from January 26, with Ringo introducing *Octopus's Garden*, which was far from complete, to George. (Ringo had briefly played the tune three days earlier prior to the arrival of George and Paul.) Harrison, standing with his acoustic guitar, strums and sings along. Ringo, who is also standing, plays some basic chords on piano. As the song moves forward, George stops and reaches down to the piano to show Ringo some new chord changes. When George Martin arrives, Harrison flashes a grin and suggests that he and Ringo

take it from the top. The rehearsal continues, and when John arrives, he moves over to the empty drum kit to fill in for Ringo, who is still on piano. The segment not only shows Harrison's uncredited contributions to the song, but also his genuine eagerness to help Ringo with his song writing.

The actual recording of *Octopus's Garden* took place at Abbey Road on April 26 during a session produced by Chris Thomas (although the recording sheet identifies the producer as "Beatles"). The group went through 32 takes with Ringo on drums and guide vocal, George on his Stratocaster through the Leslie, John on his Epiphone Casino and Paul on his Rickenbacker bass. *Anthology 3* contains Take 2, which demonstrates that the band had the arrangement worked out from the start.

Overdubs were added to Take 32 nearly three months later on July 17 and 18. These included Ringo's lead vocal with artificial double tracking, Paul's piano, additional drums and backing vocals from Paul, George and Ringo. The instrumental break with George's guitar solo was augmented with special effects, including Ringo blowing through a straw into a glass of water for bubbling sounds and Paul and George singing at a high pitch through a Leslie speaker. At the end of the July 18 session, the song was mixed for stereo. With its underwater fantasy theme and special effects, the finished master is reminiscent of *Yellow Submarine*, which was also sung by Ringo.

John's *I Want You (She's So Heavy)* is another song that dates back to the *Get Back* sessions. John introduced the *I Want You* part of the song to the group on January 28, 1969. An early runthrough of the song opens with John matching his "I want you" vocal with his distorted guitar. This funky bluesy version of the song prominently features Billy Preston on piano and response vocals and is nearly five and a half minutes long. When the group returned to the song later that day, Billy Preston shifted to organ and no longer provided vocals. John alternated between "I want you" and "I need you" verses and someone (possibly George) added a shaker. The next take featured John and George jamming on guitar. The following day, the Beatles ran through a mainly instrumental jam of the song. John played the distorted riff on his guitar and briefly sang an off-mike guide vocal. Billy Preston added keyboards and some improvised "I had a dream" vocals.

During the rooftop concert, John briefly played the song's riff. The following day, between recording Paul's ballads, the group, with John and George on guitars, Paul and Billy Preston on keyboards and Ringo on drums, returned to the song with Paul occasionally providing vocals.

The group's first proper recording of *I Want You* took place on February 22, 1969, during what would be the first session for the *Abbey Road* album. Ironically the session took place not at EMI's Abbey Road studios, but rather at Trident. With Glyn Johns serving as producer, the group, along with Billy Preston on keyboards, recorded 35 takes of the song. John sang lead on all but one take, which was sung by Paul. The next day a master was formed by editing the first part of Take 9 with the middle eight from Take 20 and the remainder from Take 32.

On April 18, at Abbey Road with Chris Thomas serving as producer, John (on his Casino) and George (on his Les Paul) overdubbed several guitar parts onto the edited master. After a reduction mix down (designated Take 1), John and George added more guitar. According to engineer Jeff Jarratt, "They wanted a massive sound so they kept tracking and tracking, over and over." Hammond organ and conga drums were overdubbed two days later.

John returned to the song on August 8 at Abbey Road with George Martin producing. Going back to the Trident master of February 23, John overdubbed sounds from the white noise generator of Harrison's Moog synthesizer, and Ringo added drums (primarily crash cymbals).

On August 11, John, Paul and George recorded their harmony vocals onto Take 1 from April 18. The vocals included the trio singing "she's so heavy" over and over again. It was at this session that the song received its full title of *I Want You (She's So Heavy)*. When John could not decide whether he preferred the August 8 version of the Trident master or the recently completed master, he had the "she's so heavy" vocals copied from the new master onto the August 8 version of the Trident master.

The song was finally completed on August 20, when both masters were remixed and then edited together. The opening 4:36 is from Take 1 (with the multi-tracked guitars from April 18 and the "she's so heavy" vocals from August 11) and the remainder of the track is from the Trident master (with the white noise and crash cymbals from August 8). The edited master originally ran over eight minutes, but John opted for a sudden surprise ending at 7:44. According to engineer Alan Parsons, "We were putting the final touches to that side of the LP and we were listening to the mix. John said 'There! Cut the tape.' Geoff [Emerick] cut the tape and that was it. End of side one!"

*I Want You (She's So Heavy)* is one of the most interesting and complex songs in the Beatles catalog. It was recorded at two studios (Trident and Abbey Road) under the supervision of three producers (Glyn Johns, Chris Thomas and George Martin) and at least six engineers (Barry Sheffield, Jeff Jarratt, John Kurlander, Tony Clark, Alan Parsons and Phil McDonald). At 7:44, it is the longest released song by the group (*Revolution 9* not really being a "song"). And while its lyrics are brief and simple, John sings the words with great passion, sometimes matching the scorching intensity heard on *Twist And Shout*. The song is also one of the group's noisiest tracks, with its tape hiss during the early stages of the song, distorted guitars throughout and white noise and crashing cymbals during the song's climatic ending. The first part of the song features a bluesy instrumental backing with changing rhythms. This is in sharp contrast to the last 3:07 of the track, which repeats the same riff over and over again, building with a sound conjuring images of powerful waves crashing with growing strength onto a rocky shoreline. Just when the listener thinks the song will never end, it stops with a harsh and jarring suddenness.

On vinyl, the abrupt end to side one of *Abbey Road* is as effective as the completely opposite long sustained chord that ends *A Day In The Life* on *Sgt. Pepper*. Unfortunately, the effect of the ending is lost on the CD, which has the bright acoustic guitar opening notes of *Here Comes The Sun* following a mere two to three seconds later.

The second side of *Abbey Road* opens with George's *Here Comes The Sun*, which is universally recognized as one of the album's highlights. In his book *I Me Mine*, Harrison states that he wrote the song "at the time when Apple was getting like school, where we had to go and be business men." It was spring of 1969, and the long English winter had finally ended. One bright morning George decided to play hooky from Apple and went to visit Eric Clapton at his house in the countryside. Inspired by the liberation from winter ("by the time spring comes you really deserve it"), as well as his escaping from Apple ("The relief of not having to go see all those dopey accountants was wonderful"), George wrote the upbeat song "while walking around the garden with one of Eric's acoustic guitars." The lyrics were finished during a June, 1969, vacation in Sardinia.

The backing track to *Here Comes The Sun* was recorded in 13 takes on July 7 with George on his Gibson J-200 acoustic guitar (played with a capo on the seventh fret) and guide vocal, Paul on his Rickenbacker bass and Ringo on drums. Harrison then rerecorded and added acoustic guitar onto Take 13. The following day George recorded his lead vocal. Backing vocal harmonies by George and Paul were double-tracked with the pair singing twice rather than relying on artificial double tracking. At the end of the session, Take 13 was given two tape reduction mixes to free up additional tracks. The second, designated Take 15, was superior and became the basis for the finished master.

On July 16, hand claps (George, Paul and Ringo) and harmonium were superimposed onto Take 15. Harrison added acoustic guitar parts on August 6 and 11. George Matin's orchestral score, consisting of four violas, four cellos, one string bass, two clarinets, two alto flutes, two flutes and two piccolos, was recorded on August 15. Harrison completed the track on August 19 by adding a few Moog synthesizer overdubs. The song was then mixed for stereo.

Harrison's upbeat track is followed by the dreamy three-part harmonies of *Because*, which Lennon based upon Beethoven's *Moonlight* Sonata. According to John, Yoko was playing the sonata on piano, and he asked her if she could play the chords backwards. He then wrote *Because* around them.

The Beatles began work on *Because* on August 1. The group recorded 23 takes with George Martin on a Baldwin spinet electric harpsichord matching notes with John on his Casino. Paul added bass on his Rickenbacker and Ringo kept the beat with his hi-hat (although this was only to guide the musicians and was not taped). John, Paul and George then added their three-part harmony onto Take 16, which was deemed the best backing track. On August 4, the three recorded their vocals two more times, thus providing a nine-part harmony for the song. Harrison added two Moog synthesizer parts on August 5. The song was mixed for stereo on August 12. *Anthology 3* contains a special remix that isolates the thrice-recorded three-part harmony vocals of John, Paul and George.

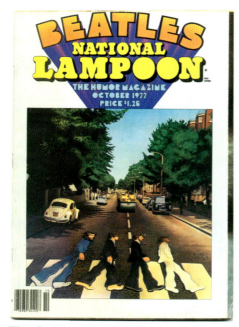

**The October, 1977, *National Lampoon* (left) satirized the *Abbey Road* cover by showing the Beatles run over by a steamroller. The October, 2000, *Mojo* (right) shows a double-decker bus bearing down on the group.**

The *Abbey Road* medley begins with Paul's *You Never Give Me Your Money*, a song consisting of three segments of its own. In Miles' *Many Years From Now*, Paul states that the first part of the song was him "directly lambasting Allen Klein's attitude to us: no money, just funny paper, all promises and it never works out. It's basically a song about no faith in the person." Next up is a nostalgic bit about being out of college with money spent, which leads into an optimistic escape ("Soon we'll be away from here. Step on the gas and wipe that tear away.") inspired by Paul and Linda's hitting the road to get away from it all.

The backing track of *You Never Give Me Your Money* was recorded on May 6, with Paul providing a guide vocal and piano, John playing a distorted guitar part on his Casino, George on his Telecaster through the Leslie and Ringo on drums. The Beatles ran through 36 takes, with Take 30 designated as the best. Several of the takes ended with an extended jam, with at least one take lasting over five and a half minutes.

Paul recorded his lead vocal on July 1 and added bass on July 11. Additional overdubs to Take 30 were made on July 15, including backing vocals from Paul, John and George, as well as chimes for the end of the song. It was during this session that the song's nursery rhyme ending ("One, two, three, four, five, six, seven. All good children go to heaven.") was recorded. Although the song was given a reduction mix and more vocals on July 30, Paul decided against using these embellishments. The following day he superimposed piano and bass to Take 30.

On August 5, Paul mixed a series of tape loop sound effects, including tubular bells, birds, chirping crickets and bubbles, onto a four-track tape for use during the crossfade of *You Never Give Me Your Money* into the medley's next selection, *Sun King/Mean Mr. Mustard*. Take 5 of the sound effects was incorporated into the stereo remix and crossfade of the tracks on August 14. Although 11 remixes were made, it was later decided that mix could be improved. Remix 12, which appears on album, was made on August 21.

According to John, *Sun King* came to him in a dream (most likely after reading Nancy Mitford's biography on France's Louis XIV, the Sun King). The song's chord progression is similar to that of the dreamy-sounding Fleetwood Mac instrumental *Albatross* (which was released as a single in late 1968 and topped the British charts in early 1969). Although *Sun King* was not properly recorded during the *Get Back* sessions, John did play bits of the song on January 2, 3 and 10. The song's brief opening lyrics consist of little more than "Here comes the Sun King" and the sentiment that everybody's laughing and happy. The song concludes with a nonsensical string of foreign and foreign-sounding words and phrases such as "Mundo paparazzi mi amore" and "tanta mucho que can eat it carousel."

*Mean Mr. Mustard* was started by John during his visit to Rishikesh in 1968. It was reportedly inspired by an article John read about a man who stored money up his rear end. John cleaned this up with the line "Keeps a ten bob note up his nose." Although Lennon's composition was part of the May, 1968, rehearsals held at Harrison's Esher home, the song was not recorded during the *White Album* sessions. The Esher demo, which appears on *Anthology 3*, contains a double-tracked Lennon vocal. Both verses were complete, although Mr. Mustard's sister was named Shirley. When the song was recorded for *Abbey Road*, John changed her name to Pam to serve as a link to *Polythene Pam*.

*Mean Mr. Mustard* was played a few times during the *Get Back* sessions. The most complete performance took place on January 8, with John on piano, George on guitar and Ringo on drums. The song was also performed on January 14, 23 and 25.

During the *Abbey Road* sessions, *Sun King* and *Mean Mr. Mustard* were recorded as a single selection in 35 takes on July 24 under the working title *Here Comes The Sun-King*. The backing track consisted of John on his Casino and guide vocal, George on his Telecaster through the Leslie, Paul on Fender Jazz Bass and Ringo on drums.

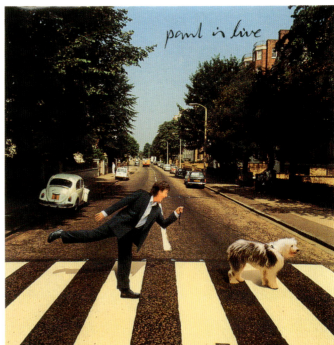

The *Abbey Road* cover has been imitated many times, including *McLemore Ave.* by Booker T & the M.G.'s (Stax 2027) (left). The LP contains R&B instrumentals of many of the songs from *Abbey Road*. McCartney and his sheepdog were digitally inserted into the famous Abbey Road crosswalk for his 1993 *Paul Is Live* album (Capitol 27704) (above).

The following day Lennon recorded his lead vocal and backing vocals along with McCartney and Harrison. George Martin added organ to *Sun King* and John overdubbed piano on *Mean Mr. Mustard*. Bongos, maracas and tambourine were also superimposed onto Take 35. As noted above, the track was mixed for stereo on August 14 and 21 as part of a crossfade with *You Never Give Me Your Money*.

The medley's next component combines John's *Polythene Pam* with Paul's *She Came In Through The Bathroom Window*. The name of the character in John's song is a slight modification of the nick name of a young Beatles fan, Pat Hodgett, who began seeing the group in the early sixties. The girl was called Polythene Pat because she had a habit of eating polythene. The weird wardrobe was inspired by an August 8, 1963, encounter with a woman introduced to Lennon by Royston Ellis, a British beat poet. In his *Playboy* interview, John stated that Ellis told him that his girlfriend Stephanie "dressed up in polythene, which she did. She didn't wear jackboots and kilts, I just sort of elaborated. Perverted sex in a polythene bag. Just looking for something to write about."

*Polythene Pam* was written in Rishikesh. As with *Mean Mr. Mustard*, the song was rehearsed at George's Esher home, but was not recorded during the *White Album* sessions, most likely because John never wrote more than two verses. The demo, which runs only 1:23, was later included on *Anthology 3*. It features John on acoustic guitar and vocals, aided and abetted by Paul, as does an impromptu performance from the January 24 *Get Back* session.

Paul's *She Came In Through The Bathroom Window* was inspired by a break-in to McCartney's house in St. Johns

Wood by a group of Apple Scruffs (female fans who constantly hung around waiting for the Beatles by their studios, Apple headquarters and sometimes their homes). Diane Ashley used a ladder found in Paul's garden to climb into an open bathroom window on the second floor of his home. The line "Tuesday's on the phone to me" refers to Paul receiving a call from a neighbor about the incident. At the end of a rehearsal of the song on January 9, Paul reenacts the phone call. "Hello, this is Tuesday speaking. Is that Paul? I'd like to have a word with you." John continues with "I've got something of interest in the garden."

Although the song may have been started as early as May, 1968, Paul was still working on the lyrics when he and Linda spent two weeks in New York after completion of *The White Album* in mid-October, 1968. During the cab ride to Kennedy Airport to head back to London at the end of the month, Paul noticed the driver identification panel displayed in the cab. The driver's photo and name, Eugene Quits, appeared above the phrase "New York Police Dept." McCartney had his guitar with him and came up with the line "And so I quit the police department and got myself a steady job."

Paul introduced *She Came In Through The Bathroom Window* to the group at Twickenham on January 6, 1969, with a series of runthroughs during which he taught John and George the chords. The group further rehearsed the song on January 7, 8 and 9 with the lineup of Paul on bass, John on piano, George on his Telecaster through the Leslie and Ringo on drums. During rehearsals on January 9, the band turned in a few humorous performances. After a German count-in, John sings the song with a thick Cockney accent,

Joe Cocker's version of *She Came In Through The Bathroom Window* was released as a single (A&M 1147) in late 1969. The 45 spent 12 weeks on the charts, peaking at number 30 on February 7, 1970. Apple recording artist Trash released its version of *Golden Slumbers/Carry That Weight* on October 15, 1969 (Apple 1811). Longtime Beatles engineer Norman Smith went on to produce and record a few discs under the name Hurricane Smith. His hit single, *Oh Babe, What Would You Say* (Capitol 3383) was released in late 1972, peaking at number three on February 17, 1973, during its 15 weeks in the *Billboard Hot 100*.

and Paul provides off-the-cuff responses. During a later performance, the vocal shenanigans continue with the following exchange:

Paul: And so I quit the police department.
John: Get a job, cop!
Paul: And got myself a proper job.
John: Bloody 'bout time too, if you ask me.
Paul: And though she tried her best to help me.
John: You bloody need it, too.
Paul: She could steal, but she could not rob.

*She Came In Through The Bathroom Window* was rehearsed during the Beatles initial Apple basement session on January 21. *Anthology 3* contains one of these performances, followed by Paul favorably discussing John's classical-sounding piano part. Although the group further rehearsed the song on January 29, these performances were not taped on the eight-track recorder.

To facilitate the intended medley concept, *Polythene Pam* and *She Came In Through The Bathroom Window* were recorded as a single track on July 25. The band recorded 39 takes with John on 12-string acoustic guitar, Paul on his Rickenbacker bass, George on his Les Paul guitar and Ringo on drums. Lennon and McCartney provided guide vocals for their separate songs. Although Take 39 was deemed the best, Ringo redid his drum part and Paul rerecorded his bass. Proper lead vocals were also recorded.

On July 28, Take 39 was embellished with additional vocals, acoustic guitar, electric guitar, piano, electric piano, tambourine, maracas and cowbell. A reduction mix, designated Take 40, was made at the end of the session to allow for additional overdubs. These were made on July 30 and included vocals, guitar and percussion. The track was mixed for stereo on August 14.

The medley continues with two of Paul's songs, *Golden Slumbers* and *Carry That Weight*, which were also recorded as a single selection. The first song was derived from the lullaby *Golden Slumbers*, which was written by Thomas

Dekker and first published in 1603. While visiting his father in 1968, Paul came across the tune in a songbook owned by his stepsister Ruth. The lyrics to Dekker's lullaby are:

Golden slumbers kiss your eyes;
Smiles awake you when you rise.
Sleep pretty wantons do not cry,
And I will sing a lullaby.
Rock them, rock them, lullaby.

Because Paul was unable to read the music, he created his own melody. He also changed a few of the words and added some of his own lyrics.

*Carry That Weight* is another of Paul's songs dealing with his growing dissatisfaction with Apple under Allen Klein. In Miles' *Many Years From Now*, Paul talked about things "getting crazier and crazier and crazier. Carry that weight a long time: like forever!" McCartney stated that the song was about the bad atmosphere at Apple, a "serious, paranoid heaviness" that was "very uncomfortable."

Paul introduced *Carry That Weight* to the *Get Back* sessions on January 6. He performed piano renditions of the *Golden Slumbers/Carry That Weight* medley on the mornings of January 7 and 9. Ringo sang with Paul on the chorus of *Carry That Weight* during the January 9 runthrough.

The rhythm track to *Golden Slumbers/Carry That Weight* was recorded in 15 takes on July 2, with Paul on piano and guide vocal, George on Fender Bass VI and Ringo on drums. During *Carry That Weight*, Paul reprises the opening to *You Never Give Me Your Money*, but with different lyrics. The next day, Takes 13 and 15 were edited to form the backing track for the master. The following overdubs were then added: a McCartney lead vocal; Harrison's Telecaster through the Leslie; rhythm guitar by Paul; a second McCartney lead vocal; and the *Carry That Weight* chorus sung by Paul, George and Ringo. Because these embellishments used up the remaining empty tracks, two reduction mixes were made at the end of the session, with Take 17 being the best.

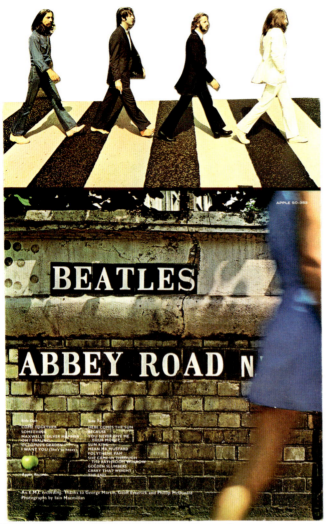

**Capitol prepared a 12" x 19" cardboard counter display combining the back cover with die cut figures of the Beatles from the front cover.**

An overdub was added during a brief session held on July 4. Overdubs made on July 31 included a vocal from Paul, drums by Ringo and timpani part (played by either Ringo or Paul). George Martin's score of 12 violins, four violas, four cellos, one string bass, four horns, three trumpets, one trombone and one bass trombone was added on August 15. The song was mixed for stereo on August 18.

The medley concludes, appropriately enough, with a song titled *The End*. Following Shakespeare's practice of placing a rhyming couplet at the end of a scene, Paul came up with "And in the end, the love you take is equal to the love you make." A fitting conclusion of which the Bard himself would be proud.

Recording of *The End* (under the working title *Ending*) began on July 23 with a backing track of John on his Casino, Paul on Rickenbacker bass and Ringo on drums. The group went through seven takes before selecting Take 7 as the best. This recording features Ringo's drumming more prominently than any other Beatles song. For the first time, Ringo was given a solo. In contrast to the long and often tedious drum solos of the late sixties, Ringo provided an effective solo lasting just over 15 seconds. In addition, his drums were recorded onto two separate tracks, thus allowing for different parts of his drumming to be placed left, right and center in the stereo mix.

Later that evening, the group added an extension to Take 7, which originally lasted for only 1:17. The backing track for the add-on features Paul on piano, John on his Casino, George on his Telecaster through the Leslie and Ringo on drums. At this stage the song was less than two minutes long, but this would be extended to 2:41 with additional overdubs. The final edit would shorten this by 36 seconds.

On August 5 and 7, the group recorded their vocals, with Paul singing lead. John, Paul and George also superimposed guitar parts on August 7. The most interesting passage begins at the 53 second mark, with the three guitarists trading solos three times over John's previously recorded churning rhythm guitar. Each solo is played for two bars and runs for approximately four seconds. Paul leads off with a tight rocking Telecaster solo, followed by George's wailing Telecaster and John's distorted Casino. The exchanging solos reach a boiling point 1:29 into the song, where Paul's piano takes over and leads into the concluding vocal couplet. The following day, Paul added bass and Ringo added drums. George Martin's orchestral score, consisting of 12 violins, four violas, four cellos, one string bass, four horns, three trumpets, one trombone and one bass trombone, was recorded on August 15. Paul added four seconds of piano preceding his ending vocal on August 18. The stereo mixing and crossfade joining of the track to the end of *Golden Slumbers/Carry That Weight* took place on August 18, 19 and 21, with Remix 4 selected for the master tape of the album. On August 25, *The End* was edited down to its final running time of 2:05.

*Anthology 3* contains a newly created mix of *The End* that starts during the opening moments of what is Ringo's drum solo on the released version of the song. The new mix reveals that guitar and tambourine parts were recorded over the drum solo, but that these additions were deleted from the final mix. The new mix has the guitar parts and orchestra more to the front. It lasts about a minute and a half, but is extended for another 80 seconds with an edit of the final chord from *A Day In The Life*.

Although *The End* is the final piece of the medley, it is not the album's last song. As explained below, the medley is followed by 14 seconds of silence and a 23-second tune titled *Her Majesty*. McCartney described the song, which was written at his farm in Scotland towards the end of 1968, as mildly disrespectful, but tongue-in-cheek, "almost like a love song to the Queen." He sang and played the song on piano at Twickenham on January 9, 1969. On January 24, Paul played the song on acoustic guitar, stretching it out for over two minutes by singing the same verse five times, with scat vocals for the first few lines of the second and fourth verses. Ringo joined in on drums and John played some rudimentary slide guitar on the Hofner Hawaiian Standard lap-steel guitar.

The song was recorded at Abbey Road in three takes as a solo McCartney song on July 2, with Paul singing a live vocal over his Martin D-28 acoustic guitar. As Paul had only written a single verse, the track lasts only 22 seconds.

*Her Majesty* nearly didn't wind up on to the album. The song was edited into the medley on July 30 between *Mean Mr. Mustard* and *Polythene Pam*. In all likelihood, the tune was placed after *Mean Mr. Mustard* to tie in with that song's line "Takes him out to look at the Queen." When the tape of the medley was played back, Paul realized that *Her Majesty* did not fit in. Although McCartney instructed engineer John Kurlander to cut the *Her Majesty* segment from the tape and throw it away, Kurtlander had been taught never to throw anything away. After Paul left the studio, Kurtlander picked the tape up off the floor, added about 20 seconds of leader tape to the end of the medley and stuck *Her Majesty* onto the end of the leader tape. The following day Mal Evans brought the tape to Malcolm Davis at Apple Studios to cut lacquers of the medley for the group. Davis, who had also been taught never to throw anything away, copied the tape complete with the gap of silence and *Her Majesty*. Upon hearing the acetate, Paul liked the surprise effect of the song popping up after the apparent end of the medley.

When the master tape for the album was banded on August 20, *Her Majesty* was placed at the end of the tape after 14 seconds of silence. Because Paul wanted to duplicate the random nature of *Her Majesty* exactly as it appeared on the July 31 acetate, he had the engineers use the actual piece of tape cut from the medley on July 30 rather than make a clean mix from Take 3 of the song. Thus, *Her Majesty* begins with the crashing final chord of *Mean Mr. Mustard* and ends abruptly without its closing chord (which was cut off as it blended with the opening chord to *Polythene Pam* in the test medley).

Both Paul and George Martin take credit for coming up with the concept of the medley; however, John was the first one to comment publicly about it. In an April, 1969, issue of *New Musical Express*, John stated "Paul and I are now working on a kind of song montage that we might do as one piece on one side." This comment shows that the idea for the medley dates back to mid-April, nearly a month before the group recorded Paul's *You Never Give Me Your Money*, which by itself comes across as a medley of three song fragments. Although John later chastised the medley, he did contribute three of its eight songs.

By July, the medley had become an important part of the sessions. While the January runthroughs of *Her Majesty* give the impression that Paul intended to write additional verses and develop the tune into a full-length song, Paul's July 2 recording of *Her Majesty* lasts a mere 23 seconds. This was all that was needed as he planned on using the song in the medley. On July 3, the group recorded *Golden Slumbers* and *Carry That Weight* as a single track. Similarly, *Sun King* and *Mean Mr. Mustard* were recorded as a single selection on July 24, as were *Polythene Pam* and *She Came In Through The Bathroom Window* on the following day. *The End* was begun on July 23.

Although only a few of the medley's component parts were complete by July 30, a test of the medley (which was then called *The Long One* or *Huge Melody*) was made that evening. The running order of the 15:30 medley was *You Never Give Me Your Money*, *Sun King/Mean Mr. Mustard*, *Her Majesty*, *Polythene Pam/She Came In Through The Bathroom Window*, *Golden Slumbers/Carry That Weight* and *The End*.

**This floor display consists of a cropped enlargement of the front cover attached to a record bin.**

The tape of the medley demonstrated that, for the most part, the songs flowed together well. An exception was *Her Majesty*, which, as discussed above, was dropped from the lineup when Paul realized the song did not fit in. The tape also revealed that the crossfade from *You Never Give Me Your Money* into *Sun King* needed embellishing. This was solved by mixing in sound effects of tubular bells, birds and chirping crickets. Extensive mixing, crossfading, editing and joining of the medley's components took place on August 14, with additional work done on August 20 and 21.

The banding session for the album took place on August 20, with all four Beatles in attendance. This was the last time the entire group was together at Abbey Road. The master tape produced during the session varied from final master in two ways: *Octopus's Garden* preceded, rather than followed, *Oh! Darling*; and, side one and side two were reversed. Had the decision not been made to switch the sides, the album would have opened with *Here Comes The Sun*, had the medley on side one and closed with the abrupt ending to *I Want You (She's So Heavy)*. While this would have worked, the final master's running order, with *Come Together* as the opening track and the medley, along with *The End* and the surprise appearance of *Her Majesty*, as the closer, is more effective.

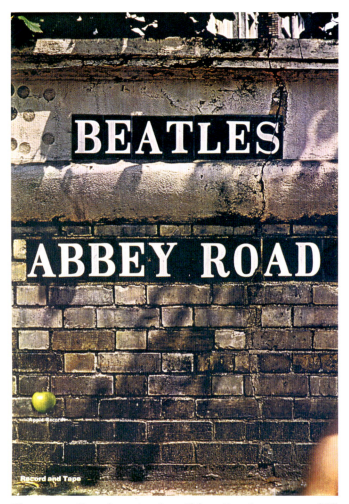

**The promotional poster for *Abbey Road* measures 23" x 33" and features a cropped enlargement of back cover without the text.**

The final master tape was completed on August 25, with minor edits to *Maxwell's Silver Hammer* and *The End*, the repositioning of *Octopus's Garden* and *Oh! Darling* and the switching of side one and side two. A copy of the master was sent to Capitol shortly thereafter.

Prior to naming the album *Abbey Road*, the Beatles considered calling the record *Everest*. This idea came from Paul's fondness of the image of Mt. Everest appearing on packs of the Everest brand cigarettes smoked by engineer Geoff Emerick. The cover was to feature the Beatles standing in front of the mountain. Although their image could have been superimposed over a picture of the famous peak, there was talk of flying to the Himalayas to do the shoot. Engineer John Kurtlander remembers one of the Beatles realizing how impractical it would be to fly to Tibet and suggesting that they shoot the cover outside the studio and name the album *Abbey Road*.

The famous cover image of the Beatles walking through the crosswalk evolved from one of Paul's sketches, which was refined by photographer Iain Macmillan. On the morning of August 8, 1969, the Beatles arrived at the studio for the picture session. While a policeman held up traffic, Macmillan stood atop a stool and shot six pictures of the Beatles walking across the street. They were shot both walking to and away from the studio entrance. Paul wore sandals for the first two pictures, but took them off for the remaining shots because his feet were hot.

After reviewing the six transparencies, Paul selected what he considered to be the best of the lot. In the image chosen for the cover, the Beatles are heading towards the studio and Paul is barefooted and holding a cigarette. One of the more interesting outtakes from the session shows a bright red double decker bus heading towards the group (see page 169).

Shortly after the album's release, the "Paul is dead" rumor started. Fans looking for clues of Paul's demise viewed the *Abbey Road* cover as proof positive that Paul was dead and had been replaced by a look-alike. John is dressed in white and represents either a priest presiding over Paul's funeral or an angel. George is dressed casually in blue jeans as would be a grave digger. Ringo is wearing a black suit, thus serving as the funeral director or mortician. The barefoot "Paul" represents the corpse as many people are buried without their shoes. And, if you look closely at his face, his eyes are shut, obviously indicating Paul is dead. Plus, the stand-in Paul is out-of-step with the others, clearly meaning he is not one of the Beatles. All of this is consistent with the trunk cover of *Yesterday And Today*, which, when turned sideways, shows Ringo (the mortician) closing the trunk (casket) on Paul (the corpse).

The other big clue on the *Abbey Road* cover was the license plate number **LMW 281F** on the Volkswagen **Beetle** parked on the street. The car was obviously a **Beatle** telling fans "**28 IF** McCartney **W**ere **L**iving." Never mind the fact that Paul "would have been" 27 at the time. Never let the truth get in the way of a good rumor.

Paul, of course, wasn't dead. But the rumor did have a positive effect on sales of Beatles albums. The November 5, 1969, Variety ran an article titled "Rumors of McCartney's Death Put Beaucoup Life Into 'Abbey Road' Sales." The interest generated by talk of Paul's demise and the hunt for clues not only sparked additional sales of *Abbey Road*, but also pushed three other Beatles albums back into the *Billboard Top LP's* chart. People were buying *Sgt. Pepper's Lonely Hearts Club Band*, *Magical Mystery Tour* and *The White Album* in hopes of learning about the clues spread throughout their covers, posters, booklets and records. While Capitol played no part in starting or even perpetuating the rumor, the company knew it had a good thing going and did nothing to dispel talk of McCartney's death.

Capitol prepared a series of promotional items for *Abbey Road*. The poster, **APP 383.P1**, measures 17" x 23" and features an altered enlargement of the back album cover. The right portion of the cover image is cropped out so that only the lower back calf of the woman's leg is visible in the lower right corner of the poster. In addition, the poster is missing most of the text on the cover, so it does not contain the song titles. It does have the Apple logo and adds the phrase "Records and Tapes" in the lower left corner.

The growing market for tape formats led to Capitol sending stores a 14"-tall, 10"-diameter cardboard octagon-shaped container, **APP 383.C1**, to hold 8-track and cassettes. The display bin's side panels alternate between text and images from the album's cover. One panel states "New! Beatles! On 8-Track Cartridge and Cassette!" and has, centered at the bottom, the Capitol logo.

Capitol also prepared a 12" x 19" cardboard counter display, **APP 383.CD1**, which has the back cover at the bottom and die-cut figures of the Beatles stepping through the crosswalk at the top.

The most elaborate and sought after *Abbey Road* promotional item is the two-piece cardboard floor display, **APP 383.FD1**. The top part of the display, which attaches to the base with a pole, is a 11½" x 27½" cropped enlargement of the album cover with die-cut figures of the Beatles in the crosswalk. The black background lower part is 27" tall and contains a record bin, which has "The BEATLES" in green on its front panel and a green apple on each of its side panels. The base has a white arrow cut through with black lines mimicking street cracks. The arrow points upward to the Beatles and the Abbey Road crosswalk.

*Abbey Road* was the first Beatles album in America packaged with print-on-board covers. These covers, **APP 383.SC1**, were manufactured by a process initiated in the United States by Shorewood Packaging, Inc. The process involves printing the cover image directly onto white posterboard, which is then folded and glued to form the album jacket. The previous Beatles album covers were constructed by affixing separately printed slicks to cardboard jackets. The new print-on-board covers were a superior looking package. Another advantage was that these covers were manufactured by one company, whereas the older style covers involved both a printer and an album fabricator. Although print-on-board covers were the norm in Europe and would later become the industry standard in America, this process was new for the United States at the time *Abbey Road* was released. Shorewood applied for a patent for its print-on-board album jackets, which it manufactured under the "Shorepak" trade name.

The *Abbey Road* covers for the East Coast were manufactured by Shorewood's Farmingdale, Long Island, New York, plant. The West Coast covers were made by Bert-Co under license from Shorewood. The jackets were initially printed onto posterboard that was coated white on both sides. The insides of these covers have a smooth white surface. After they realized there was no need to have a coated surface on the inside, they began printing onto coated one side board to save costs. These covers have a gray cardboard surface on the inside. Because the companies had leftover inventory of the two-sided posterboard, some of the later covers have smooth white interiors.

Capitol documents indicate that the album's art work was shipped to Shorewood on September 11, 1969. The first batch of covers, **SC1A**, do not list *Her Majesty* on the back. Prior to the album going on sale, Capitol had the film for the back cover revised to list *Her Majesty* after *The End*. By the time the new art work was sent to Shorewood on September 24, many covers had already been printed. Thus, the jackets listing *Her Majesty*, **SC1B**, are less common than the covers not listing the song.

*Abbey Road* ended up being the only Beatles album to have print-on-board covers upon its initial release. Although Capitol was pleased with the Shorepak jackets, future decisions regarding the mastering, packaging and advertising of Apple releases were handled directly by Apple through

The November 7, 1969, *Life* featured a cover story that cracked the case of the missing Beatle, thus assuring readers that Paul was still with us.

Abkco. Allen Klein and Allan Steckler were both very loyal individuals who had a long-standing relationship with Queens Litho solidified by the company's printing of picture sleeves and cover slicks for the Rolling Stones. Apple bypassed the Shorepak and selected Queens Litho to be the primary printer of cover slicks for future Beatles albums starting with *Hey Jude*.

When Capitol's pressing plants ran out of Shorepak covers, Apple hired Queens Litho to print slicks for additional *Abbey Road* jackets. These later covers, **APP 383.SC2A**, used slicks printed by Queens Litho and Bert-Co and were manufactured by Imperial and/or Modern Album. The back cover slicks were made from the album's original art work and accordingly do not list *Her Majesty*. The front cover image was enlarged to allow for the front slick to be wrapped around to the back cover. Thus, the picture on the front cover shows less of the crosswalk and the trees and has a larger image of the Beatles.

The initial labels prepared for *Abbey Road*, **APP 383.SR1**, do not list *Her Majesty* on Side 2. There are three layout variations of the first issue labels. All have the record and matrix numbers to the right of the spindle hole and "STEREO" to the left.

The most common label variation, **APP 383.SR1L(as)**, has the album title above the group's name (centered towards the top of the apple on Side 1 and in the upper left part of the apple on Side 2) and the side number to the right of the spindle hole. Side 1 has "Produced by George Martin" and "Recorded in England" on two lines at the bottom

Capitol mastered *Abbey Road* in early September, 1969. The engineer's notes warn that there is "distortion in spots, on original." After the entry for *I Want You*, the engineer wrote "audible hiss in intro" and "(Note: Music ends abruptly)." After *The End*, he noted that there is a 15-second pause before a track identified as "No Title." The New York production copy of the album master tape was made on September 10, 1969.

of the apple. Side 2 has the recording location in the lower left part of the apple and the production credit in the lower right part. All titles on Side 2 are below the spindle hole. The labels have light green apples and Apple perimeter print on the sliced side. They have been confirmed with Capitol Los Angeles pressings as well as Decca and RCA pressings.

A second variation, **APP 383.SR1J(as)**, has the album title and group's name on one line towards the top of the apple, the side number to the left of the spindle hole and "Produced by George Martin," "Recorded in England" and "Manufactured by Apple Records, Inc." on three lines at the bottom of the apple. The first three song titles on Side 2 are above the hole. The labels, which have light green apples and Apple perimeter print on the sliced side, were probably printed in-house by Capitol's Jacksonville factory. Jacksonville and Scranton pressings have been confirmed.

The least common variation, **APP 383.SR1S**, has amateurish-looking labels with a thin compressed font for the album title and group's name. On side 1, this information is on two lines centered at the top of the apple. On side 2, the album title is on two lines in the upper left part of the apple and the group's name is in the upper right part. The side number is to the right of the spindle hole. Side 1 has "Produced by George Martin" and "*Recorded in England*" on two lines at the bottom of the apple. Side 2 has this information in the lower right part of the apple. All titles on Side 2 are below the spindle hole. These labels, which have light green apples, were probably printed in-house by Capitol's Scranton factory. They can be found with Apple perimeter print on the sliced side, **SR1S(as)** (Scranton and non-Capitol pressings confirmed), and Capitol logo perimeter print on the sliced side, **SR1S(c)** (Winchester confirmed).

The later labels, **APP 383.SR2**, add *Her Majesty* to Side 2 and shift "Produced by George Martin" from the lower right to the upper right part of the sliced apple. All con-

firmed labels with *Her Majesty* are similar to **APP 383.SR1L**. Most have the production credit centered over the record number on Side 2, **SR2L(i)**. This layout appears on several different label backdrops: (1) Capitol logo perimeter print, **SR2L(i)(c)** (light green apple L.A. and Jacksonville pressings confirmed); (2) Apple perimeter print on the sliced side, **SR2L(i)(as)** (light green apple Scranton, Jacksonville and Winchester pressings confirmed); and (3) Apple perimeter print on the full side, **SR2L(i)(af)** (light green apple L.A. and dull dark green Winchester pressings confirmed). There is also nearly identical variation that has the production credit shifted more to the left, **SR2L(ii)**. This variation has been confirmed with Capitol logo perimeter print, **SR2L(ii)(c)** (light green apple Scranton and dark green apple Scranton and Jacksonville pressings confirmed), and Apple perimeter print on the sliced apple side, **SR2L(ii)(as)** (light green apple Scranton pressings confirmed).

There are four confirmed all rights variations, all with Apple perimeter print on the full apple side and having the same layout design as **APP 383.SR2L(i)**. The all rights variations include: (1) **APP 383.SR3A(ar)**, with the all rights language in black on two lines centered at the top of the apple on the full apple side and on five lines in the upper right part of the apple on the sliced apple side (light green apple labels) (L.A. pressings confirmed); (2) **APP 383.SR3B(ar)**, with the all rights language in black on two lines at the bottom of the apple on the full apple side and on two lines, barely legible, below the apple on the sliced apple side (light green apple labels) (Jacksonville pressings confirmed); (3) **APP 383.SR3C(ar)**, with the all rights language in green running along the lower right perimeter on the full apple side (dark green apple labels) (Jacksonville pressings confirmed); and (4) **APP 383.SR3D(ar)**, with the all rights language in green in the lower perimeter on both sides (light green apple labels) (L.A. pressings confirmed).

While *Abbey Road* is now considered one of the Beatles best albums, reviews at the time of its release were mixed. *Billboard* called the record "potent and commercial." The review described *Something* as a "driving ballad," *Come Together* as a "funky swinger" and *Maxwell's Silver Hammer* and *Mean Mr. Mustard* as "clever, typical Beatles material." Although *The New York Times* called the medley "the most impressive music they've made since *Rubber Soul*," it found the rest of the album to be an "unmitigated disaster." Reviewer Nic Cohn dismissed Harrison's songs as "mediocrity incarnate" and stated that *Come Together* was "intriguing only as a sign of just how low Lennon can sink these days." (Those upset with Cohn's put down of side one and George Harrison could snicker at his error of attributing Paul's *Oh! Darling* to John.)

The staff of *Rolling Stone* was so divided over the record that the magazine published two reviews. John Mendelssohn raved about the album, praising the first three tracks and the medley on side two, which provided "potent testimony that no, they've far from lost it, and no, they haven't stopped trying." Ed Ward called the album "garbage," labeling *Something* as vile and describing side two as a disaster. He went so far as to suggest that the group "priced it so outrageous so that fewer people would buy it" and wondered why they even bothered to release it at all.

Listening to the album today, it's hard to believe the record received negative reviews from prestigious newspapers and magazines. The opening tracks on side one rank with the best the band ever recorded. *Octopus's Garden* is charming, while *I Want You (She's So Heavy)* is a remarkable song blending simple direct lyrics with a complex musical arrangement and passionate vocals from John. Side two, with George's *Here Comes The Sun*, the beautiful harmonies on *Because* and the long medley, is an incredible showcase of the band's talents. *Abbey Road* is truly a fitting end to a remarkable recording career.

 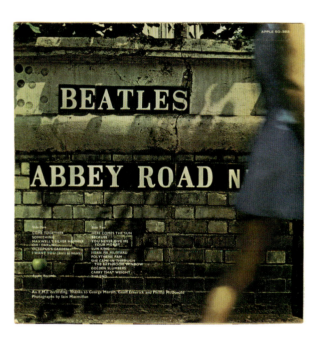

APP 383.SC1A

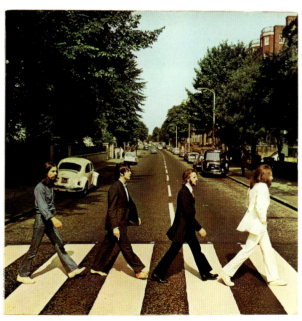 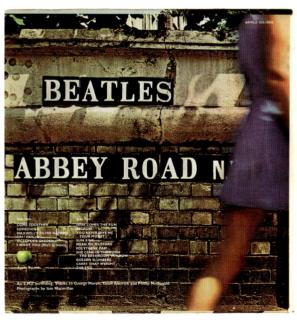

APP 383.SC2A

APP 383.SR1L(as)

APP 383.SR1J(as)

APP 383.SR1S(as)
(shown - Apple perimeter print on sliced side)
APP 383.SR1S(c) (same, except Capitol logo perimeter print on sliced apple side)

APP 383.SR2L(i)(c)

APP 383.SR2L(i)(as)
(shown)
APP 383.SR2L(i)(af) (same, except Apple perimeter print on full apple side)
(there are light apple and dark apple labels of the (af) variation)

APP 383.SR2L(ii)(c)
(shown - dark green apple label; also printed on light green apple label)
APP 383.SR2L(ii)(as) (same, except Apple perimeter print on sliced apple side)

APP 383.SR3A(ar)

APP 383.SR3B(ar)

APP 383.SR3C(ar)
(All rights only on full apple side)

APP 383.SR3D(ar)
(All rights on both sides)

## GET BACK with Let It Be and 10 other songs
## (UNRELEASED)

Side 1
1. ONE AFTER 909 (Lennon-McCartney)
   Link Tracks: ROCKER (Lennon-McCartney)
   SAVE THE LAST DANCE FOR ME (Pomus-Shuman)
2. DON'T LET ME DOWN (Lennon-McCartney)
3. DIG A PONY (Lennon-McCartney)
4. I'VE GOT A FEELING (Lennon-McCartney)
5. GET BACK (Lennon-McCartney)
6. LET IT BE (Lennon-McCartney)

Side 2
1. FOR YOU BLUE (Harrison)
2. TWO OF US ON OUR WAY HOME (Lennon-McCartney)
   Link Track: MAGGIE MAY (Public Domain)
3. DIG IT (Lennon-McCartney-Harrison-Starr)
4. THE LONG AND WINDING ROAD (Lennon-McCartney)
5. I ME MINE (Harrison)
6. ACROSS THE UNIVERSE (Lennon-McCartney)
   GET BACK (Reprise) (Lennon-McCartney)

As 1969 drew to a close, the Beatles still had not issued their *Get Back* album. The record had been put on hold so that its release would coincide with the broadcast of the TV special being edited from the January Twickenham and Apple sessions.

During this time, Allen Klein informed the Beatles that they would make more money if the documentary was distributed as a feature film. Klein also wanted to boost interest in the *Get Back* album by having it serve as the movie's soundtrack LP.

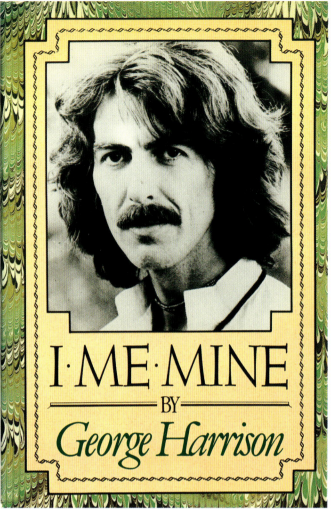

**George Harrison named his first book *I Me Mine*. The autobiography, published in 1980, contains the lyrics to George's songs, along with comments about the compositions.**

Director Michael Lindsay-Hogg's cut of the film contained a charming sequence of John and Yoko waltzing to George's *I Me Mine*. It also featured the group working through John's *Across The Universe*. Although both songs were rehearsed at Twickenham, neither was properly recorded when the sessions moved to Apple's basement studio. The desire to include these songs on the soundtrack album posed some practical problems which were solved within the first few days of January, 1970.

*I Me Mine* is George's statement "about the ego: the eternal problem." Harrison wrote the song on the evening of January 7, 1969, and introduced it to the group the following morning. Prior to the arrival of Paul and John, he sang and played the song for Ringo on John's unplugged Casino electric guitar. A portion of this initial performance appears in the film.

The Beatles rehearsed *I Me Mine* several times during the day. The tune's waltz tempo and flamenco guitar break led John to joke that the Beatles play rock 'n' roll and have no place in their playlist for a Spanish waltz. The band stayed in their standard lineup of two guitars, bass and drums for the song, although John took a break from a few of the runthroughs to dance with Yoko. During the afternoon session, Paul and George worked out harmony vocals for the chorus. Paul's suggestion that the song be made heavier by

rocking out on the instrumental break was initially rejected by George. Part of the group's final runthrough of the song was used in the film. For reasons unknown, the group did not return to George's composition during the sessions.

Nearly one year later, on January 3, 1970, George, Paul and Ringo got together with George Martin at Abbey Road to record *I Me Mine* for the soundtrack album. John was on a month-long vacation in Denmark and did not attend. Even had John been in London, he still may have missed the session as by that time he had told the others he was quitting the group.

Before Take 15, George announced to those present in Studio Two, "You all will have read that Dave Dee is no longer with us. But Micky and Tich and I would just like to carry on the good work that's always gone down in number two." Although George's remark referred to reports in the press that Dave Dee was splitting from Dozy, Beaky, Mick & Tich, his comment was full of irony as John had quit the Beatles, leaving George, Paul and Ringo to carry on.

The trio recorded 16 backing tracks of *I Me Mine* with George on his Gibson J-200 acoustic guitar and guide vocal, Paul on his Rickenbacker bass and Ringo on drums. Take 16 was then overdubbed with fresh lead vocals from George, backing vocals from George and Paul, organ, lead acoustic guitar and two distorted Les Paul guitars. The arrangement dropped the flamenco guitar instrumental break featured in the *Get Back* performances. In its place is the hard-rocking "I I me me mine" middle eight first suggested by McCartney nearly one year earlier.

The finished master, which runs a mere 1:34, was mixed for stereo by Glyn Johns at Olympic Studios on January 5, 1970. In keeping with the spirit of the other tracks on the *Get Back* album, Johns edited in Paul fooling around on bass along with some studio chatter before the start of the song:

George: Alright. Are you ready, Ringo?

Ringo: Ready, George.

Phil Spector, through the magic of editing, later extended the song to 2:25 for the *Let It Be* album. *Anthology 3* contains an unedited mix of Take 16 preceded by George's Dave Dee announcement.

Although the Beatles did not perform *Across The Universe* during the Apple basement sessions, the group had previously recorded the song back in February, 1968, at the same pre-Rishikesh session that produced *Lady Madonna*, *The Inner Light* and *Hey Bulldog*. Glyn Johns remixed this recording for his second *Get Back* album.

John considered *Across The Universe* one of his best lyrics. According to Lennon, it wasn't a matter of craftsmanship; the song wrote itself. One evening his wife Cynthia had been "going on and on about something and she'd gone to sleep." John "kept hearing these words over and over, flowing like an endless stream." Knowing that he couldn't get to sleep until he put it on paper, Lennon got out of bed and went downstairs to write. The song's verses contain beautiful and somewhat trippy imagery. The chorus mixes the Sanskrit words "Jai Guru Deva" (victory to the Guru-God) and "Om" (Hindu's most sacred mantra or holy sound) with the phrase "Nothing's gonna change my world."

*Across The Universe* made its debut on the charity compilation album *No One's Gonna Change Our World* (Regal Starline SRS 5013). The front cover (left) was drawn by Michael Grimshaw and features sketches of the recording artists and a panda bear. The back cover (right) contains a picture of and personal message from the Duke of Edinburgh and a thank you from Spike Milligan. The artists, composers, publishers and recording companies waived all fees. Royalties were donated to the World Wildlife Fund for the preservation of rare animals in danger of extinction.

The Beatles recorded six takes of the song on February 4, 1968. The first take was an instrumental track consisting of John on his Martin D-28 acoustic guitar, George on tamboura and Ringo on tom-toms. Take 2 features a beautiful Lennon vocal, John and Paul on Martin D-28 acoustic guitars, George on tamboura and Ringo on svaramandal. This pure unadulterated recording is on *Anthology 2*.

The Beatles experimented with different arrangements for Takes 4, 5 and 6 (there was no Take 3) before being satisfied with Take 7, which has John on his Martin D-28, George on tamboura and Ringo on tom-toms. All instruments were run through a Leslie speaker and subjected to artificial double tracking. John's lead vocal was then recorded with the tape running at a slower than normal speed to give it a sped-up effect upon playback.

John and Paul wanted to add falsetto vocals, but realized that the desired high harmonies were out of their range. Rather than attempt to round up professional singers on a Sunday evening, Paul merely walked outside the building and auditioned a few of the female fans hanging out by the front of the studio. He then escorted 16-year-old Lizzie Bravo and 17-year-old Gayleen Pease into Studio Three to sing "Nothing's gonna change my world" over John's previously taped lead vocal.

After the girls completed their work, Take 7 was given a reduction mix (designated Take 8) to allow for additional overdubs. One of the newly created vacant tracks was filled with backwards recordings of Paul's bass and Ringo's drums. The Beatles then recorded three takes of sound effects, which included multilayered humming, guitar and a drone-like sound. The tapes of these embellishments were played backwards and added to Take 8. A mono mix was prepared and transferred to an acetate for John. This unique mix of the song is known among collectors as the "Hums Wild" version.

On February 8, John was still experimenting with the instrumentation of the song. By the end of the session, all of the backwards additions from October 4 had been removed from Take 8 to allow for new overdubs, which included a new lead vocal from John, organ parts by Lennon and George Martin, maracas and wah-wah guitar by Harrison, piano by McCartney and backing vocals from John and Paul. The song was then mixed for mono.

Although the finished master was superb, John was not satisfied with the recording. He was against it being issued on the next single, so *The Inner Light* was selected as the B side to *Lady Madonna*.

Comedian Spike Milligan was at Abbey Road during the session and became aware of the group's decision not to issue the song. He was in the process of organizing a benefit album for the World Wildlife Fund and boldly asked the Beatles if they would be willing to contribute *Across The Universe* to the project. Much to his delight, the group agreed to do so.

John's unhappiness with the February, 1968, recording of *Across The Universe* prompted him to resurrect the song during the *Get Back* sessions. The first attempts at the song took place on January 6, 1969, and have John on his Epiphone Casino, George on his Telecaster and wah-wah pedal, Paul on his Hofner bass and Ringo on drums. John sings whatever words he can remember and Paul joins him on the choruses. These performances are miserable, suffering from a slow tempo and uninspired playing and singing. On one of the complete runthroughs, George improvises a guitar solo over the third verse as John fails to sing any lyrics. Things don't get any better after John switches to organ. When George asks him about the earlier recording, John insists it can bettered. Later attempts at the song prove him wrong.

The performances from January 7 are not much better, although John is able to sing the words when Apple's Eric Brown brings him the lyrics. After John once again expresses his dissatisfaction over the 1968 recording, George says how much he likes it. Although the earlier recording was donated to the World Wildlife Fund for inclusion on its charity album, John is concerned the album won't be issued and wants to include the song in the current project. After experimenting with different tempos and sounds (including one runthrough with George on organ), the group tries a heavier approach with Paul singing along with John. Portions of two of these performances were edited into the film. The Beatles attempted the song a few more times on January 9 with mixed results.

By the time the sessions moved to Apple's basement studio on January 21, John had apparently given up on his idea to rerecord *Across The Universe*. This decision was prompted by negative comments directed at the *Yellow Submarine* album, which was released in England on January 17. Because the full-price LP contained only four new Beatles songs, the group was accused for the first time of not giving the public good value for their money. This made John and Paul question their decision to place the four songs on an album rather than on a lesser-priced EP as they had originally planned. They decided to correct the problem by giving fans the opportunity to purchase the songs on an EP. And, to ensure that the public got good value for their money, the EP not only would contain the four new songs from *Yellow Submarine*, but also would include *Across The Universe*.

George had not been told of this decision and during the January 23 session asked John if they were doing *Across The Universe*. John replied that they were not since it was already coming out on an EP. Although a tape for the EP was compiled and banded on March 13, 1969, the idea was dropped, and the disc was never issued.

By the fall of 1969, the World Wildlife Fund album was finally taking shape. The inclusion of an unreleased Beatles recording was a real coup for the project. A line from the chorus of *Across The Universe* was modified to form the album's title, *No One's Gonna Change Our World*. Other artists included the Bee Gees, Cilla Black, Rolf Harris, the Hollies, Lulu, Spike Milligan, Cliff Richard, Bruce Forsyth, Harry Secombe and an act known as Dave Dee, Dozy, Beaky, Mick & Tich. George used the names of three members of the group (Dave Dee, Micky and Tich) in his studio announcement prior to Take 15 of *I Me Mine*.

On October 2, 1969, George Martin and engineers Jeff Jarratt and Alan Parsons gathered at Abbey Road to mix *Across The Universe* for the stereo LP. Because the song was going to open the album, it was decided to start the track with 20 seconds of sound effects: chirping birds, children at a playground and flying birds landing on water. The sound of the flying birds was also dropped in for a few moments during the song's fade out. Martin sped up the tape of Take 8, causing the song to shift up a half step from

D major to E flat. This shortened the song by ten seconds (not counting the 20 seconds of effects tagged onto the beginning) and raised the pitch of John's voice.

The following day, George Martin compiled and banded the album, which was released as Regal Starline SRS 5013. Although the record was not issued in the United States, some copies of the album were imported into the country. The Wildlife version of *Across The Universe* made its official American debut in 1980 on *Rarities* (Capitol SHAL 12060). It also appears on *Past Masters Volume Two* (Apple 90044).

By the time Glyn Johns was instructed to add *Across The Universe* to the *Get Back* album, the song had finally been released on the World Wildlife Fund LP. Thus, he had to find a way to make the recording sound different than the Wildlife album track and make it fit into the *Get Back* concept. Johns performed this task on January 5, 1970. He went back to Take 8 (without the added sound effects) and made a fresh stereo mix with the tape running at its proper speed. He mixed out the Beatles backing vocals, but did not remove the voices of Lizzie Bravo and Gayleen Pease because their vocals were part of the reduction mix of Take 7 and could not be mixed out of Take 8. The track was also faded a few seconds prior to the song's normal ending. To give the song its *Get Back* flavor, Johns left in a brief bit of studio chat that precedes the start of the song on the master tape (Lennon's "Are you alright, Ritchie?").

On January 5, 1970, Glen Johns went to Olympic Sound Studios to put together his soundtrack version of *Get Back*. After mixing *I Me Mine* and *Across The Universe*, Johns compiled and banded the album.

Because Johns was proud of his original *Get Back* album, he decided to make only minor changes. Side one was left in tact, with the only variation being the addition of *Let It Be* to the end of the side. Although Johns was aware of the embellishments added to *Let It Be* on January 4, he opted to stick with his original mix of the song. Johns did not want the sound of brass and cellos, however tasteful, to impose upon the live-in-the-studio feeling of the LP.

The running order of side two was also left alone, except for two deletions and two additions. *Teddy Boy* was dropped from the lineup because it was not shown in the film. In addition, Paul may have informed Johns that he would be recording the song for his own album. *Let It Be* was shifted to side one, thus destroying the effectiveness of Lennon's "and now we'd like to do *Hark, The Angels Come*" remark at the end of *Dig It*. The two new songs, *I Me Mine* and *Across The Universe*, were placed back to back towards the end of the side just before the *Get Back* reprise.

After *Let It Be* was selected to be the next Beatles single, the text on the album's cover was changed from "GET BACK with Don't Let Me Down and 9 other songs" to "GET BACK with Let It Be and 10 other songs." This transition is shown on page 323 of the *Anthology* book. The cover, shown on page 181 of this book, is a computer generated image of the revised cover.

Although Glyn Johns had dutifully compiled an album reflecting the film, his soundtrack version of the LP suffered the same fate as its predecessor. It was never released.

# HEY JUDE (THE BEATLES AGAIN)
## APPLE SW-385 (SO-385)

Side 1
1. CAN'T BUY ME LOVE (Lennon-McCartney)
2. I SHOULD HAVE KNOWN BETTER
   (Lennon-McCartney)
3. PAPERBACK WRITER (Lennon-McCartney)
4. RAIN (Lennon-McCartney)
5. LADY MADONNA (Lennon-McCartney)
6. REVOLUTION (Lennon-McCartney)

Side 2
1. HEY JUDE (Lennon-McCartney)
2. OLD BROWN SHOE (Harrison)
3. DON'T LET ME DOWN (Lennon-McCartney)
4. BALLAD OF JOHN & YOKO (Lennon-McCartney)

The concept behind this "new" Beatles album was simple. Take ten songs that had never appeared before on a Capitol Beatles album and let nature take its course. While the first three Beatles albums released on the Apple label in America were identical to the British records, *Hey Jude* (originally titled *The Beatles Again* and assigned number SO-385) was a throwback to Capitol albums of the sixties.

It is a uniquely configured album designed especially for the American market. The album is similar to *Yesterday And Today* in that it is a collection of songs from several different sources, but unlike the 1966 album, it offered nothing new at the time of its release. Although not a greatest hits collection, the album is full of terrific songs, including three number one hits.

At the time the *Hey Jude* LP was released on February 26, 1970, *Abbey Road* was still riding high on the charts. This, however, did not adversely affect the record's sales or airplay. The album entered the *Billboard Top LP's* chart on March 21 at number three. The following week it pushed past *Led Zeppelin II* (Atlantic 8236), but could not overtake Simon & Garfunkel's *Bridge Over Troubled Water* (Columbia 9914). *Hey Jude* held the number two spot for four straight weeks before dropping to number three for three straight weeks directly behind *Deja Vu* by Crosby, Stills, Nash & Young (Atlantic 7200). On May 16, the *Hey Jude* LP was bumped back to number four by Paul McCartney's first solo effort, *McCartney* (Apple STAO 3363). *Hey Jude* remained on the *Billboard* album charts for 33 weeks, including 11 weeks in the top ten. Although the album peaked at number two in *Billboard* and *Cash Box*, it reached number one in *Record World*. By June, 1970, the album had sold 3.3 million units.

With the exception of *Don't Let Me Down*, the *Hey Jude* album is programmed in chronological order. Side One rocks from start to finish, opening with *Can't Buy Me Love* and closing with *Revolution*. Side Two, which contains only four songs, opens with *Hey Jude* and closes with *The Ballad Of John And Yoko*.

*Can't Buy Me Love* was issued as Capitol's second Beatles single on Capitol 5150 on March 16, 1964. The song was a number one million seller. Although it is on the United Artists soundtrack record to *A Hard Day's Night* (mono UAL 3366; stereo UAS 6366) and on the Capitol compilation LP *Big Hits From England And The U.S.A.* (Capitol (D)T 2125), it had never been on a Capitol Beatles album.

*I Should Have Known Better* was the B side to the single *A Hard Day's Night* (Capitol 5222), which was released on July 13, 1964. *Billboard* charted the song separately at number 53. It appears on the United Artists soundtrack album; however, Capitol did not include the tune on its semi-soundtrack album *Something New* (Capitol (S)T 2108).

*Paperback Writer* and *Rain* were issued as Capitol 5651 on May 23, 1966. The single was a number one million seller. *Billboard* charted the B side *Rain* separately at 23.

*Lady Madonna* was the A side of Capitol 2138, which was released on March 18, 1968. Although the song sold over a million copies and received heavy airplay, it stalled at number four in the *Billboard Hot 100*.

*Revolution* was the B side of Apple 2276, which was issued on August 26, 1968, as the label's first single. *Billboard* separately charted the song at number 12. This rocking version was recorded specifically for the singles market. The original version of the song, titled *Revolution 1*, is on *The White Album*.

*Hey Jude* was the A side to Apple's first release. It topped the *Billboard Hot 100* for nine straight weeks in the fall of 1968 and sold nearly five million copies in the United States. With a running time of over seven minutes, *Hey Jude* is one of the longest songs released by the Beatles, eclipsed only by the sound collage *Revolution 9* and *I Want You (She's So Heavy)*.

George's *Old Brown Shoe* was the B side to *The Ballad Of John And Yoko* (Apple 2531), which was released on June 4, 1969. It is the only song on the album that did not make the *Billboard Hot 100*.

*Don't Let Me Down* was the flip side to *Get Back* (Apple 2490), which was released on May 5, 1969. The song charted at number 35 in the *Billboard Hot 100*. Although a different version of the song was slated to appear on the *Get Back* album, the revised *Let It Be* LP does not contain the song.

*The Ballad Of John And Yoko* only reached number eight in the *Billboard Hot 100*. The song's relatively poor performance was due to its limited airplay resulting from the song's controversial lyrics. While radio programers were reluctant to play the single, Beatles fans were not offended and purchased over one million copies of the disc.

While the *Hey Jude* LP contains ten songs making their Capitol album debut, it was not intended to fill in all the gaps. At the time the record was programmed in November, 1969, the following songs still had not appeared on a Capitol album: *Misery* and *There's A Place* (although both were on Vee-Jay's *Introducing The Beatles* LP); *From Me To You*, which was a number one hit in England, but got lost (when issued as the B side to *Please Please Me* on Vee-Jay 581) among the multitude of Beatles songs released in America in early 1964; *Sie Liebt Dich*, the German lyric version of *She Loves You*, which was released on Swan 4182 in May, 1964; *A Hard Day's Night*, which appeared on the United Artists soundtrack album; *I'm Down*, the hard-rocking flip side to *Help!* (Capitol 5476); and *The Inner Light*, the neglected B side to *Lady Madonna*.

Although *Get Back* had yet to appear on a Capitol LP, there was no reason to include the song as it was slated to be the title track to the group's next album. With only ten songs and a running time of approximately 33⅓ minutes, the *Hey Jude* album could have included all of above recordings (less *Get Back*).

Beatles historians and collectors have always assumed that Capitol Records was the driving force behind the *Hey Jude* album. This, however, is not the case. Allen Klein was anxious to have another Beatles album delivered to Capitol under the terms of the lucrative new contract signed between the parties. In late November, 1969, he asked Allan Steckler, an Abkco employee assigned to manage Apple, if there was any material available to put into a Beatles album.

Steckler reviewed the Capitol catalog to determine what songs had yet to appear on an American album. He selected ten songs covering the Beatles entire career and programmed the running order. This information was forwarded to EMI with instructions to compile a stereo master tape for the LP. Four of the pre-1969 songs had never appeared on a British album and needed to be mixed for stereo. Existing stereo mixes were used for the other selections.

*Can't Buy Me Love* and *I Should Have Known Better* were mixed for stereo on June 22, 1964, for inclusion on the stereo version of the Parlophone album *A Hard Day's Night* (PCS 3058). EMI used these mixes for the new LP.

As the stereo version of the United Artists soundtrack LP contains mono mixes of these songs, the *Hey Jude* album marked the stereo debut of these songs in America.

*Paperback Writer* was mixed for stereo on October 31, 1966, for the British hits album *A Collection Of Beatles Oldies* (Parlophone PCS 7016). For the *Hey Jude* LP, EMI used an alternate stereo mix with reversed stereo and louder backing vocals. Because the single's flip side, *Rain*, had only been issued in mono, EMI had to create a stereo mix. On December 2, 1969, George Martin, assisted by engineers Geoff Emerick and Phil McDonald, made a stereo mix of *Rain* from Take 7. A stereo mix of *Lady Madonna* from Take 5 was also made that day.

On December 5, the same crew, along with second engineer Neil Richmond, created a stereo mix for *Revolution* from Take 16. Although *Hey Jude* had been mixed for stereo on August 2, 1968, a new stereo mix was made from Take 1 on December 5. The remaining three tracks for the album had previously been mixed for stereo. EMI assembled the master tape for the LP on December 8 and sent the tape to Abkco's New York headquarters.

At the time the album was conceived in late 1969, Apple, through Abkco, was taking a more active role in the production and promotion of its releases. Apple had become increasingly frustrated with Capitol's handling of Apple product. According to Steckler, "Capitol was doing things in Capitol's best interests, not the Beatles. Advertising and release dates centered around Capitol's schedule, so things weren't getting done when Apple wanted them done." In response, Apple began placing its own advertisements in the trades and directly handling production matters previously handled by Capitol.

Although Capitol had its own mastering facilities in the Capitol Tower and in its New York studios, Steckler began taking the tapes of all Apple releases to Bell Sound Studios, Inc., 237 W. 54th Street, New York, New York, for mastering. He personally supervised the mastering, which was done by Sam Feldman. His relationship with Bell Sound dated back to 1961.

On December 11, 1969, Sam Feldman mastered two reference dubs of the album. The following day, 41 sets of lacquers, also cut by Feldman, were sent to Capitol. An additional two sets of lacquers, numbered 42 and 43,

were sent to Capitol on January 21, 1970. The trail off areas to the records generated from these lacquers have the Bell Sound machine stamped script logo and the hand etched initials "sf" for Sam Feldman.

By the time Capitol began pressing copies of the album, its new factory in Winchester, Virginia, had come on line and the Scranton plant was being phased out. First pressings of the album were manufactured by all four of Capitol's factories.

Capitol initially assigned catalog number SO-385 to the record. The "S" stands for stereo and the "O" indicates a list price of $6.98. Although *Abbey Road* had a then-high list price of $6.98, Capitol and Apple had second thoughts about charging an extra dollar for an album containing no new songs. Prior to its release, the LP was renumbered SW-385, with the "W" indicating a $5.98 list price. The trail off areas to the records generated from the original Bell Sound lacquers have the "SO" prefix. Some of the Winchester pressings have a "W" written over the "O" in the "SO" prefix.

Two counter displays were prepared to promote the record. The more basic easel-back cardboard display, **APP 385.D1**, measures 12" x 16" and features a color image of the front cover with "THE BEATLES • HEY JUDE" and the songs titles appearing in white upper case letters in a black rectangle above the cover photo. The more elaborate display, **APP 385.D2**, serves as a record bin. The gold cardboard display is 27" tall and 15" wide. The lower portion contains a black and white picture from the same session that produced the album's cover. A thin metal bar runs in front of the lower panel to hold albums in place. The top portion states "New from the Beatles!" in upper case letters. An Apple logo is used for the dot in the exclamation point.

Although the album was released as *Hey Jude*, its original title was *The Beatles Again*. At least two different covers were constructed with this title.

**The pictures used on the front and back cover of the album were taken at John's estate by Ethan Russell on August 22, 1969, in what would be the group's final photo session. This counter standee created for *Anthology 3* used another picture from the same session.**

The front cover of the first design, **APP 385.AD1**, features the picture of the band that ended up on the back of the released jacket. The color photograph was taken at John's Tittenhurst estate on August 22, 1969. Ringo and George are standing while Paul and John are sitting on the lawn. John's white house and a brick fence are in the background. The album title "BEATLES AGAIN" appears in black letters curving above a potted plant centered in the upper part of the photo. The back cover features a picture from the same session that was used for the front of the released jacket. The group is shown standing in front of the wooden front door to the estate's Victorian assembly hall. A stone bust, separated from and in front of its pillar, is on the ground to the left of the Beatles. Another stone bust perched atop a pillar is to the right. This figure is wearing George's black hat. The titles to the songs appear in black upper case letters on the marble slab in front of the door. A black and white picture of the group standing in a wooded area of John's estate is superimposed above the door. The record number Apple SO-385 is in the upper right corner and a green Apple logo is in the lower right corner. The jacket has "THE BEATLES AGAIN" and "APPLE SO-385" printed on its spine.

The second design, **APP 385.AD2,** has the same front cover as the released jacket, which uses the back cover photo from **APP 385.AD1** without the text and Apple logo. Its back cover is similar to the released back cover, which features the picture that served as the front cover to **APP 385.AD1**. The photo is surrounded by a two inch border, which contains information about the album in white letters. The record number is in the upper right corner. The border area below the picture has the song titles followed by "PRODUCED BY GEORGE MARTIN/PHOTOS BY MAL EVANS" and "Manufactured by APPLE RECORDS INC. • 1700 Broadway, New York,

**The counter display (left) has a thin metal bar in front to hold the *Hey Jude* albums in place. APP 385.D2**

N.Y. 10019." "Printed in U.S.A." is in upper case letters in the lower right corner. A green Apple logo is in the lower left corner of the picture. The differences between this design and the released back cover are: the background border is dark magenta rather than black; "BEATLES AGAIN" appears in purple above the potted plant only on this alternate design; Mal Evans' photo credit is removed; "Printed in U.S.A." is in a circle rather than in a horizontal line; and the record number has the prefix "SO" rather than "SW." The spine also has the original title and record number.

There is also an alternate back cover slick, **APP 385.AD3**,that has a gray background and an ornate white patterned design surrounding the photo. The album's new title, *Hey Jude*, appears above the photo in white upper case letters. The titles to the songs, also in white upper case letters, surround the other sides of the centered picture. The number Apple SW-385 is in the upper right corner.

The finished cover, **APP 385.SC1,** uses the same front slick as **APP 385.AD2**, except that the spine has the album's new title and number in white letters. "THE BEATLES • HEY JUDE" is towards the top of the spine and "APPLE SW-385" is at the bottom. The back slick is similar to the back of **APP 385.AD2**, except for the differences detailed above. The negatives for the cover slicks were shipped to the printers on February 7, 1970.

The *Hey Jude* album was certified gold by the RIAA on March 6, 1970. That same day Capitol had the RIAA gold record award seal added to the front cover slick. Later issue covers, **APP 385.SC2**, have the seal (shown left).

APP 385.AD1

APP 385.AD2

APP 385.SC1 (front)

APP 385.AD3 (back slick)

The covers were constructed with color front slicks that wrap around to the back of the cardboard jacket. The smaller color back slicks were pasted over the portion of the front slick that wraps around to the back. The slicks were printed by Queens Litho and Bert-Co. The covers were manufactured by Imperial and Modern Album.

Neither the group's name nor the album's title appear on the front of the jacket. Some of the covers came with a white background sticker with either red or purple ink to identify the album's title and highlight the inclusion to the Beatles mega-hit *Hey Jude*. The stickers were affixed either directly to the cover or on the shrink wrap, normally towards the top of the cover.

All of the sticker variations (shown below) have HEY JUDE surrounded by quote marks. There are three confirmed 5" x 2" stickers. **APP 385.S1** has curved quote marks and is printed in red ink. **APP 385.S2** has straight quote marks and is printed in red ink. **APP 385.S3** has straight quote marks and is similar to **APP 385.S2**, but has higher-placed quote marks and is printed in purple ink. There is also at least one variation of a 10" x 2" sticker. **APP 385.S4** has straight quote marks and is printed in red ink. Price guides mention a 10" x 2" sticker with purple ink, but this variation has not been confirmed by the author. If such a sticker exists, it will be assigned **APP 385.S5**.

The initial labels printed for the album, **APP 385.SR1**, have both the album's original title, *The Beatles Again*, and the album's original number, SO-385. There are three confirmed variations, all of which have "THE BEATLES AGAIN" and the group's name centered at the top of the apple on side one and Apple perimeter print on side two. **SR1L(as)** has the album's opening track, *Can't Buy Me Love*, above the spindle hole on side one, and the album title and group's name in the upper left part of the apple, "Produced by George Martin" in the lower left part and "Recorded in England" in the lower right part on side two. This label has been confirmed on Winchester, Scranton and

Los Angeles pressings. **SR1J(as)** has the album's opening track, *Can't Buy Me Love*, above the spindle hole on side one, and the album title and group's name centered at the top of the apple and "Produced by George Martin" and "Recorded in England" centered at the bottom of the apple on side two. This variation also has "Manufactured by Apple Records, Inc." between the production credit and recording location on both sides. These labels were pressed with Jacksonville discs. **SR1S(as)** has all the song titles below the spindle hole on side one, and the album title and group's name in the upper left part of the apple, "Produced by George Martin" in the lower left part and "Recorded in England" in the lower right part on side two. These labels were used for Scranton and some of the Winchester pressings.

There are also labels with the original album title, *The Beatles Again*, and the revised number, SW-385. Only one variation has been confirmed. It is identical to **APP 385.SR1L** except that it has the SW prefix rather than the SO prefix, **APP 385.SR2L(as)**.

After supplies of labels with the album's original title were exhausted, new labels were prepared with the corrected record number, SW-385, and the album's new title, *Hey Jude*, **APP 385.SR3**. All of the labels with this variation examined for this book have the same layout as **APP 385.SR1L**. This variation appears on three different label backdrops: Apple perimeter print on side two, **SR1L(as)**; Capitol logo perimeter print on side two, **SR1L(c)**; and Apple perimeter print on side one, **SR1L(af)**.

There are two confirmed all rights variations. **APP 385.SR4C(ar)** has the all rights language in green running along the lower right perimeter on the full apple side. These labels have dark green apples and have been confirmed on Jacksonville pressings. **APP 385.SR4D(ar)** has Apple perimeter print and the all rights language in green running in the lower perimeter on both sides. These all rights labels have light green apples and have been confirmed with Los Angeles pressings.

APP 385.D1
Hey Jude Counter Display

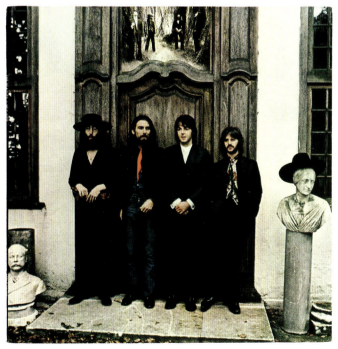

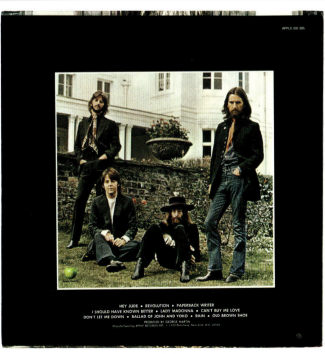

APP 385.SC1 (front)

APP 385.SC1 (back)

APP 385.SR1L(as)
APP 385.SR2L(as) (detailed left and right)

APP 385.SR1J(as)

APP 385.SR1S(as)

APP 385.SR3L(as)

APP 385.SR3L(c)
(shown)
APP 385.SR3L(af) (same, except Apple perimeter print on side one)

APP 385.SR4C(ar)
(All rights only on full apple side)

APP 385.SR4D(ar)
(All rights on both sides)

HEY JUDE • REVOLUTION • PAPERBACK WRITER
I SHOULD HAVE KNOWN BETTER • LADY MADONNA • CAN'T BUY ME LOVE
DON'T LET ME DOWN • BALLAD OF JOHN AND YOKO • RAIN • OLD BROWN SHOE
ALBUM NOW AVAILABLE • STEREO • PRODUCED BY GEORGE MARTIN

APPLE RECORDS
SW-385

Apple placed an ad for the *Hey Jude* LP on the back cover of the June 14, 1969, *Billboard.*

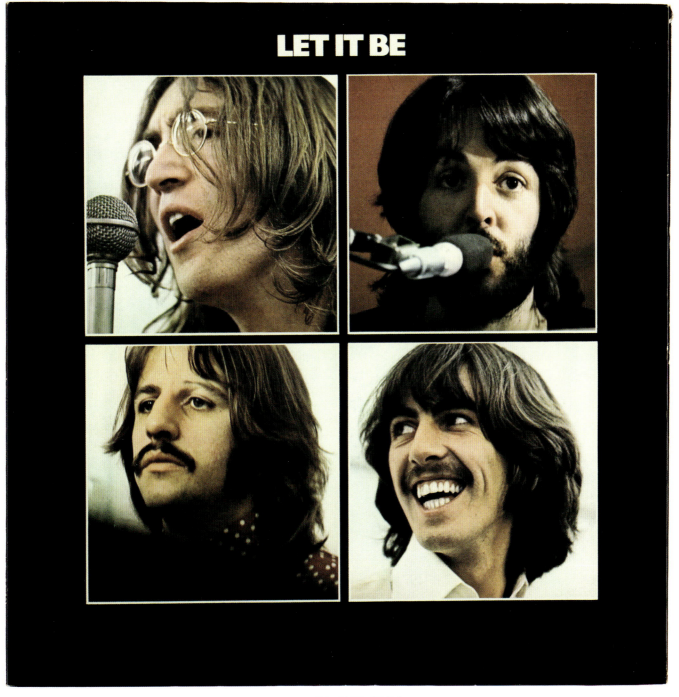

# LET IT BE
# APPLE AR 34001

Side 1
1. TWO OF US (Lennon; McCartney)
2. I DIG A PONY (Lennon; McCartney)
3. ACROSS THE UNIVERSE (Lennon; McCartney)
4. I ME MINE (Harrison)
5. DIG IT (Lennon; McCartney; Harrison; Starr)
6. LET IT BE (Lennon; McCartney)
7. MAGGIE MAE (P.D.)

Side 2
1. I'VE GOT A FEELING (Lennon; McCartney)
2. ONE AFTER 909 (Lennon; McCartney)
3. THE LONG AND WINDING ROAD
   (Lennon; McCartney)
4. FOR YOU BLUE (Harrison)
5. GET BACK (Lennon; McCartney)

This is a new phase **BEATLES** album...
essential to the content of the film, **LET IT BE** was that they performed
live for many of the tracks; in comes the warmth and the freshness of a live
performance; as reproduced for disc by **PHIL SPECTOR**

Had the liner notes from the back cover of *Let It Be* (quoted on the previous page) been subjected to truth-in-advertising law, they might have read something like this:

This is a new phase **BEATLES** album....well, actually it's the last **BEATLES** album as Paul recently announced he's quitting the band and John actually left over a half year ago, and we don't think that this is just a phase they're going through, they really mean it, the **BEATLES** are over, kaput...and as for new, well, to tell the truth, most of these recordings are over 15 months old...

essential to the content of the film, **LET IT BE**, was that they performed live for many of the tracks...well, actually, they performed live for all of the tracks in the film...we didn't tinker with the film's soundtrack, but as for this LP, well let's just say that the "new phase" approach allowed the group to abandon its original concept of making an honest live-in-the-studio album without any overdubs...

in comes the warmth and freshness of a live performance; as reproduced for disc by **PHIL SPECTOR** ...well, actually, some of you will think "in comes **PHIL SPECTOR**, out goes the warmth and freshness of a live performance; as overproduced for the disc by **PHIL SPECTOR**;" but if you can forgive him for his fruity arrangement of *Let It Be* and the excessive strings and choir on *The Long And Winding Road*, you will marvel at the warmth and freshness of *Two Of Us*, *For You Blue* and the unaltered rooftop performances.

More than 15 months after the conclusion of the *Get Back* sessions, an album containing recordings from the January, 1969, Apple basement and rooftop sessions was finally released in May, 1970. By this time the *Get Back* single was a year old, so both the album and the film were renamed *Let It Be* after the group's latest hit single.

In England, *Let It Be* was released by Parlophone as Apple PCS 7096 on May 8, 1970. The album was packaged in a box (Apple PXS 1) along with a 164-page book containing photographs by Ethan Russell and text featuring selected dialog from the film. In spite of its high list price resulting from the elaborate packaging, the album topped the British charts for three weeks. The record was not issued as a standard album without the book until November 6, 1970.

In the United States, the *Let It Be* album was released on May 18 and distributed through United Artists Records as Apple AR 34001. It did not come with the book, but rather was issued in a gatefold jacket.

*Let It Be* made its debut on the *Billboard Top LP's* chart at number 104 on May 30. The following week it moved up to the second spot behind Paul's solo album *McCartney* (Apple STAO 3363). On June 13, *Let It Be* began its four week run at the top before being replaced by the soundtrack to *Woodstock* (Cotillion SD3 500). The album was certified gold by the RIAA on May 26, 1970. The June 6 *Billboard* reported Allen Klein's claim that the LP shipped 3.2 million units in 13 days. As of 2002, the RIAA certified sales of four million units.

The early history of the *Get Back/Let It Be* project is detailed in the chapters on the unreleased *Get Back* albums. This chapter explains why and how Glyn Johns' honest live-in-the-studio album became Phil Spector's lush production.

Although Allen Klein had nothing to do with the recording of the songs or the original concept behind the project, he clearly left his mark on *Let It Be*. It was Klein who convinced the Beatles that they would earn significantly more money by releasing their documentary film as a movie rather than broadcasting it on television as originally planned. He told the group it would be stupid to waste the show on one-time broadcast deals when a movie would generate money for years to come.

Allen Klein approached United Artists with the proposition of having the documentary count as the third and final film owed by the Beatles under their 1963 agreement with United Artists. According to David Picker, who was then serving as president of United Artists, the company agreed to accept the documentary as the third film because they realized there would be no more movies like *Help!* or *A Hard Day's Night*.

Under their film agreement with United Artists, the Beatles also owed the company a soundtrack album. This is confirmed by the group's January 26, 1967, contract with EMI, which acknowledges that the Beatles "have a commitment to United Artists whereunder one LP record of a film of the [Beatles] shall be made available for United Artists for the U.S.A. only." During the film negotiations, Klein told United Artists that they would get the distribution rights for the soundtrack album in the United States.

As a result of the United Artists deal for the documentary film and its soundtrack LP, Capitol lost what was then still known as the *Get Back* album. In order to ease the blow, Klein arranged for Capitol to manufacture the records. Thus, while the album was not part of the Capitol catalog in the United States, the company did receive substantial income for pressing the discs. Because the soundtrack LP agreement was limited to the U.S.A., Capitol Records (Canada) and Discos Capitol de Mexico were not affected. Accordingly, the *Let It Be* album was distributed by Capitol's subsidiaries in Canada and Mexico.

While Klein was confident that the documentary film would be a huge success, he had concerns about the album. Abkco's Allan Steckler observed that "The Beatles had shown a marked progression in their writing, playing and production values. *Get Back* was a drastic throwback. It didn't fit in. Particularly when compared to *Abbey Road*, which was the group's most sleek production. *Abbey Road* was very slick. It slid over the speakers. By comparison, *Get Back* didn't sound finished." According to Steckler, Klein felt the same way. He wanted to bring in his old friend Phil Spector to fix it.

Phil Spector was one of the top record producers of the early and mid-sixties, best known for his famous "wall of sound" that turned pop records into mini-symphonic operas. Spector got his start in the music business as a member of the Teddy Bears, a vocal trio that had a number one hit in 1958 with his song *To Know Him Is To Love Him*

**The featured picture in the above 11" x 14" lobby card from the film shows Paul engaged in animated conversation with Ringo, John with Yoko at his side, George Harrison in the background and George Martin looking bored and concerned. Additional lobby cards are shown on page 199.**

(Dore 503). The Beatles included a gender-altered version of the song, *To Know Her Is To Love Her*, in their early stage show repertoire. *Live At The BBC* contains the Beatles July 16, 1963, recording of the song, which was broadcast on *Pop Go The Beatles* on August 6, 1963.

In May, 1960, Spector began serving an apprenticeship under famed songwriters and producers Jerry Leiber and Mike Stoller, during which time he attended sessions with acts such as the Coasters, the Drifters and Ben E. King. He not only learned production techniques at these sessions, but also contributed his ideas. Spector played guitar on some songs, including *Thumbin' A Ride* by the Coasters (Atco 6186) (later recorded by Apple artist Jackie Lomax and released on Apple 1807) and *Saved* by LaVern Baker (Atlantic 2099), a number 37 hit in early 1962. He later played the guitar solo for the Drifters *On Broadway* (Atlantic 2182), a number nine hit in April, 1963.

Spector's biggest success came when he formed Philles Records with Lester Sill in 1961. The label's early hits included: the Crystals' *He's A Rebel* (Philles 106; #1 in November, 1962), *Da Doo Ron Ron* (Philles 112; #3 in June, 1963) and *Then He Kissed Me* (Philles 115; #6 in Septem-

ber, 1963); *Zip-A-Dee-Doo-Dah* by Bob B. Soxx and the Blue Jeans (Philles 107; #8 in January, 1963); and *Be My Baby* by the Ronettes (Philles 116; #2 in October, 1963).

Spector flew to London on January 24, 1964, for a promotional visit coinciding with the Ronettes British tour. Because Philles product was distributed in England by London Records, a Decca subsidiary, Decca promotion manager Tony Hall helped arrange Spector's itinerary. Hall set up a meeting with the Rolling Stones, who recorded for Decca, and their manager/producer, Andrew Oldham. Spector attended a few of the sessions for the Rolling Stones' first album, co-wrote *Little By Little* with the group and reportedly played maracas on *Not Fade Away*, which became the band's first American hit (London 9657; #48 in July, 1964).

Famed British journalist Maureen Cleave interviewed Spector. In her *Disc Date* column for *The Evening Standard*, she reported that Spector "heard the Beatles months ago and loved them. Thought they were a great Canadian outfit. 'I would love to have a crack at recording that group,' said Mr. Spector longingly."

Hall also arranged for Phil and the Ronettes to meet the Beatles at his London home (see photo above with Phil surrounded by the Ronettes and George Harrison). Spector was on the plane with the Beatles when they flew to New York on February 7, 1964, for their first American visit. Later that year, Spector produced a recording of Lennon and McCartney's *Hold Me Tight* by the Treasures (Shirley 500).

The mid-sixties saw Spector's greatest triumph and failure. Working with Barry Mann and Cynthia Weil, he cowrote *You've Lost That Lovin' Feeling* specifically for the Righteous Brothers, Bill Medley and Bobby Hatfield, who were known for their "blue-eyed soul" style of singing. The Spector-produced epic ballad was released on Philles 124 and topped the charts for two weeks in February, 1965. According to BMI, *You've Lost That Lovin' Feeling* was the first song to be performed over eight million times.

Spector tried to repeat the magic in 1966 with Ike and Tina Turner, who he had signed to his Philles label. He cowrote *River Deep–Mountain High* with Jeff Barry and Ellie Greenwich, with whom he had collaborated with on *Da Doo Ron Ron*, *Then He Kissed Me* and *Be My Baby*. He reportedly spent over $22,000 laying down the song's dense thundering rhythm track. Tina's vocal was recorded on March 7, 1966. When released in America the following May on Philles 131, the record charted for four weeks, peaking at number 88 before falling off the charts. Although the song was a number two hit in England, Spector was crushed by the song's failure in America and began a self-imposed exile from the music business.

In 1969, Spector attempted a comeback under a deal with A&M Records. His biggest success was his production of *Black Pearl* by Sonny Charles and the Checkmates, Ltd.(A&M 1053), which reached number 13 that summer. On September 13, A&M released Ike and Tina Turner's *River Deep–Mountain High* album for the first time in the U.S. The cover to the record (A&M SP 4178) came with a

sticker proclaiming "*River Deep–Mountain High* is a perfect record from start to finish. You couldn't improve on it." The quote was followed by the signature of George Harrison.

When Spector's association with A&M ended shortly thereafter, he began planning a serious return to the record business, prompting a page one story in the December 13, 1969, *Billboard*. It was around this time that Allen Klein came up with the idea to have Phil Spector work his magic on the *Get Back* album. Rather than directly approach the Beatles about having Spector redo their album, Klein went for a more subtle approach. He arranged for Phil to meet with John and Yoko.

On January 27, 1970, John wrote a new song titled *Instant Karma! (We All Shine On)*. He wanted to record the song that evening and quickly recruited a version of the Plastic Ono Band with George Harrison on lead guitar, Klaus Voormann on bass, Billy Preston on electric piano and Alan White on drums. At Harrison's suggestion, John had Phil Spector, who was in London at the time, produce the record.

Spector's successful handling of the session led to him being invited by John and George (with Klein's blessings) to reproduce the *Get Back* album. Spector began his work on the project on March 23, 1970, at Abbey Road. He was assisted by balance engineer Peter Bown. Many of the sessions were attended by Harrison and Klein, and Ringo was recruited to play drums for the orchestral overdub session held on April 1. Spector completed his mixes for the album the following day.

Because the album had to completed quickly to coincide with the release of the movie, Spector did not wade through the multitude of tapes recorded at Apple during January, 1969. Instead, he limited his review to the *Get Back* album, other recordings previously mixed by Glyn Johns and the film itself. Although Spector added orchestration to three of the songs, he followed Glyn Johns' concept of giving the album a live-in-the-studio feeling by mixing in bits of studio chatter between the tracks.

The released album, as reproduced for disc by Phil Spector, opens with dialog from John: "*I Dig a Pigmy* by Charles Hawtrey and the Deaf-aids. Phase one in which Doris gets her oats.*" Lennon's remark is immediately followed by Ringo hitting his snare drum. This segment, which appears in the film, was taped during rehearsals for *Dig A Pony* held on January 21. Charles Hawtrey was a British actor, and deaf-aids is slang for hearing aids, although the group often used the term when referring to their amplifiers. Doris pops up elsewhere during the sessions and may have been an inside joke.

The album's first song is *Two Of Us*. While Glyn Johns chose a somewhat sluggish performance of the song from January 24,1969, Spector selected Take 11 from January 31. This up-beat rendition is clearly the best version of the song recorded by the Beatles. It was used in the film and shown on the March 1, 1970, *Ed Sullivan Show*. Spector became aware of this version of the song from watching an advance of the film and recognized that it was vastly superior to the January 24 performance picked by Johns.

Spector's March 25,1970, mix of *Two Of Us* is superb: the acoustic guitars are bright and crisp; the vocals are clean and up front; George's bass part on the upper strings of his guitar is in the background, but clearly audible; and Ringo's drumming is given emphasis at the appropriate times. Spector was able to bring out the beauty of the song as performed live by the Beatles and wisely chose not to add any embellishments.

Spector also played it pretty straight with the album's next song, *Dig A Pony*. Rather than using the ragged January 22 runthrough selected by Johns, Spector chose the superior January 30 rooftop performance of the song. Just as the song is about to begin, Ringo calls out "Hold it," so he can blow his nose. This is followed by Lennon's count-in leading into the song. Spector's March 23, 1970, mix of *Dig A Pony* completely mixes out the "All I want is ..." vocal line that opens and closes the song.

*Across The Universe* is the first song on the album heavily produced by Spector. Phil, like George Martin and Glyn Johns before him, started with Take 8 from February 8, 1968. But while Martin sped up the song and Johns left its speed alone, Spector slowed it down so that the song dropped from D to D flat and ran nine seconds longer. On March 23, he made eight mixes, none of which were used. Then, on April 1, he made a reduction mixdown from Take 8 (designated Take 9) onto an eight track tape. Separate tracks were provided for the following elements of Take 8: (1) the reduction mix of Take 7; (2) John's vocal recorded on February 8; and (3) maracas, George's wah-wah guitar and McCartney's piano recorded on February 8. That left five open tracks for overdubing an orchestral backing, a choir and fresh acoustic guitars. Later that day, Spector recorded Richard Hewson's score of 18 violins, four violas, four cellos, one harp, three trumpets, three trombones, two acoustic guitars, a 14-person choir and Ringo on drums. The orchestra was conducted by Hewson, who had served as arranger for Paul McCartney's production of *Those Were The Days* by Mary Hopkin (Apple 1801) and would later score Paul's *Thrillington* album (Capitol ST 11642), which consisted of orchestral arrangements of Paul's *Ram* LP (Apple SMAS 3375).

Spector mixed *Across The Universe* the following day. The song opens with John's acoustic guitar, which is heard as part of the reduction mix of Take 7. John's guitar disappears during the chorus and other parts of the song where the reduction mix of Take 7 is faded out. Similarly, George's tamboura is heard only during the times the reduction mix of Take 7 is brought to the front of the mix. By using John's February 8 vocal from Take 8 and acoustic guitars recorded on April 1, Spector was able to fade out the reduction mix of Take 7 during the chorus, thus eliminating the backing vocals of Lizzie Bravo and Gayleen Pease. He also mixed in maracas and Harrison's wah-wah guitar (second and third refrains only) from Take 8 during the chorus. McCartney's bass piano notes, also from Take 8, appear towards the end of the song. With the exception of John's acoustic guitar intro, the mix is dominated by Spector's trademark wall of sound, though Lennon's lead vocal is prominently featured.

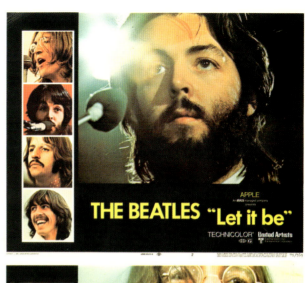

**Members of the Beatles American fan club were sent a 45 RPM record containing selections of dialog from the movie (left). The Bell Sound acetate for the dialog disc is shown right.**

George's *I Me Mine* was also given the wall of sound treatment. On March 23, Spector made his initial mix of the song from Take 16. He eliminated one of George's two lead vocals to free up a track for later overdubs and extended the song by 51 seconds with a clever edit. At the 1:21 mark, just after the line "flowing more freely than wine," the song jumps back to the :31 mark to the line "all though the day." This leads back into the hard-rocking "I I me me mine" segment and continues past "flowing more freely than wine" until the end of the song.

On April 1, Richard Hewson's orchestral score was superimposed over the extended edit of the song. Spector recorded the same musicians that played on *Across The Universe*, including Ringo on drums, but thankfully did not use the choir. His April 2 mix of *I Me Mine* keeps the orchestra in the background and allows the Beatles rocking performance to shine through.

While Spector extended *I Me Mine* from 1:34 to 2:25, he chose to shorten *Dig It*. The Glyn Johns edit was just under four and a half minutes long. Spector thought 51 seconds was enough. He faded up the song as John begins singing "Like a rolling stone" three times, followed by "Like the FBI, and the CIA, and the BBC, B.B. King, and Doris Day, Matt Busby, dig it...." He copied Glyn Johns' link from *Dig It* to *Let It Be* by crossfading into Lennon's "That was *Can You Dig It* by Georgie Wood. And now we'd like to do *Hark, The Angels Come*."

Although Phil Spector did not record any additional orchestral parts for *Let It Be*, his mix of the song was a drastic departure from both the Glyn Johns mix and the George Martin-produced single. One can't help but wonder why Spector tinkered with the single version of *Let It Be*, which was riding high on the charts at the time he remixed the song on March 26. Perhaps he wanted to create the illusion that the album contained a different performance.

Martin embellished the piano ballad with subtle orchestration and backing vocals recorded on January 4, 1970. Although Harrison recorded an additional guitar solo that same day, Martin chose not to use the raunchy-sounding new solo, instead opting for Harrison's more laid back solo recorded on April 30, 1969.

There is nothing subtle about Phil Spector's mix. Although the first verse and chorus sound similar to the other mixes, the remainder of the song has a totally different feel. During the second verse, Ringo's hi-hat is given a distracting echo effect. The next chorus has the brass blaring away. For the instrumental break, Spector mixed in Harrison's January 4 distorted solo, which is too heavy-handed for the ballad. The percussion once again becomes a distraction during the third verse with awkward drumming from Ringo and over-emphasis of the maracas. Spector extended the song from 3:50 to 4:01 by editing in an additional chorus after the third verse. The concluding choruses have Paul's vocal fighting for attention with blaring brass and George's raunchy lead guitar. Even John Lennon, who championed Spector's work on the album, admitted that Phil got "a little fruity" on *Let It Be*.

Side one concludes with *Maggie Mae*, which was also mixed by Spector on March 26. It is very similar to Glyn Johns' mix of the song.

The second side of the album opens with *I've Got A Feeling*. Phil Spector had four different Glyn Johns mixes to consider: an incomplete January 22 runthrough selected for the *Get Back* album; a more polished January 27 take from the March 13, 1969, acetate; and two rooftop performances. On March 23, 1970, Spector made mixes of the January 27 take and the first rooftop performance, which appears in the film. When banding the album, Spector went with the rooftop version, including John's post song banter, "Oh my soul...so hard."

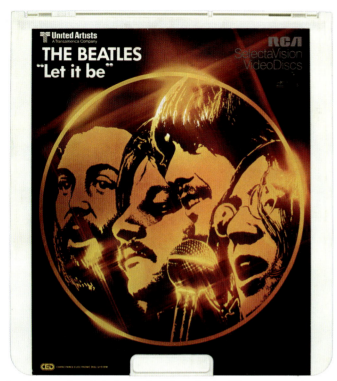 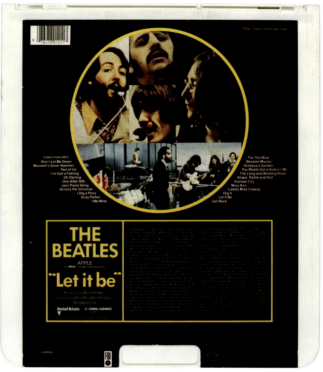

In the early eighties, the *Let It Be* film was released as a RCA SelectaVision VideoDisc. The playback-only format, which was introduced to the consumer market in 1981 and phased out from 1984 through 1986, consisted of a Capacitance Electronic Disc ("CED") stored in a thin plastic protective caddy. Unlike the competing Laserdisc format, the information stored on the carbon-loaded disc was not read by a laser, but rather by a thin titanium electrode on the player's diamond stylus. The system was a curious mix of new and old technologies. After the caddy was placed into the player, its motorized system extracted the disc from the caddy so it could be played. On some models, the machine ejected the empty caddy. The 12" discs were like old phonograph records in that they had grooves and were played by a needle while rotating at 450 revolutions per minute. Paper slicks containing pictures and information about the contents were glued onto both sides of the caddy. The *Let It Be* CED is collectible because of its unique artwork.

The album's next track, *One After 909*, is another rooftop performance mixed by Spector on March 23. This is the same take that Glyn Johns selected for the *Get Back* album; however, the mix is different. Spector retained Lennon's brief rendition of *Danny Boy* that follows the song.

The next two tracks, *The Long And Winding Road* and *For You Blue*, were issued on a single prior to the release of the album. Details regarding these songs are provided in the chapter on the single.

The album concludes with the same performance of *Get Back* that was issued for the single (and selected for the *Get Back* album), but with sufficient modifications to trick the listener into thinking it is a different take of the song. Spector starts the track with the instrumental and vocal warm-ups and banter that precede the January 27 performance selected for the single. This includes John's parody of the lyrics, "Sweet Loretta Fart, she thought she was a cleaner, but she was a frying pan," along with Paul mumbling "Rosetta" and practicing his "Sweet Loretta Mar..." opening notes, and George readying his guitar for the song's choppy rhythm guitar intro. To further add to the live feel of the track, Spector did not mix out Billy Preston's stray electric piano notes hit during the build-up instrumental intro. At the end of the performance, Spector did not cut to the January 28 coda used on the single, but rather added the post-song clapping and remarks from the end of the roof-

top concert. The album concludes appropriately with Paul's "Thanks, Mo" (to Ringo's wife Maureen for clapping the loudest) and John's "I'd like to say 'Thank you' on behalf of group and ourselves. I hope we passed the audition."

After the decision was made to change the title of the movie and the album to *Let It Be*, the *Get Back* front cover was modified by changing the text from "GET BACK With Let It Be and 10 other songs" to "LET IT BE and 10 other songs." (Apparently *Maggie Mae* didn't count as a song.) Page 323 in the *Anthology* book contains images of both of these proposed covers.

Although the original cover concept was perfect for an album featuring the Beatles getting back to their roots, the Angus McBean photo of the group in the EMI stairwell had nothing to do with the film. When the album was converted to a movie soundtrack LP, the planned cover was no longer appropriate. It was replaced with a modified version of the front cover to the *Get Back* book (see page 243).

The new jacket features the same Ethan Russell color photographs of the faces of John, Paul, George and Ringo appearing on the *Get Back* book, except that the pictures are cropped at the sides to form 4¾" squares. The background to the cover is black, with the only text being the album's title in white block letters centered above the pictures. Like its predecessors *Abbey Road* and *Hey Jude*, the album does not have the group's name on the front jacket.

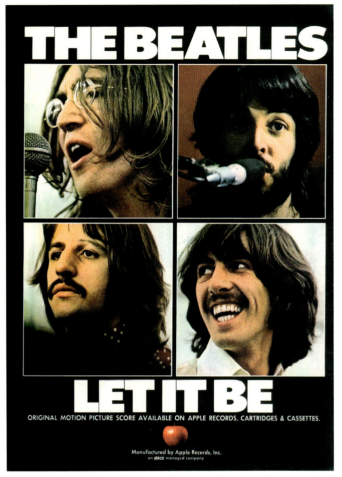

Apple placed an ad featuring the images from *Let It Be* album cover on the back of the May 23, 1970, issue of *Billboard*.

The back cover also has a black background. The text quoted at the beginning of this chapter, along with a list of the song titles, appears in white above black and white photos of each Beatle. This is followed by additional text in white: "Thanks to George Martin/Glyn Johns/Billy Preston/ Harold Seider/Mal Davies/Peter Brown/Richard Hewson/ Brian Rogers;" "Design by John Kosh;" and "Photographs by Ethan Russell." The lower part of the back cover varies among countries, with each country providing its own manufacturing information.

In the United States, the album was packaged in a gate-fold cover, **APP 34001.SC1**. The left inside panel of the open cover contains a color picture of the cavernous Twickenham soundstage shot from above. The right panel has eight color photos: a shot of the group and Yoko in the Apple basement control room; solo close-up shots of each Beatle; a rooftop picture of John and Paul; a Twickenham picture of George and Ringo; and a Twickenham picture of the group. The bottom section of the back cover has a red Apple logo and "Manufactured by Apple Records, Inc. 1700 Broadway, New York, New York 10019 an abkco managed company." (The address for Apple is the same as the address for Allen Klein's corporation, Abkco.)

In all major markets except the United States, the album was packaged in a black cardboard box containing a 164-page book of Ethan Russell photographs and text by Jonathan Cott and David Dalton. Apple wanted United Artists to issue the album with the book; however, United Art-

ists balked at the idea. Had the *Get Back* album been released by Capitol as originally planned, it would have had a list price of $10.98 to cover the additional cost of the deluxe packaging. United Artists was afraid that a $10.98 list price would negatively impact sales and refused to issue the LP with the book. A compromise was reached under which the album would come with a gatefold cover and list for $6.98. Although fans in the U.S. who knew about the deluxe packaging in other countries may have felt cheated, most Americans were unaware of the book. If the album had come with the book and listed for $10.98, sales would have been significantly lower.

United Artists prepared two promotional posters for the album. One is merely a 22" x 22" enlargement of the album's front cover with "Printed in USA" appearing in small white letters in the lower left corner, **APP 34001.P1**. The more interesting poster measures 28" x 21½" and features a 12⅜" x 12½" image of the front album cover, which is placed in the lower right corner running towards the top. The black background poster has "Now Available" printed across the top in white uppercase letters. The group's name, the album title and "Original motion picture score available on Apple records, cartridges & cassettes" appear in white upper case letters to the left of the cover. A red Apple logo, "Manufactured by Apple Records, Inc." and "an abkco managed company" appear below the cover. The poster with the text, **APP 34001.P2**, is the rarer of the two.

The labels to the album feature the same distinctive full and sliced apples as earlier releases, except that the apples are red rather than green. This has spawned collectors to speculate on the significance of the change to red. One theory is that the apples are red to match the color of the red United Artists logo. Another explanation is that all Apple soundtrack albums were to have red labels. Others theorize that the red labels signify the blood-letting death of the Beatles. A less dramatic explanation is that the label is red to signify that this was likely to be the last Beatles album. Supporters of this theory point out that the last Apple album, Ringo's *Blast From Your Past* (Apple SW 3422), has red labels.

The truth is much simpler. Allan Steckler, who was responsible for the change, said it was his belief that special albums should have special labels. He simply decided that the labels for the *Let It Be* soundtrack should have red apples. And so they did.

As was the case with *The White Album*, the label copy for all of the labels was produced from the same film. Thus, all labels have the same typesetting. Side one has the album title and the group's name centered above the center hole. On side two, this information is in the upper left part of the apple. Both sides have the record number AR 34001, the matrix number and side number at three o'clock, "STEREO" at nine o'clock and the track listings below the center hole. Side one has "Reproduced for disc by PHIL SPECTOR" and "Recorded in England" centered at the bottom of the apple. Side two has the production information in the lower left part of the apple and the recording location in the lower right. The labels have red Apple perimeter print on the full apple side.

**This United Artists 28" x 21½" promotional poster heralded the availability of the soundtrack album on records, cartridges (4-track and 8-track) and cassettes.**

The first labels for the album, **APP 34001.SR1(af)**, credit *Maggie Mae* to "(P.D.)" for public domain. The songwriters credit for *Dig It* lists Ringo's last name as "Starr." Later pressings of the record credit the arrangement of *Maggie Mae* to the band, **APP 34001.SR2(af)**. These labels list the credit as "(P.D. arr. Lennon; McCartney; Harrison; Starkey) BMI." Ringo's last name in the credit for *Dig It* appears as "Starkey." Both versions of the label list *Dig A Pony* as *I Dig A Pony* (as does the album cover).

The album was mastered at Bell Sound in New York by Sam Feldman, who also cut the multiple sets of lacquers needed to manufacture the metal parts for pressing the records. The trail off areas to both sides of the discs have the Bell Sound machine stamped script logo and Feldman's hand etched initials. The matrix number JS 17,500 is hand etched into side one, and the number JS 17,501 is hand etched into side two.

As was the case with the single pulled from the album, both sides of the record also have a script "Phil + Ronnie" hand etched in the trail off area. The inscription was added at Phil Spector's request as a tribute to his then-wife Ronnie.

This was not the first time Spector placed romantic etchings in trail off areas. For nearly one year during 1962 and 1963, the trail off areas to all records released on Spector's Philles label contained the inscription "Phil and Annette" in honor of his wife Annette Merar. When Spector signed the Ronettes to his company, he soon became enamored with lead singer Veronica "Ronnie" Bennett. When the label's first Ronettes single, *Be My Baby* (Philles 116), was issued in August, 1963, the "Phil and Annette" etching was conspicuously absent. By the time Spector became involved with the Beatles, he had moved on to "Phil + Ronnie." In April, 1971, Apple released a Ronnie Spector single, *Try Some, Buy Some* (Apple 1832), which was co-produced by Phil Spector and George Harrison.

According to Allen Klein, Apple directed Capitol to press an initial run of four million copies of the album. These discs were manufactured by Capitol's factories in Scranton, Los Angeles, Jacksonville and Winchester.

United Artists deleted the *Let It Be* album from its catalog a few years after it was issued. Counterfeiters soon stepped up to fill the void by manufacturing unauthorized fake albums. The covers to the counterfeits are relatively easy to spot due to their blurry images. Most of the fake records have fuzzy-looking labels. Some of the discs have a hand drawn ⚠ logo in their trail off areas.

The counterfeits were not designed to fool collectors. After all, the *Let It Be* album sold in the millions and is by no means rare. The counterfeiters viewed the unavailability of the album as an opportunity to meet demand and to sell a Beatles record without paying any royalties to the artists, songwriters or publishers.

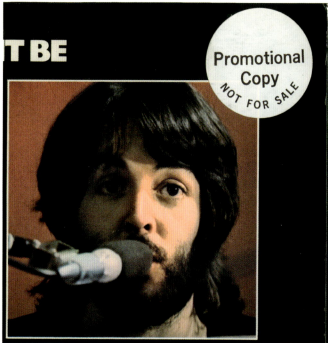

**United Artists prepared a 7" disc containing three radio commercials for the *Let It Be* film (left). Some of the albums distributed to radio stations and reviewers came with a 2" circular white sticker affixed to the front cover. The sticker (right) has "Promotional Copy NOT FOR SALE" printed in black.**

After Capitol purchased United Artists Records in 1978, it decided to add the *Let It Be* album to its catalog. To save costs, the album (Capitol SW 11922) was issued in a standard non-gatefold cover, but did come with a color poster and photo inner sleeve. The discs were pressed with purple Capitol labels.

When the *Let It Be* album was first issued in May, 1970, the reviews were mixed. While *Billboard* and other establishment-type publications focused on the quality of the songs, the more hip magazines lambasted Phil Spector's heavy handed production. *Rolling Stone* lamented that Spector had "whipped out his orchestra and proceeded to turn several of the rough gems on the best Beatles album in ages into costume jewelry."

George Martin was astonished and sickened by the final product. "It was always understood that the album would be like nothing the Beatles had done before. It would be honest, no overdubbing, no editing, truly live...almost amateurish. When John brought in Phil Spector he contradicted everything he had said before. When I heard the final sounds I was shaken. They were so uncharacteristic of the clean sounds the Beatles had always used."

Glyn Johns, who was proud of his original *Get Back* album, was Spector's harshest critic. "He totally and utterly wrecked the album. I really think he crucified what was a bloody good record."

Paul McCartney was upset with Spector's schmaltzy production of *The Long And Winding Road*. In his lawsuit to dissolve the Beatles partnership, McCartney cited Spector's addition of strings, voices, horns and drums to the song as "an intolerable interference" with his work.

John Lennon, on the other hand, praised Spector's efforts. Lennon felt the *Get Back* album had been "badly recorded...with a lousy feeling to it." John believed Spector

"made something out of it" and "did a great job." In his *Rolling Stone* interview with Jann Wenner, Lennon remembered "When I heard it I didn't puke, I was so relieved after hearing six months of this like black cloud hanging over, that this was going to go out."

*Let It Be* remains the group's most controversial album among critics and fans. Many people believe the Glyn Johns mix is charming and vastly superior to the post-session production work done by Phil Spector. They vilify Spector for his orchestral and choir additions, claiming that he made the entire album unlistenable. Others believe that Spector turned an amateurish-sounding collection of songs into a polished album that enables the listener to appreciate the quality of the songs.

The truth is somewhere in between. A comparison of the Glyn Johns mix and the Phil Spector production reveals that both have brilliant moments and flaws. Johns' decision to let well enough alone with Paul's ballads, *Let It Be* and *The Long And Winding Road*, was certainly appropriate. His inclusion of the free-wheeling performance of *Save The Last Dance For Me* into *Don't Let Me Down* is a treat. But his use of rough runthroughs from the early days of the sessions over tighter performances from January 30 and 31 is unfortunate. Phil Spector chose better takes of *Two Of Us*, *Dig A Pony* and *I've Got A Feeling*. He wisely stayed with Johns' selections for *One After 909*, *For You Blue* and *Maggie Mae*. His edit on *I Me Mine* was clever, but his lush orchestral and choir overdubs onto *The Long And Winding Road* turned a simple and reflective ballad into a schmaltzy sappy piece of muzak. His mix on the song *Let It Be* is horrendous. But as bad as his work is on the latter two songs, one should not let them ruin what overall is a very good album with some terrific songs and performances. And by the way, the band passed the audition.

United Artists prepared a series of 8" x 10" black & white stills from the film. The above pictures (obtained from the archives of United Artists) were stored in a brown paper bag with the movie's title hand-written in black ink.

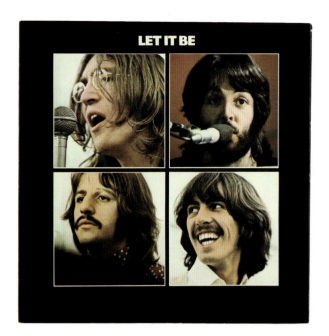 

APP 34001.SC1

APP 34001.SR1(af)

APP 34001.SR2(af) (detail)

MAGGIE MAE (P. D. arr. Lennon; McCartney; Harrison; Starkey) BMI - :39

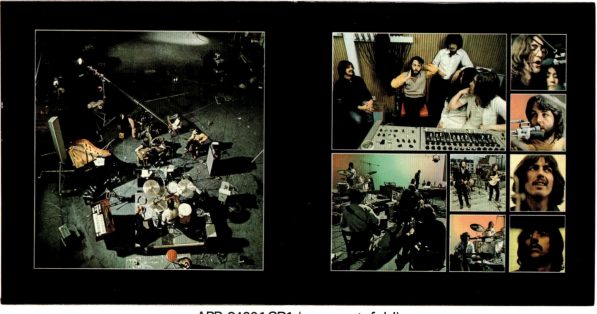

APP 34001.SR1 (open gatefold)

# THE BEATLES CHRISTMAS ALBUM
# APPLE SBC 100

Side 1
1. DEC. 1963
2. DEC. 1964
3. DEC. 1965
4. DEC. 1966

Side 2
1. DEC. 1967
2. DEC. 1968
3. DEC. 1969

Beginning in 1963, the Beatles started a holiday tradition of recording Christmas messages for their fans. The recordings were edited and issued on flexi-discs through the Official Beatles Fan Club in England. The records were not available for sale, but were distributed free to fan club members. In 1964, Beatles (U.S.A.) Ltd., the official national Beatles fan club in the United States, began sending the annual Christmas records to its members.

This tradition continued through 1969, although the last two Christmas records were not group efforts, but rather were a series of separately recorded messages from each of the Beatles. Because the group officially broke up in 1970, there was little point in assembling a new series of holiday greetings from the Beatles. Instead, the British and American fan clubs distributed albums containing all of the previously issued Christmas messages.

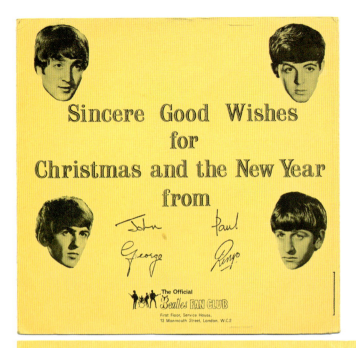

The first Beatles Christmas disc was distributed by the Official Beatles Fan Club on December 9, 1963. The disc was packaged in a yellow paper gatefold pocket (shown above). The closed front cover has a picture of a different Beatle in each corner and a holiday message. The back has a picture of the boys with the Joint Secretaries of the Fan Club (Bettina Rose and Anne Collingham) and the group meeting the Queen Mother at the November 4, 1963, *Royal Variety Show*. The open gatefold contains the Fan Club's *National Newsletter* No. 2. Lyntone Recordings pressed just over 30,000 copies of the one-sided seven inch discs (LYN 492), which have white labels with dark blue print.

The five minute Christmas message was recorded on October 17, 1963, at the session that produced the group's fourth British 45, *I Want To Hold Your Hand* b/w *This Boy*. With George Martin in control, the Beatles sang and talked their way through press agent Tony Barrow's script.

After the boys run through a brief portion of *Good King Wenceslaus*, John starts things off:

"Hello, this is John speaking with his voice. We're all very happy to be able to talk to you like this on this little bit of plastic. This record reaches you at the end of a really gear year for us and it's all due to you."

John then lists the highlights of the year: *Please Please Me* reaching number one; topping the bill at the London Palladium; and taking part in the *Royal Variety Show*. Paul also thanks the fans and states that although the group likes doing stage shows, the thing they like best is making records.

After John leads the group through a pseudo-German version of *Good King Wenceslaus*, Ringo says a few words before being coaxed into singing a bluesy version of...*Good King Wenceslaus*. George then deadpans, "Thank you Ringo, we'll phone you." George thanks the Fan Club secretaries and tells the fans "it's your reaction to our records that really matters" before singing a few lines about the good king. This evolves into the group singing a bit of *Rudolph The Red Nosed Reindeer* before signing off by wishing everyone a Merry Christmas.

The second Beatles Christmas record was issued by the Official Beatles Fan Club in December, 1964. The disc was packaged in a seven inch by seven inch cardboard sleeve (shown on following page, top row) printed and made by MacNeill Press Ltd., London. The front has a black and white picture of the group below the Fan Club logo in black and "Another Beatles Christmas Record" in red. The back has text by Tony Barrow, who wrote the liner notes to many of the band's early albums and extended play (EP) records.

The Fan Club's *National Newsletter* No. 4 (following page) was included with the holiday mailing. The single folded newsletter measures seven by seven inches and is printed on white paper. The closed front (middle row, left) has a black and white portrait of the group surrounded by their signed first names on the left and "MERRY CHRIST-MAS" on the right. The back (middle row, right) features a different photo of the boys from the same session. The open inside of the newsletter (bottom row) features a photo of each Beatle taken at Abbey Road Studio on the left side and text on the right.

According to the newsletter, Fan Club membership increased during the year from 30,000 to 65,000. Thus, Lyntone Recordings pressed approximately 65,000 copies of the 1964 Christmas record (LYN 757). The one-sided U.K. discs (shown at center) have white labels with red text. While the 1963 disc plays at 33⅓ RPM, the shorter 1964 record plays at 45 RPM.

Beatles (U.S.A.) Ltd. mailed a Record-Folder containing the year-old 1963 message (shown unfolded front and back on the second following page) to its club members. The Record-Folder was manufactured by Allied Creative Service, Inc., New York. The closed front of the folder (left column, bottom) has a black rectangle at the top with white text. The lower portion has the return address to the left and the Bulk Rate U.S. Postage permit stamp to the right with space at the bottom for the mailing label. The closed back (left column, middle) doubles as the record, with its grooves laid over a black background designed to give the appearance of a vinyl disc. The gray area of the label has "1964" in white inside a black oval at the top and "Season's Greetings from the Beatles" in black. The lower part of the label has a black banner with "the Official Beatles Fan Club" in upper case white letters. The American record plays at 33⅓ RPM.

When opened, the top panel of the record side of the folder (left column) has a cropped version of the picture appearing on the back of the British newsletter. The other side (right column) reprints *The Beatle Bulletin* in the top panel and has a photo of each Beatle in the middle panel and additional text in the lower panel, including "Season's Greetings from Seltaeb." Seltaeb (Beatles spelled backwards) was the name of their merchandising company.

The 1964 Christmas message followed the same formula as the previous year with the group running through a Tony Barrow script. It was recorded at Abbey Road during the October 26, 1964, session that produced *Honey Don't* and *What You're Doing*. With George Martin at the helm, the group went through five takes of holiday cheer, which were edited down to just over four minutes.

The record opens with the sound of marching feet leading into a version of Jingle Bells played with piano, kazoo and harmonica. Paul starts things off by thanking the fans for buying the records:

"We know you've been buying them 'cause the sales have been very good, you see. Don't know where we'd be without you really though."

To which John sneaks in:

"In the Army, perhaps."

Paul quickly continues with:

"We hope you've enjoyed listening to the records as much as we've enjoyed melting them. [Laughs] No, no, no that's wrong. Making them. We're in Number Two Studio at the moment at EMI taping this little message for you....This is the same studio we've used all along since the old days of *Love Me Do*, so many years ago it seems."

Paul then wishes everyone "a Happy Christmas and a Very New Year" before passing the proceedings over to John, who makes no secret he is reading from a script:

"Thanks all of you who bought me book. Thank you folks for buying it, it was very handy. And there's another one out pretty soon it says here. Hope you buy that too. It'll be the usual rubbish, but it won't cost much. You see, that's the bargain we're gonna strike up. I write them in my spare time it says here."

Paul then interrupts:

"Did you write this yourself?"

John responds:

"No, it's somebody's bad hand wroter. It's been a busy year Beatle peedles, one way or another, but it's been a great year, too. You fans have seen to that. Page two. Thanks a lot folks and a hap-py ah, Christmas and a merry goo year. Crimble maybe."

John then hands things over to George, who thanks the fans for going to see the film and talks about the next film:

"We start shooting it in February. This time it's a gonna be in color. [John: "Green."] It'll be a big laugh we hope."

After George wishes the listeners all the best, Ringo thanks their fans "just for being fans" and talks about the group's travels. Ringo concludes by wishing the fans all the best for Christmas and a happy new year.

This is followed by piano and the group singing "Oh can you wash your father's hair, oh can you wash it clean?" The boys then shout out "Happy Christmas" as the sound of feet running away fades with the end of disc.

Another
## Beatles Christmas Record

THIS SPECIAL RECORD IS NOT FOR PRIVATE OR PUBLIC SALE. IT IS DISTRIBUTED FREE OF CHARGE TO MEMBERS OF THE OFFICIAL BEATLES FAN CLUB. PLAY AT 45 R.P.M. USING A NORMAL LP STYLUS.

Just a year ago The Beatles made their first Christmas record for exclusive distribution to fan club members. Now at the end of another splendid period of world-wide pop supremacy our fabulous foursome have made a second equally precious recording as a Christmas gift to the club's 65,000 Beatle People. This disc will not be in the hit parade. Additional copies will never be pressed. The contents of this sleeve will make each fan club member the envy of numerous friends. Money can't buy ANOTHER BEATLES CHRISTMAS RECORD—but with membership of the most with it fan club in Britain the disc comes through your letter-box free of charge in time for yuletide parties and holiday record sessions. This is the uniquely pleasant way in which John, Paul, George and Ringo choose to say Thank You to thousands of their loyal fans throughout the nation. The Official Beatles Fan Club of Great Britain operates from special offices in Central London. Natio-

nal Secretaries Anne Collingham and Bettina Rose have a hard-working staff of full-time assistants to help run the club's affairs. And in every county throughout the British Isles there is a local Area Secretary to look after members' queries on a voluntary basis. Overseas you'll find a branch of the club in more than a score of countries scattered around the globe. Each branch is run quite independently but with the authorisation and supervision of Anne and Bettina in London.

The four boys find time to pop into the club headquarters despite their hectic schedule of tours, television appearances, recording sessions, film work and broadcasts. The girls in the office still retain vivid memories of the morning Paul dropped in for a chat, joined in with the gang to stamp up a batch of membership cards and then treated the entire staff to an excellent lunch in a nearby steakhouse!

TONY BARROW

**ISSUED IN DECEMBER 1964**

ANNE COLLINGHAM AND BETTINA ROSE WISH TO THANK E.M.I. RECORDS LIMITED FOR PERMITTING THE PRODUCTION OF THIS RECORD AND PRODUCER GEORGE MARTIN FOR SUPERVISING THE ACTUAL TAPING. THE BEATLES RECORD EXCLUSIVELY FOR THE PARLOPHONE LABEL.

THE OFFICIAL BEATLES FAN CLUB, FIRST FLOOR, SERVICE HOUSE, 13 MONMOUTH STREET, LONDON W.C.2. (Telephone—COVent Garden 2332).

Printed and made in England by MacNeill Press Ltd., London, S.E.1.

## The Official Beatles FAN CLUB

NATIONAL NEWSLETTER No. 4 CHRISTMAS 1964

First Floor, Service House, 13 Monmouth Street, London WC2 · Fan Club Telephone: London COVent Garden 2332

*Dear Beatle People,*

Along with this Newsletter comes your own personal copy of ANOTHER BEATLES CHRISTMAS RECORD—the second special gift from John, Paul, George and Ringo to their fan club members. Last year the four boys hit upon the unique idea of recording a Christmas message to be released exclusively through the club. A few weeks ago they got together to discuss plans for this year's special gift. Various suggestions were put forward but they were turned down in favour of repeating the 1963 formula by recording a second seasonal disc. Last year the club pressed a final send of just over 30,000 Christmas records. This time more than double that quantity had to be ordered—at the beginning of November the club's membership stood at 65,000 and hundreds of new Beatle People have been added to the list each week since then.

Remember that ANOTHER BEATLES CHRISTMAS RECORD is entirely exclusive to club members. It will not be sold to non-members or made available in the shops. We hope it will give you and your friends a great deal of pleasure over the holiday and party period—and if some of your mates are just a little jealous because they haven't received the gift you can tell them it is their own fault for not becoming Beatle People by joining the club during the year!

Since THE BEATLES MONTHLY BOOK contains all the latest news about our fabulous foursome (plus a Fan Club page in every issue) there is very little fresh information which we can add in this National Newsletter. From the letters we've been receiving at the club headquarters we know that Beatle People from all over Britain will be travelling to London over Christmas and New Year to see the boys in their spectacular stage

show at Hammersmith Odeon. Between the opening night (Christmas Eve) and Saturday 16 January well over 100,000 fans will attend the show. There's a star-studded cast to support The Beatles and we're sure everybody will come away from the theatre more than pleased with the exciting evening's entertainment contained in ANOTHER BEATLES CHRISTMAS SHOW. Incidentally, if you haven't been lucky enough to get tickets for the show it is still worthwhile calling at the theatre box office to see if any booking cancellations have been made. Out of a nightly audience of over 7,000 you can rest assured there will always be a few people who have to return their tickets at the last moment because of illness or other unforeseen circumstances. And your personal request for tickets at the box office might just coincide with the cancellation of someone else's seat reservations. It's well worth a try anyway!

How would you like to start up a pen-friendship with a Beatle Person in America? As you know there is a list of pen-friends in every issue of THE BEATLES MONTHLY BOOK but editor Johnny Dean just hasn't the space to print hundreds of new names each month or there'd be no room for features and photos. Therefore we have made special arrangements with Lynn Hargrave, National President of the American Fan Club branch in New York. Lynn has collected several thousand names and addresses of American club members who would love to exchange letters regularly with our members in Britain. Lynn has promised to see that every letter she receives from a club member in Britain will be forwarded to an American Beatle person with minimum delay. Why not start the ball rolling by sending a letter and/or a Christmas card? You should hear from your brand-new American pen-friend quite soon after Christmas. Here's all you want to know:

1. Write a letter giving personal details about yourself and your interests. Enclose anything you like with the letter and seal it in an envelope.

2. Place this in a second slightly larger envelope and *Airmail* to:

   British Pen-Friend Scheme,
   Lynn Hargrave,
   Beatles (U.S.A.) Ltd.,
   Box 505, Radio City Station,
   New York, N.Y. 10019,
   U.S.A.

3. Check with your local post office to make sure you use the correct value of stamps—and don't forget to send your letter *Airmail* to New York to ensure the briskest possible reply.

Our next National Newsletter will be mailed out to Beatle People throughout Britain next May. And at that time we shall be asking everyone to renew his or her membership subscription for the period June 1965 to May 1966. There is no need to send your 5/- renewal fee until you hear from us in May. In the meantime THE BEATLES MONTHLY BOOK will keep you posted with all the latest news and facts about John, Paul, George and Ringo and we'll look forward to meeting you via the Fan Club pages every month. We'd like to join with The Beatles and everyone here at the London Fan Club H.Q. in wishing you and your family a very pleasant Christmas and a healthy, happy 1965.

Lots of good Luck,

*Bettina Rose*
BETTINA ROSE

*Anne Collingham*
ANNE COLLINGHAM

*Joint National Secretaries of The Official Beatles Fan Club*

1964

*Season's Greetings*

33⅓ R.P.M.

*from the Beatles*

THE OFFICIAL BEATLES FAN CLUB

All rights of the manufacturer and of the owner of the recorded work reserved. Unauthorized public performance, broadcasting and copying of this record prohibited. Made in U.S.A.

Record-Folder
Patent Pending
Allied Creative
Service, Inc.
635 West 54 St.
New York, N.Y. 10019

# The Beatle Bulletin

## THE MAGAZINE OF THE OFFICIAL NATIONAL BEATLES FAN CLUB

### CHRISTMAS ISSUE

*December, 1964*

BEATLES (U.S.A.) LTD.
P.O. BOX 505, RADIO CITY STATION
NEW YORK, N.Y. 10019

BULK RATE
U.S. POSTAGE
**PAID**
NEW YORK, N.Y.
PERMIT NO. 788

KAREN POLLAK        N63
174 MONTELO
MEMPHIS, TENN.

# The Beatle Bulletin

December, 1964

Dear Members:

Because The Beatles could not greet each and every one of you in person, they have done the next best thing... they are sending their holiday greetings to you, in their very own voices, on the record which appears on the back of this newsletter. To hear John speak with his voice, Paul giggle, Ringo sing a Ringo-type version of GOOD KING WENCESLAUS and George being George, simply punch out the center dot, place the newsletter on your record player, set it for 33-1/3 R.P.M., and sit back and enjoy your holiday greetings from The Beatles. We here at the National Headquarters are wild about it, and we hope you will be, too.

Just to let you in on "what's 'appenin'", after the fab four left the United States, they returned to England for a recording session. On October 9th, they began a tour of England which consisted of 26 shows in as many days and which included the ABC Theatre in Hull, the Ardwick Apollo in Manchester, the Globe in Stockton and, of course, their home town, Liverpool. After the wind-up of the tour, on to preparations for THE BEATLES CHRISTMAS SHOW scheduled for the Odeon Theatre in Hammersmith from December 24th until January 16th. In February, they begin the filming of their new movie, which, we hear, is slated to be a "comedy thriller"!

For those of you who have not, as yet, heard about it, here's the story on the Brian Epstein Fan Club: Many of our members felt that some sort of tribute should be paid to the man who brought us The Beatles—and other top entertainers, as well. We agreed. The end result was the formation of THE BRIAN EPSTEIN FAN CLUB which is open, free of charge, to all members of BEATLES (U.S.A.) LIMITED. If you would like to become a member of the Brian Epstein Fan Club, send your name and address to:

THE BRIAN EPSTEIN FAN CLUB
P.O. Box 505, Radio City Station
New York, New York 10019

You will receive, in return, an 8 x 10 glossy photo of Brian, a membership card and a Fact Sheet. We hope that many of you will take advantage of the opportunity to express your appreciation for The Beatles and all the happiness and excitement they have brought to each of us.

Here's hopin' you'll enjoy this method of sending out Christmas greetings from The Beatles, and we would like to join our voices to those of John, Paul, George and Ringo to wish each and every one of you a . . .

MERRY CHRIMBLE!

Lynn Hargrave        Bernice Young

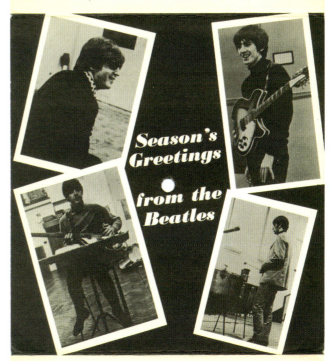

*Season's Greetings from the Beatles*

# Bulletin Board

## Fact Sheet

All members are entitled to a Beatles Fact Sheet. If you haven't already gotten yours, just send your membership card along with a self-addressed, stamped envelope to FACT SHEET, c/o Beatles (U.S.A.) Ltd., Box 505, Radio City Station, New York, New York 10019. For all non-members, the cost of the Fact Sheet is 25¢ plus a self-addressed, stamped envelope.

## Pen Pals

For those of you who have sent in for pen pals and have not, as yet, received them, please bear with us. The fact of the matter is that we received such a large response that we simply ran out of names. However, they are now coming in from England, and you will be hearing from us quite soon.

Thank you for your patience.

*Season's Greetings*

*from* **Seltaeb**

© 1964, Beatles (U.S.A.) Limited

The packaging of the Beatles third Christmas record issued by the Official Beatles Fan Club in December, 1965, was similar to the previous year's offering. It came in a seven-inch cardboard sleeve (shown on following page, top row) featuring a black and white photo of the group taken by Bob Whitaker on the set at Granada TV's Manchester studios, where the boys were taping a television special titled *The Music Of Lennon And McCartney*. The Beatles were at Granada on November 1 and 2, 1965. According to Tony Barrow's liner notes appearing on the back of the sleeve, the photo was taken just before the band launched into their "energetic performance" of *Day Tripper* (which was, in reality, lip-synced). Barrow took the opportunity to praise the group's latest album, *Rubber Soul*, commenting on the band's concentrated and extended attention to the production of the album and calling it "the most varied LP programme of their career." Both the front and back of the jacket have "The Beatles Third Christmas Record" in blue.

Once again, the record was packaged with the Fan Club's *National Newsletter* (No. 6). The front of the folded newsletter (following page, middle row, left) contains Christmas greetings from the Fan Club's National Secretary, Anne Collingham, who recaps the group's busy year and calls *Rubber Soul* the best album ever made by the group. The folded back (following page, middle row, right) has a black and white portrait of the band. The open inside (following page, bottom row) features head shots of each Beatle adorned with hand-drawn festive holiday hats. The background contains crude drawings of snow flakes, holly and round Christmas ornaments. "HAPPY CHRISTMAS Beatle People!" is written at the top center.

The flexi-disc (LYN 948) (shown center) has gold print on a white label. Due to the record's running time of nearly six and a half minutes, the disc plays at the slower speed of 33⅓ RPM.

The American Fan Club did not send out a Christmas record for 1965. *The Beatle Bulletin* from April, 1966, explained that the tape arrived too late to prepare the record.

The Beatles recorded their third Christmas record on November 8, 1965, after completing work on *Think For Yourself*. The group ran through three takes of foolishness before George Martin was satisfied that he had enough on tape to produce a respectable holiday gift from the boys.

The program begins with the group singing an off-key rendition of *Yesterday*, backed by an out-of-tune guitar. This leads into Ringo stating "Don't forget, Christmas is coming, oh that reminds me, let's do a Christmas record." The group readily agrees, and Ringo reminds them that they need to thank everyone. Paul thanks everyone for all the presents and for buying the records. John jokingly thanks the fans for the chewed up pieces of chewing gum and the

playing cards made out of knickers. George gives his thanks for "all the Christmas cards and presents and birthday cards and presents and everything, too, as well." As John mumbles additional thanks, it becomes obvious that he is reluctantly following a script.

Paul then asks "Well Ringo, what have we done this year?" After Ringo gives a brief reply, John, backed by his acoustic guitar, begins singing "Happy Christmas to ya listeners," which is followed by assorted nonsense that evolves into an Irish folk song leading into the group singing "for the sake of auld lang syne." That reminds the group that last year they were around the same old mike in the same old studio with the same old guitar and same old faces. This inspires the group to start singing the Four Tops' *It's The Same Old Song*, which had been a top ten hit during summer, 1965. Before the second line is finished, George interrupts the performance by saying "Copyright, Johnny." Paul agrees and asks "What are we going to do without a copyright?" John responds "How 'bout we'll gather lilacs in an old brown shoe?" Ringo then assures them "Yes, that's out of copyright." This bit of Christmas copyright cheer takes on an ironic twist when one considers the copyright infringement suits George and John would later face.

The group then decides to play something for the boys in the armed forces. After mimicking a radio broadcast, they break into a militarized version of *Auld Lang Syne*:

"Viet quantance be forgot and never brought behind, China. Down in Viet Nam where low cannons too. And look at all the bodies floating in the River Jordan."

As Paul says "Well that looks as though it's about it for this year," Ringo adds "Well that should cover Israel. We certainly tried our best to ah, please everybody." Paul then says, "Please everybody, if we haven't done what we could have done, we've tried."

The group then knocks out a brief Christmas song with the lyrics "Christmas comes but once a year, but when it does it brings good cheer." This develops into another off-key rendition of *Yesterday*, with some members singing "Bless you all on Christmas Day" over "I believe in Yesterday." With the guitar strumming and Paul signing "Christmas Day," John describes the past year as "one of our biggest years since we can remember, and we can remember a lot of big years." The boys then return to the off-key version of *Yesterday*, singing the last line as "Oh bless you all on Christmas Day." After another attempt at singing *Christmas Day*, Paul says "Fade it there, Charlie," and George adds, "OK, put the red lights off." John then says "And this is Johnny Rhythm just sayin' good nights to yoose all and God bless yas." Paul adds "That's got it done then, eh, what are we gonna do now?" George asks, "Has he turned it off?" as the records fades away.

The Official

Beatles FAN CLUB

33⅓ r.p.m.

Not for sale. Issued free of charge to fan Club Members in December, 1965

THE BEATLES THIRD CHRISTMAS RECORD

The Beatles record exclusively for the Parlophone label.

Lyntone Recordings

LYN 948

## The Beatles Third Christmas Record

THIS SPECIAL RECORD IS NOT FOR PRIVATE OR PUBLIC SALE. IT IS DISTRIBUTED FREE OF CHARGE TO MEMBERS OF THE OFFICIAL BEATLES FAN CLUB. PLAY AT 33⅓ R.P.M. USING A NORMAL LP STYLUS.

THE BEATLES THIRD CHRISTMAS RECORD was made immediately after The Beatles finished work on their latest album, "Rubber Soul". To complete those fourteen LP tracks John, Paul, George and Ringo spent a series of whole days and whole nights in the recording studio with George Martin. Never before have they given such concentrated and extended attention to the production of an album. The Beatles have always been perfectionists but on this occasion they spent a great deal of time creating an unusually wide range of different instrumental sounds. They set out to make "Rubber Soul" the most varied LP programme of their career and they succeeded in achieving this aim.

A special fan club record from John, Paul, George and Ringo for Christmas has become a tradition. At the same time the project remains unique in that The Beatles are the only group to make an annual gift of this kind to their truest fans. THE BEATLES THIRD CHRISTMAS RECORD cannot be bought in the shops. Copies are not available at any price to people who do not belong to The Official Beatles Fan Club Of Great Britain. That's what makes the entire venture so intriguing. Just about everything else the four boys do

—whether it is a concert tour, a recording session or a television show—becomes (more or less) public property. But these Christmas records remain personal and exclusive—collectors' gems whose value to Beatle People will increase with each year that passes.

Incidentally, I wonder how many members recognise the setting of the picture to be seen on the front of this sleeve. It was taken in Granada's Manchester television studios when the boys made their spectacular "The Music Of Lennon And McCartney". A few seconds after the photograph was taken, The Beatles launched into the energetic performance of "Day Tripper" which closes the first part of the programme.

On behalf of the boys, fan club secretary Anne Collingham writes umpteen 'Thank You' letters during the course of the year. I think it's time somebody said 'Thank You' to Anne and her hardworking staff of girls at Monmouth Street. There's never a quiet moment at the club headquarters but Anne's busy band love what they're doing and even when things get particularly hectic you'll always find them helpful if you drop in or telephone the office.

TONY BARROW

ANNE COLLINGHAM WISHES TO THANK E.M.I. RECORDS LIMITED FOR PERMITTING THE PRODUCTION OF THIS RECORD AND PRODUCER GEORGE MARTIN FOR SUPERVISING THE ACTUAL TAPING. THE BEATLES RECORD EXCLUSIVELY FOR THE PARLOPHONE LABEL.

ISSUED IN DECEMBER 1965
*Sleeve Photography* : ROBERT WHITAKER

THE OFFICIAL BEATLES FAN CLUB, FIRST FLOOR, SERVICE HOUSE, 13 MONMOUTH STREET, LONDON W.C.2. (Telephone—COVent Garden 2332)

*Printed and made in England by MacNeill Press Ltd., London, S.E.1.*

## The Official Beatles FAN CLUB

NATIONAL NEWSLETTER No. 6 CHRISTMAS 1965

First Floor, Service House, 13 Monmouth Street, London WC2 · Fan Club Telephone: London COVent Garden 2332

*Dear Beatle People,*

It is always a special pleasure for me to write my Christmas Newsletter because I know how pleased each of you will be to receive the 'extra' which accompanies it. For the third consecutive year John, Paul, George and Ringo have recorded a disc which we can send out as their personal gift to Beatle People all over the country. This year's production—THE BEATLES THIRD CHRISTMAS RECORD—is even more hilarious than those which have gone before.

I must repeat here my annual reminder to the effect that the club CANNOT supply additional copies of the Christmas Record to club members or their friends. We have just enough to go round our total membership and extra copies are not available to be given away or sold.

New Beatle People have been joining the club all through 1965. Indeed I've enrolled more new members in the past couple of months than I did during the same period of 1964. Newcomers are always welcome and it's good to know that as time goes by there are more and more people to appreciate the talents of our favourite foursome.

Some members have told me they're disappointed because the boys are not putting on a Christmas Show in London this year. On the other hand the eighteen December concerts have given people who live far from the capital an opportunity of seeing the boys on stage. In any case something like 13,000 Beatle People have been able to book seats for the tour London-area performances of the tour so, one way and another, I think this has been the fairest way of fixing things.

The Beatles have been as busy as ever throughout 1965. After completing their first colour film "Help!" they broke new ground by making first-time appearances in parts of France, Spain and Italy. During that European tour the boys established a new record for the number of people to see them in live performance on a single day. The record didn't last long — it was broken again in August when The Beatles

played to over 57,000 at New York's fantastic new Shea Stadium. That was the beginning of another sensational U.S. tour during which well over three hundred thousand American and Canadian Beatle People watched the boys sing and play in enormous arenas, stadiums and baseball parks.

During the autumn The Beatles went to work on their newest LP album, "Rubber Soul", which was released early this month via Parlophone. It's interesting to see that every one of the 14 new tracks is a beatle original — 12 fresh compositions from John and Paul plus two from George. I think this is the best album they've ever made and I know from the first letters I've been receiving on the subject that you agree with me.

To round off the year the boys lined up a series of December television appearances to coincide with the release of 'Day Tripper' and 'We Can Work It Out'. The first of these was seen the night before the tour opened when The Beatles appeared on "Top Of The Pops". Two days later they were special guests on "Thank Your Lucky Stars".

Last Christmas I mentioned the idea of Beatle People in the U.K. setting up pen-friendships with their opposite numbers in the U.S. The scheme has been working very well but for the benefit of new members I'll give you the details again. If you'd like to start writing to a member of the American club branch here's what you should do:—

1. Write a letter giving personal details about yourself and your interests. Enclose anything you like with the letter AND MAKE SURE that your own address is written CLEARLY AND IN FULL so that your reply can come through quickly. Seal your letter in an envelope.

2. Place this in a second slightly larger envelope and *airmail* to:—

British Pen-Friend Scheme,
Beatles (U.S.A.) Ltd.,
Box 505, Radio City Station,
New York, N.Y. 10019,
U.S.A.

3. Check with your local post office before mailing to make sure you use the correct value of stamps.

The circulation of THE BEATLES MONTHLY BOOK has gone up since this time last year so I know that most of you are keeping up-to-date with news of John, Paul, George and Ringo via this magazine. THE BEATLES MONTHLY BOOK contains up-to-the-minute news stories about the boys, feature articles about their tours and other appearances plus a shoal of exclusive new photographs. The boys contribute their own page — BEATLES TALK — to almost every month's issue and, of course, there's the Fan Club section to keep you posted about club activities. This month, in addition to the normal December book, you'll find a Christmas Special with full-colour cover in the shops. If you prefer to get THE BEATLES MONTHLY BOOK as early as possible by post as soon as each new issue is ready why not take out a year's subscription in advance. For details write to editor Johnny Dean at 36/38 Westbourne Grove, London W.2. Be sure to mark the outside of your envelope BEATLES BOOK SUBSCRIPTION.

I hope to see you each month on the fan club page of the Monthly but, in any case, I'll be sending you another National Newsletter next May. And that's when your club subscription of 5/- for the 1966/1967 period will become due for payment. There is no need to send in your renewal postal order until I write to you.

Everyone at Monmouth Street joins me in wishing you a very pleasant Christmas and a healthy, happy New Year.

Lots of good luck,

*Anne Collingham*
ANNE COLLINGHAM

*National Secretary of*
*The Official Beatles Fan Club*

HAPPY CHRISTMAS Beatle People!

The British Fan Club's *National Newsletter* for Christmas 1966 (shown on following page) is devoted almost exclusively to describing the recording and distribution of the Beatles Fourth Christmas Record. It also has the lyrics to two songs contained on the disc, *Please Don't Bring Your Banjo Back* and *Everywhere It's Christmas*.

As in the prior two years, the record was issued in England in a seven inch cardboard sleeve (shown on following page). But that is where the similarity ends. Rather than featuring a black and white photo of the band, the front of the 1966 sleeve is an abstract color painting designed by Paul McCartney. The record's title, *Pantomime*, is drawn in stylized red letters running across the center. The lower right corner contains the phrase "Everywhere It's Christmas." The back of the sleeve lists the titles to the eleven selections featured on the disc.

The flexi-disc (LYN 1145) (shown center) has gold print on a white label. The record has a running time of 6:40 and plays at 33⅓ RPM.

After missing 1965, Beatles (U.S.A.) Ltd. once again sent out a Christmas record in 1966. But while British fans were treated to Paul's psychedelic sleeve, Americans received a 7" x 8½" postcard with a vinyl record coated on one side and text on the other (shown lower center). The record label's silver text has the date 1966 at the top followed by "Season's Greetings" in script and "from The Beatles" in block letters. Running speed, rights information and "Made in U.S.A." appear below the spindle hole. The text side has *The Beatle Bulletin* for Christmas, 1966, and the lyrics of the two songs on the left, and space for attaching an address label on the right.

On November 24, 1966, the Beatles returned to the studio after a five month absence. That evening they recorded Take 1 of *Strawberry Fields Forever*. The creative spirit of that session was carried forward to the next day when the group gathered at Dick James Music on New Oxford Street to tape their annual holiday message. According to the *National Newsletter*, things got under way at three in the afternoon with George Martin supervising the operation along with Brian Epstein in the control room. The Fan Club flyer alerted listeners that:

"Unlike previous productions, this year's disc doesn't include actual Christmas greetings from The Beatles. Instead the boys devised this *Pantomime* idea....Each year The Beatles have gone out of their way to think up *different* ideas for this Christmas record. This time we think they've come up with their best effort yet and we're sure you'll all agree."

The record opens up with the piano driven *Everywhere It's Christmas*, a song styled in the grand tradition of English music hall tunes. This quickly segues into *Orowayna (Corsican Choir and Small Choir)*, which has the group harmonizing "Orowayna" and "in da manger" over a piano background. Ringo provides the following narration: "Our story opens in Corsica. On the veranda is a bearded man in glasses conducting a small choir."

After a bit of wind sound effects and yodeling, Ringo continues "Meanwhile, high in the Swiss Alps, two elderly Scotsmen munch on a rare cheese." This short selection, titled *A Rare Cheese (Two Elderly Scotsman)*, has the two Scotsman agreeing that the cheese is "wonderful stuff" and ends with additional yodeling. This is followed by the festivities of *The Feast*, which, according to the *National Newsletter*, sounds realistic because it is the boys and crew having a "belated lunch break with ham and cheese sandwiches, pies, Cadbury's Snacks and cups of tea being handed round!"

Crowd noises were provided by Mal Evans, Neil Aspinall, George Martin, Brain Epstein and the Joint National Secretaries of the Fan Club. Dialog includes "Tell me, are you enjoying the wine?" and "The King seems to be enjoying himself tonight." The scene then shifts to the Captain's mess on board H.M.S. Tremendous, where the sailors are proposing *The Loyal Toast* to Her Majesty.

Next up is the story of *Podgy The Bear And Jasper*, who are huddled around an unlit fire in the center of a room. When Jasper observes that there are no more matches, Podgy suggests that they make a list and afterwards go to the shop to buy matches and candles and buns. After Jasper informs Podgy that there's no more paper to write on, Podgy assures him that there's no need to worry. He opens the door and tells Jasper to keep saying "matches" while he keeps saying "candles" until they reach

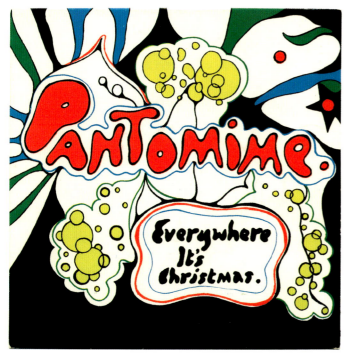

## NATIONAL NEWSLETTER ❧ Christmas 1966 ❧

*Dear Beatle People,*

THE BEATLES FOURTH CHRISTMAS RECORD was made just six days after Paul returned from Kenya and precisely one month before Christmas Day itself.

The previous evening, the boys had been working on their latest single up at the EMI Studios in St. John's Wood. Other years the first or last hour of an ordinary session has been used to get our annual Fan Club disc on tape. This time everyone agreed that there should be a separate session for the purpose and it was decided that the much smaller and more informal studio at the headquarters of Dick James Music in New Oxford Street would be the ideal setting.

Things got under way around three on the afternoon of Friday November 25 with George Martin supervising the whole operation along with Brian Epstein in the control room. There's a closed-circuit television system so that people in the control room can see what's happening in the studio which is located at the other end of a corridor. So we all watched this telly screen and listened to the boys running through the script they'd prepared and deciding who would do each of the twelve-or-so different voices involved. In the end Mal Evans was given a Special Guest Star role . . . with just one line to say towards the end of the record! Incidently Neil, George Martin and all of us were called in to make crowd-type sounds at appropriate moments. And when you hear the item called *The Feast* you needn't be surprised if it all sounds very realistic because this was the cue for everybody to take a brief and belated lunch break with ham and cheese sandwiches, pies, Cadbury's Snacks and cups of tea being handed round!

Unlike previous productions, this year's disc doesn't include actual Christmas greetings from The Beatles. Instead the boys devised this *Pantomime* idea – it's longer than any of the three earlier Fan Club records.

Each year The Beatles have gone out of their way to think up *different* ideas for this Christmas record. This time we think they've come up with their best effort yet and we're sure you'll all agree.

As you know, distribution of *Pantomime* is limited very strictly to U.K. club members and copies cannot be obtained elsewhere. This is the Beatles record which, like love (they say), money just can't buy! So please don't be mean about this, will you. Unless they're members, most of our friends won't be able to get their own copy of *Pantomime*. Don't be mean— let them hear yours and remind them that if they'd applied for membership last month they wouldn't have to keep coming round to your place for a listen!

John, Paul, George and Ringo asked us to be sure we passed on to all Beatle People via this Newsletter their sincere thanks for all your support and loyalty during 1966. And they join with us to hope that you and your families have a thoroughly happy Christmas holiday followed by a successful 1967.

Our next National Newsletter will be sent to you around the middle of the year together with your annual subscription renewal reminder. Until then don't forget to see each new issue of THE BEATLES MONTHLY BOOK for all the latest pix, news and features on John, Paul, George and Ringo. And our own Club pages will continue to appear each and every month. A lot of members have asked if it is possible to get THE BEATLES MONTHLY BOOK on annual subscription through the post. It is and for details just drop a line to the editor, Johnny Dean, at 36/38 Westbourne Grove, London W.2.

Lots of Good Luck and Tarrah for now,

*Anne Collingham*
*Freda Kelly*
Joint National Secretaries.

### THE SONGS IN PANTOMIME

**"Please don't bring your Banjo back"**
*Please don't bring your banjo back,*
*I know where it's been.*
*I wasn't hardly gone a day*
*When it became the scene.*
*Banjos, banjos all the time —*
*I can't forget that man —*
*And if I ever see another banjo*
*I'm going out to buy a big balloon!*

**"Everywhere it's Christmas"**
*Everywhere it's Christmas,*
*Everywhere it's song.*
*London, Paris, Rome, New York*
*And Tokyo, Hong Kong.*
*Everywhere it's Christmas,*
*I'm off to join the cheer,*
*Everywhere it's Christmas*
*At the end of every year*

the shop. That way, they won't have to write it down. They'll remember. When Jasper asks "Who will remember the buns, Podgy?," Podgy tells him they both will. The pair then head to the store repeating "matches" and "candles."

The next bit of dialog is titled *Felpin Mansions: Part One (Count Balder and Butler)*. After a door slams in the long dark corridors of Felpin Mansions, the shadowy figure of Count Balder appears. The listener is told that the Count is the eccentric son of Baron Lansburg, the inventor of the rack. The Count welcomes his guests to Felpin Mansions and directs the butler to show the ladies and gentlemen to their rooms. This is followed by *Felpin Mansions: Part Two (The Count and The Pianist)*. The Count knocks on the door to a room occupied by a pianist and asks if he can come in. After gaining entry into the room, the Count inquires into whether the pianist knows any "songs from the good old days." The two agree that they like the good old tunes, with the pianist observing "Well they're all

melody, aren't they?" The pianist then plays the song *Please Don't Bring Your Banjo Back*, which ends with the group repeating "And if I ever see another banjo, I'm going out to buy a big balloon."

The short but rousing rendition of *Please Don't Bring Your Banjo Back* is followed by Mal Evans stating "Yes, everywhere it's Christmas." The Beatles then break into a reprise of *Everywhere It's Christmas*, which is followed by clapping, laughter and a fitting "jolly good" to end the record.

The 1967 Beatles Christmas record follows the formula set the previous year. Rather than merely thanking their fans, the group performs a series of skits mimicking BBC radio and television programs. They also perform an original song titled *Christmas Time (Is Here Again)*.

Once again the British Fan Club packaged the disc in a seven inch cardboard sleeve (shown on following page). For the second year in a row, group members contributed to the design of the sleeve, which is credited to Julian Lennon, John Lennon and Ringo Starr. The front side is a collage of sepia-tinted portrait photos surrounding colorful sunflowers. The effect is somewhat reminiscent of the crowd of faces appearing of the *Sgt. Pepper* cover. The back side has splotches of colorful paint on its left side and text on the right, including the title *Christmas Time (Is Here Again)*. The record features "The Original Beatles with Special Guest Appearance by the feet and voice of Victor U. Spinetti and Something Else by Malcolm Lift-Evans." The production credit reads "Another little bite of the Apple: Produced by George (Is Here Again) Martin." The text ends with the nonsensical statement "Augmented Applause recorded on location in Dublin using f8 filter at 33⅓ a.s.a."

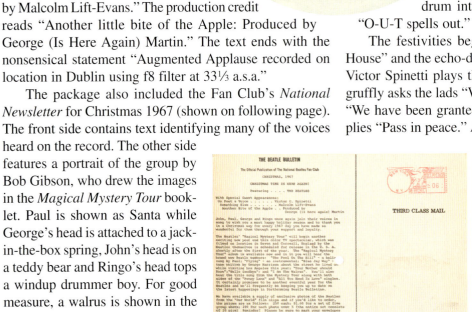

The package also included the Fan Club's *National Newsletter* for Christmas 1967 (shown on following page). The front side contains text identifying many of the voices heard on the record. The other side features a portrait of the group by Bob Gibson, who drew the images in the *Magical Mystery Tour* booklet. Paul is shown as Santa while George's head is attached to a jack-in-the-box spring, John's head is on a teddy bear and Ringo's head tops a windup drummer boy. For good measure, a walrus is shown in the lower right corner.

The flexi-disc (LYN 1360) (shown center) has red print on a white label. It is titled "Christmas Time (Is Here Again) The Beatles Fifth Christmas Record." The record has a running time of 6:10 and plays at 33⅓ rpm.

As was the case in 1966, the American Fan Club issued the Christmas message on a 7" x 8½" postcard with a vinyl record coated on one side and text on the other (shown lower center). The record label's silver text is identical to that of the 1966 label, except that it is

undated. The text side has *The Beatle Bulletin* for Christmas, 1967, which has information about the Christmas record and the *Magical Mystery Tour* film and album.

The Christmas record session took place at Abbey Road on November 28, 1967. The theme song *Christmas Time (Is Here Again)* features Paul on piano, George on acoustic guitar, John on timpani and Ringo on drums, along with double-tracked vocals from the boys, George Martin and Victor Spinetti, who starred with the Beatles in *Help!*, *A Hard Day's Night* and *Magical Mystery Tour*. Portions of the song, which is credited to Lennon-McCartney-Harrison-Starkey, appear on the disc. Although the full 6:37 version of the song has never been officially issued, the *Free As A Bird* Extended Play single and CD contains the first two minutes or so of the song. The 1967 Christmas record opens with 40 seconds of the theme song, complete with John's count in "Interplanetary Remix Take Four Hundred and Forty Four" and Ringo's drum intro. The song fades with the words "O-U-T spells out."

The festivities begin with "The boys arrive at BBC House" and the echo-drenched sound of three loud knocks. Victor Spinetti plays the part of the BBC Wise One, who gruffly asks the lads "What do you want?" After they reply "We have been granted permission, oh Wise One," he replies "Pass in peace." As the boys' footsteps are heard, the theme song is briefly faded in and out. John then does the voice of an announcer providing the details of an audition. He concludes with "Bring your own." This leads into a piano-accompanied tap dance featuring the feet of Ringo and Victor Spinetti. The audition ends with "Next please" and applause. The segment concludes with the group singing a piano-backed jingle for an imaginary product, Wonderlust: "Get Wonderlust for your trousers, get Wonderlust for your hair."

The next BBC program opens with swirling strings. Paul, serving as talk show host, tells the listeners that "Sitting with me in the studio tonight is a cross section of British youth." John, playing the part of Sir Gerald, dodges Paul's questions by insisting "There was a job to be done." This is followed by a link of the theme song and laughter leading into "On to the next round" and the pippy sound

# The Official Beatles FAN CLUB

Central London Address: P.O. Box No. 1AP, London W1    Fan Club Telephone No. (01) 734-0246

## NATIONAL NEWSLETTER ❄ Christmas 1967 ❄

*Dear Beatle People,*

EACH CHRISTMAS SINCE 1963 The Beatles have made a special record for Fan Club members and this has become their traditional way of saying an extra "Thank You" to Beatle People all over Britain. When you've listened to "*Christmas Time (Is Here Again)*" I think you'll agree that the 1967 Christmas Record is even better than those which have gone before.

I don't imagine you will have too much difficulty identifying the fantastic variety of different voices in "*Christmas Time (Is Here Again)*". At the very beginning it's John who shouts "Interplanetary Remix Take 444!" and, later on, he's heard as the Audition Announcer ("Bring your own!"), Sir Gerald, The Quizmaster and A Scottish Poet. John and Paul took it in turns to play the piano, George is the Quiz Show Prizewinner and Ringo stars as the Choked Voice in "Theatre Hour"! Incidentally the colourful Tap Dance routine (!?!) is a joint effort by Ringo and Victor Spinetti who makes several brief guest appearances during the record—for instance he's also The B.B.C. Wise One ("Pass in peace"). Mal Evans is there too—in the role of Audition Studio Man ("Are you 13 amp?") with a vaguely Glasgow (?) accent!!! At the very end that's George Martin playing the organ in the middle of a very chilly gale.

Incidentally our very sincere thanks to George Martin for producing the record and to EMI Records for allowing us to give you this seasonal gift.

By the way—if you find that the pick-up arm of your record player "jumps" now and again and misses bits of the Christmas Record *there's nothing wrong with your copy* of "*Christmas Time (Is Here Again)*". In all probability you've got a particularly *Good* record player with a very *Lightweight* pick-up arm. If this is the case the player will also have a means of adjusting the

weight *of the pickup arm* and to play our Fan Club disc you want just a little extra pressure to prevent that "jumping".

John, Paul, George and Ringo have asked me to repeat here their Good Wishes ("Thank you ALL for a Wonderful Year") and to say they hope you have a great Christmas. Everyone at the Fan Club headquarters—plus Neil and Mal—would like to join in sending you the Season's Greetings and All The Best for 1968.

It's easy to forget just how hard all the Club's voluntary Area Secretaries work throughout the year and to take their valuable services for granted. So I'd like to add my own special "Thank You" to the 40 marvellous girls, one in each county all over Britain, who put in so many hours of effort on our behalf.

As always there will be fresh Newsletters in each issue of THE BEATLES MONTHLY BOOK all the way through 1968. If you're not already a regular reader it's high time you ordered the January edition from your newsagent. Apart from the Fan Club pages and a load of new pix, the January Book will have a report from Rome about Ringo and his part in the film "Candy".

Lots of Good Luck and Tarrah for now,

*Freda Kelly*

Freda Kelly: National Secretary.

of an organ and applause. George, playing the part of a disc jockey, tells the listeners that "From the recent heavy fighting near Blackpool, Mrs. G. Evans of Solihull was gradually injured. She wants for all the people in hospital, *Plenty Of Jam Jars* by the Ravellers. And here it is." The band then takes on the identity of the Ravellers and performs the requested song, *Plenty Of Jam Jars*. The echo-laden, piano-backed recording has the sound and spirit of an English music hall tune.

In the next BBC segment, John hosts a quiz show featuring George as the prizewinner. After an exchange between the two regarding the guest's claim that he is 32 years old, the host informs the prizewinner that he has "just won a trip to Denver and five others." This leads into applause, the return of the organ and another round of Wonderlust jingle: "Get Wonderlust for your trousers, get Wonderlust

for your hair." Next up is a snippet of a show titled *Theatre Hour*, which opens with a ringing phone that is answered by Ringo. When the caller's conversation quickly gives way to a choking sound, a panicking Ringo informs the operator he's been cut off and shouts "Emergency." After a few bars of appropriately dramatic orchestration and a bit of the theme song *Christmas Time Is Here Again*, John and George continue with their quiz show, which leads to applause and laughter.

George Martin then informs the listeners that "They'd like to thank you for a wonderful year." After the group says "Thank you for a wonderful year," the laughter returns and John adds "Come in." The record concludes with a nonsensical Christmas message backed by George Martin playing *Auld Lang Syne* on Hammond organ and the sound of swirling wind.

The Beatles Christmas record for 1968 posed logistical problems. After the group finished work on their two album set, *The Beatles*, they needed a break from each other. John was spending all his time with Yoko, and George was in Los Angeles producing Jackie Lomax's album for Apple. In November, 1968, the group had no interest or desire to get together at Abbey Road for another holiday production. The problem was solved by having disc jockey Kenny Everett put together a series of separate messages taped by John, Paul, George and Ringo.

In England, the disc was issued by the Fan Club in a red, white and blue 7" cardboard sleeve (shown on following page, top row). The front side features a psychedelic patterned drawing of a woman's face and upper body. She truly appears to be a "girl with kaleidoscope eyes." The lower right corner has "Christmas 1968" in blue upper case letters. The other side has a semi-paisley patterned print in the same style and colors as that of the front drawing. The record is identified as "The Beatles Sixth Christmas Record" in small upper case blue letters. This is followed by "Happy Christmas" in red upper case letters. The blue liner notes conclude with "Non-Beatle Kenny Foreverett had a Nice Time mucking about with the tapes and deserves to be called PRODUCER although this is an unpaid position."

Due to the 7:55 length of the recording, the Christmas message, for the first time, is spread on both sides of the flexi-disc (LYN 1743/1744). Unlike prior years, the disc does not have a paper label, but rather has the text printed in silver directly on side one (following page, center left). The record is titled *The Beatles Sixth Christmas Record.* The disc was not issued with a *National Newsletter*, but rather came with an advert for Superpix Beatles photos.

After two years of shoddy postcard packaging, American Fan Club members finally received their record in a cardboard sleeve. However, it was a modified version of the 1967 British jacket. The 1968 American sleeve (following page, bottom row) was printed and manufactured in England. The art work is the same as on the earlier U.K. jacket, but most of the text has been eliminated and replaced with "The Beatles 1968 Christmas Record" in black upper case letters. The U.S. record is a two-sided flexi-disc manufactured by Americom, who pressed the Beatles pocket discs. Its label information is printed in silver directly onto the center of side one of the disc (following page, center right) and features a drawing of the group's faces. There are no text references to the Beatles or Christmas.

According to the liner notes to the British sleeve, the disc was recorded in November, 1968 "at the lush London homes of Beatle John and Beatle Paul and in the back of Beatle Ringo's diesel-powered removal van Somewhere In Surrey." George was recorded by telephone link from Los Angeles, where he was producing Jackie Lomax's album. Everett also used a bit of George's voice from a tape made earlier "in the elegant Esher home of Beatle George during rehearsal sessions for 'The Beatles' LP album set."

Side one opens with footsteps, knocking and the opening of a door, leading into "Hello, this a big 'hi' and a sincere 'Merry Christmas' from yours truly, Ringo Starr." The sound of a closing door is quickly followed by the piano intro to *Ob-La-Di, Ob-La-Da*, which is mixed with more piano. Paul, on acoustic guitar, then sings a simple holiday song with words such as "Happy New Year, Happy Christmas, Happy Easter, Happy Autumn, Happy Michaelness, Happy Christmas everybody to you." After more piano and sound effects, Paul continues with "I'd like to wish everybody Happy Christmas this year, nineteen sixty, eight, going on sixty-nine, Happy Christmas, Happy New Year, all the best to you from here." This is followed by sound effects and more of Paul's song, which fades out with clapping.

John's first segment opens with a brief orchestral piece followed by a sped-up verse of *Helter Skelter* and sound effects. John then reads a story over a piano background.

"Wonsaponatime there were two balloons called Jock and Yono. They were strictly in love...they were together, man. Unfortunatimeable they seemed to have previous experience which kept calling them one way or another. You know how it is. But they battled on against overwhelming oddities, including some of their beast friends. Being in love, they cloong together even more, man, but some of the poisonous monster of outrated busloaded *hithrowers did stick slightly and they occasionally had to resort to the dry cleaners. Luckily this did not kill them and they weren't banned from the Olympic Games. They lived hopefully ever after and who could blame them?"

The above ballad of Jock and Yono (John and Yoko) is in the style of John's books, *In His Own Write* and *A Spaniard In The Works*. It takes a not-so-subtle stab at the other Beatles, including them in a group described as "some of their beast friends." The words to this story and John's second story described below appear on the calendar with *The Plastic Ono Band - Live Peace In Toronto 1969.*

Next up is George, who gives greetings from America over holiday music and sound effects. "Well here we are again, another Fab Christmas. Christmas time is here again. Ain't been 'round since last year. And we'd like to take this opportunity, all the way from America, to say Happy Christmas to you, our faithful beloved fans all over the world who have made our life worth living." George then introduces Mal Evans, who adds "Merry Christmas, children, everywhere." Side one fades out with music and cheering.

Side two opens with a ringing telephone and Ringo engaging in a nonsensical conversation, which ends when the drummer insists "It's a private line, you know." After Ringo introduces "one of the most versatile performers in our career," Paul adds a brief snippet of his holiday song heard earlier in the program. This is followed by another of John's stories, which opens with "Once upon a pool table there lived a short-haired butcher's boy" and contains lines such as "Their father was in a long story cut short in the middle of his life sentence" and "The full meaning of Winchester Cathedral defies description." So does John's narration, which moves forward with added reverb.

George introduces Tiny Tim, who gives his holiday greetings and, in his trademark falsetto voice and accompanying ukulele, sings his unique interpretation of *Nowhere Man*. George then adds "Thank you, Tiny, thank you and God bless you, Tiny." The record ends with the sound of a church organ and the thud of Ringo's drums.

CHRISTMAS
1968

The Beatles Christmas record for 1969 followed the same formula as the previous year. Rather than gathering at the studio to record a group message or story, each Beatle supplied a tape of holiday greetings, which were once again edited by Kenny Everett (credited under his real name, Maurice Cole, on the sleeve).

As was the case in 1966 and 1967, the disc was issued in a seven inch cardboard sleeve (shown on the following page, top row) designed by a Beatle. Credited to Richard Starkey and Zak Starkey, the Ringo and son collaboration has colorful swirling images on its festive front side and a black and white drawing of people and a flowered tree on the back. The liner notes state:

"From Ascot in Berkshire, from Weybridge in Surrey, from St. John's Wood in the Borough of Marylebone and from Apple in the West End, John Ringo Paul and George send you these tapes of love and greetings soldered into a collective disc by the iron wrist of Maurice Cole. The Beatles wish all of you a happy Christmas and may the Seventies Give Peace a Chance." The last phrase is a reference to the Plastic Ono Band's single *Give Peace A Chance* (Apple 1809).

The back of the sleeve has the British Fan Club logo in the upper right corner above "Happy Christmas 1969" in pink upper case letters. The jacket was manufactured by West Brothers Printers, Limited, of London.

For the second year in a row, the length of the Christmas messages (7:42) necessitated that the recording be pressed on both sides of the flexi-disc. By coincidence, the 1969 Christmas disc is numbered LYN 1970/1971. Once again, the disc has text printed in silver on side one (following page, center left). The record is titled *The Beatles Seventh Christmas Record*.

**Apple prepared special Christmas cards like the one above to send to its friends. Another of the Apple Christmas cards is shown on the following page, bottom row.**

The American Fan Club received a shipment of the 1969 British jackets for packaging its pressing of the Christmas record, which is also a two-sided flexi-disc. The Americom-manufactured disc has its label information printed in silver on side one (following page, center right) and once again features a drawing of the group's faces. There are no text references to the Beatles or Christmas, but the date 1969 does appear.

Side one opens with John encouraging people to shout "Happy Christmas" into the tape. This is followed by a brief snippet of *Noël* on organ, which leads into Yoko interviewing John. When asked if he has any special thoughts for Christmas, John replies "eating" and says he would like corn flakes prepared by Parisian hands and blessed by a Hare Krishna mantra.

After music, sound effects and holiday greetings from George, Ringo strums a guitar and sings "Good evening to you gentleman, happy to be here/Good evening to you gentlemen, I fear, I fear, I fear/Good evening to you one and all, I hope you will enjoy/The coming sport's day of our life is mama's little boy." This is followed by a bit of *The End* from *Abbey Road* and Yoko asking John about the gardens and high walls of his new Ascot home.

Paul, on guitar, contributes another simple holiday song with lyrics such as "This is to wish you all a Merry, Merry Christmas/This is to wish you just a Merry, Merry Year." George then adds more holiday sentiments: "I'd like to say I hope everybody listening to this has a very happy time at Christmas and has a good, fortunate, lucky new year, and a good time to be had by all." The side concludes with a bit more of Paul's Christmas song.

Side two opens with an orchestral version of *Deck The Halls*, which leads into John interviewing Yoko. Responding to his questions about the seventies, Yoko is hopeful that there will be peace and "freedom of mind and everything" and that "everybody will just be flying around." As Yoko continues her answer, John begins singing the Beatles holiday favorite form their very first Christmas disc, *Good King Wenceslaus*. John and Yoko then exchange a series of "Happy Christmas" vocals. After John shouts "Take two," the pair proceed with another unique series of "Happy Christmas" vocals and an exchange of their names. Yoko sings "It's warm and nice and comfy" and "Let's put the light on the trees." John replies "well my dear, you pass me the light and I'll stick it on the tree."

Next up is Ringo, who begins saying "Merry Christmas" over and over again until it evolves into "*Magic Christian.*" He shamelessly admits "It's just a plug for the film, Ken. Try to keep it on." Ringo then wishes everybody a Merry Christmas and a very happy New Year.

The record's final contribution from a Beatle begins with John telling Yoko he'd like a big teddy. After Yoko says she will get him one, John replies "Oh thank you mommy." He promises her he will be a good boy as long as she gets him a teddy bear, a train set, a man on the moon and lots and lots and lots...." As an organ-backed choir sings *Noël*, the record ends with a bit of laughter.

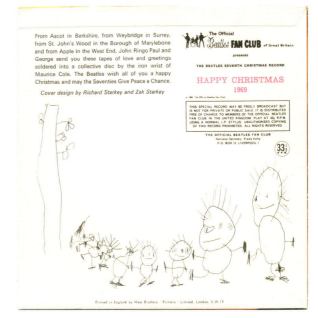

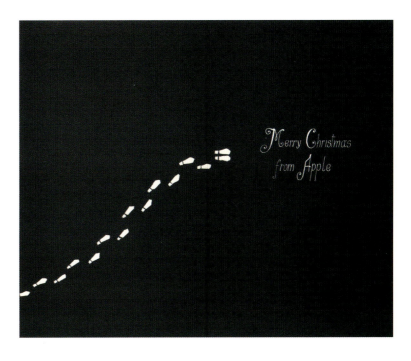

Although the Beatles breakup became public in April, 1970, the Official Beatles Fan Club continued with its activities. With the group no longer in existence, there was no chance of issuing a new Christmas disc for the 1970 holiday season. Instead, members of the British and U.S. fan clubs received an exclusive long-playing album containing the Christmas messages from the 1963 through 1969 flexi-discs. The American album was most likely shipped in the Spring of 1971.

For American Beatles fans who had faced their first yule tide season with the knowledge that the Beatles were no more, the Fan Club album was a bittersweet reminder of Christmases past. Those holiday seasons, with the exception of 1966, were highlighted by the release of a new Beatles album. Although John and George had released excellent solo albums (*John Lennon–Plastic Ono Band* and *All Things Must Pass*) in November, 1970, there was no new Beatles record in 1970 to raise holiday spirits. Instead, fans had to settle for a springtime disc of previously released holiday messages. On the plus side, the sound quality of *The Beatles Christmas Album* was vastly superior to that of the individual flexi-discs. The LP also marked the debut of the 1964 and 1965 Christmas messages in America.

Listening to the holiday tracks in chronological order demonstrates how the annual Christmas discs mirrored the ever-evolving Beatles. The 1963 recording has the Fab Four dutifully reading Tony Barrow's script, listing the highlights of the year and thanking their fans. By late 1964, the boys, particularly John, were beginning to rebel from the image carefully crafted by Brian and his staff. Although they thank their fans and follow a script, John injects humorous asides, changes words and mockingly lets the listener know he is reading from a prepared script.

The 1965 message finds the lads poking fun at the concept of recording holiday messages. After opening with an out-of-tune, off-key rendition of *Yesterday*, the group eagerly agrees to follow Ringo's suggestion to do a Christmas record. The scene is reminiscent of a typical rock movie in which someone comes up with the idea to play a song at an opportune moment. Although Paul gives the fans the usual thanks for sending presents and buying the records, John thanks the fans for pieces of chewed up gum and playing cards made of knickers. The group engages in bit of political satire with a militarized version of *Auld Lang Syne*, complete with references to Vietnam, China and bodies floating in the River Jordan. This foreshadows John's anti-war comments from 1966, in which he stated that if Americans could accept something as cruel as the war in Vietnam, then they could accept the butcher cover.

The 1966 Christmas disc was an elaborate recording that gave fans a hint of things to come. The record, which opens and closes with the song *Everywhere It's Christmas*, segues from one short skit to another. Although the stories are unrelated, they fit together under a loose overall theme. This concept Christmas record has the same framework as the group's next album, *Sgt. Pepper's Lonely Hearts Club Band*. The 1967 holiday disc follows the same format, with the group taking fans on a magical mystery tour of the BBC.

For Beatles fans, 1968 was an incredible year. Highlights included the innovative cartoon film *Yellow Submarine*, the marathon single *Hey Jude* and the double album *The Beatles*. And while the group appeared to be at their creative peak, the 1968 Christmas record was full of clues that all was not well in Pepperland. Some astute listeners viewed the Beatles latest LP as a collection of songs by John and the band, Paul and the band and George and the band. The holiday disc took it one step further by providing separately recorded solo messages edited together to form a "Beatles" record. Paul, anxious to keep the Beatles going, contributed a holiday song. George, who was pursuing other interests, was recorded by telephone hookup from Los Angeles. Ringo wished everyone a sincere Merry Christmas. John provided a story of two balloons, Jock and Yono, which was a tale of how he and Yoko had clung together despite the conduct of "some of their beast friends." This jab at the other Beatles was the most telling clue of all. Yoko's prominent presence on the 1969 Christmas record made it clear that John was more interested in being with Yoko than carrying on with the Beatles.

The American version of *The Beatles Christmas Album* was packaged in a blue background cover, **APP 100.SC1**. The front side has five rows and five columns of cubes that have black and white pictures of the Beatles. The rows feature, from top to bottom, John, Paul, George, Ringo and the entire group. Moving left to right, the columns feature pictures are from 1966, 1967, 1968, 1969 and 1970. The lower right cube does not have a 1970 picture of the band as no group pictures were taken in 1970. Instead, the cube has "The Beatles Christmas Album" in uppercase letters. The upper half of the back cover has black and white images of the front covers to the 1964 through 1969 British Christmas flexi-discs and "The Beatles" in uppercase black letters outlined in white. The lower half has "Christmas Album" in large uppercase white letters and black text in the lower left corner. Album design is credited to "GROK IT!" and photo creations to Robert Bauman.

The records, **APP 100.SR1(af)**, were pressed with standard Apple labels that have Apple perimeter print on side one. Both sides have the track selections and running times below the spindle hole. "NOT FOR SALE" and "all rights" information appears in the lower part of the apples on each side. The trail off areas contain the Bell Sound logo, the initials "sf" and a hand drawn Winchester logo, indicating that the record was mastered by Sam Feldman at Bell Sound and manufactured by Capitol's Winchester factory.

*The Beatles Christmas Album* has been frequently counterfeited. The first batch of bogus covers have blurred photos on the front. Later counterfeits have sharper images; however, some noticeable flaws remain. On legitimate covers, in the picture located in the lower left corner, both of Ringo's eyeballs are clearly visible. On all confirmed counterfeits, the right eye is covered by a dark shadow. Legitimate records were pressed by Capitol's Winchester factory and have a visible 1½"-diameter ring located ⅝" from the center hole (see image on next page). On counterfeits, the ring is much larger. There are also fake colored vinyl discs.

APP 100.SC1

APP 100.SR1(af)

British Fan Club Album

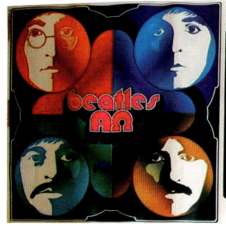

NOW AVAILABLE
The Only Authorized
Collection of
THE BEATLES

On Apple Records
and Tapes.

THE BEATLES 1962-1966                              THE BEATLES 1967-1970

LOVE ME DO
PLEASE PLEASE ME
FROM ME TO YOU
SHE LOVES YOU
I WANT TO HOLD YOUR HAND
ALL MY LOVING
CAN'T BUY ME LOVE

A HARD DAY'S NIGHT
AND I LOVE HER
EIGHT DAYS A WEEK
I FEEL FINE
TICKET TO RIDE
YESTERDAY

HELP!
YOU'VE GOT TO HIDE YOUR LOVE AWAY
WE CAN WORK IT OUT
DAY TRIPPER
DRIVE MY CAR
NORWEGIAN WOOD (THIS BIRD HAS FLOWN)

NOWHERE MAN
MICHELLE
IN MY LIFE
GIRL
PAPERBACK WRITER
ELEANOR RIGBY
YELLOW SUBMARINE

A TWO LP SET ON APPLE          A TWO LP SET ON APPLE

STRAWBERRY FIELDS FOREVER
PENNY LANE
SGT. PEPPER'S LONELY HEARTS CLUB BAND
WITH A LITTLE HELP FROM MY FRIENDS
LUCY IN THE SKY WITH DIAMONDS
A DAY IN THE LIFE
ALL YOU NEED IS LOVE
I AM THE WALRUS
HELLO GOODBYE
THE FOOL ON THE HILL
MAGICAL MYSTERY TOUR
LADY MADONNA
HEY JUDE
REVOLUTION
BACK IN THE U.S.S.R.
WHILE MY GUITAR GENTLY WEEPS
OB-LA-DI, OB-LA-DA
GET BACK
DON'T LET ME DOWN
THE BALLAD OF JOHN & YOKO
OLD BROWN SHOE
HERE COMES THE SUN
SOMETHING
OCTOPUS'S GARDEN
LET IT BE
ACROSS THE UNIVERSE
THE LONG AND WINDING ROAD

Top: Alpha Omega in-store banner. Middle: Capitol promotional poster. Bottom: *Billboard* ad, April 7, 1973.

# THE BEATLES 1962-1966
# APPLE SKBO 3403

Although Capitol planned a *Best Of The Beatles* double album in mid-1964, and Parlophone released *A Collection Of Beatles Oldies* in December, 1966 (Parlophone mono PMC 7016; stereo PCS 7016), no Beatles greatest hits album was legitimately issued in the United States until April 2, 1973, when Apple released a pair of double albums containing hits and key album tracks. The first LP, *The Beatles 1962-1966* (Apple SKBO 3403), has a red background cover featuring a picture of the group from the same Angus McBean photo session that produced the cover to the band's first album, *Please Please Me* (Parlophone mono PMC 1202; stereo PCS 3042). Its companion piece, *The Beatles 1967-1970* (Apple SKBO 3404), has a blue background cover featuring an unused photograph shot in 1969 for the G*et Back* album that mimics the cover photo from the *Please Me* LP. These collections, which are often referred to as *The Red Album* and *The Blue Album*, were both certified gold by the RIAA on March 31, two days before their release.

*The Red Album* entered the *Billboard Top LP's* chart on April 14 and peaked at number three on May 19 and 26, unable to move past *The Blue Album* and Led Zeppelin's *Houses Of The Holy* (Atlantic 7255). The LP charted for 164 weeks, including eight in the top ten. *Cash Box* reported the album at number one, while *Record World* showed a peak at four. As of 2002, the RIAA has certified sales of 15 million units (meaning 7.5 million albums as the RIAA certifies by the number of discs shipped). Chart and sales information on *The Blue Album* appears in the following chapter.

Side 1
1. LOVE ME DO (Lennon & McCartney)
2. PLEASE PLEASE ME (Lennon & McCartney)
3. FROM ME TO YOU (Lennon & McCartney)
4. SHE LOVES YOU (Lennon & McCartney)
5. I WANT TO HOLD YOUR HAND
   (Lennon & McCartney)
6. ALL MY LOVING (Lennon & McCartney)
7. CAN'T BUY ME LOVE (Lennon & McCartney)

Side 3
1. HELP! (Lennon & McCartney)
2. YOU'VE GOT TO HIDE YOUR LOVE AWAY
   (Lennon & McCartney)
3. WE CAN WORK IT OUT (Lennon & McCartney)
4. DAY TRIPPER (Lennon & McCartney)
5. DRIVE MY CAR (Lennon & McCartney)
6. NORWEGIAN WOOD (THIS BIRD HAS FLOWN)
   (Lennon & McCartney)

Side 2
1. A HARD DAY'S NIGHT (Lennon & McCartney)
2. AND I LOVE HER (Lennon & McCartney)
3. EIGHT DAYS A WEEK (Lennon & McCartney)
4. I FEEL FINE (Lennon & McCartney)
5. TICKET TO RIDE (Lennon & McCartney)
6. YESTERDAY (Lennon & McCartney)

Side 4
1. NOWHERE MAN (Lennon & McCartney)
2. MICHELLE (Lennon & McCartney)
3. IN MY LIFE (Lennon & McCartney)
4. GIRL (Lennon & McCartney)
5. PAPERBACK WRITER (Lennon & McCartney)
6. ELEANOR RIGBY (Lennon & McCartney)
7. YELLOW SUBMARINE (Lennon & McCartney)

Both of the collections were put together by Apple, through Abkco, as a way of satisfying the contractual obligation of the Beatles to provide product to Capitol. The decision to release the albums was also influenced by the success of unauthorized collections containing songs pirated from albums manufactured and distributed by Apple and Capitol.

The September, 1972, issue of *Motor Trend* magazine ran an ad for an 8-Track tape collection titled *The Story Of The Beatles* that contained about 100 performances of the Beatles as a group and as solo artists. The tapes were manufactured by Economic Consultants, Inc. An ad in the January, 1973, issue of *Oui* proclaimed: "Four ragamuffins with outrageous haircuts that woke up the world. Those four men—John Lennon, Ringo Starr, Paul McCartney and George Harrison—were the architects of what music is today. THEY SOLD MORE RECORDS THAN ANY OTHER GROUP IN HISTORY." Similar ads ran in the February, 1973, issues of *Car and Driver*, *Signature* and *Penthouse* magazines.

Even more visible was another collection that was advertised on television and radio. The TV commercial featured an image of a colorful album cover (shown on the following page) and a man with a British accent announcing "The Beatles Alpha Omega." The ad described a fabulous four record album set containing 60 Beatles songs (including a few solo recordings), all for $13.95. The announcer assured viewers that delivery was guaranteed.

Many consumers wondered how they could do it for under 14 bucks. The answer was simple. The companies behind the *Alpha Omega* collection, T.V. Products, Inc. of Cleveland, Ohio, and Audiotape, Inc. of Asbury Park, New Jersey, were not paying any royalties to the Beatles or the publishers of the songs. Although the album was sold primarily through television ads, it was carried by some retail stores for a limited time (as evidenced by the in-store banner shown on page 224).

Apple, Abkco and Capitol were rightfully concerned over the widespread distribution these unauthorized collections were enjoying. On February 16, 1973, George Harrison, Apple and Capitol filed a lawsuit in New York state court against the manufacturers of the albums as well as TV and radio stations running commercials for the collections. The stations were quickly dropped from the suit when they agreed to discontinue running the ads.

The complaint described plaintiff George Harrison as "a famous entertainer, performer and recording artist of unique talents who is worldwide renowned as a member of the entertainment group of performers and recording artists known as 'The Beatles,' known throughout the world as a 'Beatle' and under his own name." In discussing artist royalties, the suit states that the Beatles received over 19 million dollars in royalties from September, 1969, through the filing of the suit on February 16, 1973. In addition to seeking injunctive relief to halt the distribution and sales of the pirated albums and tapes, the law suit sought an award of $15,000,000 in punitive damages to Harrison. Allen Klein filed an affidavit in support of the complaint for injunctive relief and damages.

Although the court record for *George Harrison et al v. Audiotape, Inc. et al* still exists, documents pertaining to the outcome of the case are missing. One can safely assume that the case was either settled or decided in favor of Harrison, Apple and Capitol.

A Capitol press release issued on May 12, 1973, subtly referred to the illegitimate collections by emphasizing that *The Red Album* and *The Blue Album* were "an invaluable selection of Beatles hits and, to date, are the only authorized collections of the group's music." This theme was also used on the albums' 36" x 12" promotional poster (shown on page 224) and on an insert packaged with the albums.

The Apple albums were programmed by Allan Steckler, who had previously selected the tracks and running order for the *Hey Jude* LP, as well as the Rolling Stones' *Hot Rocks* collections. The songs appear in chronological order (give or take a week) based upon British release dates.

Side one of *The Red Album* opens with the Beatles first five British singles: *Love Me Do* (the album does not use the master from the British 45 with Ringo on drums, but rather has the version with Ringo on tambourine, which was a number one hit when released in America on April 27, 1964, as Tollie 9008); *Please Please Me* (a number three hit when re-released on VJ 581 in January, 1964); *From Me To You* (a song that got lost in America as the B side to VJ 581, peaking at number 41 in the *Billboard Hot 100*); *She Loves You* (a number one hit when reissued on Swan 4152 in January, 1964); and *I Want To Hold Your Hand* (the group's first number one record in the U.S. released on December 26, 1963, on Capitol 5112). The side closes with *All My Loving* (from *Meet The Beatles!* and the first song performed by the group on *The Ed Sullivan Show*) and *Can't Buy Me Love* (Capitol 5150; another number one single).

Side two opens with the title song from the Beatles first film, *A Hard Day's Night* (Capitol 5222; number one). This is followed by another song from the movie, *And I Love Her* (Capitol 5235; number 12). The second side ends with four number one songs: *Eight Days A Week* (released in England on *Beatles For Sale* on December 4, 1964, but not issued in America until February 15, 1965, as Capitol 5371); *I Feel Fine* (released on November 23, 1964, as Capitol 5327); *Ticket To Ride* (released on April 19, 1965, as Capitol 5407); and *Yesterday* (released in England on the *Help!* LP on August 6, 1965, but not issued in America until September 13, 1965, as Capitol 5498).

The third side opens with an uncredited 15-second excerpt from the *James Bond Theme* that leads directly into the title song from the Beatles second film, *Help!* This is the way *Help!* appears on the Capitol soundtrack album. The song, without the instrumental introduction, topped the charts shortly after its July 19, 1965, release on Capitol 5476. This is followed with another selection from the movie, *You've Got To Hide Your Love Away*.

The album contains eight songs recorded during the *Rubber Soul* sessions. The first two, *We Can Work It Out* and *Day Tripper*, were recorded as a double A side single and released on Capitol 5555 on December 6, 1965, the same day the *Rubber Soul* album was issued in America. *We Can Work It Out* topped the charts, while *Day Tripper* peaked at number five. *Drive My Car* was the opening track on the British version of *Rubber Soul*, but was not released in America until June, 1966, when it was featured on Capitol's *Yesterday And Today* album. Side three closes with *Norwegian Wood*, which is on both the British and American versions of *Rubber Soul*.

Side four opens with four more *Rubber Soul* tracks. *Nowhere Man* was held off the album by Capitol and released as a single on Capitol 5587 on February 15, 1966. The song stalled at number three in the *Billboard Hot 100*, but reached number two in *Cash Box* and number one in *Record World*. The next three tracks, *Michelle*, *In My Life* and *Girl*, are on both the British and American versions of the album. *The Red Album* closes with three songs recorded during the *Revolver* sessions. *Paperback Writer* was released as single on Capitol 5651 on May 30, 1966. It was another number one million seller for the group. *Eleanor Rigby* and

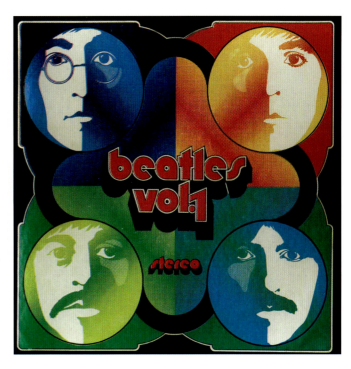

*Yellow Submarine* appeared on the album and on a double A side single (Capitol 5715), both released on August 8, 1966. *Billboard* charted *Yellow Submarine* at number two, while *Cash Box* and *Record World* reported the song at number one. *Billboard* charted *Eleanor Rigby* at 11.

Of the 26 songs appearing on *The Red Album*, a dozen topped the *Billboard Hot 100* and two more were reported at number one by other trade magazines. In addition to containing all the hit singles, the album features eight key album tracks. Although *Rubber Soul* is well represented, *Revolver* is not given proper coverage. One could also lament the omission of cover songs such as *Twist And Shout* and *Long Tall Sally*, but the decision was made to include only compositions written by members of the group. These are minor quibbles as the collection is full of one great song after another. The only legitimate criticism of the lineup is that more than 26 songs are needed to properly cover the Beatles recordings from 1962 -1966.

Unlike the *Hey Jude* album, which was compiled for Apple by EMI in London, the *Red* and *Blue* albums were put together by Capitol. The company did not obtain master tapes from EMI, but rather used what was in its vaults. Thus, some of the tracks are in mono even though stereo mixes were available.

The tracks on side one come from a variety of original sources. Although no true stereo mix for *Love Me Do* exists, George Martin made a fake stereo mix of the song for the *Please Please Me* LP. Capitol used that mix on *The Early Beatles*; however, *The Red Album* has a mono mix of the song. *Please Please Me* is the stereo mix first used by Capitol on *The Early Beatles*. A stereo mix of *From Me To You* was made by George Martin on March 14, 1963. Capitol used a mono reduction of this mix for its Star Line series issue of the song on Capitol 6063. Capitol dusted off the 1963 stereo mix for *The Red Album*. Although Capitol prepared a fake stereo duophonic mix of *She Loves You* for *The Beatles' Second Album*, the song appears in mono on *The Red Album*. Capitol did, however, use its duophonic mix of *I Want To Hold Your Hand* from its stereo *Meet The Beatles!* LP. *All My Loving* is the stereo mix from *Meet The Beatles!*, and *Can't Buy Me Love* is the stereo mix first used by Capitol on the *Hey Jude* album.

Capitol had true stereo mixes for three of the side two songs (*And I Love Her*, *Eight Days A Week* and *Yesterday*) in its vaults. The company did not bother to obtain stereo mixes from EMI for the other three. Because Capitol did not release *A Hard Day's Night* on any of its albums, it neither received a stereo mix from EMI nor created a duophonic mix of the song. *The Red Album* has the mono mix used by Capitol for the single. Capitol's fake stereo mix of *I Feel Fine* that appeared on *Beatles '65* is an echo-drenched duophonic disaster. *The Red Album* contains the superior mono single mix. *Ticket To Ride* is the duophonic mix from Capitol's *Help!* soundtrack album.

The first two selections on side three are stereo mixes from Capitol's *Help!* LP. The title track is preceded by 15 seconds of the *James Bond Theme*, while *You've Got To Hide Your Love Away* is identical to the British mix. The next two tracks, *We Can Work It Out* and *Day Tripper*, are the stereo mixes from *Yesterday And Today*. Both are different than the U.K. stereo mixes. The remaining *Rubber Soul*-era tracks appearing on sides three and four are stereo mixes from earlier Capitol albums. They are identical to the British stereo mixes. Capitol used the stereo mix of *Paperback Writer* that appeared on the *Hey Jude* LP. The album's final two selections are stereo mixes from *Revolver*.

Both *The Red Album* and *The Blue Album* contained the same 10¾" x 10¾" white paper insert listing the track selections for both albums on one side and a Beatles group and solo discography on the other. The track side boldly proclaims "These are the only authorized collections of The Beatles. On Apple Records." Each song is followed by the name of the Capitol album that it appeared on. There are a few interesting quirks with the listings. Although *From Me To You* and *A Hard Day's Night* had not previously been on a Capitol album, both are listed as being on the *Help!* LP. The rationale for this listing is that instrumental versions of each song (*From Me To You Fantasy* and *Another Hard Day's Night*) were on the soundtrack album. *Yellow Submarine* is listed as appearing on the *Yellow Submarine* album even though the song first appeared on *Revolver*. Although both *Get Back* and *Let It Be* are the single versions, *Get Back* is listed as appearing on the *Let It Be* LP, while *Let It Be* is identified as the single version.

The discography also has its quirks. The first Beatles single listed is No. 1800, *Yellow Submarine, Thingumybob*. This, of course, is not a Beatles single, but rather the Apple 45 by the Black Dyke Mills Band. By listing the discs in numerical order, the later singles *Hello Goodbye* (No. 2056) through *The Long And Winding Road* (No. 2832) appear before *I Want To Hold Your Hand* (No. 5112) through *All You Need Is Love* (No. 5964). In addition, *Yesterday, Strawberry Fields Forever* and *Baby, You're A Rich Man* are listed as A sides.

Allan Steckler realized the obvious importance of the collections and, in keeping with his philosophy that special albums deserve special packaging, brought in Tom Wilkes

to work on the project. Wilkes had previously designed the elaborate packaging for George Harrison's triple LP box sets *All Things Must Pass* and *The Concert For Bangla Desh*.

Tom Wilkes' design is based upon concepts envisioned by Allan Steckler. During a visit to Apple's London office, Steckler saw a proof of the rejected *Let It Be* cover featuring Angus McBean's 1969 recreation of the *Please Please Me* album cover. He thought that the pairing of the 1969 picture with the original 1963 photo would make a stunning combination. For the album containing the earlier recordings, the 1963 image of the Beatles is featured on the front cover, while the 1969 picture appears on the back. For the later collection, the 1969 picture appears on the front, and the 1963 photo is on the back. Although the earlier photo looks like the picture from the *Please Please Me* LP, it is actually an outtake from the same Angus McBean photo session.

Each album has a color theme. The collection of the group's earlier songs is red. The Beatles later work is their blue period. The color theme is used throughout the packaging, including the cover, the inner sleeves and the background of the record labels. As was the case with *All Things Must Pass*, the song lyrics are printed on the custom inner sleeves.

For the open inner gatefold, Steckler selected a black and white photo of the Beatles taken by Don McCullin during the July 28, 1968, "Mad Day Out" session. The picture shows the group intermixed with a crowd of onlookers of the photo session behind a wrought iron fence near the St. Pancras Old Church and Gardens in London. The presence of young children, including one standing in front of the fence, gives the package an innocent and nostalgic feeling.

Early proofs of the outside slicks show a slight variation of the concept. The 1962-1966 album has a red front cover and a blue back cover, while the 1966-1970 album has a blue front cover and a red back cover. This scheme was rejected in favor of keeping the color theme consistent throughout each album.

*The Red Album*'s gatefold cover, **APP 3403.SC1**, has a red background with "The Beatles/1962-1966" centered at the top of the front panel. The 1963 Angus McBean photo is on the front cover, and the 1969 picture is on the back The inside open gatefold has the picture from the Mad Day Out photo session, along with the track listings at the bottom. The first issue covers have a green Apple logo centered at the top of the back cover. Later issue covers from 1975 have the Capitol circle logo.

Many of the covers came with a 4" x 6" red sticker with black print, **APP 3403.S1**, affixed to the shrinkwrap. The sticker has an Apple logo centered at the top, followed by the song titles. The records are housed in custom red inner sleeves, **APP 3403.IS**, with the song lyrics printed on both sides.

The first issue records, **APP 3403.SR1(af)**, were pressed with red background Apple labels with yellow Apple perimeter print on the full apple side. The all rights labels, **APP 3403.SR2(ar)**, were used in 1975 and have yellow all rights perimeter print at the bottom on both sides.

APP 3403.SC1

APP 3403.SC1 (open gatefold)

LOVE ME DO
PLEASE PLEASE ME
FROM ME TO YOU
SHE LOVES YOU
I WANT TO HOLD YOUR HAND
ALL MY LOVING
CAN'T BUY ME LOVE

A HARD DAY'S NIGHT
AND I LOVE HER
EIGHT DAYS A WEEK
I FEEL FINE
TICKET TO RIDE
YESTERDAY

HELP!
YOU'VE GOT TO HIDE YOUR LOVE AWAY
WE CAN WORK IT OUT
DAY TRIPPER
DRIVE MY CAR
NORWEGIAN WOOD (THIS BIRD HAS FLOWN)

NOWHERE MAN
MICHELLE
IN MY LIFE
GIRL
PAPERBACK WRITER
ELEANOR RIGBY
YELLOW SUBMARINE

COMPLETE LYRICS INCLUDED INSIDE
PRINTED IN U.S.A. 3403

APP 3403.S1

APP 3403.IS

APP 3403.SR1 (af)

APP 3403.SR2 (ar)

## THE BEATLES 1967-1970
## APPLE SKBO 3404

*The Beatles 1967-1970* (Apple SKBO 3404) was released simultaneously with *The Beatles 1962-1966* (Apple SKBO 3403) on April 2, 1973. These two-disc collections are more commonly known as *The Red Album* and *The Blue Album* in recognition of their covers. While both albums performed extremely well upon their release, the collection covering the group's later years was the more popular.

*The Blue Album* entered the *Billboard Top LP's* chart on April 14 and hit number one on May 26, before being replaced the following week by Paul McCartney & Wings' *Red Rose Speedway* (Apple SMAL 3409). The LP charted for 169 weeks, including 11 in the top ten. During its final three weeks in the top ten, the number one album was George Harrison's *Living In The Material World* (Apple SMAS 3410). *Record World* also reported *The Blue Album*

at number one, while *Cash Box* showed a peak at two, being the only major trade magazine to chart *The Red Album* ahead of *The Blue Album*. As of 2002, the RIAA has certified sales of 16 million units (meaning eight million albums as the RIAA certifies by the number of discs shipped).

*The Blue Album* opens with the Beatles first single from 1967, *Strawberry Fields Forever* b/w *Penny Lane* (Capitol 5810). *Billboard* charted *Penny Lane* at number one and *Strawberry Fields Forever* at eight. This is followed by the three opening tracks from the *Sgt. Pepper* album, *Sgt. Pepper's Lonely Hearts Club Band*, *With A Little Help From My Friends* and *Lucy In The Sky With Diamonds*, and the album's final selection, *A Day In The Life*. Side one concludes with the Beatles chart topping anthem from the Summer of Love, *All You Need Is Love* (Capitol 5964).

Side 1
1. STRAWBERRY FIELDS FOREVER
   (Lennon & McCartney)
2. PENNY LANE (Lennon & McCartney)
3. SGT. PEPPER'S LONELY HEARTS CLUB BAND
   (Lennon & McCartney)
4. WITH A LITTLE HELP FROM MY FRIENDS
   (Lennon & McCartney)
5. LUCY IN THE SKY WITH DIAMONDS
   (Lennon & McCartney)
6. A DAY IN THE LIFE (Lennon & McCartney)
7. ALL YOU NEED IS LOVE (Lennon & McCartney)

Side 2
1. I AM THE WALRUS (Lennon & McCartney)
2. HELLO GOODBYE (Lennon & McCartney)
3. THE FOOL ON THE HILL (Lennon & McCartney)
4. MAGICAL MYSTERY TOUR (Lennon & McCartney)
5. LADY MADONNA (Lennon & McCartney)
6. HEY JUDE (Lennon & McCartney)
7. REVOLUTION (Lennon & McCartney)

Side 3
1. BACK IN THE U.S.S.R. (Lennon & McCartney)
2. WHILE MY GUITAR GENTLY WEEPS (Harrison)
3. OB-LA-DI, OB-LA-DA (Lennon & McCartney)
4. GET BACK (Lennon & McCartney)
5. DON'T LET ME DOWN (Lennon & McCartney)
6. THE BALLAD OF JOHN & YOKO
   (Lennon & McCartney)
7. OLD BROWN SHOE (Harrison)

Side 4
1. HERE COMES THE SUN (Harrison)
2. COME TOGETHER (Lennon & McCartney)
3. SOMETHING (Harrison)
4. OCTOPUS'S GARDEN (Starkey)
5. LET IT BE (Lennon & McCartney)
6. ACROSS THE UNIVERSE (Lennon & McCartney)
7. THE LONG AND WINDING ROAD
   (Lennon & McCartney)

---

Side two opens with both sides of the Beatles 1967 single for the Christmas season, *I Am The Walrus* and *Hello Goodbye* (Capitol 2056). *Billboard* charted *Hello Goodbye* at number one and its flip side at 56. This is followed by two more songs from the *Magical Mystery Tour* album, *The Fool On The Hill* and the title track. Next up is the group's first single from 1968, *Lady Madonna* (Capitol 2138), which inexplicitly only reached number four in *Billboard*. Side two closes with the Beatles first Apple single, *Hey Jude* b/w *Revolution* (Apple 2276). *Billboard* charted *Hey Jude* at number one for nine weeks and *Revolution* at 12.

Side three opens with three tracks from *The White Album*, the LP opener *Back In The U.S.S.R.*, *While My Guitar Gently Weeps* and *Ob-La-Di, Ob-La-Da*. This is followed by the Beatles first single from 1969, *Get Back* b/w *Don't Let Me Down* (Apple 2490). *Billboard* charted *Get Back* at number one for five weeks and the flip side at 35. The side concludes with the follow-up single, *The Ballad Of John & Yoko* b/w *Old Brown Shoe* (Apple 2531). Although limited airplay stalled the A side at number eight in the *Billboard Hot 100*, the single went on to sell over one million units.

Side four opens with four selections from the *Abbey Road* LP, *Here Comes The Sun*, *Come Together*, *Something* and *Octopus's Garden*. Two of the songs, *Come Together* and *Something*, were released on Apple 2654, which topped the *Billboard Hot 100* on November 29, 1969. The *Abbey Road* songs are followed by the single version of *Let It Be* (Apple 2764), a number one hit in April, 1970. The album concludes with two songs from the *Let It Be* album, *Across The Universe* and *The Long And Winding Road*. The latter song was issued as the group's last single on Apple 2832 and topped the charts in June, 1970.

As was the case with *The Red Album*, Capitol used tapes from its vaults to compile *The Blue Album*. Most of the tracks are stereo mixes used for stereo Capitol albums; however, there are a few anomalies. *Penny Lane* appears in the duophonic fake stereo mix from the Capitol *Magical Mystery Tour* LP; however, Capitol could have obtained a 1971 stereo mix made by EMI that was used on the German release of *Magical Mystery Tour*. Capitol inexplicably used the mono single mix of *Hello Goodbye* even though *Magical Mystery Tour* has a true stereo mix. This was almost certainly an error. For *Get Back* and *Let It Be*, the album labels list the running times of the songs as they appear on the *Let It Be* album; however, *The Blue Album* has the stereo single versions of both songs. Apparently, Capitol was originally going to use the album versions of these songs, but decided instead to go with the hit single versions.

The album's gatefold cover, **APP 3404.SC1**, has a blue background with "The Beatles/1967-1970" centered at the top of the front panel. The placement of the Angus McBean photos is the opposite of that of *The Red Album*. This collection of the group's later hits has the 1969 picture on the front cover and the 1963 picture on the back. The inside open gatefold has the same picture found on *The Red Album*, along with the track listings at the bottom. The first issue covers have a green Apple logo centered at the top of the back cover. Later issue covers from 1975 have the Capitol circle logo.

Many of the covers came with a 4" x 6" blue sticker with black print, **APP 3404.S1**, affixed to the shrinkwrap. The sticker has an Apple logo centered at the top, followed by the song titles. The records are housed in custom blue sleeves, **APP 3404.IS**, with the lyrics printed on both sides. The album also came with the same discography/track information sheet included with *The Red Album*.

The first issue records, **APP 3404.SR1(af)**, were pressed with blue background Apple labels with pink Apple perimeter print on the full apple side. Some of the labels have a bluish-gray background. The all rights labels, **APP 3404.SR2(ar)**, were used in 1975 and have pink all rights perimeter print at the bottom on both sides.

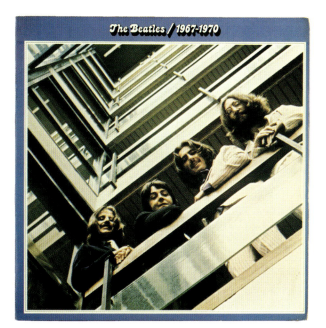

APP 3404.SC1

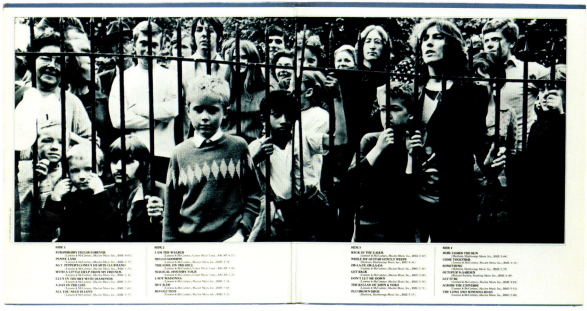

APP 3404.SC1 (open gatefold)

APP 3404.S1

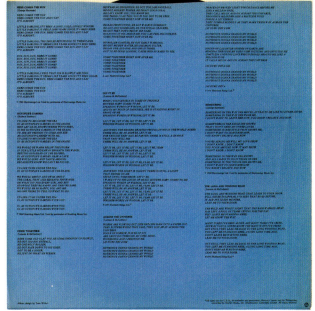

APP 3404.IS

APP 3404.SR1 (af)

APP 3404.SR1(af)
with bluish-gray background

APP 3404.SR2(ar)

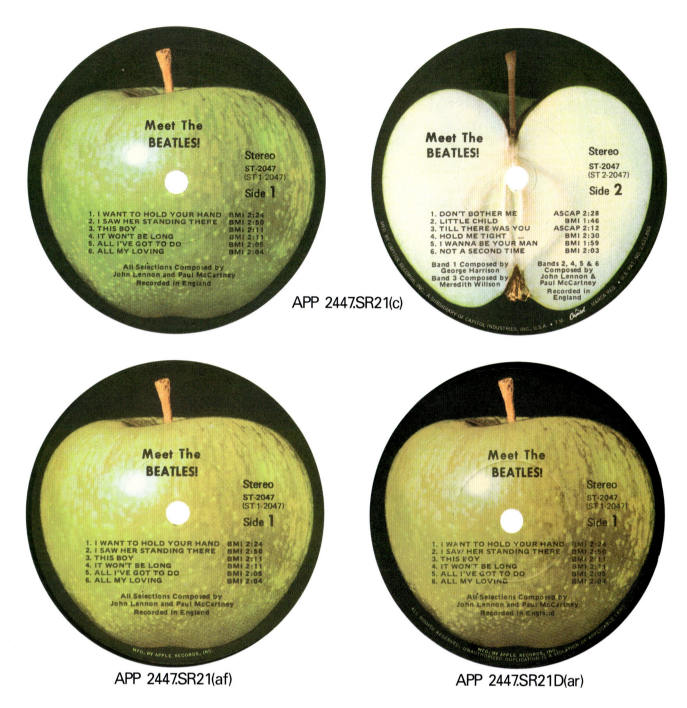

APP 2447.SR21(c)

APP 2447.SR21(af)

APP 2447.SR21D(ar)

# APPLE REISSUE ALBUMS

As detailed in the chapter "Apple Reissue Singles," Capitol began pressing its Beatles 45s and albums with Apple labels in the spring of 1971. At that time, Capitol was issuing its Beatles albums on its lime green label featuring the company's new circle logo. The pre-Apple album catalog, which includes *Meet The Beatles!* through *Magical Mystery Tour*, was pressed with Apple labels until the end of 1975, at which time Capitol switched to its then-current orange labels.

Each title in the series has three basic variations: (1) Apple labels with Capitol logo perimeter print on the sliced apple side, designated **.SR21(c)** in this book's numbering system; (2) Apple labels with Apple perimeter print on the full apple side, **.SR21(af)**; and (3) Apple labels with the all rights language used in 1975, **.SR21(ar)**. There are four basic all rights variations: (1) all rights language printed in

black at the top on both sides, **.SR21A(ar)**; (2) all rights language printed in black at the bottom on both sides, **.SR21B(ar)**; (3) all rights language appearing in green in the right side perimeter on the full apple side, **.SR21C(ar)**; and (4) all rights language appearing in green in the lower perimeter on both sides, **.SR21D(ar)**.

With the exception of differing typesetting variations appearing on small numbers of labels for some of the titles, the labels for each particular title have the same layout regardless of where and when the record was pressed. Confirmed exceptions, designated **.SR22**, include *Yesterday And Today* (title and group's name in uppercase and lowercase letters), *Rubber Soul* (spread title and band member names on two lines), *Revolver* (title and group's name in uppercase and lowercase letters) and *Magical Mystery Tour* (title on one line on both sides). There may be others.

The Apple reissue albums of the seventies are normally found with later fabricated covers. Most of these jackets have a manufacturer's identification code located in the lower right corner. Typical numbers include 12, 16, 17 and 18. (The first issue Capitol covers from the early to mid-sixties have identification numbers such as 2, 3, 4, 5 and 6.) A few of the titles sometimes appear with covers containing the RIAA gold record award seal. Confirmed pairings with RIAA seal covers include *Meet The Beatles!*, *The Beatles' Second Album*, *Beatles '65*, *Beatles VI* and *Yesterday And Today*.

Although the Apple reissue albums were pressed after the group broke up, they are still sought after by collectors. For those who first discovered the Beatles in the early seventies, the Apple label represents how they were introduced to the band. Older collectors are also attracted to these discs. Many repurchased Beatles albums in the early seventies to obtain fresh discs free from scratches developed over years of constant play. Others bought the reissues because it was cool to have the entire Beatles album catalog on the Beatles own Apple label. And besides, those green Granny Smith apples look great.

| CONFIRMED APPLE REISSUE ALBUMS | Capitol Logo | Apple | All Rights | Different Font |
|---|---|---|---|---|
| 2047 Meet The Beatles! | L | L, W | A, C, D | |
| 2080 The Beatles' Second | L, J | W | B, C, D | |
| 2108 Something New | L, J | J, W | B, C, D | |
| 2222 The Beatles' Story | L, J | J, W | A, C, D | |
| 2228 Beatles '65 | L, J | J, W | C, D | |
| 2309 The Early Beatles | L, J | J, W | C, D | |
| 2358 Beatles VI | L, J | W | A, C, D | |
| 2386 Help! | L | W | B, C, D | |
| 2442 Rubber Soul | L | L, J, W | A, C, D | J |
| 2553 Yesterday And Today | L | L, W | A, C, D | J |
| 2576 Revolver | L | J | A, C, D | W |
| 2653 Sgt. Pepper | L | L, J, W | C, D | |
| 2835 Magical Mystery Tour | L | L, W | A, C, D | J |

Confirmed Factories: L=Los Angeles; J=Jacksonville; W=Winchester
All Rights Variations: A = black at top (L); B = black at bottom (J);
C = green in right perimeter (J); D = green in lower perimeter (L)

APP 2047.SR21(af)                    APP 2080.SR21(c)                    APP 2108.SR21(af)

APP 2222.SR21(c)                    APP 2228.SR21(c)

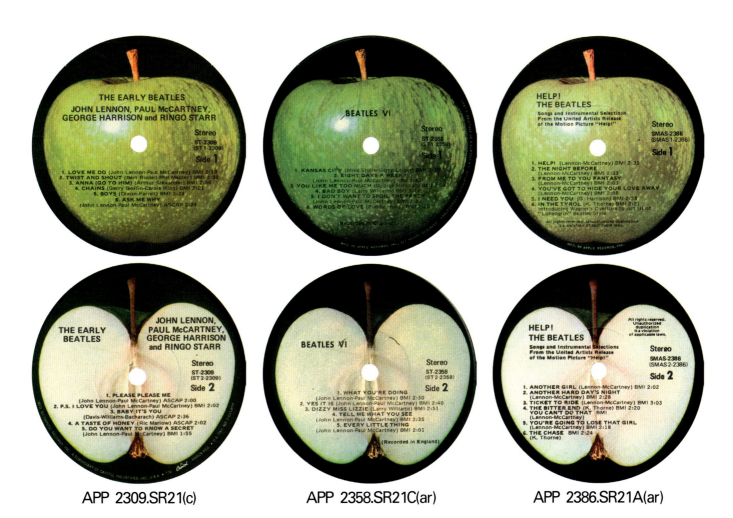

APP 2309.SR21(c)          APP 2358.SR21C(ar)          APP 2386.SR21A(ar)

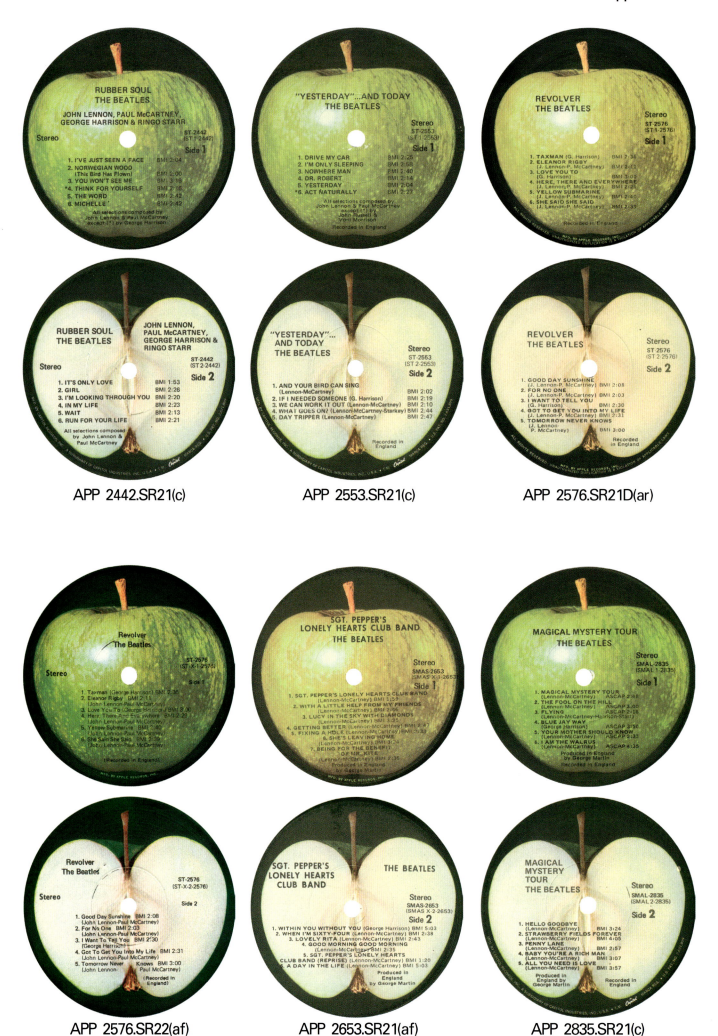

APP 2442.SR21(c)

APP 2553.SR21(c)

APP 2576.SR21D(ar)

APP 2576.SR22(af)

APP 2653.SR21(af)

APP 2835.SR21(c)

## CANADIAN & MEXICAN APPLE ALBUMS

Under the agreement reached between Apple and Capitol Records in June, 1968, Capitol Records (Canada) Ltd. obtained the rights to manufacture and distribute all Apple Records product in Canada. In addition, future Beatles releases in Canada would appear on the Apple label. With the exception of *Let It Be*, the Canadian Beatles albums on Apple were released at the same time and with the same songs as the U.S. albums prepared by Capitol.

The first Beatles album to appear on the Apple label in Canada was *The Beatles* (more commonly known as *The White Album*), which was released on November 25, 1968. The first issue Canadian albums were packaged in 12" x 12¼" gatefold covers (in comparison to the larger 12¼" x 12½" U.S. covers). The slicks were printed on Kromekote stock with "The BEATLES" embossed on the front. Unlike covers manufactured in the United States, England and many other countries, the first issue Canadian covers, **CAPP 101.SC1**, are not numbered. The jackets were not shrinkwrapped, but rather were covered with a loose-fitting polybag wrapped around the gatefold cover in a manner that allowed one to open the gatefold without cutting the protective bag.

The John Kelly color portraits were printed on 8½" x 11" Kromekote stock (as opposed to the smaller 7¾" x 10¾" U.S. pictures). The poster measures 22½" x 33¾" (compared to the slightly larger 23" x 34" U.S. posters). "Printed in Canada" appears in upper case letters inside an oval located in the lower left border of each photo and on the front and back of the poster.

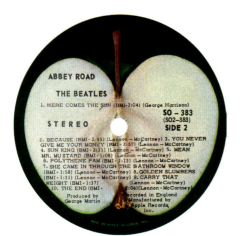

**The first-issue Canadian *Abbey Road* records do not list *Her Majesty* on the labels (Compo first pressing shown left, RCA first pressing shown middle). Later pressings added *Her Majesty* to the label (Compo later pressing shown right).**

The first issue Canadian covers, portraits and posters described above were printed by Ever Reddy Printers in Montreal, Canada. After the initial supply was exhausted, Capitol Records (Canada) imported these items from the United States to pair with Canadian-pressed discs. The covers found with Canadian discs have numbers in excess of two million. Although some covers have numbers such as **No. 2394837**, most have higher numbers such as **No. 2927644**.

The first issue Canadian records were pressed with glossy light green Apple label backdrops with Apple perimeter print on the sliced apple side. The label copy was overprinted in black from plates generated by the same film used for the U.S. labels. Capitol used two manufacturers to press its records. The albums pressed by the Compo Company Ltd. of Lachine, Quebec, **CAPP 101.SR1A**, have a one-inch diameter ring surrounding the spindle hole. The records pressed by RCA in Smiths Falls, Ontario, **CAPP 101.SR1B**, have a circular indented groove that measures 2¾" in diameter. Later RCA pressings from the seventies have labels with a different layout, **CAPP 101.SR2B**. These labels have some of the song titles above the spindle hole and "Manufactured by Capitol Records, Inc." printed in the lower part of the apple on both sides.

The *Yellow Submarine* soundtrack LP was issued on January 13, 1969. The album cover, **CAPP 153.SC1**, is virtually identical to the U.S. jacket, expect for Canadian markings. The front cover has the "ER" Ever Reddy logo followed by "Printed in Canada" running vertically along the lower left side:  Printed in Canada. The back cover has "Manufactured and distributed in Canada by Capitol Records (Canada) Ltd." followed by the oval "Printed in Canada" stamp running along the right bottom.

The records were pressed by Compo and RCA. The label copy layout varies between the two factories. The Compo discs, **CAPP 153.SR1A**, have "Recorded in England" without parenthesis. The RCA records, **CAPP 153.SC1B**, have "(Recorded in England)" at the bottom of the apple.

The album sold poorly in Canada as Canadians were still absorbing *The White Album* and were put off by the meager four new Beatles tracks on the soundtrack LP. After scores of returns, the album was quickly relegated to the cutout bins and deleted from the catalog until the late seventies. This explains why so many of the covers are found with a delete hole punched towards the upper left corner.

*Abbey Road* was released on October 1, 1969. Unlike the first issue U.S. covers, the Canadian covers were not printed directly on posterboard. Instead, they have front cover slicks that wrap around to the back. The covers also have a large split black dot wrapping over the top of the cover near the upper right corner. This is the same identification mark that appeared on U.S. and Canadian Capitol stereo albums from late 1964 through 1968. The covers do not list *Her Majesty* on the back. There are covers with, **CAPP 383.SC1A**, and without, **CAPP 383.SC1B**, the 🄴🅁 Ever Reddy logo and "Printed in Canada" running vertically along the lower left side.

The first run of labels printed for the album do not list *Her Majesty* as the last track on side two. The Compo first pressings, **CAPP 383.SR1A**, have *Here Comes The Sun* printed above the spindle hole. The RCA first pressings, **CAPP 383.SR1B**, have all song titles below the center hole. Later issue records have *Her Majesty* listed as the last track on side two. The Compo *Her Majesty* labels, **CAPP 383.SR2A**, have the first three songs on side two printed above the spindle hole. RCA *Her Majesty* labels, **CAPP 383.SR2B**, may exist, but have not been confirmed.

The *Hey Jude* album was issued on February 26, 1970. The Canadian cover is virtually identical to the U.S. cover except for the expected modifications. "Distributed in Canada by Capitol Records (Canada) Ltd" and "Printed in Canada" appear in white upper case letters at the bottom of the black background back slick. The split black dot identification mark wraps over the top upper right part of the cover. Capitol used two different printers for the album's jackets. The Ever Reddy covers, **CAPP 385.SC1A**, have the ER logo and "Printed in Canada" on the spine. The covers printed by Modern Graphics in Montreal, Canada, **CAPP 385.SC1B**, have the company's MG logo and "Litho in Canada" on the spine: 🌐 Litho In Canada.

Many of the covers came with an attractive two-inch diameter black and green round sticker with "Includes 'HEY JUDE'" printed inside an apple (shown on previous page). The stickers, **CAPP 385.S1**, were adhered to the shrinkwrap.

The initial labels for *Hey Jude* have the album's original title, *The Beatles Again* (RCA first pressing shown left). Record number SOAL 6351 appears on the labels for the *Let It Be* box set (Compo first pressing shown middle). Labels for the reissue album have record number SW 6386 (RCA reissue pressing shown right).

As was the case in the United States, the initial labels printed for the album list the title as *The Beatles Again*. The Compo first pressings, **CAPP 385.SR1A**, have the song titles left margin justified On the RCA first pressings, **CAPP 385.SR1B**, the song titles are centered. Later pressings identify the album as *Hey Jude*. There are Compo, **CAPP 385.SR2A**, and RCA, **CAPP 385.SR2B**, discs with the *Hey Jude* album title. The records were pressed with metal parts generated from lacquers cut by Sam Feldman at Bell Sound.

In the United States, the *Let It Be* LP was distributed by United Artists pursuant to a clause in the Beatles film contract. Because this provision was limited to the U.S.A., Capitol Records (Canada) retained the rights to manufacture and distribute the album. While United Artists refused to issue the album with the 164-page *Get Back* book, Capitol Records (Canada) honored Apple's wishes and prepared a cardboard outer slipcase and box tray to hold the *Get Back* book and *Let It Be* album. The packaging for the deluxe album issue was printed in Canada by Modern Graphics.

Capitol's Canadian subsidiary always used the record numbers assigned to releases by its U.S. parent. Because the album was not issued in the States by Capitol, there was no U.S. catalog number. Thus, Capitol Records (Canada) used a number in its 6000 series. The Canadian package was initially assigned SOAL 6351. The "S" indicates a stereo record, the "O" is the price code, the "A" signifies one disc and the "L" stands for libretto (indicating the package includes a book).

The deluxe package for SOAL 6351 included a black outer slipcase, **CAPP 6351.OSC**, featuring the same Ethan Russell color photos of the faces of John, Paul, George and Ringo appearing on the cover to the *Get Back* book. The rectangular pictures were cropped at the sides to form 4⅞" squares. There is no text on the front of the slipcase. The back has the record number SOAL-6351 in the upper left corner and the following information running along the bottom: "Designed by John Kosh," "Photographs by Ethan Russell," "Distributed in Canada by Capitol Records (Canada) Ltd." and the ▣ Modern Graphics logo followed by "Litho in Canada." The *Get Back* book, **CAPP 6351.B**, is housed in a black cardboard inner box tray, **CAPP 6351.BT**.

The front and back of the initial album jackets, **CAPP 6351.SC1**, match the front and back of the U.S. gatefold cover. The front cover is identical and the back cover has two modifications: the U.S. manufacturing and Abkco information is replaced with the usual Canadian manufacturing credit; and the Apple logo is green rather than red.

The Canadian records have green apple labels rather than the red apple labels that were used in the U.S. The first issue records have the number SOAL 6351 on the label. The Compo pressings, **CAPP 6351.SR1A**, have left margin justified song titles. On the RCA discs, **CAPP 6351.SR1B**, the song titles are centered. The records were pressed from metal parts generated from lacquers cut by Sam Feldman at Bell Sound. The trail off areas contain the same "Phil + Ronnie" etchings found on the U.S. discs.

By November, 1970, Capitol ceased distribution of the deluxe package and reissued the album in a standard record jacket. The album was assigned a new number, SW 6386. The reissue covers, **CAPP 6351.SC2**, have detailed information (songwriters, publishing and running times) for the songs not present on the first issue covers or the U.S. covers. Other modifications include the addition of a white border surrounding each of the four black and white photos, manufacturing and all rights information and "℗ 1970 Apple Records Inc." The green apple logo is shifted from the lower center to the lower right part of the cover. The record number SW-6386 is above the apple. The phrase "Originally released as SOAL 6351" appears below the apple.

Capitol also prepared new labels with the new record number SW 6386. The reissue labels also have "℗ 1970, Apple Records" printed in the upper part of the apple on both sides. Reissue labels have been confirmed with RCA pressings, **CAPP 6351.SR2B**.

Some copies of the Canadian *Let It Be* box set have a 7½" x 1¼" black sticker listing the songs affixed to the shrinkwrap. Because the stickers have the American spelling for "color," they may have been printed in the U.S.

The back of the album jacket packaged with the box set (left) is similar to the back of the U.S. gatefold cover. The back cover of the reissue LP (right) has several modifications. The components of the *Let It Be* box set are shown below (clockwise): outer slipcase; inside tray box; album jacket; record; and inside the *Get Back* book.

The 164-page *Get Back* book measures 8½" x 11" and features Ethan Russell's photographs (most in color) taken during the Twickenham rehearsals and recording sessions for the album. It was designed by John Kosh and contains text by David Dalton and Jonathan Cott. It was printed in England by Garrod and Lofthouse International Limited and exported to Canada. The books were also exported to Mexico.

# MEXICAN ALBUMS

Capitol's south-of-the-border subsidiary, Discos Capitol de Mexico, had the exclusive rights to issue the Beatles records in Mexico. The albums released in 1968 through 1970 were pressed with green apple labels.

While the U.S. *White Album* covers were sequentially numbered, those for the Mexican *White Album* (Apple SLEMB 134) were not. Some of the Mexican covers were printed on Kromekote stock and were embossed, while others have the group's name printed in black on a pure white slick. The album was packaged with Mexican printings of the four John Kelley portraits and the poster.

The cover to *Yellow Submarine* (Apple SLEM 138) is constructed with slicks identical to the U.S. slicks, except for the album's number and Mexican manufacturing information.

The front cover slick to *Abbey Road* (Apple SLEM 179) is printed and placed to form a white border surrounding the picture of the Beatles in the crosswalk. While the cover does not list *Her Majesty*, the song does appear on the label to side two.

The jacket to the Mexican *Hey Jude* LP (Apple SLEM 200) is virtually identical to that of the American album, except that there is no reference to Apple's New York address. The labels to the first issue discs list the album's title as *The Beatles Again*.

Discos Capitol de Mexico distributed the *Let It Be* album (Apple SLEM 216). As was the case in Canada, the soundtrack LP was initially packaged with a copy of the *Get Back* book (imported from England) housed in a black cardboard inner box tray and outer slipcase.

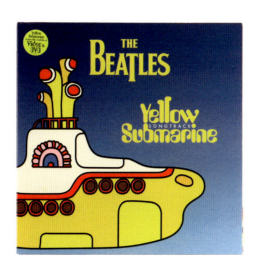

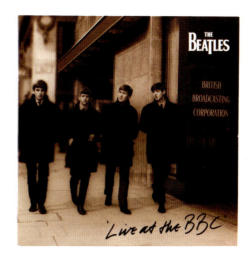

# T is for Triumphant Return

Capitol and Apple prepared a special press kit to promote *Live At The BBC*. The kit came in a 12" x 8" folder containing five 8" x 11½" sheets and four 5" x 7" black and white glossy pictures of the Beatles. The front of the folder features the same sepia-toned photograph of the Beatles as the front cover of the album and CD booklet, as well as the same graphics for the group's name and album title. The back of the folder has the same sepia-toned picture of the group as the back of the album cover and CD booklet. A small green Apple logo is in the lower right corner. The left inside panel of the open folder has twelve 2" x 2" sepia-toned pictures from the CD booklet. The right back inside panel of the folder has nine 2" x 2" photos. An 8" x 3" brown flap with the group's name and album title runs along the bottom of the inside right panel to hold the folder's contents in place.

The first unnumbered sheet is the same as the front of the folder. Page 2 combines Derek Taylor's CD and album liner notes with three small pictures from the CD booklet. Kevin Howlett's liner notes, along with seven pictures from the CD booklet, are spread over Pages 3, 4 and 5.

The press kits were first distributed at the album's launch party, which was held at the Hard Rock Café in New York City on November 22, 1994. These kits also contained bios of Beatles producer George Martin and BBC employees Brian Mathew, Alan Freeman and Kevin Howlett, additional press information and a CD sampler. The CD (Capitol DPRO-79516) contains the following nine tracks from the album: *Beatle Greetings* (dialog only); *From Us To You* (radio show theme song); *Soldier Of Love*; *Sha la la la la!* (dialog only); *Baby It's You*; *Clarabella*; *I Just Don't Understand*; *Glad All Over*; and *Matchbox*.

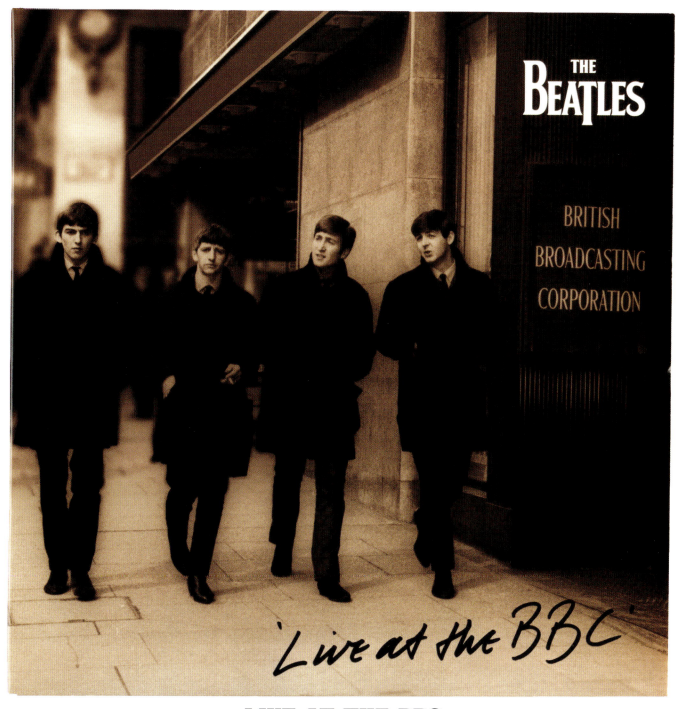

## LIVE AT THE BBC
## APPLE 31796

Less than a month before Christmas, 1994, Capitol and EMI rush released *Live At The BBC* (Apple 31796), the first album to appear on the Apple label in nearly two decades. It was the first Beatles album since 1977's *Live At The Hollywood Bowl* to contain previously unreleased material. (Although 1980's *Rarities* has a few new mixes and edits, it does not contain any new performances or outtakes.) The set contains 56 BBC performances, including 30 songs that did not appear on the group's official EMI releases. There are also 13 bits of dialog and studio banter. The album's running time of approximately 130 minutes required the set to be issued as double CD, double cassette and double record albums.

*Live At The BBC* was released in England on November 30, 1994. With first week sales of 350,000 copies, the set entered the British album chart at number one.

In America, the album was issued one week later on December 6. It entered the *Billboard* pop album chart on December 24 at number three behind Pearl Jam's *Vitalogy* and *Miracles–The Holiday Album By Kenny G*. The new Beatles album spent 24 weeks on the charts, including three in the top ten. Capitol reported initial shipments of 750,000 albums, with 500,000 back-ordered. First day sales topped 100,000 albums. On February 3, 1995, the RIAA certified sales of four million units (meaning two million albums, as the RIAA certifies by the number of discs shipped).

During Apple's inactive period, the compact disc replaced the vinyl record as the dominant music format. By the mid-nineties, record companies generally issued vinyl albums only for special artists or projects. For *Live At The BBC*, Capitol issued a limited run of 30,000 vinyl albums, which went on sale on December 13.

## Record 1

Side 1
1 Beatle Greetings (Speech)
2 From Us To You (Lennon McCartney)
3 Riding On A Bus (Speech)
4 I Got A Woman (Charles)
5 Too Much Monkey Business (Berry)
6 Keep Your Hands Off My Baby (Goffin-King)
7 I'll Be On My Way (Lennon-McCartney)
8 Young Blood (Leiber-Stoller-Pomus)
9 A Shot Of Rhythm And Blues (Thompson)
10 Sure To Fall (In Love With You) (Perkins-Claunch-Cantrell)
11 Some Other Guy (Leiber-Stoller-Barrett)
12 Thank You Girl (Lennon-McCartney)
13 Sha la la la la! (Speech)
14 Baby It's You (David-Bacharach-Williams)
15 That's All Right (Mama) (Crudup)
16 Carol (Berry)
17 Soldier Of Love (Cason-Moon)

Side 2
1 A Little Rhyme (Speech)
2 Clarabella (Pingatore)
3 I'm Gonna Sit Right Down And Cry (Over You) (Thomas-Biggs)
4 Crying, Waiting, Hoping (Holly)
5 Dear Wack! (Speech)
6 You Really Got A Hold On Me (Robinson)
7 To Know Her Is To Love Her (Spector)
8 A Taste Of Honey (Marlow-Scott)
9 Long Tall Sally (Johnson-Penniman-Blackwell)
10 I Saw Her Standing There (Lennon-McCartney)
11 The Honeymoon Song (Theodorakis-Sansom)
12 Johnny B Goode (Berry)
13 Memphis, Tennessee (Berry)
14 Lucille (Collins-Penniman)
15 Can't Buy Me Love (Lennon-McCartney)
16 From Fluff To You (Speech)
17 Till There Was You (Willson)

## Record 2

Side 1
1 Crinsk Dee Night (Speech)
2 A Hard Day's Night (Lennon-McCartney)
3 Have A Banana! (Speech)
4 I Wanna Be Your Man (Lennon-McCartney)
5 Just A Rumour (Speech)
6 Roll Over Beethoven (Berry)
7 All My Loving (Lennon-McCartney)
8 Things We Said Today (Lennon-McCartney)
9 She's A Woman (Lennon-McCartney)
10 Sweet Little Sixteen (Berry)
11 1822! (Speech)
12 Lonesome Tears In My Eyes (J and D Burnette-Burlison-Mortimer)
13 Nothin' Shakin' (Fontaine-Calacrai-Lampert-Gluck)
14 The Hippy Hippy Shake (Romero)
15 Glad All Over (Bennett-Tepper-Schroeder)
16 I Just Don't Understand (Wilkin-Westberry)
17 So How Come (No-One Loves Me) (Bryant)
18 I Feel Fine (Lennon-McCartney)

Side 2
1 I'm A Loser (Lennon-McCartney)
2 Everybody's Trying To Be My Baby (Perkins)
3 Rock And Roll Music (Berry)
4 Ticket To Ride (Lennon-McCartney)
5 Dizzy Miss Lizzy (Williams)
6 Medley: Kansas City (Leiber-Stoller)/ Hey! Hey! Hey! Hey! (Penniman)
7 Set Fire To That Lot! (Speech)
8 Matchbox (Perkins)
9 I Forgot To Remember To Forget (Kesler-Feathers)
10 Love These Goon Shows! (Speech)
11 I Got To find My Baby (Berry)
12 Ooh! My Soul (Penniman)
13 Ooh! My Arms (Speech)
14 Don't Ever Change (Goffin-King)
15 Slow Down (Williams)
16 Honey Don't (Perkins)
17 Love Me Do (Lennon-McCartney)

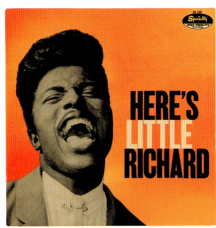

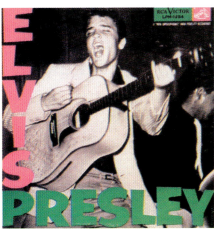
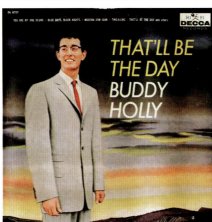

BBC producer Kevin Howlett's liner notes for the album summarize the Beatles relationship with the Beeb: "Between March 1962 and June 1965, the Beatles were featured performers in fifty-two BBC radio programmes and sang eighty-eight different songs–an amazing thirty-six never issued on disc." Of particular interest to fans and scholars are the songs that the Beatles never recorded at an EMI session. They include a Lennon-McCartney original, *I'll Be On My Way*, and numerous numbers from the band's stage show. While a few of these performances were in front of live audiences, most were recorded in BBC studios. Not realizing the historical significance of the performances, the BBC normally did not save the tapes of the studio recordings or broadcasts. Fortunately, nearly all of the shows were taped off the air on home recorders by Beatles fans.

In the early seventies, bootleggers borrowed some of these tapes and assembled albums containing BBC performances. The first two albums were *Yellow Matter Custard* and *As Sweet As You Are*, which drew its title from a line in *Don't Ever Change*. Both albums contain the following 14 songs: *I Got A Woman, Glad All Over, I Just Don't Understand, Slow Down, Don't Ever Change, A Shot Of Rhythm And Blues, Sure To Fall, Nothin' Shakin' (But The Leaves On The Tree), Lonesome Tears In My Eyes, So How Come No One Loves Me, I'm Gonna Sit Right Down And Cry Over You, To Know Her Is To Love Her, The Honeymoon Song* and *Crying, Waiting, Hoping*. Although the sound quality was less than stellar, the LPs gave Beatles scholars and fans 13 songs that had never been released by the Beatles.

The BBC began combing its archives for interviews with and performances by the Beatles. In addition, tapes were obtained or copied from fans. Other performances were lifted from bootlegs. Then, on March 7, 1982, in celebration of the twentieth anniversary of the first Beatles radio broadcast, the BBC aired a 3-hour special program titled *The Beatles At The Beeb*. The show blended contemporary interviews of BBC hosts, engineers and producers with performances and banter from the original broadcasts. It opened with *The Hippy Hippy Shake* and ended with *Ticket To Ride*.

The program was syndicated in the United States and broadcast on 350 stations over Memorial Day weekend. The May 31, 1982, issue of *Time* magazine previewed the program, commenting that "the musical trajectory is astounding" and calling the songs "simple, lively and made of magic." The article further raved that the "songs all have the blind energy, nerve and joyful rowdiness of genius before history took over." After warning that thorny copyright problems would probably keep the BBC material from ever making it to record, the writer gave the same advice Bruce Springsteen used to tell home listeners of radio broadcasts of his concerts: "Roll them tapes!"

More radio specials covering the Beatles BBC shows were broadcast during the eighties. These programs provided additional source material for bootleggers, who issued several records and CDs of BBC performances in the late eighties and early nineties. In 1994, Great Dane Records issued a nine-CD, 257-song set titled *The Complete BBC Sessions*, which was packaged in a 12" x 12" box (shown upper right) and came with a 36-page color booklet.

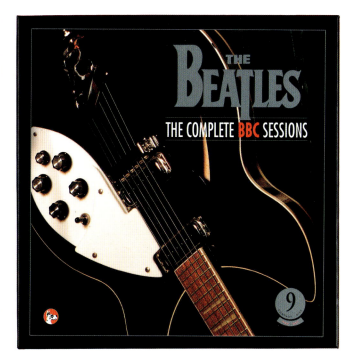

Meanwhile, George Martin and EMI, working with Apple and the BBC, assembled an official collection of BBC recordings for issuance on the Apple label. The album was tentatively set for release in the summer of 1994, but was dropped from the schedule. Then, on October 28, EMI announced that *Live At The BBC* would be issued on November 30 in England and on December 6 in America.

The BBC performances on the album provide wonderful insights regarding the songs and artists that influenced the Beatles. There are eight Chuck Berry songs, five tunes recorded by Carl Perkins, four songs associated with Elvis, four Little Richard rockers and two songs recorded by R&B singer Arthur Alexander. The Beatles also cover songs by the Coasters, Buddy Holly, Smokey Robinson and the Miracles, the Crickets, the Everly Brothers and Ann Margret, as well as songs associated with the girl group sound, including tunes by the Teddy Bears, Little Eva and the Shirelles.

*Live At The BBC* opens with a bit of dialog from each Beatle titled *Beatle Greetings*. These sound bites were recorded on October 9, 1963, and broadcast on the BBC magazine program *The Public Ear* on November 3. This leads into the brief theme song from the Beatles BBC show *From Us To You*. The tune, a modified version of *From Me To You*, was recorded on February 28, 1964, at BBC Paris Theatre in London. This is followed by a segment, titled *Riding On A Bus*, from a Brian Mathew interview of the group that aired on *Top Gear* on November 26, 1964.

The first regular song on the album is *I Got A Woman*, which the Beatles played twice for the BBC. The performance on the album was recorded on July 16, 1963, for broadcast on the August 13 *Pop Go The Beatles*. The song was written by singer/pianist Ray Charles and Renald Richard and recorded by Charles at Radio Station WGST, Georgia Tech, in Atlanta, Georgia, on November 18, 1954. It was released on Atlantic 1050 as *I've Got A Woman* in December. The song entered the *Billboard* R&B singles charts on January 22, 1955, spending 20 weeks on the charts and reaching number one on the *Most Played in Juke Boxes* chart. The Beatles arrangement is based on the guitar-driven Elvis Presley cover of the song, called *I Got A Woman*, which was recorded at RCA Studios, Nashville, Tennessee, on January 10, 1956, and appeared on the singer's first album, *Elvis Presley* (RCA LPM-1254). The Beatles performance features John on lead vocal and acoustic guitar.

*Too Much Monkey Business* is the first of eight Chuck Berry songs on *Live At The BBC*. The song was recorded by Berry on April 16, 1956, and released on Chess 1645. Although it was not a pop hit, the song entered the *Billboard* R&B singles charts on October 6, 1956, spending six weeks on the charts and peaking at number four on the *Most Played in Juke Boxes* chart. The BBC album contains the group's fourth and final BBC performance of the song, which was recorded on September 3, 1963, and aired on *Pop Go The Beatles* on September 10. John handles the lead vocal.

*Keep Your Hands Off My Baby* was written by Gerry Goffin and Carole King. It was recorded by Little Eva in 1962 as the follow-up to her number one smash *The Loco-Motion*. The song was issued on Dimension 1003 and entered the *Billboard Hot 100* on November 3, 1962, peaking at number 12 during its 12-week stay. It also charted on the *Billboard Hot R&B Singles* chart for ten weeks, topping out at number six. The Beatles recorded the song on January 22, 1963, for broadcast on the January 26 *Saturday Club*, with John on lead vocal backed by Paul and George. Unfortunately, the surviving tape of the performance is of poor quality. George Martin and crew significantly improved the low fidelity recording and added a nonexistent drum introduction. Although the February 22, 1963, *Musical Express* reported that the Beatles recorded the song at the February 11 session for their first album, the recording sheets from the sessions do not list the song.

One of the many highlights of the album is the group's recording of *I'll Be On My Way*, a Lennon-McCartney song that was given to Billy J. Kramer and the Dakotas for use as the B side to their first single, *Do You Want To Know A Secret* (Parlophone R 5023). The song was recorded on March 21, 1963, at a George Martin-produced session at Abbey Road, and the single was released on April 26. The Beatles version of the song was recorded on April 4, 1963, and broadcast on the June 24 *Side By Side* program.

*Young Blood* was written by Jerry Leiber, Mike Stoller and Doc Pomus. It was recorded by the Coasters in February, 1957, and released the following April as the flip side to *Searchin'* (Atco 6087). As part of a double-sided smash, *Young Blood* peaked at number eight during its 24 weeks in the *Billboard* pop charts. The song remained on the R&B charts for 17 weeks, reaching the top spot in the *Billboard R&B Best Sellers In Stores* chart. The Beatles recorded the song during their Decca audition held on January 1, 1962. The BBC version was recorded on June 1, 1963, for broadcast on the June 11 *Pop Go The Beatles*. George handles the lead vocal, aided and abetted by John and Paul.

*A Shot Of Rhythm And Blues* was recorded by one of John's favorite singers, Arthur Alexander, who holds the distinction of having his songs recorded by the Beatles, the Rolling Stones and Bob Dylan. The song, written by Terry Thompson, was the flip side of *You Better Move On* (Dot 16309), a number 24 hit in 1962 that was later recorded by the Stones. The Beatles, with Lennon on lead vocal, performed *A Shot Of Rhythm And Blues* three times for the BBC. The album version was recorded on August 1, 1963, and aired on the August 27 *Pop Go The Beatles*.

*Sure To Fall (In Love With You)* was written by Carl Perkins, along with Claunch and Cantrell, and appeared on *Dance Album Of Carl Perkins* (Sun LP 1225). While most of the Perkins songs performed by the Beatles were rockabilly, this one is pure country. Paul takes the lead with John and George provided backing harmonies. Harrison's lead guitar is full of country twang. The group performed the song four times for the BBC, with this version being their initial recording of June 1, 1963, which aired the June 18 *Pop Go The Beatles*.

*Some Other Guy* was recorded by Richie Barrett and released on Atlantic 2142 in April, 1962. The song was written by Barrett along with Jerry Leiber and Mike Stoller. Although the song was not a hit, it was included in the repertoire of several Liverpool bands. Granada Television filmed the Beatles performing the song in the Cavern Club on August 22, 1962. The Beatles played *Some Other Guy* three times for the BBC. The album contains their performance before a live audience at the Playhouse Theatre, London, on June 19, 1963, which was broadcast on *Easy Beat* on June 23.

The Beatles performed *Thank You Girl* three times for the BBC. The album version has the same recording and broadcast history as the previous track. It was the flip side to the Beatles then-current single, *From Me To You*.

The Shirelles' *Baby It's You* was recorded by the Beatles for their first British LP, *Please Please Me*. This group performed the song twice for the BBC. The version selected for the album was recorded at BBC Paris Theatre in London on June 1, 1963, and broadcast on the first *Pop Go The Beatles* show on June 11. The song is preceded by Lee Peters' introduction, which is listed as a separate track titled *Sha la la la!*

The first side of record one closes with three songs recorded on July 2, 1963, for broadcast on the July 16 *Pop Go The Beatles* show. *That's All Right* was written and originally recorded by Arthur "Big Boy" Crudup and released in 1947 on RCA Victor 20-2205. The Beatles, with Paul on lead vocal, had long been performing the Elvis Presley version of the song, which was recorded on July 5, 1954, and released as his first single on Sun 209.

Chuck Berry's *Carol* was recorded on May 2, 1958, and released on Chess 1700. It entered the *Hot 100* on August 25 and peaked at 18 during its ten weeks on the chart. The song also reached number nine on the *Billboard Most Played R&B by Jockeys* chart. John sings lead on the song, which was also recorded by the Rolling Stones for their first album.

*Soldier Of Love* is another Arthur Alexander song featuring John on lead vocal. It was written by Buzz Cason and Tony Moon and served as the flip side to *Where Have You Been (All My Life)* (Dot 16357), which charted at number 58 in 1962.

ATLANTIC
45 R.P.M.
45-1050
VOCAL
Pub., Progressive, BMI
Time: 2:48
A-1383 SP
I'VE GOT A WOMAN
(Ray Charles)
RAY CHARLES
AND HIS BAND
MFG. BY ATLANTIC RECORDING CORP., 1841 BROADWAY, NEW YORK, N.Y.

CHESS
RECORD CORP.
8111
ARC
Vocal
B. M. I.
TOO MUCH MONKEY BUSINESS
(C. Berry)
CHUCK BERRY
and his combo
1635
MANUFACTURED BY CHESS RECORD CO. CHICAGO, ILL.

DIMENSION
ALDON MUSIC, INC.
BMI 10004
1003
TIME: 2:29
KEEP YOUR HANDS OFF MY BABY
(GOFFIN - KING)
LITTLE EVA
PRODUCED BY GERRY GOFFIN
FOR NEVINS-KIRSHNER
DIVISION OF NEVINS-KIRSHNER ASSOC., INC.

45 RPM
ATCO
RECORDS
VOCAL QUARTET
57C-187
45-6087
Pub., Tiger, BMI
Time: 2:15
YOUNG BLOOD
(Leiber-Stoller-Pomus)
THE COASTERS
MFD. BY ATLANTIC RECORDING CORP., N.Y.

ULTRA HIGH FIDELITY
Dot
Fame Pub. Co.
BMI
Time 1:44
45-16309
MW-16390
A SHOT OF RHYTHM AND BLUES
(Terry Thompson)
ARTHUR ALEXANDER
12-61
DOT RECORDS, INC., HOLLYWOOD 28, CALIF. TRADEMARK REGISTERED IN U.S. PAT. OFF.

ATLANTIC
45 RPM
45-2142
VOCAL
Pub., Trio, BMI
Time: 2:19
A-6057
SOME OTHER GUY
(Leiber-Stoller-Barrett)
RICHIE BARRETT
A Leiber-Stoller Production

BABY IT'S YOU
(Mack David-Barney Williams-Bert Bacharach)
SCEPTER
RECORDS
Dolfi Music, Inc. (ASCAP)
2:40
1227 A
THE SHIRELLES
Arranged by Bert Bacharach
SCEPTER MUSIC INC., NEW YORK, N.Y.

SUN
Wabash
BMI
209
Vocal
U-12E
"THAT'S ALL RIGHT"
(Arthur Crudup)
ELVIS PRESLEY
SCOTTY and BILL
MEMPHIS, TENNESSEE

"CAROL"
(Chuck Berry Music Inc.)
CHESS
Arc Music
BMI
U-8868
Time 2:21
CHUCK BERRY
1700
MANUFACTURED BY CHESS PRODUCING CORP., CHICAGO ILLINOIS, U.S.A.

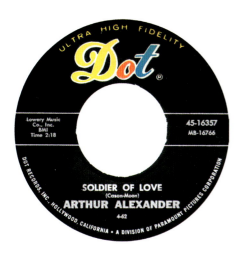

ULTRA HIGH FIDELITY
Dot
Lowery Music Co. Inc.
BMI
Time 2:18
45-16357
MB-16766
SOLDIER OF LOVE
(Cason-Moon)
ARTHUR ALEXANDER
4-62
DOT RECORDS, INC., HOLLYWOOD, CALIFORNIA · A DIVISION OF PARAMOUNT PICTURES CORPORATION

Capitol
Myers Music
ASCAP-2:00
F3588
Vocal Chorus-
Marshall Lytle
(45-21235)
CLARABELLA
(Frank Pingatore)
THE JODIMARS
MANUFACTURED BY CAPITOL RECORDS, INC., HOLLYWOOD, CALIFORNIA, U.S.A.

RCA VICTOR
47-6638
45 RPM
"NEW ORTHOPHONIC"
HIGH FIDELITY
Royal Music Corp.
BMI
G2WW-1254
I'M GONNA SIT RIGHT DOWN
AND CRY (Over You)
(Thomas-Biggs)
ELVIS PRESLEY
2:01
RADIO CORPORATION OF AMERICA, CAMDEN, N.J. MADE IN U.S.A.

The second side of record one opens with a bit of dialog titled *A Little Rhyme*, which consists of John reading a fan letter and introducing Paul singing *Clarabella*. The song was written by Frank Pingatore and recorded in 1956 by the Jodimars, a group made up of former members of Bill Haley's backing band, the Comets. It was released on Capitol F3588. The dialog and song have the same recording and broadcast history as the previous three tracks.

*I'm Gonna Sit Right Down And Cry (Over You)*, written by Joe Thomas and Howard Biggs, was originally recorded by Roy Hamilton and released on Epic 9015 in 1954. The Beatles were familiar with Elvis Presley's version, which appeared on his first RCA album. The song was released as a single on RCA 6638 on September 8, 1956. The Beatles version, featuring Paul and John on vocals, was recorded on July 16, 1963, and aired on the August 6 *Pop Go The Beatles*.

*Crying, Waiting, Hoping* was written and recorded by Buddy Holly as a demo shortly before his death in a plane crash on February 3, 1959. After backing vocals and instruments were added to the recording, the song was released on Coral 62134 on July 27, 1959. The Beatles version features George on lead vocal backed by John and Paul. The song was performed by the group as part of their January 1, 1962, Decca audition. The BBC version has the same recording and broadcast history as the previous track.

*Dear Wack!* is another bit of dialog with John reading a fan letter, this time backed by piano and guitar. It leads into John, backed by Paul and George, singing *You Really Got A Hold On Me*. The song was written by Smokey Robinson and recorded by Robinson with his group the Miracles. Released on November 19, 1962, on Tamla 54073, the song peaked at number 8 during its 16 weeks in the *Billboard Hot 100* and reached number one on the *Billboard Hot R&B Singles* chart. The Beatles performed the song four times for the BBC, including the album's July 30, 1963, recording that aired on the August 24 *Saturday Club*. The group recorded the song on July 18, 1963, for inclusion on its second British album, *With The Beatles*. In America, Capitol placed the track on *The Beatles' Second Album*.

*To Know Her Is To Love Her* is a gender-altered version of the Teddy Bears' *To Know Him Is To Love Him*. The song was written by group member and future legendary producer Phil Spector. Released on Dore 503, the song topped the *Hot 100* for three weeks in December, 1958, during its 23 week stay on the charts. The Beatles performed the song at their Decca audition. The BBC version, featuring John on lead vocal, was recorded on July 16, 1963, and aired on the August 6 *Pop Go The Beatles*.

*A Taste Of Honey* was featured in the 1960 Broadway play of the same name. The Bobby Scott-Ric Marlow tune came to the Beatles attention by way of Lenny Welch's 1962 recording of the song released on Candence 1428. The Beatles version of the song first appeared on the *Please Please Me* album in England and on *Introducing The Beatles* in America. The Beatles, with Paul on lead vocal, performed song six times for the BBC. The album version contains the July 10, 1963, recording, which was broadcast on the July 23 *Pop Go The Beatles*.

Little Richard's *Long Tall Sally*, co-written by the singer with Enotris Johnson and Robert "Bumps" Blackwell, was recorded on February 8, 1956, at J&M Studio in New Orleans and released on Specialty 572. It entered the *Billboard* charts on April 7, 1956, and went on to become Little Richard's biggest hit and a certified million seller. The song spent 16 weeks on the *Rhythm & Blues Records* charts, including eight weeks at number on the separate *Best Sellers*, *Juke Box* and *Jockey* charts. In addition, the rocker remained in the *Billboard* pop charts for 19 weeks, peaking at number six in the *Best Sellers in Stores* chart. The Beatles, with Paul on lead vocal, performed the song four times for the BBC, including a July 16, 1963, recording broadcast on the August 13 *Pop Go The Beatles* that appears on the album. The EMI recording of the song was first issued in America on *The Beatles' Second Album* and in England on the *Long Tall Sally* EP.

*I Saw Her Standing There* was the lead track from the Beatles first British album, *Please Please Me*. In addition to being issued as the B side to the group's first Capitol single, the song hold the distinction of being the only track to appear on both Vee-Jay's *Introducing The Beatles* and Capitol's *Meet The Beatles!* The Beatles played the song 11 times for the BBC. The version included on the album was recorded before a live audience at the Playhouse Theatre in London on October 16, 1963, and broadcast on the October 20 *Easy Beat* show.

*The Honeymoon Song*, written by Mikis Theodorakis and William Sansom, was from the film *Honeymoon*. Paul's vocal version of the song was based on the 1959 recording by Marino Marini and his Quartet. The song was released in the U.S. by Manuel on Capitol 4306. Paul later produced Mary Hopkin's recording of the song.

Chuck Berry's *Johnny B. Goode* was recorded on December 29-30, 1957 and released on Chess 1691. It entered the *Billboard* pop charts on April 28, 1958, peaking at number 8 on the *Top 100 Sides Chart* during its 15 weeks on the charts. The song was a number two hit on the *Billboard Most Played R&B by Jockeys* chart. The Beatles recorded the song on January 7, 1964, for broadcast on the February 15 *Saturday Club*.

*Memphis, Tennessee* is another Chuck Berry rocker. It was recorded by Berry in September, 1958, and issued in mid 1959 as the flip side of *Back In The U.S.A.* on Chess 1729. The Beatles recorded the song five times for the BBC, including their first performance on the Beeb. The album contains the group's July 10, 1963, recording, which was broadcast on the July 30 *Pop Go The Beatles*.

*Lucille*, written by Little Richard with Albert Collins, was recorded by Little Richard on July 30, 1956. Released on Specialty 598 in 1957, the song topped the *Billboard Most Played R&B in Juke Boxes* chart for two weeks. It peaked at number 21 during its 21-week run in the *Billboard* pop charts. The Beatles recorded the song twice for the BBC. The album contains the September 7, 1963, performance, which was broadcast on the October 5 *Saturday Club*. Although host Brian Mathew credits the song to the Everly Brothers (who were also guests on the show), the Beatles arrangement features Paul at his Little Richard best.

CRYING, WAITING, HOPING
(Buddy Holly)
BUDDY HOLLY

YOU'VE REALLY GOT A HOLD ON ME
(Wm. Robinson)
THE MIRACLES
T-54073

TO KNOW HIM, IS TO LOVE HIM
(Phillip Spector)
THE TEDDY BEARS
45-503

A TASTE OF HONEY
B. Scott-R. Marlow-L. Morris
LENNY WELCH

LONG TALL SALLY
(E. Johnson)
LITTLE RICHARD
And His Band

"JOHNNY B. GOODE"
(C. Berry)
CHUCK BERRY
1691

MEMPHIS, TENNESSEE
(Chuck Berry Music, Inc.)
CHUCK BERRY
From The Hal Roach Motion Picture
"GO JOHNNY GO"
1729

LUCILLE
(Penniman-Collins)
LITTLE RICHARD
And His Band
598
(5045)

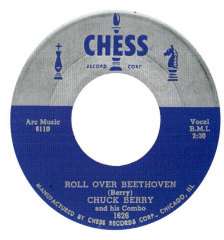

ROLL OVER BEETHOVEN
(Berry)
CHUCK BERRY
and his Combo
1626

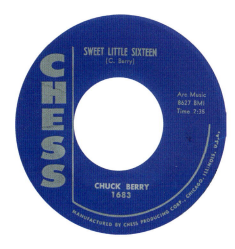

SWEET LITTLE SIXTEEN
(C. Berry)
CHUCK BERRY
1683

NOTHIN' SHAKIN'
(But The Leaves On The Trees)
(Fontaine-Colacrai-Lampert-Gluck)
EDDIE FONTAINE
ARNIE GOLAND
(orch.)

THE HIPPY HIPPY SHAKE
(R. Romero)
CHAN ROMERO
4119

Record one concludes with two songs and dialog recorded on February 28, 1964, and broadcast on the March 30 *From Us To You* program. *Can't Buy Me Love* (performed three times for the BBC) was the group's current worldwide single at the time the show was broadcast. The song topped both the British and American charts.

*From Fluff To You* consists of interplay between host Alan "Fluff" Freeman, Paul and John. As McCartney tells Fluff he was influenced by Elvis, Chuck Berry, Carl Perkins and Marvin Gaye, Lennon can be heard in the background shamelessly plugging his recently released book *In His Own Write*.

*Till There Was You* was written by Meredith Wilson as part of his book, music and lyrics for the Broadway hit show *The Music Man*. Peggy Lee's rendition of the tune on her album *Latin ala Lee!*, with its jazz-styled lead guitar, served as the basis for the Beatles version of the song, which features Paul on lead vocal. The ballad appeared on *With The Beatles* in England and *Meet The Beatles!* in America. Four of the group's seven BBC recordings of the song were broadcast prior to the release of the British album. *Till There Was You* was the second song performed on the Beatles historic *Ed Sullivan Show* appearance of February 9, 1964.

Record two opens with *A Hard Day's Night*, surrounded by two bits of dialog, recorded on July 14, 1964, and broadcast on the July 16 *Top Gear* program. *Crinsk Dee Night* is an interview with host Brian Mathew about the Beatles first film. This leads into a BBC recording of the title song from the movie, which contains a drop-in edit of George Martin's piano solo from the EMI master tape because Martin did not show up for the session as expected. At the song's end, the Beatles do a protracted fade to prove that Brian Mathew is not merely playing the record. *Have A Banana!* is nothing more than Mathew tossing Ringo a banana and yelling "Catch!"

The next three songs, along with a dialog track, were recorded on February 28, 1964, and aired on the March 30 *From Us To You*. First up is *I Wanna Be Your Man*, a Lennon-McCartney tune sung by Ringo. The song was given to the Rolling Stones for their second single. The Beatles version of the song is on *Meet The Beatles!* and *With The Beatles*.

*Just A Rumour* starts with host Alan Freeman asking George if it's true he is a connoisseur of the classics. When George replies that "it's just a rumor," Freeman asks him if he enjoys playing Beethoven. This leads into the next selection, *Roll Over Beethoven*.

Chuck Berry recorded *Roll Over Beethoven* on April 16, 1956. Released on Chess 1626, the song entered the *Billboard* pop charts on June 30, peaking at number 29 in *The Top 100* during its five weeks on the chart. It entered the *Billboard* R&B singles charts on June 9, spending seven weeks on the charts and peaking at number two on the *Most Played in Juke Boxes* chart. The Beatles performed the song seven times for the BBC. The EMI recording of the song was released in England on *With The Beatles* and in the U.S. on *The Beatles' Second Album*.

The Beatles performed *All My Loving* four times for the BBC. The song was released in the U.S. on *Meet The Beatles!* and in England on *With The Beatles*. It was the

first song performed by the Beatles on their first *Ed Sullivan Show* appearance.

*Things We Said Today* was released in England on *A Hard Day's Night* and in America on *Something New*. The Beatles performed the song twice for the BBC, including this July 14, 1964, recording that was broadcast on the July 16 *Top Gear* program.

*She's A Woman* was the flip side of *I Feel Fine*. It was a hit in its own right, peaking at number four in the *Billboard Hot 100*. The group performed the song three times for the BBC. The album version was recorded on November 17, 1964, for broadcast on *Top Gear* on November 26, the day before the single was issued in England.

The next three songs, along with a dialog track, were recorded on July 10, 1963, and broadcast on the July 23 *Pop Go The Beatles*. Chuck Berry's *Sweet Little Sixteen* was recorded during a December 29-30, 1957, session and issued on Chess 1683. The song entered the *Billboard Top 100 Sides* chart on February 17, 1958, holding down the number two spot for three weeks during its sweet 16-week run on the charts. The song was a number one hit for three weeks on both the *R&B Best Sellers in Stores* and *Most Played R&B by Jockeys* charts. John handles the lead vocal and George provides an excellent lead guitar solo on this spirited BBC performance.

*1822!* serves as John's introduction to the next song, which he claims was recorded on the group's first album back in 1822. *Lonesome Tears In My Eyes* was written by Johnny and Dorsey Burnette, along with Paul Burlison and Al Mortimer. It was recorded by the Johnny Burnette Trio and released on the LP *Johnny Burnette and the Rock 'n' Roll Trio* (Coral CRL 57080) in 1956. John handles the lead vocals.

*Nothin' Shakin'* was recorded by Eddie Fontaine, who co-wrote the song with Cirino Calacrai, Dianne Lampert and Gluck. It was originally released on Sunbeam 105, though it received national distribution as Argo 5309. The song charted at number 64 in 1958. George sings lead on this rockabilly classic.

*The Hippy Hippy Shake* was written and recorded by Chan Romero and released on Del-Fi 4119 on July 6, 1959. The Beatles, with Paul on lead vocal, performed the song five times for the BBC, including this July 10, 1963, performance that aired on the July 30 *Pop Go The Beatles*. In 1964, the Swinging Blue Jeans' cover of the song (Imperial 66021) reached number 24 in the *Billboard Hot 100* and was a number two hit in England.

*Glad All Over* was recorded by Carl Perkins and released on Sun 287 in late 1957. The tune was written by Roy Bennett, Sid Tepper and Aaron Schroeder. The Beatles, with George on lead vocal, performed the song twice for the BBC. The July 16, 1963, recording, which aired on the August 20 *Pop Go The Beatles*, is on the album.

*I Just Don't Understand*, written by Marijohn Wilkin and Kent Westberry, was a number 17 hit for Swedish-born actress Ann-Margret in the summer of 1961 on RCA Victor 7894. The Beatles recorded the song on July 16, 1963, for broadcast on the August 20 *Pop Go The Beatles*. John supplies the lead vocal.

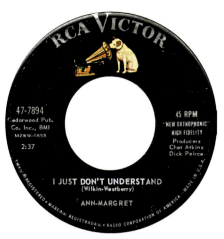

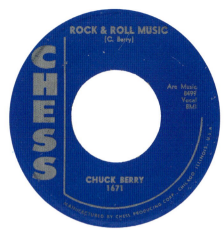

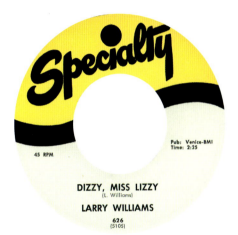

*So How Come No One Loves Me* was written by Felix Bryant and Boudaloux Bryant and is on the 1960 album *A Date With The Everly Brothers* (Warner Brothers WB 1395). The Beatles recorded the song on July 10, 1963, for the July 23 *Pop Go The Beatles*.

The first side of the second record closes with *I Feel Fine*, which was a number one hit for the Beatles in late 1964. The Beatles first of two BBC performances of the song was recorded on November 17, 1964, for broadcast on *Top Gear* on November 26, the day before the single was issued in England.

The group performed *I'm A Loser* three times for the BBC. The version included on the album has the same recording and broadcast history as the previous track. The song was issued in England on *Beatles For Sale* and in America on *Beatles '65*.

*Everybody's Trying To Be My Baby* was written and recorded by Carl Perkins. The tune came to the attention of the Beatles by its inclusion on *Dance Album Of Carl Perkins* (Sun LP 1225). An early live version of the song by the Beatles is on the *Live At The Star Club* album, which was recorded in Hamburg, Germany, during the Christmas season of 1962. The group, with George on lead vocal, performed the song four times for the BBC. The version included on the album was recorded on November 17, 1964, and broadcast first on the November 26 *Top Gear* and then later on the December 26 *Saturday Club*. It was issued in England on *Beatles For Sale* and in the United States on *Beatles '65*.

Chuck Berry's *Rock & Roll Music* was recorded in May, 1957, and released on Chess 1671. The song entered the *Billboard Top 100 Sides* chart on November 11, 1957, peaking at eight during its 19-week stay on the charts. It reached number six on the *Billboard R&B Best Sellers in Stores* chart. The Beatles recorded *Rock And Roll Music* on November 25, 1964, for the December 26 *Saturday Club*. Like the previous two tracks, it was issued in England on *Beatles For Sale* and in America on *Beatles '65*.

The next two selections were recorded on May 26, 1965, and broadcast on June 6 on a special program titled *The Beatles Invite You To Take A Ticket To Ride*. This would be the last show featuring BBC recordings. *Ticket To Ride* was the group's current single, a number one hit in England and the United States. *Dizzy Miss Lizzy*, written and recorded by Larry Williams, was released on Specialty 626. It entered the *Billboard Top 100 Sides* chart on April 14, 1958, and peaked at number 69 during its four-week run. The Beatles recorded their version of the song specifically for the Capitol album *Beatles VI*. When the group ran short of original songs for their British *Help!* LP, the song was inserted into the lineup.

The so-called Little Richard medley of *Kansas City/Hey! Hey! Hey! Hey!* is actually Little Richard's November 29, 1955, recording of Jerry Leiber and Mike Stoller's *Kansas City* with a call and response segment at the end. Little Richard later developed the segment into a full length song titled *Hey-Hey-Hey-Hey*, which he recorded nearly six months later on May 9, 1956. It was released on Specialty 624 as the B side to *Good Golly Miss Molly* in early 1958.

His 1955 recording of *Kansas City* was not released until 1959, when it was issued on Specialty 664 to compete with Wilbert Harrison's version of the song. The Beatles performed the song four times for the BBC. The version included on *Live At The BBC* was recorded on July 16, 1963, for broadcast on the August 6 *Pop Go The Beatles*. The group later recorded the song for *Beatles For Sale*. It was issued in America on *Beatles VI*.

*Set Fire To That Lot!* is a bit of vocal interplay between Ringo and host Rodney Burke that leads into Ringo singing lead on *Matchbox*, which was recorded on July 10, 1963, for the July 30 *Pop Go The Beatles*. The group performed the song an additional time for the BBC before recording it at Abbey Road on June 1, 1964, for inclusion on the *Long Tall Sally* EP. Capitol added the song to its *Something New* album and issued it as a single on Capitol 5255 on August 24, 1964. The song peaked at number 17 in the *Billboard Hot 100*. *Matchbox* is a traditional blues song that was recorded by Blind Lemon Jefferson in 1927 and Leadbelly in 1934. The Beatles rendition is based on Carl Perkins' 1957 recording, which was issued on Sun 261.

*I Forgot To Remember To Forget*, written by Stanley Kesler and Charles Feathers, was recorded by Elvis Presley and released on Sun 223 in August, 1955. George sings lead on the Beatles BBC recording from May 1, 1964, which was broadcast on *From Us To You* on May 18.

In *Love These Goon Shows!* John claims he's going to play a harp. He actually plays guitar and harmonica and sings lead vocal on Chuck Berry's *I Got To Find My Baby*. The band recorded the song twice for the BBC, including this May 1, 1964, performance that was broadcast on the June 11 *Pop Goes The Beatles*. Chuck Berry's version of the song was recorded on either February 12 or March 29, 1960, and released on Chess 1763.

*Ooh! My Soul* was written and recorded by Little Richard and released on Specialty 633. The song peaked at number 31 in the *Billboard Best Selling Pop Singles in Stores* chart on June 30, 1958, and reached 15 in the *Billboard R&B Best Sellers in Stores* chart. The Beatles BBC recording, which features a fabulous Paul vocal, was recorded on August 1, 1963, and aired on *Pop Go The Beatles* on August 27. *Ooh! My Arms* is a bit of dialog between host Rodney Burke and the group that links *Ooh! My Soul* to the next Beatles performance, *Don't Ever Change*. The song, written by Gerry Goffin and Carole King, was recorded by the Crickets, who had several hits with Buddy Holly. It was released in 1962 on Liberty 55441. Although the single did not chart in the U.S., it was a top five hit in England. The Beatles version of the song features John and Paul on lead vocals.

*Slow Down* was written and recorded by Larry Williams. It was released in the spring of 1958 as the B side to *Dizzy, Miss Lizzy* on Specialty 626. The Beatles, with John on lead vocal, performed the song for the BBC on July 16, 1963, for the August 20 *Pop Go The Beatles*. The group later recorded the song on June 1, 1964, for inclusion on the *Long Tall Sally* EP. Capitol placed the song on *Something New* and paired it with *Matchbox* on Capitol 5255. *Slow Down* peaked at number 25 in the *Billboard Hot 100*.

*Honey Don't* was written and recorded by Carl Perkins and issued as the flip side to *Blue Suede Shoes* on Sun 234 in 1956. The Beatles recorded the song on October 26, 1964, with Ringo singing lead. Prior to that time, John had handled the lead vocal on the song. It was turned over to Ringo to give the drummer his requisite lead vocal for *Beatles For Sale*. The group performed the song four times for the BBC. The version included on *Live At The BBC* was recorded on August 1, 1963, nearly 15 months prior to the EMI session, and broadcast on the September 3 *Pop Go The Beatles*. It features John on lead vocal.

The album ends with the Beatles first single, *Love Me Do*, which was released in England on Parlophone 45-R 4949 on October 5, 1962. The group's debut effort stalled at number 17 on the charts. Capitol Records passed on the song, and it was not issued as a single in the United States until Vee-Jay Records released the song on its Tollie subsidiary as Tollie 9008 on April 27, 1964. American fans and disc jockeys hungry for a "new" Beatles 45 pushed the song to the top of the *Billboard Hot 100*. The Beatles performed *Love Me Do* nine times for the BBC, including this July 10, 1963, recording that aired on the July 23 *Pop Go The Beatles*.

The vinyl edition of *Live At The BBC* was issued in a double side-opening gatefold cover, **APP 31796.SC1**. In contrast to the Beatles albums of the sixties and seventies, the cover is not made of slicks pasted over cardboard. Instead, the images are printed directly onto posterboard. The package was designed by Richard Ward/The Team in London.

The front cover features a digitally-altered sepia-toned photograph of the Beatles outside the entrance to BBC Paris Theatre located on Lower Regent Street in London. The picture was taken by Dezo Hoffman on April 4, 1963. Richard Ward and The Team tightly cropped the original photo and cloned out the following images to enhance the Beatles presence: a sign appearing above John's head, tiles on the outside strip of the building's overhang and a protruding sign in the background between the heads of George and Ringo. In addition, the background in the upper left quadrant was blurred. The Beatles classic extended T logo appears in white in the upper right corner. The album's title is handwritten in black and runs along the right bottom of the cover.

Even more digital trickery was used for the back cover. Images of each Beatle were lifted from another Dezo Hoffman photograph taken the same day at the same location. The boys were then pasted over the same digitally-altered background appearing on the front cover. All four were placed closer to the building's entrance and closer to each other. Drop shadows were added. There is, however, one amusing glitch. A blurred image of Ringo's head and upper left body left over from the front cover can be seen to the left of Ringo's head. The entire back cover was given as washed effect to allow for the overprinting of black text, which includes: the Beatles logo and album title in the upper left corner; album credits and copyright information in the lower right corner; and the track listings for each side running over the images of the boys.

The white-background inside gatefold contains a sepia-toned photo of each Beatle and liner notes by Derek Taylor and BBC Radio producer Kevin Howlett. Both sets of notes were written in September, 1994, and are the same as those printed in the CD booklet.

The discs are packaged in white background custom inner sleeves that open on the side. The sleeve for record one, **APP 31796.IS1**, has 15 sepia-toned photos of the group on one side and details regarding each track on the other. The sleeve for record two, **APP 31796.IS2**, has 16 sepia-toned pictures on one side and selection details on the other. These are the same photos that appear in the CD booklet, although they are cropped differently to form 2" x 2" squares on the sleeves. The information regarding each track is also the same as CD text.

By the time *Live At The BBC* was issued, Capitol was no longer manufacturing vinyl records at any of its factories. Capitol contracted with Specialty Records in Olyphant, Pennsylvania, to press the 12" discs for the album. (Specialty Records Corporation was founded in 1950. It originally manufactured only 45 RPM singles and had no relationship with the California-based Specialty Records label. In 1978, the company was acquired by Warner Communications Inc. and was folded into the newly formed WEA Manufacturing Inc.)

Capitol engineer Wally Traugott cut the masters for the vinyl records at the Capitol Tower in Hollywood, California. He hand etched "Wally" in the trail off areas to the discs. Additional trail off area markings include hand-etched matrix numbers, a machine-stamped "Mastered by Capitol" and the SRC logo of Specialty Records Corporation.

The records, **APP 31796.SR1**, were pressed with cream-colored background Apple label backdrops. The full apple side has the Beatles logo at the top of the apple and the album title and "See booklet for details" at the bottom. These items are white, with all other text appearing in small black letters to the left and right of the center hole. The layout for the sliced apple side is the same, with all overprinting in black. The reference to the booklet is an error resulting from the use of the text appearing on the CD, which is packaged with a booklet. The record label text should have said "See inner sleeve for details." Only 25,000 copies of the vinyl album were pressed, thus making the vinyl much more collectible than the multi-platinum-selling CD.

*Live At The BBC* was deleted from the Capitol catalog on October 30, 1995, in anticipation of the release of *Anthology 1* three weeks later on November 21. The BBC album remained out of circulation for over five years until its welcomed reinstatement on June 5, 2001.

The album's 130-minute running time presented a challenge for Wally Traugott as each side of the two record set runs for over 30 minutes, with the longest side clocking in at 34. (Vinyl records normally do not have more than 25 minutes of music per side.) Because the album is entirely mono, its grooves could be cut thinner than if the disc had been stereo. Still, Traugott had to cut the masters at a low volume level to keep the grooves small enough to fit on the disc. Because the later *Anthology* albums had stereo selections, they had to be spread out over three vinyl LPs.

APP 31796.SC1

APP 31796.SC1 (open gatefold)

APP 31796.IS1

APP 31796.IS2

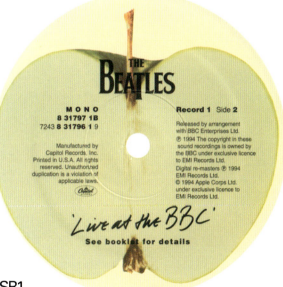

APP 31796.SR1

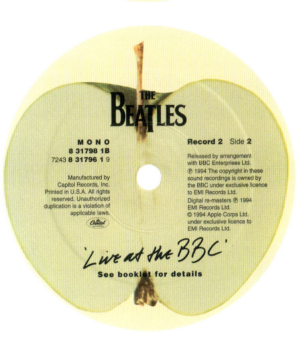

# BABY IT'S YOU (APPLE 58348)

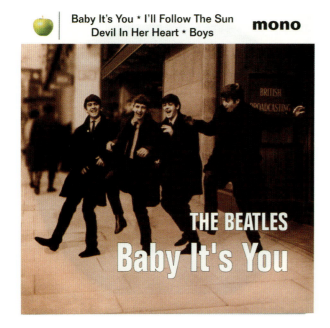

On March 23, 1995, Capitol issued an extended play release with four BBC performances. The EP (Apple 58348) was issued in the CD, cassette and seven-inch vinyl record formats. It features the album track *Baby It's You*, along with three songs not on the album: *I'll Follow The Sun*, *Devil In Her Heart* and *Boys*. The *Baby It's You* EP entered the *Billboard Hot 100 Singles* chart on April 22 at number 67, while Montell Jordan's *This Is How We Do It* was firmly entrenched at the number one spot. Although the song was designated the "Hot Shot Debut," it dropped to 79 the following week, before falling further to 89 and 99 during its brief four weeks on the charts.

In England, *Baby It's You* was released on March 20, 1995. The song was a surprise hit, peaking at number seven.

Each of the songs on the EP features a different Beatle on lead vocal: *Baby It's You* (John; recorded June 1, 1963, for the June 11 *Pop Go The Beatles*); *Ill Follow The Sun* (Paul; recorded November 17, 1964, for the November 26

*Top Gear*); *Devil In Her Heart* (George; recorded July 16, 1963, for the August 20 *Pop Go The Beatles*); and *Boys* (Ringo; recorded June 17, 1963, for the June 25 *Pop Go The Beatles*).

The record was packaged in a side-loader picture sleeve, **APP 58348.PS1**, featuring the altered Dezo Hoffmann photograph used on the back cover to *Live At The BBC*. The back of the sleeve has Kevin Howlett liner notes and descriptions of each track. The sleeve, which was designed by Richard Ward/The Team, mimics the Beatles EP sleeves from the early sixties.

The masters for the vinyl EP were cut at the Capitol Tower by Kevin Reeves, who etched "KEV" in the trail off area to side 1 and "Scotty Man" in the trail off area to side 2. The 7" records, **APP 58348.01**, were pressed by Specialty and have a full-size center hole. The label backdrops have the same creme-colored background as those used on the album.

# ANTHOLOGY 1 - APPLE 34445
# ANTHOLOGY 2 - APPLE 34448
# ANTHOLOGY 3 - APPLE 34451

Even before *Live At The BBC* was released, there was talk of Apple and EMI issuing a series of albums in conjunction with a planned *Beatles Anthology* video series. In a late 1993 press conference, George Martin stated that the albums would complement and parallel the video and would include private recordings, test recordings, outtakes, newly-created versions, broadcasts and bootleg selections. When the albums were issued in 1995 and 1996, they contained all that and more.

The music component of *Anthology* consists of three separately issued albums titled *Anthology 1*, *Anthology 2* and *Anthology 3*. Each was issued as a double CD, double cassette and three-record vinyl set. The first installment,

containing recordings from 1958 through 1964, covers the band's formative years through the initial surge of Beatlemania. It opens with *Free As A Bird*, a John Lennon demo from the seventies enhanced by newly-recorded contributions from Paul, George and Ringo. The second album also starts with a "new" Beatles song, *Real Love*, before continuing with the band's remarkable development as recording artists. This phase begins in February, 1965, and ends three years later with a pair of songs recorded days before the Beatles journey to Rishikesh, India, in February, 1968. The final installment covers the Apple years from 1968 through 1970. The albums were produced and directed by George Martin and remixed by Geoff Emerick.

# ANTHOLOGY 1

**Side 1**
1. Free As A Bird
2. "We were four guys ... that's all"
3. That'll Be The Day
4. In Spite Of All The Danger
5. "Sometimes I'd borrow ... those still exist"
6. Hallelujah, I Love Her So
7. You'll Be Mine
8. Cayenne
9. "First of all ... it didn't do a thing here"
10. My Bonnie
11. Ain't She Sweet
12. Cry For A Shadow

**Side 2**
1. "Brian was a beautiful guy ... he presented us well"
2. "I secured them ... a Beatle drink even then"
3. Searchin'
4. Three Cool Cats
5. The Sheik Of Araby
6. Like Dreamers Do
7. Hello Little Girl
8. "Well the recording test ... by my artists"
9. Besame Mucho
10. Love Me Do
11. How Do You Do It
12. Please Please Me

**Side 3**
1. One After 909 (sequence)
2. One After 909 (complete)
3. Lend Me Your Comb
4. I'll Get You
5. "We were performers ... in Britain"
6. I Saw Her Standing There
7. From Me To You
8. Money (That's What I Want)
9. You Really Got A Hold On Me
10. Roll Over Beethoven

**Side 4**
1. She Loves You
2. Till There Was You
3. Twist And Shout
4. This Boy
5. I Want To Hold Your Hand
6. "Boys, what I was thinking ..."
7. Moonlight Bay
8. Can't Buy Me Love

**Side 5**
1. All My Loving
2. You Can't Do That
3. And I Love Her
4. A Hard Day's Night
5. I Wanna Be Your Man
6. Long Tall Sally
7. Boys
8. Shout
9. I'll Be Back (Take 2)
10. I'll Be Back (Take 3)

**Side 6**
1. You Know What To Do
2. No Reply (demo)
3. Mr. Moonlight
4. Leave My Kitten Alone
5. No Reply
6. Eight Days A Week (sequence)
7. Eight Days A Week (complete)
8. Kansas City/Hey-Hey-Hey-Hey!

The selections surrounded by quotation marks are vocal-only tracks. These include excerpts from interviews, Brian Epstein reading from his book, *A Cellarful Of Noise* and a brief discussion from *The Morecambe And Wise Show*. Sides one, two and three have the same tracks as compact disc one. Sides four, five and six have the same tracks as compact disc two.

---

*Anthology 1* was released in America on November 21, 1995. It debuted at the top of the *Billboard* album chart on December 9, based on first-week sales of 855,797 copies reported by SoundScan. An additional 200,000 copies were sold in outlets not monitored by SoundScan. Thus, *Anthology 1* sold over one million units in its first week of release. The album stayed at the top for three weeks before being replaced by Mariah Carey's *Daydream*. It remained on the charts for 29 weeks, including six in the top ten. On December 19, 1996, the RIAA certified sales of eight million units (equating to sales of four million copies of the double CD and cassette). Although Capitol did not arrange for the album to be pressed in vinyl, it imported 25,000 British copies of the three-record set, which went on sale on December 5. In England, the album peaked at number two.

*Anthology* opens with *Free As A Bird*, a song John recorded as a home demo on cassette some time around 1977. Paul and Yoko began discussions in early 1994 about having some of John's unreleased songs on the record. After Paul inducted John into the Rock 'n' Roll Hall of Fame on January 19, 1994, he visited Yoko at the Dakota to listen to three songs selected by Yoko: *Grow Old With Me*, *Free As A Bird* and *Real Love*. Paul took an immediate liking to *Free As A Bird*. That February and March, he got together with George and Ringo to add overdubs to the Lennon demo.

In an Allan Kozinn interview appearing in *Beatlefan*, Paul stated that their attitude was "Let's pretend John's gone on holiday, and he sent us a cassette and said, 'finish this up, I trust you, just do your stuff on it, finish it up for me.'" As John had not completed the lyrics to the middle eight, he and George ending up writing their own words for that part of the song. John's piano and vocal were augmented with acoustic guitar, piano and bass from Paul, acoustic guitar, electric lead guitar and slide guitar from George and drums by Ringo. All three contributed vocals and George added a ukulele part at the end.

The song's credits read "Original composition by John Lennon, Beatles version by John Lennon, Paul McCartney, George Harrison and Ringo Starr." The production credit is given to John Lennon, Paul McCartney, George Harrison, Richard Starkey and Jeff Lynne. Geoff Emerick served as engineer. The overdubs were recorded in February and March, 1994, at Mill Studio on Paul McCartney's farm.

The chronological musical history of the Beatles is preceded by John's comment from his December 8, 1970, interview with Jann Wenner of *Rolling Stone*. According to Lennon, "We were four guys...I met Paul, I said 'you wanna join me band,' you know, and then George joined, and then Ringo joined. We were just a band who made it very, very big, that's all."

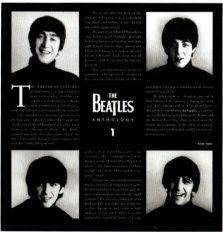

In 1958, the Quarry Men recorded the Crickets' *That'll Be The Day* with John on lead vocal. *Anthology 1* also contains a 1960 rehearsal of the Beatles doing Ray Charles' *Hallelujah, I Love Her So*. The group's instrumental backing to Tony Sheridan's recording of *My Bonnie* was first issued in the U.S. in 1962 on Decca 31382.

John's understatement is followed by a pair of 1958 recordings by Lennon's pre-Beatles group, the Quarry Men. At the time the songs were recorded at Phillips Sound Recording Service in Liverpool, the band consisted of John, Paul and George on guitars, John Lowe on piano and Colin Hanton on drums. The two songs were recorded on tape and transferred to a shellac 78 RPM disc. *That'll Be The Day*, released by the Crickets on Brunswick 55009, charted for 22 weeks, topping the *Billboard Best Sellers in Stores* chart on September 23, 1957. The song was written by Buddy Holly, the group's leader, chief vocalist and guitarist, along with drummer Jerry Allison and producer Norman Petty. The Quarry Men version features John Lennon on lead vocal backed by Paul. *In Spite Of All The Danger*, written by Paul and George, also has a Lennon lead vocal. Although the sound quality is poor, the recordings are included for their historical importance.

Paul, in a November 3, 1994, interview with Mark Lewisohn, then explains that sometimes he'd borrow a tape recorder to record the band's practice sessions. His statement that the songs are in "very bad quality" prepares the listener for what follows.

The next three songs were taped in 1960 at a rehearsal at Paul McCartney's home in Liverpool. The band consisted of John Lennon, Paul McCartney and George Harrison on guitars and Stuart Sutcliffe on bass. The group had no regular drummer at that time. *Hallelujah, I Love Her So* was written and recorded by Ray Charles. It was released on Atlantic 1096 and reached number five on the *Billboard R&B Best Sellers in Stores* chart. The Beatles arrangement, with Paul on lead vocal, is based on Eddie Cochran's 1960 cover version. *You'll Be Mine* is an early Lennon-McCartney original in which Paul and John ham it up on the vocals. John's spoken passage in the middle eight is delivered in a deep bass voice and contains the phrase "National Health eyeball." *Cayenne* is an instrumental written by Paul.

The history lesson continues with comments from Paul about the group's recording session with Tony Sheridan in Hamburg, Germany. In the interview, which was recorded on October 27, 1962, McCartney mentions that *My Bonnie* got to number five in Germany, but didn't do a thing in England.

The next three selections were recorded on June 22 at Friedrich-Ebert-Halle during the Beatles 1961 visit to Hamburg, Germany. The session was produced by Bert Kaempfert, who signed the Beatles to a contract primarily to serve as the backing band for British singer Tony Sheridan, who was developing a following in the German club scene. The group backed Sheridan on six songs, including a rocking rendition of the traditional ballad *My Bonnie*. When the song was released in the United States in 1962 on Decca 31382 (credited to Tony Sheridan and the Beat Brothers), it failed to chart. After Beatlemania exploded in America, the single was issued on MGM K 13213 on January 27, 1964, and credited to the Beatles with Tony Sheridan. Riding the popularity of the group, the record charted at number 26 in the *Billboard Hot 100*.

The next two songs were recorded by the Beatles without Tony Sheridan. *Ain't She Sweet*, written by Jack Yellen and Milton Ager, was a standard among Vaudeville singers. The Beatles arrangement of the song is loosely based on Gene Vincent's 1956 recording of the song, although the group's version is much more of a rocker. It features John on rhythm guitar and lead vocal, George on lead guitar, Paul on bass and Pete Best on drums. The song was released in America on Atco 6308 on July 6, 1964, and charted at 19 in the *Billboard Hot 100*, at a time when the Beatles had four other songs on the charts. During the *Abbey Road* sessions, the Beatles ran through the song during a jam that included two other Gene Vincent songs. This July 24, 1969, recording of *Ain't She Sweet* is on *Anthology 3*.

*Cry For A Shadow* was written by the one-time-only songwriting team of John Lennon and George Harrison. The instrumental track is a Beatles only performance with George on lead guitar, John on rhythm guitar, Paul on bass and Pete Best on drums. The song opens with John's choppy chords on his treble-toned guitar. He is quickly joined by a Pete Best drum roll, Paul's thumping bass and George's wailing and harmonic lead guitar playing, Paul provides intermittent background shouts. The song is probably Pete Best's best performance on a Beatles record. It was issued in America on March 27, 1964, on MGM K 13227 as the B side to *Why*, a song featuring Tony Sheridan on lead vocal. *Billboard* charted *Why* for one week at number 88.

After Beatlemania exploded in the United States, MGM and Atco issued all eight of the Beatles Hamburg recordings on singles. Pictured above are the labels to the three songs included on the *Anthology* album: *My Bonnie* (MGM K 13213); *Ain't She Sweet* (Atco 6308); and *Cry For A Shadow* (MGM K 13227).

The next selections are speech tracks. The first contains an excerpt from John's October, 1971, interview with David Wigg, which was broadcast on the BBC in November, 1971. Lennon tells him that "Brian was a beautiful guy." This leads into a segment of an October 13, 1964, recording of manager Brian Epstein reading from his autobiography *A Cellarful Of Noise*. Brian's description of how he secured the band an audition with Decca Records leads into five songs from the 15 song audition held at Decca Studios, London, on January 1, 1962, before producer Mike Smith.

*Searchin'* and *Three Cool Cats* were both written by Jerry Leiber and Mike Stoller and recorded by the Coasters. *Searchin'* was released in April, 1957, on Atco 6087. The song charted for 26 weeks in the *Billboard* pop charts, peaking at number three, and held down the number one spot on the *Billboard R&B Best Sellers in Stores* chart for 12 weeks. The single's flip side, *Young Blood*, was also a huge hit and was later recorded by the Beatles for the BBC. *Three Cool Cats* was the B side to *Charlie Brown* (Atco 6132), a number two hit from early 1959. *Searchin'* featured Paul on lead vocal, while George, aided and abetted by John and Paul, sang lead on *Three Cool Cats*.

Harrison was also the featured vocalist on *The Sheik Of Araby*. The tune originated in the Broadway musical *Make It Happen* and appeared in the 1940 film *Tin Pan*

*Alley*. The Beatles rock version of the song was based on Joe Brown's recording.

The other two selections from the Decca audition are Lennon-McCartney originals. *Like Dreamers Do* features Paul on lead vocal. John and Paul share vocals on *Hello Little Girl*, which was the first song written by Lennon. While the songs were not considered strong enough for the Beatles to record, they were given to other Brian Epstein-managed acts. The Fourmost recorded *Hello Little Girl* in 1963, and the Applejacks laid down their version of *Like Dreamers Do* the following year.

The next track consists of more Brian Epstein reading from his autobiography, this time telling of the disappointment over Decca's rejection of the group and the securing of an audition with George Martin. This leads into two songs recorded during the June 6, 1962, audition at Abbey Road. *Besame Mucho*, written by Consuelo Velazquez and Sunny Skylar, was a number one hit in 1944 for the Jimmy Dorsey Orchestra. The Beatles were familiar with the song through the Coasters two-part cover version issued in 1960 on Atco 6163. While *Part I* charted a number 70 in the *Billboard Hot 100*, the Beatles drew more from *Part II* and added a "Cha-cha-boom" refrain. Paul handles the lead vocal on the song, which was also recorded at the group's Decca audition.

The Beatles performed three songs recorded by the Coasters at their January 1, 1962, Decca audition: *Three Cool Cats*, *Searchin'* and *Besame Mucho*. The first two are on *Anthology 1*. The group's rendition of *Besame Mucho* from their June 6, 1962, Parlophone audition is also on the album.

The performance of *Love Me Do* from the Parlophone audition has Pete Best on drums. This early version of the song reveals why George Martin advised Brian that Best would not be allowed to play drums on the band's studio recordings. His drumming is weak, particularly in the middle eight where it sounds like he falls off the bridge.

*How Do You Do It* was recorded by the Beatles at their first official EMI recording session on September 4, 1962. George Martin insisted that the band learn the song, which was written by songwriter Mitch Murray, because he was not convinced that the group had written any songs strong enough to be a hit single. The Beatles worked out a suitable arrangement of the tune, but told Martin that they wanted their own songs issued on their first single. After Martin agreed to place to Lennon-McCartney originals on the 45, he gave the song to Gerry and the Pacemakers, who had a number one British hit with the song in 1963. In the States, the single was ignored when first issued on Laurie 3162 in 1963, but became a number nine hit when re-released on Laurie 3261 during the Beatles-led British Invasion in the summer of 1964.

The version of *Please Please Me* on the *Anthology* album was recorded on September 11, 1962, at a session in which Ron Richards served as producer in place of George Martin. After *P.S. I Love You* and a remake of *Love Me Do* had been recorded with session drummer Andy White on drums, the group began recording *Please Please Me* when Martin arrived at the session. According to Martin, the song was "a very dreary song," which "was like a Roy Orbison number, very slow, bluesy vocals." He told the group to speed up the tempo and work out tight vocal harmonies. Following Martin's advice, the group recorded the song at a quicker pace, but failed to nail it down. This early version is interesting, but suffers in comparison to the released single. Conspicuously absent from this version are John's distinctive harmonica and John and Paul's Everly Brothers style harmonies. It is presumed that Andy White played drums on this run through of the song.

The Beatles first attempted to record *One After 909* on March 5, 1963, after completing work on their third single, *From Me To You* b/w *Thank You Girl*. The album contains a sequence containing bits of Takes 3, 4 and 5, none of which were complete. This is followed by an edit of Takes 4 and 5 to form a complete version of the song. The Beatles dusted off this oldie for the *Get Back/Let It Be* sessions.

*Lend Me Your Comb* was recorded by the band at BBC Maida Vale Studios, London, on July 2, 1963, for broadcast on the July 16 *Pop Go The Beatles* program. The song, written by Kay Twomey, Fred Wise and Ben Weisman, was recorded by Carl Perkins and was the flip side to *Glad All Over* on Sun 287, released in late 1957. The Beatles version of the song, which was not included on *Live At The BBC*, features John and Paul on lead vocals.

*I'll Get You* is taken from the group's October 13, 1963, appearance on the popular British variety TV show *Val Parnell's Sunday Night At The London Palladium*. This exciting performance, complete with screams from the fans in the audience, is followed by an excerpt from John's December 8, 1970, interview with Jann Wenner of *Rolling Stone*. Lennon describes the band's early performances and states: "What we generated was fantastic when we played straight rock. And there was nobody to touch us in Britain, you know."

The next five songs were recorded live before a studio audience at Karlaplansstudion in Stockholm, Sweden, on October 24, 1963, for broadcast on Sveriges Radio on November 11. The group provides spirited performances of *I Saw Her Standing There*, *From Me To You*, *Money (That's What I Want)*, *You Really Got A Hold On Me* and *Roll Over Beethoven*.

Next up are three songs from the group's appearance at the 1963 Royal Command Performance on November 4. *Anthology* includes *She Loves You*, *Till There Was You* and *Twist And Shout*. Before the group launches into its final number of the show, John makes his famous request that charmed the affluent audience at London's Prince of Wales Theatre. "Would the people in the cheaper seats clap your hands? And the rest of you, if you'll just rattle your jewelry."

The next selections are from the Beatles December 2, 1963, appearance on *The Morecambe And Wise Show*, a popular British television comedy program. The band performs both sides of its then-current single, *This Boy* and *I Want To Hold Your Hand*. After a brief discussion, the group joins hosts Eric Morecambe and Ernie Wise singing the Tin Pan Alley standard *Moonlight Bay*.

*Can't Buy Me Love* was recorded on January 29, 1964, at EMI's Pathé Marconi Studios in Paris, France. The *Anthology* version of the song (Take 2, with the guitar solo from Take 1 edited into the instrumental break) reveals that Paul originally envisioned the song as having a blues feeling. This early version of the song is one of the more fascinating outtakes on *Anthology* in that it demonstrates the band's ability to transform musical ideas in the studio. Its verses contain wonderful backing vocals by John and George which are not present on the finished master. During the last verse, Paul forgets the lyrics and improvises a scat vocal that Louie Armstrong would have been proud of.

The Beatles historic performance on *The Ed Sullivan Show* on February 9, 1964, is represented by the first song played that evening, *All My Loving*. The track contains a brief introduction Ed Sullivan and screams from the audience.

*You Can't Do That* was recorded on February 25, 1964. *Anthology* includes Take 6, a complete runthrough with a John Lennon guide vocal.

Prior to recording *And I Love Her* as an "unplugged" ballad featuring John on acoustic guitar, George on nylon-stringed acoustic guitar, Paul on bass and Ringo on bongos, the band recorded the song with George on electric guitar and Ringo on drums. Take 2 from February 25, 1964, shows how different the song originally sounded.

Take 1 of *A Hard Day's Night*, recorded on April 16, 1964, is a rough but fun runthrough of the song. The initial arrangement lacks the immaculate instrumental break featuring the tandem of George Harrison on his twelve string Rickenbacker guitar and George Martin on piano. In its place is a crude Harrison solo.

The Beatles performed their version of Carl Perkins' recording of *Lend Me Your Comb* for the BBC radio program *Pop Go The Beatles*. The Isley Brothers' *Shout* was recorded by the band on April 19, 1964, at IBC Studios, London, for lip syncing on the BBC television special *Around The Beatles*. Little Willie John's *Leave My Kitten Alone* was recorded for *Beatles For Sale*, but did not make the cut.

The next four selections, *I Wanna Be Your Man*, *Long Tall Sally*, *Boys* and *Shout*, were recorded on April 19, 1964, at IBC Studios, London, for lip syncing on the BBC television special *Around The Beatles*. For *Anthology*, the songs were mixed for stereo from the original three-track tapes. This performance of *Boys* was not included in the program when it aired on May 6. *Shout* is of particular interest as the Beatles never recorded the song for EMI or for their BBC radio shows. Each Beatle sings lead for a segment of song, which was a number 47 hit for the Isley Brothers in 1959 on RCA Victor 47-7588.

*I'll Be Back* was recorded on June 1, 1964, in 16 takes. Anthology contains the second and third takes of the song, which was first attempted as a waltz in 3/4 time. After Take 2 breaks down, John confesses it's "too hard to sing." For Take 3, the band switched the tempo to 4/4 time.

The next two tracks are demos that were recorded on June 3, 1964, the day before the group began their summer tour. Ringo was not present at the Abbey Road session as he became sick that morning, missing the opening dates of the tour and being temporarily replaced on drums by Jimmy Nicol. *You Know What To Do* is a George Harrison composition that had been long forgotten until its misfiled tape was discovered in 1993. The song features George on lead vocal backed by his guitar, Paul's bass and John on tambourine. *No Reply*, which was later recorded for *Beatles For Sale* and ended up on *Beatles '65* in America, has John and Paul on vocals, John on rhythm guitar, Paul on bass and possibly George on drums. Although the *Anthology* booklet speculates that this recording was intended as a demo for Tommy Quickly, that theory is probably incorrect. The recording ends in a bit of laughter from the band.

The version of *Mr. Moonlight* released on *Beatles For Sale* and *Beatles '65* was recorded on October 18, 1964. *Anthology* contains Takes 1 and 4, which were recorded two months earlier on August 14. The first take instantly breaks down after John misfires on the song's vocal introduction. Take 4 is complete and features an interesting-sounding guitar solo from George rather than Paul's Hammond organ solo found on the released master. The song was first recorded by Dr. Feelgood and the Interns

and released as the B side to *Dr. Feel-Good* (Okeh 4-7144) on January 15, 1962. Although the original issue of the single gave writer's credit to "R. Stevens - R.C. Stevens," *Mr. Moonlight* was written by the band's guitarist, Roy Lee Johnson, Jr. who also sang the tune. Dr. Feelgood was Willie Perryman, who had previously recorded under the name Piano Red.

*Leave My Kitten Alone* is a spirited rocker originally recorded by Little Willie John and released on King 5219 in the summer of 1959. The song charted for nine weeks in the *Billboard Hot 100*, peaking at number 60, and for nine weeks in the *Billboard Hot R&B Sides* chart, peaking at 13. When Johnny Preston released a cover version of the song on Mercury 71761 in early 1961, King reissued the single. Preston's version only got to number 73, while John once again reached number 60. The song was written Little Willie John along with Titus Turner and James McDougal. The Beatles recorded five takes of the song with John on lead vocal and rhythm guitar, Paul on bass, George on lead guitar and Ringo on drums. Overdubs to Take 5 included a second Lennon vocal, Paul on piano and Ringo on tambourine. The Beatles recording of the song was slated to appear on the aborted *Sessions* album in 1984. It was also scheduled to be the lead single from the LP.

The song *No Reply* appears on *Anthology* for a second time as Take 2 from September 30, 1964. This performance has more of a bluesy feeling than the finished master.

Next up is an edit of Takes 1, 2 and 4 of *Eight Days A Week* (recorded on October 6, 1964), which gives the flavor of how the song's intro was initially conceived–John and Paul singing a sequence of harmonized "Ooohs" over hand claps and acoustic guitar, with Paul's walking bass and Ringo's drums falling into place. This is followed by the complete Take 5, which varies considerably from the finished master, with the vocals having different emphasis, phrasing and harmonies.

*Anthology 1* concludes with Take 2 of *Kansas City*. The Beatles, accompanied by George Martin on piano, recorded the song on October 18, 1964. Take 1 was selected for inclusion on *Beatles For Sale* and appeared on *Beatles VI* in America.

# ANTHOLOGY 2

**Side 1**
1. Real Love
2. Yes It Is
3. I'm Down
4. You've Got To Hide Your Love Away
5. If You've Got Trouble
6. That Means A Lot
7. Yesterday
8. It's Only Love

**Side 2**
1. I Feel Fine
2. Ticket To Ride
3. Yesterday
4. Help!
5. Everybody's Trying To Be My Baby
6. Norwegian Wood (This Bird Has Flown)
7. I'm Looking Through You
8. 12-Bar Original

**Side 3**
1. Tomorrow Never Knows
2. Got To Get You Into My Life
3. And Your Bird Can Sing
4. Taxman
5. Eleanor Rigby (Strings Only)
6. I'm Only Sleeping (Rehearsal)
7. I'm Only Sleeping (Take 1)
8. Rock And Roll Music
9. She's A Woman

**Side 4**
1. Strawberry Fields Forever (Demo Sequence)
2. Strawberry Fields Forever (Take 1)
3. Strawberry Fields Forever (Take 7 & Edit Piece)
4. Penny Lane
5. A Day In The Life
6. Good Morning Good Morning
7. Only A Northern Song

**Side 5**
1. Being For The Benefit Of Mr. Kite! (Takes 1 And 2)
2. Being For The Benefit Of Mr. Kite! (Take 7)
3. Lucy In The Sky With Diamonds
4. Within You Without You (Instrumental)
5. Sgt. Pepper's Lonely Hearts Club Band (Reprise)
6. You Know My Name (Look Up The Number)

**Side 6**
1. I Am The Walrus
2. The Fool On The Hill (Demo)
3. Your Mother Should Know
4. The Fool On The Hill (Take 4)
5. Hello, Goodbye
6. Lady Madonna
7. Across The Universe

Sides one, two and three have the same tracks as compact disc one. Sides four, five and six have the same tracks as compact disc two.

---

*Anthology 2* was released on March 19, 1996. Like its predecessor, it debuted at number one, earning its place at the top of the April 6 *Billboard* album chart by virtue of SoundScan-reported sales of 441,000 copies. The following week it was replaced by *Jagged Little Pill* by Alanis Morissette (Maverick 45901). The album spent four weeks in the top ten during its 37 week run on the charts. The RIAA certified sales of four million units (equating to sales of two million copies of the double CD).

Capitol prepared a limited edition run of the album on vinyl, with engineer Kevin Reeves cutting the masters for the discs at the Capitol Tower. The records were pressed by Specialty Records Corporation in Olyphant, Pennsylvania, with light tan background Apple label backdrops.

*Anthology 2* had originally been slated for release on February 27; however, a last minute change in the album's running order necessitated more time to reprint CD booklets and other items. The delay was caused by Paul McCartney, who decided that the album's chronological running order should be varied by moving *I'm Down* from the sixth spot to the third. This decision resulted in the destruction of millions of components, such as CD booklets and J-card/booklets for the cassette version of the album. Unconfirmed reports at the time stated that McCartney agreed to pay $2,000,000 to EMI and Capitol to cover the costs of the change. It was speculated that Paul revised the order so that his first lead vocal would appear earlier in the lineup and would be a strong rocker as opposed to the inferior *That Means A Lot*.

The album's first track is *Real Love*, another new recording involving Paul, George and Ringo embellishing an unfinished John Lennon demo from about 1979. The cassette provided by Yoko contained John's live vocal and piano, with overdubs of a drum-machine and a second vocal. Because the tape was full of clicks and background hum, it was decided not to record over the tape. Instead, the trio laid down a backing track, and John's vocal was cleaned up and dropped in over the newly-recorded backing. Paul played acoustic guitar, electric bass and stand-up double bass (the same one used by Bill Black on Elvis Presley songs including *Heartbreak Hotel*). George played acoustic guitar, a Model T Hamber guitar for the solos and fills and a Fender Stratocaster for the slide guitar solo at the end. Ringo added drums. Paul recorded a lead vocal to match John's vocal, and Paul and George added backing vocals and harmonies. All three contributed percussion. Jeff Lynne produced the February, 1995, session (with John, Paul, George and Ringo also receiving credit as producers in the liner notes). Geoff Emerick and Jon Jacobs served as engineers.

*Yes It Is* was recorded on February 16, 1965, during the *Help!* sessions. Although not selected for the film, the song was used as the B side for *Ticket To Ride*. The *Anthology* version of *Yes It Is* combines Take 2, which features John's guide vocal and breaks down midway, with the last part of the finished master (Take 14) featuring the three-part harmony of John, Paul and George.

*I'm Down* was recorded in seven takes on June 14, 1965. The album contains Take 1, an exciting performance with Paul singing, hollering, barking and whooping it up. After completing the song, Paul mutters "plastic soul, man, plastic soul." Apparently Paul was observing that the song wasn't a real soul shouter, but rather a plastic imitation of soul music. This phrase may have inspired the title to the group's next album, *Rubber Soul*.

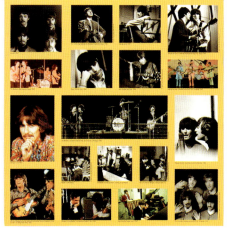

*You've Got To Hide Your Love Away* was recorded on February 18, 1965. *Anthology* contains John's studio chat before and after Take 1's false start, including his announcement that "Paul's broken a glass." This is followed by Take 5, which is complete, but does not have the overdub of the flute solo present on the finished master.

*If You've Got Trouble* was written by John and Paul to serve as Ringo's vocal contribution to the *Help!* album. It was recorded in one take on February 18, 1965, and is not one of the group's better efforts. During the instrumental break, Ringo shouts out, "Rock on, anybody," perhaps sensing the song is going nowhere. The Beatles decided that the tune was not worthy of release.

*That Means A Lot* is another song that was recorded during the *Help!* sessions that was not released. *Anthology* contains Take 1, which was recorded on February 20. The Beatles attempted a different approach to the song with a remake on March 30, but this also proved unsatisfactory. The tune was then turned over to P.J. Proby, who had a number 24 British hit with the song in the Fall of 1965.

*Yesterday* was recorded on June 14, 1965. A string quartet was overdubbed onto Take 2 to form the finished master. The album contains Take 1, to which strings were never added. Paul reverses the first two lines of the second verse.

*It's Only Love* was recorded on June 15, 1965. It was issued in England on the *Help!* LP and in America on *Rubber Soul*. The album contains Take 2, which is missing George's overdubbed lead guitar.

The next four tracks, *I Feel Fine*, *Ticket To Ride*, *Yesterday* and *Help!*, are from the Beatles August 1, 1965, appearance on the British television program *Blackpool Night Out*. George introduces *Yesterday* with "And so for Paul McCartney of Liverpool, opportunity knocks." After Paul performs the song backed only by his acoustic guitar and strings, John deadpans "Thank you Ringo, that was wonderful."

The next track, *Everybody's Trying To Be My Baby*, is from the group's August 15, 1965, concert at Shea Stadium. This performance was not included in the television program *The Beatles At Shea Stadium*, which was broadcast in England on BBC1 on March 1, 1966, and in America on the ABC television network on January 10, 1967.

The version of *Norwegian Wood (This Bird Has Flown)* appearing on *Rubber Soul* is a remake recorded on October 21, 1965. *Anthology* contains Take 1 from October 12. The backing track was subjected to numerous overdubs and features John's lead vocal, John and Paul's backing harmonies, John's acoustic guitar, Paul's bass, George's double-tracked sitar and Ringo's finger cymbals, tambourine and maracas.

*I'm Looking Through You* is another song that went through a complete remake. Take 1 was recorded on October 24, 1965, and was embellished with numerous overdubs. This terrific performance features a great vocal from Paul, backed by acoustic and electric guitars, bass, organ, maracas and extremely effective hand claps. Unlike the remake included on *Rubber Soul*, Take 1 does not have any lyrics on the bridge.

*12-Bar Original* is an instrumental recorded during the *Rubber Soul* sessions on November 4, 1965, but not released. The song, credited to Lennon, McCartney, Harrison and Starr, has John and George on electric guitars, Paul on bass, Ringo on drums and George Martin on harmonium. Take 2, which is over six and a half minutes long, was edited down to 2:54 for *Anthology*.

Take 1 of *Tomorrow Never Knows* was recorded on April 6, 1966. It is a dense, echo-drenched dirge dominated by Ringo's drumming and the same melody line played over and over on guitar. John's vocal is buried under a wall of sound murkier than anything achieved before by Phil Spector. It sounds like it was recorded deep inside a cave at the bottom of an ocean.

Take 5 of *Got To Get You Into My Life*, recorded on April 7, 1966, also varies significantly from the released master. The song opens with George Martin on organ and Ringo's hi-hat. John and George are on acoustic guitars and Paul on bass. Paul sings a bluesy lead vocal, backed by John and George.

*And Your Bird Can Sing* is another song that went through a complete remake. *Anthology* contains Take 2 from April 20, 1966, which has a backing track of lead and rhythm guitars and drums. Overdubs included tambourine, bass and several vocal parts by John, Paul and George. During one of the vocal overdubs, John and Paul get the giggles and end up laughing their way through much of the song while the previously recorded voices continue unabated behind them.

*Taxman* was recorded on April 21, 1966, and embellished with overdubs on May 16. *Anthology* includes Take 11 prior to the later overdubs. The backing vocals in the last verse have a fast-paced gibberish "Anybody got a bit of money, anybody got a bit of money?" refrain rather than the stately references to political leaders Mr. Wilson and Mr. Heath heard in the finished master. The song also lacks the cow bell overdub and ends with a hard break, which would later be edited with a repeat of the song's guitar solo for a fade out ending.

The instrumental backing for *Eleanor Rigby*, consisting of George Martin's score of four violins, two violas and two cellists, was recorded on April 28, 1966. *Anthology* contains a strings only remix.

The backing track to *I'm Only Sleeping* was recorded on April 27, 1966. *Anthology* contains selections from an April 29 session during which the group attempted a remake of the song. During an instrumental rehearsal, the song was performed with vibraphone, acoustic guitar and drums. Fortunately, a brief portion of this rehearsal was preserved at the end of the tape containing the proper takes from the session. Take 1 of the remake features John and Paul sharing live lead vocals backed by acoustic guitars and percussion.

Two of the Beatles five concert performances at Nippon Budokan Hall in Tokyo, Japan, were taped for broadcast by the Japanese television company NTV. The album contains two songs from the evening show of June 30, 1966: *Rock 'N' Roll Music* and *She's A Woman*.

**Capitol's Creative Services Department prepared a beautiful promotional poster for *Anthology 2* that combined a picture of the Beatles sticking up through the roof of the *Magical Mystery Tour* bus with a cloud background sent to Capitol by Rick Ward of The Team in England. Two sizes were printed: 36" x 24" and 30" x 20".**

The second compact disc and fourth side of the vinyl record each open with three tracks tracing the development of *Strawberry Fields Forever*. First up is an edited sequence of demos recorded by John in November, 1966, at his home in Weybridge. This is followed by Take 1, which was recorded on November 24. The song is an exquisite blend of mellotron (a new electronic instrument capable of duplicating the sounds of string instruments) played by Paul, guitar, slide guitar and creative drumming topped with John's dreamy lead vocal. Although Take 1 is a truly remarkable performance, John was not satisfied. The group recorded two additional arrangements of the song before a finished master was completed by editing the first part of Take 7 with the second part of Take 26. (The full recording history of the song is detailed in the book *The Beatles' Story on Capitol Records, Part One: Beatlemania and The Singles*.) *Anthology* contains the mono mix of Take 7, along with an expanded edit and remix of the ending of Take 26. The new mix clearly reveals John twice saying "cranberry sauce." People looking for clues of McCartney's death claimed that John was mumbling "I buried Paul" during the song's fade out ending.

*Penny Lane* was recorded over a series of sessions held from December 29, 1966, through January 17, 1967. The album contains a new edit and mix that features Paul's single-tracked vocal, cor anglais and trumpets on the bridge and an extended B-flat piccolo trumpet solo at the end. At the song's conclusion, Paul can be heard saying "A suitable ending, I think."

*Anthology* contains an interesting sampling of *A Day In The Life* at different stages of the song's development. The track opens with studio talk, the testing of the alarm clock and John's "sugar plum fairy, sugar plum fairy" count-in from Take 1 recorded on January 19, 1967. This leads to Take 2, which features John's lead vocal backed by his acoustic guitar, Paul's piano, George Harrison on maracas and Ringo on bongos. As John sings "I'd love to turn you on," Mal Evans' echo-drenched voice is heard counting the 24 measures that would later be filled with the orchestral buildup. The track then switches to an acetate made of Take 6 on January 30, which contains Paul's first attempt at singing the "woke up, fell out of bed" segment, complete with an expletive after he flubs the lyrics. After returning to Take 2 for the final verse, the track switches to a new mix of the song's orchestral climb which abruptly stops at the top without the song's final chord. The track ends with Paul commenting about the use of the orchestra.

The rhythm backing for *Good Morning Good Morning* was recorded on February 8, 1967, in eight takes, with rhythm guitar and Ringo's drums each given a separate track. John's lead vocal and Paul's bass were added to the remaining empty tracks on February 16. At this stage the song contained none of the "Good morning, good morning" backing vocals, horns or sound effects that would later give the song its unique sound. The unadorned Take 8 is highlighted by Ringo's excellent drumming and Paul's hyperactive yet melodic bass playing.

Although it ended up on the *Yellow Submarine* soundtrack, *Only A Northern Song* was recorded during the *Sgt. Pepper* sessions. *Anthology* contains a new stereo mix utilizing elements from sessions held on January 13 and 14, 1967, and April 20, 1967. This version has different lyrics and sound effects than the finished master.

The backing track of *Being For The Benefit Of Mr. Kite!* was recorded on February 17, 1967. *Anthology* contains Takes 1 and 2, both of which quickly break down, followed by Take 7, the backing used for the finished master. It consists of John's guide vocal (later erased) backed by George Martin on harmonium, Paul on bass and Ringo on drums. The special *Anthology* mix adds organ and the special effects calliope tape as John concludes his vocal towards the end of the song.

*Anthology* contains a unique mix of *Lucy In The Sky With Diamonds* combining elements of Takes 6, 7 and 8 recorded on March 1 and 2, 1967. Its basic track is Take 6, with tamboura added from Take 7 and the chorus vocals from Take 8. The main interest in this new mix is John's guide vocal.

George's *Within You Without You* was recorded on March 15, 16 and 22 and April 3, 1967. *Anthology* contains a remixed version of the backing instrumental track.

*Sgt. Pepper's Lonely Hearts Club Band (Reprise)* was recorded in nine takes during one long session on April 1, 1967. The album contains Take 5, a high-energy performance complete with Paul's rough guide vocal.

Although the backing track to *You Know My Name (Look Up The Number)* was recorded on May 17 and June 7 and 8, 1967, and vocals were added on April 30, 1969, the song was not released until March 11, 1970, when it surfaced as the B side to *Let It Be* (Apple 2764). *You Know My Name* is a humorous piece of nostalgic night club nonsense concocted by John that would not have fit comfortably on any Beatles album. On November 26, 1969, John made a mono mix and then edited the six-minute plus track down to 4:19 for intended release as a Plastic Ono Band single; however, the record was not issued when EMI and/or the other Beatles objected. *Anthology* contains a new version of the song that restores much of what John edited. The song is in stereo for the first time and runs 5:42, thus presenting more of the song's infectious humor.

The backing track to *I Am The Walrus* was recorded in 16 takes on September 5, 1967, and later embellished with elaborate overdubs. The album contains the unadorned Take 16, a stark-sounding track consisting of John's electric piano, mellotron and vocal, George's Stratocaster guitar, McCartney's Rickenbacker bass and Ringo's drums.

Paul's demo for *The Fool On The Hill* was recorded at Abbey Road on September 6, 1967. The track, featuring Paul's live vocal and piano, has a campy ending not present on the finished master.

The first session for *Your Mother Should Know* took place at Chappell Recording Studios on August 22 and 23, 1967. Paul was not satisfied with the results, so he ran the band through a remake of the song at Abbey Road on September 16. On this version, the sound and style of Ringo's snare drum is similar to that of a drummer in a military marching band. Paul's lead vocal is backed by harmonium and piano, the latter recorded to sound like a harpsichord. Paul didn't get the sound he was looking for, so this arrangement was not used. *Anthology* contains Take 27 from the remake session.

The Beatles first attempt at *The Fool On The Hill* took place on September 25, 1967. The backing track included acoustic guitar, Paul's piano and John and George on harmonicas. The third take was mixed down to a single track to allow the addition of Paul's lead vocal and recorder solo and Ringo's drums. This version, Take 4, is on *Anthology*. Its lyrics vary from the finished master, for which the group rerecorded many of the instruments.

The basic rhythm track for *Hello, Goodbye* was completed in 14 takes on October 2, 1967. It includes piano, organ, drums and numerous percussion instruments. Guitars and vocals were superimposed over the backing track on October 19. The album contains Take 16, which has subtle differences from the finished master.

The Beatles recorded *Lady Madonna* at Abbey Road on February 3 and 6, 1968, just before leaving for Rishikesh, India. *Anthology* contains a special remix of the song comprised of portions of Takes 3 and 4, along with saxophone overdubs. This stripped-down version of the song contains Paul's vocal before double-tracking, as well as Ringo's brush drumming prior to the addition of his stick drumming. There is also a unique saxophone solo in the middle eight. After the line "Listen to the music playing in your head," hand claps are followed by vocals imitating brass instruments. At the end of the song, there is a brief saxophone ad-lib.

The album closes with Take 2 of *Across The Universe*, which was recorded on February 4, 1968. It features a beautiful Lennon vocal, John and Paul on Martin D-28 acoustic guitars, George on tamboura and Ringo on swaramandal.

# THE BEATLES ANTHOLOGY 2 SAMPLER

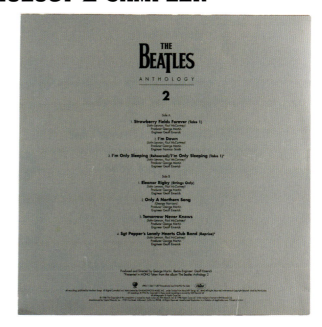

Although CD promotional samplers were prepared by Capitol for each volume of *Anthology*, only *Anthology 2* had a vinyl sampler (Apple SPRO-11206/11207). The promotional record was distributed on March 14, 1996, primarily to college radio stations. Side 1 contains *Strawberry Fields Forever*, *I'm Down* and *I'm Only Sleeping (Rehearsal)/I'm Only Sleeping (Take 1)*. Side 2 has *Eleanor Rigby (Strings Only)*, *Only A Northern Song*, *Tomorrow Never Knows* and *Sgt. Pepper's Lonely Hearts Club Band (Reprise)*. Its track selection is unique, with only three songs in common with the ten-song CD sampler. The vinyl sampler has more of a psychedelic and rock edge to it, foregoing melodic tunes such as *You've Got To Hide Your Love Away*, *Yesterday* and *I'm Looking Through You* found on the CD sampler. The inclusion of *Sgt. Pepper* was a last-minute substitute for *I Am The Walrus*. All mixes are identical to those on the album except *Only A Northern Song*, which is mixed with less stereo spread. The vinyl was reportedly limited to 3,500 units.

The record is packaged in a posterboard jacket, **APP 11206.SC1**. The front cover has a black and white *Revolver* era photo placed over a psychedelic silver paisley background. The picture was taken by Robert Whitaker at Abbey Road on May 19, 1966, the day the indoor footage for the *Paperback Writer* and *Rain* promotional videos were shot. The group is shown looking at color transparencies of Whitaker's photos taken at the infamous March 25, 1966, Somnambulant Adventure session that produced the picture for the Butcher cover. The cover's paisley background appears to have been lifted from John's shirt. The back cover has the track listings and other information over a silver background.

The 12" record, **APP 11206.DJ1**, has black background Apple label backdrops. The label copy includes the song titles, copyright and manufacturing information, a reference to the *Anthology 2* album and the Beatles logo. The disc was mastered by Wally Traugott at the Capitol Tower and pressed by Specialty.

# ANTHOLOGY 3

Side 1
1. A Beginning
2. Happiness Is A Warm Gun
3. Helter Skelter
4. Mean Mr. Mustard
5. Polythene Pam
6. Glass Onion
7. Junk
8. Piggies
9. Honey Pie
10. Don't Pass Me By
11. Ob-La-Di, Ob-La-Da
12. Good Night

Side 2
1. Cry Baby Cry
2. Blackbird
3. Sexy Sadie
4. While My Guitar Gently Weeps
5. Hey Jude
6. Not Guilty
7. Mother Nature's Son

Side 3
1. Glass Onion
2. Rocky Raccoon
3. What's The New Mary Jane
4. Step Inside Love/Los Paranoias
5. I'm So Tired
6. I Will
7. Why Don't We Do It In The Road
8. Julia

Side 4
1. I've Got A Feeling
2. She Came In Through The Bathroom Window
3. Dig A Pony
4. Two Of Us
5. For You Blue
6. Teddy Boy
7. Medley: Rip It Up/Shake, Rattle And Roll/Blue Suede Shoes

Side 5
1. The Long And Winding Road
2. Oh! Darling
3. All Things Must Pass
4. Mailman, Bring Me No More Blues
5. Get Back
6. Old Brown Shoe
7. Octopus's Garden
8. Maxwell's Silver Hammer

Side 6
1. Something
2. Come Together
3. Come And Get It
4. Ain't She Sweet
5. Because
6. Let It Be
7. I Me Mine
8. The End

Sides one, two and three have the same tracks as compact disc one. Sides four, five and six have the same tracks as compact disc two.

---

*Anthology 3* was released on CD and cassette on October 29, 1996, with a three-record vinyl set appearing in stores two weeks later on November 12. As was the case with the first two installments in the series, the album debuted at number one on November 16. The next week it dropped to number five while *The Don Killumineti - The 7 Day Theory* by Makaveli (2 PAC) (Death Row 90039) topped the chart. The album remained on the charts for 16 weeks. Capitol reported first day sales of 100,000 copies. SoundScan monitored first week sales of 238,000. On February 21, 1997, the RIAA certified sales of 3,000,000 (equating to sales of 1,500,000 copies of the double CD and cassette). In England, the album debuted at number four and peaked at two.

The vinyl discs were mastered at the Capitol Tower by Kevin Reeves. Capitol reportedly ordered a press run of 40,000 record albums from Specialty. The discs have black background Apple label backdrops.

Unlike the prior two albums, *Anthology 3* does not open with a "new" Beatles song. Although Paul, George and Ringo had worked on a few additional tracks, none was satisfactorily completed. Instead, the album appropriately starts with an instrumental track titled *A Beginning*. The tune, written and scored by George Martin, was recorded at, and using the same musicians as, the orchestral overdub session for *Good Night* held on July 22, 1968. The 48-second passage was conceived as a possible introduction to Ringo's *Don't Pass Me By*.

The first Beatles song on the album is the Esher demo version of John's *Happiness Is A Warm Gun*. The song,

along with over two dozen others, was recorded at George's home in Esher in May, 1968, prior to the group entering the studio to record their next LP. This demo is discussed in the chapter on *The White Album*.

The mood shifts drastically for the next track, a loud raucous version of *Helter Skelter* recorded on July 18, 1968. This is a 4:30 mono edit of Take 12, which ran over 12 minutes. The song moves along at a slower pace than the finished master, which was recorded as a remake on September 9.

The next six selections are additional Esher demos: *Mean Mr. Mustard, Polythene Pam, Glass Onion, Junk, Piggies* and *Honey Pie*. The first two songs were not recorded during the sessions for *The White Album*, but rather became part of the *Abbey Road* medley. These demos are discussed in the *Abbey Road* chapter. *Junk* is a Paul McCartney tune that was also passed over. Instead, Paul recorded the song for his first album, *McCartney*. The demo shows that although the basic acoustic guitar arrangement was in place, Paul had yet to complete the lyrics. The remaining three songs were recorded for *The White Album*. These demos are discussed in that chapter.

The next seven tracks are variations of songs appearing on *The White Album*: a stark version of *Don't Pass Me By* highlighted by vocal ad-libs from Ringo not present on the finished master; the rejected reggae version of *Ob-La-Di, Ob-La-Da*; a charming rehearsal of *Good Night* with Ringo backed by John on piano and George on percussion, which is crossfaded into the finished master's orchestral

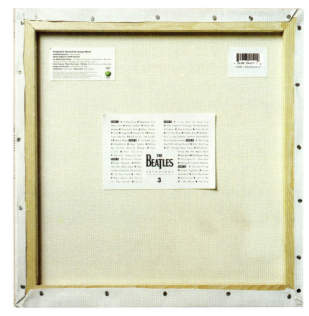

ending; Take 1 of *Cry Baby Cry*, highlighted by John's guide vocal and acoustic guitar; Take 4 of *Blackbird*, featuring Paul's solo vocal and acoustic guitar; Take 6 of *Sexy Sadie*, which has a totally different feel than the finished master recorded one month later at a faster tempo and with different instruments; and a beautiful unplugged version of *While My Guitar Gently Weeps*. The latter recording is one of the highlights of the album, featuring George on acoustic guitar and vocal, with Paul adding harmonium towards the end. This acoustic version of the song has a verse with lyrics differing from the Kinfauns demo and the finished master.

Prior to recording the master take for *Hey Jude* on July 31, 1968, on Trident Studios' eight-track machine, the Beatles performed live rehearsals of the song at Abbey Road on July 29 and 30. *Anthology* contains a slightly edited version of one of the rehearsal takes from the first evening featuring Paul on piano and vocal, John on acoustic guitar, George on electric guitar and Ringo on drums. Prior to the start of the song, John announces, "From the heart of Black Country" (England's industrial region). Paul then breaks into an improvised tune singing "When I was a robber, in Boston place, you gathered 'round me, with your fond embrace." During the extending ending of *Hey Jude*, George can be heard playing lead guitar in the background.

*Not Guilty* was written by George in response to the grief he was getting from John and Paul over the Beatles recent involvement with the Maharishi Mahesh Yogi. In an interview with Timothy White for *Musician* magazine, George explained, "I said I wasn't guilty of leading them astray in our all going to Rishikesh to see the Maharishi." The song also appears to be a commentary on George's desire to have his songs placed on Beatles albums. Harrison sings "Not guilty of getting in your way, while you're trying to steal the day" and "I only want what I can get." It also has a clever pun with "I won't upset the apple cart."

The song was written shortly after George's return from India and was recorded in demo form at Kinfauns in late May, 1968. On August 7, the Beatles went through 46 attempts to record a successful backing track with George on his Les Paul guitar, John on electric piano, Paul on Rickenbacker bass and Ringo on drums. Of the 46 takes, only five were complete. The next evening the group ran through Takes 47 through 101, this time with John on harpsichord. Take 99 was judged the best and was given a reduction mix (designated Take 102) the following night to allow for overdubs, which included additional drums by Ringo, bass by Paul and rhythm guitar by George. Harrison then recorded his solo played on his Les Paul through a Fender Twin-Reverb amplifier placed in an echo chamber, with the microphone located across the room to pick up the ambient sound. George sat in the control room and had his guitar chord run to the echo chamber. Harrison also recorded his lead vocal from the control room on August 12. Although the song was given a mono mix that evening, it was not mixed for stereo and was not selected for the album. In 1984, Geoff Emerick made a stereo mix of the song, which was slated to appear on the aborted *Sessions* album in 1985. George rerecorded *Not Guilty* for his 1979 album *George Harrison*.

Paul recorded *Mother Nature's Son* on the evening of August 9, 1968, after the other Beatles had gone home. *Anthology* contains Take 2, featuring Paul singing live over his Martin D-28 acoustic guitar.

This is followed by a bizarre mono mix of *Glass Onion* made by John on September 26, 1968, while George Martin was away on holiday. John mixed in special effects, including a ringing telephone, a sustained organ note, BBC soccer commentator Kenneth Wolstenholme shouting "It's a goal" over the sound of a roaring crowd and the sound of breaking glass. These effects were later deleted, and the song was embellished by George Martin's score of four violins, two violas and two cellos.

*Rocky Raccoon* was recorded on August 15, 1968, with Paul on vocal and acoustic guitar, John on harmonica and Fender Bass VI and Ringo on drums. *Anthology* contains Take 8, in which Paul flubs the lyrics, having the doctor "sminking" of gin. This causes him to laugh and ad-lib his way through the rest of the verse.

Although *What's The New Mary Jane* is credited to Lennon-McCartney, it was written by John with an assist from self-proclaimed electronic genius Alex Mardas, the madcap inventor who headed Apple Electronics. The song, like Magic Alex's inventions, doesn't work. Its "hook" consists of little more than John singing "What a shame Mary Jane had a pain at the party."

*What's The New Mary Jane* was recorded on August 14, 1968, in a session during which John and George were the only Beatles in the studio. Although the song sounds improvised, the Kinfauns demo shows that John had actually worked out its arrangement months in advance. Four backing tracks, featuring John on vocal and piano and George on his Gibson J-200 acoustic guitar, were recorded. Take 4, which rambled on for over six and one-half minutes, was deemed the best and embellished with a second vocal and piano part from John and more acoustic guitar from George. Also present in the studio were Mal Evans and Yoko, who each contributed vocals and percussion. Additional overdubs included harmonium, tin whistles, xylophone, handbells and piano strings being plucked and scraped. At the end of the tape, John says "Let's hear it, before we get taken away." The song was mixed for mono at the end of the session. A stereo mix was made on October 14, thus indicating that John wanted the track on *The White Album*. Fortunately, Paul and George Martin were able to convince John there wasn't space for the song on the LP.

In November, 1969, John decided that if the Beatles wouldn't release *What's The New Mary Jane* and *You Know My Name (Look Up The Number)*, he would put the songs out as a Plastic Ono Band single. On November 26, John, serving as co-producer with Geoff Emerick, remixed and edited the songs at Abbey Road. During the second stereo remix of Take 4 of *What's The New Mary Jane*, John and Yoko added more vocals and sound effects directly to the two-track stereo tape. This was designated Remix 5, which was later edited to form Remix 6.

Although Apple announced that the two songs would be released in England as APPLES 1002 on December 5,

One of the most visual *Anthology* promotional items is the stackable set of three 17" cubes (shown on page 279). Two of the side panels of the middle cube are shown above. The photo on the left was shot by Ethan Russell on August 22, 1969. The one on the right was taken by Bruce McBroom on April 9, 1969.

the single was put on hold and never issued. In 1984, Geoff Emerick made a new stereo mix of the song, with a running time of about six minutes, for the aborted *Sessions* album. Emerick's remix for *Anthology* is similar to his *Sessions* mix.

*Step Inside Love/Los Paranoias* is an edit of a pair of impromptu performances taped between takes of *I Will* on September 16, 1968. The session was produced by Chris Thomas and featured Paul on vocals and acoustic guitar, Ringo on maracas and cymbals and John on temple blocks. *Step Inside Love* was written by Paul to serve as the theme song for Cilla Black's BBC TV show, *Cilla*, which debuted on January 30, 1968. *Los Paranoias* is a jam with silly made-up-on-the-spot lyrics. The song is credited to all four Beatles even though Harrison did not attend the session.

*I'm So Tired* was recorded in 14 takes on October 8, 1968. *Anthology* contains an edit of Takes 3, 6 and 9.

*I Will* was recorded on September 16, 1968. Paul's first attempt at the song, Take 1, is included on *Anthology*.

Take 4 of *Why Don't We Do It In The Road* is a solo Paul McCartney performance from October 9, 1968. Paul, accompanied by his acoustic guitar, alternates between gentle and gritty vocals. Towards the end of the song, he changes the line "No one will be watching us" to "People will be watching us."

The first CD and side 3 each conclude with *Julia*, which was recorded in three takes on October 13, 1968, as the last new song for *The White Album*. Take 2 is a mostly instrumental runthrough with John on acoustic guitar that breaks down past the midway point.

The second CD and side 4 each open with a January 22, 1969, performance of *I've Got A Feeling* that breaks down just before the final verse when John realizes he's playing too loud. This spirited version of the song was selected by Glyn Johns for the *Get Back* album.

Although *She Came In Through The Bathroom Window* ended up on *Abbey Road*, Paul introduced the song to the group during the *Get Back* sessions held at Twickenham Film Studios. *Anthology* contains a rehearsal of the song most likely recorded in the makeshift Apple basement studio on January 21, 1969.

The *Anthology* version of John's *Dig A Pony* was recorded on January 22, 1969. At the conclusion of the song, Paul enthusiastically says "Ah, you see, you see, we improve with time, like a fine wine really." John knows the song still needs work and tells Paul "You're not talking to Ricky and the Red Streaks, you know." This is a reference to Paul's earlier suggestion that the Beatles go on the road to perform a series of impromptu concerts booked as Ricky and the Red Streaks.

Next up is a charming runthrough of *Two Of Us* recorded on January 24, 1969. After the first middle eight, Paul calls out "Take it Phil" to John. This reference to Phil Everly is an acknowledgment of the Everly Brothers' influence on the group's vocal harmony style.

George's upbeat *For You Blue* was recorded on January 25, 1969, with George on acoustic guitar, Paul on piano, Ringo on drums and John on a Hofner Hawaiian Standard lap-steel slide guitar. *Anthology* contains Take 1.

Although *Teddy Boy* was slated for the first *Get Back* album and was later mixed by Phil Spector for possible inclusion on the *Let It Be* LP, the song did not appear on a Beatles album until *Anthology*. The version included here is an edit of 1:15 from a January 28, 1969, runthrough followed by 2:00 from a January 24, 1969, rehearsal. The latter performance, complete with John's square dance calls, was selected by Glyn Johns for the *Get Back* album. Paul recorded the song for his first solo album, *McCartney*, which was released one month prior to the *Let It Be* LP.

During the Get Back sessions, the Beatles ran through numerous oldies. *Anthology* contains an exciting medley of three classics from the fifties. *Rip It Up*, written by Robert Blackwell and John Marascalco, was recorded by Little Richard in 1956 and released on Specialty 579. The song entered the *Billboard* pop charts on July 7, 1956, peaking at number 17 on the *Best Sellers in Stores* chart during its 18 week run. It topped the *Billboard R&B Best Sellers in Stores* chart for two weeks. John later recorded the song as part of a medley with the single's flip side, *Ready Teddy*, for his *Rock 'N' Roll* album (Apple SK 3419). *Shake, Rattle And Roll*, written by Charles Calhoun, was recorded by Joe Turner in 1954 and released on Atlantic 1026. It topped the *Billboard Most Played in Juke Boxes* R&B chart for three weeks. A cover version by Bill Haley and his Comets on Decca 29204 was a million seller number seven pop hit later that year. *Blue Suede Shoes* was written and recorded by Carl Perkins. When released on Sun 234 in early 1956, the song charted for 21 weeks on the *Billboard* pop charts, including four weeks at the number two spot on the *Most Played in Juke Boxes* chart. It also held down the number two spot for four weeks on the R&B *Most Played in Juke Boxes* chart and topped the Country & Western *Most Played in Juke Boxes* chart for three weeks. John's concert performance of the song was released on *The Plastic Ono Band–Live Peace In Toronto 1969* (Apple SW 3362).

The *Rip It Up/Shake, Rattle And Roll/Blue Suede Shoes* medley is an edit of two segments of the Beatles running through some oldies recorded on January 26, 1969. The lineup is the same one used for Paul's piano ballads: Paul on piano, George on electric guitar, John on the Fender Bass VI, Ringo on drums and Billy Preston on Hammond B-3 organ. Glyn Johns mixed these songs on March 13 and included them on an acetate. *Anthology* uses 1:13 of Johns' 2:05 recording of the first two songs edited to 1:55 of the 2:06 tape of *Blue Suede Shoes*.

The medley opens with John and Paul singing a few lines of *Rip It Up* a capella before being joined by the band for the chorus. During George's guitar solo, John and Paul begin singing lines from *Shake, Rattle And Roll*, causing the spirited rocker to mutate into the latter song. As the performance comes to an end, the medley continues with John singing the opening verse of *Blue Suede Shoes*. This is followed by a Harrison guitar solo, Paul joining John on the second verse and a Billy Preston organ solo. John then takes over the vocals and leads the song to its conclusion.

The version of *The Long And Winding Road* appearing on the *Let It Be* album and issued as the group's last American single is a heavily orchestrated Phil Spector production. *Anthology* contains the basic recording of the song from January 26, 1969, selected by Glyn Johns for his version of the *Get Back* LP and later embellished by Spector.

*Oh! Darling* is another song from the *Get Back* sessions that ended up on *Abbey Road*. The *Anthology* version is a 4:07 edit of a January 27, 1969, take featuring Paul on vocal and bass, John on vocal and guitar, George on guitar, Ringo on drums and Billy Preston on electric piano. When the song appears to come to an end, John announces that

Yoko's divorce has gone through and states "Free at last." As John sings "I'm free... this morning, Baby told the lawyer it's OK," the band falls back into the song.

George introduced *All Things Must Pass* to the *Get Back* sessions on January 2, 1969. The Beatles went through numerous runthroughs of the song the following day, most with George on lead vocal and electric guitar, John on Hammond B-3 organ, Paul on bass and Ringo on drums. Rehearsals for the song continued on January 6 and 8, with Paul and John working out harmony parts to sing on the chorus. Towards the end of the latter session, John switched from organ to piano. Although *All Things Must Pass* was given significant rehearsal time at Twickenham, the Beatles did not return to the song during the Apple basement sessions until January 28. On this and the following day, the band, with Billy Preston on organ, went through a couple of performances, none of which were recorded on the studio's eight-track. The first day runthroughs are notable for the extra vocals thrown in by John and Paul.

On February 25, 1969 (his 26th birthday), George recorded solo demos of three of his compositions, including *All Things Must Pass*. The *Anthology* LP contains this demo, which features George's vocal and doubled-tracked guitar.

*Mailman, Bring Me No More Blues*, written by Ruth Roberts, Bill Katz and Stanley Clayton, was recorded by Buddy Holly in 1957 and appeared as the B side to *Words Of Love* (Coral 61852). The group included *Words Of Love* on *Beatles For Sale*. During the *Get Back* sessions, John led the group through the flip side on January 29, 1969.

The Beatles final rooftop runthrough of *Get Back* was the last song the group played before an audience. *Anthology* contains this historic January 30, 1969, performance.

*Mailman, Bring Me No More Blues* was recorded by Buddy Holly and released on Coral 61852 in June 1957. Paul gave Cilla Black *Step Inside Love,* which was released in England on Parlophone R-5674 on March 8, 1968. Badfinger's recording of *Come And Get It* (Apple 1815) duplicated Paul McCartney's demo of the song.

*Old Brown Shoe* is another Harrison demo from February 25, 1969. George recorded his vocal and piano live and then overdubbed two guitar parts.

The Beatles went through 32 takes of *Octopus's Garden* on April 26, 1969, with Ringo on guide vocal and drums, John and George on guitar and Paul on bass. *Anthology* combines Take 2, a charming performance, with Ringo's comment from the end of Take 8, "Well that was superb."

The backing track to *Maxwell's Silver Hammer* was recorded on July 9, 1969, with Paul on piano and guide vocal, George on the Fender Bass VI and Ringo on drums. *Anthology* contains Take 5, which has Paul vocalizing the instrumental passages.

*Something* is the third demo from George's February 25, 1969, birthday solo session. It features George on vocal backed by his electric guitar and contains extra lyrics not present on the *Abbey Road* version of the song.

The backing track to *Come Together*, featuring an exciting John Lennon guide vocal, was recorded on July 21, 1969. *Anthology* contains Take 1, which is described in detail in this book's chapter on the single.

*Come And Get It* was written by Paul as the theme for the film *The Magic Christian. Anthology* contains Paul's demo, which was recorded on July 24, 1969. After singing and playing piano, McCartney overdubbed two vocal tracks, maracas, drums and bass guitar, all within an hour. He gave the demo to the Iveys, an Apple act that would soon change its name to Badfinger, with instructions to learn the song exactly as it appeared on the demo. On August 3, he produced Badfinger's recording of the song, which was issued in America on Apple 1815 on January 12, 1970. The song peaked at number seven in the *Billboard Hot 100* and was a number four hit in England.

*Ain't She Sweet* was first recorded by the Beatles in Hamburg, Germany, on June 22, 1961. More than eight years later, on July 24, 1969, the band revisited the song during a jam that featured it and two other songs recorded by Gene Vincent: *Be-Bop-A-Lula* and *Who Slapped John?*

John, Paul and George recorded their vocals for *Because* on August 1 and 4, 1969. After recording their three-part harmony on August 1, two more sets of three-part harmonies were overdubbed on the 4th. *Anthology* contains a new mix that isolates the vocals in all their splendor.

The version of *Let It Be* on *Anthology* is from January 25, 1969, and is detailed in the chapter on the single. It is followed by John's "let's track it" remark from the conclusion of January 31's Take 25.

*I Me Mine* was recorded by George, Paul and Ringo on January 3, 1970. It was the last song recorded by the band. The version appearing on the *Let It Be* LP was extended and embellished by Phil Spector. This is the 1:34 master that Glyn Johns included on his second *Get Back* album.

The final *Anthology* album ends appropriately with a new mix and edit of *The End*. The new mix restores guitar and tambourine parts that were recorded over Ringo's drum solo, but deleted from the final mix. It also has the dueling guitar solos and orchestra more to the front, and is extended with an edit of the final dramatic chord from *A Day In The Life*. In the words of Paul, it is "a suitable ending."

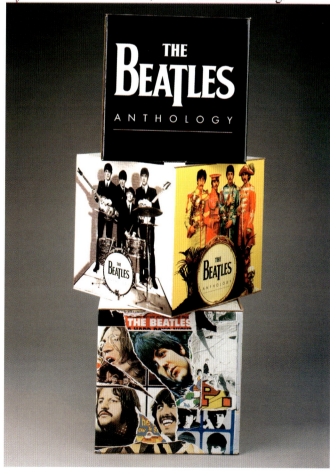

# FREE AS A BIRD (APPLE 58497)

*Free As A Bird* was released as a single in the CD and cassette formats on December 12, 1995. The vinyl 7" single was released one week later on December 19.

The song debuted in the *Billboard Hot 100* on December 30 at number ten and peaked at number six during its 11 weeks on the charts. SoundScan reported sales of 60,093 during its first week of release. The single was certified gold by the RIAA on July 8, 1996, indicating sales of over 500,000 units. In England, the single peaked at number two on the charts.

The CD, cassette and vinyl record contain a non-album song selected to tie-in with the holiday season release of the single. *Christmas Time (Is Here Again)* is a three minute track consisting of the first two minutes or so of the theme song recorded for the group's 1967 Christmas fan club record (see pages 214-215), season's greetings from each Beatle and nonsensical seasonal babbling from John over the sound of a Hammond organ and swirling wind.

The Maxi CD Single contains two additional tracks not found on the album. *I Saw Her Standing There* (Take 9) is

an energetic outtake from the February 11, 1963, *Please Please Me* album session. Paul's famous "One, two, three, faaa!" count-in from Take 9 was edited to the start of the released master. *This Boy* is represented by two incomplete attempts at the song, Takes 12 and 13, recorded on October 17, 1964, complete with studio banter.

The masters for the vinyl single, **APP 58497.01**, were cut by Kevin Reeves at the Capitol Tower. Capitol ordered 25,000 records, which were pressed by Specialty Records in Olyphant. Pennsylvania. The discs have a small spindle hole rather than the U.S. standard 1½" punch-out center hole to allow for the single's extensive label copy. The singles were pressed with creme-colored background Apple label backdrops. The picture sleeve, **APP 585497.PS1**, features a John Lennon drawing that previously appeared on the dedication page of Lennon's first book, *In His Own Write*. It is a caricature of Pete Shotton (a member of John's pre-Beatles band, The Quarry Men) surrounded by birds. The back of the sleeve has the same canvas back motif as the back covers to the albums. The sleeve is a side loader.

# REAL LOVE (APPLE 58544)

The *Real Love* single was scheduled for release in CD and cassette formats on February 5, 1996; however, like the *Anthology 2* album, its release was pushed back. Although the official release date was rescheduled for March 5, many stores put the single on sale as early as March 1. The vinyl 7" single was issued on March 12.

*Real Love* entered the *Billboard Hot 100* on March 23 at its peak position of 11. Although the song received limited airplay, it remained on the charts for seven weeks. SoundScan monitored sales of 67,000 copies during its first week. The single was certified gold by the RIAA on July 8, 1996, indicating sales of over 500,000 units. In England, the single debuted at number 4 on the sales-only chart. Airplay was a problem as BBC Radio One refused to play it.

All three formats include a track not included on *Anthology 2*. *Baby's In Black* was recorded live at band's August 30, 1965, Hollywood Bowl concert. John's humorous introduction to the "slow waltz" is from the previous night's show at the same venue. The song was not included on the 1977 album *The Beatles At The Hollywood Bowl*.

The Maxi CD Single contains two additional tracks not found on the album. *Yellow Submarine* is presented in a new and interesting mix made from the May 26 and June 1, 1966, sessions for the song. It begins with a previously unheard spoken introduction by Ringo. The mix contains more sound effects than the released version of the song. The CD closes with a newly created edit and mix of *Here, There And Everywhere*, which was recorded for the *Revolver* album on June 16, 1966. It begins with Take 7 (the backing track with Paul's guide vocal) and concludes with a remix of the backing harmonies superimposed onto Take 13.

The masters for the vinyl single, **APP 58544.01**, were cut by Kevin Reeves. Capitol ordered 50,000 records, which were pressed by Specialty. The singles have a small center hole and black background Apple label backdrops. The side-loader sleeve, **APP 58544.PS1**, features a late 1965 Robert Whitaker color photo of the boys on the front and the canvas back motif on the back. A special heart-shaped red apple logo appears on both sides, designed as a tie-in with the single's original Valentine's Day holiday season release date.

# ANTHOLOGY HISTORY

The *Anthology* albums evolved out of two separate projects: a video history of the Beatles, initially titled *The Long And Winding Road*, and a planned album of Beatles outtakes known as *Sessions*. In late 1969 or early 1970, Apple's managing director, Neil Aspinall, began compiling concert, interview and promotional footage for a documentary film on the Beatles. At the time, Apple was being managed by Allen Klein, and Aspinall no longer had the time consuming responsibility of running the company. The archiving of Beatles film and video gave Aspinall something productive to do. An article in *The New York Times* (February, 1970) reported that Apple would be releasing two new films, *Let It Be* and *The Long And Winding Road*. The latter project was Aspinall's documentary.

In a 1995 interview with Allan Kozinn appearing in *Beatlefan*, Aspinall revealed that his first rough cut of the film ran about one hour and 45 minutes. He sent copies of his work product to each of the Beatles. Although they reportedly liked the film, it was put on the shelf for nearly 20 years as many other things were going on.

As the eighties came to a close, Neil contacted Paul, George, Ringo and Yoko about the project. He suggested that the documentary be structured as a series of home videos rather than a theatrical release. He believed that visual documentaries did not work well in the theater and knew that the Beatles story could not be adequately told in a mere hour and a half.

Aspinall wanted interviews with John, Paul, George and Ringo to be a significant part of the documentary. He explained to Kozinn that he "didn't want a mid-Atlantic voice to tell their story" and "thought that they'd be much better at doing that themselves." He hired Nell Burley to begin researching and assembling footage and tapes on a worldwide basis. After she had organized everything, Aspinall line up Geoff Wonfer to direct and Chips Chipperfield to produce the videos.

The scope of the project then expanded rapidly. Someone suggested that the videos could be edited down and broadcast on television as a mini-series. From this followed the need for a soundtrack, so George Martin was brought in to direct and produce the *Anthology* albums. The extensive new interviews with Paul, George and Ringo, along with tapes of interviews of John, provided more dialog than could possibly be used in the video. It was only natural to combine the words with pictures from Apple's vast archive to produce a book.

The idea of releasing an official album of Beatles outtakes dates back to the aborted *Sessions* album. In 1984, EMI prepared an album consisting of 13 previously unreleased tracks: *Come And Get It, Leave My Kitten Alone, Not Guilty, I'm Looking Through You, What's The New Mary Jane?, How Do You Do It?, Besame Mucho, One After 909, If You've Got Trouble, That Means A Lot, While My Guitar Gently Weeps, Mailman Blues* and *Christmas Time (Is Here Again)*. The songs were remixed for the album by Geoff Emerick, who would a decade later remix the *Anthology* tracks. Capitol assigned number ST-12373 to the LP, which was scheduled for release on February 22, 1985. Capitol's Album Status report for January 3, 1985, indicates that the record was put on "Legal Hold." It was never issued.

The *Anthology* albums are more than a collection of EMI outtakes. *Anthology 1* contains demos, live recordings and songs from the 1961 Hamburg sessions and the 1962 Decca audition. To tie in with the video and help the listener get past some of the rough recordings, George Martin added bits of dialog to *Anthology 1*. The second album also has some live recordings, while the final installment is exclusively EMI outtakes. Some of the tracks are edited versions of outtakes.

ABC paid Apple 20 million dollars for the American broadcast rights for the *Anthology* mini-series. The program ran in three two-hour segments shown on November 19, 22 and 23, 1995. The first night of the program ended with the world premiere of *Free As A Bird*. ABC began running promotional spots for *Anthology*, which it dubbed "the television event of a lifetime," eight weeks in advance. In a move reminiscent of radio stations during the height of Beatlemania, the network began calling itself "A-Beatles-C."

Although the *Anthology* mini-series had good ratings, the numbers were much less than ABC had hoped for. The first night drew the largest audience. Nielsen reported a 26% share of the viewing audience and a 17.4 rating. ABC equated this to 47 million viewers. The television network estimated that 22.4 million people watched the entire mini-series and that 60 million people watched at least part of the program. While these numbers are respectable, they pale in comparison to the 73 million people who watched the Beatles on their first *Ed Sullivan* appearance.

In the end, *Anthology* evolved into much more than its original concept of a theatrical documentary. George Harrison described it best. "It is both a record, a video, a television program, a book and, no doubt, somewhere down the line it will also be a T-shirt."

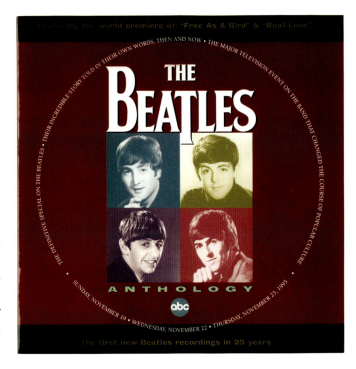

# ANTHOLOGY PACKAGING

Apple was impressed with the art work done by Rick Ward and The Team for *Live At The BBC*. When it came time to start planning the packaging for *Anthology*, Apple hired Ward to serve as the project's art director.

Several artists were considered for *Anthology*, including Peter Blake, who designed the cover for *Sgt. Pepper*. Blake turned down the work because of prior commitments.

Klaus Voormann, the artist for the group's *Revolver* cover, was contacted by Apple managing director Neil Aspinall in June, 1995. Aspinall told him that at this stage Apple was kicking around ideas with seven other artists and had yet to commit to an individual or a particular concept. Apple was looking for a design that represented the entire career of the band, from 1960 through 1970.

In a 1996 interview with Matt Hurwitz, Voormann confessed that he didn't think he would get the job. He sketched out a few ideas, which he faxed to Apple. One early sketch showed images of the band members coming together in a braid and then separating into four individuals. It was an interesting idea, but not exactly what Apple had in mind.

By July, Klaus came up with a concept that appealed to Apple. His idea was to depict images of the group in a manner simulating torn handbills posted on a brick wall. He presented his sketches at a meeting with Aspinall, Derek Taylor, Rick Ward and David Saltz, who represented ABC. They liked what they saw, and Klaus was given the go ahead.

Voormann was instructed to develop art for three covers, with each featuring images from the time period covered by the album. His initial idea was to do the covers in a layered approach, with each successive cover adding more posters on

top of the posters shown on the previous cover. This concept proved unworkable, particularly when Apple added that the art work would need to be divided not only in three parts for the albums, but also in eight pieces for the eight-part video. The layered approach was scrapped in favor of a long rectangle that could be more easily divided.

Aspinall asked Klaus to complete his design at Apple, where he would have access to the images of the band in the company's vast archives and be able to get immediate feedback from Aspinall. On September 6, 1995, Voormann arrived at Apple. Two days later, his layout was complete.

Voormann's work consisted of drawings and photocopies assembled on a rectangular poster board. Although Ward liked the design, he wanted the artwork painted. This would fit in with his concept of having the back covers of each album appear to be the back of a canvas painting wrapped around and tacked onto a wooden frame. Aspinall, concerned about time, was against the idea, but eventually was convinced by Ward and Voormann that a painting would be special.

Voormann told Aspinall that he could not complete the work in time by himself. He recruited fellow German artist Alfons Kiefer. Voormann then returned to Germany with his posterboard mock-up. The pair worked at Kiefer's Munich studio, using water-based, water-resistant paints.

In order to give the viewer a clear perception of the scale of the posters painted on the covers, they added bricks to the background. The complete painting (see page 245) shows more of the wall and adds a fire hydrant and bicycle.

The cover has some mischievous touches. *Anthology 1* features the album cover of an unauthorized collection of 1961 German recordings titled *The Savage Young Beatles*. The part of that cover with Pete Best is torn away, exposing Ringo's face from the *Please Please Me* album cover.

The artists managed to sneak themselves into their work. The cover to *Anthology 2* shows slivers of the *Sgt. Pepper* and *Revolver* covers. Alfons Kiefer's head appears as a face in the *Sgt. Pepper* crowd next to the actor Tom Mix (who is wearing a cowboy hat). Klaus appears through the courtesy of his self-portrait on the *Revolver* cover. A larger section of the *Revolver* cover is shown on *Anthology 3*, but this time Voormann's 1966 portrait is replaced with a current image of the aging artist.

The *Anthology* vinyl albums were packaged in attractive triple gatefold covers (shown on pages 263, 269 and 275). The covers contain Derek Taylor's liner notes and Mark Lewisohn's track descriptions from the CD booklets, as well as many of the photographs from the booklets. *Anthology 2* came with a 5" x 1⅛" magenta sticker affixed to the shrinkwrap. *Anthology 3* had a 4" x 1" yellow sticker.

# THE LAUNCH OF THE BEATLES ANTHOLOGY PROJECT

Capitol Records recognized the tremendous potential of *Anthology*. In the summer of 1995, the company educated its sales representatives about the project with an elaborate 35-page spiral-bound booklet containing its marketing report. The cover (shown below) identifies the booklet as a "Confidential Internal Document" and features an image of the back of a canvas painting showing a wooden inner frame and the Beatles *Anthology* logo. This basic design would later appear on the back of the *Anthology* albums and CDs. *Anthology* is described as "The Biggest Thing Since The Beatles..."

The booklet contains 20 numbered pages of text and 15 pages with pictures, including five in full color. The splash pages to each of the 14 sections in the booklet are preceded by a clear plastic sheet.

Section I describes *Anthology*'s mission statement. "The Beatles' Anthology is the most important event in modern musical history. The unprecedented synergies created by prime time network broadcast, previously unreleased albums, artist merchandise and a multi-volume home video release, will allow Capitol to assemble the most significant

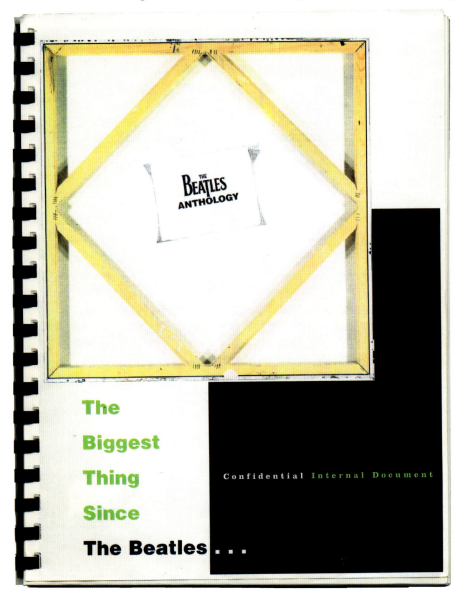

marketing and promotional team, who will initiate an innovative, year long multimedia campaign to rival anything ever put together in the entertainment industry."

Section II gives an overview of *Anthology*, which is described as "The definitive story of The Beatles by The Beatles told in three distinct ways." A separate paragraph is devoted to the ABC television miniseries, the three double CDs of previously unreleased recordings and the home videos. The overview concludes with a description of the game plan. "Every aspect of this release will work in tandem with the other and every window of opportunity will be leveraged against the next to create a cohesive campaign. For the next year, plan on Capitol to pull out all the stops, throw away the rule book and push every marketing button available to us."

To paraphrase the booklet's cover, Capitol viewed the Beatles *Anthology* Campaign as the biggest thing since its Beatles Campaign promoting the label's initial Beatles releases in the winter of 1963-1964. For details regarding the company's first marketing plan for the Beatles, see "The Beatles Campaign" chapter in the author's book *The Beatles' Story on Capitol Records, Part One: Beatlemania & The Singles*.

Section III of Capitol's booklet contains the project's projected release timetable, broken into five phases. Under Phase I, Capitol and ABC were set to begin their teaser/set up campaign in August, 1995. September is listed as the time "Formal publicity and marketing launch begins." This leads up to the November 19 airing of the first two hours of the ABC miniseries, featuring the debut of *Free As A Bird*, followed by subsequent two-hour broadcasts on November 22 and 23. The street date for the *Anthology 1* double CD is listed as November 20, with the *Free As A Bird* single set for December 4 release. Due to ABC's inflexible broadcast schedule, Apple and Capitol more or less stuck to the plan, with the double CD coming out one day later and the single one week later.

Phase II heralded the release of the *Real Love* single on January 22, 1996, with *Anthology 2* set for February 6. These dates were pushed back to March 5 and 19. Phase III optimistically listed Spring, 1996, as the street date for *Anthology 3;* however, it was not released until October 29, 1996. Phase III also listed Spring, 1996, as the release date for the *Anthology* video, which was not issued until September 6, 1996.

Phase IV stated that "The Beatles Anthology coffee table book from Apple" would be issued during the summer of 1996. This date proved to be a mirage as the book's release was pushed back several times before finally being published in October, 2000, a delay of over four years. This prompted American late night TV host Jay Leno to joke that Ringo was a slow typist.

Phase V called for the release of a special, unique home video box set in Fall, 1996. This idea was abandoned and the eight video tapes were released in a simple cardboard slipcase.

The booklet's release schedule also mentions an audio box set described as "a unique and special box set featuring: 6 single CDs, or 6 single LPs, or 6 single cassettes, with hard back book and special inserts." The box set was cancelled when it became obvious that by the time the *Anthology* book was ready, all serious Beatles fans would already have purchased all of the *Anthology* music. The release timetable also listed 26 hours of Beatles *Anthology* radio shows as "To Be Scheduled." The radio shows were also scrubbed.

Capitol hired Strategic Record Research to survey 10,000 people about the Beatles. The highlights of the research demonstrate the overpowering demand and recognition for the group: 78% of the United States is familiar with the music of the Beatles, the highest rating of any artist ever researched; familiarity is greatest among males and females in their thirties and forties; the Beatles strongest sales regions are the mid-Atlantic and the Pacific, heavily weighted to large cities; 90% of radio listeners know the Beatles music; and, the Beatles are the favorite artist of all time among VH-1 viewers and second among MTV viewers.

The booklet stated that the *Anthology* packaging objective was "to create a timeless and classic presentation of the highest possible quality, reflecting the essence of The Beatles for a global audience of music lovers." The publicity objective was "to wage a global publicity campaign prior to the launch of the first release through Christmas '96, targeting both hard core Beatles fans and all mainstream music consumers" as well as "to position The Beatles as a vital and credible band with today's rock and alternate music consumer." The promotion objective was "to create multi-format exposure of The Beatles culminating in a major hit single and video, and to create awareness of the Anthology and all Beatles product via major promotions that target The Beatles consumer."

Under the "Sales & Distribution" section, key account presentation was set to begin on August 14, 1995, with full-blown solicitation starting on October 16. October 24 was listed as the reissue date for the Beatles 13 core albums on vinyl in limited quantities "sure to become prized collectibles." The schedule indicates that *Live At The BBC* would be deleted from the Capitol catalog on October 30, 1995. How this was supposed to enhance the *Anthology* Campaign is not explained and remains a mystery. *Live At The BBC* was added back to the catalog in the summer of 2001. The booklet highlighted the unique overnight delivery of *Anthology 1* to stores set for November 20. This was implemented to prevent stores from selling the CDs prior to the official release date.

The book also details merchandising plans, including elaborate point of purchase displays, and advertising campaigns. It concludes by emphasizing the importance of the Beatles. "Capitol/EMI has an unprecedented opportunity to create the musical event of the century. All of our resources are geared to synergize the record release, network broadcast, and home video release to promote The Beatles' Anthology as both a celebration and a look behind the scenes at the genius that made up The Beatles. This is just the start of a campaign that will keep The Beatles' music and legacy in the minds of the consumer for the *next* 30 years."

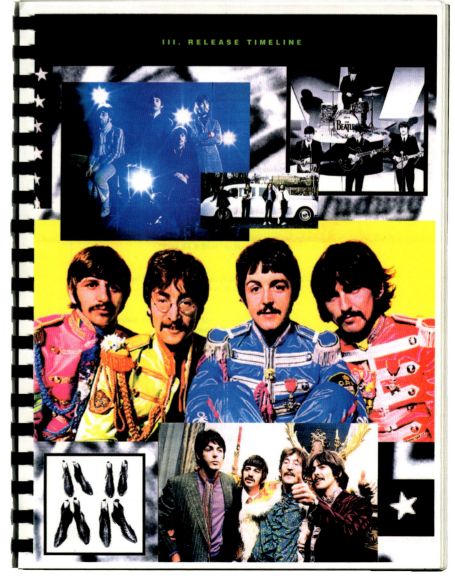

# THE ANTHOLOGY HOME VIDEO

Capitol and Turner Home Entertainment created an attractive promotional box for the Anthology home video containing a loose leaf binder of informational material and a sneak preview VHS tape. The binder and tape are housed in a colorful 12½" x 12½" x 3½" flip top box designed to look like a stack of Beatles albums with the front cover to *Meet The Beatles!* on top and the back cover to *Let It Be* on the bottom. Although Apple forced Capitol to delete its uniquely configured albums from its catalog in the late eighties, nearly all of the cover spines depicted on the left side of the box are Capitol albums from the sixties. The entire package came in a brown box containing a black and white sticker stating "Open Immediately/The Beatles' Anthology/ Sneak Preview."

The complete package was sent to video and record stores for promotional purposes. When the video box set went on sale, some stores received extra copies of the flip top box (without the binder or sample VHS tape) to give to customers. The Beatles *Anthology* video was released on VHS tape and Laserdisc on September 6, 1996.

## YELLOW SUBMARINE SONGTRACK
## APPLE UK 21481

Side 1
1. Yellow Submarine
2. Hey Bulldog
3. Eleanor Rigby
4. Love You To
5. All Together Now
6. Lucy In The Sky With Diamonds
7. Think For Yourself
8. Sgt. Pepper's Lonely Hearts Club Band
9. With A Little Help From My Friends

Side 2
1. Baby You're A Rich Man
2. Only A Northern Song
3. All You Need Is Love
4. When I'm Sixty Four
5. Nowhere Man
6. It's All Too Much

Released simultaneously with the video reissue of the *Yellow Submarine* cartoon on September 14, 1999, *Yellow Submarine Songtrack* contains the six Beatles songs from 1969's soundtrack LP plus nine more songs featured in the film. The album is an excellent collection of songs beginning with the October, 1965, *Rubber Soul* sessions through the recording of the last song for the film on February 11, 1968, just before the Beatles left for India. The album's most striking feature is the sound quality of the songs, all of which were given new stereo mixes using technology unavailable when the songs were recorded over 30 years earlier.

*Yellow Submarine Songtrack* entered the *Billboard* album chart on October 2 at number 15, its peak position, during its 15 weeks on the charts. SoundScan reported first-week sales of 67,939 copies. On November 2, 1999, the RIAA certified the album gold, indicating sales of 500,000.

Capitol released the album in the CD and cassette formats, but chose neither to manufacture nor to import vinyl records. Beatle fans and collectors in America were left to seek out imported copies of the British album.

The *Yellow Submarine Songtrack* album was an outgrowth of the re-release of the cartoon. The story begins in 1995 when Bruce Markoe, vice-president with MGM-UA, sought a video copy of the cartoon movie to show his five-year-old daughter. The home video had been deleted from the catalog since 1987; however, Markoe was able to rent a laserdisc copy. After seeing the cartoon, he was disappointed in how the film looked and sounded. Markoe wanted to "renovate" the film by "improving it while remaining true to the integrity of the original piece."

When he inquired into whether MGM-UA still had the video rights to the film, Markoe learned that his company was involved in a legal dispute with Apple over the rights. He convinced United Artists president John Calley that the film should be re-released, and Calley instructed his business affairs department to settle the litigation. Once the companies settled their differences, he pitched his renovation project to MGM-UA and Apple.

In a *Goldmine* interview with Mark Wallgren, Markoe explained that he had an extensive background in sound and knew "there was so much more we could do with the sound in this movie using today's technology and what audiences were accustomed to, with six-track sound in movie theaters and on DVD." He got Apple to agree to the remastering of the songs used in the film "with the caveat that if Apple didn't like it or if the Beatles didn't like it, nobody would ever hear it."

Fortunately for Beatles fans, Apple and the Beatles liked what they heard. According to Markoe, "once Apple and everybody realized the importance of the remixing and remastering of the songs, and once that was heard in terms of the quality of the new mixes, I think Apple and Capitol said, 'Let's do this *Songtrack*.'"

The job of preparing the 5.1 surround mixes of the songs for the film was turned over to EMI engineer Peter Cobbin, who was experienced in pop and orchestral music as well as 5.1 surround mixing. Cobbin, assisted by Paul Hicks and Mirek Stiles and project coordinator Allan Rouse, began mixing the songs at Abbey Road in 1997.

All of the songs used in the film were originally recorded on four-track tape. In many cases, instruments and/or vocals were recorded onto separate tracks and then given a reduction mix onto one track, thus leaving up to three open tracks for overdubs. Once a reduction mix had been made, there was no way to separate the instruments and vocals that had been mixed together and transferred onto one track when making the final mix of the song.

For example, when the backing instrumental track for *Eleanor Rigby* was recorded on April 28, 1966, the eight string instruments (four violins, two violas and two cellos) were recorded with a pair of instruments allocated to each of the four tracks. It took 14 takes to get a satisfactory backing track. At the end of the session, a reduction mix of the four tracks of Take 14 was made to one track to allow for the recording of the vocals over the three remaining tracks. This mix was designated Take 15 and was embellished with vocal overdubs recorded over the empty tracks the following evening and on June 6. When the song was later mixed for stereo, George Martin could not spread the various string instruments separately between the left and right stereo tracks. His mix was limited to spreading the string instruments as a block along with the separate vocal tracks.

For *Anthology*, George Martin and Geoff Emerick went back to Take 14 (before the reduction mix) and created a new "strings only" stereo mix from the four tracks. Peter Cobbin, using the latest in recording technology, took the process a step further. He transferred the four instrumental tracks from Take 14, along with the three separate vocal tracks from Take 15, to multitrack tape. All seven tracks were then synchronized. This enabled Cobbin to draw from all seven tracks when creating his new mixes. Thus, each pair of instruments could be placed separately in the mix.

In some cases, separate instruments were recorded on the same track in different parts of a song. For example, a single track might have vocals at the beginning, a guitar solo in the middle eight and piano towards the end. Cobbin had the separate instruments split off and put on separate tracks to give him greater control over the mix.

Bruce Markoe attended the initial 5.1 mixing sessions for the film. During Markoe's week at Abbey Road, Cobbin completed four songs. After spending a month completing the 5.1 mixes, Cobbin did fresh stereo mixes for the album.

The results of Cobbin's efforts are stunning. *The New York Times*' Allan Kozinn commented that "Many of Mr. Cobbin's remixes have a revelatory freshness that even Beatles purists may find surprising."

The album's opening track, *Yellow Submarine*, demonstrates the care and thoroughness put into the remixes. Staying true to the original stereo mix, the acoustic guitar in the song's introduction is first heard over the word "town" rather than from the very beginning as in the mono mix. However, the tight placement of John's response vocals towards the end of the song duplicates the mono version. According to Cobbin, he normally went with elements from the more familiar stereo mixes, but his reference point, if there was a question or if he thought there was a mistake, was the mono mix. Cobbin's remix brings the background effects and vocals more to the front, thus enhancing the party atmosphere.

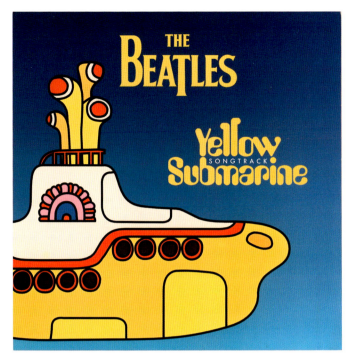
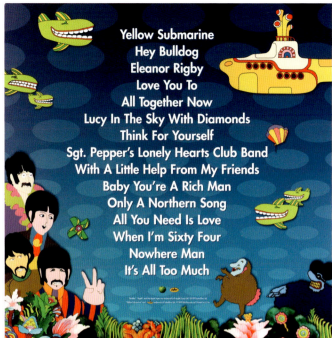

**Capitol prepared 12" x 12" promotional flats featuring the front cover on one side and colorful images from the film and the song titles on the other side.**

On the original *Yellow Submarine* album, *Hey Bulldog* has a muddy-sounding mix, perhaps intended to give the song a heavy metal edge. The remix cleans things up, allowing the listener to appreciate John's hard driving piano and Paul's innovative bass riff. John's voice and the vocal shenanigans are also brought more to the front.

*Eleanor Rigby* benefits from the stereo separation given to the strings and vocals. *Love You To* has the Indian instruments featured more prominently than in the original mono and stereo mixes. *All Together Now* adds more punch to the acoustic guitars and reveals additional percussion barely audible on the earlier mixes. *Lucy In The Sky With Diamonds* is highlighted by enhancements to John's vocal and Ringo's drumming. Paul's fuzz bass on *Think For Yourself* pounds through the remix with a new sharpness.

The remixes of *Sgt. Pepper's Lonely Hearts Club Band* and *With A Little Help From My Friends* give an added presence to the guitars and lead vocals. *Baby You're A Rich Man* follows the mono mix by having the piano more in the background. *Only A Northern Song* appears in true stereo for the first time. The orchestral ending on *All You Need Is Love* is clearer than on prior mixes. The remix on *When I'm Sixty Four* brings added clarity to the clarinets.

On the stereo mix from the British *Rubber Soul* LP, the vocals to *Nowhere Man* are isolated on one channel. The remix effectively spreads the harmonies throughout the mix.

The album concludes with George's *It's All Too Much*. The odd array of instruments used by the Beatles on the song sound different than on the original 1969 album, making the song even more of a psychedelic listening experience than before. Unfortunately the remix has the same edit as the previously released version rather than the still unreleased full take of the song.

The British album has a blue background continuous gatefold cover, **UKAPP 5214811.SC1**, which was designed by Fiona Andreanelli. The outside front panel shows the

periscope and front sections of the submarine, beginning in the lower left corner with the periscope running nearly to the top. A yellow Beatles logo is centered towards the top. The *Yellow Submarine* logo appears above the front hull of the submarine, with "SONGTRACK" sandwiched between "Yellow" and "Submarine" in thin white letters. The back panel shows the tail section of the submarine with its rudder and propeller. The song titles are listed on the left side running from the top to about two-thirds down. The side numbers and song numbers are white, and the song titles are yellow. All are in the same font as the *Yellow Submarine* logo. Credits, as well as copyright information, run along the bottom left side in small white print. The inside gatefold is a colorful drawing full of images from the film along with the song titles in the *Yellow Submarine* font.

Many of the covers have a 1⅜" yellow background sticker adhered directly to the upper left corner of the front panel. The sticker reads "Yellow Submarine feature film available on Video & DVD" in blue letters.

First issues of the album were pressed in yellow vinyl, **UKAPP 5214811.SR1**, at EMI's pressing plant in Hayes, Middlesex, England. The labels to both sides have the front cover image. The album's side number is in white below the album title. The song titles do not appear on the labels. Later issues are black vinyl, **UKAPP 5214811.SR2**.

Paul McCartney was very pleased with the album, stating "it's great you can buy all the songs that were in the movie on this one new songtrack album." Perhaps still sensitive to criticism that the original *Yellow Submarine* LP contained only six Beatles songs, Paul further commented that the Beatles "always try to give people good value for money...and pack the albums with good stuff so you don't feel cheated." *Yellow Submarine Songtrack* certainly gave listeners good value for their money and demonstrated how much better the Beatles catalog will sound when it is eventually remixed and remastered using the latest technology.

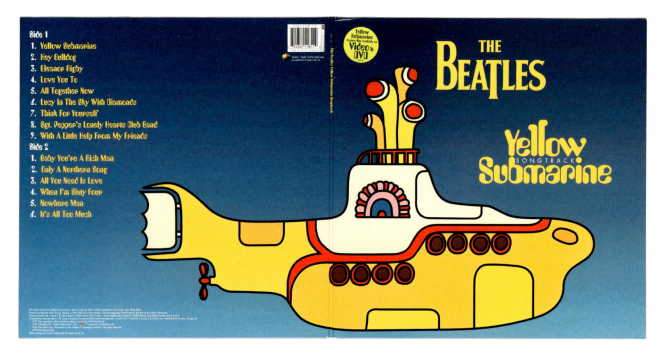

Side 1
1. Yellow Submarine
2. Hey Bulldog
3. Eleanor Rigby
4. Love You To
5. All Together Now
6. Lucy In The Sky With Diamonds
7. Think For Yourself
8. Sgt. Pepper's Lonely Hearts Club Band
9. With A Little Help From My Friends
Side 2
1. Baby You're A Rich Man
2. Only A Northern Song
3. All You Need Is Love
4. When I'm Sixty Four
5. Nowhere Man
6. It's All Too Much

## BEATLES 1
## APPLE UK 29325

In the spring of 2000, Apple announced that it would be issuing a brand new Beatles collection containing all of the group's number one hits in England and the United States. Many Beatles fans, collectors and scholars treated the news with emotions ranging from ho-hum boredom to contempt for what was viewed as an excuse for Apple to make fans re-buy old recordings.

What truas the point? All of the songs were available on the red and blue collections. And by limiting the selections to number one hits, many of the Beatles best recordings would not be on the disc. There would be no songs from three of the group's best albums: *Rubber Soul*, *Sgt. Pepper* and *The White Album*. And, because the song credited with starting Beatlemania in England failed to reach the top spot

in *Record Retailer* (the U.K. benchmark for the project) or *Billboard* (the U.S. standard), *Please Please Me* would not be included. Even worse, no *Strawberry Fields Forever*. Just what was Apple thinking?

And hadn't this been done before nearly 20 years earlier? In 1982, Capitol put out a collection of the 20 U.S. number one *Billboard* hits titled *20 Greatest Hits*. That album barely got to number 50 on the charts. Why would it be any different this time around? Oh sure, collectors would buy the disc to keep their collections complete, but who else would want this album?

When *Beatles 1* was released in America on November 14, 2000, the answer quickly became apparent. Everyone wanted the album.

Side 1
1 Love me do
2 From me to you
3 She loves you
4 I want to hold your hand
5 Can't buy me love
6 A hard day's night
7 I feel fine
8 Eight days a week

Side 2
1 Ticket to ride
2 Help!
3 Yesterday
4 Day tripper
5 We can work it out
6 Paperback writer
7 Yellow submarine
8 Eleanor Rigby

Side 3
1 Penny Lane
2 All you need is love
3 Hello, goodbye
4 Lady Madonna
5 Hey Jude

Side 4
1 Get Back
2 The ballad of John and Yoko
3 Something
4 Come together
5 Let it be
6 The long and winding road

All songs composed by
Lennon/McCartney except
Side 4 track 3 by Harrison

*Beatles 1* debuted at number one in *The Billboard 200* album chart cover-dated December 2, 2000, based upon SoundScan-reported first week sales of 594,666 units. Although sales increased to 662,077 the following week, the album dropped to number two behind the Backstreet Boys' *Black & Blue*. It remained in the second spot for another week with sales of 606,809. The Beatles album then reclaimed the top spot on the December 23 chart (by selling 670,673 copies) and remained number one for an additional six weeks (before being replaced by Jennifer Lopez's *J.Lo*). During the week before Christmas, *Beatles 1* proved to be the ideal last-minute present, selling 1,258,670 copies.

The album's performance led to a quick multi-platinum certification by the RIAA. On December 15, 2000, the RIAA certified sales of five million. An additional two million sales were certified on February 2, 2001. As of December 19, 2001, the RIAA certified sales of eight million.

*Billboard* named *Beatles 1* its Album of the Year for 2001. The disc was also the year's Top Internet Album. In addition, *Billboard* named the Beatles the number one group for 2001, as well as number one album artists and top internet artists. As of November 2, 2002, *Beatles 1* was in its 101st week on the charts.

In England, *Beatles 1* sold over 59,000 copies its first day of release (November 13) and debuted on the album chart at number one. It held the top spot for nine straight weeks.

It was the same throughout much of the world. *Beatles 1* reached the number one spot in 34 countries. Capitol reported that the album had sold over 23 million copies worldwide in its first two months.

The magnitude of the album's success caught everyone off-guard. Magazines, newspapers and television all jumped on the story and searched for explanations of why *Beatles 1* was selling to people of all ages. Most missed the point, focusing on how the Beatles had affected our culture and influenced musicians in styles of music ranging from rap to rock to heavy metal to folk to country.

The answer to the album's success was much simpler – price, and, most important of all, the quality of the music.

Prior to the release of *Beatles 1*, those wanting to purchase the Beatles hit singles on CD needed to buy *The Red Album* and *The Blue Album*. These double CD collections were selling for about $32 each, thus requiring an outlay of $64 plus tax. *Beatles 1*, on the other hand, was available in the $13 to $18 range. This made the music affordable to consumers of all ages. But price was only a facilitator as people do not buy for price alone.

In the sixties, the youth of America were attracted to the Beatles for numerous reasons. The freshness and excitement of the music was undeniable, but there was more to it than that. The Beatles were cool. They were British. They were charming. They had long hair. And later on they sang of love and peace. The Beatles were both trend setters and reflectors of what was going on in the sixties.

But the importance of the Beatles in the sixties was not the reason people were buying *Beatles 1*. In today's global village, the fact that the Beatles were British is no big deal. And the hair certainly didn't sell any extra albums. People bought *Beatles 1* because of the quality of the music. Consumers were able to purchase 79 minutes and 12 seconds of hit after hit after hit, all on one CD.

And while some people complained that limiting the album to number one hits meant that many of the Beatles best songs were not on *Beatles 1*, Apple's simplistic approach made sense. It provided a totally objective standard of what to include on the album. After all, if 100 Beatles fans and experts were asked to program eighty minutes of what they each considered to be the best Beatles music, you would have 100 different lineups. And while presenting the songs in chronological order took no imagination, it was the right decision as it enables the listener to follow the incredible development of the Beatles as songwriters and recording artists.

The first three selections on the disc are mono, with the remaining tracks stereo. The songs were digitally remastered by Peter Mew, assisted by Peter Cobbin and Steve Rooke, at Abbey Road.

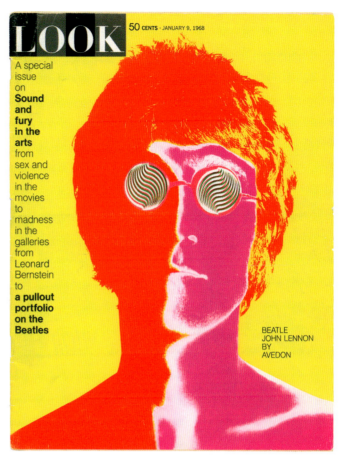

On October 15, 1982, Capitol released *20 Greatest Hits*, with 20 Beatles songs that topped the U.S. charts. Although the album stalled at number 50 on *Billboard Top LP's & Tapes* chart, it eventually sold over two million units. The January 9, 1968, *Look* has Richard Avedon's portrait of John Lennon on its cover.

Apple decided against remixing the songs for the album and did not include the remixed versions of *Yellow Submarine*, *Eleanor Rigby* and *All You Need Is Love* from *Yellow Submarine Songtrack*.

The album was designed by Rick Ward and The Team. The front cover features a painted yellow "1" over a bright red background. A light pink Beatles extended 'T' logo is in the upper left corner. The attractive packaging features four colorful psychedelic Richard Avedon portraits of the group taken in London on August 17, 1967, as well as a series of picture sleeves from the collections of Joachim Noske and Bruce Spizer.

Capitol limited its release of *Beatles 1* to the CD and cassette formats. Once again, American fans looking for a vinyl copy of the album had to purchase the British disc.

The British double album has a red gatefold cover, **APP 29325.SC1**. The front cover is the same as that of the CD. The back cover has the song titles in yellow. The Avedon portraits appear on the inside gatefold. The records, **APP 29325.SR1**, have custom labels featuring the same graphics as the front cover and are packaged in custom inner sleeves, **APP 29325.IS1** and **29325.IS2** (see pages 296-297).

The double record set also includes 8¼" x 11¼" reproductions of the four Richard Avedon portraits and a 24" x 36" poster displaying 126 picture sleeves from the collections of Joachim Noske and Bruce Spizer. The deluxe packaging of the vinyl album, with its four portraits and poster, is reminiscent of that of *The White Album*.

Capitol prepared an attractive brochure detailing its marketing plan for *Beatles 1*. Events related to the CD's release included the publication of the Beatles *Anthology* book on October 5, a two-hour primetime ABC television special (titled *Revolution* and airing on Friday, November

17) and a Beatles radio special. Capitol took out over 5,000 television spots running from pre-release through Christmas. The company also ran more than 600 radio spots and several print ads in top national publications. A variety of point of purchase displays were distributed to stores: dump bins, counterpieces, banners, window acetates, posters and bin cards. When fully opened, the brochure displayed the four Avedon portraits and 84 picture sleeves. Its back cover is shown on page 298.

The brochure contains quotes from each Beatle explaining the group's success.

**John** "In spite of all things, The Beatles really could play music together...I though we were the best group in the goddamn world."

**Paul** "For all our success, The Beatles were always a great little band. Nothing more, nothing less. Forget about all your MBEs and recording careers, it was really down to being a good band."

**George** "The Beatles can't ever really split up, because as we said at the time we did split up, it doesn't really make any difference. The music is there. Whatever we did is still there and always will be."

**Ringo** "I felt with us four it was magical and it was telepathy. When we were working in the studio sometimes it was just...it's indescribable, really. Although there were four of us, there was one of us; all of our hearts were beating at the same time."

The above quotes all focus on why the Beatles were so popular: the music. And it is the timeless quality of the music that explains the phenomenal success of *Beatles 1* and why people will still be listening to the Beatles hundreds of years from now. As George put it best, "The music is there. Whatever we did is still there and always will be."

The British vinyl version of the *Beatles 1* came with 8¼" x 11¼" reproductions of the colorful Richard Avedon posters of the group. The pictures were taken by Avedon in London on August 17, 1967, and were first published in the January 9, 1968, issue of *Look* magazine. The four 22½" x 31" posters, along with a 42" x 16" black and white portrait banner of the group, were available from *Look* for $5.95 plus 25¢ postage and handling. The British album also came with a 24" x 36" poster featuring 126 of the picture sleeves from the CD booklet to *Beatles 1.* The sleeves are from the collections of Joachim Noske and Bruce Spizer.

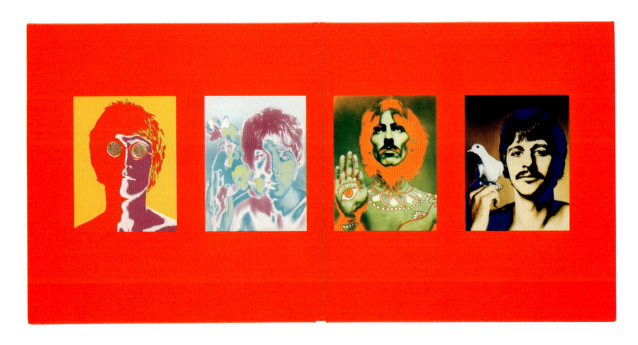

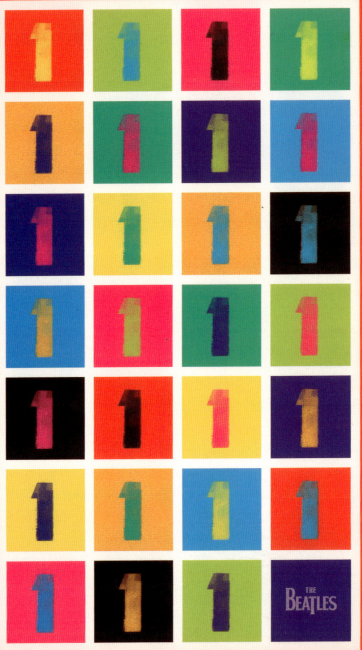

# B is for Bibliography

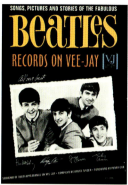

*The Beatles Records on Vee-Jay,*
Bruce Spizer

*The Beatles' Story on Capitol
Records, Part 1,* Bruce Spizer

*The Beatles' Story on Capitol
Records, Part 2,* Bruce Spizer

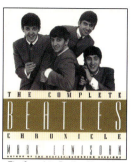

*The Complete Beatles Chronicle,*
Mark Lewisohn

*The Beatles Recording Sessions,*
Mark Lewisohn

*The Beatles as Musicians - The
Quarry Men through Rubber Soul,*
Walter Everett

*The Beatles as Musicians - Revolver
through the Anthology,* Walter
Everett

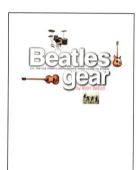

*Beatles Gear,* Andy Babiuk

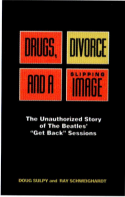

*Drugs, Divorce and a Slipping
Image,* Doug Sulpy and Ray
Schweighardt

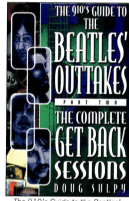

*The 910's Guide to the Beatles'
Outtakes, Part Two, The Complete
Get Back Sessions,* Doug Sulpy

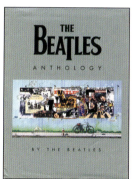

*The Beatles Anthology,* The Beatles

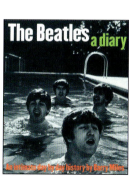

*The Beatles a diary,* Barry Miles

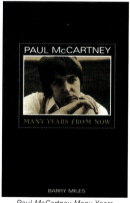

*Paul McCartney Many Years
From Now,* Barry Miles

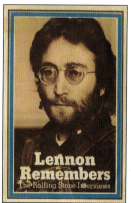

*Lennon Remembers
The Rolling Stone Interviews*

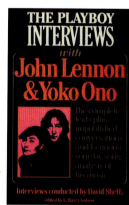

*The Playboy Interviews with John
Lennon & Yoko Ono,* David Sheff &
G. Barry Golson

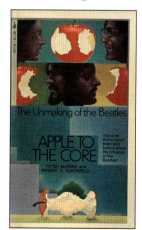

*Apple to the Core,* Peter McCabe
and Robert D. Schonfeld

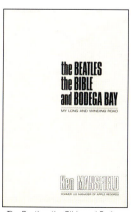

*The Beatles, the Bible and Bodega
Bay,* Ken Mansfield

*Those Were The Days,*
Stefan Granados

*The Longest Cocktail Party,*
Richard DiLello

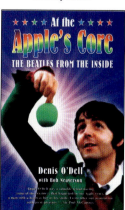

*At the Apple's Core - The Beatles
from the Inside,* Denis O'Dell

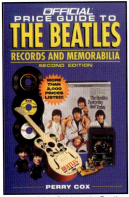
*Official Price Guide to the Beatles Records & Memorabilia*, Perry Cox

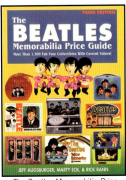
*The Beatles Memorabilia Price Guide*, Jeff Augsburger, Marty Eck & Rick Rann

*With a Little Help from My Friends*, George Martin

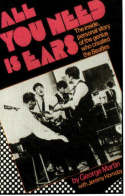
*All You Need Is Ears*, George Martin

*All Together Now*, Harry Castleman and Walter J. Podrazik

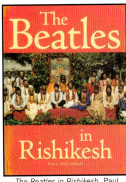
*The Beatles in Rishikesh*, Paul Saltzman

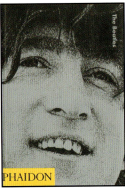
*The Beatles*, Allan Kozinn

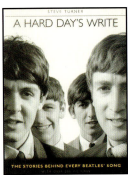
*A Hard Day's Wrote*, Steve Turner

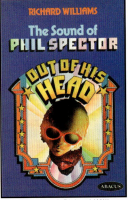
*Out of His Head*, Richard Williams

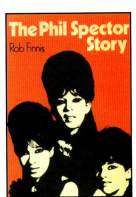
*The Phil Spector Story*, Rob Finnis

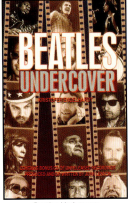
*Beatles Undercover*. Kristofer Engelhardt

*The Beatles at the Movies*. Roy Carr

*Hello Goodbye - The Life and Times of Alistair Taylor*, George Gunby

*The Beatles on Record*, Mark Wallgren

*Abbey Road/ Let It Be/ The Beatles*. Peter Doggett

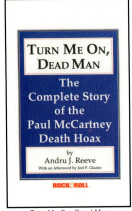
*Turn Me On, Dead Man*. Andru J. Reeve

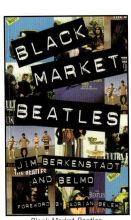
*Black Market Beatles*. Jim Berkenstadt and Belmo

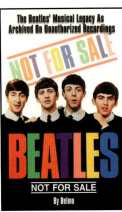
*Beatles Not For Sale*, Belmo

*The Beatles Japanese Record Guide*, Jason Anjoorian

*The Beatles at the BEEB*, Kevin Howlett

*Reference books from Joel Whitburn's Record Research:*

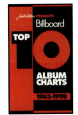
*Billboard Top 10 Album Charts*

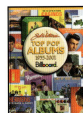
*Top Pop Albums*

*Top Pop Singles*

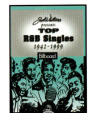
*Top R&B Singles*

*The Billboard Hot 100 Charts*

# C is for Checklist

# Beatles Singles on Apple

## APPLE 2276  HEY JUDE b/w REVOLUTION

- ⃝ APP 2276.01L(i)(as) — Hey Jude @ 9 o'clock/vertical Revolution/no GM or England or master #
- ⃝ APP 2276.01L(ii)(as) — Hey Jude @ 9 o'clock/vertical Revolution/GM and England/no master #
- ⃝ APP 2276.01L(ii)(c) — Hey Jude @ 9 o'clock/vertical Revolution/GM and England/no master #
- ⃝ APP 2276.01S(i)(as) — Hey Jude @ 9 o'clock/vertical Revolution/no GM or England or master #
- ⃝ APP 2276.01S(ii)(as) — Hey Jude @ 9 o'clock/vertical Revolution/master #/no GM or England
- ⃝ APP 2276.01S(iii)(as) — Hey Jude @ 9 o'clock/vertical Revolution/master #/GM/England
- ⃝ APP 2276.01S(iii)(c) — Hey Jude @ 9 o'clock/vertical Revolution/master #/GM/England
- ⃝ APP 2276.02L(c) — Hey Jude and Revolution in upper left apple
- ⃝ APP 2276.03L(as) — Thick Hey Jude @ 9 o'clock/Revolution in upper left apple/light apple
- ⃝ APP 2276.03L(c) — Thick Hey Jude @ 9 o'clock/Revolution in upper left apple/light apple
- ⃝ APP 2276.03S(c) — Thick Hey Jude @ 9 o'clock/Revolution in upper left apple/dark apple
- ⃝ APP 2276.03J(af) — Thick Hey Jude @ 9 o'clock/Revolution in upper left apple/dark dull apple
- ⃝ APP 2276.04W(af) — Hey Jude @ 9 o'clock/Revolution in lower left apple
- ⃝ APP 2276.11L(ar) — Hey Jude @ 9 o'clock/Revolution in lower left apple
- ⃝ APP 2276.12J(ar) — Thick Hey Jude @ 9 o'clock/Revolution in upper left apple

## APPLE 2490  GET BACK b/w DON'T LET ME DOWN

- ⃝ APP 2490.01L(i)(c) — Regular label copy/Beatles below center/no time
- ⃝ APP 2490.01L(ii)(c) — Regular label copy/Beatles below center
- ⃝ APP 2490.01J(ii)(af) — Regular label copy/Beatles below center/medium dull apple
- ⃝ APP 2490.02S(c) — Bold label copy/Beatles below center
- ⃝ APP 2490.02L(af) — Bold label copy/Beatles below center
- ⃝ APP 2490.02L(ab) — Bold label copy/Beatles below center
- ⃝ APP 2490.03S(c) — Thin compressed label copy/Beatles in upper right apple/no time
- ⃝ APP 2490.11L(ar) — Bold label copy/Beatles below center/light apple
- ⃝ APP 2490.11J(ar) — Bold label copy/Beatles below center/dark apple

## APPLE 2531  THE BALLAD OF JOHN AND YOKO b/w OLD BROWN SHOE

- ⃝ APP 2531.PS1A — Picture sleeve · Straight cut top
- ⃝ APP 2531.PS1B — Picture sleeve · Curved cut top
- ⃝ APP 2531.DJ1 — White label with hand written information
- ⃝ APP 2531.01L(c) — Bold label copy/Beatles below center/light apple
- ⃝ APP 2531.01L(af) — Bold label copy/Beatles below center/light apple
- ⃝ APP 2531.01S(c) — Bold label copy/Beatles below center/dark apple
- ⃝ APP 2531.01J(af) — Bold label copy/Beatles below center/dark apple
- ⃝ APP 2531.02S(c) — Thin label copy/Beatles in upper right apple/Mfd by Capitol
- ⃝ APP 2531.11L(ar) — Bold label copy/Beatles below center

## APPLE 2654  SOMETHING b/w COME TOGETHER

- ⃝ APP 2654.01L(as) — Bold label copy/song titles and Beatles below center/light apple
- ⃝ APP 2654.01L(af) — Bold label copy/song titles and Beatles below center/light apple
- ⃝ APP 2654.01J(af) — Bold label copy/song titles and Beatles below center/dark apple
- ⃝ APP 2654.02S(as) — Thin label copy/song titles left of center/info on right loosely spaced
- ⃝ APP 2654.03S(as) — Thin bold label copy/song titles left of center/info on right tightly spaced
- ⃝ APP 2654.04J(af) — Bold label copy/song titles at top
- ⃝ APP 2654.04J(c) — Bold label copy/song titles at top
- ⃝ APP 2654.11L(ar) — Bold label copy/song titles and Beatles below center/light apple

## APPLE 2764  LET IT BE b/w YOU KNOW MY NAME (Look Up The Number)

- ⃝ APP 2764.PS1A — Picture sleeve · Straight cut top
- ⃝ APP 2764.PS1B — Picture sleeve · Curved cut top
- ⃝ APP 2764.01L(as) — Let It Be and Beatles below center/light apple
- ⃝ APP 2764.01L(c) — Let It Be and Beatles below center/light apple
- ⃝ APP 2764.01J(af) — Let It Be and Beatles below center/dark apple
- ⃝ APP 2764.01L(af) — Let It Be and Beatles below center/light apple
- ⃝ APP 2764.02S(c) — Let It Be to left of center/dark apple
- ⃝ APP 2764.02S(as) — Let It Be to left of center/dark apple
- ⃝ APP 2764.03J(c) — Let It Be to left of center/dark apple/Mfd. by Apple/no stereo
- ⃝ APP 2764.11L(ar) — Let It Be and Beatles below center/light apple/time on left on Let It Be side
- ⃝ APP 2764.12J(ar) — Let It Be and Beatles below center/dark apple/time on right on Let It Be side

## APPLE 2832  THE LONG AND WINDING ROAD b/w FOR YOUR BLUE

- ⃝ APP 2832.PS1A — Picture sleeve · Straight cut top
- ⃝ APP 2832.PS1B — Picture sleeve · Tab cut top
- ⃝ APP 2832.01L(c) — A side title below center/light apple
- ⃝ APP 2832.01L(af) — A side title below center/light apple
- ⃝ APP 2832.02S(as) — A side title to left of center/dark apple
- ⃝ APP 2832.03J(as) — A side title above center/tight Lennon-McCartney/dark apple
- ⃝ APP 2832.04J(as) — A side title above center/spaced Lennon-McCartney/dark apple
- ⃝ APP 2832.04J(af) — A side title above center/spaced Lennon-McCartney/dark apple
- ⃝ APP 2832.11L(ar) — A side title below center/light apple

## APPLE 58348  BABY IT'S YOU EP

- ⃝ APP 58348.PS1 — EP jacket
- ⃝ APP 58348.01 — Cream colored background Apple label

## APPLE 58497  FREE AS A BIRD b/w CHRISTMAS TIME (IS HERE AGAIN)

- ⃝ APP 58497.PS1 — Picture sleeve
- ⃝ APP 58497.01 — Cream colored background Apple label

## APPLE 58544  REAL LOVE b/w BABY'S IN BLACK

- ⃝ APP 58544.PS1 — Picture Sleeve
- ⃝ APP 58544.01 — Dark background Apple label

## POCKET DISCS

- ⃝ APP 2276.PD — HEY JUDE b/w REVOLUTION
- ⃝ APP 2490.PD — GET BACK b/w DON'T LET ME DOWN
- ⃝ APP 2531.PD — THE BALLAD OF JOHN AND YOKO b/w OLD BROWN SHOE

This book uses the same numbering system for cataloging and identifying records that appears in previous books of this series. A separate identification number is assigned for each significant variation. For example, the first single listed in the checklist is **APP 2276.01L(i)(as)**. The first part of the number, **APP 2276**, refers to the record number assigned by Capitol, 2276. This is followed by a decimal point and additional numbers and letters.

For Apple singles, the two-digit number following the decimal point identifies the label by its layout design. This is followed by a letter that refers to the primary Capitol factory that pressed the records using that particular layout variation. (**L** = Los Angeles; **S** = Scranton; **J** = Jacksonville; and **W** = Winchester). In cases where the label copy used by the Los Angeles factory is the same for other pressing plants, the letter **L** is often used as the default letter because the film that generated the label copy was most likely prepared for Capitol by Barclay in Los Angeles. Some labels have a number following the letter to indicate the addition of more information to the label. The numbers and letters for the first single listed above is **01L(i)**. The **01** signifies the first layout variation. The **L** indicates that this variation appears primarily on records pressed by Capitol's Los Angeles factory. The **(i)** signifies that this is the first run of this layout variation. In this case, the first labels did not list the master number or identify George Martin as producer or indicate that the song was recorded in England. Label **01L(ii)** added the production and recording location information, but otherwise is the same.

The final parenthetical letters provide the following additional information about the label backdrops: **(c)** = Capitol logo perimeter print on the sliced apple side; **(as)** = Apple perimeter print on the sliced apple side; **(af)** = Apple perimeter print on the full apple side; **(ab)** = Apple perimeter print on both sides; and **(ar)** indicates that the label contains the all rights language added in 1975.

The descriptions following the number in the checklist sometimes have abbreviations. **GM** indicates that the label states "Produced by George Martin." **England** indicates that the label states "Recorded in England." Mfd by Capitol indicates that "Manufactured by Capitol Records, Inc." is typed on the label and "Mfd by Apple" indicates that "Manufactured by Apple Records, Inc." is typed on the label.

# Beatles Albums on Apple

**APPLE SWBO 101   THE BEATLES (THE WHITE ALBUM)**

| | | |
|---|---|---|
| ○ | APP 101.SC1 | Numbered and embossed/no copyright notice/number of 2,250,000 or less |
| ○ | APP 101.SC2 | Numbered and embossed/copyright notice/number over 2,250,000 |
| ○ | APP 101.SC3 | Numbered and embossed/copyright notice/number over 2,900,000 |
| ○ | APP 101.SC4 | Embossed/no number/copyright notice |
| ○ | APP 101.SC5 | No number/not embossed/title in gray or black |
| ○ | APP 101.SR1(c) | Bungalow Bill · short title |
| ○ | APP 101.SR2(c) | Bungalow Bill · full title |
| ○ | APP 101.SR2(as) | Bungalow Bill · full title |
| ○ | APP 101.SR2(af) | Bungalow Bill · full title |
| ○ | APP 101.SR3(c) | Record 1 & 2 designation |
| ○ | APP 101.SR3(af) | Record 1 & 2 designation |
| ○ | APP 101.SR4A(ar) | All rights in black at top of apple |
| ○ | APP 101.SR4B(ar) | All rights in black at bottom of apple/record 1 & 2 designation |
| ○ | APP 101.SR4C(ar) | All rights in green in lower right perimeter |
| ○ | APP 101.SR4D(ar) | All rights in green in lower perimeter |

**APPLE SW 153   YELLOW SUBMARINE**

| | | |
|---|---|---|
| ○ | APP 153.SC1 | Images from cartoon film |
| ○ | APP 153.SR1L(c) | Yellow Submarine in small print/light apple |
| ○ | APP 153.SR1S(c) | Yellow Submarine in bold print/dark apple |
| ○ | APP 153.SR1L(af) | Yellow Submarine in small print/light apple |
| ○ | APP 153.SR2A(ar) | All rights in black at top of apple |
| ○ | APP 153.SR2C(ar) | All rights in green in lower right perimeter |
| ○ | APP 153.SR2D(ar) | All rights in green in lower perimeter |

**APPLE SO 383   ABBEY ROAD**

| | | |
|---|---|---|
| ○ | APP 383.SC1A | Print-on-board cover/no Her Majesty |
| ○ | APP 383.SC1B | Print-on-board cover/Her Majesty |
| ○ | APP 383.SC2A | Cover constructed with slicks/no Her Majesty |
| ○ | APP 383.SR1L(as) | No Her Majesty/Abbey Road above The Beatles on both sides |
| ○ | APP 383.SR1J(as) | No Her Majesty/Abbey Road and The Beatles on same line/Mfd. By Apple |
| ○ | APP 383.SR1S(as) | No Her Majesty/Thin compressed print |
| ○ | APP 383.SR1S(c) | No Her majesty/Thin compressed print/ |
| ○ | APP 383.SR2L(i)(c) | Her Majesty/GM centered above record number |
| ○ | APP 383.SR2L(i)(as) | Her Majesty/GM centered above record number |
| ○ | APP 383.SR2L(ii)(c) | Her Majesty/GM above left of record number |
| ○ | APP 383.SR2L(ii)(as) | Her Majesty/GM above left of record number |
| ○ | APP 383.SR3A(ar) | All rights in black at top of apple |
| ○ | APP 383.SR3B(ar) | All rights in black at bottom of apple |
| ○ | APP 383.SR3C(ar) | All rights in green in lower right perimeter |
| ○ | APP 383.SR3D(ar) | All rights in green in lower perimeter |

**APPLE SW-385   HEY JUDE**

| | | |
|---|---|---|
| ○ | APP 385.SC1 | Group in front of John's home |
| ○ | APP 385.SR1L(as) | The Beatles Again/SO prefix/Can't Buy Me Love above holer |
| ○ | APP 385.SR1J(as) | The Beatles Again/SO prefix/Can't Buy Me Love above hole/Mfd. by Apple |
| ○ | APP 385.SR1S(as) | The Beatles Again/SO prefix/Can't Buy Me Love below hole |
| ○ | APP 385.SR2L(as) | The Beatles Again/SW prefix/Can't Buy Me Love above center |
| ○ | APP 385.SR3L(as) | Hey Jude/SW prefix/Can't Buy Me Love above center |
| ○ | APP 385.SR3L(c) | Hey Jude/SW prefix/Can't Buy Me Love above center |
| ○ | APP 385.SR3L(af) | Hey Jude/SW prefix/Can't Buy Me Love above center |
| ○ | APP 385.SR4C(ar) | All rights in green in lower right perimeter |
| ○ | APP 385.SR4D(ar) | All rights in green in lower perimeter |

**APPLE AR 34001   LET IT BE**

| | | |
|---|---|---|
| ○ | APP 3400.SC1 | Gatefold cover |
| ○ | APP 3400.SR1(af) | Red apple label/Maggie Mae credited to P.D. |
| ○ | APP 3400.SR2(af) | Red apple label/Maggie Mae credited to group |

**APPLE SBC 100   THE BEATLES CHRISTMAS ALBUM**

| | | |
|---|---|---|
| ○ | APP 100.SC1 | Blue background cover |
| ○ | APP 100.SR1(af) | Dark green apple |

**APPLE SKBO 3403   THE BEATLES 1962-1966 (THE RED ALBUM)**

| | | |
|---|---|---|
| ○ | APP 3403.SC1 | Gatefold cover with Apple logo |
| ○ | APP 3403.SR1(af) | Red background Apple label |
| ○ | APP 3403.SR2(ar) | All rights in lower perimeter |

**APPLE SKBO 3404   THE BEATLES 1967-1970 (THE BLUE ALBUM)**

| | | |
|---|---|---|
| ○ | APP 3404.SC1 | Gatefold cover with Apple logo |
| ○ | APP 3404.SR1(af) | Red background Apple label |
| ○ | APP 3404.SR2(ar) | All rights in lower perimeter |

**APPLE 31796   LIVE AT THE BBC**

| | | |
|---|---|---|
| ○ | APP 31796.SC1 | Gatefold cover |
| ○ | APP 31796.SR1 | Cream colored background Apple label |

**APPLE 34445   ANTHOLOGY 1**

| | | |
|---|---|---|
| ○ | APP 3445.SC1 | Gatefold cover |
| ○ | APP 3445.SR1 | Dark background Apple label |

**APPLE 34448   ANTHOLOGY 2**

| | | |
|---|---|---|
| ○ | APP 3448.SC1 | Gatefold cover |
| ○ | APP 3448.SR1 | Cream colored background Apple label |

**APPLE 34451   ANTHOLOGY 3**

| | | |
|---|---|---|
| ○ | APP 3451.SC1 | Gatefold cover |
| ○ | APP 3451.SR1 | Dark background Apple label |

**APPLE UK 21481   YELLOW SUBMARINE SONGTRACK**

| | | |
|---|---|---|
| ○ | APP 21481.SC1 | Gatefold cover |
| ○ | APP 21481.SR1 | Yellow vinyl |
| ○ | APP 21481.SR2 | Black vinyl |

**APPLE UK 29325   BEATLES 1**

| | | |
|---|---|---|
| ○ | APP 29325.SC1 | Gatefold cover |
| ○ | APP 29325.SR1 | Custom red labels |

The numbering system for the Apple albums is similar to the one for the singles. A separate identification number is assigned for each significant variation of an album's cover and the labels to the records. For example, all items pertaining to *Abbey Road* start with the number **APP 383**, which refers to the record number assigned to the album, SO 383. This is followed by a decimal point and additional letters and numbers.

For album covers, **SC** is used to identify a stereo cover. This is followed by a number to distinguish among variations of the cover, if any. For *Abbey Road*, **SC1A** is the first run print-on-board cover without *Her Majesty*. **SC1B** is the later print-on-board cover that adds *Her Majesty*. **SC2A** identifies covers constructed with slicks.

For the records, **SR** indicates a stereo disc. The number after **SR** categorizes the label by its printed information. This is followed by a letter that identifies the label by its layout design. The letter refers to the primary Capitol factory that pressed the records with labels using that particular layout variation (L = Los Angeles; S = Scranton; J = Jacksonville; and W = Winchester). In cases where the label copy layout used by the Los Angeles factory is the same for other pressing plants, the letter **L** is often used as the default letter because the film that generated the label copy was most likely prepared for Capitol by Barclay in Los Angeles. For **APP 101**, there is no letter for the labels used prior to the all rights language being added because there are no layout variations as all labels were generated from the same film. Some labels have a number following the letter to indicate a minor variation.

For *Abbey Road*, **SR1** is used to identify the first run labels, which did not include *Her Majesty*. The numbers **SR1L**, **SR1J** and **SR1S** categorize the first run labels by the Los Angeles, Jacksonville and Scranton factories. The labels with *Her Majesty* are listed as **SR2**. The **L** layout has two slight variations distinguishable by the location of the George Martin production credit (abbreviated as **GM** in the checklist description). **SR2L(i)** identifies labels where the credit is centered above the record number and **SR2L(ii)** identifies labels where the credit is above and to the left of the record number.

The final parenthetical letters provide the following additional information about the label backdrops: (c) = Capitol logo perimeter print on the sliced apple side; (as) = Apple perimeter print on the sliced apple side; (af) = Apple perimeter print on the full apple side; (ab) = Apple perimeter print on both sides; and (ar) indicates that the label contains the all rights language added in 1975.

The letters for the all rights labels do not refer to the factories, but rather to one of four primary variations. Thus, the letters **L**, **S**, **J** and **W** are not used for all rights labels. The four variations are identified as follows: **A** has the all rights language overprinted in black at the top of the apple; **B** has the all rights language overprinted in black at the bottom of the apple; **C** has the all rights language in green running along the lower right perimeter on the full apple side; and **D** has the all rights language in green in the lower perimeter on both sides.

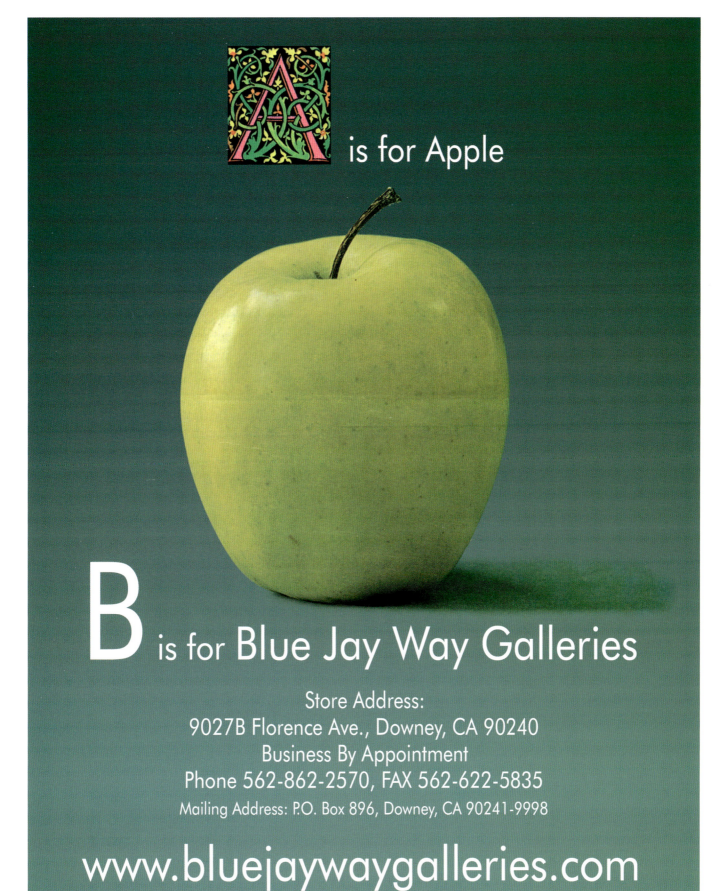

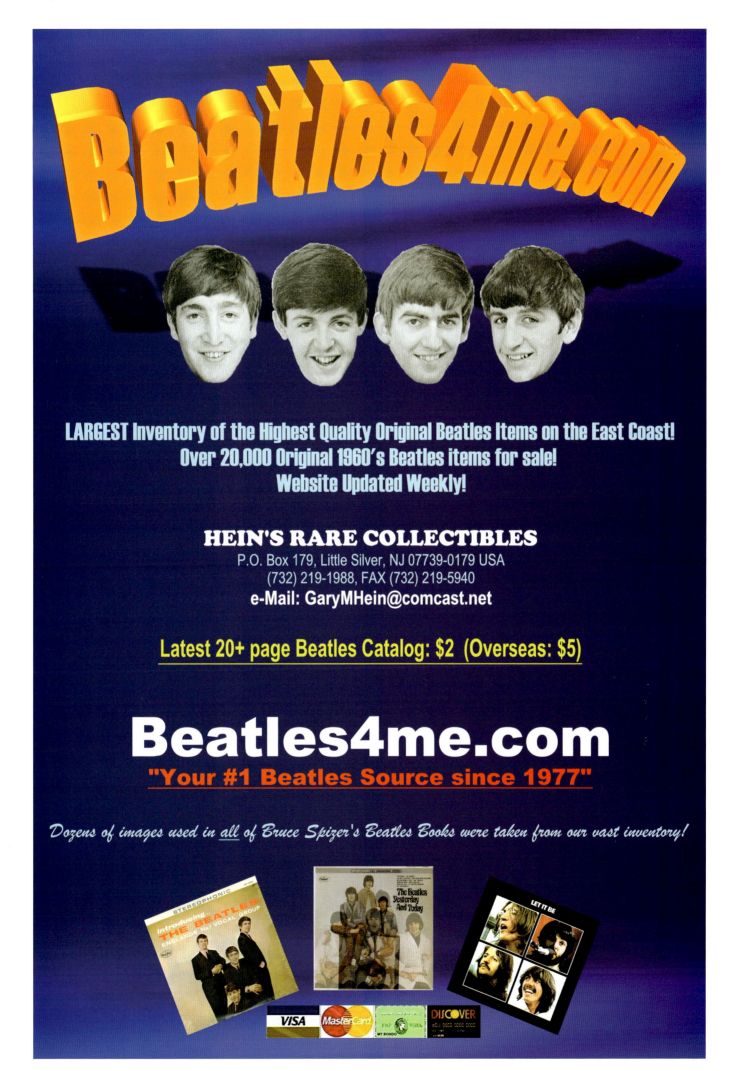

# Beatlology is...

## The study of all things Beatle-related…

*Beatlology Magazine* is *the* magazine for fans and collectors alike and is the official magazine of Joe Johnson's *Beatlebrunch Radio*. Feature articles by well-known Beatles collectors, exclusive interviews, detailed accounts of The Beatles' recording sessions, auction reports, news and reviews all in a glossy, full colour format make *Beatlology Magazine* the premiere magazine for fans and collectors around the world. Published six times a year, the magazine is available at all Towers Music stores worldwide and by subscription for $24US per year. Call us Monday to Friday, 9–5 EST or mail a cheque, money order, VISA or Mastercard info to the address below.

*Beatlology Online Auctions* is an online marketplace Beatles collectors use to safely buy and sell authentic collectibles. This categorized and moderated auction environment ensures that only legitimate items are offered and are described with utmost accuracy. Check our web site for more details.

*Beatlology Publishing* is a multi-media publishing company created in the spirit of The Beatles' own Apple Corps. We are looking authors and creators who want to publish their own projects but don't want to have to deal with big companies that dictate how the project is produced. Check our web site for more details.

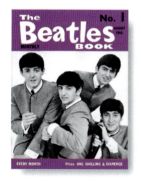

P.O. Box 90, 260 Adelaide Street East, Toronto, Ontario  M5A 1N1
Tel.: 416-360-8902  Fax: 416-360-0588  Toll-free: 1-888-844-0826

# www.beatlology.com

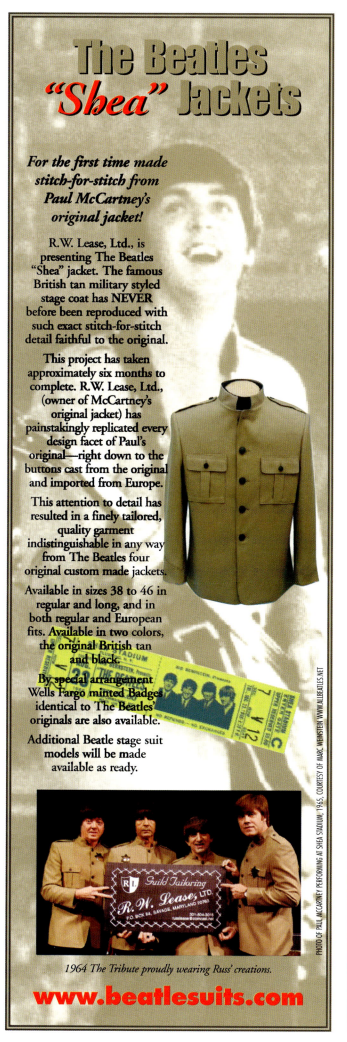

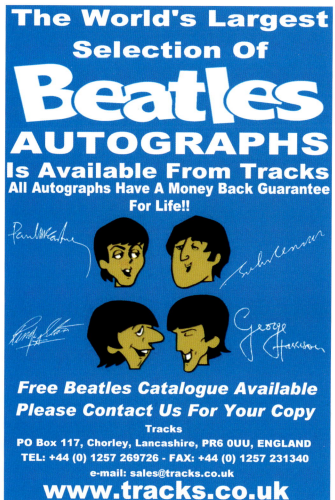

# THE BEATLES ON

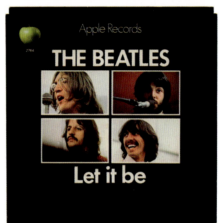

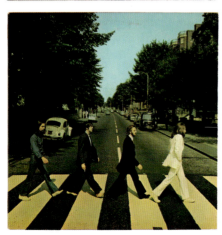